THE DEMOGRAPHY OF ARMED CONFLICT

International Studies in Population

Volume 5

The International Union for the Scientific Study of Population (IUSSP)

The IUSSP is an international association of researchers, teachers, policy makers and others from diverse disciplines set up to advance the field of demography and promote scientific exchange. It also seeks to foster relations between persons engaged in the study of demography and population trends in all countries of the world and to disseminate knowledge about their determinants and consequences. The members of the IUSSP scientific group responsible for this book were chosen for their scientific expertise. This book was reviewed by a group other than the authors. While the IUSSP endeavors to assure the accuracy and objectivity of its scientific work, the conclusions and interpretations in IUSSP publications are those of the authors.

International Studies in Population (ISIP) is the outcome of an agreement concluded by IUSSP and Springer in 2004. The joint series covers the broad range of work carried out by IUSSP and includes material presented at seminars organized by the IUSSP. The scientific directions of the IUSSP are set by the IUSSP Council elected by the membership and composed of:

The Demography of Armed Conflict

Edited by

HELGE BRUNBORG

Statistics Norway,
Oslo, Norway

EWA TABEAU

International Criminal Tribunal for the former Yugoslavia,
The Hague, Netherlands

and

HENRIK URDAL

Centre for the Study of Civil War,
International Peace Research Institute, Oslo (PRIO)
Oslo, Norway

Springer

A C.I.P. Catalogue record for this book is available from the Library of Congress.

ISBN-10 1-4020-5134-4 (HB)
ISBN-13 978-1-4020-5134-0 (HB)

Published by Springer,
P.O. Box 17, 3300 AA Dordrecht, The Netherlands.

www.springer.com

Printed on acid-free paper

CONTENTS

PREFACE

HELGE BRUNBORG
EWA TABEAU
HENRIK URDAL

The study of the demography of armed conflict has not been a prominent and well-developed field, despite strong public interest and the potentially important contributions that demographers could make. This was the initial motivation for establishing a Working Group on the Demography of Conflict and Violence under the auspices of the International Union for the Scientific Study of Population (IUSSP), chaired by Helge Brunborg, and for organising a seminar intended to provide a state-of-art overview of current research related to demographic aspects of armed conflict. The seminar, titled "Demography of Conflict and Violence", was held near Oslo, Norway, 8–11 November 2003.

While planning the 2003 seminar, the organisers initially feared that the attendance would be rather small and narrow. However, the call for papers received an overwhelming response, with more than 90 abstracts submitted. The largest number of proposals focused on demographic consequences of conflict, especially deaths and forced migration. Another but much smaller group of abstracts was devoted to the role of demographic factors in conflict, a few of them explicitly discussing demographic causes of conflict. Some abstracts proposed studies of methods and data sources to be used in peace research. There were also several case studies, including studies of genocide. While the majority of proposals came from researchers in the fields of demography or peace research, the interdisciplinary interest in the field became apparent as proposals were submitted by people with a wide variety of backgrounds, including political science, economics, psychology, anthropology, philosophy, law, geography, sociology, ecology and statistics.

Out of 90 submitted abstracts, 40 were invited, and 34 papers presented at the 2003 seminar. The seminar turned out to be an exciting and meaningful event and a stimulating tool for exchanging experience between researchers working in this area. The many discussions not only brought researchers of conflict and violence together, but also allowed for a very useful overview of on-going work in the field, as well as providing landmarks for future work. At the seminar, the first steps were taken towards "populating" a new field, the Demography of Armed Conflict.

In 2005, two international journals published special issues based on papers presented at the seminar, the *Journal of Peace Research* (*JPR*)[1], associated with the International Peace Research Institute in Oslo (PRIO), and the *European Journal of Population* (*EJP*)[2], issued under the auspices of the European Association for Population Studies (EAPS) and affiliated with the Netherlands Interdisciplinary

Demographic Institute (NIDI) in The Hague, and the Institut National d'Études Démographiques (INED) in Paris.

The present volume brings together all fifteen articles from the two special issues, of which twelve were presented at the seminar, as well as one related article previously published in *EJP*. They address demographic processes both as a cause and as a consequence of armed conflict. All articles, including those by the editors, were subject to the normal anonymous peer-review process of the two journals.

Besides the two special journal issues, a number of activities bear testimony to the growing interest in the intersection between conflict research and demography since the 2003 seminar: a session on Demography of Conflict and Violence at the IUSSP General Conference in Tours in July 2005 (with 29 proposals for presentation), and similar sessions at the annual meetings of the Population Association of America in 2004 and 2005. The IUSSP Council decided in 2006 to continue to focus on this area by establishing a Panel on the Demography of Armed Conflict as an extension of the Working Group on the Demography of Conflict and Violence.

There is also a steadily growing number of journal articles and books about armed conflict and demography, many of them referred to in the articles in this book. We hope that this volume will stimulate continued research in the field of demography and armed conflict.

Notes

[1] Special Issue on the Demography of Conflict and Violence, *Journal of Peace Research*, Volume 42, No. 4 (July 2005). Guest editors: Helge Brunborg and Henrik Urdal.

[2] Special Issue on Demographic Perspectives on Violence and Conflict, *European Journal of Population*, Volume 21, No. 2–3 (September 2005). Guest editors: Helge Brunborg and Ewa Tabeau.

ACKNOWLEDGEMENTS

HELGE BRUNBORG
EWA TABEAU
HENRIK URDAL

We are grateful to the International Union for the Scientific Study of Population (IUSSP) for establishing the Working Group on the Demography of Conflict and Violence and for continued encouragement and support. For organising the seminar in Norway we are grateful for the assistance of the two other members of the IUSSP Working Group, Holly Reed (National Academy of Sciences, Washington, DC) and Gustav Feichtinger (ORG Vienna University of Technology), as well as Silje Vatne Pettersen of Statistics Norway and Nils Petter Gleditsch of the International Peace Research Institute, Oslo (PRIO).

Financial and technical support for the seminar was provided by the IUSSP, the Research Council of Norway, Statistics Norway and the Centre for the Study of Civil War at PRIO.

We would especially like to thank Nils Petter Gleditsch for initially proposing the special issue of the *Journal of Peace Research* (JPR) and for encouragement and comments. Information about the IUSSP, the Working Group and the Seminar may be found at http://www.iussp.org/ Activities/con-index.php. We are also grateful to the *Journal of Peace Research* and SAGE Publications as well as to the *European Journal of Population* (Springer) for allowing reprints of the articles in the two special issues, and to Springer for agreeing to publish it. Finally, we would like to express our appreciation for the IUSSP support for organising the seminar and publishing this book, especially Mary Ellen Zuppan, Mary M. Kritz and David Coleman, the last also for comments on the introduction.

INTRODUCTION

HELGE BRUNBORG
EWA TABEAU
HENRIK URDAL

1. Background

War and conflict, whether internal or international, remain pervasive phenomena affecting most regions of the world and particularly low-income countries. Demographic *consequences*, especially death and forced migration, are among the gravest costs of war and receive much attention in mass media, although are often difficult to quantify. Demographic factors like population pressure on natural renewable resources, migration, differential population dynamics by ethnic or religious group, or the number of young persons in a population, have also been suggested as potential *causes* of conflict. Despite the obvious importance of both demographic causes and consequences of armed conflict, research on the demographic aspects of conflict is scarce. While there have been several important historical accounts of demographic consequences of major warfare (e. g. Winter, 1976, 1977; Parker, 1988; Ronsin, 1995; Landers, 2003), recent armed conflicts have rarely been studied from this perspective, despite the grave humanitarian consequences. In part, this may be because demographic analyses of war cannot be easily conducted by using standard demographic sources and methods. Wars and conflict are always associated with destruction, not only of people, property, order, culture, institutions and infrastructure, but also of archives and data. New data collection efforts are often impossible due to war activities and conflict. As a consequence, good and reliable data are usually unavailable for countries affected by conflict. Clearly, there is a need to evaluate and develop methods and sources for use in the study of demographic aspects of armed conflict.

The lack of a broader research field on the demography of conflict was the motivation for establishing, under the auspices of the International Union for the Scientific Study of Population (IUSSP), the Working Group on Demography of Conflict and Violence. The Working Group organized a seminar on this topic near Oslo in November 2003, meant to provide a state-of-art overview of the current research related to demographic aspects of wars and conflict. The call for papers for the seminar outlined a number of research questions on the demography of violence and conflict, which may be used to classify research as well as pointing out areas for future research:

Helge Brunborg et al. (eds.), The Demography of Armed Conflict, 1–16.

(1) *Demographic factors as causes of conflict*
   (a) The impact of population composition or change on the risk of armed conflict, such as youth bulges, skewed sex ratios, population growth and density, domestic and international migration, differential growth rates between ethnic groups, HIV/AIDS and rapid urbanization.
   (b) The role of ethnicity, religion and other group characteristics in structuring conflict, including the potentially exacerbating role of population policies.
   (c) Interaction of demographic factors with economic, political and environmental conditions in affecting risks of armed conflict.

(2) *Demographic consequences of conflict*
   (a) Consequences of conflict for morbidity, mortality and disability.
   (b) Impact of conflict, through, for example, psychosocial effects among combatants and civilians, on fertility, reproductive health, nuptiality and household composition.
   (c) Consequences of conflict in terms of forced migration and other types of internal or international mobility, as well as the demographic repercussions of forced migration.

(3) *Data and methods to measure the population impact of conflict and violence*
   (a) Identification of problems in collecting data on the demographic consequences of conflict and war, and the types of data useful for assessing the demographic impact.
   (b) Development of indirect methods of demographic estimation, that is, methods based on incomplete or deficient data, to measure the demographic impact of conflict.
   (c) Use of estimates of war casualties for prosecuting war crimes or informing truth commissions, including the role of forensic demography.

(4) *Special cases of violence and conflict and their demographic determinants and effects*
   (a) Assessments of the direct (e.g. mortality) and indirect (e.g. migration, fertility) demographic effects of terrorism, and the possible impact of demographic factors, for instance age composition or ethnic heterogeneity, on the risk of terrorism.
   (b) Defining and characterising genocide; examination of the long-term demographic and other consequences on the population that experienced genocide.

The term "war crimes" is perhaps intuitively clear but defining it legally is complex. Going into legal details is far beyond this chapter and even beyond this book but a basic explanation is required.

Throughout this book we use the expression "war crimes" for crimes committed during, or in relation to, an armed conflict whether international or non-international. War crimes are in the first place related to violations of the laws and customs of war and to failures to adhere to rules and procedures of battle. They also comprise acts such as, for example, mistreatment of prisoners of war or civilians. In addition to this war crimes sometimes include instances of mass murder and genocide, which are broadly covered as crimes against humanity. Note that crimes against humanity *embrace particularly odious offences or serious attacks on human dignity*, whereas genocide relates to the intentional killing, destruction or extermination of groups or members of groups as such. Summing up, the following crimes are understood in this book as war crimes:

i) grave breaches of the Geneva Conventions of 1949,
ii) violations of the laws and customs of war,
iii) genocide, and
iv) crimes against humanity.

Crimes listed under i) and ii) are often referred to in legal texts as violations of International Humanitarian Law (IHL), which was originally developed with a military perspective (narrow approach). Sometimes IHL can be seen, however, as additionally covering also categories iii) and iv), i.e. genocide and crimes against humanity (broad approach). More details on these crimes (i–iv) can be found at www.un.org/law/icc and http://www.un.org/icty/legaldoc-e/index.htm.

In this book we generally use the term "war crimes victims" for victims of serious violations of IHL (its broad definition) and committed during (or in relation to) an armed conflict, whether international or non-international. The article by Fenrick in Part III contains some explanation of legal concepts related not only to combat casualties but also to IHL as well as some legal references. However, a majority of the articles in this book represent the social science perspective and concentrate on war-related casualties, which are not necessarily the same as war crime victims (the latter concept being much narrower than the former). One article (by Midlarsky) discusses genocide cases committed in the absence of armed conflict, and several articles investigate post-conflict (but still conflict-related) demographic consequence (e.g. Li and Wen, Verwimp and Van Bavel).

2. This Book

The importance of advancing research on the demography of conflict and violence is obvious because of the enormous human suffering associated with conflict and violence. Research in this field is challenging, however, both from a human and from a professional point of view. Besides the serious human consequences, the data needed to estimate these consequences are often destroyed, intentionally or not, during acts of war. Thus, there is a need for non-standard methods to estimate and analyze demographic consequences of conflict.

The study of demographic *consequences* of conflict is not merely of academic interest, but has also a practical application in providing evidence for the prosecution of people suspected of war crimes as well as establishing facts for post-war truth commissions and for the future writers of history. Agreeing on the basic facts, such as the number of people killed in a conflict, is important for the reconciliation process, bringing together old enemies and reducing post-war tension. The other strand of studies presented in this book, on the demographic *causes* of conflict, may hopefully increase the capability of preventing conflicts from breaking out in the future.

Our own interest in the demography of conflict and violence started with work for the International Criminal Tribunal for the former Yugoslavia (ICTY), where we were involved in a project to estimate the demographic consequences of the armed conflicts in Bosnia and Herzegovina during the period 1992–1995, to be used as background material and evidence in trials against perpetrators. Some of this work has been published, such as Brunborg (2001), Brunborg et al. (2003) and Tabeau and Bijak (2005). A few expert reports are available on Internet, e.g. Brunborg and Urdal (2000) and Tabeau et al. (2002, 2003a, 2003b), while results still remain confidential. Another demographer involved in the analysis of casualties of the Yugoslav conflicts for use in ICTY trials is Patrick Ball (Ball et al., 2002). The work in this area at ICTY has added a new reason for doing demographic analysis of conflict and violence, i.e. supporting legal systems operating in the area of justice and human rights by providing reliable statistics and analyses of the number of victims in a conflict.

Work on the demographic consequences of armed conflict may benefit the *ad hoc* criminal courts established in recent years as well as the International Criminal Court (ICC), also based in The Hague. The ICC will most likely, sooner or later, need demographic evidence in the prosecution of serious violations of International Humanitarian Law (Brunborg, 2003; Spirer and Seltzer, 2005). A plan for developing demographic analysis capacity was formulated when this new and permanent court was established and recently (in March 2006) the ICC advertised for the first time for a statistician that would work in the area of conflict casualties. Another recent example of using demographic expert reports in court proceedings comes from the International Court of Justice (ICJ) in The Hague, where such reports were referred to in the case of Bosnia and Herzegovina (BH) versus Serbia and Montenegro (SM) during the testimony of the French demographer Jean-Paul Sardon, see http://www.icj-cij.org/icjwww/idocket/ibhy/ibhyframe.htm.

This anthology consists of articles from recent special issues of two highly recognized international journals, one in demography, the *European Journal of Population*, and one in peace research, the *Journal of Peace Research*. The articles are quite different in character, as is the field itself. Although we encourage the search for developments and characteristics that are similar between conflicts, we agree with Lubkemann and Randall that one cannot talk about a coherent field of demography of conflict. In order to understand or even predict responses in specific conflict situations, it is essential to have both general knowledge as well as particular information about a given conflict and area. We believe that the articles in this book together represent such a broad approach.

The demography of conflict and violence, as it has been defined by the IUSSP Working Group, is primarily concerned with *political* conflict. This is also the reason for continuing this work under a new name, the Scientific Panel on the Demography of Armed Conflict. Thus, other types of conflict, such as criminal and household violence, are excluded. However, the distinction between political and other forms of violence may be blurred. For instance, during armed conflict some forms of criminal violence, such as looting or rape, may be widespread.

The articles in this volume have been written by demographers or demographically oriented researchers from other fields, such as peace research, economics, anthropology, sociology geography, history or political science.

The book contains five parts:

Part I. Demographic Causes of Conflict
Part II. Conflict and Mortality: The Broader Picture
Part III. Estimating Victims of Conflict for the Prosecution of War Crimes
Part IV. Demographic Consequences of Conflict: Case Studies
Part V. Post-conflict Demographic Responses: Case Studies

Part I includes four articles, by Midlarsky, Besançon, Urdal and Ware, which all focus on the *causes* of violent conflict, in particular on demographic causes. Midlarsky and Ware present detailed comparative case studies, Midlarsky on the demographic driving forces explaining different genocidal trajectories among German allies and occupied areas during World War II, and Ware on conflict and state failure in Pacific island states. Besançon and Urdal use global time-series statistical models to address inequality and population pressure, respectively, as causes of conflict.

Part II describes historical trends in conflict mortality. Landers takes the distant historical perspective of pre-industrial Europe, and assesses how the gunpowder revolution changed the financial and human costs of war. Lacina and Gleditsch present recent trends in warfare by type of conflict and region, showing that the decline in the number of conflicts globally is paralleled (and even was preceded) by a decline in total number of war deaths. Li and Wen address the short- and long-term sex-specific mortality from different forms of conflict.

The theme of measuring the number of victims is continued in Part III, which is devoted to requirements of and methods for counting conflict casualties conducted for the needs of the prosecution of war crimes (Fenrick; Brunborg et al.; Tabeau and Bijak). Fenrick introduces the major principles of international humanitarian law, and the remaining two articles are examples of how this type of counting is done in practice.

The next three articles in Part IV (Neupert and Prum; Bocquier and Maupeu; Lubkemann) are case studies that primarily attempt to estimate mortality, the last one dealing mostly with migration, as a consequence of conflict in Cambodia, Kenya and Mozambique. Lubkemann's article on Mozambique also elaborates on the specific and local circumstances that influence the reactions to conflict.

Finally, Part V contains three case studies (Singh et al.; Verwimp and Van Bavel; Randall) addressing post-conflict conditions and responses of populations from Uganda/Sudan, Rwanda and Mali.

3. Articles in this Book

In the first article in Part I, Midlarsky investigates the seriousness of the genocide against Jews in some German allied or occupied countries during the Second World War. He argues that territorial loss and the related influx of refugees produced a shrinking socio-economic space in many of the countries that later followed the genocidal path. This was the case in Italy, Vichy France and Romania, as well as Germany and Austria. Furthermore, two German allies that experienced an expansion of their borders in the early phases of the Second World War, Finland and Bulgaria, opposed the genocidal policies and succeeded in saving most of their Jewish populations. Midlarsky finds support for his hypothesis not only cross-sectionally, but also temporally within countries.

Besançon suggests a possible explanation to the puzzle why previous rigorous studies have failed to convincingly support a relationship between inequality and armed conflict (Collier and Hoeffler, 2004). Disaggregating internal armed conflicts into ethnic wars, revolutions and genocides, she finds in a series of statistical models that economic inequality increases the likelihood of revolution, but decreases the risk of ethnic war. Thus, while countries experiencing vertical, or class-structured economic inequality appear to be at greater risk of deprivation-driven violent conflict, Besançon suggests, although not testing the hypothesis directly, that ethnic group violence is more likely when horizontal inequalities are small, meaning that ethnic groups are more equal in terms of economic resources. On the other hand, she finds that social inequality, measured by human capital inequality, seems to be a greater contributor to ethnic war. Together, this suggests that greater political and social inequalities increase the risk of inter-ethnic violence when groups have more equal access to economic resources. For genocide, the effect of inequality is more ambiguous.

Urdal investigates the neo-Malthusian claim that high population pressure on renewable resources increases the risk of armed conflict. In a cross-national time-series study he finds no support for the suggestions that high population growth, high population pressure on potentially arable land, rapid urbanization or large refugee populations should be associated with the onset of internal armed conflict. While there is some support for a resource-optimistic view that population density in itself may have a long-term pacifying effect, the interaction of high population growth and land scarcity appears to increase the risk of conflict somewhat. But neither finding is very robust. A claim that population pressure on land resources should have become a more salient cause of conflict after the end of the Cold War is unsupported. The sum of findings leads to the conclusion that security is not an important macro rationale for reducing global population growth.

Finally, in a comparative study of Pacific island states, Ware finds that rapid population growth combined with the lack of unemployment opportunities for youths, rather than environmental degradation, represents a considerable risk of civil violence and 'failed states'. Many Pacific island states have relatively weak governments and small military or law-enforcement units, making them vulnerable to militias consisting of young deprived men.[1] This is particularly the case in states where migration opportunities are greatly constrained, as they are for the Melanesian region, in contrast to most of Polynesia and Micronesia. Melanesia is also the region that has experienced the most serious civil violence events. To prevent future conflict and state failure, Ware suggests a dual strategy of faster economic growth and opportunities for migration for the entire region.

In Part II, Landers discusses the demographic impact of warfare in pre-industrial Europe. Warfare mortality among both soldiers and civilians alike was almost entirely due to epidemic disease. Landers reviews historical estimates for causes of death among troops in major wars from the early seventeenth to the late nineteenth century, where disease was always the leading cause of death and sometimes accounted for more than eighty per cent of mortality among the militaries. The main demographic impact of warfare, however, was due to increased civilian mortality resulting from the spread of pathogens combined with economic and social disruption. Civilian mortality was the greatest where the disruption was most severe when rulers, in order to reduce the cost of warfare, allowed military brokers to raise mercenary armies who lived off the civilian population. Landers argues that high levels of population growth produced an increased supply of cheap recruits, but that the growth in armies and the increasing costs of equipping soldiers when firearms were generally adopted put a great financial burden on many European powers leading to mounting national debts. In France, this eventually resulted in the introduction of a mass-conscription system and an increasing destructiveness of warfare.

A leading promise of the article by Lacina and Gleditsch, the second contribution in Part II, is the opinion that a proper understanding of trends in warfare across time or space requires consistent measures of deaths due to armed conflict (i.e. *war deaths*). The authors consequently begin by introducing a classification of war deaths into four categories. While soldiers and civilians killed in combat are considered *battle-related*, increased mortality from one-sided violence (for example, execution of war prisoners or a genocidal campaign), criminal and unorganised violence, or indirect causes such as diseases and starvation, are seen as *non-battle deaths*. Each of these categories may serve to answer different questions, depending on the objectives of the research, examples of which are generously given in the text. The authors use a new series of "cleaned" battle deaths to present, for the first time, new estimates of trends in global and regional warfare over time (1946–2002) and by region. They conclude that battle violence has declined over the past fifty years due to a decline in major interstate conflicts and large internationalised civil conflicts. However, many conflicts are characterized by high numbers of non-violent deaths due to humanitarian crises that far surpass the lives lost in combat.

[1] In a global statistical study, Urdal (2006) finds that large youth cohorts, or youth bulges, increase the risk of armed conflict and other forms of political violence.

One of the essential points raised by the authors is that classification of war-related deaths may often involve normative issues, such as, for example, the distinction between combatant and non-combatant deaths as satisfying (or not) the proportionality requirement (discussed below). This distinction is critical in court proceedings related to cases of serious violations of International Humanitarian Law. These issues are beyond the scope of the article by Lacina and Gleditsch, but are central in the review paper by Fenrick (Part III).

Li and Wen takes a new approach by looking at deaths *following* a conflict, both in the short and in the long run, without having any information about the deaths being directly caused by the conflict or not. They do not differentiate between battle and non-battle deaths, or between civilian and military deaths. Neither do they limit their study to deaths during the conflict period. To analyse this they pool data on conflicts and deaths, as well as a number of covariates or explanatory variables, over time (1962–98) and over space (84 countries). They find that the *type* of conflict is important for the long-term effects. Civil conflicts have much stronger immediate mortality effects than interstate conflicts, while the reverse is the case for the lingering effects. Moreover, and not surprisingly, they find that severe conflicts have much stronger mortality effects than weak conflicts, and conclude that it is important to prevent conflicts into escalating.

Before we move on towards the issues summarized by Fenrick in his overview of major notions of the law regulating the illegitimacy of combat victims, it is useful to explain the meaning of the rule of proportionality. This rule is a legal concept formulated in the framework of the law of war (see e.g. Human Rights Watch, 1991). The law of war, or the International Humanitarian Law (IHL), has developed over centuries. In modern times, the four 1949 Geneva Conventions, several more recent UN resolutions, and customary laws of war should be seen as the primary legal sources governing the conduct of a war. The first codification of the customary rule of proportionality as it relates to collateral (i.e. unavoidable) civilian casualties and damage to civilian objects is available from Protocol I of the 1949 Geneva Conventions, art. 51(5) and 57(2), (a) (iii) and (b):

> An attack which may be expected to cause incidental loss of civilian life, injury to civilians, damage to civilian objects, or a combination of thereof, which would be excessive in relation to the concrete and direct military advantage anticipated (Human Rights Watch, 1991).

Obviously, the term "*excessive damage*" is a relational concept, not quantifiable in terms of a fixed number of civilians dead or injured, or houses destroyed. Such damage does not need to be great. Rather, its avoidance requires a good-faith balance of anticipated collateral damage and the relative importance of a particular military target.

Contrary to demographic research, legal proceedings of serious violations of International Humanitarian Law are restricted to a much narrower approach. Their approach is regulated by the IHL principles, which are intended to reduce net human suffering and net damage to civilian objects in armed conflict. In his article, Fenrick focuses on some major IHL concepts and their application in the legal practice of major international institutions, especially the International Criminal Tribunal for the former Yugoslavia (ICTY). In particular, he reviews the law regulating combat and discusses which of combat casualties can be viewed as war crimes victims.

In Part IV, Fenrick begins by saying that "War inevitably involves death and destruction. The only way to avoid death and destruction in war is to avoid the war", and he ends by concluding that "The fact that people are killed or injured as a result of combat activities does not automatically mean that a crime has been committed." Fenrick further explains that deliberate killing of combatants is illegitimate if the combatants surrender or are disabled and hence do not participate in the fighting. The killing of civilians who do not directly take part in hostilities is illegitimate if civilian losses are disproportionately high compared to the military objective of an action.

Obviously, IHL-based counting of casualties of combat is characterised by a complexity that goes beyond the usual demographic standards of counting deaths. Applying the IHL principles in practise is hard and requires studying all individual deaths on a case-by-case basis. As of today, only a limited number of demographic studies of this type have been completed and presented in international or national criminal courts. A few unique examples from ICTY are included in this anthology.

Fenrick focuses combat casualties only, not on victims of crimes against humanity, which are often responsible for large numbers of victims. This latter category includes the following acts committed against a civilian population during an international or internal armed conflict: a) murder; b) extermination; c) enslavement; d) deportation; e) imprisonment; f) torture; g) rape; h) persecutions on political, racial and religious grounds; i) other inhumane acts (ICTY Statute, 1993). Genocide, not explicitly mentioned in the above list, may be regarded as the supreme crime against humanity (see Fenrick). It does not need to occur during an armed conflict, however. According to the ICTY Statute, genocide "... means any of the following acts committed with intent to destroy, in whole or in part, a national, ethnical, racial or religious group, such as: a) killing members of a group; b) causing serious bodily or mental harm to members of the group; c) deliberately inflicting on the group conditions of life calculated to bring about its physical destruction in whole or in part; d) imposing measures intended to prevent births within the group; e) forcibly transferring children of the group to another group". Note that in media and common language the term 'genocide' is sometimes inappropriately used just for describing large numbers of victims (i.e. deaths). Such misnomer should be avoided in scientific research on the demography of violence and conflict. In fact, a person may be found guilty of genocide by killing one person only.

A first example of counting victims made partly along the IHL lines, is given by Brunborg et al., who studied the victims after the UN 'Safe area' of Srebrenica in Bosnia and Herzegovina was over-run by Bosnian Serb forces in July 1995. The attack was followed by the killing of a large number of male Bosnian Muslim civilians in what has been characterised as the worst massacre in Europe since World War II. The authors, formerly with the International Criminal Tribunal for the former Yugoslavia, estimated the minimum number of missing and dead persons from Srebrenica from independently collected lists of missing persons and other sources of pre- and post-war population data. Their estimate of Srebrenica victims (7,475) was presented in the Krstić case at ICTY in June 2000. Since then it has often been referred to in other ICTY trials cases and in the media as the baseline standard on Srebrenica deaths.

We had planned to include a new article with an update on Srebrenica, summarizing the findings that have been obtained since the 2003 article. Due to the ongoing trials related to Srebrenica no further results on Srebrenica may yet be published, however. Briefly, we can only say, based on publicly available sources, that the number of persons registered as missing or dead after the fall of Srebrenica in July 1995 has not increased significantly and that a large number of names of the identified persons also appear on the list of missing or dead persons that the 2003 article was based on. This shows that the list was almost complete, that it was not made up of false reports on missing persons, and that most of the missing persons were indeed killed. The list was compiled in 1999–2000 and first presented in the trial against Radislav Krstić (June 2000) and later against Vidoje Blagojević (Feb. 2004) and Slobodan Milošević (Feb. 2004). The identification process has recently progressed fast. On 10 July 2005, at the memorial ceremony in Potočari marking the tenth anniversary of the fall of Srebrenica, representatives of the International Commission for Missing Persons (ICMP) noted that out of the 7,789 Srebrenica victims registered in the ICMP database, for whom family members have come forward and donated a blood sample for DNA identification, 2, 079 had been identified up to the present (closed cases only, i.e. excluding the cases under review; according to the ICMP News Archive, 10 July 2005, http://www.ic-mp.org/home.php). In September 2005, the total of all unique DNA profiles identified from the remains exhumed from Srebrenica-related sites already covered 2,600 individuals and in March 2006 3,600 persons. A majority of these cases was also registered as missing in connection with the fall of Srebrenica. This is a strong indication that all or most of the missing persons were in fact killed. Thus, the information that has become available since the first ICTY study of the missing from Srebrenica shows that collecting and analysing data on victims of serious violations of IHL is a process that may last for a long time, perhaps never-ending. Conclusions on the number of victims of armed conflicts should take this into account.

Tabeau and Bijak, also affiliated with ICTY, put forward an example largely consistent with the IHL framework. They propose an analytical framework and a new estimate of deaths for the conflict in Bosnia and Herzegovina 1992–95. Their assessment is concentrated on victims whose death (or disappearance) may be linked to war operations in a straightforward manner. The estimate is based on carefully selected sources analysed jointly at the level of individual records, allowing for identity verification of victims, elimination of duplicates within each source, and exclusion of overlapping records between the sources. They consider their estimate to be much better founded than any other estimates that have been made, but believe that due to some yet unavailable sources the estimate is still incomplete and their project should be seen as work in progress.

The approach proposed by Tabeau and Bijak has frequently been used not only at the ICTY but also outside it, including Bosnian authorities, such as the Research and Documentation Centre in Sarajevo[2] led by Mirsad Tokača, or the Bosnian Serbs Commission for Srebrenica, that submitted their final report on Srebrenica in October 2004.

Counting conflict-related deaths in this way is usually very difficult, due to among other things, the lack, incompleteness, and deficiencies of data sources. Often demographic projection is the only way to produce such numbers. Neupert and Prum (Part IV) show how they obtained such estimates for Cambodia, by using the well-known cohort component approach, with assumptions formulated according to the demographic developments in the years preceding and following the turbulent 1970s. Several projection variants were made—most notably that the 1980 population was projected twice, both backwards and forwards—to estimate the effects of crisis versus continued normal mortality. The result of comparing the two different projection variants is about 2 million excess deaths in the 1970s. This coincides well with the violent periods of warfare and the terror regime of Khmer Rouge. The authors stress that excess deaths are just one of the many demographic consequences of the tragic decade: non-returning migrants, birth deficit, and distortions in the age composition of the population are other examples of the legacy of these years. In addition to giving a broad picture of the tragic decade, they offer a complex study of population development in Cambodia since the early 1960s up to the year 2020.

The next article in this section, by Bocquier and Maupeu, is a proposal to use an unusual source, namely press reports, to evaluate specific causes of death in Kenya. In the absence of reliable and unbiased sources in most African countries, press reports could be carefully inspected for this purpose, on condition that a political analysis of the relation between the press and the political power is conducted. Tested on data from a leading Kenyan newspaper, the method proposed here is used to conduct a historical and geographical analysis of deaths due to police violence, community clashes and banditry.

Finally, Lubkemann documents how migration during the civil war in Mozambique was organized primarily as a response to micro-level political struggles rather than merely to hostilities between national-level political actors. The populations of different local areas reacted very differently towards the war, including the support to the warring factions. The article provides convincing evidence

---

[2] The Research Centre is the successor of the BH State Commission for Gathering Facts on War Crimes. The Commission was established in 1992 and ceased its existence a few years after the war ended in 1995.

for the need to study local conditions and that anthropological approaches can make important contributions to the demographic analysis of forced migration.

The next three articles (Part V) are survey-based case studies related not only to mortality but also to other late consequences of war. The study by Singh et al. uses 1999–2000 data from North-western Uganda and Southern Sudan to analyse how forced migration and resulting residential arrangements impact under-five mortality for both the long-term displaced and the host populations. The analysis reveals that over the long run forced migration and living in refugee camps did not significantly affect under-five mortality.

Verwimp and Van Bavel explore the cumulated fertility of Rwandan refugee women and the survival of their children, using a national survey conducted in 1999–2001 of 6,420 former refugee and non-refugee households. Their findings support the old-age security theory of reproductive behaviour: refugee women have higher fertility but their children have lower chances of surviving. Moreover, newborn girls suffer more than boys.

In the final case study, Randall analyses the post-conflict demography of the Malian Tuareg in the context of historical demographic relationships and conflict-induced social, political and economic changes. In her study the post-conflict data collected in 2001 and the pre-conflict data from 1981 demonstrate a remarkable stability in the fertility and marriage regimes alongside declining child mortality. Randall concludes that an important demographic consequence of persecution and conflict may be an entrenchment of demographic behaviour, which reinforces the population's demographic and cultural identity.

4. Closing Remarks

This book takes a broad approach by bringing different contributions and disciplines together. It includes issues such as demographic causes and consequences of conflict, development of conflict and its impact over time and space, and counting casualties for prosecution of war crimes. The focus is, however, more on the demographic consequences of conflict than the causes of conflict. We would have liked to include more articles of demographic causes but the study of this is still in its infancy. We hope, however, that the four articles by Midlarsky, Besançon, Urdal and Ware with this approach will contribute to an increased interest in research on how demographic factors may be related to armed conflict. This is an exceedingly important area, where the results of research may have profound impact.

Of the demographic consequences of conflict, most contributions to this volume deal with mortality. There are multiple ways of assessing deaths from violent conflict, and estimates may vary greatly with the purpose of the analysis and the assumptions and definitions employed. While this is well documented in Landers' account of the indirect effects of war on mortality through increased disease, the majority of deaths in modern-day conflicts may also be primarily due to indirect causes. Severe under- and malnutrition, the collapse of health care infrastructure, and the spread of diseases like HIV/AIDS may have profound indirect effects on mortality in war-torn societies.

In their new dataset on conflict deaths, Lacina and Gleditsch limit the numbers to battle (or combat) deaths among both soldiers and civilians. While this is often regarded as a very restrictive approach, estimations used to prosecute war crimes may take an even narrower and more cautious perspective (Brunborg et al.; Fenrick). Demographers, on the other hand, often prefer to include both combat and non-combat war-related deaths, and war-related deaths which resulted, or not, from war crimes (Tabeau and Bijak). Demographic studies may also aim at estimating the overall impact of conflict, including indirect deaths due to disease and deteriorating living conditions and health services (Li and Wen; Neupert and Prum; Singh et al.; Verwimp and Van Bavel). A distinction is often made by the type of conflict, especially whether it is an inter-state conflict or a civil war. Li and Wen include both types, finding quite different mortality effects over time. Finally, genocide and ethnic cleansing are special cases of violent deaths that are not always related to armed conflict (Midlarsky); these deaths are usually not included in estimates of combat or other war-related deaths but represent deaths resulting from crimes against humanity. Thus, a simple definition of conflict-related deaths does not exist and depending on the goals of the analysis this definition might become broader or narrower.

Besides the problem of defining conflict-related deaths, it is usually difficult to measure the number of deaths, due to the chaotic circumstances in a war situation. Violent conflicts often destroy the very data that are needed to estimate their own consequences, such as vital statistics systems, statistical offices and so the most obvious possibilities for conducting censuses and surveys (Tabeau and Bijak; Bocquier and Maupeu). An extreme example is Stalin's execution of the persons in charge of the 1937 census of the Soviet Union to avoid publishing the embarrassing result of massive population losses due to one of the most catastrophic state-engineered harvest failures in history (Blum and Mespoulet, 2003).

Because of problems with standard statistical sources in conflict situations, a variety of methods and data are employed to estimate the number of deaths due to a conflict, from comparison of censuses before and after a conflict (Heuveline, 1998; Neupert and Prum), to collecting names and other personal characteristics of missing and killed persons (Brunborg et al.; Tabeau and Bijak). Other data sources include sample surveys (Verwimp and Van Bavel; Singh et al.), anthropological data (Lubkemann), and press reports (Boquier and Maupeu). The methods of analysis also vary tremendously, from standard demographic methods such as forwards and backwards projections (Neupert and Prum), matching of individual records (Brunborg et al.; Tabeau and Bijak), historical source criticism (Landers) and detailed comparative case studies (Midlarsky; Ware), to anthropological methods emphasizing the importance of local context (Lubkemann; Randall), as well as multivariate statistical analyses (Besançon; Li and Wen; Singh et al.; Urdal; Verwimp and Van Bavel).

Some of the results presented in this book challenge popular perceptions. Besançon challenges previous studies on inequality and conflict, suggesting that economic inequalities increase the likelihood of revolutionary war, but decrease the likelihood of ethnic war. Social inequalities, on the other hand, greatly increase the risk of ethnic war. Urdal finds that countries experiencing high population growth rates and pressure on land resources are not more susceptible to low-scale armed conflict, contrary to some of the influential case study literature in the field. On the other hand, several of the articles support previous findings. Landers support previous historical accounts when he shows that in pre-industrial Europe about three quarters of the deaths of soldiers were due to disease, that the soldiers had a much higher mortality due to disease than civilians, and that most of the civilians also died from epidemics and not from direct conflict-related killings and injuries. Supporting similar research from other settings, Singh et al. show that over the long run forced migration did not significantly impact under-five mortality in refugee camps in Uganda, which was *not* found to be higher than the mortality of non-refugee children living in the same area and also not higher than where they came from in Sudan.

Consequences of violent conflict other than deaths are less frequently studied but still several examples of these consequences are given in this book. As mentioned above, Lubkemann documents how migration during the civil war in Mozambique was organized primarily as a response to micro-level political struggles, while. Randall analyses the marital behavour of the Tuareg in Mali before, during and after conflict. The effects of conflict on fertility is studied in the context of the Cambodia conflict (Neupert and Prum).

With these summarising remarks, we hope that not only demographers working on conflict and violence, but also other demographers as well as researchers from other disciplines, particularly in peace research, will find these articles an exciting and worthwhile introduction to the subject.

References

Ball, P., W. Betts, F. Scheuren, J. Dudukovich, and J. Asher, 2002. 'Killings and Refugee Flow in Kosovo March–June 1999. A Report to the International Criminal Tribunal for the former Yugoslavia', 3 January 2002. Washington, DC: American Association for the Advancement of Science (AAAS) and American Bar Association Central and East European Law Initiative (ABA/CEELI).

Besançon, M.L., 2005. 'Relative Resources: Inequality in Ethnic Wars, Revolutions, and Genocides', *Journal of Peace Research* 42(4): 393–415.

Blum, A. and M. Mespoulet, 2003. '*L'Anarchie bureaucratique. Statistique et pouvoir sous Staline*', Paris: Editions La Découverte.

Bocquier, P. and H. Maupeu, 2005. 'Analysing low intensity conflict in Africa using press reports', *European Journal of Population* 21(2–3): 321–345.

Brunborg, H., 2001. 'Contribution of statistical analysis to the investigations of the international criminal tribunals', *Statistical Journal of the United Nations Economic Commission for Europe* 18: 227–238.

Brunborg, H., 2003. 'Needs for demographic and statistical expertise at the International Criminal Court'. Contribution to an expert consultation process on general issues relevant to the ICC Office of the Prosecutor. http://www.icc-cpi.int/otp/brunborg.pdf.

Brunborg, H., T.H. Lyngstad and H. Urdal, 2003. 'Accounting for genocide: How many were killed in Srebrenica?', *European Journal of Population* 19(3): 229–248.

Brunborg, H. and H. Urdal, 2000. 'Report on the number of missing and dead from Srebrenica'. Expert report prepared for the case of MILOSEVIC / BOSNIA (IT-02-54). http://hague.bard.edu/icty_info.html.

Collier, P. and A. Hoeffler, 2004. 'Greed and grievance in civil war', *Oxford Economic Papers* 56/4): 563–595.

Fenrick, W.J., 2005. 'International Humanitarian Law and combat casualties', *European Journal of Population* 21(2–3): 167–186.

Heuveline, J.H., 1998. 'Between one and three million: Towards the demographic reconstruction of a decade of Cambodian history (1970–79)'. *Population Studies*, 52, 49–65.

Human Rights Watch (HRW), 1991. *Needless Deaths in the Gulf War. Civilian Casualties During the Air Campaign and Violations of the Laws of War*, New York: Human Rights Watch.

ICTY Statute – Statute of the International Criminal Tribunal for the Former Yugoslavia (ICTY), 1993, American Society of International Law, 1993, *International Legal Materials*, 32, 1192–1201, Washington, D.C. (*"ICTY Statute"*).

Lacina, B. and N.P. Gleditsch, 2005. 'Monitoring trends in global combat: A new dataset of battle deaths', *European Journal of Population* 21(2–3): 145–166.

Landers, J., 2003. *The Field and the Forge: Population, Production and Power in the Pre-industrial West*. Oxford: Oxford University Press.

Landers, J., 2005. 'The destructiveness of pre-industrial warfare: political and technological determinants', *Journal of Peace Research* 42(4): 455–470.

Li, Q. and M. Wen, 2005. 'The immediate and lingering effects of armed conflict on adult mortality: A time-series cross-national analysis', *Journal of Peace Research* 42(4): 471–492.

Lubkemann, S.C., 2005. 'Migratory coping in wartime Mozambique: An anthropology of violence and displacement in 'fragmented wars'', *Journal of Peace Research* 42(4): 493–508.

Midlarsky, M.I., 2005. 'The demographics of genocide: refugees and territorial loss in the mass murder of European Jewry', *Journal of Peace Research* 42(4): 375–391.

Neupert, R.F. and V. Prum, 2005. 'Cambodia: Reconstructing the demographic stab of the past and forecasting the demographic scar of the future', *European Journal of Population* 21(2–3): 217–246.

Parker, G., 1988. *The Military Revolution*. Cambridge: Cambridge University Press.

Randall, S., 2005. 'The demographic consequences of conflict, exile and repatriation: A case study of Malian Tuareg', *European Journal of Population* 21(2–3): 291–320.

Ronsin, F., 1995. 'Guerre et nuptialité. Réflexions sur l'influence de la seconde Guerre mondiale et de deux autres, sur la nuptialité des Français', *Population* 50(1): 119–148.

Singh, K., U. Karunakara, G. Burnham and K. Hill, 2005. 'Forced migration and under-five mortality: A comparison of refugees and hosts in North-western Uganda and Southern Sudan', *European Journal of Population* 21(2–3): 247–270.

Spirer, H.F. and W. Seltzer 2005. 'Obtaining Evidence for the International Criminal Court Using Data and Quantitative Analysis. Revised draft, 22 November 2005.

Tabeau, E. and J. Bijak, 2005. 'Casualties of the 1990s War in Bosnia and Herzegovina: A critique of previous estimates and the latest results', *European Journal of Population* 21(2–3): 187–215.

Tabeau, E., J. Bijak, and N. Loncaric, 2003a. Death toll in the siege of Sarajevo, April 1992 to December 1995: A study of mortality based on eight large data sources. Expert report prepared for the case of MILOSEVIC/ BOSNIA (IT-02-54). http://www.un.org/icty/bhs/cases/milosevic/documents/docpros/expert/mil-rep030818b.htm.

Tabeau, E., M. Żółtkowski and J. Bijak, 2002. Population losses in the siege of Sarajevo, 10 September 1992 to 10 August 1994. Expert report prepared for GALIC (IT-98-29-I). http://www.un.org/icty/bhs/cases/milosevic/documents/docpros/expert/mil-rep-tabeau020513b.pdf

Tabeau, E., M. Żółtkowski, J. Bijak, and A. Hetland, 2003b. Ethnic Composition in and Internally Displaced Persons and Refugees from 47 Municipalities of Bosnia and Herzegovina, 1991 to 1997. Expert report prepared for the case of MILOSEVIC / BOSNIA (IT-02-54). http://hague.bard.edu/icty_info.html.

Urdal, H., 2005. 'People vs. Malthus: Population Pressure, Environmental Degradation, and Armed Conflict Revisited', *Journal of Peace Research* 42(4): 417–434.

Urdal, H., 2006.'A Clash of Generations? Youth Bulges and Political Violence', *International Studies Quarterly* 50(3): 607–629.

Verwimp, P. and J. Van Bavel, 2005. 'Child survival and fertility of refugees in Rwanda after the genocide', *European Journal of Population* 21(2–3): 271–290.

Ware, H., 2005. 'Demography, migration and conflict in the Pacific', *Journal of Peace Research* 42(4): 435–454.

Winter, J. M., 1976. 'Some aspects of the demographic consequences of the First World War in Britain', *Population Studies* 30(3): 539–552.

Winter, J. M., 1977. 'Britain's 'Lost generation' of the First World War'; *Population Studies* 31(3): 449–466.

PART I. DEMOGRAPHIC CAUSES OF CONFLICT

CHAPTER 1. THE DEMOGRAPHICS OF GENOCIDE: REFUGEES AND TERRITORIAL LOSS IN THE MASS MURDER OF EUROPEAN JEWRY*

MANUS I. MIDLARSKY
Department of Political Science, Rutgers University, USA

Abstract. This study seeks to distinguish between instances where genocide occurred and others where it might have been expected to occur but did not. Territorial loss, a corollary refugee influx, and a resulting contraction of socio-economic space are suggested to provide that distinction. Four analytic perspectives based on emotional reactions, class envy, prospect theory, and territoriality indicate the critical importance of loss. The theory is examined in the context of the mass murder of European Jewry including, of course, Germany and Austria, and all European German allies that allowed an indigenous genocidal impulse, willingness to comply with German genocidal policies, or an ability to resist German pressures for Jewish deportation. Three instances of perpetrating states—Italy, Vichy France, and Romania—emerge from the analysis. The latter two governments willingly collaborated with the Germans in victimizing their own Jewish citizenry, while Italy was on a genocidal path just prior to the German occupation. All five states mentioned above were found to experience considerable territorial loss and a contraction of socio-economic space. Bulgaria and Finland, on the other hand, actually expanded their borders at the start of the war and saved virtually all of their Jewish citizens. The importance of loss is demonstrated not only cross-sectionally, in the comparison between the five victimizers, on the one hand, and Bulgaria and Finland, on the other, but also diachronically, in the changing behavior over time of the genocidal and perpetrating states.

1. Introduction

Why does genocide occur in some instances, but not in others in which it might be expected to occur? This article examines one factor that can distinguish between the two. It examines the consequences of demographic change, especially refugee influx, frequently associated with territorial loss, on the propensity for states to commit or participate in genocide. Refugees fill up the state's territory, thereby shrinking the population's spatial environment; territorial loss has the same appearance of contraction. Refugees from the lost territories or neighboring states also can signify a status reversal vis-à-vis competing groups. If that reversal also implies the loss of political power, then genocide can ensue. However, if territorial loss and a corollary refugee influx are absent, then genocide would be far less likely to occur.

This article centers on the mass murder of European Jewry during 1941–45—the principal genocidal component of the Holocaust—both in its origins in Germany and Austria, and in its implementation in Nazi-dominated Europe. At

This chapter was previously published in *Journal of Peace Research*, vol. 42, no. 4, 2005, pp. 375–391.

Helge Brunborg et al. (eds.), The Demography of Armed Conflict, 19–38.

least four analytically distinct theoretical perspectives inform this study. First, as physical space contracts, the presence of considerable numbers of refugees may lead to an emotional reaction that in turn can result in brutality or even murder. As Blakeslee (2001) puts it: "People who are emotionally wrought by anger or disgust, say over ... the condition of the downtrodden, may decide that certain brutal actions are morally acceptable." This conclusion is based on recent findings that decisions having moral import are far more likely to be based on emotional reactions than on reasoned deliberation (Greene et al., 2001). Identification with the downtrodden because of ethno-religious commonality may lead to brutal actions against those, often of a different ethnicity, who are perceived to be at fault in generating the refugee influx.

Additional evidence is found in studies indicating that anger, in contrast to sadness or a neutral emotion, increases the probability of negative reactions to people of a different ethnicity (Bodenhausen, Sheppard and Kramer, 1994; DeSteno et al., 2004). External threat can stimulate anger, which in turn is most frequently directed against members of a group different from one's own.

Second, if those perceived to be at fault also arrive as refugees or are viewed as comfortable and wealthy, then they can be targeted for massacre or, ultimately, genocide. The intersection of migration, ethno-religious identity, and social class is combustible. Refugees sharpen an existential contrast with the "other" (Jews as the anti-German), especially if the victims are, on the whole, wealthier and/or more visible than the majority. Competing for the same resources in a shrunken environment, refugees and "native" populations can come to see each other as inevitable opponents in a contracting socio-economic space (Midlarsky, 1999).

Introducing the element of social class in the context of refugees competing with the "other", Hitler himself remarked, "our upper classes, who've never bothered about the hundreds of thousands of German emigrants or their poverty, give way to a feeling of compassion regarding the fate of the Jews whom we claim the right to expel" (Hitler, [4 April 1942] 2000: 397).

Third, prospect theory also tells us that losses are valued more highly than gains (Kahneman and Tversky, 1979, 2000; Levy, 2000). Experimental evidence has consistently demonstrated the asymmetry between losses and gains, even to the extent that, in contrast to gains, losses can generate extreme responses. Losses as the result of a shrinking spatial environment, therefore, may have a magnified role in the public consciousness, out of all proportion to the real-world consequences of loss. Again, brutality may be justified in the mind of the observer.

Fourth, the importance of territoriality in its own right should not be minimized, especially if the presence of refugees serves as a continual reminder of the territorial loss. Territory is so fundamental to state security that massive brutalities may be justified in the name of the state. When compared with general foreign policy disputes and those involving contrasting regime types, territorial disputes have a higher probability of escalating to war (Senese and Vasquez, 2004; Vasquez, 2000; Vasquez and Henehan, 2001; Huth, 1996). This suggests the fundamental importance of territoriality, even in comparison with other issues that are typically thought to be critical in fomenting conflict.

A contributing element to the importance of territoriality stems from the signaling of state weakness associated with territorial loss in time of war. Territory can be used to protect the state, as in a buffer zone between the state core and its enemies. When that territory is lost, state weakness can be perceived by both defenders of the state and its external opponents. Under certain conditions, that weakness can lead to elimination of internal "enemies" in order to buttress the newly vulnerable state (Midlarsky, 2000).

In addition to Germany and Austria, included in the analysis are states within the Nazi orbit that enjoyed considerable domestic autonomy in policymaking at the time of the German pressures for Jewish deportation. These states turn out to be German allies in Europe.

An examination of all such European German allies shows that governments of countries that experienced substantial contraction, like France or Romania, or Italy in mid-1943, tended to be more complicit with the Germans than others such as Bulgaria and Finland, which actually expanded in 1940–41. When truncated to the borders of the rump Vichy regime, France, the traditional home of continental liberalism, in its own anti-Jewish laws actually *preceded* Germany in promulgating anti-Semitic legislation within the occupied zone. Hungary in 1919 and Romania in 1940, experiencing severe territorial losses, would, like France, for the first time in the interwar period also promulgate anti-Semitic legislation. Indeed, for France, this would be the first anti-Semitic legislation since the time of Napoleon I. Bulgaria and Finland, on the other hand, expanding their borders, saved the vast majority of their Jews.

2. Demographic and social antecedents of the Holocaust in Germany and Austria

In the case of Germany after World War I, the dimension of loss is magnified by the appearance of refugees from the lost territories. A contraction of socio-economic space had been effected with visible consequences. If, as did many Germans, one measures the territorial losses from June 1918 when much of Eastern Europe and Ukraine, and portions of France and Belgium, were under German and Austro-Hungarian authority, then the contraction would appear to be immense (Evans, 2004: 52–53). While in the German election of 1912, it became apparent that anti-Semitic political parties had lost virtually all of their influence (Melson, 1992: 119), the same certainly could not be said of the post-World War I period.

Eastern territories lost to Poland gave rise to German-identified refugees, as did the Baltic states now governed by indigenous populations unwilling to continue experiencing German land ownership. Many of these Baltic Germans, including the Nazi ideologist Alfred Rosenberg, were to become rabid supporters of the Nazi cause. These migrations and expulsions continued down to the start of World War II. According to the German consul-general at Thorn, writing to the Foreign

Office in October 1938:

> In view of the severe pressure to which the German minority in Poland is subjected, for [sic] it finally sees no alternative but to emigrate to the Reich.... The continual measures oppressive [sic] of the Polish administration as recently evinced in the expulsions from the frontier zone and in the closing of schools, etc., are sufficient evidence that it is impossible for the Germans to continue living here, and that they must leave the country if they are to survive. The prospects of waging a successful battle against the Polish authorities, without considerable active support from home, is so poor that the enormous emigration of earlier days and again of the past two years has seriously weakened the German community here. (German Foreign Office, 1940: 141)

At the same time, many Jews crossed into Germany fleeing the pogroms of Petlyura and other Ukrainians, as well as White Russian nationalists. The image of both the German and the Jew on an equally uprooted footing must have been anathema to the traditional German, indeed ubiquitous European Christian view, that the Jew was to be held in a subordinate position.

Immigration of Eastern Jews into German-speaking lands had a tortuous history. As early as the 17th century, German rulers clearly distinguished between native and immigrant Jews, often requiring the former to keep out the would-be newer arrivals. During the Imperial period, if a German woman married an alien, she lost her citizenship (Wertheimer, 1987: 159). Both German Christians and Jews looked down upon the *Ostjuden.* Upon returning from a trip to Russian-ruled Poland, Hugo Ganz described the "repulsive" Jews:

> Their laziness, their filth, their craftiness, their perpetual readiness to cheat cannot help but fill the Western European with very painful feelings and unedifying thoughts, in spite of all the teachings of history and all the desire to be just. The evil wish arises that in some painless way the world might be rid of these disagreeable objects, or the equally inhuman thought [arises] that it would really be no great pity if this part of the Polish population did not exist at all. Either we must renounce our ideas of cleanliness and honesty or find a great part of Eastern Hebrews altogether unpleasant. (Wertheimer, 1987: 148)

Speaking as a German Jew, Lion Wolff remarked: "The Russian Jews have multiplied in Germany like frogs... they serve as cantors, functionaries, etc. But they do not know the language of the state, and therefore they evoke a justified German hatred for Jews.... The first and true cause of German anti-Semitism is known to all but no one dares to reveal it: It is the coming of foreigners... to Germany" (Wertheimer, 1987: 158). Russian Jewish students were rapidly entering German universities, prompting Chancellor von Bülow to declare in 1904 that Germany "will not be led by the nose by such *Schnorrers* [sic] and conspirators" (Wertheimer, 1987: 65).

A contrast between German Jews and their East European co-religionists is found in their differential fertility rates. Whereas in 1910, German Jewish females had an average of 1.23 children under the age of 15 in their households, the corresponding figure for East European Jews in Germany was more than twice as high, 2.96 (Wertheimer, 1987: 85).

By 1925, the German Jewish population had grown to 565,000. But more important, at least for the Nazis, was its prominence. As of 1930, Jews owned approximately two-thirds of Germany's larger department and chain stores and almost half of Germany's textile firms. At least half of the German industry in Upper Silesia, including its largest steel manufacturer, was owned or managed by Jews. The two largest publishing houses (Ullstein and Mosse) were owned by Jews. In addition to prominence in journalism as well as in the arts and sciences, more than half of the lawyers in Berlin were Jewish (Sachar, 2002: 242).

As bad as the situation was in Germany before World War II, it was worse in Austria, especially Vienna, site of Hitler's early political education and a target for Jewish immigrants from Galicia and elsewhere within the Austro-Hungarian Empire. Post-World War I Austria, of course, was a rump state vastly shrunken in size from its prewar imperial expanse. During World War II, a disproportionately large number of concentration camp guards and SS men were Austrian.

A common political framework greatly facilitated migration from one part of the Empire to another. Between 1860 and 1910, the Jewish population of Vienna rose from 6,200 to 175,300, roughly a quadrupling from 2.2% to 8.7% (Hamann, 1999: 326). By the end of World War I, their number had increased beyond 10%, because of both a somewhat larger number of Jews (200,000) and a smaller total Viennese population (1,865,000) as the result of the privation and emigration stemming from the war (Sachar, 2002: 179).

Because of the tolerant reign of Franz Josef II until his death in 1916, Austro-Hungarian Jews were protected, even rewarded with medals and titles by the monarch, grateful for their contribution to the imperial economy and society (Hamann, 1999: 327–328). Wealthy Jews occupied newly constructed mansions in Vienna that were the envy of the aristocracy. In 1912, almost half of the secondary school population of Vienna was Jewish (47.4%). Nearly one-third of all university students were Jewish; in 1913, Jews constituted more than 40% of all medical students in Vienna. In excess of 25% of the law students were Jewish. To gauge the rapidity of this demographic change, one has only to note that of 681 lawyers in Vienna in 1889, over half, 394, were Jewish. Two decades earlier, the number was 33. By the mid-1930s, Jews constituted 62% of Vienna's lawyers and 47% of physicians. A minimum of 70% of the city's wholesale and retail businesses were in Jewish hands (Sachar, 2002: 179).

In Germany, a sign of the times was a 1919 memorandum from the Reichsbank to the Interior Minister:

> Because of their shrewdness, their connections with one another and with third parties, and their skill in using loopholes in the regulations... to get around the legal requirements, a complete success against their mischief is unlikely to be achieved... unless it proves possible to keep these unwanted foreign guests, whose presence from a political as well as from a food and housing perspective is not exactly advantageous, out of Germany. (Feldman, 1993: 201–202)

After World War I, over 70,000 recent Jewish immigrants from the east were found in Berlin alone, most of them illegal. Many of these Jews, without proper means of support, along with large segments of German society, were engaged in black marketeering, which further alienated many Germans already inclined to anti-Semitic thinking. "By 1920, the term *Volksschädling* had become a widely accepted code word for the Jew, a term used to identify those who injured the people but which also suggested a noxious insect whose elimination could only serve the public good" (Feldman, 1993: 203).

In Vienna in that year, there occurred a concerted campaign against Vienna's Eastern Jews, many of them recently arrived, including physical violence. And in 1923, all Jews who had settled in Bavaria since 1914 were expelled—principally, of course, the Eastern Jewish refugees. Between 5 November and 8 November 1923, the 20th century's first German pogrom occurred. In Berlin's ghetto, Jews were robbed and beaten by a rampaging mob estimated to be approximately 10,000 in size (Aschheim, 1982: 242–243). Soon, German and Austrian battlefield losses during World War II, beginning in August 1941, would signal that the losses of World War I had not ended in 1918, but would likely be amplified by the unfolding of vicious combat on the Eastern Front (Burrin, 1994; Midlarsky, 2005).

3. Perpetrators and exceptions

Contraction of socio-economic space as part of the domain of losses can help us understand not only the onset of genocide in certain instances, but even the extent of collaboration with the initiators. In the following analysis, states to be examined are those with indigenous governments unfettered by military occupation and having some freedom of policy choice. Perpetrators are states which openly collaborated with the Nazis in victimizing their own Jewish citizenry. Exceptions are states that did not do so. I choose these cases because only here can we observe (1) the indigenous genocidal impulse, (2) willingness to comply with German genocidal policies, or (3) the ability to resist German pressures for Jewish deportation. These instances stand in contrast to cases of direct occupation or absolute dependence on the genocidal state that pre-ordain the policy outcome.

All European states in the Nazi orbit (Hilberg, 1985: 544; Fein, 1979: 40–41; Murray and Millett, 2000) were examined for the extent of their decisionmaking autonomy in regard to their own citizenry. All countries directly occupied by German forces ultimately dedicated to the slaughter were excluded. These include Czechoslovakia (March 1939), Poland (September 1939), Norway (April 1940), Belgium, the Netherlands, and Luxembourg (May 1940), Greece and Yugoslavia (April 1941), the Soviet Union (June 1941; partial occupation), Denmark (August 1943), Albania (September 1943), and Hungary (March 1944).

Although Hungary was an ally of Germany, with considerable domestic autonomy that even protected Hungarian Jews stranded in Germany during the war, in addition to Jewish citizens within Hungary itself, that policy was reversed after the German occupation (Braham, 1981: 255). The Danes, with Swedish help, did rescue almost the entire Jewish community of Denmark, but not as a consequence of policy choices made by Danish governmental leaders who had already been removed from office by the German occupying forces (Goldberger, 1987).

Successor states such as Slovakia and Croatia explicitly created by the Nazis in their subjugation respectively of Czechoslovakia and Yugoslavia also were excluded. Not only were these states thoroughly dependent on their creator, Nazi Germany, but their fictive independence was emphasized by the United States' non-recognition, before US entry into the war (*Keesing's Contemporary Archives; Foreign Relations of the United States 1940–1942*). In contrast, the United States did recognize Vichy France as a sovereign entity (Burrin, 1996: 77). All genuinely neutral states also were excluded.

These exclusions leave the set of European German allies (including the formally neutral but militarily constrained Vichy France), Italy, Romania, Bulgaria, and Finland, which were allowed substantial leeway in their domestic policies by the Germans in order to maintain their support for the war.

3.1. ITALY: A GENOCIDAL TRAJECTORY

Although the entirety of Jewish genocidal victimization in Italy occurred after German occupation, Italy nevertheless deserves comment because its behavior just prior to German occupation is suggestive of the central importance of loss. Because of Italy's status as Germany's principal European great-power ally, it was, like Finland, allowed substantial freedom in its domestic policies. Yet, German pressure was repeatedly placed on the Italian government to release Jews for deportation. One of these sources of pressure emanated from the presence of Jews in Italian-administered areas of former Yugoslavia. Appalled by the deadly brutality of the Croatian fascist Ustaše toward Serbs and Jews, Italian military forces interceded to protect as many as they could from the Ustaše, and then later from the Germans intent on Jewish deportation. A second source of German pressure was the relatively large concentration of free Jews in Italian-occupied France in the area of Nice.

It has been suggested that this early experience in protecting endangered populations under Italian rule, beginning in 1941, led to their continued refusal to allow German deportation of Jews throughout Mussolini's tenure in office prior to German occupation (Carpi, 1977: 505; Steinberg, 1990: 133). Perhaps this fact, more than any other, led to the positive view among scholars of Italy's record during the Holocaust, a view that was actually well deserved prior to the Allied invasion of Sicily.

This relatively benign situation changed, however, after the experience of territorial loss, first in North Africa and then in Sicily. On 13 May 1943, the Axis forces surrendered in Tunis, leading to a reported loss of morale among Italian troops in Yugoslavia (Steinberg, 1990: 138). On 10 July, the Allies invaded Sicily, making rapid advances on all fronts. By 15 July, Guido Lospinoso, an Italian police officer charged with Jewish affairs in Italian-occupied France, was ordered by his superiors in Rome to deport 1,000–1,200 Jews. According to Zuccotti (2000: 132), "Such a direct and unequivocal order could not have been issued without Mussolini's approval, and Lospinoso would not have been able to evade it. The Jews concerned were saved only by Mussolini's fall a few days later".

Prior to this time, Mussolini had wavered on all German requests for deportation, ultimately declining to deport the Jews. Now, in the midst of experiencing the loss of nearly 10% of core Italian territory in Sicily, his position was unequivocal. State weakness, signaled by the loss of Sicily and an expected immediate Allied invasion of the Italian peninsula, ultimately proved decisive. German military support would be required to salvage his regime, and so the Germans had to be propitiated by deporting the foreign Jews. Given the extent of Italian state weakness, had Mussolini stayed in office, it is most likely that he would have extended the deportation to Italian Jews as well, especially in the light of his agreement with Jewish deportation in his later tenure as leader of the rump northern Italian state under German occupation (Zuccotti, 2000: 291–292). Among these Italian Jews was the young Primo Levi, a future Nobel laureate, and a suspected suicide many years after his Auschwitz experience.

3.2. VICHY FRANCE

Shortly after formation of the regime, in August 1940, Vichy repealed the *loi Marchandeau* (Marchandeau law), which had outlawed any attack in the press on a specific group of people on account of race or religion and designed to arouse hatred against them (Marrus and Paxton, 1995: 3). Repeal of this law opened the floodgates to much anti-Semitic writing in the press.

In October, a series of laws directed specifically at Jews was enacted. On 3 October, the *Statut des Juifs* defined who was Jewish according to the state, and then proceeded to exclude Jews from top positions "in the public service, from the officer corps and from the ranks of noncommissioned officers, and from professions that influence public opinion: teaching, the press, radio, film, and theater" (Marrus and Paxton, 1995: 3). As Marrus and Paxton (1995: 7) comment, "Without any possible doubt, Vichy had begun its own antisemitic career before the first German text appeared, and without direct German order".

But this tawdry beginning was not to be the end of it. When the deportations to the east began in the summer of 1942, the Vichy police cooperated fully, indeed as the Germans requested. The Germans simply did not have the manpower to carry out the required administrative functions, including those involving Jews, throughout all of France. Vichy was created, in part, to serve these functions, while maintaining political neutrality in the war. According to Heinz Röthke, the SS lieutenant in charge of Jewish affairs within the German police hierarchy in France, "The entire operation in the southern French territory was much more dependent on the French police than in the formerly occupied territory. The German strike force there could only exercise a weak supervision over the operation" (Levendel, 1999: 236).

Vichy neutrality was not a mere fictive creation of the Nazi regime. On all matters of internal administration, negotiations were required between the Germans in the occupied zone and the Vichy authorities. Yet, in the matter of the deportations, the Germans could rely on a rival homegrown anti-Semitism to effect the required cooperation. Little if any "arm-twisting" was required.

The extent to which Vichy cooperation was required may be gleaned from the following statistics. Under conditions of full cooperation from Vichy, in the summer and autumn of 1942 when the deportations began, approximately 42,000 Jews were sent to their deaths. Roughly one-third of these were sent at Vichy's initiative from the unoccupied zone. In 1943, after forced labor of European youth required, in the end, 750,000 French males in Germany and a consequent diminution of French enthusiasm for cooperation with the Germans, only 22,000 Jews were deported. And in 1944, after the Germans were left more to their own devices, 12,500 were deported.

Alois Brünner, an SS captain with a formidable reputation for efficiency in his earlier successful actions in deporting Jews from Vienna and Salonika, Greece, failed almost entirely in late 1943 without the support of the French police. After the Italian war effort collapsed in the summer of 1943, Brünner was sent to the Italian zone of occupation in the Côte d'Azur to arrest and deport the Jews that heretofore had enjoyed the protection of the Italian authorities. Left with only the support of his German staff, only 1,900 Jews of the estimated 25,000 in the region were found and deported (Webster, 1991: 170–171).

Inescapably, one arrives at the conclusion that (1) there was considerable initial enthusiasm for the deportations on the part of the Vichy government, and (2) the Germans absolutely required the cooperation of that government. As the German consul in Vichy remarked in February 1942, after many conversations with Vichy leaders, "the French government would be happy to get rid of the Jews somehow, without attracting too much attention" (Burrin, 1996: 156).

Why should this have been the case? One answer is to be found in an acute contraction of socio-economic space, much as we saw in the histories of Germany, Austria, and territorial losses in Italy prior to their genocidal activities. Three-fifths of France was occupied by the Germans, and the remaining two-fifths was limited as to political maneuverability (required neutrality), size of the armed forces, and availability of resources for the German war effort. This was a major contraction from France's former status as a European great power and one that only 21 years earlier had, with the other victors, dictated the Peace of Versailles to the defeated Germans.

Indeed, the preceding large outbreak of anti-Semitism in France occurred after the first modern French contraction upon the defeat of 1871 and the loss of Alsace-Lorraine to the new united Imperial Germany. French Jews fled the conquered territories, and according to Webster (1991: 10), "There was a flood of what were to become familiar caricatures of hook-nosed, repulsively ugly, rapacious Jews barely able to make themselves understood through thick German accents—images that were copied by Pétain's propaganda services".

Refugees are a significant indicator of socio-economic contraction and a strong provocation in their own right. Here, in the case of Vichy, they performed a similar function. Almost immediately after constitution of the Vichy regime, Germany was dumping its unwanted Jews across the demarcation line into the unoccupied zone, even over fierce French objections. Only the most intense French protests prevented over 270,000 Jews from being transported into Vichy France. Some trains containing Jews were simply sent back to the occupied zone by the French authorities. On their own, many French Jews fled the occupied zone for what was perceived to be the relative safety of Vichy.

Jews were prominent in politics, with Léon Blum as premier leading the Popular Front coalition of 1936, and in industry, with Henri Citroën establishing a leading car company and Bloch heading an aviation manufacturer that later, after the war, was to become Dassault, Europe's largest exporter of combat aircraft. All of the ills plaguing French society during the 1930s, and there were many—parliamentary disorder, a declining birthrate, and economic decline—would be attributed to the Jewish presence.

Even before establishment of the Vichy regime, France had experienced large-scale immigration and refugee arrival. Now, with the contraction of French socio-economic space—territorially, economically, and in a radically diminished international stature—foreigners, especially Jews, could be convenient targets. For this reason, the Vichy French insisted on filling the early German deportation requirements with foreign or recently naturalized Jews. Initially, the Germans went along with this French preference, but later, many French-born Jews also went to their deaths with their foreign-born co-religionists. By mid-1942, the Germans had no interest in distinguishing between native or foreign Jews; all were targeted for extinction. Nevertheless, to placate the French, whose cooperation they required, the earliest transports contained few French Jews. Later, when the internment camps containing the foreign Jews (built by Vichy) had been emptied and deportation quotas still had to be filled, French Jews were routinely included in the transports to the east.

3.3. ROMANIA

Romania also confirms the importance of truncation as a key stimulant to domestic anti-Semitism, leading ultimately to the perpetration of mass murder. While Hungary was truncated after World War I and, for the first time since 1867, promulgated anti-Semitic legislation, Romania was expanded at that time and, for the first time, ceased its earlier anti-Jewish campaigns. Later, however, just prior to its entry into World War II, when it too experienced territorial and population losses, the first anti-Semitic legislation of the interwar period was passed. The case of Romania, therefore, is important, because it provides a longitudinal demonstration that territorial gain after World War I was associated with liberal policies towards minorities, while losses in 1940 were associated first with anti-Semitic legislation and then with widespread massacre.

After World War I and the dismemberment of Austria-Hungary (complete) and Imperial Russia (partial), Romania was one of the states that gained most from this process. As of 1920, the territory of Romania doubled, absorbing Transylvania, Bessarabia, Bukovina, and Cişana, and in the process, Romania was transformed from a relatively homogenous state to one with 28% of its population composed of non-Romanian minorities. They included Magyar, German, Jewish, Ukrainian, Bulgarian, and Turko-Tatar minorities (Jelavich, 1983: 122–124). The addition of these territories was to accentuate the prominence and visibility of Jews. As in Hungary, neither the feudal aristocracy nor the peasantry was prepared to engage in economic development. This was left to the Jews as an entrepreneurial middle class. Thus,

> By the middle of the interwar era, Jews controlled the bulk of the private capital in the export, transportation, insurance, textile, leather, electrotechnical, chemical, housing, printing, and publishing industries. Though their access to the universities was restricted by statutory limitations and extralegal violence, they were also strongly represented in the legal, medical, dental, journalistic, and banking professions. Though only 4.2% of the total population, they constituted 30.1, 27, and 23.6%, respectively, of the town populations of Bukovina, Bessarabia and Moldavia, and 14.3% of the entire country's urban population. In such cities as Chişinău (Kishinev) and Cernăusţi, . . . where the Jews accounted for 52.6 and 44.9% of the population, most store signs were in Hebrew letters. (Jelavich, 1983: 160)

Even in Regat (historic) Romania, the Jewish population of Iaşi, the largest city in Moldavia, numbered 42% of the total (Boia, 2001: 173). As in Hungary, the Jews were disproportionately visible economically and socially. "In the textile industry 80% of the engineers were Jews, in the Army Medical Corps 1,960 doctors were Jewish, 460 belonged to other minority groups, and only 1,400 were Romanian; 70% of journalists were Jews; and in the universities, where, in 1925, 27% of the student body had been of foreign origin, the proportion in 1934 had risen to 43%" (Weber, 1965: 529).

The sense of foreign, especially Jewish domination was palpable. According to a poet of the Iron Guard, the premier Romanian fascist organization,

> You've come with foreign laws
> To steal my stock, my song, my poverty;
> Out of my sweat you've built your property,
> And taken from our children for your whores.
> (Weber, 1965: 529)

The "foreign laws" mentioned by the poet most likely were elements of the 1923 constitution, promulgated at the behest of the Allied powers, granting Jews citizenship rights equal to all other Romanians (Nagy-Talavera, 2001: 357).

According to loanid (2000: 12), "The period between 1923 and 1938 represented a golden age of human rights in Romania". But the rise of anti-Semitic movements, such as the Christian National Defense League and the Iron Guard, clouded the horizons. Nevertheless, no anti-Semitic legislation was proposed until the actual takeover of Romanian territory, first by the Soviet Union (Bessarabia and northern Bukovina, June 1940), then by Hungary (northern Transylvania, August 1940), and finally by Bulgaria (southern Dobrudja, September 1940) (Jelavich, 1983: 226). Just as Hungary earlier was forced by the victorious Allies to cede territory at the Trianon Palace in 1920, so too now in 1940 Romania was forced to cede territory by the allied Soviet and Nazi governments, united now in their eastern policies by the Nazi–Soviet pact of June 1939. When the Romanians consulted the Germans upon the receipt of Soviet territorial demands, they were advised to acquiesce (Jelavich, 1983: 225). Germany also was instrumental in effecting the losses to Hungary and Bulgaria.

These cessions "caused enormous public indignation, especially the surrender of the Transylvanian lands" (Jelavich, 1983: 226). As a contemporary Romanian historian, Iosif Drăgan, put it without embellishment, "With the support of the Soviet army, Party activists were brought in, under new, Romanianized names, people like Ana Rabinovici-Pauker, Leonte Răutu (Rotmann), Mihail Roller, Silviu Brucan, Teoharia Georgescu, Lászlo Lukács (Vasile Luca) and the Bulgarian Borilă, etc.... The leadership of the Party was monopolized by these allogenic elements" (Boia, 2001: 172).

Now the Romanian truncation to the boundaries of the Old Kingdom (Regat) existing prior to World War I would yield anti-Semitic legislation. The law of 8 August 1940 defined Jews racially in even more draconian fashion then did the Nazis. Another law forbade marriage between Jews and gentiles, while directly citing the 1935 Nuremberg laws as precedent (Ioanid, 2000: 20–22). Further legislation restricted Jewish access to education and entry into both the medical and military professions. Economic legislation severely limited Jewish business activity and further restricted Jewish life circumstances. Jewish rural property was nationalized, and Jewish civil servants were purged.

Iaşi was the location of the first large-scale massacre of the Holocaust on Romanian soil. In addition to its anti-Semitic traditions of over a century, because of its proximity to the Soviet frontier, "it became the focus of many of the anti-Semitic measures that accompanied plans to join Germany's invasion of the USSR" (Ioanid, 2000: 63). The terms "Jew" and "Communist" were virtually inter-changeable, as in the order by Ion Antonescu, the Romanian head of state, to compile lists of "all Jews, Communist agents, or sympathizers in each region" (Ioanid, 2000: 4). Worse was Order No. 4147, issued at about the same time, which demanded the expulsion of all Jews between the ages of 18 and 60 from northeastern Moldavia (the Iaşi region) in expectation of fighting in the region.

The presence of large numbers of Jews in the region was displeasing to both the German and Romanian officials (Ioanid, 2000: 64). Iaşi alone held nearly 50,000 Jews. In cooperation with the German Gestapo and the SD (intelligence arm of the SS), the Romanian Secretariat of the Secret Intelligence Service (SSI) prepared the expulsions. At the same time, former Iron Guardists were informed of the impending expulsions and likelihood of a pogrom.

A raid against Iaşi by the Soviet air force provided the spark for the pogrom. Damage was minor but rumors spread that the entire Jewish population of Iaşi was in league with the Red Army. Further rumors of Iaşi natives flying Soviet aircraft fanned the flames still further. On 20 June, four days after the beginning of Operation Barbarossa, the pogrom began in earnest. It lasted several days until 29 June. Although it is difficult to gain accurate estimates of the number of Jews killed, the minimum is probably about 900, with more forthright testimony from a witness estimating the number of dead at 3,000–4,000 (Ioanid, 2000: 77).

Iaşi was only the first of many massacres of Jews that were to take place in nearby Bessarabia and Bukovina, territories that had been transferred to Soviet control in 1940 but were now under German and Romanian authority. Mihai Antonescu, a relative of Ion Antonescu and deputy premier, supported the forced "migration" of Jews from Bessarabia and Bukovina. This attitude of "blame" for the loss of these territories in 1940 was to characterize much of Romanian Jewish policy. Frequent massacres occurred immediately after the German invasion of the Soviet Union.

Jews were now interned in transit camps throughout Bessarabia. In October, deportations to Ukraine began. During the first months of the war, it is estimated that at least 65,000 Jews from Bessarabia and Bukovina were killed in mass murders, in the transit camps and during deportation (Ioanid, 2000: 172–173). If we add the number of Jews deported who died in southwestern Ukraine, the number reaches approximately 130,000. Adding to this the number of native Ukrainian Jews in Odessa and elsewhere killed by the Romanian and German authorities, the number reaches approximately 250,000 murdered under Romanian jurisdiction. According to Hilberg (1985: 759), "no country, besides Germany, was involved in massacres of Jews on such a scale".

3.4. BULGARIA: AN EXCEPTION

Instead of relinquishing territory at the start of World War II, Bulgaria actually gained. Indeed, territories lost in 1913 at the end of the Second Balkan War, and at the end of World War I, were mostly recouped. As the result of German intercession on its behalf in 1940, Bulgaria received southern Dobrudja; after Bulgaria's adherence to the Axis in March 1941, one month later the Bulgarians assumed control (but not annexation) of Macedonia and Thrace (Todorov, 2001: 4–5). And in contrast to Italy, France, and Romania, virtually the entire Bulgarian Jewish community was saved.

Several reasons were advanced for the failure of the Nazi plan. First, King Boris III appeared to play a significant role in refusing to allow the deportation of Bulgaria's Jews (Chary, 1972: 184). Here the analysis focuses on the very top of the decisionmaking hierarchy to explain the absence of deportations. Second, also focusing on the apex of the hierarchy, are those who credit the Bulgarian Orthodox Church, especially Metropolitan Stefan and others who followed his lead, such as Kiril of Plovdiv and Neofit of Vida. Kiril was especially adamant in his opposition to anti-Semitism, promising to lie down on the tracks before the deportation trains if the deportations were actually carried out (Chary, 1972: 90). Stefan's frequent messages to the king opposing the deportations are said to have been influential.

Third, the Bulgarian National Assembly is said to have been influential in mustering a protest against the deportations that led to their postponement and ultimate cancellation. Here, a minority of parliamentarians, although a sizeable one from the government's own party, protested this operation, never achieving abrogation of the decree, but postponing it just enough for other political forces to emerge that would render the temporary permanent (Chary, 1972: 190).

More recently, the focus has shifted to an emphasis on one member of the National Assembly in particular, its vice-chairman, Dimitâr Peshev. It was he who organized the petition signed by one-third of the government's own party members. When he heard of a roundup of Jews in his own electoral district, the town of Kyustendil, he acted. Attempting to speak to Bogdan Filov, the prime minister, he was allowed to see the minister of internal affairs, Petâr Gabrovski, in charge of the deportations. Peshev pointed out to Gabrovski that these unpublicized deportations violated Bulgarian constitutional law; Gabrovski initially denied any knowledge of this operation. Peshev and his colleagues Mikhalev, Ikonomov, and other deputies refused to leave Gabrovski's office until all telephone or telegraph contacts had been made that were necessary to free the Jews who had been arrested (Todorov, 2001: 37).

In order to ensure that the arrests would not shortly resume, Peshev organized the parliamentary petition that ultimately led to his removal as vice-chairman of the National Assembly, but postponed further any deportation plans to the more distant future (Todorov, 2001: 39). By then, the war would nearly be over, and even the thought of such mass killing was abhorrent.

Yet, not denying the goodness that Todorov attributes to Peshev, this is not the whole story. It is instructive to examine the manner in which Peshev was informed. When Bulgarians in Kyustendil heard of the arrests, they quickly made plans to send 40 of their number to the National Assembly in Sofia. After deliberation, they chose only four, all non-Jews, to plead the case of their Jewish townspeople (Todorov, 2001: 9–10). Although Peshev had already heard of the arrests through other avenues, he was heartened by the concern of his non-Jewish constituents. Thus, in addition to the basic decency of the man and his supporters in the National Assembly, we must consider the milieu that made it possible. Why, in contrast to France and Romania, not to mention Germany and Austria, was Bulgaria so free of anti-Semitism that it could yield Peshev's success?

One answer, of course, is the absence of territorial loss and its accompanying refugee influx. Without the large number of refugees of like ethno-religious identity, sympathy can be extended to others of a different identity, who through no fault of their own are subject to deportation and probable death. Thus, according to Peshev,

> As I was trying to understand what was happening and why, I received a visit from Dimitâr Ikonomov, the deputy of the National Assembly from the town of Dupnitsa ... He told me that he had just returned from a visit there and was extremely depressed by what he had witnessed taking place in the street. He described a distressing scene—Thracian Jews, old people, men, women, and children, carrying their belongings, defeated, desperate, powerless people, begging for help as they crossed the town on foot, dragging themselves towards some unknown destination. He was saddened and utterly outraged to see helpless people being sent to some destination that could only be surmised, to a fate that conjured up everyone's darkest fears. He spoke of the effect of this horrible scene on the residents of Dupnitsa, their anger and outrage, their inability to remain indifferent to the tragedy that was unfolding before their eyes: This multitude of women and children and old people who were being taken who knows where. To hear Ikonomov tell it, the townspeople's despair was so great that many had been moved to tears. (Todorov, 2001: 158)

Here, Peshev refers to a failure of Bulgaria to protect the Jews of Macedonia, Thrace, and a small portion of Serbia, now under Bulgarian authority. The Germans demanded these deportations and in order to placate them, the Bulgarian government complied, at the same time asserting that these were residents of newly occupied territory, not Bulgarian citizens subject to Bulgarian constitutional law. In all, 11,393 Jews from these regions were deported to Poland, almost all perishing in the extermination camps (Chary, 1972: 127). Yet, despite being evacuated from the capital, Sofia, as were non-Jews later during the Allied bombing, the 45,000 Jews of Bulgaria (48,000 according to Boyadjieff, 1989: 1) were not deported from the country and survived the war.

Finally, in our cases of genocidal or perpetrating states such as Vichy France and Romania, victim prominence has been cited. But in Bulgaria, this element is decidedly absent. In an open letter to the National Assembly deputies, journalist and politician Christo Punev remarks,

> The vast majority of Jews in Bulgaria are working-class people: small grain merchants, pushcart vendors, retail tradesmen, labourers and maids, all of them working for a living and all of them going hungry. Have you not walked by the children of Yuchbunar on the streets of the capital? Little children and students, have you not seen them, famished, jaundiced, wasted and ragged, marching alongside Bulgarian children on Cyril and Methodius' Day? ... We are seven million people, yet we so fear the treachery of 45,000 Jews who hold no positions of responsibility at the national level that we need to pass exceptional laws to protect ourselves from them. ... And then what? (Todorov, 2001: 51)

The combustible mix of migration, ethno-religious identity, and social class is absent, as is outright collaboration in the genocide of a state's own citizenry.

3.5. FINLAND: AN EXCEPTION

The Jewish community of Finland numbered approximately 2,000 in the early 1930s, before the addition of several hundred foreign Jews who had been granted asylum. Nearly all escaped deportation.

After an extended analysis, Rautkallio (1987: 170) concludes that the visits of Hitler and Himmler to Finland, respectively in June and July of 1942, "proved how much the Führer valued the contribution of Finland as a co-belligerent fighting a common enemy in the East.... The Jewish Question was therefore left in the background of Finnish–German relations; in fact, this issue was never brought forcefully to the attention of the Finns". German pressure was minimal, hence the Finns could act with considerable latitude in regard to their Jewish residents, including support for their civil liberties. Why the absence of anti-Jewish animus? One answer is found in territorial expansion.

As in the case of Bulgaria, Finland gained territory prior to its brush with genocide. At the start of the later Continuation War with the Soviet Union, by December 1941 the Finns had regained all of the territory lost to the Soviets in the Peace of Moscow of March 1940 ending the earlier Winter War (Polvinen, 1986: 282). Now, instead of losing one-ninth of their territory as in 1940, the Finns regained it all plus a substantial amount. They were to retain this territory until June 1944, well after the period during which even minor German pressure for deportation had ended (Kirby, 1979: 141).

Equally, if not more important, was the status of refugees. In 1940, 11% of the total population was relocated westward on newly created holdings, a process that proved to be a colossal undertaking (Jutikkala and Pirinen, 1974: 279). After the territorial advances of 1941, these refugees returned to their old homes. Instead of refugees streaming into the country invoking feelings of anger and identification with their unfortunate ethnic kin, the nation could feel satisfied that this earlier wrong had been corrected. We would expect, as in the case of Bulgaria, a sympathetic response to other refugees in Finland, many of them Jewish.

And this is what we find. Despite the absence of "forceful" German pressure, in October 1942 the Finnish government did plan to deport foreign Jews. When the plan became known, 200 citizens of the town of Pietarsaari signed a petition asking that the government not deport these Jews (Cohen and Svensson, 2001: 205). This effort parallels that which occurred in the Bulgarian town of Kyustendil, as we saw in the preceding section. After a public dispute leading to a reduction in the number of deportees, on 6 November, eight Jews including two children were deported to Tallinn in Estonia and then to Auschwitz. Only one person from this group, an adult, survived the war (Cohen and Svensson, 2001: 205).

Although seemingly incomparable in one respect—the sacrifice of foreign Jews in Bulgaria and their attempted rescue in Finland—this difference is more apparent than real. Foreign Jews in Finland resided on Finnish territory and had been granted asylum. Thracian and Macedonian Jews deported by Bulgaria did not reside on Bulgarian territory, and had not been acknowledged in any way by the Bulgarian government. Similar dynamics were at work in a population outraged by the prospect of violating Finnish hospitality and horrified by the treatment of the Thracian and Macedonian Jews. Without the popular anger that might have erupted over treatment of their own indigenous refugees, had they existed at the time, the routine sympathies of ordinary people could be activated.

4. Conclusion

In the context of the Holocaust, territorial contraction and its corollary of refugee influx are important progenitors of mass killing. In our genocidal states and two of the perpetrating states, Vichy France and Romania, the mix of territorial loss, refugees, and issues of social class was prominent. In Italy, the state itself was threatened by the ongoing territorial loss. Only in Bulgaria and Finland, where the vast majority of Jews were saved, were these elements absent.

At the same time, this conclusion does not exclude the possible impact of other independent variables, or intervening ones between territorial loss and refugee migration on the one hand, and the genocidal outcome on the other. The purpose of this inquiry has been to establish the foundations of a theory of loss, a suggested important consequence, and its initial empirical examination in the context of a salient historical event.

One may argue that a large proportion of France's Jewish population, although not as large as Bulgaria's, also survived the war, and France did indeed suffer severe truncation and territorial loss. Yet until World War II, France was the home of continental European liberalism, never having promulgated an anti-Semitic law after the time of Napoleon I. Pogroms in France were unknown. Bulgaria, on the other hand, had experienced episodic pogroms including the most famous one in Pazardzhik (1895), as well as Sofia (1884), Vratsa (1890), Lom (1903), and Kyustendil (1904). Most were sparked by rumors of ritual Passover murders by Jews, the infamous blood-libel (Chary, 1972: 32). Thus for France, the leap to state-supported anti-Semitism and complicity in Jewish deportation, including many French citizens, was far greater than that for Bulgaria, and certainly Romania. Although Romania did take that plunge into the abyss, as did Vichy France, Bulgaria ultimately declined.

As it does not differentiate effectively between Vichy France and Bulgaria, emphasis on a history of anti-Semitism as a potential explanation for genocidal behavior (e.g., Fein, 1979: 72–73) also does not distinguish between Italy and Finland. In both instances, before the 1930s, widespread anti-Semitism was virtually unknown in the modern period, yet the outcomes differed in the two cases.

Romania, in its 20th-century history, like France, demonstrated radically different behaviors upon expansion and later after contraction. Only after substantial shrinkage of the Romanian state in 1940 did it embark on its genocidal path. These considerations suggest that one must examine a perpetrating state's behavior not only in comparison with others, as in the comparisons among Italy, Vichy France, Romania, Bulgaria, and Finland, but also in the light of its own history. The behaviors of these states, as well as those of Germany and Austria, suggest enormous changes in state policy regarding Jews only after the experience of territorial loss and, in four of these states, Germany, Austria, Vichy France, and Romania, refugee migration. Political elites concerned with state security may be more directly sensitive to territorial loss in itself, as was Mussolini, while refugee migration, often associated with territorial loss, can lead to mass disaffection and popular violence directed against targeted minorities.

Finally, there is the issue of symbolic representation. For many French people and as a percentage, many more Romanians, as for many Germans, there was the indelible but vastly exaggerated connection between Jews and Communism. Any gains for the Soviet Union—for example, territories that Romania was forced to cede to it in 1940—were frequently laid at the Jewish doorstep. Elsewhere (Midlarsky, 2005), in a more extended comparison with the Armenian and Tutsi genocides, I show that the civilian victims also were falsely blamed for the respective Ottoman and Hutu losses. Thus, in addition to the psychosocial implications of loss suggested by prospect theory, identification with the downtrodden of one's own ethnicity, anger at the presumptive "other", and economic competition within a shrunken spatial environment, there are issues of political responsibility that emanate from territorial transfers. Jews were to pay a heavy price for an unwarranted culpability emerging from the national experience of loss, made palpable in the everyday lives of people by the often ubiquitous presence of refugees.

Note

* I am grateful to the guest editors and several anonymous referees for their helpful comments.

References

Aschheim, Steven E., 1982. *Brothers and Strangers: The East European Jew in German and German Jewish Consciousness, 1800–1923.* Madison, WI: University of Wisconsin Press.

Blakeslee, Sandra, 2001. "Watching how the brain works as it weighs a moral dilemma", *New York Times*, 25 September: F3.

Bodenhausen, Galen V., Lori A Sheppard and Geoffrey P. Kramer, 1994. "Negative affect and social judgment: The differential impact of anger and sadness", *European Journal of Social Psychology* 24(1): 45–62.

Boia, Lucian, 2001. *History and Myth in Romanian Consciousness*, trans. James C. Brown. Budapest: Central European University Press.

Boyadjieff, Christo, 1989. *Saving the Bulgarian Jews in World War II.* Ottawa: Free Bulgarian Center.

Braham, Randolph L., 1981. *The Politics of Genocide: The Holocaust in Hungary,* Vol. 1. New York: Columbia University Press.

Burrin, Philippe, 1994. *Hitler and the Jews: The Genesis of the Holocaust*, trans. Patsy South-gate. London: Edward Arnold.

Burrin, Philippe, 1996. *France Under the Germans: Collaboration and Compromise*, trans. Janet Lloyd. New York: New Press.

Carpi, Daniel, 1977. "The rescue of Jews in the Italian zone of occupied Croatia", in Yisrael Gutman and Efraim Zuroff (eds), *Rescue Attempts During the Holocaust.* Jerusalem: Yad Vashem (465–525).

Chary, Frederick B., 1972. *The Bulgarian Jews and the Final Solution, 1940–1944.* Pittsburgh, PA: University of Pittsburgh Press.

Cohen, William B. and Jürgen Svensson, 2001. "Finland", in Walter Laqueur (ed.), *The Holocaust Encyclopedia.* New Haven, CT: Yale University Press (204–206).
DeSteno, David, N., Nilanjana Dasgupta, Monica Y. Bartlett and Aida Cajdric, 2004. "Prejudice from thin air: The effect of emotion on automatic intergroup attitudes", *Psychological Science* 15(5): 319–324.
Evans, Richard J., 2004. *The Coming of the Third Reich.* New York: Penguin.
Fein, Helen, 1979. *Accounting for Genocide: National Responses and Jewish Victimization during the Holocaust.* New York: Free Press.
Feldman, Gerald D., 1993. *The Great Disorder: Politics, Economics, and Society in the German Inflation, 1914–1924.* New York: Oxford University Press.
Foreign Relations of the United States 1940–1942. Washington, DC: US Government Publications Office, Superintendent of Documents.
German Foreign Office, 1940. *Documents on the Events Preceding the Outbreak of the War.* New York: German Library of Information.
Goldberger, Leo (ed.), 1987. *The Rescue of the Danish Jews: Moral Courage Under Stress.* New York: New York University Press.
Greene, Joshua D., R. Brian Sommerville, Leigh E. Nystrom, John M. Darley and Jonathan D. Cohen, 2001. "An fMRI investigation of emotional engagement in moral judgment", *Science* 293(5537): 2105–2108.
Hamann, Brigitte, 1999. *Hitler's Vienna: A Dictator's Apprenticeship*, trans. Thomas Thornton. New York: Oxford University Press.
Hilberg, Raul, 1985. *The Destruction of the European Jews.* New York: Holmes and Meier.
Hitler, Adolf, [1942] 2000. *Hitler's Table Talk, 1941–1944: His Private Conversations*, trans. Norman Cameron and R. H. Stevens, intro. Hugh R. Trevor-Roper. New York: Enigma.
Huth, Paul K., 1996. *Standing Your Ground: Territorial Disputes and International Conflict.* Ann Arbor, MI: University of Michigan Press.
Ioanid, Radu, 2000. *The Holocaust in Romania: The Destruction of Jews and Gypsies Under the Antonescu Regime, 1940–1944*, foreword Elie Wiesel. Chicago, IL: Ivan R. Dee.
Jelavich, Barbara, 1983. *History of the Balkans,* Vol. 2. Cambridge: Cambridge University Press.
Jutikkala, Eino and Kauko Pirinen, 1974. *A History of Finland*, rev. edn, trans. Paul Sjöblom. New York: Praeger.
Kahneman, Daniel and Amos Tversky, 1979. "Prospect theory: An analysis of decision under risk', *Econometrica* 47(2): 263–292.
Kahneman, Daniel and Amos Tversky (eds), 2000. *Choices, Values, and Frames.* Cambridge: Cambridge University Press.
Keesing's Contemporary Archives. London: Keesing's.
Kirby, D. G., 1979. *Finland in the Twentieth Century.* Minneapolis, MN: University of Minnesota Press.
Levendel, Isaac, 1999. *Not the Germans Alone: A Son's Search for the Truth of Vichy.* Evanston, IL: Northwestern University Press.
Levy, Jack S., 2000. "Loss aversion, framing effects, and international conflict: Perspectives from prospect theory", in Manus I. Midlarsky (ed.), *Handbook of War Studies II.* Ann Arbor, MI: University of Michigan Press (193–221).
Marrus, Michael R. and Robert O. Paxton, 1995. *Vichy France and the Jews.* Stanford, CA: Stanford University Press.
Melson, Robert, 1992. *Revolution and Genocide: On the Origins of the Armenian Genocide and the Holocaust.* Chicago, IL: University of Chicago Press.
Midlarsky, Manus I., 1999. *The Evolution of Inequality: War, State Survival, and Democracy in Comparative Perspective.* Stanford, CA: Stanford University Press.
Midlarsky, Manus I., 2000. "Identity and international conflict", in Manus I. Midlarsky (ed.), *Handbook of War Studies II.* Ann Arbor, MI: University of Michigan Press (25–58).
Midlarsky, Manus I., 2005. *The Killing Trap: Genocide in the Twentieth Century.* Cambridge: Cambridge University Press.
Murray, Williamson and Allan R. Millett, 2000. *A War To Be Won: Fighting the Second World War.* Cambridge, MA: Belknap.
Nagy-Talavera, Nicholas M., 2001. *The Green Shirts and the Others: A History of Fascism in Hungary and Romania.* Iaşi: Center for Romanian Studies.

Polvinen, Tuomo, 1986. *Between East and West: Finland in International Politics, 1944–1947*, (eds) and trans. D. G. Kirby and Peter Herring. Minneapolis, MN: University of Minnesota Press.

Rautkallio, Hannu, 1987. *Finland and the Holocaust: The Rescue of Finland's Jews*, trans. Paul Sjöblom. New York: Holocaust Library.

Sachar, Howard M., 2002. *Dreamland: Europeans and Jews in the Aftermath of the Great War.* New York: Vintage.

Senese, Paul D. and John Vasquez, 2004. "Alliances, territorial disputes, and the probability of war: Testing for interactions", in Paul F. Diehl (ed.), *The Scourge of War: New Extensions on an Old Problem.* Ann Arbor, MI: University of Michigan Press (189–221).

Steinberg, Jonathan, 1990. *All or Nothing: The Axis and the Holocaust 1941–1943.* London: Routledge.

Todorov, Tzvetan, 2001. *The Fragility of Goodness: Why Bulgaria's Jews Survived the Holocaust*, trans. Arthur Denner. Princeton, NJ: Princeton University Press.

Vasquez, John, 2000. "Reexamining the steps to war: New evidence and theoretical insights", in Manus I. Midlarsky (ed.), *Handbook of War Studies II.* Ann Arbor, MI: University of Michigan Press (371–406).

Vasquez, John and Marie T. Henehan, 2001. "Territorial disputes and the probability of war, 1816–1992", *Journal of Peace Research* 38(2): 123–138.

Weber, Eugen, 1965. "Romania", in Hans Rogger and Eugen Weber (eds), *The European Right: A Historical Profile.* Berkeley, CA: University of California Press (501–574).

Webster, Paul, 1991. *Pétain's Crime: The Full Story of French Collaboration in the Holocaust.* Chicago, IL: Ivan R. Dee.

Wertheimer, Jack, 1987. *Unwelcome Strangers: East European Jews in Imperial Germany.* New York: Oxford University Press.

Zuccotti, Susan, 2000. *Under His Very Windows: The Vatican and the Holocaust in Italy.* New Haven, CT: Yale University Press.

CHAPTER 2. RELATIVE RESOURCES: INEQUALITY IN ETHNIC WARS, REVOLUTIONS, AND GENOCIDES*

MARIE L. BESANÇON
Program on Intrastate Conflict, John F. Kennedy School of Government, Harvard University, USA

Abstract. Political scientists and economists have exhaustively examined the nexus between economic inequality and political conflict (EI–PC nexus) in aggregated civil wars. This article revisits the nexus and its related theories, empirically and parsimoniously testing the effects of inequality on disaggregated intrastate conflicts. The results buttress the notion that traditionally deprived identity groups are more likely to engage in conflict under more economically equal conditions, while class or revolutionary wars fall under the conditions of greater economic inequality and war. Of the three types of conflicts tested—ethnic conflicts, revolutions, and genocides—economic inequality seems to have the most ambiguous bearing on genocides. Support follows for recent findings that political and social equalities are of greater importance in mitigating ethnic violence and that greed factors might exacerbate violence in all civil conflicts, including genocides. The theoretical argument proposes that the context within which intrastate violence takes place affects the requisite level of relative resources needed for the escalation of violence between groups. The results have policy implications for ethnically divided states that are in the process of equalizing their income differential, but neglect the substantial inclusion of all groups within the political process and the distribution of public goods. The social contracts between the governors and the governed then require careful crafting for a peaceful coexistence of diverse identity groups.

1. Introduction

The threat of spreading civil wars, along with their implications for regional stability and escalated terrorism, has allied economists, political scientists, and practitioners in re-examining an old question: is inequality one of the causal factors in civil wars? Extending that question, what kind of inequality might be pertinent, and in what kind of civil wars?

Political scientists, for decades, have argued that there is a nexus between economic inequality and political violence, yet these decades of studies have empirically challenged this view. Rarely have statistical studies resulted in a robust relationship between the two variables, and the results have often been contradictory and inconclusive.[1] The inequality data themselves, as well as the dependent variable measuring civil wars, have been partly culpable. Furthermore, comparing different conflict processes in all intrastate wars inherently contains an equivalence problem (Moore, Lindström and O'Regan, 1996). So far, the data problems have been addressed more than the equivalence issues.

This chapter was previously published in *Journal of Peace Research*, vol. 42, no. 4, 2005, pp. 393–415.

Helge Brunborg et al. (eds.), The Demography of Armed Conflict, 39–65.

Recent studies of civil conflict have broadened to such causal variables as economic growth, geographical terrain, elite manipulation of the masses, exploitable diamond and fuel resources, renewable resources, degrees of heterogeneity among languages, religions, and shape, size, and color shades of *homo sapiens*, while hesitating to focus too much on economic inequality. Indeed, one could say that "the poor will always be with us", that we are not quite sure what economic inequality has to do with conflict, and move on to other factors such as greed, corruption, governance, globalization, and democracy.[2]

Because of spurious findings from these many empirical studies, scholars have suggested disaggregating political violence into particular types of civil conflict or case studies for further investigation as reasonable approaches, in that causes for all types of civil wars are not necessarily parallel.[3] In addition to the case studies that have been produced, Sambanis (2001) and Robinson (2001) have uncovered some evidence that identity wars may have different causes than revolutions—giving credence to the non-equivalence suggestions from earlier literature. It is clear that alternate specifications for the dependent variable are required to interpret the conditions under which inequality may lead to civil political conflict, and why past studies have yielded such variations in results. Furthermore, inequalities between ethnic groups rather than class groups have not been well defined cross-nationally.

Theoretically, combining different approaches in the IR and comparative fields, the concept here is to expand the economic inequality-political conflict nexus and propose that within different societies and groups, members have different opportunities and resources for mobilization relative to each other, different histories of deprivation, and different kinds of deprivation, and therefore are likely to have different propensities for violence and different perceptions of inequality leading to deadly conflict. Additionally, given a certain economic inequality threshold beyond which dissatisfied groups resort to violence, a relative minimum resource threshold is required before certain groups or subgroups will risk fighting. Furthermore, the threshold for violence in ethnic wars may not be an economic inequality grievance.

Consideration is given to the literature on other factors germane to political violence, and a few of the most parsimonious are controlled for, while testing the effects of two Gini Indexes and a Human Capital Gini measure (based on education inequality) on intensity of conflict and on the presence or absence of conflict in *ethnic wars, genocides*, and *revolutions*. These models result in distinct anomalies between the types of intrastate violence and different patterns of economic, political, and social divergences contributing to the violence—informing previous difficulties with the economic inequality–political conflict nexus in aggregated intrastate conflict studies.

2. A chimera of theories

Though the many theories on inequality and political violence propose arguments that seem contradictory—when they are applied to disaggregated civil wars—they can explain a continuum of reasoning behind economic inequality and conflict in different kinds of intrastate violence. If the conjecture that testing aggregate internal conflicts produces an equivalence problem is true, then logically the effect of income inequality might be different for different types of internal violence. While the relationship may yet exist, disaggregating the dependent variable to types of civil violence should show differences in magnitude, significance, or direction of the effect of inequality on political violence.

The proposal here is to integrate components of relative deprivation arguments for internal conflict (De Tocqueville, 1887; Davies, 1962; Gurr, 1970; Nagel, 1974; Inglehart, 1990) and power arguments for systemic wars (Blainey, 1975; Organski and Kugler, 1980; Tammen et al., 2000) with institutional bargaining reasoning (Knight, 1992, 1995), augmented with thoughts on the hierarchy of needs (Popkin, 1979; Maslow, 1954) and risk and utility (Bueno de Mesquita, 1985; Grossman, 1991) to explain why internal factors might affect the requisite relative economic inequality levels for different kinds of civil wars to inflate, or for conflict to occur.

2.1. DEPRIVATION, EQUALITY, RISK

Without belaboring these much-traveled theoretical paths, deprivation and group perceptions of this phenomenon are at the forefront of one sphere of intrastate conflict theory. At the national and groups levels of analysis, the theoretical approach of Gurr (1970) argues that discontent arising from the perception of relative deprivation is the basic, instigating condition for participants in collective violence. At the extreme end of the spectrum on deprivation, Bueno de Mesquita (1985) shows that those who have nothing will risk conflict because they have nothing to lose. Davies's (1962: 5) conceptualization of relative resources and conflict suggests that revolutions will most likely occur after a "prolonged period of objective economic and social development is followed by a short period of sharp reversal". Grossman's (1991) equilibrium model for insurrections also implies that the very deprived have an expected income gain from fighting. The end results of these theories are that economic inequality produces conflict.

Knight (1995) believes that asymmetries in the ownership of resources affect the willingness of actors or groups to accept the bargaining demands of other actors. He argues that those who are the most deprived will be risk averse and will bargain with those having a greater economic base rather than demand greater equality and political representation. Based on the matrix of his institutional bargaining theory, greater resources would mean greater propensity for actors to fight for their political demands. Nagel (1974) proposes that comparison is negatively related to the degree of income disparity. If there is a large gap between groups, they will have a smaller tendency to compare than if they are closer in resources. This also implies that groups closer to each other are in a position to compare, and have a greater impetus to rebel. For Popkin (1979) and Maslow (1954), those who are the most deprived are thinking foremost of survival and have nothing left for conflict. The systems theorists expand this "glimpse of victory" to improve understanding of when global wars occur.

At the global systems level of analysis (Organski and Kugler, 1980; Tammen et al., 2000), power parity theory introduces the concept of equality and conflict, proposing that when nations approach equality and are discontent with the existing conditions, they are most likely to fight. A nation growing in resources and population can credibly challenge a formerly dominant nation when it achieves adequate resources to do so. Blainey (1975) has a similar concept with his theory of victory, in that there must be a belief in the ability to win in order to choose violent rebellion. This proposal applies globally and regionally (Lemke, 2002) and could be applied within nations and between groups. These theories are not incompatible with De Tocqueville (1887) or Denzau and North (1994). On an individual actor level, Denzau and North (1994: 8) ask "to what extent does the individual believe that his own choice can affect the real outcomes". Extending the systems theory and the individual beliefs theory, groups will be more likely to challenge each other when there is a greater parity in resources, or some other factor that increases the group's belief in their chances of winning. Ellingsen (2000) shows this parity theory to be true with group size and rebellion between ethnic groups.

The above disparate theories have the common chord of discontent with circumstances, sometimes producing rebellion, sometimes concessions. The proposals primarily address economic inequality while ignoring other inequalities such as participation in rule and public goods. Taken individually, each theory has logic and merit, but each allows for violence to occur at very different levels of relative deprivation or equality.

In situations where the major standing grievances occur between ethnic, religious, or cultural groups, with longstanding abuse and repression in many areas—social and political as well as economic—greater economic equality might be a facilitating factor for rebellion. Given a background of repression, self-esteem issues, and identity group exclusion from rule and privileges, institutional bargaining theory, power parity theory, and the theory of victory would infer that ethnic identity groups might perceive inequality in ways other than economic, but would require greater economic equality in order to perceive a higher probability of winning. Therefore:[4]

H1: Increasing economic equality coincides with increasing levels of ethnic intrastate conflict.

The relative deprivation theories have traditionally maintained that violence occurs at greater economic inequality thresholds in situations where the major standing grievances are heavily economically based with large disparities in income, and thus inequality is a causal factor. Given income inequality (particularly in the absence of ethnic or identity groups), relative deprivation, risk, and utility theories imply that discontent arising from increasing economic inequality is endemic to revolutions, and since groups might perceive that there is nothing to lose and everything to gain, greater economic inequality should lead to conflict.

H2: Increasing economic inequality coincides with increasing levels of violence in revolutions.

This study does not attempt to examine theoretically the complexity of reasons for a state to sponsor violence against a particular group (as defined by the State Failures Task Force), or one identity group to carry out systematic killing of another group. No hypothesis for economic inequality's effect on genocide is inferred here by the various inequality theories on conflict. However, the effects of the explanatory inequality variables on genocide are reported, given the clear divergence from the other two types of intrastate conflict. The results imply that genocides are caused by other factors addressed in a growing body of literature on that subject (Krain, 1997; Harff, 2003; Midlarsky, 2005) and that the disaggregated data provide an avenue for further testing. The models give a clear differentiation between causes and effects on all different types of civil wars.

3. Methods[5]

The State Failures Task Force is the single publicly available source for disaggregated civil war data compiled cross-nationally, and thus it forms the basis for the dependent variable—number of deaths in ethnic wars, revolutions, and genocides (and the absence or presence of conflict in the disaggregated wars). The data, which include only the cases with positive results for conflict measured, were extended to include nonviolent country-years as described below.

3.1. DEPENDENT VARIABLES

The dependent variable for political conflict is specified as deaths caused by insurgent activity (see definition in following section) in ethnic wars, in revolutions, or in genocides, and is measured on a Guttman scale. The MAGFATAL variable in the State Failures Data Set (Marshall, Gurr and Harff, 2002) is used for ethnic war deaths (*ethnic*) and revolution deaths (*revolutions*), and the DEATHMAG variable is employed for genocide deaths (*genocide*). These data, taken from the State Failures Data Set, span from 1960 to 2001. The magnitude of deaths from ethnic conflicts and revolutions is subdivided between zero and four (rounded up to whole numbers), and the magnitude of deaths for genocide is subdivided between zero and five (rounded up to whole numbers) in Table 1. The zero values for nonviolent

Table 1. Categories of number of deaths

Ethnic/revolution deaths	Genocide deaths
$0 \leq 100$	$0 \leq 300$
$1 = 100$–1,000	$1 = 300$–2,000
$2 = 1{,}000$–5,000	$2 = 2{,}000$–8,000
$3 = 5{,}000$–10,000	$3 = 8{,}000$–32,000
$4 \geq 10{,}000$	$4 = 32{,}000$–128,000
	$5 \geq 128{,}000$

country-years were added with the aid of Taylor and Jodice (1983), newspapers, and other sources. Admittedly, this is not complete, but provided adequate data for eliminating the dependent variable being only non-zero country-years.[6] The data were also converted to binary variables (war being greater than 100 deaths for ethnic wars and revolutions and greater than 300 deaths for genocides) for secondary assays with a logit model testing for war, or no war.

The definitions of the types of civil wars disaggregated by the State Failures Project are as follows (Gurr and Harff, 1997):

3.1.1. *Ethnic wars*

"Episodes of violent conflict between governments and national, ethnic, religious, or other communal minorities (ethnic challengers) in which the challengers seek major changes in their status.... Rioting and warfare between rival communal groups is not coded as ethnic warfare unless it involves conflict over political power or government policy".

3.1.2. *Revolutions*

"Episodes of violent conflict between governments and politically organized groups (political challengers) that seek to overthrow the central government, to replace its leaders, or to seize power in one region".

3.1.3. *Genocide*

"The promotion, execution, and/or implied consent of sustained policies by governing elites or their agents—or in the case of civil war, either of the contending authorities—that result in the deaths of a substantial portion of a communal group or politicized non-communal group".[7]

3.2. INDEPENDENT VARIABLES

The two major inequality variables are from datasets that use predicted variables based on hard data, the Gini Index and the Human Capital Gini. The third inequality variable, the World Bank Gini, was tested with the logit and probit models as a control matrix for comparison. They are as follows:

3.2.1. *Gini index*

The Gini Index for economic inequality measures derives from Feng's (Feng, Kugler and Zak, 2005) time-series. Feng uses the Deininger and Squire (1996) data as a base and *predicts* the missing values and country-years with an OLS (Ordinary Least Squares) model using GDP per capita, literacy rate, RPE (relative political extraction), and regional control variables. The data span from 1960 to 1992. These data have a wider coverage than the World Bank Data, show less outlier variance, and cover countries not included in the World Bank Gini.[8]

3.2.2. *Human capital Gini index*

Castelló and Doménech (2002) formulate a human capital inequality measure based on education attainment levels from Barro and Lee (2001) for 108 countries (every five years from 1960 to 1999). They claim more robust results than income inequality measures in estimating growth and investment equations. Their data are not highly correlated to the above Gini Index (0.49) that derives from Deininger and Squire. The Human Capital Gini used here is the measure for ages 15 and above, and the missing data are imputed with "ipolate" in Stata. The index is scaled to a non-fraction (percent) to be comparable to the Gini Index and the World Bank Gini Index.

3.2.3. *World Bank Gini*

The World Bank Gini Index used here was taken from the "all Gini" column in the referenced web-based dataset with missing values interpolated using Stata.[9] These data are intermittent depending on the country. Some extend from 1960 to 1999, and others end much earlier or start later, thus producing fewer variables than the predicted Gini dataset. These data are noted to have marked variances; for example, Ecuador measures 41 in 1995 and 52 in 1998, and Denmark jumps from 31 in 1976 to 40 in 1978.

3.3. CONTROL VARIABLES

Overall prosperity (as measured by real GDP per capita) is included in all models, as previous work has shown robustly that the more prosperous a nation is overall, the less likely it is to be plagued with civil wars (e.g., Fearon and Laitin, 2003). Furthermore, since the dependent variable is ordered and measures numbers of deaths in increasing categories, the model includes a control variable for size of the population, since an exact ratio of deaths per population cannot be derived.

As a proxy for elites in a society, the measure for tertiary education is used to simulate a test for elite or entrepreneurial influences toward violence (Grossman, 1991; Addison and Murshed, 2001). Lastly, the variable which Collier and Hoeffler (2004) use as a proxy for "greed" is included, to test whether its effects are greater than the inequality variables within the models, or if they cancel out the inequality effects, and to test results in disaggregated wars. They reason that "lootable" resources are a much greater cause of civil wars than inequality between groups.

Sambanis (2001) shows that politics have a greater causal effect on "identity" wars than on "non-identity" wars. As the democracy effects have been well investigated in civil wars (Horowitz, 1994; Gurr, 1994; Rummel, 1994, 1995; Hegre et al., 2001; Reynal-Querol, 2002), the political/institutional measure "Parcomp" is included, from the Polity IV data, that captures a different aspect of representation from the democracy variable—that of non-elite representation. Lichbach (1989: 75) suggests that the "real explanation of dissent lies in the (a) component (the conditions) and not the (b) component (economic inequality) of EI–PC propositions". The independent variables that cast the essential background to the inequality measures are as follows:

3.3.1. *Tertiary*

The percentage of population enrolled in tertiary education. This measure is used (rather than the traditional secondary education measure) as a proxy measure for the number of elites in society as well as the educated (World Bank, 2000).

3.3.2. *Non-elite representation*

The extent to which non-elites are able to access institutional structures for political expression. The most unregulated is 0, and the most competitive is 5 (Parcomp: Marshall, Jaggers and Gurr, 2004).

3.3.3. *Greed*

Primary commodities exports/total exports from Collier and Hoeffler (2004). This series extends from 1960 to 1995 in five-year intervals. Interpolation of missing data was computed in Stata.

3.3.4. *Ln real GDP per capita*

Ln real GDP per capita = Natural log of real GDP per capita (Heston, Summers and Aten, 2002, supplemented with Easterly and Yu, 2000).

3.3.5. *Ln population*

Ln population = Natural log of the population from Easterly and Yu (2000).

3.4. MODEL

An ordinal probit model is employed to test empirically the effects that the chosen social, political, and economic variables have on disaggregated intrastate violence using data from 108–142 countries (depending on explanatory variable availability). The data are time series from 1960 to 1992, 1995, or 1999, as constrained by the limits of the available country-year data.

The models examine the effects of inequality variables, institutional variables, threshold variables, and a greed variable on the probability of deaths caused by ethnic violence, revolutions, and genocide. A scaled "number of deaths" is used as the dependent variable rather than the presence or absence of conflict, thereby lending a measure of "conflict intensity", or "severity of war", rather than the presence or absence of a specific number of threshold deaths and above (these vary: 25, 100, or 1,000 depending on the dataset). Since much previous work has been done testing inequality and other causal variables against the presence or absence of war rather than level of violence, the logit version of the model is also employed to test war or no war.

The simpler version of the ordinal probit model estimate is as follows:

$$y^* = \beta' x + \varepsilon \tag{1}$$

where y^* is the unobserved dependent variable for level of violence, β' is a coefficient vector, x is a vector of the independent variables (in this case the political, social, and economic control variables as well as the income convergence variables), and ε is a stochastic error term (Elder and Rudolph, 1999). However, we do observe values of y from the data that correspond to levels of deaths from each of the three types of internal violence. The levels vary from 0 to 4 for revolutions and ethnic conflicts and 0 to 5 for genocides. The level of deaths corresponds to a set of parameters, μ, that partition the distribution of y^*. The estimation procedure thus determines the probability that the value y^* falls into the range of μ's as established by the observed values of y for the levels of violence (Elder and Rudolph, 1999).

The estimations for the probabilities of y falling into the μ range for each category with multiple independent variables are as follows. The first threshold parameter μ_1 is normalized to zero, giving one less parameter to estimate (Liao, 1994: 43–47).

$$\text{Prob}\,(y = 1) = \phi \cdot \left[-\sum_{k=1}^{K} \beta_k x_k \right],$$

$$\text{Prob}\,(y = 2) = \phi \cdot \left[\mu_2 - \sum_{k=1}^{K} \beta_k x_k \right] - \phi \cdot \left[-\sum_{k=1}^{K} \beta_k x_k \right],$$

$$\text{Prob}\,(y = 3) = \phi \cdot \left[\mu_3 - \sum_{k=1}^{K} \beta_k x_k \right] - \phi \cdot \left[\mu_2 - \sum_{k=1}^{K} \beta_k x_k \right],$$

$$\text{Prob}\,(y = J) = 1 - \phi \cdot \left[\mu_{J-1} - \sum_{k=1}^{K} \beta_k x_k \right],$$

where Φ is the standard normal cumulative distribution function. The coefficient β_k estimates the unknown μ parameters and estimates the marginal effect of the corresponding χ_k on the probability of event 0–4 (or 5) occurring. The y's are dependent variable categories.

The crucial questions are why do intrastate conflicts begin at a particular time, what is the background, and how does inequality factor in the conflicts? Communities can live together for long periods of time as unequal and separate entities, without necessarily killing each other. Inequality in more than the economic realm provides important clues to discontent, though Collier and Sambanis (2002: 3) observe that "if conflict has a substantial economic dimension, economists can make a positive contribution to conflict analysis".

3.4.1. *What the tests show*

What about relative deprivation? Does it increase, decrease, or have no effect on intrastate violence? To whom do groups compare, and what kind of deprivation causes what kind of violence? As suggested from the initial discussion, results for the causal variables differed for ethnic deaths, revolutions, and genocides, which explains some of the previous ambiguous findings in the aggregate economic inequality–political violence studies. The de-aggregation of types of political violence proves to be a useful and interesting exercise and leads to fairly robust results for the different measures of relative deprivation. Furthermore, the different specifications for inequality also expand understanding of inequality's effect on civil wars.

3.5. ECONOMIC INEQUALITY

The central finding is that the most adverse effects from economic inequality grievances occur in revolutions (Table 2, Models 2 and 5; Figures 1 and 2; Appendix D). Conversely, economic inequality's effect on ethnic conflict is much weaker, and opposite for ethnic wars when measured with the Gini Index. Table 2 (Models 1 and 4) shows that in ethnically divided societies, higher levels of conflict occur where there is a greater degree of equality. Using another inequality measure (not shown here), where the upper income quintile is divided by the lower one (as in Bollen and Jackman, 1985; Perotti 1996), conflict is twice as likely in ethnic conflicts, given a ten-fold increase in equality.

While the predicted probit models graphed three-dimensionally in Figure 1 illustrate very nicely the distinctly varying patterns of inequality's effects on the levels of violence in the three divisions of intrastate conflict, the overall impact of change in economic inequality on the probability of each level of death is relatively low. Nevertheless, the positive and non-linear effects of economic inequality on revolutions, the slighter but negative effects on ethnic wars, and the comparatively far lesser effects on genocides are very clear. The probit specification shows that Hypotheses 1 and 2 have robust merit when tested against the Gini Index. These results are not entirely model-dependent, particularly for revolutions. If all of the independent variables are lagged both one and two periods on the dependent variables, the results remain essentially the same for ethnic wars and revolutions. Furthermore, including a lagged y for one and two periods in the revolutionary war model (probit models: Figure 2, Models 2 and 5) decreases the Gini Index coefficient slightly, while the sign and significance remain the same. At lag period five years, the coefficient returns to its original model value. Including a lagged y as an independent variable for one and two periods in the ethnic war model (probit models: Figure 2, Models 1 and 4) initially renders the Gini Index insignificant, though the sign remains the same; however, the Gini Index effect returns to significance when the y lag is five years. Lagging the dependent variable for one, two, and five years and testing it on the right side of the equation in the World Bank Gini models

Table 2. Gini index and conflict intensity in disaggregated civil wars, 1960–92, using an ordinal probit model: robust results

Model	Ethnic 1	Revolutions 2	Genocide 3	Ethnic 4	Revolutions 5	Genocide 6
Ln real GDP per capita	−0.394	−0.123	−0.213	−0.461	−0.051	−0.283
Z-value	−7.18	−2.23	−3.24	−13.81	−1.43	−7.06
Std. error	0.055	0.055	0.066	0.033	0.036	0.040
$P > z$	0.000	0.026	0.001	0.000	0.154	0.000
Marginal effects	0.112	0.022	0.036	0.111	0.009	0.038
Ln population	0.332	0.277	0.244	0.294	0.227	0.261
Z-value	12.57	7.46	8.02	14.73	9.42	12.16
Std. error	0.026	0.037	0.030	0.020	0.024	0.021
$P > z$	0.000	0.000	0.000	0.000	0.000	0.000
Marginal effects	0.095	0.050	0.041	0.071	0.040	0.035
Non-elite representation	−0.049	−0.017	−0.116			
Z-value	−1.79	−0.53	−2.93			
Std. error	0.027	0.033	0.040			
$P > z$	0.073	0.599	0.003			
Marginal effects	0.014	0.003	0.019			
Gini Index	−0.034	0.081	0.016	−0.018	0.060	0.028
Z-value	−4.06	7.75	1.73	−2.43	6.81	3.31
Std. error	0.008	0.011	0.009	0.007	0.009	0.009
$P > z$	0.000	0.000	0.083	0.015	0.000	0.001
Marginal effects	0.010	0.015	0.003	0.004	0.010	0.004
Tertiary education	−0.017	0.013	−0.014			
Z-value	−3.11	2.59	−1.78			
Std. error	0.006	0.005	0.008			
$P > z$	0.002	0.010	0.083			
Marginal effects	0.005	0.002	0.002			
Greed	0.011	0.012	0.009			
Z-value	3.53	3.09	2.52			
Std. error	0.003	0.004	0.003			
$P > z$	0.000	0.002	0.011			
Marginal effects	0.003	0.002	0.001			
N	2,474	2,474	2,476	3,683	3,692	3,686
Wald χ^2	(6)450	(6)154	(6)226	(3)470	(3)129	(3)239
Prob > χ^2	0.000	0.000	0.000	0.000	0.000	0.000
Pseudo R^2	0.180	0.100	0.118	0.166	0.081	0.11

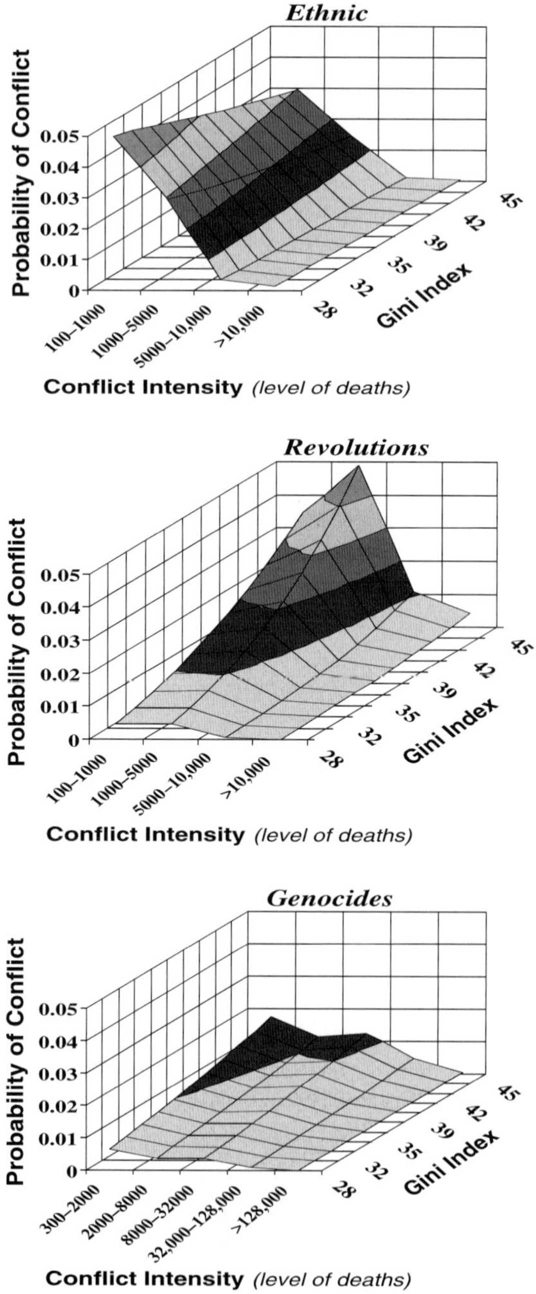

Figure 1. Predicted probability of deaths with changing values of Gini index. (From probit models with two controls: *Ln population* and *Ln real GDP per capita* held at their means.)

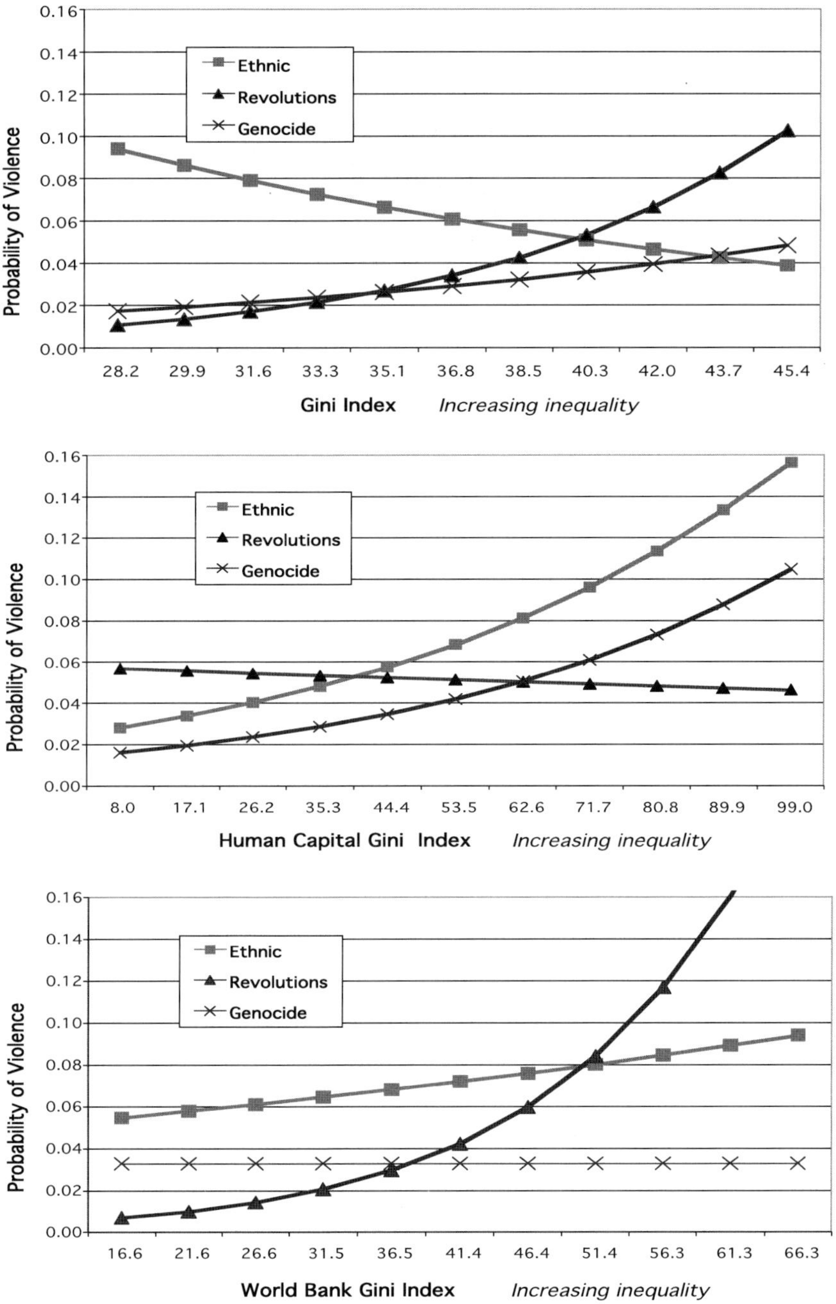

Figure 2. Predicted probability of conflict with changing values of Gini index, human capital Gini index, and World Bank Gini index. (From logit models with two controls: *Ln population* and *Ln real GDP per capita* held at their means.)

(Appendix D, Models 13 and 14) does not change the effects for ethnic wars, or for revolutions.

The majority of economic inequality testing on civil wars has been either on the initiation of war or on the absence or presence of intrastate violence rather than level of violence. Therefore, assays using logit models were also performed for the economic and human capital variables (Appendix E, available at http://www.prio.no/jpr/datasets). This does not necessarily mean that the causes for war and for increasing levels of violence are the same. It simply tests the effects of resource inequality and human capital inequality on the different dependent variables.

Predicted probability models for intrastate wars using binary dependent variables, graphed in Figure 2, clearly illustrate that as economic inequality increases from the least unequal to the most unequal as measured by the Gini Index (28–45), the predicted probability of revolutions increases five-fold. The results from the World Bank Gini measure also demonstrate that economic inequality profoundly impacts revolutions, with an eight-fold increase in predicted likelihood of conflict if a country is three times more unequal.

The striking two-dimensional pictures also show that as inequality increases within the same range of the Gini Index (28–45) for ethnic wars, the likelihood of conflict significantly decreases by almost half. The World Bank Gini Index shows a slight but insignificant increase in the likelihood of conflict with more inequality, and it appears to have no impact on genocides.

The two differently derived measures of economic inequality demonstrate that when types of civil wars are distinguished, in fact economic inequality does exacerbate revolutions, giving further credence to Hypothesis 2. Gurr, Davies, Bueno de Mesquita, and Grossman have quite accurate theories for revolutions. Furthermore, if ethnic societies require more economic equality for conflict, or at least ethnic conflict occurs with greater likelihood in more economically equal societies than revolutions, then ethnic groups might require greater resources to fight, as Knight, Blainey, Popkin, Maslow, and Tammen et al. would predict, rendering Hypothesis 1 also correct in the continuum.

Owing to the spate of criticisms of model dependence in past literature, the same logit models were assayed with cubic splines created using the methods of Beck, Katz and Tucker (1998) to control for the years of no war prior to war years. Again, the positive and significant effect of economic inequality on revolutions remains robust for both the Gini Index measure and the World Bank Gini Index (see http://www.prio.no/jpr/ datasets for Appendix F, Models 29 and 35, and Appendix G). The addition of cubic splines changes the sign and significance of the effect of the Gini Index on ethnic wars (Appendix F, Model 28) but has no effect on the World Bank Gini's already insignificant effect. The end result for the logit models is that Hypothesis 2 is model dependent—that is, when cubic splines are included, inequality no longer has a negative and significant effect on ethnic wars. What does not change, however, as shown in Figure 2 and Appendix G, is that ethnic wars do occur in more equal societies, whereas inequality consistently coincides with violence in revolutions.

3.6. HUMAN CAPITAL INEQUALITY

Castelló and Doménech's (2002) measure for human capital inequality is a comparatively recent and useful tool for viewing social grievance situations through a different lens from economic inequality. De Soysa and Wagner (2003: 25) argue that this measure captures some of the logic of ethnic inequality under the assumption that dominant ethnic groups control the resources of the state and use education policies to discriminate. This social inequality measure yielded unexpected and opposing results for inequality's effect on ethnic violence and revolutions. Inequality in the human capital realm (Table 3), indicates a greater likelihood of higher levels of violence for ethnic wars. The predicted logit model in Figure 2 shows that a ten-fold increase in human capital inequality in ethnic wars parallels a greater than ten-fold increase in the predicted probability of violence. These results hold with the cubic spline controls (Appendix F).

Though revolutions are more likely in economically unequal societies, inequality in the human capital realm renders a low and insignificant predicted probability of violence. While economic factors are not radically significant in genocides, educational inequality appears to be a significant causal factor for higher levels of genocides.

3.7. THE COMPONENT VARIABLES

Access to political institutions by non-elites (Table 2) lowers the levels of violence in genocides at a significance level of less than 0.005 and somewhat less significantly for ethnic wars (0.073). The fact that non-elites having access to political institutions mitigates the severity of civil wars most significantly in genocides and identity wars indicates that the measure captures an aspect of discontent that could be attributed to exclusion of a particular group from rule, though it does not necessarily distinguish between opposing ethnic groups.

The *greed* variable affects all three types of civil unrest positively and significantly when included with the Gini Index (Table 2); however, the average marginal effects are extremely low. Interestingly enough, social inequality is a more important warexacerbating factor than greed in ethnic wars as shown in Model 7 (Table 3), and the significance of greed disappears when all of the probit models are tested with lags of the *y* variable included among the independent variables.

This study does not attempt to theoretically approach ethnic entrepreneurs; nevertheless, the results for the elite proxy of *tertiary education* give fodder for future studies. Societies where a greater percentage of the population is enrolled in tertiary education predict lower levels of violence in ethnic wars and genocides, but slightly higher levels in revolutions. Though this is not the variable of secondary education generally applied in the literature, it has significance and introduces a new avenue of investigation for elite influence on political violence. Better proxies for elite control using a political constraints variable such as Henisz's (2004) "POLCON" variable might show some of these effects more clearly.

Table 3. Human capital Gini and conflict intensity in disaggregated civil wars, 1960–99, using an ordinal probit model: robust results

Model	Ethnic 7	Revolutions 8	Genocide 9	Ethnic 10	Revolutions 11	Genocide 12
Ln real GDP per capita	−0.203	−0.276	−0.107	−0.217	−0.273	−0.198
Z-value	−3.57	−4.38	−1.64	−5.58	−6.97	−4.42
Std. error	0.057	0.063	0.064	0.039	0.039	0.045
$P > z$	0.000	0.000	0.100	0.000	0.000	0.000
Marginal effects	0.052	0.062	0.017	0.053	0.058	0.028
Ln population	0.400	0.073	0.155	0.384	0.139	0.196
Z-value	16.65	2.81	5.76	19.40	8.01	10.01
Std. error	0.024	0.026	0.027	0.020	0.017	0.020
$P > z$	0.000	0.005	0.000	0.000	0.000	0.000
Marginal effects	0.101	0.017	0.024	0.094	0.030	0.027
Non-elite representation	−0.012	−0.056	−0.123			
Z-value	−0.37	−1.84	−3.07			
Std. error	0.033	0.030	0.040			
$P > z$	0.711	0.066	0.002			
Marginal effects	0.003	0.013	0.019			
Human Capital Gini	0.011	−0.003	0.007	0.012	−0.0007	0.011
Z-value	4.29	−1.36	2.67	−5.78	0.34	4.93
Std. error	0.003	0.002	0.003	0.002	0.002	0.002
$P > z$	0.000	0.173	0.008	0.000	0.734	0.000
Marginal effects	0.003	0.0008	0.001	0.003	0.0001	0.002
Tertiary education	−0.011	0.006	−0.012			
Z-value	−2.17	1.46	−1.72			
Std. error	0.005	0.004	0.007			
$P > z$	0.030	0.145	0.085			
Marginal effects	0.003	0.001	0.002			
Greed	0.0002	−0.005	−0.003			
Z-value	0.06	−1.52	1.81			
Std. error	0.004	0.003	0.004			
$P > z$	0.951	0.129	0.353			
Marginal effects	0.00006	0.001	0.0005			
N	2,414	2,408	2,408	3,438	3,446	3,422
Wald χ^2	(6)593	(6)144	(6)237	(3)454	(3)231	(3)226
Prob > χ^2	0.000	0.000	0.000	0.000	0.000	0.000
Pseudo R^2	0.204	0.043	0.098	0.185	0.054	0.098

4. Discussion

The maxim of a *relative minimum resource threshold* is built as a continuum tying relative deprivation theory, risk, and utility to institutional bargaining theory and power parity, proposing that the context within which the violence takes place affects the requisite level of resources needed for violence escalation. Furthermore, with different histories and in different types of uprisings, inequality takes on meanings that encompass more than economic inequality.

In ethnic uprisings, these results indicate that more economic *equality* in a society precedes escalation of violence and suggests that the perception of inequality is not necessarily confined to economic deprivation—discontent derives from other sources, and the opportunity costs of rebellion are greater. This parallel of greater equality with higher levels of violence also supports the theoretical proposal that belief in the possibility of winning is an important prerequisite of war. Stewart (2000) analyzes inequality in terms of horizontal and vertical inequality, defining ethnic, cultural, and religious groups as "horizontal groups" and purely economic or class distinctions as "vertical" inequalities. She suggests that in addition to economic inequality, a group's relative social and political dimensions are causes for instability. She also addresses the issues of self-image and beliefs within groups. Cramer (2003: 397), while asking if inequality causes conflict, states that it is "important to focus on the variety of ways in which inequalities are managed by societies, and the significance of varying kinds of equality".

Given that the results are negative (or insignificant) for inequality's effect on ethnic wars, and given that there must be at least two groups (within a nation) with either religious differences, language differences, historical differences, or some physical difference for an "ethnic war" to occur, it is not a stretch to say that identity groups will have a greater probability to fight as they approach greater economic equality, but lack political and education equality. Granted, these data do not actually measure the resources of each identity group; however, societies that have resources that are available to the discontent groups will allow the opportunity for rebellion. These resources will not be in the exclusive control of the elite, but will be in the hands of a greater portion of the population. When hope springs forth for the possibility of change, then there is an impetus to fight. De Soysa and Wagner's (2003) reasoning that Castelló and Doménech's (2002) Human Capital Index proxies horizontal inequalities seems to support Stewart's proposals that social inequalities are cause for instability in these models. Inequality of a different sort breeds conflict in ethnic wars.

Nepal, a state with rebellion that is both horizontal and vertical in nature, elegantly exemplifies the two inequality measure results (Murshed and Gates, 2005). While the Maoist struggle is a revolutionary struggle ideologically, the rebelling groups are from different ethnic and different class groups. The overall average Gini measures (34 for the Gini Index and 37 for the World Bank Gini) do not indicate the most extreme economically unequal society overall, thought certainly a more unequal measure than the developed nations. On the other hand, Nepal stars in education inequality at 87 (mean value for 39 years), predicting the highest rates of conflict probability.

"Nafziger and Auvinen (2002: 154) make the relative deprivation argument for violence in vertical group (class wars or revolutions) and horizontal group (regional or ethnic wars) conditions, but they also contend that "ruling elites can expand rent-seeking opportunities for existing political elites, contributing to further economic stagnation that can threaten the legitimacy of the regime and increase the probability of regime turnover". This argument fits for the increase in elites (as proxied by tertiary education) in this study coinciding with increase in conflict intensity in revolutions, though it is perhaps a weak proxy. Like Collier and Hoeffler (1998), they then extend the argument to political elites using "repression to suppress discontent or to capture a greater share of the majority's shrinking surplus", which would imply decreasing violence (Nafziger and Auvinen, 2002: 154). Increasing the number of tertiary-educated population may follow this argument and mitigate violence in genocides and ethnic wars concomitant with a greater social equality in education. The intuitive interpretation of a greater number of the population enrolled in tertiary education is an overall advancement in a society, and the implication, along with greater prosperity and a higher GDP per capita, is that there would be less violence. However, these models do not show that to be the case for revolutions.

Though the purpose here is not to reiterate the conditions for revolutions in all of the revolution literature, the results for an increase in economic inequality being significant in conflict increase demonstrate a different structural mechanism for class wars and a larger gap in income between the high and the low—and therefore a lower relative minimum resource threshold (see Figures 1 and 2). Revolutionary groups are not necessarily financed in the same way as identity group wars, and comparison is not happening between horizontal groups who are close, but at the extremes.

Van de Walle (2004) maintains that beliefs and ideologies are important in civil wars and that countries need to use primary commodities to finance long-term wars. He argues that the greed and crime notion put forth by Collier and Hoeffler (2004) is exaggerated. Lags of the dependent variable (tested on the right-hand side of the equations) weaken the effect of greed to insignificance on all civil conflicts. The implication here is that the greed factor is more an element of financing rather than causing civil wars. This greed measure, nevertheless, does not capture leadership exploitation and size of bank accounts in Luxembourg or Switzerland.

Certainly, ideologies between revolutionary uprisings and ethnic wars do differ, and economic inequality might be more important in some conflicts, while inclusion in the governing process and the social contract is more important in others. The ideologies in revolutions can encompass class and economic issues, while in ethnic wars, the issues of sovereignty, representation, and social welfare may be the type of inequality of paramount importance. Institutions including all groups in the governing process and equal distribution of public goods are essential when divisions are ascriptive rather than economic.

5. Conclusions

Borooah and McGregor (1991: 1) suggest that policy should ensure that "persons of different sex, ethnic background, religion, color, etc. are treated fairly when they enter the labor market". For example, the Fair Employment Act of 1976 in Northern Ireland demonstrated that the state's guaranteeing employment rights for the Catholics and the state's guaranteeing the underprivileged group access to government processes had some mitigating effect on violence.

Horowitz's and Gurr's notion that ethnic violence is more likely in democracies appears to hold upon superficial examination of the countries with ethnic violence included in the dataset. However, the variable used for *non-elite representation* shows that a high degree of access to government processes for non-elite groups is significantly related to mitigating deaths in genocides. Perhaps better measures of ethnic group representation could demonstrate that ascriptive groups are not satisfied with just income equality, but as in the cases of Northern Ireland and Sri Lanka, the underprivileged groups demand access to governmental processes, social and citizenship privileges such as access to education, and the perception of equal treatment. More recent studies indicate that democracies must be institutionally well established to ensure stability and the effect on conflict is curvilinear. Gurr (2000) says that a trend in accommodating ethnic demands, allowing them rights formerly denied such as political participation, sometimes autonomy, and cultural recognition, has been instrumental in decreasing the number of ethnic groups using violent tactics in the last decade.

Midlarsky states that "the distribution of vastly greater inequality is associated with state formation and interestingly, under different conditions, with the dissolution of states'. He reiterates the previous problems in the literature in finding robust relationships between economic inequality and political violence, yet explains its importance in that "these investigations will yield outcomes that are relevant to policy making in democracies and their survivability" (Midlarsky, 1999: 6). Extrapolating the results of this study, equality in ethnically diverse nations holds implications for destabilizing weak democracies. In a more economically equal society with a fairly large middle class (statistical results not shown here), the oppressed groups will have more access to resources and a closer idea of what privileges they have been missing, particularly political ones. Groups are both cognizant of missed privileges and empowered to bargain for more by violent means. Better measures for horizontal inequalities, such as life-expectancy differences between groups and human development measures that Murshed and Gates (2005) and Stewart (2000) employ in their case studies, entrench the perils of inequality in ethnically divided nations.

Specific countries, particularly where both ethnic strife and revolutions occur, either concurrently or with one sparking the other, concur that equality comes in many flavors. Examples include the Democratic Republic of Congo (DRC) (mean Gini Index 45, Human Capital Gini Index 65) and Nigeria (mean Gini Index 45, mean Human Capital Gini Index 65). All three types of intrastate conflicts have continually devastated the DRC for the last few decades while social, political, and economic equality have been *absent.* Current news reports on the violence and terror in Sudan (mean Gini Index 45, mean Human Capital Gini Index 79) indicate violence of both ethnic and nascent revolutionary natures.

Increasing economic equality as a mitigating factor in countries subject to revolutions might then, in turn, create conditions for ethnic combat, making institutional inclusion of the major ethnic groups a priority. Addressing political inequality and the maintenance of an equitable social contract between the governors and the governed must go hand in hand with rectifying economic grievances.[10]

Notes

* Many thanks to Jacek Kugler for guidance with the theories and to Yi Feng for his Gini dataset. My great appreciation to Robert Rotberg and Jane Mansbridge for mentoring at Harvard. Special thanks to Ismene Gizelis for considerable intellectual input to the theory with regard to gender inequalities and civil wars. Thanks to Brian Efird for coining the phrase and Siddharth Swaminathan for assistance with the cubic spline tests. Thanks to the editors and reviewers for their very helpful comments and particularly Henrik Urdal for his encouragement and support of the article. The dataset and Appendices E, F, and G are available at http://www.prio.no/jpr/datasets.

[1] Lichbach (1989) identified more than 40 studies using cross-sectional data, with most resulting in a positive relationship between economic inequality and political violence, some with a negative relationship, and some with no relationship. Nagel (1974) found a concave curvilinear relationship between the Gini Index of landholdings across South Vietnamese provinces and its effect on control. Russett (1964) observed the lack of specification for the dependent variable of instability and measures of inequality and proposed a Gini Index of land concentration as a reasonable measure of inequality. Russett reported a positive correlation between Gini and violent political deaths. Muller et al. (1989) criticized the use of Gini measures and found ambiguous relationships between land inequality and violence.

[2] Toft (2003) and Rotberg (2004) deal with territory and failed states as being reasons for conflict.

[3] Alker (1994) expressed doubts as to whether or not general models from cross-sectional data can predict ethnic conflict and proposed that microanalysis of individual cases is useful.

[4] Stewart (2000) defines horizontal groups as “culturally formed groups” and argues that consideration of inequalities between groups—economically and politically—are important. She also discusses cultural differences, group identity, and self-esteem issues as having fundamental influence on group decisions.

[5] The analysis was conducted using Stata.

[6] King and Zeng (2001:628) derive another method for correcting selection on the Y term, by subtracting the $\ln[1 - \tau)]/[\bar{y}/1 - \bar{y})]$ from the estimated constant term.

[7] Neither Correlates of War nor the Uppsala conflict data refer to genocide (“one sided violence”) as civil war.

[8] As the paper is still under review, the SAS file showing the method for predicting this Gini can be obtained from Yi Feng.

[9] http://www.worldbank.org/research/inequality/data.htm.

[10] Addison and Murshed (2001: 2) define the social contract as the “agreed upon rules of the game that govern the distribution of resources and obligations across society—and the concomitant mechanisms for settling disputes”.

Appendix A: Correlation matrix

	Ethnic	Revolutions	Genocide	Ln real GDP per capita	Non-elite representation	Gini index	Human Capital Gini	World Bank Gini	Greed
Ethnic	1.000								
Revolutions	0.216	1.000							
Genocide	0.371	0.197	1.000						
Ln real GDP per capita	−0.272	−0.101	−0.145	1.000					
Non-elite representation	−0.170	−0.089	−0.144	0.690	1.000				
Gini index	−0.051	0.144	0.023	−0.666	−0.501	1.000			
Human Capital Gini	0.241	0.019	0.123	−0.727	−0.620	0.493	1.000		
World Bank Gini	−0.078	0.147	−0.024	−0.386	−0.329	0.682	0.345	1.000	
Greed	−0.110	−0.012	0.014	−0.026	−0.186	0.225	0.098	0.195	1.000
Tertiary	−0.222	−0.011	−0.149	0.706	0.605	−0.526	−0.626	−0.370	−0.231

Appendix B: Frequency distribution on the dependent variables

	Frequency	Percent	Cumulative percent
Ethnic wars			
0	4,351	87.88	87.88
1	279	5.64	93.52
2	225	4.54	98.06
3	52	1.05	99.11
4	44	0.89	100.00
Total	4,951	100.00	
Revolutions			
0	4,625	93.66	93.66
1	108	2.19	95.85
2	140	2.84	98.68
3	44	0.89	99.57
4	21	0.43	100.00
Total	4,938	100.00	
Genocides			
0	4,681	95.10	95.10
1	74	1.50	96.61
2	45	0.91	97.52
3	67	1.36	98.88
4	46	0.93	99.82
5	9	0.18	100.00
Total	4,922	100.00	

Appendix C: Summary statistics

Variable	Observations	Mean	Std. dev.	Min.	Max.
Ethnic deaths	4,951	0.214	0.655	0.00	4.00
Revolution deaths	4,938	0.122	0.518	0.00	4.00
Genocide deaths	4,922	0.121	0.596	0.00	5.00
Ln real GDP per capita	5,615	7.945	1.232	2.90	10.98
Non-elite representation	5,092	2.712	1.603	0.00	5.00
Tertiary education	4,238	14.02	15.31	0.00	97.70
Ln population	6,228	15.406	1.945	10.62	20.96
Gini index	4,261	38.277	6.484	28.16	55.00
Human Capital Gini	4,094	43.52	23.52	8.04	98.98
World Bank Gini	2,366	40.37	9.68	15.90	66.25
Greed	5,001	16.81	18.40	0.20	213.9

Appendix D: World Bank Gini and conflict intensity in disaggregated civil wars, 1960–99, using a probit model: robust results

Model	Ethnic 13	Revolutions 14	Genocide 15	Ethnic 16	Revolutions 17	Genocide 18
Ln $RGDP_PC$	−0.320	−0.165	−0.319	−0.269	−0.250	0.026
Z-value	−9.39	−4.80	−9.28	−4.19	−3.57	0.30
Std. error	0.034	0.034	0.034	0.064	0.070	0.084
$P > z$	0.000	0.000	0.000	0.000	0.000	0.761
Marginal effects	0.089	0.027	0.044	0.071	0.040	0.003
Ln population	0.354	0.214	0.180	0.356	0.231	0.191
Z-value	14.31	8.48	6.97	11.34	6.47	5.33
Std. error	0.025	0.025	0.026	0.031	0.036	0.036
$P > z$	0.000	0.000	0.000	0.000	0.000	0.000
Marginal effects	0.099	0.035	0.025	0.094	0.037	0.020
Non-elite representation				0.019	−0.127	−0.185
Z-value				0.53	−2.75	4.10
Std. error				0.037	0.046	0.045
$P > z$				0.597	0.006	0.000
Marginal effects				0.005	0.020	0.020
World Bank Gini	0.006	0.0359	−0.0002	0.008	0.039	−0.005
Z-value	1.34	8.31	−0.04	1.68	7.45	−0.90
Std. error	0.005	0.004	0.005	0.005	0.005	0.006

(*Continued*)

Appendix D: ***(Continued)***

Model	Ethnic 13	Revolutions 14	Genocide 15	Ethnic 16	Revolutions 17	Genocide 18
$P > z$	0.180	0.000	0.966	0.093	0.000	0.368
Marginal effects	0.002	0.006	0.00003	0.002	0.006	0.0005
Tertiary education				−0.018	0.020	−0.031
Z-value				−2.90	4.33	−2.45
Std. error				0.006	0.005	0.013
$P > z$				0.004	0.000	0.014
Marginal effects				0.005	0.003	0.003
Greed*				−0.007	0.007	0.0005
Z-value				−1.41	1.46	0.10
Std. error				0.005	0.005	0.005
$P > z$				0.159	0.145	0.919
Marginal effects				0.002	0.001	0.00005
N	2,042	2,048	2,040	1,601	1,600	1,601
Waldχ^2	(3)310	(3)140	(3)149	(3)377	(3)137	(3)144
Prob > χ^2	0.000	0.000	0.000	0.000	0.000	0.000
Pseudo R^2	0.175	0.084	0.096	0.203	0.098	0.140

Spearman's test for *tertiary education* and *Ln real GDP per capita* $P > t = 0.000$.
Spearman's test for *Ln real GDP per capita* (LnRGDP$_P$C) and *non-elite representation* $P > t = 0.000$.
**Greed* variable limits the model's time span from 1960 to 1995.

References

Addison, Tony and S. Mansoob Murshed, 2001. "From conflict to reconstruction: Reviving the social contract", *WIDER Discussion Paper No.* 2001/48, http://www.wider. unu.edu/publications/dps/dp2001-48.pdf.

Alker, Hayward R., 1994. "Early warning models and/or preventative information systems?", in Ted Robert Gurr and Barbara Harff, (eds), Special Issue on Early Warnings of Communal Conflicts and Humanitarian Crises, *Journal of Ethno-Development* 4(1): 117–123.

Barro, Robert J. and Jong-Wha Lee, 2001. "International data on educational attainment updates and implications", *Oxford Economic Papers* 53(3): 541–563.

Beck, Nathaniel; Jonathan N. Katz and Richard Tucker, 1998. "Taking time seriously: Time-series-cross-section analysis with a binary dependent variable", *American Journal of Political Science* 42(4): 1260–1288.

Blainey, Geoffrey, 1975. *The Causes of War.* New York: Free Press.

Bollen, Kenneth and Robert Jackman, 1985. "Political democracy and the size distribution of income", *American Sociological Review* 50 (August): 371–400.

Borooah, Vani K. and Patrick McGregor, 1991. "The measurement and decomposition of poverty: An analysis based on the 1985 family expenditure survey for Northern Ireland", *Manchester School of Economic & Social Studies* 59(4): 357–377.

Bueno de Mesquita, Bruce, 1985. "The war trap revisited", *American Political Science Review* 79(1): 156–177.

Castelló, Amparo and Rafael Doménech, 2002. "Human capital inequality and economic growth: Some new evidence", *Economic Journal* 112 (478 March): C187–200.

Collier, Paul and Anke Hoeffler, 1998. "On economic causes of civil war", *Oxford Economic Papers* 50(4): 563–573.

Collier, Paul and Anke Hoeffler, 2004. "Greed and grievance in civil war", *Oxford Economic Papers* 56(4): 563–595.

Collier, Paul and Nicholas Sambanis, 2002. "Understanding civil war: A new agenda", *Journal of Conflict Resolution* 46(1): 3–12.

Cramer, Christopher, 2003. "Does inequality cause conflict?", *Journal of International Development* 15(4): 397–412.

Davies, James, 1962. "Toward a theory of revolution", *American Sociological Review* 27(1): 5–19.

Deininger, Klaus and Lyn Squire, 1996. "Measuring income inequality: A new data set", *World Bank Economic Review* 10(3): 565–591.

Denzau, Arthur and Douglass North, 1994. "Shared mental models: Ideologies and institutions", *Kyklos* 47(1): 3–31.

de Soysa, Indra and Angelika Wagner, 2003. "Global market, local Mayhem? Foreign investment, trade openness, state capacity, and civil war, 1989–2000", Center for Development Research, University of Bonn. http://www.dgroups.org/groups/globaliz ation/index.cfm?op=main&cat_id=2751&sor t=title.

De Tocqueville, Alexis, 1887. *L'Ancien Régime et la Revolution* [The Old Regime and the French Revolution]. Paris: Lévy.

Easterly, William and Hairong Yu, 2000. "Global development network growth database", *World Bank.* http://www.worldbank.org/ research/growth/GDNdata.htm.

Elder, Harold and Patricia Rudolph, 1999. "Does retirement planning affect the level of retirement satisfaction?", *Financial Services Review* 8(2): 117–127.

Ellingsen, Tanja, 2000. "Colorful community or ethnic witches" brew? Multiethnicity and domestic conflict during and after the cold war", *Journal of Conflict Resolution* 44(2): 228–249.

Fearon, James and David Laitin, 2003. "Ethnicity, insurgency, and civil war", *American Political Science Review* 97(1): 75–90.

Feng, Yi, Jacek Kugler and Paul Zak, 2005. "Demographic transition, income distribution and politics. A model of economic development" (under review: *Contemporary Economic Policy*).

Grossman, Herschel I., 1991. "A general equilibrium model of insurrections", *American Economic Review* 81(4): 912–921.

Gurr, Ted, 1970. *Why Men Rebel.* Princeton, NJ: Princeton University Press.

Gurr, Ted, 1994. "Peoples against states: Ethno-political conflict and the changing world system", *International Studies Quarterly* 38 (September): 347–377.
Gurr, Ted, 2000. "Ethnic warfare on the wane", *Foreign Affairs* 79(3): 52–64.
Gurr, Ted and Barbara Harff, 1997. "Internal wars and failures of governance, 1954–1996", *State Failure Task Force*. http://www.bsos. umd.edu/cidcm/stfail/sfcodebk.htm.
Harff, Barbara, 2003. "No lessons learned from the holocaust? Assessing risks of genocide and political mass murder since 1955", *American Political Science Review* 97(1): 57–73.
Hegre, Håvard; Tanja Ellingsen, Scott Gates and Nils Petter Gleditsch, 2001. "Toward a democratic civil peace? Democracy, political change, and civil war, 1816–1992", *American Political Science Review* 95(1): 33–48.
Henisz, Witold Jerzy, 2004. "Political institutions and policy volatility", *Economics & Politics* 16(1): 1–27.
Heston, Alan; Robert Summers and Bettina Aten, 2002. "*Penn world table version* 6.1", Center for international Comparisons, University of Pennsylvania (CICUP).
Horowitz, Irving Louis, 1994. "How to think democracy", *Freedom Review* 25(2): 37–38.
Inglehart, Ronald, 1990. *Culture Shift in Advanced Industrial Society.* Princeton, NJ: Princeton University Press.
King, Gary and Langche Zeng, 2001. "Improving forecasts of state failure", *World Politics* 53 (July): 623–658.
Knight, Jack, 1992. *Institutions and Social Conflict.* Cambridge: Cambridge University Press.
Knight, Jack, 1995. "Models, interpretations, and theories: Constructing explanations of institutional emergence and change", in Jack Knight and Itai Sened, (eds), *Explaining Social Institutions.* Ann Arbor, MI: University of Michigan Press (95–121).
Krain, Matthew, 1997. "State-Sponsored mass murder: The onset and severity of genocides and politicides", *Journal of Conflict Resolution* 41(3): 331–360.
Lemke, Douglas, 2002. *Regions of War and Peace.* Cambridge: Cambridge University Press.
Liao, Tim Futing, 1994. *Interpreting Probability Models: Logit, Probit and Other Generalized Linear Models.* London: Sage.
Lichbach, Mark, 1989. "An evaluation of 'does economic inequality breed political conflict?'", *World Politics* XLI(4): 431–472.
Marshall, Monty G. Ted Robert Gurr and Barbara Harff, 2002. "*Internal Wars and Failures of Governance,* 1955–2002". http://www.cidcm.umd.edu/inscr/stfail.
Marshall, Monty G., Keith Jaggers and Ted Robert Gurr, 2004. Polity IV: http://www.cidcm.umd.edu/inscr/polity/.
Maslow, Abraham, 1954. *Motivation and Personality.* New York: Harper.
Midlarsky, Manus, 1999. *The Evolution of Inequality: War, State Survival and Democracy in Comparative Perspective.* Stanford, CA: Stanford University Press.
Midlarsky, Manus, 2005. *The Killing Trap: Genocide in the Twentieth Century.* Cambridge: Cambridge University Press.
Moore, William, Ronald Lindström and Valerie O'Regan, 1996. "Land reform, political violence and the economic inequality–political conflict nexus: A longitudinal analysis", *International Interaction* 21(4): 335–363.
Muller, Edward N.; Mitchell A. Seligson, Hungder Fu, Manus I. Midlarsky, 1989. "Inequality and political violence", *American Political Science Review* 83(2): 577–596.
Murshed, S. Mansoob and Scott Gates, 2005. "Spatial–Horizontal inequality and the maoist insurgency in Nepal", *Review of Development Economics* 9(1): 121–134.
Nafziger, Wayne and Juha Auvinen, 2002. "Economic development, inequality, war, and state violence", *World Development* 30(2): 153–163.
Nagel, Jack, 1974. "Inequality and discontent: A nonlinear hypothesis", *World Politics* 26(4): 453–472.
Organski, A. F. K. and Jacek Kugler, 1980. *The War Ledger.* Chicago, IL: University of Chicago Press.
Perotti, Roberto, 1996. "Growth, income distribution, and democracy: What the data say", *Journal of Economic Growth* 1(2): 149–187.
Popkin, Samuel, 1979. *The Rational Peasant.* Berkeley, CA: University of California Press.
Reynal-Querol, Marta, 2002. "Ethnicity, political systems, and civil wars", *Journal of Conflict Resolution* 46(1): 29–54.
Robinson, James A., 2001. "Social identity, inequality and conflict", *Economics of Governance* 2(1): 85–99.

Rotberg, Robert, 2004. *When States Fail: Causes and Consequences.* Princeton, NJ: Princeton University Press.
Rummel, Rudolph J., 1994. "Power, genocide and mass murder, *Journal of Peace Research* 31 (February): 1–10.
Rummel, Rudolph J., 1995. "Democracy, power, genocide, and mass murder (Theory of Democide)", *Journal of Conflict Resolution* 39 (March): 3–26.
Russett, Bruce, 1964. "Inequality and Instability, The relation of land tenure to politics", *World Politics* XVI (October–July): 442–470.
Sambanis, Nicholas, 2001. "Do ethnic and nonethnic civil wars have the same causes? A theoretical and empirical enquiry (Part 1)", *Journal of Conflict Resolution* 46(1): 259–282.
Stewart, Frances, 2000. "Crisis prevention: Tackling horizontal inequalities", *Oxford Development Studies* 28(3): 245–262.
Tammen, Ronald, et al., 2000. *Power Transitions: Strategies for the 21st Century.* New York: Chatham House.
Taylor, Charles and David Jodice, 1983. *World Handbook of Political and Social Indicators III.* Vol. 2. New Haven, CT: Yale University Press.
Toft, Monica, 2003. *The Geography of Ethnic Violence.* Princeton, NJ: Princeton University Press.
Van de Walle, Nicolas, 2004. "The economic correlates of state failure", in Robert Rotberg, (ed.), *When States Fail: Causes and Consequences.* Princeton, NJ: Princeton University Press (94–115).
World Bank, 2000. *World Development Indicators*, computer file: http://www.world bank.org/research/inequality/data.htm.

CHAPTER 3. PEOPLE VS. MALTHUS: POPULATION PRESSURE, ENVIRONMENTAL DEGRADATION, AND ARMED CONFLICT REVISITED*

HENRIK URDAL
Centre for the Study of Civil War, International Peace Research Institute, Oslo (PRIO), Norway

Abstract. Demographic and environmental factors have claimed a dominant position in the post-Cold War security discourse. According to the neo-Malthusian conflict scenario, population pressure on natural renewable resources makes societies more prone to low-intensity civil war. On the contrary, resource-optimists concede that agricultural land scarcity caused by high population density may be a driving factor behind economic development, thus causing peace in a long-term perspective. These notions are tested in a quantitative cross-national time-series study covering the 1950–2000 period. The results do not provide strong support for either perspective. Countries experiencing high rates of population growth, high rates of urbanization, or large refugee populations do not face greater risks of internal armed conflict. There is some indication that scarcity of potential cropland may have a pacifying effect. However, where land scarcity combines with high rates of population growth, the risk of armed conflict increases somewhat. This trend is particularly marked for the 1970s, the decade that saw the great rise in neo-Malthusian concerns. Claims that the world has entered a "new age of insecurity" after the end of the Cold War, where demographic and environmental factors threaten security and state stability, appear to be unfounded. Overall, the robustness of the empirical support for both paradigms is low. A strong emphasis on security as a macro rationale for reducing global population growth thus seems unwarranted.

1. Introduction

The social and human implications of armed conflict are enormous. The number of people dying from indirect causes of conflict such as under- and malnutrition, or diseases that could easily be treated if medicines were available, can be much higher than the number of battle-related deaths.[1] In the 1998–2001 civil war in the Democratic Republic of Congo, the ratio of indirect to direct casualties was roughly six to one (Roberts et al., 2003).[2] Armed conflict is further harmful to people's quality of life through negative effects on economic development and the environment. Collier (1999) has shown that conflict can tear down levels of economic development that took decades to achieve. He argues that spinoff effects continue to hamper economic growth for a long period following the termination of conflict.

Domestic armed conflicts and civil wars are now far more frequent than interstate conflicts. While there was a peak in conflict occurrence in the mid-1990s, the number of domestic conflicts has fallen slightly to equal approximately the level

This chapter was previously published in *Journal of Peace Research*, vol. 42, no. 4, 2005, pp. 417–434.

Helge Brunborg et al. (eds.), The Demography of Armed Conflict, 67–86.

of the 1980s. In 2001, 33 internal armed conflicts with more than 25 battle-related casualties took place in 28 different countries. Eleven conflicts inflicted more than 1,000 battle casualties (Gleditsch et al., 2002).

This article addresses the *neo-Malthusian* concern that countries with rapidly growing populations will experience degradation and scarcity of natural resources such as cropland, fresh water, forests, and fisheries, increasing the risk of violent conflict over scarce resources. Although already rising as a security issue in the 1960s and 1970s, a renewed and more pronounced neo-Malthusian concern over security arrived in the 1990s. Explanations for this have been twofold. First, a general environmental awareness increased in Western popular opinion in this period, and environmental protagonists succeeded in "securitizing" central environmental issues, thereby attracting the attention of policymakers (Levy, 1995: 44). In the United States, vice president Al Gore initiated the "State Failure Task Force" project in 1994, aimed at revealing environmental, political, and social causes of state failure. Second, the end of the Cold War left a void in security policy, and Western national security establishments sought ways to legitimize their continued existence (Gleditsch, 2001: 259).[3]

Some argue that demographic and environmental factors have become *more important* as causes of conflict after the end of the Cold War. A widely cited article states that "West Africa is becoming *the* symbol of worldwide demographic, environmental and societal stress", potentially leading to anarchy and dissolution of nation states in the future (Kaplan, 1994: 46, emphasis in original). According to de Soysa (2002a: 3), some of the environmental security literature argues that ecological and demographic pressures represent a "new age of insecurity" after the end of the Cold War.

Much of the empirical literature on population, environment, and conflict is based on single-case studies, and these are frequently criticized for lack of methodological rigor. In this article, I have put neo-Malthusian notions to an empirical test in a large-*N* model covering all states and dependent areas in the international system for the past 50 years, using several different indicators of population pressure.

2. Population, environment, and conflict

Malthus (1803/1992) assessed that food production would grow arithmetically, while the human population would grow exponentially, at some point causing serious food shortages and human misery. History has to a considerable extent proven Malthus wrong. Food production has increased more than he foresaw, while population has grown more slowly. However, the idea survived that the human population cannot continue to grow indefinitely without at some point reaching and exceeding the carrying capacity of the earth. At the end of the 1960s and the beginning of the 1970s, a wave of alarmist "neo-Malthusian" literature emerged, predicting that the rapidly growing world population would soon exceed the resource base and lead to serious environmental destruction, widespread hunger, and violent conflicts.[4]

Attempts to foresee future development are a prominent feature of much of the neo-Malthusian literature. In 1968, Ehrlich stated that "the battle to feed humanity is over. In the course of the 1970s the world will experience starvation of tragic proportions—hundreds of millions of people will starve to death" (Ehrlich, 1968: xi). Like many other alarmist predictions, Ehrlich's did not hold. The focus on potential future resource wars in much of the resource pessimist literature has been criticized for not being testable (Gleditsch, 2001). Since the argument that population-induced resource scarcity can cause violent conflict has such a long history, I assume that the argument does not apply only to future conflicts, but also to the past. The neo-Malthusian conflict scenario should be expected to stand up to empirical testing.

The view that population pressure and resource scarcity can cause conflict is met by counter-arguments on several grounds from a research tradition often referred to as cornucopians, resource optimists. Believing that the world is continuously improving by both human and environmental standards, cornucopians offer three main challenges to the neo-Malthusian paradigm. First, they claim that most debated natural resources are not really scarce, at least not in a global context, and that we are not going to experience a major resource crisis even in the face of continued population growth (e.g., Lomborg, 2001).

Second, if some resources are getting scarcer, humankind is able to adapt to these challenges. Market mechanisms are believed to reduce the demand for scarce resources through higher pricing. Furthermore, natural resource scarcity may even work as a catalyst to trigger technological innovation, making scarcity ever less likely in the future. Boserup argues that population pressure on natural resources is actually the key to development and implementation of new techniques in agricultural production (Boserup and Schultz, 1990). The higher population density is relative to the resource base, the more societies are forced to adopt new technologies. Boserup sees the relatively low agricultural effectiveness of many African states as a result of the continent's low population density (Boserup and Schultz, 1990). The third point made by cornucopians is that it is abundance of valuable natural resources, rather than scarcity, that leads to violent conflict. Income from rich natural resources such as gems, tropical timber, cash crops, and drugs may be regarded as an incentive for armed conflict ("greed") or as a means to finance warfare ("opportunity"). The empirical support for this argument is strong (e.g., Collier, 2000; Le Billon, 2001; de Soysa, 2002a).[5] While often portrayed as competing, the scarcity and abundance hypotheses are not theoretically mutually exclusive and may in fact coexist (Renner, 2002).

2.1. THE MODERATE NEO-MALTHUSIAN POSITION

Although some of the alarmist literature may have discredited the neo-Malthusian position, few scholars would argue that resource scarcities never occur or that they are irrelevant for conflict behavior. Natural resources that are essential to human life and welfare are unevenly distributed between and within states, and scarcities of certain natural resources may arise and persist locally, at least temporarily. The most influential scholar moderating the neo-Malthusian position has been Thomas Homer-Dixon and his "Project on Environment, Population, and Security" at the University of Toronto.[6] Homer-Dixon and associates distinguish between different sources of resource scarcity.[7] Population growth is an important source to *demand-induced scarcity* (Homer-Dixon, 1999: 48). If a resource base is constant, the availability of resources per person will diminish as an increasing number of persons have to share it. Such scarcity can also arise from an increase in demand per capita.

Most armed conflicts and wars are over objectives that can broadly be defined as resources (Gleditsch, 2001: 252). Neo-Malthusians are primarily concerned with resources that are essential to food production. Homer-Dixon and Blitt (1998) argue that large populations in many developing countries are highly dependent on four key resources: fresh water, cropland, forests, and fisheries. The availability of these resources determines people's day-to-day well-being, and scarcity of such resources can, under certain conditions, cause violent conflict (Homer-Dixon and Blitt, 1998: 2). It has been proposed that the resource scarcity and conflict scenario is more pertinent to developing countries, owing to generally lower capacity to deal with environmental issues and less ability to cope with and adapt to scarcity (Homer-Dixon, 1999: 4–5; Kahl, 2002: 258).

Homer-Dixon argues that increased environmental scarcity is likely to cause social effects that increase the risk of internal violent conflict. Environmental scarcities can lead to constrained agricultural and economic productivity, causing migration and widespread poverty. Grievances may result in violence provided two conditions exist. First, the aggrieved individuals need to participate in some sort of ethnic, religious, or class-based collective that is capable of violent action against the authorities. Second, the political structure must fail to give these groups the opportunity to peacefully express their grievances at the same time as it offers them the openings for violent action.

Some more recent contributions, particularly by Kahl and Matthew, further moderate the neo-Malthusian position. Kahl (2002: 266) refutes the critique that neo-Malthusian models are deterministic, and claims that they are rather under-specified. He criticizes much neo-Malthusian writing for failing to identify clearly which intervening variables are most important. Referring to the assumption of "state weakness" as a necessary precondition for environmentally induced conflict in the works of Homer-Dixon and of Goldstone (e.g., 2002), he contends that such conflicts can also arise under conditions of. "state exploitation", when powerful elites exploit rising scarcities and corresponding grievances in order to consolidate power. Conflicts in Kenya and Rwanda are claimed to be examples of the latter (Kahl, 2002: 265).

Matthew (2002: 243) provides two important critiques of the simple neo-Malthusian thesis. First, it understates the capacity to adapt to scarcities that are manifest in many societies. Second, it does not adequately deal with historical and structural dimensions of violence, like globalization and colonial influence. Matthew's approach shifts the focus to why some states succeed while others fail to adapt to scarcities of renewable resources.

Among the more moderate neo-Malthusian contributions, there are few apocalyptical claims of large-scale warfare over scarce resources. Dalby (2002: 95) concedes that "the likelihood of large-scale warfare over natural resources is small". And while claims of future "water wars" proliferate, Homer-Dixon (1999: 5) concludes that interstate scarcity wars are not very likely. He rather predicts that the most likely forms of violent conflict to erupt from resource scarcities are ethnic clashes and civil strife. In order to address the proposition that scarcity is more likely to produce low-level domestic violence, this study investigates whether population pressure may increase the risk of internal armed conflict with at least 25 battle-related deaths, a threshold well below the 1,000-deaths criterion conventionally set for civil war.

2.2. NEO-MALTHUSIAN POPULATION PRESSURE AND ARMED CONFLICT

If there is something to the neo-Malthusian causal scheme, I would expect to find that countries experiencing a high population pressure would have an increased risk of armed conflict, all other factors being equal.[8] The concept of population pressure, however, contains several different aspects. The traditional Malthusian focus has been on *population growth*. The concern has been that high population growth would outstrip growth in revenues from natural resources. Population would then eventually exceed the productive capacity of natural resources, a situation often referred to as overpopulation. I thus assume the following:

H1: Countries with high population growth are more likely to experience domestic armed conflict than countries with low population growth.

Another measure that is often argued to be an indicator of population pressure is *population density*. However, the conventional density measure, the number of people per square kilometer, says very little about the ratio between population and the resource base. High density is more of a problem in arid areas than in fertile. Partly on these grounds, Ehrlich and Ehrlich (1996: 70) criticize the use of population density as a measure of population pressure, calling it the "Netherlands fallacy". If density instead is measured as population relative to the area that potentially could be used for food production, what I term *potential cropland*, one is able to measure the population pressure relative to what is perhaps the single most important renewable natural resource. Population density then resembles a measure of *cropland scarcity*. I expect the following:

H2: Countries with high population density relative to potential cropland are more likely to experience domestic armed conflict than countries with low density.

Population density is a static measure that tells us little about the current pressure on natural resources. Countries that have been densely populated for a longer period, and now experience moderate or low population growth, may have had sufficient time and opportunity to adapt to and overcome scarcities. By contrast, population growth in itself is a dynamic measure that is decoupled from actual resource availability. Population growth can also happen in countries with a plethora of natural resources, thus not causing scarcity. While one could question separately the validity of each of these indicators, I expect that the coexistence of the two factors, high population growth in a context of already scarce per capita cropland, would indicate an extraordinary strain on natural resources.

H3: The higher population density relative to potential cropland a country experiences, the stronger is the conflict-conducive effect of high population growth.

Urbanization is often added to the "litany of emerging challenges" to state stability (Brennan-Galvin, 2002: 123). Rapid urbanization may be the result of rural resource scarcity (Homer-Dixon, 1999: 155), but urbanization may also produce severe scarcities of certain commodities, in particular fresh water (Klare, 2001: 140). While acknowledging that past studies have found "surprisingly little correlation between urban growth and civil strife", Homer-Dixon (1999: 155–156) claims that "in interaction with . . . other factors [including economic crisis and weakening of the state], it appears much more likely to contribute to violence". According to Goldstone (2002: 14), urban growth that is not matched by increased economic growth and job creation is associated with an increased risk of political violence.

H4: The stronger the growth of the urban population, the more likely a country is to experience domestic armed conflict.

A final form of population pressure addressed by this study is *migration*. While Homer-Dixon is mainly concerned with how migration can be the outcome of resource scarcity, large groups of migrants can also be a source of serious environmental degradation in the receiving area. This is especially the case with large refugee camps (ECHO, 1995: 5). The impact that migrants have on the environment in the receiving area depends on their total number, the degree of concentration, and whether the movement of people is sudden or long term.[9] Refugee movements are likely to produce more acute and sudden social and environmental challenges than population growth, beyond the aspect of numbers. Refugees may have a short-term perspective, reducing incentives to handle resources in a sustainable manner; they may lack information about fragile ecological balances in the area of refuge, and may be regarded as competitors from the point of view of original inhabitants.

H5: Countries that host large refugee populations are more likely to experience domestic armed conflict than countries that do not.

3. Research design

This study takes the form of a large-*N* quantitative survey. The unit of analysis is the country-year, and the dependent variable is armed conflict onset. With a dichotomous dependent variable, logistic regression is chosen as the statistical method.

Included in the analysis are all sovereign states in the international system and all politically dependent areas (colonies, occupied territories, and dependencies) for the whole period 1950–2000.[10] The logit model is specified as

$$ln(p_{it}/(1 - p_{it})) = \alpha + \beta X_{it} + e_{it}$$

where α is the intercept, βX is a set of explanatory variables with corresponding coefficients, and e is the random error term, for country i at time t.

3.1. PREVIOUS EMPIRICAL WORK

There has been little systematic comparative empirical research on the causal effects of population pressure on war and armed conflict. A few studies have addressed the population aspect briefly by including one or more measures of population pressure into more general models. Overall, they seem to find some support for neo-Malthusian concerns. Tir and Diehl (2001) find a significant and positive effect of population growth on the likelihood of interstate war, while there is no such effect of population density. Hauge and Ellingsen (2001) and de Soysa (2002b) find that high population density slightly increases the likelihood of domestic conflict. De Soysa further concludes that renewable resource scarcity, measured by the per capita stock of total renewable resources, does not condition the effect of density. Both studies apply the same low-intensity conflict data (at least 25 deaths per year) as this study does, covering mainly the 1980s and the 1990s, respectively. Collier and Hoeffler (1998) find no significant effects of population growth or density on civil war (more than 1,000 deaths).

3.2. OPERATIONALIZATIONS

The conflict data are drawn from the PRIO–Uppsala dataset (Gleditsch et al., 2002). This dataset has been published annually in *Journal of Peace Research* since 1993 but has only recently been extended beyond the post-Cold War period. Shorter series, mostly for the post-Cold War era, have been analyzed in earlier studies (Hauge and Ellingsen, 2001; de Soysa, 2002b). Colonial wars are defined here as domestic conflicts.[11]

The PRIO–Uppsala dataset defines a relatively low threshold for conflict, a minimum of 25 battle-related deaths per year. According to the PRIO–Uppsala criteria, an armed conflict is further defined as a contested incompatibility concerning government and/or territory, between at least two parties, of which one is the government of a state, using armed force (Gleditsch et al., 2002: 619). An armed conflict onset is consequently coded 1 for the first year of a domestic conflict. Subsequent years in conflict (including new conflict onsets when a previous conflict is still active) as well as years in peace are coded 0. If a conflict falls below the threshold of 25 deaths for at least two years and then resumes with the same parties and over the same incompatibility, this is coded as a separate conflict onset.[12]

A substantial number of the conflicts registered in the PRIO—Uppsala dataset broke out at a time when there was already at least one other conflict going on in the same country. Typically, large countries like India and Indonesia have experienced several local conflicts taking place at the same time. The number of such overlapping conflicts is greater for the PRIO—Uppsala data than for most other conflict datasets, owing to the low-intensity threshold. During the 1950–2000 period, a total of 192 conflict onsets from a state of peace were identified. Another 42 onsets happened when a country was already experiencing another armed conflict. For the alternatively coded dependent variable, all country-years experiencing a conflict onset are coded 1, irrespective of whether a previous conflict is active. Overlapping conflicts pose a methodological challenge, since studies of armed conflict usually focus on transitions from peace to war, omitting consecutive years of war. While this study follows the conventional approach, a separate model using the alternative dependent variable will be run for comparison.

Data on *population growth* are estimated from UN total population size estimates of the *World Population Prospects* (UN, 1999).[13] For states with populations under 150,000 in 1995 (in the following referred to as "small states"), data were collected from the *Demographic Yearbook* (UN, annual) and the *Statistical Abstract of the World* (Reddy, 1994). The measure is lagged by five years to account for the presumably slow-moving process of population-induced resource scarcity.

A measure of *population density* relative to the total area of a country, as applied by Hauge and Ellingsen (2001), misses the important aspect that countries differ significantly with respect to the productive capacity of their land.[14] This study aims to establish a measure of per capita *cropland scarcity*: population density relating the number of people in a country to the area that is potentially suitable for food production, here termed *potential cropland*. I define potential cropland as all of a country's land that falls into the following land use categories: arable land, permanent crops, permanent pastures, and forests and woodland (CIA, annual). Land that is excluded from this definition includes, but is not limited to, urban areas, mountains, roads, and deserts. Owing to lack of reliable time-series estimates, the potential cropland measure is based on a single observation per country only, dating from the 1993–2001 period, ignoring the potential problem of changing land use over time. Data on total land area (in square kilometers) were collected from the *World Development Indicators* (World Bank, 2003), the *World Factbook* (CIA, annual), and the *Encyclopedia Britannica* (Britannica, annual). Data on total population size originate from UN (1999), and from the *Demographic Yearbook* (UN, annual) and the *Statistical Abstract of the World* (Reddy, 1994) for small states. The population density variable is log-transformed in order to reduce the huge variation.

The population data from the *World Population Prospects* are assumed to be the most reliable and comparable available. For more developed countries, the availability of reliable data on population size and dynamics is high, although data on international migration flows are generally inadequate (UN, 2000: 175). For many less developed countries and regions, data are less available and sometimes of inferior quality (ibid.). The UN Population Division uses a well of different sources to assess consistency between them and employs demographic estimation techniques to arrive at reasonable estimates. For some extreme cases where no or only outdated information exists, estimates are derived by inferring levels and trends from those experienced by countries in the same region that have a socio-economic profile similar to the country in question (UN, 2000: 176).

Data on *urbanization* covering the 1960–2000 period have been collected from the *World Development Indicators* (World Bank, 2003) and measure the annual increase in urban populations. *Refugee* data are drawn from statistics of the United Nations High Commissioner for Refugees (UNHCR, 1998, 1999, 2000). Refugee data are generally of low reliability. While the ideal would be to assess both total size and flows of refugees, building a more reliable dataset for refugees is beyond the scope of this article.[15] As a very crude first test of the refugee proposition, this study employs a dummy variable taking on the value 1 for countries that hosted more than 100,000 refugees in a given year, and 0 otherwise. Data on refugee populations are available for the years 1988–99 only. All estimates are as of 31 December, and the variable is lagged by one year.

3.3. CONTROL VARIABLES

Existing conflict literature suggests a broad variety of control variables that can explain the onset of domestic armed conflict. A number of previous empirical studies have found level of *development* to be strongly associated with conflict (Collier and Hoeffler, 1998; de Soysa, 2002a; Hauge and Ellingsen, 2001; Hegre et al., 2001; Henderson and Singer, 2000). This study applies the infant mortality rate (IMR) as a proxy for development, as previously done by the State Failure Task Force group (Esty et al., 1998).[16] While conventional development proxies, like GDP or energy consumption per capita, focus heavily on economic aspects, IMR better captures the diverse aspects of development. The IMR is defined as the fraction of live-born children who die before the age of one year. Data are gathered from the *World Population Prospects* (UN, 1999), and the *Demographic Yearbook* (UN, annual) for small states.

Regime type is another variable assumed to be associated with conflict. While the democratic peace hypothesis argues that democracies never fight each other, democracy is also found to have a pacifying effect on the domestic arena (Hegre et al., 2001). The impact of regime type is generally believed to take an inverted U-shaped form, meaning that stark autocracies and fully developed democracies are both less likely to experience conflict than intermediate and unstable regimes. I use the Polity IV data (Marshall and Jaggers, 2000) to measure regime type, and the variable ranges from –10 (most autocratic) to 10 (most democratic).[17] I also include a squared term in order to measure the assumed inverted U-shaped effect of regime on armed conflict.

Regardless of the absolute level of wealth of a country, economic performance is assumed to influence the legitimacy of a government. If *economic growth* is low, leading to decreasing levels of wealth and rising unemployment, this is likely to cause grievances and anti-government sentiments. Economic growth is measured as average annual percentage change in GDP per capita over the five-year period prior to the year of observation. The estimates are based on PPP adjusted GDP per capita data from Heston, Summers and Aten (2002).[18]

To account for differences in conflict propensity potentially embedded in the size of a country, a variable measuring *total population* size is included.[19] The larger the size of a state's population, the greater the likelihood of a large geographical area, and the greater the chance of linguistic, religious, ethnic, or cultural fractionalization. Data are drawn from the *World Population Prospects* (UN, 1999), and from the *Demographic Yearbook* (UN, annual) for small states. The variable is log-transformed, as I expect the marginal effect of population size to be small for populous countries. I also include controls for political *dependency* status, a dummy variable coded 1 for political dependent areas and 0 for sovereign states. The data were gathered from Gleditsch and Befring (1986), the *Encyclopedia Britannica* (Britannica, annual), and the *World Factbook* (CIA, annual).

3.4. CONTROLS FOR STATISTICAL DEPENDENCY

A number of previous empirical studies applying country-years as the unit of observation have noted that such an approach, if uncorrected, leads to serially correlated errors (Beck, Katz and Tucker, 1998: 1263). Obviously, a country that experiences conflict over several years will find subsequent years of conflict to be heavily dependent on the first year. This problem of *time-dependence* is usually dealt with by omitting all observations of conflict, except for observations of the onset of conflict given that the country was at peace at $t - 1$. But omitting consecutive years of war does not solve the problem of time-dependence entirely, because the same statistical dependence prevails for consecutive years of peace. To account for temporal dependence, this study applies a control variable measuring the number of years in peace since the previous conflict, termed *brevity of peace.* It is generally assumed that the risk of experiencing a new conflict is high in the period immediately after an armed conflict and that this risk diminishes as time goes by. I follow Hegre et al. (2001) and assume that the effect of a previous conflict is decaying over time according to the formula $\exp\{(-\textit{years in peace})/X\}$.[20] In this formula, "years in peace" is the number of years since a country experienced the end of armed conflict, while the value of X determines the rate of decay of the effect of a previous armed conflict. Here, the value chosen for X is 4, implying that the risk of conflict is halved approximately every three years.[21] The brevity of peace variable takes on values close to 1 immediately after the end of a conflict and converges towards 0 over time.

In the model allowing for simultaneous conflicts, the brevity of peace variable is substituted for a *brevity of conflict* variable. This variable decays according to the same formula as brevity of peace and counts the time since a country experienced the most recent conflict onset. If a country did not experience a conflict since 1950, the variable is coded 0. I expect this variable to be positive, assuming that the risk of a new conflict breaking out is decreasing as time passes since the previous conflict onset. Since, in this model, consecutive years of a conflict are not censored, and several conflicts in a country can occur simultaneously, I also apply a dummy variable, *ongoing conflict in country*, taking the value 1 if a country is currently experiencing conflict.[22] I expect small countries to be particularly likely to have "space" for only one conflict at a time, and include an interaction term between *total population* and *ongoing conflict in country.*

4. Results

The empirical results from Table 1 provide only limited, and not very robust, support for both neo-Malthusian and cornucopian propositions. High population growth is by itself not associated with armed conflict. The estimated effect is in fact negative in most models, and it is consequently statistically insignificant. Land scarcity, measured by population density, is mostly negatively associated with armed conflict.[23] In a few models (1, 3, and 6), population density has a significant negative impact on conflict.[24] However, the robustness of this finding is low; the effects turn insignificant if only the restricted sample of sovereign states is considered.[25] Where land scarcity combines with high population growth, there is generally a positive association with conflict, and this relationship is statistically significant when longer periods of peace are required before coding a new onset (Model 6). But again, the relationship is not particularly robust and becomes statistically insignificant when only sovereign states are included.

Interaction effects between population pressure variables and IMR in Model 1 were not significant, speaking against the proposition that developing countries are more susceptible to violence generated by population pressure and resource scarcity. Urbanization is not significantly related to armed conflict in any of the models. Furthermore, an interaction term between urbanization and economic growth[26] was not significant, running counter to the expectation that urbanization may cause violence when interacting with economic crises.

4.1. A GOLDEN AGE OF NEO-MALTHUSIANISM?

The importance that neo-Malthusian factors have been ascribed in the security discourse has changed over time. In particular, the 1970s and the 1990s saw the emergence of such security concerns. Could it be that the impact of population pressure on conflict propensity has changed over time? In Table 2, I investigate whether indicators of neo-Malthusian population pressure perform differently over the five decades covered by this study.

Stratifying the model on decades does not provide considerable support for the neo-Malthusian conflict scenario, but for the 1970s the interaction term between

Table 1. Risk of armed conflict by neo-Malthusian population pressure variables

	Full sample	Restricted sample	Full sample			
Explanatory variables	Model 1 β st. error	Model 2 β st. error	Model 3 β st. error	Model 4 all onsets β st. error	Model 5 β st. error	Model 6 onset 2 β st. error
Population pressure variables						
Population growth[a]	−0.009	0.074	−0.020	0.003	−0.013	−0.019
	(0.062)	(0.071)	(0.062)	(0.058)	(0.071)	(0.063)
Population density[a]	−0.088*	0.002	−0.156***	−0.074	−0.068	−0.113**
	(0.053)	(0.061)	(0.052)	(0.049)	(0.060)	(0.055)
Growth* density[a]	0.042	−0.017	0.061	0.041	0.014	0.081**
	(0.039)	(0.050)	(0.041)	(0.036)	(0.045)	(0.037)
Urban growth					−0.025	
					(0.041)	
Control variables						
Total population[a]	0.269***	0.207***	0.266***	0.323***	0.289***	0.285***
	(0.047)	(0.055)	(0.047)	(0.043)	(0.055)	(0.050)
Dependency	−0.890**	−0.663	−1.167***	−0.855	−0.933**	
	(0.381)		(0.716)	(0.354)	(0.538)	(0.394)
Infant mortality rate[a]	0.006***	0.006***		0.006***	0.010***	0.006***
	(0.001)	(0.002)		(0.001)	(0.002)	(0.002)
GDP per capita (Ln)			−0.663***			
			(0.102)			
Missing GDP data			0.408			
			(0.729)			
Regime	0.006	0.005	0.009	0.003	0.015	0.011
	(0.014)	(0.014)	(0.014)	(0.012)	(0.015)	(0.014)
Regime, squared	−0.014***	−0.013***	−0.013***	−0.014***	−0.014***	−0.015***
	(0.003)	(0.003)	(0.003)	(0.003)	(0.003)	(0.003)
Missing regime data	−0.259	−0.009	−0.313	−0.114	−0.311	−0.235
	(0.314)	(0.331)	(0.317)	(0.274)	(0.346)	(0.332)
Economic growth					−0.054**	
					(0.024)	
Missing economic growth data					0.296	
					(0.245)	
Controls for statistical dependency						
Brevity of peace	1.819***	1.725***	1.763***		1.691***	1.124***
	(0.275)	(0.285)	(0.278)		(0.304)	(0.325)
Brevity of conflict				1.366***		
				(0.318)		
Ongoing conflict in country[a]				−1.218***		
				(0.351)		
Ongoing conflict* total population[a]				0.304**		
				(0.118)		
Constant	−6.078***	−5.385***	−2.273**	−3.845***	−6.302***	−6.157***
	(0.488)	(0.569)	(0.944)	(0.206)	(0.599)	(0.513)
N	7,752	5,490	8,065	8,691	5,851	7,730
Log likelihood	−793.33	−700.47	−795.95	−963.45	−631.85	−733.86
Pseudo R^2	0.107	0.080	0.112	0.096	0.113	0.089

* $p < 0.10$, ** $p < 0.05$, *** $p < 0.01$.

[a] Singular terms are centered to avoid multicollinearity when introducing interaction terms (Kleinbaum, Kupper and Muller, 1998: 206–212).

Table 2. Risk of armed conflict by neo-Malthusian population pressure variables and decades, full sample

Explanatory variables	Model 6 1950–59 β st. error	Model 7 1960–69 β st. error	Model 8 1970–79 β st. error	Model 9 1980–89 β st. error	Model 10 1990–2000 β st. error	All decades β st. error
Population pressure variables						
Population growth[a]	0.030	0.134	−0.024	0.150	−0.126	−0.009
	(0.250)	(0.193)	(0.099)	(0.184)	(0.086)	(0.062)
Population density[a]	0.009	−0.386***	−0.080	−0.246*	0.064	−0.088*
	(0.137)	(0.142)	(0.115)	(0.136)	(0.106)	(0.053)
Growth* density[a]	−0.017	0.094	0.129**	−0.065	0.040	0.042
	(0.096)	(0.099)	(0.057)	(0.096)	(0.075)	(0.039)
Urban growth					−0.112**	
					(0.046)	
Refugees[b]					0.424	
					(0.346)	
Control variables						
Total population	0.409***	0.431***	0.344***	0.272**	0.228**	0.269***
	(0.130)	(0.126)	(0.103)	(0.133)	(0.106)	(0.047)
Dependency[c]	−0.332	−1.005	−0.416			−0.890**
	(0.824)	(0.723)	(0.996)			(0.381)
Infant mortality rate	0.001	0.012***	0.011***	0.013**	0.021***	0.006***
	(0.004)	(0.004)	(0.003)	(0.005)	(0.005)	(0.001)
Regime	−0.018	0.006	0.028	0.060*	−0.0001	0.006
	(0.041)	(0.036)	(0.029)	(0.034)	(0.027)	(0.014)
Regime, squared	−0.016**	−0.006	−0.005	−0.015*	−0.022***	−0.014***
	(0.008)	(0.007)	(0.007)	(0.008)	(0.006)	(0.003)
Missing regime data	−0.069	1.254*	0.310	−0.127	−2.140***	−0.259
	(0.823)	(0.689)	(0.764)	(0.943)	(0.705)	(0.314)
Controls for statistical dependency						
Brevity of peace	2.376***	1.534**	1.101	0.058	1.716***	1.819***
	(0.726)	(0.681)	(0.714)	(1.046)	(0.467)	(0.275)
Constant	−7.265***	−9.160***	−7.433***	−6.304***	−5.691***	−6.078***
	(1.283)	(1.441)	(1.143)	(1.562)	(1.087)	(0.488)
N	1,483	1,578	1,519	1,423	1,680	7,752
Log likelihood	−118.26	−143.21	−165.94	−133.47	−194.43	−793.33
Pseudo R^2	0.149	0.147	0.103	0.083	0.197	0.107

* $p < 0.10$, ** $p < 0.05$, *** $p < 0.01$.

[a] Centered variable.

[b] Data on refugees are available only for the 1990s.

[c] For the periods 1980–89 and 1990–2000, no dependent country-years that were analyzed experienced an armed conflict onset; thus, the dependency variable is omitted from the analysis for these periods.

population growth and density is positive and significant (Model 8). Thus, in the decade in which neo-Malthusian literature exploded, countries that experienced high population growth and cropland scarcity combined did experience a higher risk of armed conflict, other factors being equal. This relationship is quite robust, but as in Model 5, it turns insignificant when the model is applied to a restricted sample of only sovereign states. For the period of the second wave of environmental security literature, the post-Cold War era, there is no support for neo-Malthusian claims. Population density is found to be negative and significantly associated with conflict in the 1960s and 1980s (Models 7 and 9).[27] Urbanization is associated with a significantly decreased risk of conflict for the 1990s, and is insignificant for all other periods. Data for refugee populations is available only for the post-Cold War period. The refugee term has the expected positive sign but is not statistically significant.

4.2. CONTROL VARIABLES

Among the control variables, countries with larger populations are clearly more exposed to the risk of armed conflict, while economic growth and political dependency act to reduce conflict propensity. High levels of development, as measured by either infant mortality or GDP per capita, strongly reduce the risk of armed conflict. This study also reconfirms the inverted U-curved relationship between regime type and conflict; intermediary regimes seem to be most conflict prone. The more recent the termination of a previous conflict, the higher is the risk of a new armed conflict onset. An ongoing conflict is associated with a reduction in conflict propensity (Model 5). This may be explained by several factors. First, since the army is already mobilized, a government is able to crack down on subsequent rebel attempts. Second, governments of countries that experience an ongoing conflict will probably be likely to increase surveillance of potential rebel elements. Third, observing the negative effects of the ongoing conflict may act as a deterrent to the initiation of another.

5. Conclusion

After the end of the Cold War, demographic and environmental factors have increasingly been regarded as security issues. According to neo-Malthusian theorizing, population growth is an important source of natural resource scarcity. Societies experiencing such scarcity are likely to perform worse in terms of food production and economic development and are assumed to have an increased risk of domestic armed conflict.

This study has not found strong empirical support for neo-Malthusian concerns. Countries experiencing high population growth are generally not experiencing a greater risk of conflict compared to countries with low levels of population pressure. There is some support for "cornucopian" expectations that scarcity of potentially productive land is associated with a decreased risk of armed conflict. These results generally back up a development scheme proposing that densely populated areas are forced to develop in order to overcome resource scarcity, thereby eventually reducing the risk of conflict. However, as cornucopians concede, peace is likely to be a long-term effect of land scarcity. Some of the empirical evidence provided here suggests that countries experiencing the demographic transition, still facing high rates of population growth, may be under a somewhat greater risk of armed conflict if productive land is already scarce. Neither of these relationships are very robust, though, suggesting that high population pressure on natural resources is not a strong predictor of domestic armed conflict, nor of peace.

When assessing differences over time, it is interesting that the neo-Malthusian proposition is supported only for the 1970s. It could be that the great rise in environmental security concerns in this decade reflected a greater significance played by neo-Malthusian factors. In the 1965–80 period, the less developed regions of the world experienced the highest levels of population growth ever. This was particularly the case in many parts of Asia where population density was already high. In a period of strong superpower involvement in armed conflicts around the globe, the attention paid to demographic and environmental factors may have influenced the superpowers' perceptions of what would be fertile ground for military engagement. There is, on the contrary, no support for claims that the post-Cold War period represents a new era of insecurity, or an erupting state of anarchy due to demographic pressure and resource scarcity. Rather, the post-Cold War era is marked by the strong statistical significance of conventional explanations of conflict such as level of development, regime type, and geography. Although often portrayed as an emerging challenge to security, countries with high levels of urban growth are significantly less prone to armed conflict in this period. A very crude measure for refugee populations is not associated with conflict.

When controlling for trade, de Soysa (2002a,b) finds that population density is positively associated with armed conflict. One possible interpretation is that when a country is trading less, land scarcity becomes a more pertinent issue and may instigate armed conflict. The possibly conditioning effect of a bad macroeconomic environment on the relationship between land scarcity and armed conflict may be a promising avenue for further research. But a strong emphasis on security as a macro rationale for reducing global population growth seems unwarranted. Although the looting of cropland and cattle may be observable in violent conflicts in agrarian societies like Rwanda, natural resource scarcity is not necessarily a root cause of conflict. As Ferguson (1992: 61) notes, "even when people do acquire land through war, they actually go to war for other reasons".

The attempt to establish a measure of population density that would be more sensitive to the availability of cropland than the conventional measurement did not produce very different outcomes. GIS tools and more detailed information on land quality can improve the density measure further. While a first assessment addressing refugee populations and conflict did not result in any significant relationship, future studies taking a more cautious approach will most certainly add to our understanding of this relationship. Such studies should also aim to take into account issues of migration and internal displacement. A third future avenue for testing neo-Malthusian claims are meso-level quantitative studies of selected countries, aimed at revealing possible conflict-conducive effects of neo-Malthusian population pressure at a local level.

Neo-Malthusians may well claim that the aggregated data used here to test population pressure hypotheses fail to reflect local population pressure causing local conflict. However, similar criticism should also then be directed to much neo-Malthusian literature. Four of the five cases investigated in Homer-Dixon and Blitt (1998) deal with whole countries, while only one case study is limited to a region within a country.[28] In all these cases, Homer-Dixon and associates argue that overall population growth in a country contributes to resource scarcity. My study indicates that the relationship between population-induced scarcity and conflict that was found for some of the cases presented in Homer-Dixon and Blitt (1998) does not seem to represent a strong general trend among countries over time.

Notes

* I gratefully acknowledge the financial support of the Research Council of Norway and the Norwegian Trust Fund for Environmentally and Socially Sustainable Development (NTFESSD). I am indebted to Nils Petter Gleditsch, Øystein Kravdal, Nico Keilman, Indra de Soysa, Håvard Hegre, Håvard Strand, Eric Neumayer, Han Dorussen, three anonymous referees, and countless conference participants for great suggestions, ideas, and corrections to previous drafts. The data and correlation matrix (Appendix B) are posted at http://www.prio.no/jpr/datasets. (Because the author is one of the guest editors of this issue, the review process for this article was handled by *JPR* Associate Editor Han Dorussen.)

[1] See Lacina and Gleditsch (2005) for a discussion of different war mortality measurements.

[2] Of around 2.5 million deaths due to the conflict, 350,000 followed acts of violence (Roberts et al., 2003).

[3] See Hughes (1997: 11) for an excellent example.

[4] For a selection of alarmist literature, see Ehrlich (1968), Hardin (1968), and more recently Myers (1993), Renner (1996), and Ehrlich and Ehrlich (1996).

[5] Lujala, Gleditsch and Gilmore (2005) find that this relationship is not straightforward. While deposits of easily extractable secondary diamonds increase the risk of some forms of violence, primary diamonds do not have a similar effect.

[6] Gleditsch and Urdal (2002) provide a review of Homer-Dixon's work on population, environment, and conflict.

[7] I prefer the term "resource scarcity" over Homer-Dixon's "environmental scarcity".

[8] Homer-Dixon and associates do not provide a stringent definition of "civil violence" and do include cases of violence that would not qualify as "organized armed conflict" as defined in this article.

[9] For data reasons, I focus on refugees crossing an international border and do not address the equally interesting aspect of internally displaced persons or migrants more generally.

[10] I have also run analyses on a more restricted set of countries that qualify as members of the interstate system as defined by Small and Singer (1982).

[11] I see no reason to treat armed conflicts between a liberation army and the representatives of a colonial power any differently than other forms of organized armed opposition against an autocratic regime.

[12] The choice of number of years in peace before coding resumed fighting between the same parties as a new onset is not guided by any theoretical justification. I follow Buhaug and Gates (2002), coding a new onset after at least two years of peace, but have also coded alternative dependent variables employing one and five years of peace. The slightly different results arising from alternative specifications are discussed below.

[13] For colonial powers, only the population of the territory proper, and not that of colonial territory, forms the basis for the population variables. All dependent areas, both historical and current, are treated as separate units of analysis.

[14] De Soysa (2002b) measures population density relative to arable land, which includes all land currently used for agricultural production.
[15] A better understanding of the dynamics between refugees and armed conflict will evolve as new work in this field moves forward.
[16] For the sake of comparison, I will also apply a development measure of log-transformed GDP per capita adjusted for purchasing power parities collected from Heston, Summers and Aten (2002).
[17] In order not to lose a lot of observations, I assign the value for the sample average for units with missing values. I add a dummy variable, *missing regime data*, controlling for imputed values.
[18] As for regime type, I have imputed the sample average for missing values.
[19] This is merely a control for state size, and is not a population pressure indicator.
[20] This form of time-dependency control is very similar to that suggested by Beck, Katz and Tucker (1998). I prefer the Hegre et al. (2001) approach as it is directly interpretable.
[21] This value for a half-life of conflict is also used by Toset, Gleditsch and Hegre (2000). Three years after the end of conflict, the value is approximately halved: $\exp(-3/4) = 0.47$. The analyses of this article are extremely robust over different specifications of this function. Assuming half-lives of 5, 10, or 16 years does not change the results.
[22] The variable is coded 0 for the first year of a conflict erupting from a state of peace.
[23] These results are virtually unchanged when using a conventional density measure.
[24] However, when running this model on the restricted sample only, population density turns insignificant.
[25] If the interaction term is excluded from Models 1–6, the only change in the main explanatory variables is that population density turns insignificant in Model 1.
[26] The test was performed for both short- and long-term economic growth.
[27] However, when using the conventional density measure, the variable turns statistically insignificant.
[28] The countries studied in Homer-Dixon and Blitt (1998) are Gaza (included in this study as a separate entity), South Africa, Pakistan, and Rwanda. The region is Chiapas, Mexico.

Appendix A: Descriptive statistics

	N	Mean	St. dev.	Min.	Max.	Measurement unit
Population pressure variables						
Population growth	9,183	2.07	1.71	−32.3	16.66	Annual growth rate (%), lagged by five years.
Population density, potential cropland (Ln)	9,004	4.29	1.89	0	13.98	Inhabitants per square km productive land. Log-transformed.
Population density, all land (Ln)	9,159	3.76	1.71	0	10.07	Inhabitants per square km total land. Log-transformed.
Growth* density (potential cropland, Ln)	9,004	8.61	9.49	−172	103	
Urban growth	6,776	3.67	2.75	−44.2	23.4	Annual percentage growth in urban population.
Refugees	2,340	0.14	0.35	0	1	1 if country hosts >100,000 refugees.
Control variables						
Total population (Ln)	9,183	8.01	2.20	1.79	14.06	Population in thousands.

(Cont.)

Appendix A: (*Continued*)

	N	Mean	St. dev.	Min.	Max.	Measurement unit
GDP per capita (Ln)	9,183	8.32	0.94	5.62	10.74	GDP per capita in PPP adjusted US$. Log-transformed.
Missing GDP data	9,183	0.20	0.40	0	1	1 if missing.
Regime type	9,183	−0.25	6.39	−10	10	Polity score, 10 if full democracy.
Regime type, squared	9,183	40.90	37.63	0	100	Squared polity score.
Missing regime data	9,183	0.31	0.46	0	1	1 if missing.
Economic growth	9,183	2.05	3.21	−23	50	Average percentage growth in PPP-adjusted GDP per capita over past five years.
Missing economic growth data	9,183	0.35	0.48	0	1	1 if missing.
Controls for statistical dependency						
Brevity of peace	9,183	0.15	0.33	0	1	Function of time since the end of previous conflict.
Brevity of conflict	9,183	0.07	0.17	0	0.78	Function of time since last conflict onset.
Ongoing conflict in country	9,183	0.10	0.30	0	1	1 if ongoing.
Ongoing conflict* total population (Ln)	9,183	0.95	2.87	0	13.83	

Number of country-years with originally missing values in parentheses: Regime type (2,866), Economic growth (3,169), Purchasing Power Parities adjusted GDP per capita (1,866).

References

Beck, Nathaniel, Jonathan N. Katz and Richard Tucker, 1998. "Taking time seriously: Time-series-cross-section analysis with a binary dependent variable", *American Journal of Political Science* 42(4): 1260–1288.

Boserup, Ester and T. Paul Schultz, (eds), 1990. *Economic and Demographic Relationships in Development.* Baltimore, MD: Johns Hopkins University Press.

Brennan-Galvin, Ellen, 2002. "Urbanization crime and violence", *Journal of International Affairs* 56(1): 123–145.

Britannica, annual. *Britannica Book of the Year.* Chicago, IL: Encyclopedia Britannica.

Buhaug, Halvard and Scott Gates, 2002. "The geography of civil war", *Journal of Peace Research* 39(4): 417–433.

CIA, annual. *The World Factbook.* Washington, DC: Central Intelligence Agency, 2001 edition available at http://www.odci.gov/ cia/publications/factbook/index.html.

Collier, Paul, 1999. "On the economic consequences of civil war", *Oxford Economic Papers, New Series* 51(1): 168–183.

Collier, Paul, 2000. "Doing well out of war: An economic perspective", in Mats Berdal and David M. Malone, (eds), *Greed and Grievance: Economic Agendas in Civil Wars.* Boulder, CO and London: Lynne Rienner (91–111).

Collier, Paul and Anke Hoeffler, 1998. "On economic causes of civil war", *Oxford Economic Papers* 50(4): 563–573.

Dalby, Simon, 2002. "Security and ecology in the age of globalization", *Environmental Change and Security Project Report* 8: 95–108.

de Soysa, Indra, 2002a. "Paradise is a bazaar? greed, creed, and governance in civil war, 1989–99", *Journal of Peace Research* 39(4): 395–416.

de Soysa, Indra, 2002b. "Ecoviolence: Shrinking pie or honey pot?", *Global Environmental Politics* 2(4): 1–36.
ECHO, 1995. *Environmental Impacts of Sudden Population Displacements.* Brussels: European Community Humanitarian Office: Expert Consultation on Priority Policy Issues and Humanitarian Aid.
Ehrlich, Paul R., 1968. *The Population Bomb.* New York: Ballantine.
Ehrlich, Paul R. and Anne H. Ehrlich, 1996. *Betrayal of Science and Reason: How Anti-Environmental Rhetoric Threatens Our Future.* Washington, DC: Island.
Esty, Daniel C., Jack A. Goldstone, Ted Robert Gurr, Barbara Harff, Marc Levy, Geoffrey D. Dabelko, Pamela Surko and Alan N. Unger, 1998. *State Failure Task Force Report: Phase II Findings.* McLean, VA: Science Applications International, for State Failure Task Force.
Ferguson, R. Brian, 1992. "The general consequences of war: An amazonian perspective", in Giorgio Ausenda, (ed.), *Effects of War on Society.* San Marino: AIEP (59–86).
Gleditsch, Nils Petter, 2001. "Armed conflict and the environment", in Paul F. Diehl and Nils Petter Gleditsch, (eds), *Environmental Conflict.* Boulder, CO: Westview (251–272).
Gleditsch, Nils Petter and Totto Befring, 1986. *The Composition of the International System*, 1945–86. Manuscript. Oslo: International Peace Research Institute, Oslo (PRIO).
Gleditsch, Nils Petter and Henrik Urdal, 2002. "Ecoviolence? links between population growth, environmental scarcity and violent conflict in Thomas Homer-Dixon's work", *Journal of International Affairs* 56(1): 283–302.
Gleditsch, Nils Petter, Peter Wallensteen, Mikael Eriksson, Margareta Sollenberg and Håvard Strand, 2002. "Armed conflict 1946–2001: A new dataset", *Journal of Peace Research* 39(5): 615–637.
Goldstone, Jack A., 2002. "Population and security: How demographic change can lead to violent conflict", *Journal of International Affairs* 56(1): 3–21.
Hardin, Garrett, 1968. "The tragedy of the commons", *Science* 162: 1243–1248.
Hauge, Wenche and Tanja Ellingsen, 2001. "Causal pathways to conflict", in Paul F. Diehl and Nils Petter Gleditsch, (eds), *Environmental Conflict.* Boulder, CO: Westview (36–57).
Hegre, Håvard, Tanja Ellingsen, Scott Gates and Nils Petter Gleditsch, 2001. "Toward a democratic civil peace? democracy, political change, and civil war, 1816–1992", *American Political Science Review* 95(1): 33–48.
Henderson, Errol A. and J. David Singer, 2000. "Civil war in the post-colonial world, 1946–92", *Journal of Peace Research* 37(3): 275–299.
Heston, Alan, Robert Summers and Bettina Aten, 2002. *Penn World Table Version 6.1.* Center for International Comparisons, University of Pennsylvania (CICUP), October. http://pwt.econ.upenn.edu/php_site/pwt_index.php.
Homer-Dixon, Thomas F., 1999. *Environment, Scarcity, and Violence.* Princeton, NJ and Oxford: Princeton University Press.
Homer-Dixon, Thomas F. and Jessica Blitt, (eds), 1998. *Ecoviolence: Links Among Environment, Population and Security.* Lanham, MD: Rowman and Littlefield.
Hughes, Patrick M., 1997. *Global Threats and Challenges to the United States and Its Interests Abroad.* Statement for the Senate Select Committee on Intelligence, 5 February, and the Senate Armed Services Committee on Intelligence, 6 February. Washington, DC: Defence Intelligence Agency. http://www.fas.org/irp/congress/1997_hr/s970205d.htm.
Kahl, Colin H., 2002. "Demographic change, natural resources and violence", *Journal of International Affairs* 56(1): 257–282.
Kaplan, Robert D., 1994. "The coming anarchy", *Atlantic Monthly* 273(2): 44–76.
Klare, Michael T., 2001. *Resource Wars: The New Landscape of Global Conflict.* New York: Metropolitan.
Kleinbaum, David G., Lawrence L. Kupper and Keith E. Muller, 1998. *Applied Regression Analysis and Other Multivariable Methods*, 3rd edn. Pacific Grove, CA: Duxbury.
Lacina, Bethany and Nils Petter Gleditsch, 2005. "Monitoring trends in global combat: A new dataset of battle deaths", *European Journal of Population* 21(2–3): in press.
Le Billon, Philippe, 2001. "The political ecology of war: Natural resources and armed conflicts", *Political Geography* 20(5): 561–584.
Levy, Mark, 1995. "Is the environment a national security issue?", *International Security* 20(2): 35–62.
Lomborg, Bjørn, 2001. *The Skeptical Environmentalist: Measuring the Real State of the World.* Cambridge: Cambridge University Press.

Lujala, Päivi, Nils Petter Gleditsch and Elisabeth Gilmore, 2005. "A diamond curse? Civil War and a lootable resource", *Journal of Conflict Resolution* 49(4): in press.

Malthus, Thomas Robert, 1803/1992. *An Essay on the Principle of Population.* Cambridge: Cambridge University Press.

Marshall, Monty G. and Keith Jaggers, 2000. *Polity IV Project: Political Regime Characteristics and Transitions, 1800–1999.* CIDCM, University of Maryland. codebook and data: http://www.cidcm.umd.edupolity/index.html.

Matthew, Richard A., 2002. "Environment, population and conflict", *Journal of International Affairs* 56(1): 235–254.

Myers, Norman, 1993. *Ultimate Security: The Environmental Basis of Political Stability.* New York: Norton.

Reddy, Marlita A., (ed.), 1994. *Statistical Abstract of the World.* Detroit, MI: Gale Research.

Renner, Michael, 1996. *Fighting for Survival: Environmental Decline, Social Conflict, and the New Age of Insecurity.* Environmental Alert Series. New York: Norton.

Renner, Michael, 2002. "The anatomy of resource wars", *Worldwatch Paper* 162. Washington, DC: Worldwatch Institute.

Roberts, Les, Pascal Ngoy, Colleen Mone, Charles Lubula, Luc Mwezse, Mariana Zantop and Michael Despines, 2003. *Mortality in the Democratic Republic of Congo: Results from a Nationwide Survey.* Bukavu and New York: International Rescue Committee.

Small, Melvin and J. David Singer, 1982. *Resort to Arms: International and Civil Wars, 1816–1980.* Beverly Hills, CA: Sage for list extended to 1997: http://pss.la.psu.edu/ intsys.html.

Tir, Jaroslav and Paul F. Diehl, 2001. "Demographic pressure and interstate conflict", in Paul F. Diehl and Nils Petter Gleditsch, (eds), *Environmental Conflict.* Boulder, CO: Westview (58–83).

Toset, Hans Petter Wollebæk, Nils Petter Gleditsch and Håvard Hegre, 2000. "Shared rivers and interstate conflict", *Political Geography* 19(8): 971–996.

UN, 1999. *World Population Prospects: The 1998 Revision.* New York: United Nations.

UN, 2000. *World Population Prospects: The 1998 Revision. Volume III: Analytical Report.* New York: United Nations.

UN, annual. *Demographic Yearbook.* New York: United Nations.

UNHCR, 1998. "Refugees and others of concern to UNHCR: 1997 statistical overview". Geneva: United Nations High Commissioner for Refugees. http://www.unhcr.ch.

UNHCR, 1999. "Refugees and others of concern to UNHCR: 1998 statistical overview". Geneva: United Nations High Commissioner for Refugees. http://www. unhcr.ch.

UNHCR, 2000. "Refugees and others of concern to UNHCR: 1999 statistical overview". Geneva: United Nations High Commissioner for Refugees. http://www. unhcr.ch.

World Bank, 2003. *World Development Indicators on CD-ROM.* Washington, DC: World Bank.

CHAPTER 4. DEMOGRAPHY, MIGRATION AND CONFLICT IN THE PACIFIC

HELEN WARE
International Agency Leadership (Peace Building), University of New England, Australia

Abstract. This article explores the relationships between demography and internal conflict in the Pacific Island countries, focusing on the three subregions Polynesia, Micronesia and Melanesia. These countries confront distinctive challenges and opportunities because of their unique cultures and non-militarized status, combined with very small size and remote locations. The use of the MIRAB model of island economies based on migration, remittances, aid and bureaucracy is extended to examine its impact on social cohesion and the avoidance of internal conflict. For Polynesia, MIRAB is found to be a sustainable development strategy. Continuous emigration from Polynesia serves to reduce population pressure and communal tensions. Further, remittance income supports the Polynesian economies, and this also reduces the potential for conflict. For Micronesia, except Kiribati and Nauru, migration access to the USA is assured. In contrast, for the Melanesian countries, there is minimal emigration, rapid population growth and considerable intercommunal tension, which has resulted in several coups and one "failed state". Demographic pressure created by rapid population growth results in a lack of employment opportunities for youths (who provide the majority of participators in civil unrest and conflicts) rather than in direct pressure on land and other natural resources.

1. Introduction

Until the 1987 coup in Fiji, it was a commonplace that the Pacific was indeed pacific. The small islands of the Pacific face unique challenges of demography and government. With annual population growth rates varying from −3.1% to +3.4%, their governments range from a near absolute monarchy, to a number of the developing world's longest surviving successful democracies, to at least one "failed" state and a number allegedly tottering on the brink of collapse. Some states draw half of their income from migrants' remittances. Others have seen rapid population growth lead to steep declines in per capita incomes. This article examines the extent to which emigration acts as a safety valve to reduce the risk of conflict in the Pacific, while, inversely, internal migration and urbanization often exacerbate social and ethnic tensions. Conflict is multi-causal, and depending on the direction of its impact on population growth, migration can be a significant factor for good or evil in that causation. International migration is very important for the region because there are very few alternative economic opportunities for potential migrants.

This chapter was previously published in *Journal of Peace Research*, vol. 42, no. 4, 2005, pp. 435–454.

Helge Brunborg et al. (eds.), The Demography of Armed Conflict, 87–108.

2. Objective

There is a considerable literature on the relationships between population factors and conflict and security risks (see citations in Choucri, 2002; Goldstone, 2002; Kahl 2002). Studies of the potential impact of population changes in promoting conflict have moved away from simple deterministic models, which significantly over-predicted the likelihood of conflict because, as the neoclassical economists argued, such models ignored the potential for economic and technical developments to ameliorate the impacts of population pressures (see discussion in Kahl, 2002: 260). Instead, researchers have moved on to examine the precise political and economic conditions under which societies find it most difficult to adjust to particular forms of population pressure (de Sherbinin, 1995). In a classic review of the literature, Goldstone (2002: 4) summarized these more nuanced findings thus: "while overall population growth and population density do not generally predict political risks, a number of distinct kinds of demographic changes—rapid growth in the labor force in slow-growing economies, a rapid increase in educated youth aspiring to elite positions when such positions are scarce, unequal population growth rates between different ethnic groups, urbanization that exceeds employment growth and migrations that change the local balance among major ethnic groups—do appear to increase the risks of violent internal political and ethnic conflicts". One example of how the analysis of possible linkages between population factors and violence has become increasingly sophisticated relates first to the isolation of "youth bulges" as a possible causal factor and then to defining the circumstances when, and the mechanisms through which, youth bulges are linked to violence (Mesquida and Wiener, 1999; Collier and Hoeffler, 2000; Urdal, 2004).

Much of the study of the relationship between migration and conflict has tended to focus on internal migration and urbanization as developments which can create hot spots of particular tension. In the case of links between international migration and conflict, much of the emphasis has been on the impact of migrants on recipient countries (see Choucri, 2002, for an overview of the literature). However, there is also a tradition, now more than a century old, of regarding emigration as a safety valve for the sending countries or districts (Turner, 1893). This has survived more as a popular belief than a rigorous academic theory. Over time, governments from Italy to Mexico and the Caribbean have seen emigration as a means of reducing both the numbers and the political impact of the unemployed at home (Bertozzi, 2002; Bean, 1997; Levine, 1995). The Catholic church has also argued for the migration "safety valve" as a correlate of the human right to emigrate (Pontifical Council, 2000).

Partly because many multinational datasets exclude countries with very few inhabitants, Pacific Island countries have been omitted from most studies in political demography. The aim here is to restore the Pacific Islands to the picture, taking advantage of the fact that they provide a sample of 22 countries and territories whose demography differs in the main because of different emigration patterns (see Tables 1 and 2). Drawing upon insights from studies of other regions, and especially

Table 1. Demographic characteristics of members of the Pacific community

Country/territory and year of observation	Population size	Natural growth rate	TFR	Net growth rate[a]	Net immigration rate (per 1,000)	Urbanization[b]		Density, circa 2000[c]
Melanesia	6,475,900	2.3	4.6	2.3	−0.4	21	3.6	12
Fiji 1996	775,077	1.9	3.3	1.6	−3.7	46	2.6	45
New Caledonia 1996	196,836	1.6	2.6	1.8	2.4	71	2.1	11
Papua New Guinea 2000	5,190,786	2.3	4.8	2.3	0.0	15	4.1	10
Solomon Islands 1999	409,042	3.4	5.7	3.4	0.0	13	6.2	16
Vanuatu 1999	186,678	3.0	5.3	3.0	0.0	21	4.3	16
Micronesia	516,100	2.4	4.1	2.3	−1.2	48	2.8	161
Federated States of Micronesia 2000	107,008	2.5	4.9	1.9	−5.9	27	0.4	168
Guam 2000	154,805	2.1	3.8	1.0	−10.8	38	1.9	274
Kiribati 2000	84,494	2.5	4.5	2.5	0.0	37	2.2	112
Marshall Islands 1999	50,840	3.6	5.7	2.0	−20.0	65	1.8	286
Nauru 1992	9,919	1.8	4.4	1.8	−0.2	100	1.8	545
Northern Mariana Islands 2000	69,221	2.2	2.1	5.5	33.5	90	5.6	163
Palau 2000	19,129	1.4	2.6	2.2	8.1	71	2.9	39
Polynesia	613,100	2.0	3.6	1.2	−8.4	39	1.7	75
American Samoa 2000	57,291	2.3	4.5	2.9	2.7	48	4.6	321
Cook Islands 1996	19,103	1.6	3.7	−0.5	−21.7	59	0.5	79
French Polynesia 2000	245,405	1.6	2.6	1.6	0.0	53	1.4	66
Niue 2001	1,788	1.2	3.0	−3.1	−43.2	35	1.2	7
Pitcairn Islands 1999	47	—	—	0.0	—		None	1
Samoa 2000	176,848	2.4	4.5	0.6	−17.6	21	1.2	58
Tokelau 2001	1,537	2.5	5.7	0.0	−24.9		None	125
Tonga 1996	97,748	2.1	4.2	0.6	−15.1	32	0.8	154
Tuvalu 2002	9,561	1.4	3.7	0.9	−5.2	42	4.8	381
Wallis and Futuna 1996	14,166	1.5	3.1	0.7	−8.7		None	57

Source: SPC Demographic Data Base (because of varying dates, totals for regions differ from totals for individual countries and territories).
TFR: total fertility rate, i.e. an estimate of children born per woman at current fertility rates.
[a] Estimate used in SPC projections based on the previous 5 years' experience of births, deaths and net migration.
[b] The first figure is the percentage urban using the local definition and the second figure the annual inter-censal urban growth rate (%).
[c] Number of persons per square kilometre.

Table 2. Status, migration rights and GNI of members of the Pacific community

Country/ territory	Year of independence	Status	Migration opportunities	GNI PPP[a] 2004	Currency
Melanesia					
Fiji	1970	Republic		$5,410 [$2,360]	Fiji$
New Caledonia	—	French territory in transition; vote due 2014–18	Full access to France	N/A	Pacific Franc/ Euro
Papua New Guinea	1975	Constitutional monarchy[b]		$2,240 [$510]	Kina
Solomon Islands	1978	Constitutional monarchy[b]		$1,630 [$600]	SI$
Vanuatu	1980	Republic		$2,880 [$1,180]	Vatu
Micronesia					
Federated States of Micronesia	1986	Constitutional govt. in free association with USA	Full access to USA	[$2,150]	US$
Guam	—	Organized and unincorporated territory of USA	Full access to USA	N/A	US$
Kiribati	1979	Republic	Special deal with Japanese merchant marine	$960 [$880]	Aus$
Marshall Islands	1986	Republic in free association with USA	Full access to USA	[$2,330]	US$
Nauru	1968	Republic		[$2,860]	Aus$
Northern Mariana Islands	—	Self-governing commonwealth in political union with USA	Full access to USA	N/A	Aus$
Palau	1994	Republic in free association with USA		[$7,500]	US$
Polynesia					
American Samoa	—	Unincorporated and unorganized territory of USA	Full access to USA	High	US$

Table 2. (*Continued*)

Country/ territory	Year of independence	Status	Migration opportunities	GNI PPP[a] 2004	Currency
Cook Islands	—	Self-governing in free association with NZ	Full access to NZ	[$3,020]	NZ$
French Polynesia	—	Overseas territory of France	Full access to France	High	Pacific Franc
Niue	—	Self-governing in free association with NZ	Full access to NZ	[$2,220]	NZ$
Pitcairn Islands	—	Overseas territory of UK	Full access to NZ	N/A	NZ$
Samoa	1962	Constitutional monarchy (Chief)	1,100 annual quota to NZ	[$1,600]	Tala
Tokelau	—	Self-administering territory of NZ	Full access to NZ	[$980]	NZ$
Tonga	1970	Constitutional monarchy (King)		$6,890 [$1,490]	Pa'anga
Tuvalu	1978	Constitutional monarchy[b]	Special deal with German merchant marine	[$1,140]	Aus$
Wallis and Futuna	—	Overseas territory of France	Full access to France	N/A	Pacific Franc

Source: Data from http://www.spc.int/prism/social/demog.html, except for GNI, which is from http://www.worldbank.org/data/databytopic/ GNIPC.pdf.
N/A: Not available.
[a] GNI PPP: Gross National Income adjusted by purchasing power parity. GNI for small states varies from year to year and is exceptionally unreliable. Figures in brackets are "atlas method" figures from the World Bank, which are more widely available than GNI PPP.
[b] Constitutional monarchy with Governor-General appointed by Queen Elizabeth on advice of Prime Minister.

from Goldstone's (2002) overview, the objective of this article is to examine the role of migration in the creation and alleviation of tensions within the Pacific Island countries. It starts with a region-wide overview of the role of emigration as a safety valve and moves on to illustrate the interactions between migration and conflict with country case studies of Fiji, the Solomon Islands and Vanuatu. These three countries were chosen to examine causation patterns in countries where violence has already threatened the stability of their governments. The theory examined here is that emigration acts as a safety valve via three mechanisms: first, by reducing the number of young people in search of employment; second, by the departure of many of those most likely to attack those in power; and, third, by raising family and national incomes through remittances. While, as noted above, the concept of migration as a safety valve has a long history, its functioning in relation to conflict in the Pacific Island states has not previously been examined. Population densities in the region are still generally low (Table 1); thus, the areas of demographic stress to be examined are in relation to available economic opportunities—rather than to direct pressure on the environment. The State Failure Task Force established by US Vice President Al Gore, which omitted countries with populations less than 500,000, found that the urbanization-to-development ratio was a good predictor of political risk (Esty et al., 1998). Inter-island and rural-urban migration within states may be preparatory steps to emigration or a final move. Where there is little subsequent emigration, such movements often create high population densities in localized areas, especially bordering the national capitals, which can result in inter-ethnic tensions between the original inhabitants and the immigrants, unless there is sufficient economic growth to provide ample economic opportunities for both groups (for a Western comparison, see Teitelbaum and Winter, 1998).

3. The study area: Melanesia, Micronesia and Polynesia

The 22 countries and territories of Oceania included in this overview are the members of the Pacific Community, a regional organization based in Noumea, New Caledonia, which was formerly known as the South Pacific Commission and retains the acronym SPC. Since, as noted, many worldwide databases exclude less populous countries, the SPC database is the best source of information for Oceania as a whole and for the three geographical sub-regions of Melanesia, Micronesia and Polynesia (see the map in Figure 1). While lively debate continues over exact boundaries and the routes by which these groups arrived in the Pacific, Melanesians, Polynesians and Micronesians are genetically, linguistically and historically distinct groups (Gibbons, 2001). The Melanesians arrived in the Pacific some forty to fifty thousand years ago, while the Polynesian and Micronesian movements into outer Oceania occurred only some three to four thousand years ago (Irwin, 1992). Over the past two centuries, the impositions of colonialism have interacted with earlier political and cultural differences to mould their contemporary societies (Sahlins, 1963; Thomas, 1989). The strength and survival of pre-colonial differences can be judged from the fact that the Micronesian inhabitants of Kiribati and the Polynesian inhabitants of Tuvalu, who were united under a single colonial administration as the Gilbert and Ellice Islands, voted to become separate countries at independence, even though Tuvalu had less than 10,000 inhabitants. All of the island countries face similar social and economic challenges associated with the lack of economies of scale, remoteness from major markets and, in most cases, the difficulties of providing services across chains of islands separated by long stretches of ocean.

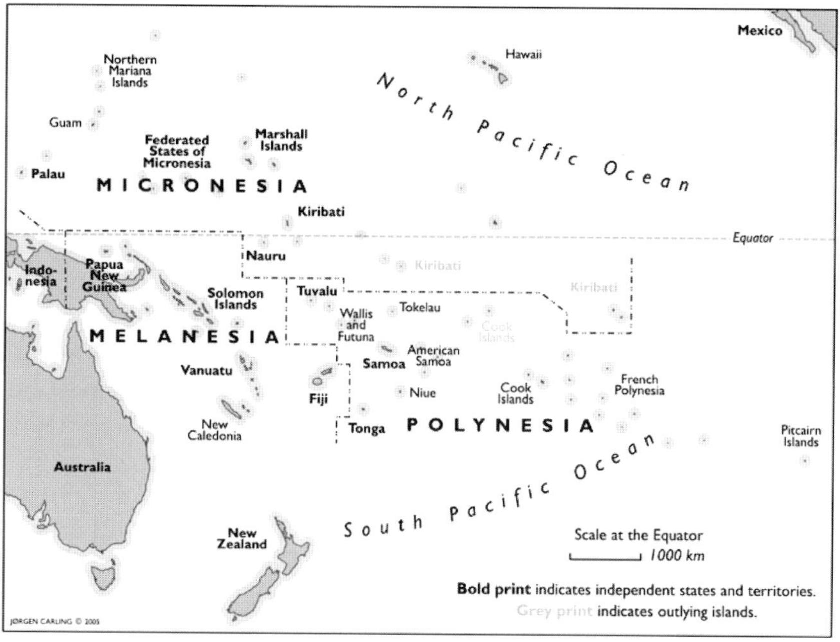

Figure 1. Map of Melanesia, Micronesia and Polynesia.

Table 1 summarizes the demography of the SPC countries and territories. It shows that fertility and thus natural growth rates remain relatively high across the region. However, while for Melanesia the natural growth rate is almost the same as the growth rate net of migration, for Micronesia major movements out of Guam and the Marshall Islands are counterbalanced by movements into the Northern Mariana Islands, and for Polynesia net growth is significantly lower than natural growth because of emigration, often at national rates of above 1% per annum. Table 2 indicates something of the complexity of political and legal statuses, and Table 3 presents estimates of Pacific migrants in receiving countries, showing that proportionally Polynesians are much more likely to emigrate than Melanesians, while almost one in five of all Micronesians are resident in the USA.

4. Civil conflict in the region

Until the first coup in Fiji in 1987 stunned its neighbours, the Pacific presented a unique case of a region emerging from colonial rule, without a single military coup. Pacific countries generally maintain law and order through their police forces, and most of them do not have military forces. Tonga is the only non-Melanesian island state with an army—of 350 persons for royal ceremonies. Within Melanesia, Fiji has 3–4,000 soldiers who are often exported to assist in UN peacekeeping; Papua New Guinea has 4,400; and Vanuatu has a small group of 300 paramilitary police. The lack of armies removes a major potential drain on governmental budgets. However,

Table 3. Pacific islanders across the region

Country (self-declared)	At home (census year)	In Australia (2001) Birthplace	In Australia (2001) Ancestry	In New Zealand (2001) Birthplace	In New Zealand (2001) Ethnicity	In USA (2000) Race
Melanesia	6,475,900	62,258	27,141	27,654	7,500	14,156
Fiji	775,077 (1996)	44,261		25,722		
Fijians	395,000	15,000[e]	16,620	7,197	6,978	13,581
Fijian Indians	336,597	27,048		12,108		
Solomon Islands	380,000 (1999)	1,326	769	507		25
Papua New Guinea	5,180,000 (2000)	15,773[e]	9,441	1,149		224
Vanuatu	182,900 (1999)	898	311	276		18
Micronesia	516,100	450	640	588	500	115,247
Kiribati	83,000 (2000)	407	358	504		
Polynesia	885,400	27,195	125,390	602,150	762,498	180,000
American Samoa	51,000 (2000)	152		399		133,281 (all Samoans)
Samoa	170,900 (2001)	13,254	28,090	47,118	115,017	
Cook Islands	17,500 (2001)	4,742	8,154	15,222	52,569	
New Zealand Maori	526,281 (2001)		72,956	513,128 Language: 494,679	526,281	
Nauru	9,919 (1992)	465		222		
Niue	1,600 (2001)	491	1,301	5,328	19,776	
Tokelau	1,500 (2001)	262		1,662	6,204	574
Tonga	97,400 (1996)	7,692	14,889	18,054	40,716	36,840
Tuvalu	9,300 (2002)	97		1,017	1,935	

Sources: 2001 Census of Australia; 2001 Census of New Zealand; 2000 Census of USA; Pacific Island countries' national censuses.
[e]estimate. Owing to missing data and varying definitions, totals for regions need to be used with caution.
Polynesian figures for the USA exclude 401,162 native Hawaiians.
The 2001 Canadian Census recorded 22,340 people born in Fiji, plus 14,160 people born in "Other Oceania".

it is still possible for armed groups to attempt to change the government in power. As in the Solomon Islands and Vanuatu, it is possible for dissatisfied youths to form illegal militias or for the police to use force to pressure the government to step down.

To date, the geographic and cultural coordinates of conflict in the Pacific are clear. In Polynesia, there are only three independent countries—Samoa, Tonga and Tuvalu—none of which has experienced major civil violence or a coup since independence. Micronesia, with the exception of Kiribati and Nauru, is so much within the US sphere of influence that the United States implicitly guarantees civil order, since it would almost certainly intervene were there to be any civil upheaval involving violence. Civil conflict in Oceania has essentially been confined to Melanesia. In Melanesia, there are four independent countries and one French territory. Of these independent countries, Papua New Guinea experienced civil war in Bougainville from 1988 to 1997, Fiji experienced three coups from 1987 to 2000, the Solomon Islands parliament had to invite in a regional armed force to re-establish order in 2003, and Vanuatu experienced a revolt of its paramilitary police and had a series of near-coup changes of government. In the territory of New Caledonia, the French reaction to the pro-independence movement in the 1980s led to bloodshed, and there are fears of further violence associated with the independence referendum due between 2014 and 2018. In summary, all of Melanesia, except Vanuatu, has experienced civil violence with multiple civilian deaths.

Looking at the population growth rates in Table 1, together with the dimensions of the diasporas in Table 3, there would appear to be a simple relationship: Polynesia and Micronesia have built up large-scale emigration safety valves and have not experienced civil conflict. Melanesia (excluding Fijian Indians before the coups and Fijian Islanders since the coups) has few such safety valves, and all but one of its countries and territories has experienced significant civil violence. However, this analysis ignores the possibly confounding factor that the cultures of the subregions are different (Thomas, 1989). Whereas Polynesian societies are strongly hierarchical, "Melanesian societies were famously stateless" (Larmour, 1996: 2). Traditionally, Melanesians had no central government and order was maintained by face-to-face interactions backed by the threat of supernatural sanctions (Taylor, 1982; Larmour, 1998). Melanesian statelessness may partly be attributed to very early arrival in the region as well as to frequently living in mountainous areas where communication is very difficult. One draft constitution for Melanesian Vanuatu dispensed with all state functions except protection against external force, decentralizing all other roles to local chiefs (Larmour, 1996). In contrast, Polynesians arrived in canoe parties, organized in lineages that are still celebrated in folklore. Polynesians had well-established state-like governance structures in pre-colonial times. Tonga was a kingdom, and elsewhere, including the mixed culture of Fiji, high chiefs controlled significant areas with the ability to extract tribute and young men for warfare. The Polynesian countries are also characterized by linguistic and ethnic unity: each country speaks a single language such as Tongan or Samoan, while the Melanesian countries are famed as "islands of Babel" with probably the highest ratio of languages to inhabitants to be found anywhere in the world. For example, Vanuatu has one language—not dialect—per two thousand inhabitants. Such linguistic diversity is a significant factor dividing the population in ethnic conflict and making nation-building difficult (Reilly, 2000).

5. The demography of the Pacific Island states

In discussing Pacific demography and economic options, it is important to realize just how few citizens there are in each Pacific country (Table 1). In many areas, options are circumscribed by the sheer practical constraints of governing or living in a country with less than 200,000 people scattered over a range of islands. States so small that they must depend on the good will and financial support of the international community for their continued existence have been called quasi-states (Jackson, 1990; Armstrong and Read, 2000). The Pacific abounds in quasi-states. Tuvalu, an independent country and United Nations member, has a population of 9,000 spread across eight inhabited islands, while 30% of its total paid labour force works overseas in New Zealand or in the German merchant marine. Even the more populous Pacific island countries face continuing issues of sustainability.

Thus, in many ways, the core viability of the Pacific Island countries depends on their demography. This is true at both ends of the spectrum. On some islands, at the current level of economic development, there are too many people in a small area for the land and sea to sustain the population, with a consequent strong likelihood of internal conflict. On other islands, there are too few people to support basic services, with a consequent risk of a downward spiral of continuing emigration moving towards total depopulation. Certainly, sustained economic development (perhaps through tourism) and technical advances could make it possible to support larger numbers of people even on the coral atolls, but rapid *rates* of population growth are in themselves one of the many factors impeding economic investment and development.

One adaptive strategy is simply to leave. Niue is a vast coral island becoming depopulated as Niueans can migrate freely to New Zealand. The 2001 Census of New Zealand showed ten times more Niueans in New Zealand than at home (Table 3). Being small and remote greatly limits the economic options available to both individuals and governments. Fiji is the most populous of the Pacific Island countries with 800,000 people. (Papua New Guinea, with a population of 5 million sharing a mainland with Indonesian-held West Papua, is a member of the SPC but is not a Pacific Island country and merits more extensive discussion than can be provided here. It is included in the Tables for comparative purposes as the fourth of the independent Melanesian countries.)

All of the SPC countries still have relatively high natural rates of population growth. However, emigration often cuts back net growth rates (see Table 1). High growth rates are challenging since, in a simple arithmetical relationship, if the rate of population growth exceeds the rate of economic growth, per capita incomes will decline. Conversely, in the Pacific, as in Africa, it appears that: "the higher is the rate of growth of per capita GDP and the lower is the rate of population growth, the lower is the risk of conflict" (Collier and Hoeffler, 2000: 4), Thus, in the absence of economic growth, rates of population growth can create demographic pressure on the economy even where, as is common across the Pacific, national population densities remain low in relation to the natural resource base (Table 1). In the economic sphere, demographic pressure is characterized by, and can be measured in terms of, declining per capita incomes and more people looking for work than can find remunerative jobs or self-employment. Thus, demographic pressure can be reduced either by economic growth and the expansion of income-earning opportunities or by a reduction in population numbers through out-migration. This applies both at the national level and in relation to economically disadvantaged regions within countries (Birdsall et al., 2003). High birth rates also result in youthful populations, which place particular pressure on education facilities and entry into the labour market (Urdal, 2004).

Demographically, the core distinction between Polynesia and Melanesia is that the Polynesian countries have developed a safety valve through emigration, which has kept down their population growth rates to levels that limit social tensions (Table 1 shows migration rates). Young people who are dissatisfied at home can use their ethnic networks to explore new horizons in the developed world. In turn, those who stay behind draw very significant economic benefit from the remittances sent home by the emigrants. Education levels are quite high, and younger couples are adopting family sizes closer to those of the developed world. Micronesian population pressures are either released through migration to the mainland United States or through sending young men overseas as sailors. In contrast, for Melanesia, there is minimal emigration. This is because the country of birth and its history determines the legal and practical possibilities for islander migration to a first world country. (Table 2 presents the situation for each of the Pacific countries, and Table 3 presents data on the size of overseas diaspora.) Some Polynesians have an automatic right of entry to New Zealand. Furthermore, since New Zealand citizens do not need visas to enter Australia, step-wise migration to Australia is possible. Citizens of the Micronesian states and territories, except for Kiribati and Nauru, have a right of entry to the United States. In contrast, Melanesian countries do not have any special political relationships with the Pacific Rim countries which could allow automatic entry, and low literacy levels make their citizens less attractive as labour recruits. Also, while most Polynesians are fully literate in English or French, only a minority of Melanesians are comfortable speaking English or French and fewer can write either language. Melanesians from New Caledonia are represented in the French and European parliaments and can go to France, but few can afford the fare. For the Solomon Islanders, even an airfare from their capital to Sydney costs more than twice the annual per capita GNI. Diasporic communities often help with fares for new migrants, but Melanesian countries do not have such established communities. Movement is also easier where sending and receiving areas share a common currency (Table 2).

The sheer numbers of those using the emigration safety valve is striking (Table 3). At the 2001 census, apart from indigenous Maoris, there were close to 220,000 other ethnic Polynesians resident in New Zealand, including 89,000 overseas-born Polynesians. The Samoan diaspora around the rim out-numbers the Samoan populations of American Samoa and Samoa combined (276,000 versus 222,000). In sharp contrast, less than 5% of people from the Solomon Islands are to be found overseas.

Migration within the Pacific Island countries is widespread and usually involves movement from the outer islands into the main island where the capital is located. This inter-island migration (commonly referred to as urbanization by government officials and statisticians, see Table 1) is a significant cause of actual or potential conflict. Most land-holding rights across the Pacific are based on traditional communal law. Provisions for outsiders to settle on urban fringe lands often require in-marriage or depend upon highly contestable informal arrangements. As in the Solomon Islands, if an urban immigrant group as a whole is rejected by the host ethnic group, the result can be massive social dislocation and conflict. Describing urbanization, the late president of Fiji, Ratu Sir Kamisese Mara, saw "an erosion of cultural values, growing unemployment and the attendant restlessness, increased crime and other ills which plague large urban centres" (Mara, 1994, quoted in Connell, 1996: 43).

The many islanders who continue to leave their home islands and villages to move to the capitals, even though there is no work for them there, provide the strongest evidence that the subsistence life-style in the islands is no longer acceptable to many. One extreme case would be South Tarawa, the capital island of Kiribati, where the population density in 2004 was as high as 2,400 per square kilometre, peaking at 6,000 people plus their pigs on Betio Islet. To find space for a new Parliament for Kiribati, the Japanese had to construct an artificial island to put it on. Here land-holding kin-groups used to repel immigrants with violence and there are still fist-fights and even murders over land disputes (Thomas, 2002).

6. Migration's economic impact: the MIRAB system

A number of the Polynesian countries are noted for being MIRAB economies, that is countries whose economies are based upon a system of Migration, Remittances, Aid and Bureaucracy, with aid and remittances providing the funding for bureaucratic employment of significant proportions of island populations (Bertram and Watters, 1987; Bertram, 1999). MIRAB is a national strategy intended to keep Polynesian economies viable and to avoid conflict through maintaining economic returns to a wide cross-section of the population and opportunities for young people to explore the world.

Some economists predict that MIRAB will fail because familial remittances will dry up over time. Others claim that it is not a viable strategy because the remittances are not used for productive investments at home (the debate is covered in Hayes (1991) and Brown (1998)). Yet, it is the very lack of productive opportunities for investment that causes continuing emigration. Instead, remittances are invested in the education of the next generation of potential emigrants. Indeed, education in nursing is preferred as providing such highly exportable skills (Brown and Connell, 2004). It is government policy in Samoa and Tonga to train more professionals than can be employed locally in order to boost remittance income.

Relatively little is known of the impact that exporting large numbers of young people has on the political and social structure or environment of the sending, as opposed to the much-studied receiving, countries. There is a need for research on the possibility of the alleviation of population pressure on the resource base through out-migration (Curran and Agardy, 2004: 17). Social remittances, exchanging visits and ideas have resulted in some questioning of gerontocratic Polynesian traditions. But there is little evidence of overseas groups sponsoring political changes at home (Huffer and So'o, 2003). Perhaps this is because unlike Sri Lankans and Cape Verdeans, for instance, overseas Polynesians have no voting rights at home. Tongans have given some support to the pro-democracy movement via the website http://www.planet-tonga.com (with a million hits a month), but their radicalism is constrained by their church links (Lee, 2004). The diaspora of the Indian Fijians has also been remarkably politically quiescent (Spoonley, 2000: 15).

For some Polynesian and Micronesian countries, remittances represent 30–50% of GDP (Spoonley, 2000: 8). In 1990, declared remittances provided Tonga with four times the revenue earned through exports or 60% of GDP (Lee, 2004). Undeclared remittances may represent an additional 40% of recorded remittances (Bedford, 2000). Without this emigration outlet, Tonga would face legal difficulties, since Tongan law provides that every male citizen is entitled to a set allocation of 3.3 hectares of rural land (USP, 2003). Currently, even with the majority of Tongans resident overseas, there is simply not enough dry land in the kingdom to meet this basic requirement. Remittances are not all unidirectional. Micronesians send crabs to their relatives in the USA to maintain a claim on future favours (Naylor et al., 2002). Many emigrants intend to retire home once they leave the workforce, but there are very few statistics on return migration or home visits that might help to clarify how far this expectation is met and how strong the linkages remain. Sociological studies suggest that linkages for the second generation do remain significant, especially for those who can speak Tongan (Lee, 2004).

Kiribati and Tuvalu both have government policies to train seamen to work on foreign fleets. They deliberately share such employment around on an informal roster so as to avoid violent conflict at home (Simati and Gibson, 1999). Kiribati is now extending this policy to overseas nursing employment for women. National remittance income remains relatively constant, as emigrants both support their families and accumulate resources for retirement and are joined by a steady flow of new emigrants (Brown, 1998; Simati and Gibson, 1999).

There are concerns that the Pacific Rim countries may be less willing to accept islander immigrants in future because of declining requirements for unskilled labour. However, the ageing of Rim populations will make importation of labour for the service industries, and especially care for the aged, increasingly attractive. Currently, the Australian trade unions are working with the Fijian unions to establish a guest-worker scheme for Fijians to work in seasonal agriculture as a means of relieving poverty and potential conflict in Fiji. Dobell (2003) has argued that Australia should move to special short-term migration provisions rather than aid for the island states—this view was strongly supported by the report of a bipartisan committee of the Australian Senate (2003).

MIRAB apart, there is little governmental population policy in the Pacific (McMurray, 2001). Most governments have low-key, health-focused family planning programs but they are hampered by the strong sexual conservatism and patriarchal ideals of the powerful churches, which tax one-tenth of their members' incomes, and a lack of employment opportunities for married women. The strongest demand for contraception often comes from unmarried young people, but the churches deny them access (thereby potentially exposing youth to HIV/AIDS as well as pregnancy).

7. Demographic causal factors in conflict in the Pacific

Since the days of Malthus, theories linking demographic factors with conflict have focused on issues of resource scarcity. Before large-scale international fishing fleets, land was the critical resource factor in the Pacific. Now, because of rising expectations, formal sector employment also looms large. Indeed, it could be queried whether the young men who riot in the streets over land issues from Port Moresby to Honiara and Suva would actually want to go and farm the land if it were given to them. In most places in the Pacific it is still possible to live a relatively comfortable semi-subsistence lifestyle. There are coconuts and fish to eat and the sun still shines. However, schooling requires money for books and clothes, even where it is officially free, and is not designed for manual workers (Ware, 2004). The problem is that young men are increasingly unwilling to see their future as being subsistence fishers, sugar cane/vanilla farmers or copra cutters (Connell, 1996).

Relationships between population impact, migration and the environment are extremely complex (Curran and Agardy, 2004; Kahl, 2002; Mearns, Leach and Scoones, 1998). Population pressures result in violent conflict in the Pacific, not because of a lack of enough land to grow crops on, nor because elites exclude the poor from access to land, but because population growth makes it difficult to create enough job opportunities for the increasing numbers of youths who leave school each year (McGavin, 1997). Very high rates of Pacific urbanization (Table 1) are driven by the pulls of education, potential employment, public services and entertainment rather than, as yet, push factors from environmental degradation.

With this background on the general interrelationships across the Pacific, it is possible to examine three case studies of Pacific Island countries that have experienced conflict.

8. Fiji: ethnic conflict or class war?

Fiji presents a revealing case study where one group, the Indo-Fijians, had established routes and links for emigration and the other group, the Fijian islanders, had not. From a surface view, the coups in Fiji in 1987 (two in one year) and 2000 present a classic case of changes in the demographic/electoral balance resulting in a political transition that was unacceptable to the disadvantaged ethnic group, who then seized government by force. In reality, the Indians' demographic majority, first achieved in 1946, had been steadily declining since the 1960s owing to emigration and lower fertility than the Fijians. What changed in 1987 was a new Indian ability to create class-based political coalitions, which gave their parties political predominance through the inclusion of poor, urban Fijians. For the first time, electoral victory was based on a coalition of the disadvantaged rather than ethnic Fijian loyalties. Thus, it was actually a breakdown in the ethnic barriers that resulted in conflict, Although many factors are involved, a strong case can be made that the coups in Fiji were led by men motivated by a desire for power as a means to maintain their status and control of valuable resources (greed), while their followers were motivated by perceived grievances and the frustrations of unemployment and low incomes (see Goldstone's "elite leadership" [2002: 8]). The leaders could play the ethnic-rivalry card because opportunities for Fijians were visibly more limited than for Indians. Since the army was more than 98% ethnically Fijian, once force was invoked, the Fijians held an unassailable position. Indeed, one motivation for the first 1987 coup was a proposal to create greater ethnic balance within the army. Fiji is not an example of state weakness resulting in civil violence. The state machinery of the army and the police in Fiji is very powerful; the problem has been that the elected politicians do not necessarily have a strong hold on this Fijian-dominated machinery, especially if they are Indians.

An extensive review of the more than one hundred academic studies of the 1987 Fiji coups shows four core explanations: the racial explanation, the class explanation, the custom explanation and a range of explanations involving special interests supporting the greed motivations of particular groups (Ewins, 1992). None of these explanations highlights demographic factors (beyond the numerical imbalance between Indians and Fijians), although most acknowledge the importance of the cohorts of unemployed Fijian youths in providing active support for pro-tradition and anti-Indian sentiment. In the lead-up to 1987, total numbers of paid workers in Fiji were actually declining, while the population continued to grow and Indians had the links to emigrate while Fijians did not (McGavin, 1997: Table 5.1).

It was only too easy for coup leaders to play the "Fiji for Fijians" card. Land is an intensely emotive issue ("*vanua*" in Fijian means cultural identity as well as physical territory), and many of the Indian leases were coming up for renewal by 2000. The tragedy was that sugar, the country's major export crop, is grown by Indian leaseholder farmers on exclusively Fijian-owned land. The real threat in 1987 was that Indians and commoner Fijians, especially those who had migrated to the towns and discovered that work was poorly paid and hard to find, were beginning to unite. Poor Fijians questioned why the chiefs should automatically get 23% of all rents for Fijian lands. "It is the changing attitude among indigenous Fijians that the chiefly aristocracy fear as the primary threat to their power and authority, not the Indians" (Robie, 1987: 12).

Again in 2000, there were clear divisions between the avowed motives of the leaders and their actual objectives and between the motivations of the leaders and of their followers. George Speight, the non-Fijian-speaking coup leader, educated in Australia and of mixed Fijian and European descent, was an unlikely nationalist. However, as chair of the Fiji Hardwood Corporation, he was intent on maintaining control of the rights to log Fiji's vast mahogany plantations. Most of his followers were unemployed young urban males: members of the "*Taukei*", (which means "owners of the land") movement. Since unemployment was 25%, reaching close to 40% among those under 25, there was a large pool of potential supporters (Gounder, 2002). Although the 2000 coup plotters were ultimately arrested after two months of holding the parliament hostage, the first Indian-led government, which had been deposed by the coup, was not reinstated, and its replacement is still led by a Fijian technocrat who has to maintain the many Fijians who supported the coup as part of his political support base.

Demographically, the crisis in Fiji is being partially solved by the out-migration of skilled Indo-Fijians. In the decade following the 1987 coups, some 5,000 people (or 0.6% of the national total) migrated from Fiji every year; 95% of these emigrants were Indo-Fijians, thus securing the electoral majority for the ethnic Fijians. Far from regretting this skills haemorrhage, many welcomed it as a simple measure of unemployment reduction. After the 2000 coup, emigration by skilled ethnic Fijians also grew, acting as a barometer of fear of further conflict at home (Narayan and Smyth, 2003). The prospect of emigration directly curbs violence in Fiji, since individuals need clean police records to be accepted overseas. This applies both to Indians moving as teachers and nurses and to potentially undisciplined Fijian youths, recruited to comparatively well-paid positions in the British Army, working to keep the peace in Northern Ireland and former Yugoslavia.

9. Solomon islands: rapid population growth and state failure

For many, the Solomon Islands represents the Pacific's first "failed" state, with failure being defined as the collapse of the government's ability to control the police and thus to control street violence and maintain law and order (Roughan, 2002). Quite unlike Fiji, the Solomon Islands state has always been very weak. This is a country with very rapid population growth, doubling in 20 years; internal migration across ethnic boundaries, both resulting from and causing land shortages; no emigration safety valve; and very little in the way of a social or economic safety net. Traditionally, the archipelago comprised a series of village communities with no higher level of government than the village. Apart from football, the sense of statehood remains embryonic. Of the 30 local languages, none has a word for state. The pidgin word "governmen" means the people who collect taxes and should deliver services in return. Many Melanesians "do not imagine the state as a reified entity or transcendent abstraction" (Foster, 1996: 92). Of little interest to the British colonial authorities, the Solomon Islands have always been very weakly resourced with physical infrastructure and people trained to run the country. Since independence in 1978, the government, although democratic, has not developed a party structure based on ideological differences. Instead politics is personality driven and corrupt, as loyalty to political chiefs is bought and exchanged for favours. Electors are willing to re-elect politicians, knowing them to be corrupt, believing that the benefits of corruption will be shared with local electorates that are otherwise starved of basic services. "Big men" flourish, often to the severe detriment of the environment through logging and over-fishing (Hviding and Bayliss-Smith, 2003). A tradition of monetary compensation (originally with strings of shell money) for wrongs such as the killing of a relative has become highly corrupted with the use of modern paper money and the government being held to ransom at gunpoint by ethnic gangs.

The capital, Honiara, is a small town on the island of Guadalcanal. Its population is largely made up of immigrants from other islands and their locally-born children (at the 1986 census, 88% of the adult population of the capital had been born elsewhere; Gagahe, 2000). The population with higher education mainly comes from Malaita, a more heavily populated island, and the Malaitans have predominated in the public service. As land on Guadalcanal became more valuable for plantations and urban uses, conflict arose over Malaitans living and working there. This climaxed in 1999 with riots in which over 20,000 Malaitans were forced to flee their homes owing to armed terrorism and intercommunal fighting on Guadalcanal (Naidu, 2001). Rebellion was a simple matter for the militias of opposing "freedom fighters"/unemployed youths, who seized police guns and paid themselves by levying tribute at road blocks. The prime minister was forced to resign at gunpoint.

Finally, in July 2003, surrounded by 200 ex-militants demanding "goodwill" payments, the Solomons' parliament was convened to pass a motion endorsing an Australian-led regional assistance mission (RAMSI) of 2,000 troops and police to restore law and order. RAMSI's first objective was to round up the guns; the second objective was to assist the police and bureaucracy to restore order and services to provide the setting for hoped-for economic recovery for a country that had experienced a 14% decline in GNI in one year. The Solomon Islanders are fortunate that, in contrast to any country in Africa, it is realistic to insist that no civilians own guns (new laws make the penalty for holding a gun up to 10 years in prison). Since there is no army, the only guns should be in the hands of a reformed, honest and ethnically diverse police force.

From a statistical analysis at a distance, the Solomons' case might well appear to be one of greed fuelling revolt, since the country has rich resources of timber and fish and had a newly opened gold mine. However, from close up, the young men with guns were preoccupied with grievances against members of the opposing ethnic group and were insufficiently organized to contemplate taking over the government. Their focus was on seizing cash rather than securing a continuing income stream, and they made no attempt to seize the gold mine or get it reopened. Many saw the mine as raping agricultural land (Banks, 2002). Kahl (2002) has reviewed the debate relating to demographic change, natural resources and violence. He contrasts the neo-Malthusian arguments relating to pressures on states and societies, and hypotheses relating to deprivation, state weaknesses and state exploitation with the neoclassical economists' arguments on adaptation and the "honey pot" and "resource curse" hypotheses. In the case of the Solomons, a selection of these arguments are relevant and no single explanation is sufficient. The speed of population growth has placed pressure on the society through urbanization and on the state through the difficulties of providing education and other services for rapidly growing numbers. In the case of neighbouring Bougainville, Kahl (2002: 273) concludes that "strife . . . stemmed from the direct and indirect effects of demographic and environmental stress on economic, social and political conditions". This would also be a fair summary for the Solomon Islands.

With civil order restored by RAMSI, future visions range from a new federal constitution of separate island communities to the other extreme of a Pacific Union following the model of the European Union. Whatever the political solution, the demographic issues still need to be resolved. Implementing a federal constitution will not create jobs. Absent new technologies, Malaitans will still need space beyond their overcrowded island and all kinds of development will be easier to achieve with slower population growth. Solomon Island mothers' groups played an active peacebuilding role. However, individual women, some of whom found the conflict quite liberating, will only adopt contraception when they have significantly more access to educational, health and economic opportunities.

10. Vanuatu: the politics of survival

Looking for the most fragile economy and the weakest government, most pundits have nominated Vanuatu as the next site of political violence in the Pacific (Dobell, 2003; ASPI, 2002). Vanuatu has much in common with the Solomon Islands. It is Melanesian with great ethnic diversity; education levels are low; population growth is rapid; and central government is weak. Unemployment levels among young people are over 40%, and emigration prospects are minimal. Furthermore, society is divided along the Anglophone/Francophone divide of the old Condominium. In terms of the Pacific predictive factors for civil conflict, Vanuatu is in much the same position as the Solomon Islands (Henderson and Bellamy, 2002). The difference is that a succession of elected governments of Vanuatu have demonstrated remarkable skills in creating a series of coalitions to survive a national public service strike, insurrection by the paramilitary police and multiple constitutional crises (Ambrose, 1996). Although government ministers are frequently simultaneously personally corrupt and collectively naive in the pursuit of implausible get-rich-quick schemes, the democratic state has successfully staggered on from crisis to crisis in pursuit of 'a unified, peaceful, self-reliant and democratic nation, upholding the rule of law, Melanesian values and Christian principles' (Vanuatu constitution quoted in Crossland, 2000: 4).

For Vanuatu, the combination of high population growth and weak economic growth has resulted in an average annual 1.8% decline in per capita incomes over the past decade (Asian Development Bank figures from 2004). Young people still flock to the capital without any realistic prospect of finding paid work. Formal employment opportunities would need to grow at 10% per annum to absorb all the young people who want paid jobs when they leave school. The tiny elite who graduate from formal vocational training cannot all find work, and life is much harder for the majority who never finished primary school. Yet, Vanuatu is not overpopulated in any conventional sense, with rich volcanic soils and a national population density of only 16 persons per square kilometre. It is the rates of population growth and urbanization that present the challenge, rather than the absolute numbers.

11. Conclusion

The 22 Pacific Island countries and territories are small and often ignored in a post-Cold War world. Yet, 12 of them are members of the United Nations (Table 2; Schwarzberg, 2003). If their governments should lose control, they have the potential to disturb the neighbourhood, although less with terrorists than with contraband guns, drugs and illegal immigrants. This is why the Australian government has changed its attitude towards internal conflicts from deploring them from a distance to favouring direct intervention in regional countries when the breakdown of law and order results in local anarchy, as in the Solomon Islands (Dobell, 2003).

With countries whose populations are counted in the millions, there often appears to be little that the international community can realistically do to help to prevent or resolve internal violent conflicts. However, when national populations are counted in the hundreds of thousands or less, as in the Pacific, then the international community can play a significant role in conflict mitigation. Thus, this article argues for allowing continued emigration as a safety valve for social and economic discontents in micro-states. It also stresses that, while population pressures on land, sea and other natural resources can be mediated by social arrangements (Curran and Agardy, 2004), Pacific island countries are still prone to violent conflict where governments are weak and population growth has outstripped economic growth and thus employment opportunities. Education and global media exposure renders youths unwilling to foresee life as bounded by subsistence fishing or agriculture. Youth suicide is growing under the palm trees (Booth, 1998). Young people who are deprived of the "dream" of migration lose hope (Macpherson, 1990). Young men who join illegal rogue militias demonstrate a similar hopelessness. The Pacific saw its first "failed" nation with no government capable of securing law and order in the Solomon Islands and, while controls on small arms will help (IANSA, 2004), the real answers lie in faster economic growth to provide jobs and entrepreneurial opportunities and slower demographic growth (through emigration and declining birth rates) to relieve the constant pressure to provide more education and create new jobs.

Elsewhere in the developing world, the slogan is often "trade not aid"; in the Pacific it should be "migration rights for the poor not hand-outs for the rich". Because the numbers are so small, less than two million people in total (excluding Papua New Guinea), Australia and New Zealand, who regularly absorb some 200,000 immigrants a year, could readily take all those who wish to come in from the Pacific (especially if short-term migrant worker schemes are accepted). Migration access has demonstrably helped Polynesia to stay stable. Skilled migrants retiring to their home islands, in a reverse brain drain, may even be able to make Polynesian economies more self-sustaining. For Melanesia's less educated and internationally mobile peoples, the picture is less clearcut. However, bringing ethnically mixed teams of youths to Australia and New Zealand for short-term work contracts during which they would learn to work together and receive both pay and utilizable skills training would be a highly worthwhile initiative. In the meantime, in the interests of both slowing population growth and preventing the spread of HIV/AIDS, island governments could be assisted to make barrier contraceptives available to youths irrespective of sex or marital status.

References

Ambrose, David, 1996. 'A coup that failed? recent political events in Vanuatu', *State, Society and Governance in Melanesia Project, Paper 3*. Canberra: Australian National University.

Armstrong, Harvey and Robert Read, 2000. "Comparing the economic performance of dependent territories and sovereign microstates", *Economic Development and Cultural Change* 48(2): 285–298.

Australian Senate, 2003. Report on Australia's *Relationship with the South West Pacific*. Canberra.

ASPI, 2002. *Our Failing Neighbour: Australia and the Future of the Solomon Islands*. Canberra: Australian Strategic Policy Institute.

Banks, Glenn, 2002. "Mining and the environment in Melanesia", *Contemporary Pacific* 14(1): 39–67.

Bean, Frank D., Rodolfo de la Garza, Bryan Roberts and Sidney Weintraub, (eds), 1997. *At the Crossroads: Mexico and U.S. Immigration Policy*. New York: Rowman and Littlefield.

Bedford, Richard, 2000. "Meta-societies, remittance economies and Internet addresses", in David Graham and Nana Poku (eds), *Migration, Globalisation and Human Security*. London: Routledge (110–137).

Bertozzi, Andrea, 2002. "Italy's recent change from an emigration country to an immigration country", speech to the Cicero Foundation, Rome, 15 November.

Bertram, Geoffrey, 1999. "The MIRAB model twelve years on", *Contemporary Pacific* 11(1): 105–123.

Bertram, Geoffrey and Ray Watters, 1987. "The MIRAB economy in pacific microstates", *Pacific Viewpoint* 26(3): 497–519.

Birdsall, Nancy, Allan C. Kelley and Steven W. Sinding (eds), 2003. *Population Matters: Demographic Change, Economic Growth, and Poverty in the Developing World*. Oxford: Oxford University Press.

Booth, Heather, 1998. *Pacific Island Suicide in Perspective*. Canberra: Australian National University.

Brown, Richard, 1998. "Do pacific island migrants' remittances decline over time?", *Contemporary Pacific* 10(1): 107–151.

Brown, Richard and John Connell, 2004. "Occupation-specific analysis of migration and remittance behaviour: Pacific Island nurses", *Beyond MIRAB: The Political Economy of Small Islands in the 21st Century Conference, Wellington, 23–25 February*.

Choucri, Nazli, 2002. "Migration and security: some key linkages", *Journal of International Affairs* 56(1): 97–125.

Collier, Paul and Anke Hoeffler, 2000. *On the Incidence of Civil War in Africa*. Washington, DC: World Bank.

Connell, John, 1996. "Urbanization and settlement in the pacific", *Resettlement Policy and Practice in Southeast Asia and the Pacific*. Manilla: Asian Development Bank (43–53).

Crossland, Kavel, 2000. "The ombudsman role: Vanuatu's experiment", *State, Society and Governance in Melanesia Project, Paper 5*. Canberra: Australian National University.

Curran, Sara and Tundi Agardi, 2004. "Considering migration and its effects on coastal ecosystems", in Jon Unruh, Maarten Krol and Nurit Kliot, (eds), *Environmental Change and its Implications for Population Migration* (Chapter 10). Berlin: Springer.

de Sherbinin, Alex, 1995. "World population growth and US national security", in Woodrow Wilson Center, *Environmental Change and Security Project Report* 1 (Spring): 24–39.

Dobell, Graeme, 2003. "The reluctant pacific nation: Policy taboos, popular amnesia and political failure", *Quadrant* 396 (May): 16–23.

Esty, Daniel, Jack Goldstone, Ted Robert Gurr, Barbara Harff, Marc Levy, Geoffrey Dabelko, Pamela Surko and Alan Unger, 1998. *State Failure Task Force Report, Phase II Findings*. McLean, VA: Science Applications International.

Ewins, Rod, 1992. *Colour, Class and Custom: The Literature of the 1987 Fiji Coup*. Canberra: Australian National University.

Foster, Robert, 1996. "State ritual: voting in Namatanai", in Yaw Saffu (ed.), *The 1992 PNG Election*. Canberra: Australian National University (144–167).

Gagahe, Nick, 2000. "The process of internal movement in Solomon islands", *Asia Pacific Population Journal* 15(2): 53–75.

Gibbons, Ann, 2001. "The peopling of the pacific", *Science* 291(5509): 1735–1737.

Goldstone, Jack A., 2002. "Population and security: how demographic change can lead to violent conflict", *Journal of International Affairs* 56(1): 3–23.

Gounder, Rukmani, 2002. "Political and economic freedom, fiscal policy, and growth nexus: some empirical results for Fiji", *Contemporary Economic Policy* 20(3): 234–245.

Hayes, Geoffrey, 1991. "Migration, metascience and development policy in Polynesia", *Contemporary Pacific* 3(1): 1–58.

Henderson, John and Paul Bellamy, 2002. "Prospects for further military intervention in melanesian politics", *World Affairs* 164(3): 124–134.

Huffer, Elise and Asofou So'o, 2003. "Consensus versus dissent: democracy, pluralism and governance in Samoa", *Asia-Pacific Viewpoint* 44(3): 281–304.

Hviding, Edvard and Tim Bayliss-Smith, 2003. *Islands of Rainforest: Agro Forestry, Logging and Ecotourism in Solomon Islands*. Aldershot: Ashgate.

IANSA (International Action Network on Small Arms), 2004. http://www.iansa.org.

Irwin, Geoffrey, 1992. *The Prehistorical Exploration and Colonization of the Pacific*. Cambridge: Cambridge University Press.

Jackson, Robert, 1990. *Quasi-States, Sovereignty, International Relations and the Third World*. Cambridge: Cambridge University Press.

Kahl, Colin, 2002. "Demographic change, natural resources and violence: the current debate", *Journal of International Affairs* 56(1): 257–282.

Larmour, Peter, 1996. "Research on governance in weak states in Melanesia", *State, Society and Governance in Melanesia Project*. Canberra: Australian National University.

Larmour, Peter, 1998. "Migdal in Melanesia", in Peter Dauvergne (ed.), *Weak and Strong States in Asia-Pacific Societies*. Sydney: Allen and Unwin (77–92).

Lee, Helen, 2004. "Second generation tongan transnationalism", *Asia Pacific Viewpoint* 45(2): 235–254.

Levine, Daniel H., 1995. Migration from the Caribbean: Issues for the 1990s', *Journal of the International Institute* 3(1): 1–3.

McGavin, Paul, 1997. *Labour Resource Utilisation in Melanesia*. Canberra: Australian National University.

McMurray, Chris, 2001. *Population and Development Planning in the Pacific*. Noumea: Secretariat of the Pacific Commission.

Macpherson, Cluny, 1990. "Stolen dreams: Some consequences of dependency for western Samoan youth", in John Connell (ed.), *Migration and Development in the South Pacific*. Canberra: Australian National University (107–120).

Mearns, Robin, Melissa Leach and Ian Scoones, 1998. *The Institutional Dynamics of Community-Based Natural Resource Management: An Entitlements Approach*. Washington, DC: World Bank.

Mesquida, Christian G. and Neil I. Wiener, 1999. "Male age composition and severity of conflicts", *Politics and the Life Sciences* 18(2): 113–117.

Naidu, Vijay (ed.), 2001. *Current Trends in South Pacific Migration*. Wollongong: APMRN, University of Wollongong.

Narayan, Paresh and Russell Smyth, 2003. "The determinants of emigration from Fiji to New Zealand", *International Migration* 41(5): 33–58.

Naylor, Rosamund, Kimberly Bonine, Katherine Ewel and Erick Waguk, 2002. "Migration, markets, and mangrove resource on kosrae, FSM", *Ambio* 31(4): 340–350.

Pontifical Council for the Pastoral Care of Migrants and Itinerant People, 2000. *I Was a Stranger and You Made Me Welcome*. Vatican: Roman Curia.

Reilly, Ben, 2000. "The africanization of the pacific", *Australian Journal of International Affairs* 54(3): 263–273.

Robie, David, 1987. "Why the Fiji plot theory is gaining ground", *Fiji Times on Sunday*, 12 July.

Roughan, John, 2002. "*Pacific First: A Failed State*", http://rspas.anu,edu.au/melanesia/solomonsarticles, htm#21.

Sahlins, Marshall, 1963. "Poor man, rich man, big man, chief: political types in Melanesia and Polynesia", *Comparative Studies in Society and History* 5(3): 285–303.

Schwartzberg, Joseph, 2003. "Entitlement quotients as a vehicle for United Nations reform", *Global Governance* 9(1): 81–115.

Simati, Aunese and John Gibson, 1999. "*Do Remittances Decay? Evidence from Tuvaluan Migrants in New Zealand*", Department of Economics, University of Waikato, Auckland.

Spoonley, Paul, 2000. "*Reinventing Polynesia: The Cultural Politics of Transnational Pacific Communities", Working Paper* 2K 14, Humanities and Social Sciences, Massey University, Auckland.

Taylor, Michael, 1982. *Community, Anarchy and Liberty*. Cambridge: Cambridge University Press.

Teitelbaum, Michael and Jay Winter, 1998. *A Question of Numbers: High Migration, Low Fertility and the Politics of National Identity*. New York: Hill and Wang.

Thomas, Frank, 2002. "Self-reliance in Kiribati: contrasting views of agriculture and fisheries production", *Geographical Journal* 168(2): 163–177.

Thomas, N. and commentators, 1989. "The force of ethnology: origins and significance of the Melanesia—Polynesia division", *Current Anthropology* 30(1): 27–41.

Turner, Frederick Jackson, 1893. "*The Significance of the Frontier in American History*", paper read to the American Historical Association, Chicago, IL.

Urdal, Henrik, 2004. "*The Devil in the Demographics: The Effect of Youth Bulges on Domestic Armed Conflict, 1950–2000", Social Development Papers* 14. Washington, DC: Conflict Prevention and Reconstruction Unit, World Bank. http://www-wds.worldbank.org/servlet/WDSContentServer/WDSP/IB/2004/07/28/000012009_20040728162225/Rendered/PDF/29740.pdf.

USP (University of the South Pacific), 2003. Legal website http://www.vanuatu.usp.ac.fj.

Ware, Helen, 2004. "*Current Issues in Education in the Pacific*", Australian Population Association, http://acsr.anu.edu.au/APA2004/program.html.

PART II. CONFLICT AND MORTALITY: THE BROADER PICTURE

CHAPTER 5. THE DESTRUCTIVENESS OF PRE-INDUSTRIAL WARFARE: POLITICAL AND TECHNOLOGICAL DETERMINANTS

JOHN LANDERS
All Souls College, University of Oxford, United Kingdom

Abstract. This article is concerned with the demographic impact of warfare in pre-industrial Europe and the consequences of the adoption of firearms from the early 16th century. The scale of warfare and its costs both increased, but the demographic impact depended on rulers' strategies for meeting or evading these costs, rather than the scale of warfare itself. War-induced mortality was almost entirely due to epidemic disease precipitated by economic and social disruption. The impact was primarily regional, but diseases such as bubonic plague could trigger supraregional crises, as they did in 17th-century Germany. Gunpowder weapons initially reduced military costs, but this trend was reversed as warships and fortifications became more expensive and armies acquired more sophisticated sub-unit organization. Rulers cut their outgoings by using "military brokers" to raise mercenary units who lived off the resources of the war zones, resulting in extreme damage to civilian life and property. As a reaction, highly organized, well-disciplined standing armies with their own supply organizations emerged after 1670. These were much less destructive to civilians but were very expensive to maintain, partly because the new level of organization allowed larger forces to be coordinated effectively. European rulers became increasingly indebted, and in France, the *ancien régime* collapsed as a result. Its revolutionary successor sustained campaigns of predatory expansion with a military system based on mass conscription. The result was an increase in the scale and destructiveness of warfare, before France succumbed to a hostile coalition financed by the wealth of England's industrializing economy.

1. Introduction

The costs of raising, equipping and fielding troops loom large in histories of early-modern (and subsequent) public finance, but are only one part of the total costs war imposed on men and women who lived through it. Costs arise wherever something valued is destroyed, lost or otherwise foregone, and beyond the "immediate" costs of war lay the "consequential" costs—psychological as well as material or demographic—arising from war's impact on civilian economic and social life. Material and demographic costs were closely interrelated, not least because the threat or reality of material destruction was mainly responsible for wartime demographic crises. Demographic costs form a natural point of entry to this nexus, if only because they are, in principle at least, more readily quantifiable, and will be the main focus of this article.

The immediate costs of war were financial by definition, but its consequential costs took many forms, not all of which were tangible or expressible in monetary terms. The two categories are thus incommensurable but were closely interrelated

This chapter was previously published in *Journal of Peace Research*, vol. 42, no. 4, 2005, pp. 455–470.

Helge Brunborg et al. (eds.), The Demography of Armed Conflict, 111–129.

nonetheless; the more rulers evaded their military ambitions' immediate costs—which they did for much of our period—the more consequential costs increased, eventually reaching unsustainable levels. The military reforms of Europe's *ancien régime*—as its 18th-century political systems are commonly termed—ameliorated war's consequential costs but thereby drove up its immediate costs, to the point of ultimate fiscal collapse. The scale of military destructiveness thus reflected political choices, but both the choices and their demographic outcomes were constrained by deeper economic and epidemiological structures, and the occasion of choice was itself forced on rulers by technological innovation—in the shape of gunpowder weaponry—whose consequences were initially unforeseeable and which no one prince or general was in a position to control.

2. Economics, epidemiology and the demography of war

Two sets of structural relationships limited the collective material welfare of populations, in Europe and elsewhere, until well into the 19th century. One followed from the almost exclusive reliance on organic energy and raw material inputs in production and transportation. The limits of material life, in what Wrigley terms "organic economies" (Wrigley, 1988), were thus the limits of animal and plant production, and this had three direct consequences. Energy scarcity kept labour productivity and living standards near the subsistence minimum and liable to fall below it, should harvests fail. Second, long-distance overland bulk transport was so inefficient that most people had to live near where their staple foods or raw materials were produced. The geographical scale of economic life was regional if not local, and its spatial structure characteristically one of areal dispersal. Finally, as the agricultural labour force grew beyond a certain point, input shortages and land use conflicts depressed labour's marginal productivity still further. Where labour and product markets existed wages fell relative to prices, unemployment grew and demand for non-essential commodities reduced. In family-based systems, with farms or workshops inherited as indivisible units, prolonged growth generated a population of "surplus sons" and daughters condemned to survival on the margins of the productive economy.

These constraints had military and political implications. Armies depended on organic inputs for logistics, transport and communications, and pre-gunpowder weaponry also relied on muscle-power. Economic geography shaped strategy, since controlling productive assets dispersed across the countryside required a corresponding dispersal of military force. Indirect constraints were probably even more important. Low productivity restricted the size of the resource base, thereby setting physical limits to what rulers could appropriate, but such limits were rarely reached in practice.

What really mattered was not how big the cake was, but how big a slice any ruler could actually get his hands on, and here the immediate problem was the endemic weakness of the "means of appropriation". Levying efficient taxation involved assessing the resource base, calculating and distributing liabilities and then imposing them against actual or potential resistance. Doing all this required a network of competent, uncorrupt officials reaching into the localities and resistant to local or sectional pressures, and coercive forces able to withstand the political or even military strength of the social elite. Few medieval or early-modern rulers could afford an apparatus of this kind, and so they were unable to appropriate large shares of national wealth, because they were too poor to afford the means of doing so.

Without an effective salaried bureaucracy, early-modern government commonly devolved responsibilities to individuals outside the formal state apparatus, or to office-holders acting in a personal capacity and using private resources in exchange for rewards that might be economic, political or purely symbolic. Devolution reduced rulers' outgoings but brought a damaging and potentially dangerous loss of central political control. Devolved taxation required accommodations with the wealthy elite that limited rulers' political options and shifted burdens disproportionately on to the poor and powerless (Thompson, 1976; Bonney, 1995, 1999; Landers, 2003, ch. 15).

Devolution also featured prominently in military affairs. Feudalism provided one model, but as monetary economies reemerged, European rulers sought for greater operational flexibility without incurring the unsustainable costs of a standing army. One solution was to commission regional magnates to raise troops from their clienteles, but the 16th century saw the rise of "military brokers" able to supply units ranging from companies to entire armies by tapping a growing pool of mercenary manpower (Hale, 1985; Anderson, 1988). Devolution offered rulers a cheap and effective means of recruitment but shifted soldiers' loyalty towards their immediate commanders, thereby reducing central control in a manner that was mainly responsible for the heavy consequential costs of contemporary warfare and, particularly, for its demographic costs.

This responsibility worked out in the way it did because of the second of the two structural continuities referred to earlier. This was epidemiological and followed from the absence of effective life-saving medical techniques,[1] which meant the only sure protection from life-threatening infections was to avoid them, or to be immune following prior exposure. This circumstance shaped the demographic outcomes of military decisions by making mortality levels acutely sensitive to changes in exposure to infection (Landers, 1993, ch. 1); increased disorder, vagabondage, overcrowding or the prevalence of dirt and squalor led to increased deaths from endemic or epidemic disease.

The structure of war-related mortality reflected the shared epidemiological vulnerability of soldier and civilian and the limited destructive capacity of contemporary weaponry. Table 1 shows disease to have caused nearly 70% of deaths among British troops in Napoleonic Spain and Portugal. Such data are rare before the 1790s, but corresponding proportions are unlikely to have been much lower; the early-modern Swedish estimate is appreciably above 75% and probably indicates contemporary conditions more broadly. Military disease deaths on this scale arose from the same proximate causes as they did among civilians: exposure to infection, owing to overcrowded, unhygienic and insanitary conditions.

Table 1. Causes of death among troops in wartime

Army	Combat (%)	Disease (%)	Source
Sweden, 1620–1719	12.0	88.0	Lindegren (2000)
British, 1793–1815*	18.7	81.3	Hodge (1857)
Peninsular Campaign, (1810–14)	30.8	69.2	Hodge (1857)
French, 1803–15	22.4	77.6	Houdaille (1972)
Russia, 1854–56	31.4	68.6	Kozlovski (1912)
French, 1854–56	21.2	78.8	Kozlovski (1912)
British, 1854–56	20.7	79.3	Kozlovski (1912)
USA, 1861–65	30.6	69.4	Livermore (1957)
Confederacy, 1861–62	44.0	56.0	Livermore (1957)
Austria, 1866	31.9	68.1	Dumas and Vedel-Peterson (1923)
Prussia, 1866	37.6	62.4	Dumas and Vedel-Peterson (1923)
German, 1870–71	30.6	69.4	Kozlovski (1912)
Russia, 1877–78	21.6	78.4	Kozlovski (1912)

*Includes deaths of soldiers on United Kingdom territory.

Logistical failures exposed soldiers in the field to inadequate, rotten or otherwise contaminated food and water, but deployment to unhygienic camps or barracks away from the fighting also promoted infection. Finnish garrisons in the Baltic suffered an annual mortality of 37.3 per thousand over the years 1662–74. This was probably twice the mortality of the surrounding civilians and inflated by rural recruits' vulnerability to urban infections (Lindegren, 2000: 143, n. 15). Houdaille found non-combat deaths among three French regiments in 1782–93 to have been double those expected among civilians, while some coast-guard companies had a 40% excess in 1803–14 (Houdaille, 1977). Disease mortality among troops in Britain reached 18.4 per thousand in 1801–05 and apparently ran at 15.9 per thousand in the 1850s (Hodge, 1857: 160). These levels are likely to have been 50–100% above those of contemporary civilians (Landers, 2003: 340, n. 10).

Military deaths on this scale drove up young adult male mortality but made only secondary contributions to wars' total demographic cost since around half of males died in childhood. Half a million Swedish and Finnish troops are estimated to have died in wars during the years 1620–1719, during which 30% of males surviving to age 20 died as soldiers (Lindegren, 2000). But these deaths only exceeded six per thousand per year of the general population in the decade 1700–09, and only in four other decades did they exceed four per thousand. Lindegren puts Castilian military deaths at 300,000 out of a total of 6 million over the years 1618–59. This implies that around 10% of adult males died as soldiers but equates to only an annual 1.3 deaths per thousand of population. Houdaille estimates that, of the roughly 1.8 million

Frenchmen in the birth cohorts 1790–95 who reached the age of 20, 45% served in Napoleon's armies and 20% died in them (Houdaille, 1970), but only the truly massive mortalities of 1812–14 translated into major falls in male life expectation relative to females (Meslé and Vallin, 1989).

Military losses on the scale of early-modern Sweden's had appreciable demographic consequences, but they were very unusual, and war's main demographic impact occurred through increased civilian mortality. Here, too, infectious disease played the major role. Soldiers did kill civilians in early-modern wars; rural looting and devastation claimed lives, but such violence mostly occurred when cities fell to assault or after a long siege, as at Magdeburg in 1631. Such atrocities horrified contemporaries, but their wider demographic impact was minimal, and Outram (2001: 157) describes the direct contribution of military violence to civilian mortality during the Thirty Years War as "quantitatively quite insignificant". Epidemic disease represented the main wartime danger to civilians in besieged cities and elsewhere, and social disruption, due to the threat or reality of violence and destruction, was its main precipitator. This arose in three main ways: the simple presence or passage of troops through a region placed demands on civilian supplies and accommodation—made in a more or less destructive fashion—and introduced pathogens from outside; the civilian economy was deliberately targeted as an act of policy; and undisciplined troops wrought havoc on their own initiative.

These assaults triggered mortality crises through the same mechanisms that operated during peacetime harvest failures and the ensuing subsistence crises. Such crises caused great suffering but led to mortality crises only when increased exposure to infection—due to vagabondage, overcrowding, hygienic collapse, or the intrusion of external pathogens—led to epidemic disease.[2] The damage inflicted on regional social and economic structures by poorly organized troops created just such conditions, and it was this that accounted for their destructive demographic impact. The prevalence of such events in early-modern Europe itself reflected a growing mismatch between rulers' political ambitions, the demands of contemporary military technology and the resources available to fulfil them. The fundamental problem was that military technology had undergone a revolutionary change that generated new demands, unmatched by comparable changes in the spheres of production or transportation.

3. The gunpowder revolution and the Habsburg century

The general adoption of firearms in European warfare marked the first application of chemical energy to a major sphere of human activity. The consequences of this 16th-century "gunpowder revolution" included long-term increases in both troop strengths and costs per man, but the initial rise in numbers—occurring roughly from the early 16th century to the 1640s—probably owed more to population growth than to anything specifically military. The wars of this "Habsburg Century", as I shall term it after its main dynastic protagonist, were fought by old-style campaign armies that were raised when needed and disbanded when the fighting was over.[3] Poorly documented in the surviving sources, their size evidently fluctuated week by week, but the major powers are generally agreed to have fielded forces with peak strengths of over 100,000 men by the second quarter of the 17th century (Glete, 2002: 30–36; Landers, 2003: 319–321).[4] This expansion was disproportionate to the previous century's population growth, but it was not sustained, and numbers fell between the 1630s and 1670s.

The reasons for this increase remain controversial, but it probably reflected the organic economy's inability to absorb manpower on the scale generated by contemporary demographic expansion. The "marginal" component of underemployed and landless men consequently mushroomed, and having few choices beyond soldiering or vagrancy, they could be recruited for the promise of subsistence wages or simply the chance to loot. An ample supply of very cheap recruits seems to have produced similar results at the crest of the medieval demographic wave (Landers, 2003: ch. 13), but early-modern circumstances differed in two respects. Whereas the high-medieval infantryman was poorly trained and largely ineffective, the 16th-century hand-gunner, however cheaply recruited, held a weapon that could dominate the battlefield if properly deployed. Moreover, as the century wore on, the trend of per capita cost reduction was reversed.

Some of the ensuing cost increases arose from new-style fortifications and warships (Duffy, 1979; Pryor, 1988; Gardiner, 1992), but field armies were affected too, as unit costs rose by up to 40% (Thompson, 1995: 281–282). These had declined earlier as the proportion of cavalry fell and cheaper arque-busiers and pistol-armed horsemen replaced pikemen and heavy cavalry. But these changes ran their course by the later 16th century, and some were reversed, while increased proportions of officers and NCOs raised infantry unit costs by as much as 15% (Thompson, 1995: 281), reflecting the need to inculcate the "drill" underlying the new technique of synchronized volley fire and the higher level of battlefield supervision that this technique required.

3.1. MEETING THE COSTS

The supply of cheap recruits provided an opportunity for increased army size, but realizing this opportunity required increased numbers of intermediate and lower-level commanders. The resulting combination of increased numbers and higher costs per man was historically very unusual, if not unparalleled, and placed a potentially crippling burden on national treasuries (Landers, 2003: ch. 12).[5] The fact that it could be shouldered at all, even in the short term, was due to the large expansion of public credit permitted by the increasing sophistication of contemporary financial networks (Körner, 1995). In principle, wartime debts could be repaid at leisure out of peacetime revenues or the profits of war, but even where these were forthcoming, there were two intrinsic dangers: borrowing necessarily raised costs to a further and potentially hazardous degree, by attracting interest payments, and, by freeing rulers from "current account" constraints, it removed an essential barrier to overspending. In practice, militarily ambitious rulers, however successful, burdened their successors with debts that eventually had to be met by expedients ranging from default to the lynching of creditors.

The political and military muscle princes could bring to bear against mere money-lenders made such expedients feasible in the short term, but only made matters worse in the long term, as future creditors loaded "risk premia" on to interest rates which were already high. Debt service charges plus direct military costs eventually ranged up to 80–90% of total government expenditure. Again, in principle, rulers could conscript their subjects at lower wages than were needed to attract volunteers. Conscription was used to varying degrees throughout the period but rarely worked well. Rulers could no more afford the means of tapping demographic resources effectively than they could economic resources. They devolved the task to community bodies, landowners or magistrates who commonly used it to rid themselves of criminals, troublemakers and the mentally or physically infirm. Such men were rarely fit to be soldiers, and those who might have been usually deserted before they reached their unit (Landers, 2003: 284–285).

A more practical expedient was to default on wages and money for supplies and equipment. This was so frequent that published wage scales degenerated into book-keeping fictions, with morale and discipline both deteriorating as armies were forced to live at the expense of surrounding civilians. The destructive consequences were aggravated by the third cost-cutting expedient, which was the extensive resort to devolution and the use of military brokers in order to raise and maintain armies. Reliance on mercenary troops and commanders motivated wholly by material rewards created the worst problems. Such commanders had little interest in the welfare of their employers' subjects or the fate of civilian life and property and made few efforts to control their troops off the battlefields.

3.2. DEMOGRAPHIC COSTS

The basic problem was that brokers furnished troops relatively cheaply but did so by ignoring most of the costs needed to establish effective administrative organization, off-battlefield discipline or logistical support. These costs could be ignored, but this did not make them go away; instead, they were taken out on the civilian population as consequential costs, in the form of material and demographic destruction. The increased size of armies made things worse, because living off the land now required the establishment of territorial control over large areas, with a corresponding dispersal of force. This resulted in a pattern of low-level warfare waged by small local forces and readily sliding into simple banditry. Poorly documented by its nature, its prevalence emerges from some 17th-century figures. In 1632, Sweden's main field army contained only 20,000 of their 150,000 troops, with the balance divided roughly equally between regional field armies and 98 permanent garrisons. In 1639, around half of Spain's Army of Flanders, some 33,000 men, was scattered among 208 garrisons ranging from a thousand to only ten men (Parker, 1972: 11).

Prolonged low-level warfare was very destructive to civilian life and property,[6] not least because local detachments generally had to provision both themselves and their main force from the surrounding countryside, and settlements could face simultaneous exactions from multiple garrisons owing allegiance to either belligerent.[7] In these circumstances, civilians' first response to the approach, or simply the rumour, of troops was frequently to take flight. Between 1572 and 1609—in the early decades of the Dutch Revolt against Habsburg rule—nearly all communities in Brabant and Flanders lost 50–65% of their people, and only an estimated 1% of the rural population remained continuously on the land through the 1580s (Parker, 1975), a decade in which the cultivated area fell by 92%.

If country districts could rapidly empty out, they could also recover very quickly because most cultivators faced destitution away from their holdings. The extent of recovery depended largely on the duration of the crisis. Where it was brief, the demographic effects were often brief as well, but protracted crises could wreck a region's economic and social structure; capital assets were destroyed, arable land reverted to over-grown waste, and skills were lost owing to death or migration. Where persisting insecurity prevented cultivators from planting in the confidence they would ever harvest their crops, progressive demographic and economic collapse might occur on a scale that destroyed the logistical foundation of regional defence and turned it into a depopulated no-man's land. Such conditions prevailed in parts of 17th-century Germany, creating a self-perpetuating downward spiral with those inhabitants who did not take flight being forced to join armies or bandit gangs in order to survive.[8]

Population loss was due to flight and mortality in proportions that are notoriously difficult to determine exactly, though emigration predominated in most regional cases, while mortality played a greater role in major supraregional losses. Nonetheless, it is clear that war's material and demographic consequential costs were unusually severe in the century after 1550. Northern France may have lost 20% of its people between 1580 and 1600 (Benedict, 1985), but things were at their worst in the second quarter of the 17th century, where recent work suggests that Germany's population fell from some 15–16 million to around 10 million, mostly as a result of mortality crises due to epidemic typhus and bubonic plague (Stier and Von Hippel, 1996; Outram, 2001).

Plague disappeared from north and west Europe by the 1680s, and from east Europe a century later, so there are few reliable data on its military incidence, but urban epidemics could kill 25–40% of the inhabitants, and military death rates doubtless ranged as high (Benedictow, 1987). Contemporary accounts describe plague as having "almost entirely exterminated" the Swedish and Imperialist armies campaigning in Silesia in 1633 and to have killed "most" of a Spanish army of 20,000 men sheltering in the Alpine foothills the following winter (Prinzing, 1916: 47; Parker, 1984: 132). In a better-documented outbreak of 1828–29, plague accounted for most of the 50,000 or more deaths that occurred among 68,000 Russian troops fighting the Turks in the Balkans (Dumas and Vedel-Peterson, 1923: 40–41). Baggage trains are likely to have harboured the rats and infected fleas thought to have spread the disease (Slack, 1985: 11–12), and, given the nature of early-modern armies and their interactions with civilians, the transmission of infection was almost inevitable. According to Ladurie, the 6,000 French soldiers sent from La Rochelle to the War of Mantuan Succession triggered an outbreak which killed over a million people throughout northern Italy (Prinzing, 1916: 74–75; Le Roy Ladurie, 1981: 14).

Typhus fever arises from infection by rickettsial micro-organisms spread primarily by body lice, and transmission normally requires physical contact with infected individuals or articles (Zinsser, 1935). Typhus was a scourge of early-modern armies, and civilians became infected as they looted abandoned camps or stripped the dead on battlefields (Prinzing, 1916: 53), but more important than any specific route of transmission were the general conditions of wartime disruption and the physical movement to which it gave rise. The destructive consequences of logistical failures and mercenary indiscipline, aggravated by default of pay, were ultimately responsible for this. As Outram (2001: 181) concludes:

> It is the wanton destruction of the peasants' means of livelihood and their frequent flight from their fields that explains how the 15 million people of Germany were unable to support armies of perhaps 210,000 (less than 2% of their number) without repeated episodes of starvation. It is flight from violence and atrocity and the conditions they endured in their places of refuge that explain the exceptionally high mortality from epidemic disease.

3.3. THE ANCIEN RÉGIME

Damage on the scale inflicted by the Habsburg century's worst conflicts deprived military victors of much economic or political gain, and the consequent military reforms of *ancien régime* Europe made its armies much more effective political instruments (Childs, 1982; Anderson, 1988). Large numbers of men were retained in permanent peacetime regiments; the ratio of commanders to soldiers was increased; and tight discipline was imposed off the battlefield. Elements of the old logistical system—or lack of it—remained, but the soldiers of the new "standing armies" were substantially equipped, fed, clothed and housed by, and at the expense of, a state apparatus into which the army was bound ever more closely. Armed forces began to resemble "total institutions" in which obedience to regulations, including sanitary regulations, could be readily enforced (Goffman, 1968), and as they did so the refinement of military and naval medicine allowed barracks, and particularly ships, to be treated as "natural laboratories" for testing hygienic and sanitary measures.

Typhus receded from central and western European warfare, and plague entirely disappeared from the region after the 1670s. The growing use of military depots and supply trains to support campaigns greatly ameliorated the damage that these inflicted on rural economies (Lynn, 1993), and tighter discipline reduced the amount of looting.[9] More direct measures were also put in place to reduce warfare's destructive effects, particularly in the area of siege craft. Siege conditions necessarily produced shortages of accommodation, food, water and fuel of a severity varying with geographical location and the extent of prior preparation. Since fortified towns and cities were natural places of refuge, conditions were commonly exacerbated by a rural influx, all of which produced ideal conditions for epidemic disease.

The situation apparently deteriorated following the gunpowder revolution, as military forces expanded and sieges grew in length and frequency.[10] The *ancien régime*'s organizational improvements, paradoxically, threatened to aggravate the problem, since defeated armies, rather than breaking up, were better able to disengage and withdraw into fortified towns whose population could be multiplied several times over. Military authorities responded with an elaborate code of conduct intended to minimize the duration of sieges and the likelihood that they would culminate in a bloody assault. Defending commanders were offered repeated opportunities for honourable surrender without penalty from either the enemy or their own superiors. Only if all were refused and the city fell to assault could the defeated commander be executed and the troops turned loose on the inhabitants.

3.4. ESCALATION: QUALITY AND QUANTITY

These improvements in organization and equipment made armies correspondingly more expensive per capita, though we cannot say just how much more because the Habsburg century's military strengths and finances are so poorly documented. Increases in unit costs need not surprise us, given that civilian productivity was rising as population pressure eased, but what is remarkable is that numbers also expanded substantially at a time when civilian real wages were holding up, if not actually rising. Sweden and the Netherlands both fielded more native troops around 1700 than they had against the Habsburgs, while the French fielded as many as 250,000 men, at times, in the 1670s and 340,000 in the 1690s. Britain's rulers were paying at least 75,000 and perhaps as many as 120,000 men (including foreign units) by 1712 (Landers, 2003: 3231–3232). Military demands were now moving dangerously out of step with what the demographic conjuncture was best suited to offer, and British and French numbers declined around mid-century, although further expansion occurred in central and eastern Europe, above all in Prussia.

The numerical growth of *ancien régime* armies was linked to the period's organizational changes and the crystallization of a new kind of tactical system that was based on musketeer battalions supported by squadrons of sword-armed cavalry and mobile artillery batteries. This "musket and sabre" system marked an important break with the structure of relative advantages that characterized the pre-gunpowder era. This era's diverse tactical systems displayed interlocking strengths and weaknesses, which meant that even the most successful possessed an inherent vulnerability to some other system (Landers 2003, ch. 7); like the choices in the "scissors, paper, stone" game, the relationship between the major systems was generally non-transitive. This changed with the gunpowder revolution. Once fully developed, the musket and sabre system was unbeatable in all but the most exceptional circumstances, and the armies of 1914 went to war with a technology that was its recognizable lineal descendant. Gaining a systematic advantage in European conflicts, therefore, required either a better musket and sabre army or a much bigger one. Better weaponry provided an initial means of boosting overall quality, but the scope for incremental development was exhausted around 1700, with the adoption of the flint-lock and socket bayonet. A long period of technological conservatism ensued, which left better organization or greater numbers as the sole means to greater military power, and in practice, the two were interrelated.

The armies of the early 17th century were already becoming better organized on the battlefield, but the ratio of leaders to fighters remained low and the organizational hierarchy poorly developed; they were prone to disorganization in victory and rapid dispersal in defeat. The battlefield organization of *ancien régime* armies differed dramatically from their predecessors, and its basis was a transformation in the nature and function of drill. The old firing drill was elaborated into a system of "evolutions" or manoeuvres that enabled several hundred men to deploy and change formation as a single unit under fire. This, in turn, allowed forces running into tens, and eventually hundreds, of thousands to manoeuvre effectively, to sustain combat for days at a time and to withdraw from the field as a coherent force if defeated. This elaboration was bound up with the structural development of military units as these became permanent institutions with a complex hierarchy of rank and organization. Companies were subdivided with more officers and NCOs. Permanent regiments were maintained, incorporating formally established battalions and deployed into ad hoc higher formations on the battlefield. Army commanders ceased to double up as regimental, or even company, commanders and acquired supporting staffs. From the 1790s, units were organized into permanent divisions and then into army corps of 10,000–20,000 men. Overall, the proportion of leaders rose substantially—in Frederician Prussia it has been put at 10% (O'Connell, 1989)—and with it the size of the wage bill.

The fundamental requirement of this new tactical sophistication was the inculcation and maintenance of a discipline that meant more than self-control off the battlefield. Drill "had to become so automatic and obedience so complete that troops performed their duties regardless of danger, that they suffered and endured without losing their effectiveness or resolution on the battlefield" (Lynn, 1997: 525). The barrack blocks that proliferated at this time functioned, in Jones's (1995) phrase, as "discipline factories", in which training became a semi-permanent condition. But it was a training that had little to do with skill-formation. Once the soldier had learnt to load, fire, march in step and turn about on the appropriate word of command, nothing more was expected than that he remain steady and obedient under fire. It was a foundation of *ancien régime* military thinking that this achievement required long periods on the parade ground and, above all, on the battlefield.

Veterans were valued, but valued not for what they knew but for what they had become: well-drilled cogs in a machine that required only unthinking obedience and whose supreme virtue was endurance. *Ancien régime* armies that had not benefited from such organization investments had little chance against those that had, but the process gave little scope for balancing numerical disadvantages against higher "man for man" troop quality; the formation of a veteran could not be "fast-tracked" by spending more money. Beyond a relatively early point in the process, the principal tactical benefit conferred by organization investment was to allow bigger armies to be used effectively on the battlefield. Combined increases in both army size and costs per man, therefore, continued into the early decades of the 18th century, and the financial burden on Europe's treasuries increased accordingly.

4. The crisis of the ancien régime

The *ancien régime*'s reforms reduced the consequential costs born by the civilian population, but they were correspondingly burdensome to the central treasury—all the more so because of the increase in the numbers of troops and in the length of time for which they served. The ultimate problem was that the new tactical system, and the technology on which it was based, allowed resources to be committed on a scale that the old productive technology could not sustain, but the proximate problem was that the means of appropriation were insufficient to command even what was available. Rulers who maintained or expanded their military establishments risked long-term financial collapse, but to cut back was to court immediate politico-military disaster. The continental powers continued to borrow against revenue, helped by the availability of cheaper long-term credit instruments, but burdened by inherited debts and the risk-premia stemming from earlier defaults.

What these rulers needed was a system of direct taxation able to tap the major concentrations of private wealth, but this required a powerful fiscal apparatus answerable directly to themselves, and this was precisely what they could not afford. By the end of the 18th century, Europe's fiscal systems reached breaking point; the first casualty was the most fiscally efficient of early-modern regimes, the United Provinces, but the biggest was Bourbon France. Successive 18th-century ministries managed the French debt relatively well, but servicing it was expensive, and the tax system on which it rested proved unreformable; the costs of successful intervention in the American Revolutionary War delivered the final blow.

Louis XVIII's consequent need for extra revenue forced the summoning of the long-suspended Estates General, with fatal consequences for both monarch and regime. Its revolutionary successors faced an unprecedented crisis in the shape of war with their monarchical neighbours, the disintegration of the old army and the mass defection of its officer corps. The revolutionaries' solution was a new military-fiscal system based on ideological zeal, backed up by compulsion at home and sustained by the exploitation of conquered territories. The mass levies of 1793 furnished the new Republic with an army of at least three-quarters of a million men (Forrest, 1989: 20–36), and, in 1798, a regular system of conscription—based on registration by age-classes—was introduced in time to provide Napoleon with manpower.

Compulsion itself was not new, but its scale increased massively, and there was a qualitative improvement in its effectiveness. Under the 1798 system, the members of each class were liable for service at the age of twenty, and the required proportion was selected by ballot (Forrest, 1989: 34–42). In relatively peaceful years, some 78,000 men were taken, but much larger numbers could be drafted by drawing on younger classes and re-balloting classes from previous years. In the crisis of 1813, some 800,000 Frenchmen were conscripted, including many underage adolescents or "Marie-Louises", and Napoleon was able to replace the half million or so casualties from the previous year's Russian campaign more easily than he could the dead horses (Esdaile, 1995: 52, 268–276). In all, more than 40% of French males born in the years 1790–95 are thought to have served in Napoleon's army (Houdaille, 1972).

The Revolution's nemesis, Britain, also sustained its struggle with a new system of appropriation, but it was one based on the appropriation of wealth rather than manpower. Eighteenth-century ministries funded their wars by borrowing against taxation, in much the same way as continental powers. They were helped by a more efficient fiscal system and freedom from an inherited debt mountain. This gave Britain the vital margin of advantage that underwrote its military and naval victories, but by the 1790s that margin had largely been consumed, and the old system failed when tested against revolutionary France. The central problem was that British indirect taxation bore relatively heavily on the middle classes, but its direct taxes did little better than continental systems at tapping elite wealth (O'Brien, 1988, 2001). By the end of the decade, the screws were as tight as they would go, and there was still not enough revenue to stave off a collapse of credit, which would threaten both the regime's war effort and its survival.

The introduction of income tax resolved the crisis. It was the first direct tax to bear effectively on the major source of wealth and something no organic economy had previously been able to sustain. The first measure was relatively weak but covered the vital margin needed to sustain public credit, and successive reforms generated enough cash to fund unprecedented amounts of wartime expenditure out of revenue. National debt trebled during the war years, but nearly 60% of additional government income came from taxation. By 1815, Britain was the most heavily taxed nation in Europe, and expenditure was almost equalled by revenue—nearly 30% of which came from direct taxation (as against 18% in 1790). The fruits sustained an army of 500,000 men and a navy of unprecedented size. Equally important, it enabled Westminster to subsidize its continental allies on a scale that kept them in the war against Napoleon, despite the virtual collapse of their own public finances.

French and British systems were distinct, and distinctly innovative, but they nonetheless had something in common; each depended on a necessary conjunction of ideology and administrative innovation. In France, patriotic defence of the imperilled motherland combined with support for revolutionary ideals to provide a necessary condition for national mobilization, but free-rider problems meant that this condition was insufficient in itself. Effective mobilization also required a means of enforcing conscription with an administrative apparatus reaching from the centre into local communities; and unlike its predecessors, the revolutionary regime was able to sustain this. The British system also depended on being accepted as legitimate by those it most affected, and here the spectre of revolution readied the propertied classes to dig into their own pockets (O'Brien, 1988: 22). Once again, however, free-rider problems made collective self-interest a necessary but insufficient condition for long-term success. The new tax also required an administrative and coercive apparatus that no organic economy had ever sustained and, I believe, a level of economic and social complexity that no purely organic economy could ever have sustained.

The French system, based on the appropriation of manpower directly, rather than of funds to pay volunteers, was simpler to administer, as long as the regime and its wars retained popular legitimacy, but it produced forces on a scale that neither the administrative nor the economic resources of the country could support. The solution was to make war feed war, by keeping the army outside France and supporting it from foreign resources. As early as September 1793, the National Convention declared that its generals should "exercise the customary rights of war" on conquered territory (Blanning, 2002: 115–117). Costs were further cut, and operational flexibility enhanced, by dispensing with the *ancien régime's* elaborate logistical systems on campaign and living off the land. Damage to the civilian economy increased as a result and was aggravated by the citizen armies' looser discipline that allowed plundering to become "the most obtrusive, ubiquitous, constant—and hated—feature of revolutionary warfare" (Blanning, 2002: 118).

The new ideology also legitimated old methods of appropriation, on the principle that "the people" should contribute to the cost of their liberation from monarchical tyranny. But underlying everything, in Blanning's words, was the revolutionaries' conviction that "they were fighting a war quite different from anything in the past... So important was their cause that *anything* could be done to ensure its victory", and the consequence was "the liberation of the state from those former constraints of law, custom, and religion that had restrained its ambition" (Blanning, 2002: 116). The worst results ensued where revolutionary forces encountered organized civilian resistance, which was punished by the destruction of settlements, mass killing and a descending spiral of reprisal and counter-reprisal (Blanning, 2002: 127–131).

The Revolution also saw a retrogression in siege warfare; the revolutionaries repudiated the old conventions, and sieges were increasingly pursued to the bitter end with correspondingly brutal consequences (Landers, 2003: 303, n. 22). Longer sieges, and increased army size under Napoleon, led to increased levels of epidemic disease. Prinzing, in his *Epidemics Resulting from Wars*, catalogued instances from the last campaigns of the Napoleonic Wars when fugitive French Corps were besieged in cities across Germany. At Danzig, a population of 40,000 was more than halved between January and November 1813, with nearly 5,600 recorded civilian deaths. Torgau, with a civilian population of 5,000, witnessed 30,000 deaths during a four-month siege; among them were 678 civilians—an annualized civilian death rate of over 400 per thousand. A six-month siege saw typhus claim 17,000–18,000 of Mayence's 30,000-man garrison together with 2,445 of around 24,500 civilians—equivalent to an annualized civilian death rate of some 200 per thousand; all the gravediggers died, leaving thousands of bodies in heaps awaiting burial.

5. Conclusion

The conjunction of early-modern population growth, the gunpowder revolution and the availability of public credit set off a process of military escalation whose immediate costs were unsustainable given the limited fiscal apparatus of early-modern states. This conjunction did not itself dictate the subsequent course of historical events but, given the political, economic and epidemiological structures of the period, it was both a necessary and sufficient condition for the cost outcomes that occurred. It was necessary because these outcomes could not have occurred without it, and it was sufficient inasmuch as any plausible counterfactual starting from such conditions must also incorporate such outcomes. Unless, of course, it is a counterfactual in which Europe's rulers were prepared to live and fight within their means.

As it was, no such willingness was forthcoming, and the unmet costs were taken out in the form of material and demographic destruction visited on the population of the war zones. Consequential costs rose to a level that comprised war's utility as a political instrument, and rulers' self-interest as much as their humanity dictated the radical changes in military administration characterizing *ancien régime* warfare. Consequential costs were reduced, but immediate costs rose to a level that required unsustainable borrowing, and the era of organic economies ended with a struggle between two new kinds of military-fiscal regime: one founded on the economic and administrative resources of an emerging mineral economy and the other on ideologically mediated coercion at home and predatory expansion abroad. In their different ways, each offered a window on the future.

Notes

[1] Preventive measures against smallpox form a late and partial exception to this generalization (Razzell, 1977; Sköld, 1996).

[2] Malnutrition sometimes aggravated mortality by lowering resistance to infection, but this was generally less important than increased exposure during early-modern crises. There is insufficient evidence to judge the relative contributions of exposure and resistance to mortality crises in earlier periods: see Flinn (1981), Post (1990), Dupâquier (1989), Walter and Schofield (1989) and Landers (1993: ch. 1).

[3] For general introductions to contemporary military developments, see Hale (1985), Tallett (1992) and Anderson (1988). Recent work has been dominated by Parker's hypothesized "military revolution": see Parker (1988) and, for critical evaluations, Black (1990) and Rogers (1995).
[4] See Parrott (2001: ch. 3) and Lynn (1995) for case studies of the relatively abundant French sources and the problems of extracting numerical estimates.
[5] Cavalry equipment grew heavier and more expensive as armies grew in size over the 13th and the early 14th century, but, in England at least, this was offset by an increase in the proportions of cheaper infantry; see Prestwich (1996: 115–119) and Landers (2003: 295–296).
[6] This kind of fighting seems to have been endemic in later-medieval warfare, and particularly the Hundred Years War between England and France, from which many of the most destructive examples derive. See Rogers (2002) for a discussion of damage inflicted on French country-dwellers by both aggressors and "defenders".
[7] It seems also to have been particularly bloody relative to the numbers involved. Carlton tabulated 84,830 fatalities from 645 "incidents" in England's 17th-century civil wars. Only 15% of deaths occurred in nine major battles, with nearly half falling in encounters that cost less than 250 lives. The three regions with the largest total deaths also had a ratio of deaths per incident that was less than 60% of the ratio in the three with the lowest total (129 as opposed to 217). In Carlton's words (1992: 207), much of the civil war "consisted of small-scale, localised fighting, of sudden attacks with minor losses yet all too often fatal results".
[8] The mercantile and industrial cities of southern Germany and the Rhineland also suffered from the destruction of long-range economic linkages, which led to a persisting "regionalisation" of the German economy at all levels (Stier and Von Hippel, 1996: 242; François, 1990).
[9] Deliberate devastation remained a threat to civilian life and property, and larger, better organized armies were capable of even more damage than their predecessors. French commanders razed over 20 towns and numerous villages across the Rhineland Palatinate in 1688–89 (Lynn, 2002)—but the technique was little used thereafter, possibly because of the revulsion this episode triggered—although in 1704, the British burned some 400 villages in an attempt to force the Bavarian Elector into making peace (Chandler, 1979: 139).
[10] Epidemics accompanied siege warfare from ancient times when Thucydides gave a vivid account of the "plague" outbreak in Athens during the Spartan siege. Unfortunately, Thucydides' very celebrity made his text a model for later writers, some of whose accounts of similar outbreaks may represent conformity to a literary convention rather than historically accurate narrative (Longrigg, 1992; Bray, 1996). The actual incidence of epidemic disease mortality in ancient and medieval sieges remains obscure.

References

Anderson, M. S., 1988. *War and Society in the Europe of the Old Regime, 1618–1789*. London: Fontana.

Benedict, Philip, 1985. "Civil war and natural disaster in Northern France", in Peter Clark (ed.), *The European Crisis of the 1590s: Essays in Comparative History*. London: George Allen and Unwin (84–105).

Benedictow, O. J., 1987. "Morbidity in historical plague epidemics", *Population Studies* 41(3): 401–431.

Black, Jeremy, 1990. *A Military Revolution? Military Change and European Society 1550–1800*. Basingstoke and London: Macmillan.

Blanning, T. C. W., 2002. "Liberation or occupation? Theory and practice in the french revolutionaries' treatment of civilians outside France", in Grimsley and Rogers (111–135).

Bonney, Richard (ed.), 1995. *Economic Systems and State Finance: The Origins of the Modern State in Europe*. Oxford: European Science Foundation, Clarendon.

Bonney, Richard (ed.), 1999. *The Rise of the Fiscal State in Europe c1200–1815*. Oxford: Oxford University Press.

Bray, R. S., 1996. *Armies of Pestilence: The Effects of Pandemics on History*. Cambridge: Lutterworth.

Carlton, Charles, 1992. *Going to the Wars: The Experience of the British Civil Wars, 1638–1651*. London: Routledge.

Chandler, David, 1979. *Marlborough as Military Commander*. London: Batsford.

Childs, John, 1982. *Armies and Warfare in Europe 1648–1789*. Manchester: Manchester University Press.

Duffy, Christopher, 1979. *Siege Warfare: The Fortress in the Early Modern World 1494–1660*. London: Routledge and Kegan Paul.

Dumas, Samuel and K. O. Vedel-Peterson, 1923. *Losses of Life Caused by War*. Oxford: Clarendon.

Dupâquier, Jacques, 1989. "Demographic crises and subsistence crises in France, 1650–1789", in John Walter and Roger Schofield (eds), *Famine Disease and the Social Order*. Cambridge: Cambridge University Press (189–200).

Esdaile, Charles J., 1995. *The Wars of Napoleon*. London: Longmans.

Flinn, Michael W, 1981. *The European Demographic System 1500–1820*. Brighton: Harvester.

Forrest, Alan, 1989. *Conscripts and Deserters: The Army and French Society During the Revolution and Empire*. Oxford and New York: Oxford University Press.

François, Etienne, 1990. "The German urban network between the sixteenth and eighteenth centuries: Cultural and demo-graphic indicators", in Ad van der Woude, Jan de Vries and Akira Hayami (eds), *Urbanization in History*. Oxford: Clarendon (84–100).

Gardiner, Robert (ed.), 1992. *The Line of Battle: The Sailing Warship, 1650–1840*. London: Conway Maritime.

Glete, Jan, 2002. *War and the State in Early Modern Europe: Spain, the Dutch Republic and Sweden as Fiscal-Military States, 1500–1660*. London: Routledge.

Goffman, Erving, 1968. *Asylums*. Harmondsworth: Penguin.

Grimsley, Mark and Clifford J. Rogers (eds), 2002. *Civilians in the Path of War*. Lincoln, NB and London: University of Nebraska Press.

Hale, J. R., 1985. *War and Society in Renaissance Europe*. London: Fontana.

Hodge, William Barwick, 1857. "On mortality arising from military operations", *Assurance and Journal of the Institute of Actuaries* 6: 80–90, 151–217, 275–285.

Houdaille, Jacques, 1970. "Le Problème des Pertes de Guerre" [The problem of War Losses], *Revue d'histoire moderne et contemporaine* 17(iii): 411–423.

Houdaille, Jacques, 1972. "Pertes de l'armée de Terre sous le Premier Empire, d'après les Registres Matricules" [Army Losses Under the First Empire, According to the Nominal Rolls], *Population* 27(1): 27–50.

Houdaille, Jacques, 1977. "La Mortalité (Hors Combat) des Militaires Français à la Fin du XVIIième Siècle et au Debut du XIXième Siècle" [French Military Mortality (Outside Combat) from the End of the 17th Century to the Beginning of the 19th Century], *Population (num spec)*: 481–497.

Jones, Colin, 1995. "The military revolution and the professionalisation of the French army under the ancien regime", in Clifford J. Rogers (ed.), *The Military Revolution Debate: Readings in the Military Transformation of Early-Modern Europe*. Boulder, CO: Westview (149–167).

Körner, Martin, 1995. "Public credit", in Richard Bonney (ed.), *Economic Systems and State Finance*. Oxford: European Science Foundation, Clarendon (507–538).

Kozlovski, N., 1912. "Statistical data concerning the losses of the Russian army from sickness and wounds in the war against Japan", *Journal of the Royal Army Medical Corps* 18: 330–346.

Landers, John, 1993. *Death and the Metropolis: Studies in the Demographic History of London* 1670–1830. Cambridge: Cambridge University Press.

Landers, John, 2003. *The Field and the Forge: Population, Production and Power in the Pre-industrial West*. Oxford: Oxford University Press.

Le Roy Ladurie, Emmanuel, 1981. "History that stands still", in *The Mind and Method of the Historian*. Brighton: Harvester (1–27).

Lindegren, Jan, 2000. "Men, money and means", in Philippe Contamine (ed.), *The Origins of the Modern State in Europe*. Oxford: European Science Foundation, Clarendon (129–162).

Livermore, Thomas L., 1957. *Numbers and Losses in the Civil War in America, 1861–1865*. Bloomington, IN: Indiana University Press.

Longrigg, James, 1992. "Epidemics, ideas and classical athenian society", in Terence Ranger and Paul Slack (eds), *Epidemics and Ideas: Essays on the Historical Perception of Pestilence*. Cambridge: Cambridge University Press (21–44).

Lynn, John A., 1993. "Foods, funds and fortresses: Resource mobilization and positional warfare in the campaigns of Louis XIV", in John A. Lynn (ed.), *Feeding Mars: Logistics in Western Warfare from the Middle Ages to the Present*. Boulder, CO: Westview (137–159).

Lynn, John A., 1995. "Recalculating french army growth during the grand siècle, 1610–1715", *French Historical Studies* 18(4): 881–906.

Lynn, John A., 1997. *Giant of the Grand Siècle: The French Army 1610–1715*. Cambridge: Cambridge University Press.

Lynn, John A., 2002. "A brutal necessity? The devastation of the Palatinate, 1688–1689", in Grimsley and Rogers (79–110).

Meslé, France and Jacques Vallin, 1989. "Reconstitution de Tables annuelles de Mortalité pour la France au XIXe Siècle" [Reconstitution of 19th-Century French Annual Mortality Tables], *Population* 44(6): 1121–1158.

O'Brien, Patrick K., 1988. "The political economy of British taxation, 1660–1815", *Economic History Review (2nd series)* 41(1): 1–32.

O'Brien, Patrick K., 2001. "*Fiscal exceptionalism: Great Britain and its European rivals: From civil war to Triumph at Trafalgar and Waterloo", Working Paper No.* 65/01. London: London School of Economics, Department of Economic History.

O'Connell, Robert. L., 1989. *Of Arms and Men*. New York: Oxford University Press.

Outram, Quentin, 2001. "The socio-economic relations of warfare and the military mortality crises of the thirty years' war", *Medical History* 45(2): 151–184.

Parker, Geoffrey, 1972. *The Army of Flanders and the Spanish Road 1567–1659*. Cambridge: Cambridge University Press.

Parker, Geoffrey, 1975. "War and economic change: The economic costs of the Dutch revolt", in J. M. Winter (ed.), *War and Economic Development*. Cambridge: Cambridge University Press (49–71).

Parker, Geoffrey (ed.), 1984. *The Thirty Years' War*. London: Routledge and Kegan Paul.

Parker, Geoffrey, 1988. *The Military Revolution*. Cambridge: Cambridge University Press.

Parrott, David, 2001. *Richelieu's Army: War, Government and Society in France*, 1624–42. Cambridge: Cambridge University Press.

Post, J. D., 1990. "Nutritional status and mortality in eighteenth-century Europe", in Lucille F, Newman (ed.), *Hunger in History: Food Shortage, Poverty and Deprivation*. Cambridge, MA and Oxford: Basil Blackwell (241–280).

Prestwich, Michael, 1996. *Armies and Warfare in the Middle Ages: The English Experience*. New Haven, CT and London: Yale University Press.

Prinzing, Friedrich, 1916. *Epidemics Resulting from Wars*. Oxford: Clarendon.

Pryor, John H., 1988. *Geography, Technology, and War: Studies in the Maritime History of the Mediterranean 649–1571*. Cambridge: Cambridge University Press.

Razzell, P. E., 1977. *The Conquest of Smallpox*. Firle Sussex: Caliban.

Rogers, Clifford J. (ed.), 1995. *The Military Revolution Debate: Readings in the Military Transformation of Early-Modern Europe*. Boulder, CO: Westview.

Rogers, Clifford. J., 2002. "By fire and sword: *Bellum hostile* and 'civilians' in the hundred years' war", in Grimsley and Rogers (73–78).

Sköld, Peter, 1996. *The Two Faces of Smallpox: A Disease and Its Prevention in Nineteenth-Century Sweden*. Umeå: Demographic Data Base.

Slack, Paul, 1985. *The Impact of Plague in Tudor and Stuart England*. London: Routledge and Kegan Paul.

Stier, Bernhard and Wolfgang Von Hippel, 1996. "War, economy and society", in Sheilagh Ogilvie (ed.), *Germany: A New Social and Economic History*. Vol. 2 *1630–1800*. London: Arnold (233–262).

Tallett, Frank, 1992. *War and Society in Early-Modern Europe, 1495–1715*. London: Routledge.

Thompson, I. A. A., 1976. *War and Government in Habsburg Spain*. London: Athlone.

Thompson, I. A. A., 1995. "'Money, money and yet more money!' finance the fiscal-state and the military revolution", in Clifford J. Rogers (ed.), *The Military Revolution Debate: Readings in the Military Transformation of Early-Modern Europe*. Boulder, CO: Westview (273–298).
Walter, John and Roger Schofield, 1989. "Famine, disease and crisis mortality in early modern society", in John Walter and Roger Schofield (eds), *Famine Disease and the Social Order*. Cambridge: Cambridge University Press (1–73).
Wrigley, E. A., 1988. *Continuity, Chance and Change: The Character of the Industrial Revolution in England*. Cambridge: Cambridge University Press.
Zinsser, Hans, 1935. *Rats, Lice and History*. London: Routledge.

CHAPTER 6. MONITORING TRENDS IN GLOBAL COMBAT: A NEW DATASET OF BATTLE DEATHS*

BETHANY LACINA
Stanford University, USA
Centre for the Study of Civil War (CSCW),
International Peace Research Institute Oslo (PRIO), Norway

NILS PETTER GLEDITSCH
Centre for the Study of Civil War (CSCW),
International Peace Research Institute Oslo (PRIO)
Norwegian University of Science and Technology, Norway

Abstract. Both academic publications and public media often make inappropriate use of incommensurate conflict statistics, creating misleading impressions about patterns in global warfare. This article clarifies the distinction between combatant deaths, battle deaths, and war deaths. A new dataset of battle deaths in armed conflict is presented for the period 1946-2002. Global battle deaths have been decreasing over most of this period, mainly due to a decline in interstate and internationalised civil armed conflict. It is far more difficult to accurately assess the number of war deaths in conflicts both past and present. But there are compelling reasons to believe that there is a need for increased attention to non-battle causes of mortality, especially displacement and disease in conflict studies. Therefore, it is demographers, public health specialists, and epidemiologists who can best describe the true human cost of many recent armed conflicts and assess the actions necessary to reduce that toll.

1. Introduction

Estimating how many deaths a war has caused is an exercise of obvious importance but surprising complexity.[1] Of course, relevant information is frequently concealed by parties to the conflict, destroyed in the course of the war, or never recorded at all. But an additional layer of confusion arises due to the complex and contradictory schemes that are used to account for war losses. Few who go in search of such statistics pay close attention to the maze of categories that militaries use to classify combat losses, and those formal schemes are often difficult to apply or even irrelevant in the context of civil wars or wars against informally organised insurgents. The result is that inaccurate or misleading fatality figures are frequently circulated widely, gaining credibility through mere repetition. One example is the oft-repeated observation that 90% of the casualties in today's wars are civilians (Sivard, 1996, p. 17), as against only 5% in World War I (Chesterman, 2001, p. 2). Yet, the 5% figure for World War I is far lower than the range cited by most historians (Clodfelter,

This chapter was previously published in *European Journal of Population*, vol. 21, no. 2–3, 2005, pp. 145–166.

Helge Brunborg et al. (eds.), The Demography of Armed Conflict, 131–151.

2002, p. 479), while the source of the estimate of 90% civilian casualties in modern wars has long vanished (Mack, 2005).

In order to understand trends in warfare across time or space, we need data that measure deaths due to armed conflicts in a consistent manner. This article begins by distinguishing three principal ways of counting war fatalities: combatant deaths, battle (or combat) deaths, and war deaths. These three measures are appropriate for answering different research questions, and we suggest some of the possibilities and limitations of each. We also clarify the distinction between battle deaths and one-sided violence. We then present a new dataset of battle deaths in state-based armed conflicts for the period after World War II (1946–2002). The new data have been gathered for conflicts recorded in the Uppsala/PRIO dataset of armed conflicts (Gleditsch et al., 2002; Harbom and Wallensteen, 2005). Versions of the data are also available for use with the Correlates of War (COW) data on wars 1900–1997 (Sarkees, 2000) and data on civil wars 1945–1999 compiled by Fearon and Laitin (2001). After presenting the data, we display our estimate of the trends in global and regional battle deaths 1946–2002. Battle violence has declined over the past 50 years due to a decline in major interstate conflict and large internationalised civil conflicts. However, in our final section, we point out that many conflicts are characterised by numbers of non-violent deaths due to humanitarian crisis that far surpass the lives lost in combat. For that reason, demographers, epidemiologists and others who specialise in the scientific study of population will play an important role in investigating the relationship between conflict and humanitarian crisis and making recommendations on appropriate international responses.

2. Distinguishing among fatality statistics

War fatality statistics may be compiled with very different research needs in mind and there are a number of classification schemes for doing so. In this article, however, we seek to distinguish three of the most common: counts of combatant deaths, battle deaths (which we use synonymously with combat deaths), and war deaths. The theoretical uses of each of these measures can be quite different. We explain each term as we proceed, but Appendix A contains the formal definition of battle deaths used to code our dataset.

Among political scientists, military experts, and legal scholars one of the most commonly sought war fatality figures is that of combatant deaths. For example, the Correlates of War (COW) dataset on interstate wars, widely used by political scientists in quantitative study of conflict, records for each state involved "the number of battle-connected fatalities among military personnel" (Sarkees 2000, p. 128). Other compilations expand this definition somewhat and account for soldiers who are not formally attached to any state's military.

Figures on combatant losses can be used to answer questions of strategy. Comparing the parties' battle losses may reveal their military capacity and effectiveness, and be useful for evaluating their preparation for and execution of a war and their capacity to continue fighting it. Counting the number of non-violent deaths among combatants can be important to a study of campaign conditions, or to comparing militaries' culture or organisational sophistication.

Comparisons of combatant to non-combatant deaths are also often used to illuminate normative questions. Such an accounting of war losses implies a distinction between legitimate targets in a war (combatants) and all other persons (such as captured soldiers and civilians). The laws of war contained in international treaties such as the Fourth Geneva Convention offer a degree of protection for civilians that is not extended to combatants and hold military forces responsible for the safety of civilians in the areas they control. Thus, investigation of war crimes can turn on accounts of war deaths that distinguish between combatants and civilians (e.g. Brunborg et al., 2003). Just war theory sets the benchmark of proportionality in order to evaluate the conduct of war by weighing the military objectives achieved against 'collateral damage' to non-combatants (Walzer, 1977). This kind of a balancing analysis can be used to criticize certain modes of warfare as particularly indiscriminate, inhumane, or unjustifiably devastating to civilians.

By contrast, the measure we refer to as battle deaths includes all people, soldiers and civilians, killed in combat. Measuring battle deaths answers the question of how many people were killed in military operations during a war and, therefore, it is the best measure of the scale, scope, and nature of the military engagement that has taken place. It reflects the degree of military parity between the sides, how heavily armed they are, and how frequently and widely they engage each other.

Data on battle deaths are empirical measures of the size of combat operations. They lack the normative concerns of an accounting of combatant deaths that seeks to distinguish between legitimate and illegitimate targets and participants. For this reason, the concept of battle deaths is readily applied across a variety of types of conflicts. In today's dominant forms of conflict—civil wars, wars of insurgency, and asymmetric conflicts—the distinction between combatants and non-combatants may be very unclear or even entirely fluid, in sharp contrast to an idealised model of a conflict fought between formally organised state militaries. Even in wars fought by state militaries there is an increasing reliance on private military firms, whose personnel are not traditionally defined as combatants (Keefe, 2004). Thus a focus on combatant deaths rather than battle deaths could seriously underestimate the scope of military combat in many, if not most, of today's wars.

The number of battle deaths provides an exhaustive measure of how many have died in combat operations. But it does not provide a remotely adequate account of the true human costs of conflict. War kills people in less direct (but highly predictable) ways, especially when it causes the collapse of a society's economy, infrastructure of health and human services, and public safety systems. As Figure 1 lays out, the toll of a war is comprised of not only battle deaths but deaths due to upsurges in one-sided violence (e.g. the execution of prisoners of war or a genocidal campaign such as the Holocaust or the Armenian Genocide); increases in criminal violence (e.g. an upsurge in crime following the collapse of local policing, as

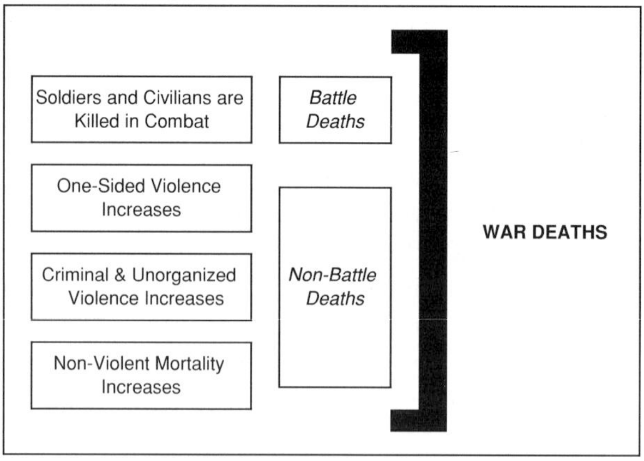

Figure 1. Sources of war deaths.

in post-Baathist Iraq); increases in unorganised violence (e.g. deadly food riots); and increases in non-violent causes of mortality such as disease and starvation. A complete accounting of the true human costs of conflict would include—in addition to fatalities—non-fatal injuries, disability, reduced life expectancy, sexual violence, psychological trauma, displacement, loss of property and livelihood, damage to social capital and infrastructure, environmental damage, destruction of cultural treasures. Tallying the cost of a war quickly defies straightforward accounting.[2]

An account of war deaths must record all people killed in battle as well as all those whose deaths were the result of the changed social conditions caused by the war. Thus, measuring war related deaths involves comparing the number of deaths that occurred due to a conflict against the counterfactual scenario of peace (Li and Wen, 2005).[3] It is necessary to judge whether certain events—such as a famine or riot—would not have happened at all if peace had prevailed, and to measure the degree of elevation (or depression) in peacetime risks of mortality from factors like crime or malnutrition. Making such estimates becomes quite difficult when there is no meaningful peacetime benchmark to compare measured mortality rates against—as in Burma, where civil war has been more or less continuous since independence—or when a complex sequence of events that includes armed conflict lies behind certain events or social changes. For example, conflict may have abetted the spread of HIV/AIDS in Africa (Elbe, 2002), but the epidemic has other causes as well. Separatist conflict in the Caucasus has fed into black market economies and increased violent crime, but so has the difficult transition to a market economy. Finally, when measuring war deaths it is difficult to determine the relevant time frame. Indirect causes of higher mortality will continue after the battles have stopped. How many years of elevated mortality due to, for instance, depressed economic performance, environmental degradation, or the spread of sexually transmitted diseases should be attached to the terminated war and can those impacts be measured in a reliable way?

Despite the definitional ambiguities of trying to account for war deaths, study of the linkages between human insecurity and conflict and between humanitarian crisis and conflict is vital. Throughout history wars have been associated with humanitarian crisis. Even the most devastating instances of battle violence in human history—World Wars I and II—are estimated to have led to nearly as many non-battle deaths as combat fatalities, and perhaps more (Clodfelter, 2002, p. 479 and 581). But although the elevated mortality caused by war is predictable, attempts to prevent or ameliorate non-battle impacts of war are too often thwarted by the political and security dynamics of the conflict itself and by international indifference or clumsiness. Also, the linkages between warfare, humanitarian crisis, and human insecurity have not been as widely studied as the political and military factors that lie behind battle and battle deaths.

Some recent work has discussed or estimated the long-term public health consequences of war (Krug et al., 2002; Murray et al., 2002; Black et al., 2003; Ghobarah et al., 2003). There is also an increasing amount of original research on specific populations in conflict by scholars in a variety of disciplines, including recent studies of Afghanistan (Sliwinski, 1989; Benini and Moulton, 2004), Bosnia–Herzegovina (Brunborg et al., 2003), the Democratic Republic of Congo (Roberts, 2000; Roberts et al., 2001, 2003), Guatemala (Ball et al., 1999), and Rwanda (Verwimp, 2003). Relevant health and demographic data are also continually being gathered by many humanitarian agencies, such as the International Committee of the Red Cross (ICRC) or Epicentre, which works with Médecins Sans Frontières, in order to assess the humanitarian needs of war-affected populations. The World Health Organization's (WHO) Collaborating Centre for Research on Epidemiology and Disasters (CEDAT) is currently building a repository for scientific studies of conflict-affected populations, and promises to become an important resource for those interested in this topic. The second volume of the *Human Security Report* published by the Centre for Human Security at the Liu Institute for Global Issues, University of British Columbia will focus on 'the war/disease nexus' (Mack, 2005).[4]

3. Distinguishing battle deaths from one-sided violence

Our definition of battle deaths includes a distinction between battle deaths and one-sided violence. It may be necessary to explain in more detail why we do not define one-sided violence to be battle-related, even though it may be of a political character and intimately related to the issues at the heart of an ongoing conflict. Examples of such one-sided violence include security forces firing on unarmed protestors, summary executions of prisoners, and genocide.

Following most studies of armed conflict, we have conceived battle as a two-sided phenomenon. Combat is political violence against any target, military or civilian, in which the perpetrator faces the immediate threat of lethal force being used by the opposing forces against him/her and/or allied fighters. Again, our definition of battle deaths is empirical rather than normative. Rather than judging the legitimacy of certain targets or tactics for collective violence as in humanitarian law (Schabas, 2001), we focus on the degree of meaningful armed resistance. Thus, for example, terrorist attacks against civilians were included as battle acts in our dataset because the perpetrators must take measures to avoid opposing security forces. The execution of kidnapped civilians was excluded because these acts are carried out in an environment of impunity. Words such as 'massacre' are sometimes used to describe very lop-sided battle outcomes or attacks against soft targets. In general, we consider such events to be battle violence. We judge fatal incidents to be one-sided violence—and thus exclude them from our count of battle deaths—only when there is evidence of sustained destruction of non-combatants taking place outside of the context of any reciprocal threat of lethal force. The Cambodian and Rwandan genocides fall into this category.

We have attempted to make this distinction between battle violence and onesided violence because we believe that battle deaths are the best measure of combat intensity. Battle deaths are not a representation of the human costs of war, which should obviously include all violent death caused by the conflict, nor the basis for a normative evaluation of war. Data on one-sided violence is of critical importance for scholarship on genocide and politicide; for investigations of war crimes and crimes against humanity by courts and truth commissions; and for evaluation of the trends in one-sided violence and the effects of changing international norms and institutions for evaluating and prosecuting war crimes.[5]

Battle deaths data, however, provide a more accurate measurement of the scope and scale of contested military engagement. On the one hand, we do not recommend using a very narrow definition of combat deaths based on the legitimacy of targets and tactics in order to measure the intensity of battle violence. For example, although terrorist attacks against civilians are not a sanctioned mode of warfare they are important to understanding the degree of armed contest taking place in many conflicts.

On the other hand, by defining one-sided violence by the absence of armed resistance it is possible to gain both a clear idea of the amount of military engagement taking place (the number of battle deaths) and to study the relationship of combat to one-sided violence. Measurements of the two are not simply proxies for each other. For example, it has been argued that the 1994 genocide of Rwandan Tutsis could have been halted within a week by even a small but credible United Nations force (Feil, 1998), suggesting that the perpetrators lacked the capacity to continue their program of terror in the face of even limited effective resistance. Demographic study has shown that the intensity of the Rwandan genocide was greatest in those areas removed from battles between the Hutu and Tutsi armies where Hutu Interhamwe could act with impunity (Verwimp, 2003). Because one-sided violence often depends on minimal threat of resistance or retaliation, battle violence and one-sided violence have often varied inversely rather than directly, suggesting that the relationship between them deserves careful study. Kalyvas (2004) finds that selective execution of civilians during the Greek Civil War was suppressed in areas of the highest combat intensity. The Khmer Rouge began its ethnic and political terror, while it was still a rebel group, but the genocide began in earnest when it won full military control of the country.

4. A new dataset of battle deaths

Several datasets have tracked fatalities in war. The best known is the list of wars produced by the COW Project (Sarkees, 2000), which includes interstate, intrastate, and extra-systemic (more commonly called colonial or imperial) wars in which more than 1000 combatant deaths occurred (1000 deaths per year in the case of interstate conflict). The COW data estimate combatant deaths by state participant, but do not disaggregate their data into annual estimates. A related project, the Militarized International Dispute Dataset, estimates the death toll among state militaries in smaller scale clashes of a purely interstate nature. In the past, the COW and the MID projects have drawn criticism for their exclusive focus on deaths among states' armed forces (Henderson, 2002). However, Lacina et al. (2005) demonstrate that the COW data suffers from a more serious limitation: supposedly comparable figures actually vary indiscriminately between recording combatant, battle, and war deaths. For interstate wars, the COW project has tended to record the number of military personnel killed in battle or the number of military deaths from all causes, while for many extra-systemic and intrastate wars the COW dataset estimates all war deaths, including those due to disease and starvation. The result is that the COW data cannot be accurately compared between types of war, decades, or regions.

Similar problems of comparability occur in fatality compilations that attempt to record war deaths (Eckhardt, 1996; Rummel, 1997; Leitenberg, 2003). In these cases, the most serious problem is that reliable information on war deaths in many long-terminated conflicts is simply not available and that experts in conflict studies are often ill-equipped to estimate non-battle levels of mortality. Reliable accounts of the earliest conflicts that appear in such compilations are sparse or non-existent, let alone scientific demographic and mortality data. For example, although the number of Herero and Nama destroyed by the German military in south-western Africa in 1904–1905 was of genocidal proportions (Hull, 2003), scholars can only speculate on the number of people who were killed outright or forced into the desert to starve because no pre-war census of the population was ever taken (Pakenham, 1992, pp. 614–615). There is necessarily great uncertainty in any compilation of war deaths that attempts even modest backdating.

We present here a dataset of estimates for battle deaths in armed conflicts from 1946 to 2002. It is, we believe, the first fatality compilation for use in the study of armed conflict that focuses on battle deaths rather than combatant or war deaths. As we argued above, battle deaths are the most appropriate measure of the scale of military combat taking place in a conflict, especially given the fluidity of the lines between combatants and civilians in so many armed conflicts. Tracking trends in the number of battle deaths is of great interest to those who study patterns of combat activity world-wide and in the context of certain eras, regions, and cases.

The new dataset was collected for the dataset produced by the Uppsala/PRIO Conflict Data Project (Gleditsch et al., 2002; Harbom and Wallen-steen, 2005), which records state-based armed conflicts that claim at least 25 battle deaths per year. Conflicts may be extra-systemic, interstate, internal (i.e. civil), or internationalised internal struggles (for additional information see the codebook: Strand et al., 2003). The new battle deaths data have also been adapted for use with the Correlates of War data on extra-systemic, interstate, and intrastate wars from 1900–1997 in which at least 1000 combatants died (Sarkees, 2000) and with the Fearon and Laitin (2001) dataset of civil wars 1945–1999 that killed at least 1000 persons.

Our dataset draws on leading compendia of casualty statistics (e.g. Harff and Gurr, 1988; Laffin, 1994; Bercovitch and Jackson, 1997; Rummel, 1997; Brogan, 1998; Clodfelter, 2002; Ghosn and Palmer, 2003; State Failure Task Force, 2003); on conflict monitoring projects (e.g. International Institute for Strategic Studies, 2003; Project Ploughshares, 2003); on the annual tables of major armed conflicts in the SIPRI Yearbooks (see, most recently, Wiharta and Anthony, 2003); as well as consultations with regional experts. These sources were augmented with studies of individual cases (e.g. Ball et al., 1999; Sutton, 2001); archival materials from government sources (e.g. Anušaukas, 2000); media sources and published studies based on compiled media data (e.g. Mueller, 1995; Dunlop, 2000); and original demographic and epidemiological work where it was available.[6]

5. Global trends in battle deaths: good and bad news

There has been a great deal of alarmist writing about the bloody post-Cold War era, often painted in the media as a world of unprecedented internecine conflict. Snow (1996, pp. 1-2, 105-113) holds, for instance, that armed conflicts of the 1990s, which he calls "uncivil wars," were less principled, less focused on political goals, and therefore bloodier than many in the past. Sarkees et al. (2003, p. 65) strike a similar note of pessimism, arguing that the risk of suffering death in battle has trended neither up nor down since the Napoleonic wars. Such remarks are surprising given that organisations that monitor the global incidence of armed conflict have found that the late 1990s and first years of the twenty-first century enjoyed a downward trend in warfare between and within states (Gleditsch et al., 2002; State Failure Task Force, 2003).

What do global trends in battle deaths tell us about the amount of armed combat taking place in the world today? Figure 2 provides our estimate of the global trend in battle deaths from 1946 to 2002 in state-based armed conflicts, while Table 1 notes the five conflicts that inflicted the largest numbers of battle deaths during that era. Figure 2 reveals that the long-term trend in battle deaths has been sharply downward. The late 1940s and early 1950s were very grim; the combined impact of the Chinese Civil War and the Korean War were augmented by the French

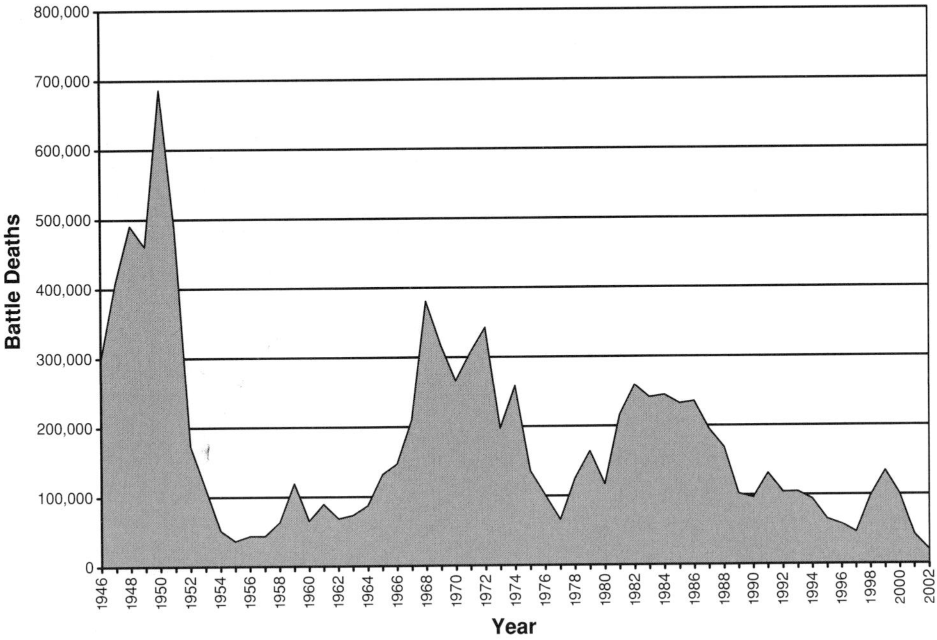

Figure 2. Battle deaths worldwide, 1946–2002.

Indochina War (estimated to have killed 365,000 in battle) and the Greek Civil War (154,000 battle deaths). The Vietnam War forms the next hump in the dataset, and the combined impacts of the Iran-Iraq war and the Soviet intervention in Afghanistan constitute the third peak. In the mid-1990s, the world seemed to enter another trough in the number of battle deaths, until the war in the Democratic Republic of Congo (DRC), with an estimated 145,000 battle deaths in 1998–2001, and the interstate war between Ethiopia and Eritrea that killed 50,000 from 1998 to 2000. Each peak is significantly lower than the previous one and the trough in 2002 is the lowest for the entire period.[7]

Table 1. Conflicts with the largest battle death totals

Conflict	Years	Best estimate of battle deaths*
Vietnam War	1955–1975	2,097,705*
Korean War	1950–1953	1,254,811*
Chinese Civil War	1946–1949	1,200,000
Iran–Iraq War	1980–1988	644,500
Afghan Civil War	1978–2002	562,995*

*The precision of these figures is due to exact accounting of Western losses; the accuracy should be regarded as spurious.

Thus, the good news about battle deaths since World War II is that although there have been multiple major international security crises their military scale has progressively diminished. This may reflect increasingly pacific behavior among the great powers, who possess the resources and the military technology (such as aerial power and heavy artillery) to inflict large numbers of battle deaths in the wars they start, join, or provide with support. Each of the five largest conflicts identified was a war of this type. The Korean War and the Vietnam War were massive Cold War confrontations, and the Chinese Civil War was also fed by superpower military assistance. The wars between Iran and Iraq and the Soviet invasion of Afghanistan were also driven in part by the logic of Cold War politics and the parties were armed by the US and USSR. By contrast, declining tension between the superpowers hastened the de-escalation of the Soviet war in Afghanistan and slowed rates of battle deaths there in the late 1980s (Sliwinski, 1989, pp. 40–41). And while the recent war in the DRC involved regional armies, it was not a proxy war for major military powers. The most cataclysmic battles of the past half-century were related to the now defunct ideological polarisation between East and West.

The very large conflicts that these peaks represent almost overwhelm the rest of the curve: together, the five conflicts in Table 1 constitute more than half of the estimated toll of global battle deaths in the period 1946–2002, accounting for about 5.76 million battle deaths out of a total of about 10 million. The five wars with the highest number of battle deaths, especially the Vietnam and Korean Wars, are such outliers that they eclipse most of the rest of the story of global warfare. Figure 3

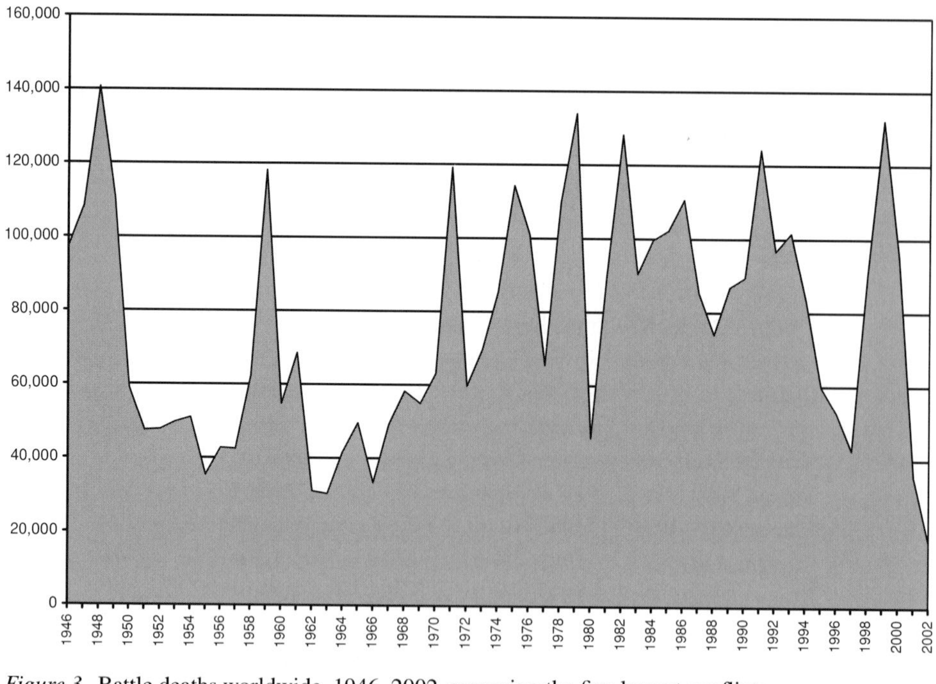

Figure 3. Battle deaths worldwide, 1946–2002, removing the five largest conflicts.

Table 2. Battle deaths by time period and conflict type

	Comparing Cold War vs. Post-Cold War conflict			
	All conflicts		Internal conflicts*	
Statistic	1946–1989	1990–2002	1946–1989	1990–2002
No. of conflict-years	1213	526	993	510
Mean	7430	2070	4250	1980
Median	500	300	439	308
Comparing types of conflict				
Statistic	Extrasystemic and interstate		Internal conflicts*	
No. of conflict-years	236		1503	
Mean	20,620		3480	
Median	945		373	

*Includes internationalised internal wars.

shows the graph of global battle deaths with those five largest conflicts excluded. What seemed like a downward trend in battle violence vanishes and the world seems to fluctuate between high and low war intensity years (although the final year is the lowest for the entire period). Thus, the bad news about global battle deaths is that, although the now-terminated Cold War played a devastating role in driving major battle death events, there is a persistence of smaller scale, more diverse conflicts, the trend in which is less obvious.

Even so, the data by no means support the sombre picture painted by Sarkees et al. (2003) of a world of basically constant total rates of combat. Table 2 shows

Table 3. Share of battle deaths that occurred in internal conflicts (%)

Years	Battle deaths in internal conflicts*
1946–1949	87
1950s	8
1960s	29
1970s	43
1980s	67
1990s	92
2000–02	93
1946–2002	52

* Includes internationalised internal conflicts.

that the mean and median numbers of battle deaths in a year of conflict after the Cold War era were significantly lower than during the Cold War. Nor do we find support for Snow's hypothesis of increasingly bloody civil conflicts, at least when measured according to the number of battle deaths; the mean and median number of combat fatalities in a year of internal or internationalised internal conflict have fallen dramatically since the end of the Cold War.

Civil war has been the dominant form of conflict for several decades, as Table 3 demonstrates. For the whole period after World War II just over half the battle deaths occurred in internal conflicts, but during the three decades in the middle of the Cold War, there were more deaths in interstate and extra-systemic conflicts.[8] Table 2 shows that the mean values for interstate and extra-systemic conflict-years are much larger than for internal conflicts, although the median value is less dramatically so. The fact that such conflicts are increasingly rare no doubt accounts for some of the downward trend in global battle deaths.

Figure 4 gives a regional picture of the trend in battle deaths (see Appendix B for regional definitions). This is a stacked graph, in which each region is represented by the area between those below and above it. The sum of the stacked regional data provides the global estimate of battle deaths. The most remarkable transformation in the security status of any region is that of East and South East Asia. The greatest battle violence of the past 50 years took place in China, Korea, and the Indochinese peninsula. By contrast, since the 1980s, the region has been increasingly free of

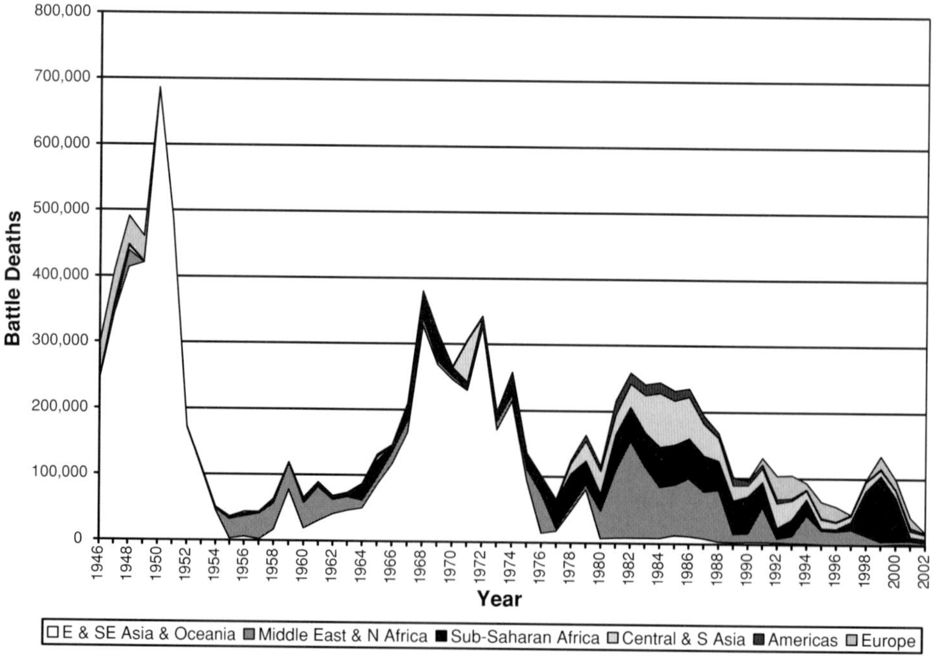

Figure 4. Battle deaths by region, 1946–2002.

combat due to the de-escalation of Cold War conflict in Indochina and the Western rapprochement with China.

In the most recent years, Sub-Saharan Africa and Central and South Asia are the primary drivers of battle deaths. The most common conflict scenario today is civil war and/or state failure in an impoverished society governed, if at all, by a very weak post-colonial regime (Collier et al., 2003; Fearon and Laitin, 2004; Mack, 2005). Most of these conflicts are neglected by major powers, and the combatants often remain relatively ill-organised and poorly equipped when compared to those who fought in the civil conflicts that turned into proxy wars during the Cold War. The amount of actual military engagement (rather than tactics of insurgency or banditry) in many modern civil wars has been quite limited and sporadic, even desultory (Mueller, 2003). Thus these civil conflicts, though often intractable and devastating, have produced fewer battle deaths than their Cold War counterparts.

6. Winning the battles and losing the wars?

Battle deaths do not tell the full story of the human cost of war. Although it seems plausible to expect that the global downturn in battle violence over the past half-century has been accompanied by some amelioration in numbers of war deaths, we do not have the scientific data on war deaths available to test this contention or provide a sufficient account of how war has affected human populations over the past decades.

We suspect that war-related deaths were less severe in the late 1990s than in previous decades primarily because the number of ongoing conflicts declined. At the same time, it seems likely that the post-Cold War environment has been more effective in reducing the incidence of conflict and battle deaths than in addressing the scourge of non-battle fatalities in those conflicts that do occur. Excess mortality is probably increased because most armed conflicts now take place in poor countries with a weak infrastructure and limited medical facilities.

Table 4 lists nine African conflicts that caused very large numbers of nonviolent war deaths due to insecurity, displacement, deprivation, and disease. The estimates of battle deaths come from our dataset, the estimates of total war related deaths are figures that are widely cited in media and conflict literature, although, to our knowledge, only the figures for the Democratic Republic of Congo (DRC) are based on a scientific study of the affected population.

In the DRC, the International Rescue Committee conducted a series of household surveys in order to estimate the impact of the internationalised civil war fought there from 1998–2001 (Roberts, 2000; Roberts et al., 2001, 2003). The researchers estimate that roughly 350,000 persons died due to violence in that time period, while the total toll of war-related deaths, primarily driven by disease, is estimated at 2.5 million, a ratio of roughly one to six. Combat deaths constitute an even smaller category than violent fatalities; our best estimate of battle deaths in the DRC is 145,000 (see the DRC conflict report within International Institute for Strategic

Table 4. Deaths in selected conflicts in Africa

Country	Years	Estimates of total war deaths	Battle deaths	Percentage battle dead
Sudan (Anya Nya rebellion)	1963–1973	250,000–750,000	20,000	3–8%
Nigeria (Biafra Rebellion)	1967–1970	500,000 to 2 million	75,000	4–15%
Angola	1975–2002	1.5 million	160,475	11%
Ethiopia (not inc. Eritrean insurgency)	1976–1991	1–2 million	16,000	<2%
Mozambique	1976–1992	500,000 to 1 million	145,400	15–29%
Somalia	1981–1996	250,000 to 350,000 (to mid-1990s)	66,750	19–27%
Sudan	1983–2002	2 million	55,500	3%
Liberia	1989–1996	150,000–200,000	23,500	12–16%
Democratic Republic of Congo	1998–2001	2.5 million	145,000	6%

Studies, 2003).[9] If these figures are accurate, battle deaths constituted only about 6% of the fatalities due to the war. Table 4 suggests that this disparity between battle deaths and war deaths is not unique. Although there is great uncertainty associated with these data, they strongly suggest that protracted conflicts in poor countries claim the vast majority of their victims off the battlefield. This is especially dramatic in cases where conflict causes famine, as has occurred in Ethiopia and the Sudan.

Although poorly equipped and organised armies may have relatively little capacity to cause large numbers of battle deaths or limited will to engage other combatants, they may still be able to cause high numbers of war deaths. In a very poor nation with weak state structures, it may not require great military capacity to collapse the infrastructure of health and human security and cause a full-blown humanitarian crisis. For example, a small force can cut transportation links vital to food security, as demonstrated by the relatively limited military intervention required to break the siege of Mogadishu and relieve famine in Somalia in 1992–1993 (United Nations, 1996). With a greater percentage of contemporary wars being internal conflicts in poor states, it is likely that the number of global battle deaths has fallen far more precipitously than the count of war deaths. All of the conflicts in Table 4 occurred in Africa, the region that now accounts for the greatest share in global battle violence. In other regions, such as Central and South Asia and Europe, it has also been weak and poor states that have fallen prey to conflict.

Despite optimism in the early 1990s regarding the prospects for peace enforcement by the newly unified community of major powers acting through the United Nations, experiences with preventing the massive humanitarian crises caused by war have been mixed. The UN deployment to Somalia ended in humiliation, as did missions to the Balkans and Rwanda, dimming enthusiasm for multilateral international intervention in civil conflicts. The major powers have few strategic interests in many of the most conflict-prone regions, and major humanitarian crises in West Africa and the DRC have been largely ignored. In the summer of 2004 and early 2005, the grim scenario of a displaced population at risk and a humanitarian relief process stymied by insecurity and international inattention was playing out again in the Darfur region of the Sudan. Today the nexus between conflict, one-sided violence, and humanitarian crisis seems more important than ever.

7. Improving knowledge about deaths in war time

Media reports, government accounts, military data, and the analysis of historians and political scientists all play a role in establishing statistics for conflict deaths. However, the fields of demography and epidemiology are better equipped to scientifically examine and describe the impacts of armed conflict on human population, especially studying impacts beyond mortality such as changes in fertility or migration. The tools of scientific studies of population have already been used to provide data on a few recent conflicts that is of a precision and clarity far beyond that offered by other sources.

Where possible, we have made use of such data to compile a dataset of battle deaths over the past half-century. The results reveal interesting trends in global battle violence, considered both in terms of the impacts of the end of the Cold War and the changing fortunes of geographic regions. The declining numbers of major interstate conflicts and internationalised civil wars have led to a decline in global battle deaths. Presently, most warfare is in the form of civil conflict and wars of state failure taking place outside of areas of the major powers' strategic interest. We expect that many of these conflicts will be characterised more by severe humanitarian crises than combat of the intensity seen during the Cold War. Thus, we are encouraged to see an increasing number of studies on the demography of conflict and conflict and public health. Security and conflict analysts will increasingly require such expertise in order to understand and address the true human costs of war.

Notes

* The work reported here has been carried out in collaboration with a number of colleagues at the Centre for the Study of Civil War, the Uppsala Conflict Data Project, and the Centre for Human Security at the Liu Institute for Global Issues, University of British Columbia. We are grateful to our colleagues at all these three institutions as well as to Andy Mack, Daniel Muños-Rojas, Michael Spagat, and Juan Vargas for their comments, encouragement, and constructive criticisms. The referees and editors of this journal also provided valuable comments. Our work has been funded mainly by the Research Council of Norway, with additional contributions from the Centre for Human Security. The dataset described here, along with detailed documentation, can be downloaded from www.prio.no/cscw/cross/battledeaths.

[1] Throughout this article, we will use the terms 'armed conflict,' 'conflict,' and 'war' as synonyms. We also use 'battle' and 'combat' synonymously to refer to the act of military contest taking place within an armed conflict. For the more precise definition of state-based armed conflict upon which our dataset of battle deaths draws see Appendix A.
[2] For discussion of the long-term economic consequences of civil war, see the World Bank report on civil war (Collier et al., 2003) as well as Murdoch and Sandler (2002). For a project that undertakes comprehensive estimates of the impacts of war, see State Failure Task Force (2003).
[3] Of course, an estimate of battle deaths also involves comparison with a counterfactual. For example, mortality rates among U.S. soldiers during the first Gulf War may actually have been lower than those among similar cohorts living in the U.S. (Wolfson and Smith, 1993). In most cases, however, the counterfactual scenario can probably be ignored when analyzing figures for battle deaths.
[4] A planning report for the second volume of the Human Security Report (Mack, 2005) discusses the need to bring demography, public health, and epidemiology into conflict studies. See Centre for Human Security (2004).
[5] While studies of genocide and politicide (Harff, 2003) find relationships with some of the same factors that predict to the onset of internal war (Fearon and Laitin, 2001; Hegre et al., 2001), the explanatory models are not identical. See also Valentino et al. (2004) on why civil wars involve differing amounts of targeting of civilians.
[6] The dataset may contain much that is incomplete or inaccurate, but it has been compiled in the hope of constant improvement based on users' feedback. We have documented our source materials and coding decisions for each armed conflict. In some cases, we provide low and high estimates of battle deaths in a conflict, along with our best estimate.
[7] The invasion and occupation of Iraq will undoubtedly form a new peak in the incidence of battle deaths beginning in 2003. It is not clear whether the final toll in battle deaths will surpass that in the DRC. On the basis of a sample survey, Roberts et al. (2004) estimate total excess death among Iraqis in the 18 months following invasion at 100,000. This is seven times the number of Iraqi citizens killed by coalition forces according to the leading monitoring project based on press reports (www.iraqbodycount.net), but far less than the millions estimated killed by all war-related causes in the DRC. However, the war in Iraq seems to have claimed a far higher percentage of its victims through violence, especially aerial strikes.
[8] This figure is strongly influenced by the coding of the Vietnam War. In the Uppsala/PRIO data this conflict is an internal war from 1955–1964 and an interstate war from 1965–1975.
[9] The authors of the IRC reports are quite explicit in emphasizing the criminal and/or one-sided character of most deaths through violence they investigated.
[10] A detailed list of references to sources used in compiling the dataset (but not cited in this article) is found on www.prio.no/cscw/cross/battledeaths.

Appendix A: Definition of battle deaths

Our definition of *battle deaths* closely follows the definition of *conflict* used to create the Uppsala/PRIO Armed Conflict Dataset (Gleditsch et al., 2002; Harbom and Wallensteen, 2005). According to codebook for the Uppsala/PRIO dataset (Strand et al., 2003, pp. 3–4):

- "An *armed conflict* is a contested incompatibility that concerns government and/or territory where the use of armed force between two parties, of which at least one is the government of a state, results in at least 25 battle-related deaths."

- The separate elements of the definition are operationalised as follows:
- *Use of armed force:* use of arms in order to promote the parties' general position in the conflict, resulting in deaths.
- *Arms:* any material means, e.g. manufactured weapons but also sticks, stones, fire, water, etc.
- *25 deaths:* a minimum of 25 battle-related deaths per year and per incompatibility.
- *Party:* a government of a state or any opposition organisation or alliance of opposition organisations.
- *Government:* the party controlling the capital of the state.
- *Opposition organisation:* any non-governmental group of people having announced a name for their group and using armed force.
- *State:* a state is an internationally recognised sovereign government controlling a specified territory, or an internationally unrecognised government controlling a specified territory whose sovereignty is not disputed by another internationally recognised sovereign government previously controlling the same territory.
- *Incompatibility concerning government and/or territory:* the incompatibility, as stated by the parties, must concern government and/or territory.
- *Incompatibility:* the stated generally incompatible positions.
- *Incompatibility concerning government:* incompatibility concerning type of political system, the replacement of the central government, or the change of its composition.
- *Incompatibility concerning territory:* incompatibility concerning the status of a territory, e.g. the change of the state in control of a certain territory (interstate conflict), secession, or autonomy (internal conflict).

The Lacina and Gleditsch dataset defines the following terms:

- *Battle deaths* are deaths resulting directly from violence inflicted through the use of armed force by a party to an armed conflict during contested combat.
- *Contested combat* is use of armed force by a party to an armed conflict against any person or target during which the perpetrator faces the immediate threat of lethal force being used by another party to the conflict against him/her and/or allied fighters. Contested combat excludes the sustained destruction of soldiers or civilians outside of the context of any reciprocal threat of lethal force (e.g. execution of prisoners of war).
- *Timeframe:* we have collected annual battle deaths data which includes both deaths during combat and deaths from wounds received in combat. Some of those considered dead of wounds may have died in a year following that in which combat actually took place, especially in the case of battles taking place late in the calendar year. These deaths were included, however, if they were the direct and immediate result of injuries sustained during combat violence. Long-term reduction in life expectancy because of wounds or disability was not included.

Appendix B: Regional definitions

- *Africa, Sub-Saharan:* Angola, Benin, Botswana, Burkina Faso, Burundi, Cameroon, Cape Verde, Central African Republic, Chad, Comoros, Congo (Brazzaville), Democratic Republic of Congo (Zaire), Côte d'Ivoire, Djibouti, Equatorial Guinea, Eritrea, Ethiopia, Gabon, Gambia, Ghana, Guinea, Guinea-Bissau, Kenya, Lesotho, Liberia, Madagascar, Malawi, Mali, Mauritania, Mauritius, Mozambique, Namibia, Niger, Nigeria, Rwanda, Senegal, Sierra Leone, Somalia, South Africa, Swaziland, Tanzania, Togo, Uganda, Zambia, Zanzibar, Zimbabwe.
- *Americas:* Argentina, Bahamas, Barbados, Belize, Bolivia, Brazil, Canada, Chile, Colombia, Costa Rica, Cuba, Dominican Republic, Ecuador, El Salvador, Guatemala, Guyana, Haiti, Honduras, Jamaica, Mexico, Nicaragua, Panama, Paraguay, Peru, Suriname, Trinidad and Tobago, United States of America, Uruguay, Venezuela.
- *Asia, Central and South:* Afghanistan, Armenia, Azerbaijan, Bangladesh, Bhutan, Georgia, India, Kazakhstan, Kyrgyzstan, Nepal, Pakistan, Sri Lanka, Tajikistan, Turkmenistan, Uzbekistan.
- *Asia, East and Southeast and Oceania:* Australia, Brunei, Cambodia, China, East Timor, Fiji, Indonesia, Japan, People's Republic of Korea (North Korea), Republic of Korea (South Korea), Laos, Malaysia, Maldives, Mongolia, Myanmar (Burma), New Zealand, Papua New Guinea, Philippines, Singapore, Solomon Islands, Taiwan, Thailand, Democratic Republic of Vietnam (North Vietnam), Republic of Vietnam (South Vietnam).
- *Europe:* Albania, Austria, Belarus, Belgium, Bosnia Herzegovina, Bulgaria, Croatia, Cyprus, Czech Republic, Czechoslovakia, Denmark, Estonia, Finland, France, German Democratic Republic (East Germany), German Federal Republic (West Germany), Greece, Hungary, Iceland, Ireland, Italy, Latvia, Lithuania, Luxembourg, Macedonia, Malta, Moldova, Netherlands, Norway, Poland, Portugal, Rumania, Russia (Soviet Union), Slovakia, Slovenia, Spain, Sweden, Switzerland, Ukraine, United Kingdom, Yugoslavia (Serbia and Montenegro).
- *Middle East and North Africa:* Algeria, Bahrain, Egypt, Iran, Iraq, Israel, Jordan, Kuwait, Lebanon, Libya, Morocco, Oman, Qatar, Saudi Arabia, Sudan, Syria, Tunisia, Turkey, United Arab Emirates, Yemen (Arab Republic), Yemen (People's Republic).

References[10]

Anušaukas, A., 2000. 'A comparison of the armed struggles for independence in the Baltic States and Western Ukraine', in A. Anušaukas (ed.), *The Anti-Soviet Resistance in the Baltic States.* Du Ka: Vilnius, 63–70.

Ball, P., Kobrak, P. and Spirer, H. F., 1999. *State Violence in Guatemala, 1960–1996: A Quantitative Reflection.* Annapolis, MD: American Association for the Advancement of Science.

Benini, A. A. and Moulton, L. H., 2004. 'The distribution of civilian victims in an asymmetrical conflict: Operation Enduring Freedom, Afghanistan', *Journal of Peace Research* 41(4): 403–422.

Bercovitch, J. and Jackson, R., 1997. '*International Conflict: a Chronological Encyclopedia of Conflicts and their Management 1945–1995*'. Washington, DC: Congressional Quarterly.

Black, R., Morris, S. and Bryce, J., 2003. 'Where and why are 10 million children dying every year?', *Lancet* 361: 2226–2234.

Brogan, P., 1998. *World Conflicts.* Lanham, MD: Scarecrow.

Brunborg, H., Lyngstad, T. H. and Urdal, H., 2003. 'Accounting for genocide: how many were killed in Srebrenica?', *European Journal of Population* 19(3): 229–248.

Centre for Human Security, 2004. Deadly connections: the war/disease nexus workshop report, Liu Institute for Global Issues, University of British Columbia, http://www.humansecuritycentre.org/Deadly%20 Connections%20Meeting%20Report.doc.

Chesterman, S., 2001. 'Introduction: global norms, local contexts', in S. Chesterman (ed.), *Civilians in War.* Boulder, CO: Lynne Rienner.

Clodfelter, M., 2002. *Warfare and Armed Conflicts: A Statistical Reference to Casualty and Other Figures, 1500–2000.* Jefferson, NC.: McFarland.

Collier, P., Elliott, L., Hegre, H., Hoeffler, A., Reynal-Querol, M. and Sambanis, N., 2003. *Breaking the Conflict Trap: Civil War and Development Policy.* Oxford: Oxford University Press.

Dunlop, J., 2000. 'How many soldiers and civilians died during the Russo-Chechen war of 1994–1996?', *Central Asian Survey* 19(3/4): 329–339.

Eckhardt, W., 1996. 'Wars and war-related deaths, 1900–1995', in R. L. Sivard (ed.), *World Military and Social Expenditures 1996.* Washington, DC: World Priorities, 17–19.

Elbe, S., 2002. 'HIV/AIDS and the changing landscape of war in Africa', *International Security* 27(2): 159–177.

Fearon, J. D. and Laitin, D. D., 2001. 'Ethnicity, insurgency, and civil war', *American Political Science Review* 97(1): 75–90.

Fearon, J. D. and Laitin, D. D., 2004. 'Neotrusteeship and the problem of weak states', *International Security* 28(4): 5–43.

Feil, Col. S. R., 1998. *Preventing Genocide: How the Early Use of Force might have Succeeded in Rwanda.* Washington, DC: Carnegie Corporation of New York.

Ghobarah, H.A., Huth, P.K. and Russett, B., 2003. 'Civil wars kill and maim people–long after the shooting stops', *American Political Science Review* 97(2): 189–202.

Ghosn, F. and Palmer, G., 2003. Militarized interstate dispute data, version 3.0, Correlates of War 2 Project, http://cow2.la.psu.edu.

Gleditsch, N. P., Wallensteen, P., Eriksson, M., Sollenberg, M. and Strand, H., 2002. 'Armed conflict 1946–2001: a new dataset', *Journal of Peace Research* 39(5): 615–637.

Harbom, L. and P. Wallensteen, 2005. 'Armed conflict and its international dimensions, 1946–2004', *Journal of Peace Research* 42(5): 623–635.

Harff, B., 2003. 'No lessons learned from the holocaust? Assessing risks of genocide and political mass murder since 1955', *American Political Science Review* 97(1): 57–73.

Harff, B. and Gurr, T. R., 1988. 'Toward empirical theory of genocides and politicides: identification and measurement of cases since 1945', *International Studies Quarterly* 32(3): 359–371.

Hegre, H., Ellingsen, T., Gleditsch, N. P. and Gates, S., 2001. 'Towards a democratic civil peace? Democracy, political change and civil war, 1816–1992', *American Political Science Review* 95(1): 33–48.

Henderson, E., 2002. *Democracy and War: The End of an Illusion.* Boulder, CO: Lynne Rienner.

Hull, I. V., 2003. 'Military culture and the production of final solutions in the colonies: the example of Wilhelminian Germany', in R. Gellately and B. Kiernan (eds), *The Specter of Genocide: Mass Murder in Historical Perspective.* Cambridge: Cambridge University Press, 141–162.

International Institute for Strategic Studies, 2003. Armed conflict database, International Institute for Strategic Studies, http://acd.iiss.org/armedconflict/.

Kalyvas, S., 2004. Techniques of violence in Greece and Vietnam. Unpublished paper presented at the Workshop on Techniques of Violence in Civil War, Centre for the Study of Civil War, PRIO, Oslo, 20–21 August.

Keefe, P. R., 2004. 'Iraq: America's private armies', *The New York Review of Books* LI(13): 48–50.

Krug, E. G., Dahlberg, L. L., Mercy, J. A., Zwi, A. B. and Lozano, R., 2002. *World Report on Violence and Health.* Geneva: World Health Organization.

Lacina, B., Gleditsch, N. P. and Russett, B., 2005. The declining risk of death in battle. Unpublished paper presented at the 2005 Annual Convention of the International Studies Association, Honolulu, HI, 1–5 March, www.prio.no/cscw/cross/battledeaths.

Laffin, J., 1994. *The World in Conflict: War Annual 6.* London: Brassey's.

Leitenberg, M., 2003. *Death in Wars and Conflicts Between 1945 and 2000.* Ithaca, NY: Cornell University.

Li, Quan and Ming Wen, (2005). 'The immediate and lingering effects of armed conflict on adult mortality: a time-series cross-national analysis', *Journal of Peace Research* 42(4): 471–492.

Mack, A. (ed.), 2005. *Human Security Report.* New York: Oxford University Press, two volumes, in press.

Mueller, J., 1995. 'The perfect enemy: assessing the Gulf War', *Security Studies* 5(1): 77–117.

Mueller, J., 2003. 'Policing the remnants of war', *Journal of Peace Research* 40(5): 507–518.

Murdoch, J. C. and Sandler, T., 2002. 'Economic growth, civil wars, and spatial spillovers', *Journal of Conflict Resolution* 46(1): 91–110.

Murray, Ch. J. L., King, G., Lopez, A. D., Tomijima, N. and Krug, E. G., 2002, 'Armed conflict as a public health problem', *BMJ* 324(7333): 346–349.

Pakenham, T., 1992. *The Scramble for Africa, 1876–1912.* London: Weidenfeld and Nicolson.

Project Ploughshares, 2003. Armed conflicts report 2003, Project Ploughshares, http://www.ploughshares.ca/content/ACR/ACR00/ACR00.html.

Roberts, L., 2000. *Mortality in Eastern DRC: Results from Five Mortality Surveys.* Bukavu/New York: International Rescue Committee.

Roberts, L., Hale, Ch., Belyakdoumi, F., Cobey, L., Ondeko, R., Despines, M., IRC DRC Bukavu/Kisangani and Keys, J., 2001. *Mortality in Eastern Democratic Republic of Congo: Results from Eleven Mortality Surveys.* Bukavu/New York: International Rescue Committee.

Roberts, L., Ngoy, P., Mone, C., Lubula, Ch., Mwezse, L., Zantop, M. and Despines, M., 2003. *Mortality in the Democratic Republic of Congo: Results from a Nationwide Survey.* Bukavu/New York: International Rescue Committee.

Roberts, L., Lafta, R., Garfield, R., Khudhairi, J. and Burnham, G., 2004. 'Mortality before and after the invasion of Iraq in 2003', *The Lancet* 364(9448): 1857–1864.

Rummel, R. J., 1997. *Statistics of Democide: Genocide and Mass Murder since 1900.* Rutgers, NJ: Transaction Publishers.

Sarkees, M. R., 2000. 'The Correlates of War data on war: an update to 1997', *Conflict Management and Peace Science* 18(1): 123–144.

Sarkees, M. R., Wayman, F. W. and Singer, J. D., 2003. 'Inter-state, intra-state, and extra-state wars: a comprehensive look at their distribution over time, 1816–1997', *International Studies Quarterly* 47: 49–70.

Schabas, W. A., 2001. *Introduction to the International Criminal Court.* Cambridge: Cambridge University Press.

Sivard, R. L., 1996. *World Military and Social Expenditures 1996.* Washington, DC: World Priorities.

Sliwinski, M., 1989. 'Afghanistan: the decimation of a people', *Orbis* 33(1): 39–56.

Snow, D. M., 1996. *Uncivil Wars: International Security and the New Internal Conflicts.* Boulder, CO: Lynne Rienner.

State Failure Task Force, 2003. State failure problem set, 1955–2001. Center for International Development and Conflict Management at the University of Maryland and Integrated Network for Societal Conflict Research, http://www.cidcm.umd.edu/inscr/stfail/sfdata.htm.

Strand, H., Wilhelmsen, L. and Gleditsch, N. P., in cooperation with Wallensteen, P., Eriksson, M. and Sollenberg, M., 2003. Armed conflict dataset codebook, version 2.0.: International Peace Research Institute, http://www.prio.no/cwp/ArmedConflict/current/Codebook_v2_0.pdf.

Sutton, M., 2001. An index of deaths from the conflict in Northern Ireland. ARK: Northern Ireland Social and Political Archive: Conflict Archive on the Internet (CAIN), http://cain.ulst.ac.uk/sutton/index.html.

United Nations, 1996. *The United Nations and Somalia, 1992–1996.* United Nations, New York: Department of Public Information.

Valentino, B., Huth, P. K. and Balch-Lindsay, D., 2004. 'Draining the sea: mass killing and guerilla warfare', *International Organization* 58(2): 375–407

Verwimp, P., 2003. 'Testing the double-genocide thesis for Central and Southern Rwanda', *Journal of Conflict Resolution* 47(4): 423–442.
Walzer, M., 1977. '*Just and Unjust Wars: A Moral Argument with Historical Illustrations*'. New York: Basic Books.
Wiharta, S. and Anthony, I., 2003. 'Major armed conflicts', in: *SIPRI Yearbook 2003: World Armaments and Disarmament.* Oxford University Press, Oxford 87–125.
Wolfson, M. and Smith, R., 1993. 'How not to pay for the war', *Defence Economics* 4(4): 299–314.

CHAPTER 7. THE IMMEDIATE AND LINGERING EFFECTS OF ARMED CONFLICT ON ADULT MORTALITY: A TIME-SERIES CROSS-NATIONAL ANALYSIS*

QUAN LI
Department of Political Science, Pennsylvania State University, USA

MING WEN
Department of Sociology, University of Utah, USA

Abstract. This research investigates the effect of armed conflict on adult mortality across countries and over time. Theoretical mechanisms are specified for how military violence influences adult mortality, both immediately and over time after conflict. The effects of aggregate conflict, interstate and intrastate conflicts, and conflict severity are explored. The Heckman selection model is applied to account for the conflict-induced missing data problem. A pooled analysis across 84 countries for the period from 1961 to 1998 provides broad empirical support for the proposed theoretical expectations across both genders. This study confirms the importance of both the immediate and the lingering effect of military conflict on the mortality of the working-age population. The immediate effect of civil conflict is much stronger than that of the interstate conflict, while the reverse applies to the lingering effect. Both the immediate and the lingering effects of severe conflict are much stronger than those of minor conflict. While men tend to suffer higher mortality immediately from intrastate conflict and severe conflict, women in the long run experience as much mortality owing to the lingering effects of these conflicts. The mortality data show a strong data selection bias caused by military conflict. The research findings highlight the imperative for negotiating peace. Preventing a contest from escalating into a severe conflict can produce noticeable gains in saved human lives.

1. Introduction

Mortality is one of the most important aspects of population health. While military violence is known to cause killings and have deleterious consequences for public health, there has not been any systematic longitudinal analysis of the effect of military conflict on population mortality in a cross-national design. Most scholars of public health and demography have focused on the impact of economic variables in the cross-national analysis. For example, both GDP per capita and income inequality are found to be associated with life expectancy (e.g., Wilkinson, 1996). These scholars have typically ignored the impact of armed conflict on key demographic outcomes such as life expectancy and mortality rate. In contrast, conflict scholars who examine the consequences of military violence have limited their attention to a few issues such as trade, economic growth, and democracy.[1] They also have largely ignored the impact of military conflict on population health.

This chapter was previously published in *Journal of Peace Research*, vol. 42, no. 4, 2005, pp. 471–492.

Helge Brunborg et al. (eds.), The Demography of Armed Conflict, 153–176.

As Murray et al. (2002) point out, little attention has been devoted to the question of exactly how military conflict affects mortality across countries and over time. The analysis by Ghobarah, Huth and Russett (2003) is an exception. They analyze the effect of civil war during the period 1991–97 on death and disability in 1999. They find that the effect of civil war is strong. But they do not examine the effect of interstate conflict. Moreover, their cross-sectional analysis does not address simultaneously the short-term and the long-term effects of conflict on public health. In this article, we analyze how various attributes of military violence influence mortality across countries, not only in the short term but also over time.

We believe that understanding the effect of military conflict on mortality has important policy and theoretical implications. If prolonging population life expectancy is a desirable policy objective, we need to better understand the causal determinants of mortality, in order to formulate effective policies. While military violence is known to kill, a narrow focus on the direct killings of war is likely to understate its deleterious consequences for human welfare. A rigorous analysis of how armed conflict affects mortality will help illuminate the real costs of war and offer an additional rationale for promoting peace. In addition, to the extent that national economic conditions are related to military conflict, analyses of mortality that narrowly focus on economic variables are likely to suffer from the omitted-variable bias and incorrectly estimate their effects. Finally, a thorough analysis of the consequences of military conflict for mortality allows the public, policymakers, and conflict scholars to appreciate the costs of war on human life in ways that may ultimately inform the decisions to use force. Hence, a theoretical dialogue between public health and conflict scholars is mutually beneficial.

The article proceeds as follows. The first section presents our theoretical argument on how military conflict affects mortality across countries and over time. The second section discusses the research design for our empirical analysis. The third section presents the statistical findings. The final section summarizes our findings and discusses their policy implications.

2. Theoretical argument

How does military violence affect mortality across countries over time? We argue that military conflict increases mortality both immediately and over time after conflict. In addition, the types of military conflict (e.g., intrastate or interstate; minor or severe) modify the ways in which conflict increases mortality.

2.1. IMMEDIATE AND LINGERING EFFECTS OF MILITARY VIOLENCE

Our theoretical argument starts with the premise that military violence influences mortality through the following six direct or indirect mechanisms. First, obviously, warfare causes people to die. That is, military conflict causes casualties to soldiers and civilians and kills humans. Thus, military conflict directly reduces the overall life expectancy and immediately increases the mortality level in a population.

Second, military conflict affects mortality by influencing the national economy. War and conflict are costly and destructive. They use huge amounts of economic resources while destroying public and private property. Wars frequently result in widespread homelessness, forced migration, economic recession, and deterioration of public health. A weakened economy also causes unemployment to rise. Even during peace, unemployment is a stressful life-event, leading to deterioration of both psychological and physical health and causing self-destructive behaviors such as alcoholism and suicide (Durkheim, 1951; Montgomery et al., 1999; Morris, Cook and Shaper, 1994; Warr, 1984). As many studies (see e.g., Moser, Fox and Jones, 1984; Preti and Miotto, 1999; Pritchard, 1990) show, the risk of committing suicide is higher among the unemployed at the individual level, and the unemployment rate is often positively correlated with the suicide rate at the society level. Detrimental consequences of unemployment are often worse following a war, during which the economic infrastructure may have been destroyed and the social security system disrupted. Poverty, recession, unemployment, and massive migration may also cause the re-emergence of infectious diseases that lead to premature death.

Third, military conflict often damages health-related facilities and infrastructure. In military conflict, heavy bombings often destroy hospitals and kill doctors and nurses. Roads and highways also are often damaged, obstructing the transportation of the sick, the wounded, medicine, and medical equipment. Water is often polluted, making accessing sanitary water difficult. Diseases that are easily treated during peace often turn out to be lethal during war. Life expectancy is shortened, and mortality increases as a result.

Fourth, war and preparing for war crowd out health-related private investment and government spending on public health. While government tax revenues are limited, warfare is expensive, requiring resources and increased spending on military equipment and personnel. A large literature (see e.g., Keynes, 1963; Heijdra and Ligthart, 1997; Chan, 1986; Knight, Loayza and Villanueva, 1996) suggests that as public spending including defense expenditures increases, government borrowing bids up the interest rate in the credit market, crowding out private investment and reducing private spending on education, health, transportation, and other goods and services. This leads to deterioration of health-care services. In addition, expenditures on warfare represent public expenditures that could have been used for any number of other purposes, including promoting public welfare (e.g., through public health measures). Waging war means that government spending on health services may have to be reduced or cut. Poor people who rely on government health-care services have to scramble for means to deal with their illnesses, causing mortality to rise. Finally, a tightened government budget may also lead to loosened regulation of public health hazards. For example, reducing the number of government inspectors and deregulating the meat-processing industry often cause an increase in contaminated meat and poultry, eggs with *E. coli*, and salmonella bacteria (Link and Phelan, 1995). The ensuing bacterial infection can cause infectious disease-related deaths to rise.

Fifth, military conflict affects mortality by influencing social cohesion. Since Durkheim (1951), sociologists have argued that the degree of social integration can account for variations in the suicide rate—a special type of mortality—across countries and regions. Durkheim's theory also applies to other health-related outcomes such as violence, crime, homicide, and cardiovascular diseases (see e.g., Berkman et al., 2000). While social relationships may have both positive and negative effects on health, the majority of the research community agrees that social integration is beneficial for health (Berkman et al., 2000). Military conflict can have competing effects on social cohesion. Military conflict may motivate people toward nationalism and enhance social cohesion, especially in the presence of foreign aggression (Durkheim, 1951). However, to the extent that military violence intensifies the struggle for survival and deepens social cleavages, conflict erodes social cohesion. Hence, the effect of military conflict on social cohesion may be indeterminate, depending on the nature of the conflict.

Sixth, military violence causes traumatic experience and psychological distress in a population, raising mortality. While studies on extreme situations, including natural disasters such as earthquakes, tornados, and hurricanes, find little evidence of incapacitating and long-lasting psychological reactions to catastrophes, these events tend to be short in duration and limited in scale (Cockerham, 2003). Presumably, large-scale unnatural disasters such as war may have long-lasting effects. War-related distress is a specific form of post-traumatic stress that involves such responses as fear, hopelessness, or horror, causing distress or impairment in daily functioning (American Psychiatric Association, 1994). A study conducted immediately after the civil war in Croatia between 1991 and 1995 finds that 33% of the subjects reported that they had recurrent and bothersome thoughts or memories about a traumatic war-related event, 37% of the subjects reported a persistent sense of a foreshortened future, and one person in ten reported significant impairment in social, occupational, or other important areas of functioning (Kunovich and Hodson, 1999). Mental distress and physical illness often go hand in hand because they are affected by the same circumstances and feed on each other (Mirowsky, Ross and Reynolds, 2000). Mental illness, such as psychological distress and depression, can make people hopeless, listless, and worried, impairing their ability or desire to follow a healthy lifestyle. Psychological stress can also directly damage health via biological pathways. Specifically, psychological stress triggers neuroendocrine and immune response, disturbs the body's internal status quo, and rouses patho-physiological changes that are eventually manifested in organ impairment, leading to morbidity and mortality (Brunner and Marmot, 1999).

While each of these causal mechanisms is worth independent investigation, we do not study them individually in this article. Data on key variables such as unemployment rate, health infrastructure and facilities, and government health spending are extremely limited cross-nationally and over time, while data on social cohesion and psychological distress are currently unobserved in cross-national settings over time. The theoretical discussion of these six mechanisms above, however, suggests an important implication that we examine in this article. That is, through these various direct and indirect causal paths, warfare undermines population health, causing higher mortality. These effects have varying temporal characteristics. Some effects are immediate but dissipate quickly as conflict concludes, such as direct killings caused by conflict. Other effects linger beyond conflict, such as the effect on social cohesion and psychological distress. Eroded social cohesion and psychological trauma resulting from involvement in military violence require considerable time to recover and heal. Social cohesion and psychological health may never return to the prewar level. Many effects may operate both immediately and over time after conflict, such as the indirect effects of conflict operating via the economy, health facilities, government health spending, and psychological distress. Damage to the economy and health-related infrastructure can cause the death toll to rise immediately, even as war occurs. It also exerts a lingering effect on mortality because such damage is expensive and time-consuming to repair or replace. Therefore, we hypothesize that military conflict increases mortality both immediately and over time after conflict.

2.2. EFFECTS OF DIFFERENT TYPES OF MILITARY CONFLICT

Military conflicts are heterogeneous. Some conflicts occur between sovereign states or alliances of sovereign states, while others occur between factions within a country. Some conflicts are minor in terms of the death toll and damage, while others are severe. We believe that to understand how military violence affects mortality, one has to examine the immediate and lingering effects of different types of military conflict on mortality. Doing so helps us identify more nuanced patterns in the effect of conflict.

Differences between minor and severe conflicts are straightforward. To the extent that all conflicts kill, both minor and severe conflicts increase mortality immediately during and after conflict. But the level of manpower input may differ greatly between minor and severe conflicts. Severe conflict often involves more salient issues than minor conflict. Because the stakes are higher, leaders often commit more manpower and financial resources in severe conflict. They also are less likely to give in or compromise. Hence, relative to minor conflict, severe conflict ends up killing more people during and immediately after conflict.

Both minor and severe conflicts also produce a lingering effect on mortality. Both types of conflict can cause economic recession and damage a country's infrastructure. They also can weaken social cohesion and increase post-traumatic psychological problems in a society. Severe conflict, however, is likely to cause more economic, physical, and psychosocial damage than minor conflict. More severe conflict involves more participants and the use of possibly more lethal weapons, producing more casualties and depleting a country's financial resources more quickly and more deeply. Hence, while both types of conflict increase mortality over time after conflict, severe conflict tends to have a larger lingering effect.

The differences between the effects on mortality of intrastate and interstate conflicts are more subtle. Both types of conflict directly kill humans and cause damage to national economy and health facilities, a decline in government health spending, and a rise in psychological distress. They both cause mortality to rise immediately. Intrastate conflict, however, often results from society-wide class, ethnic, religious, and/or ideological cleavages, which in turn lead to massive migration, destruction of infrastructure, repression, even mass killing and genocide. A tragic example is the mass killing, genocide, and massive migration that occurred in Sudan in 2004. In contrast, interstate conflict often involves territorial claims and border skirmishes, resulting in a low death toll and ending with a compromise on the negotiation table. While large-scale interstate conflict is particularly damaging, worldwide catastrophic wars such as World War I and World War II are typically rare. In addition, to the extent that interstate conflict is restricted in scope (e.g., to border areas), their damages to the national economy and health facilities may be limited. To the extent that interstate conflicts raise the demand for the production of military-related goods and services, they may even encourage the growth of certain economic sectors that benefit from such demand increases. More surprisingly, statistics have shown that the most rapid improvements in life expectancy in Britain during last century occurred during the two world wars (Wilkinson, 1996). Such rapid improvement has been largely attributed to greater egalitarianism and the related higher level of social cohesion in Britain during those times (Wilkinson, 1996). Hence, while we expect both types of conflict to cause mortality to rise immediately, the short-term effect of the intrastate conflict on mortality should be larger than that of the interstate conflict.

In terms of the lingering effect, both intrastate and interstate conflicts are expected to cause human mortality to rise over time after conflict. Damages to the national economy and health facilities are not easy to repair, and conflict-related psychological distress heals slowly and with difficulty. The difference in the lingering effect of the two types of conflict, however, is difficult to predict *a priori*. This is so particularly because the effect of interstate conflict on social cohesion can change dramatically and become inconsistent over time. Interstate conflict may encourage social cohesion in a country that faces foreign aggression or is engaged in a war that its citizens widely regard as just. For example, Durkheim (1951: 208) argued that "great social disturbances and great popular wars rouse collective sentiments, stimulate partisan spirit and patriotism, political and national faith, alike, and concentrating activity toward a single end, at least temporarily cause a stronger integration of society". The positive effect of interstate conflict on social cohesion, however, may disappear once the conflict is over and the threat of foreign aggression subsides. Old conflicts of interest resume, while new conflicts of interest emerge. Soldiers coming back from the battlefield (e.g., the Vietnam War veterans) find it difficult to fit into a society they are no longer familiar with and which may not be entirely welcoming. Hence, locating possible differences in the lingering effects of interstate and intrastate conflicts will be less of a theoretical issue and more a matter of empirical analysis.

Table 1. Expected effects of military conflict on adult mortality

		Immediate effect of conflict occurrence	Lingering effect of conflict history
Aggregate conflict		+	+
Conflict type	Intrastate conflict	+	+
	Interstate conflict	+	+
	Difference of (intrastate – interstate)	>0	Not clear
Conflict severity	Severe	+	+
	Minor	+	+
	Difference of (severe – minor)	>0	>0

Table 1 summarizes the expected signs of the immediate and lingering effects of military conflict on human mortality. Because these theoretical expectations concern patterns across different types of conflict and over time, they should be assessed in a longitudinal analysis.

3. Research design

To assess the effects of armed conflict on mortality across countries over time, we employ a pooled time-series cross-sectional design, covering all countries with available data from 1961 to 1998. In this analysis, we focus on the mortality rate of the working-age population from 15 to 64, a commonly used age range that includes most people of working ages. Working-age adult mortality tends to have more deleterious effects for families, communities, and societies because working-age adults constitute the most productive group in society, regardless of the national wealth level. Because we are interested in evaluating the effect of armed conflict on mortality over time and across countries, we need data covering enough years and countries to reach valid generalizations. The mortality data for the adult population are the most comprehensive.

We separate the empirical analysis for males and females, a standard practice in the public health literature. Men tend to have higher mortality than women in almost all societies (Cockerham, 2003). Men and women are different in terms of physiological dynamics and gender roles within society in general, the military and labor markets in particular.

3.1. DEPENDENT VARIABLE

The dependent variable is the age-standardized sex-specific death rate for age group 15 to 64 years old. To construct this variable, we use official national statistics on age-sex-cause-specific deaths and age-sex-specific total population counts from the data provided in the WHO Mortality Database (WHO, 2004). The data in this database comprise deaths registered in national vital registration systems, with the underlying cause of death coded by the relevant national authority. They are reported directly to the WHO by the responsible authorities of each country. We aggregate total deaths across the underlying causes and compute the sex-specific death rate of population ages 15 to 64, standardized on age. Age groups 15–24, 25–34, 35–44, 45–54, and 55–64 are used to generate the standardized death rate using direct standardization.[2] The variable is log transformed to correct for its skewed distribution.

3.2. KEY INDEPENDENT VARIABLES

To test our hypotheses, we design several groups of conflict-related variables. Data on all conflict variables either come directly from or are simple transformations of measures found in the Armed Conflict Database from 1946 to 2001 by Gleditsch et al. (2002). In the database, an armed conflict is defined as "a contested incompatibility that concerns government and/or territory where the use of armed force between two parties, of which at least one is the government of a state, results in at least 25 battle-related deaths".

To test the immediate effect of conflict, we create five different dummy variables. *Conflict dummy* is coded 1 if a country is engaged in any type of armed conflict in year ($t - 1$) and 0 otherwise. The variable measures the immediate effect of any conflict, regardless of its type. To assess the effects of different types of conflict, *interstate* (or *intrastate*) *conflict dummy* is coded 1 if a country is involved in an interstate (or intrastate) conflict in year ($t - 1$) and 0 otherwise. *Minor* (or *severe*) *conflict dummy* is coded 1 if a country is involved in any conflict with fewer (or more) than 1,000 battle deaths in year ($t - 1$) and 0 otherwise. We lag these conflict dummy variables one year behind the dependent variable to control for possible reverse causality, because unnatural mortality weakens a country's manpower and in turn influences its decision to use force.

To capture the lingering effect of conflict history on mortality, we create five continuous variables. *Conflict history* is the percentage of years a country has been involved in any armed conflict from 1946 to year ($t - 2$), capturing the lingering effect of past conflict on mortality in year t. *Interstate* (or *intrastate*) *conflict history* is the percentage of years the country has been involved in any interstate (or intrastate) conflict from 1946 to year ($t - 2$), which measures the lingering effect of the interstate (or intrastate) conflict history on adult mortality. *Minor* (or *severe*) *conflict history* is the percentage of years the country has been involved in any minor (or severe) conflict from 1946 to year ($t - 2$), reflecting the lingering effect of the minor (or severe) conflict history on adult mortality.

3.3. CONTROL VARIABLES

Income inequality within a country may affect its adult mortality. Since the early 1990s, ecological work has suggested that the extent of income inequality in a society negatively affects its average population health (Wilkinson, 1992, 1996). Higher income inequality implies that a greater proportion of the population is in the low income category and below the poverty line. The marginalized population group is less able to afford needed medical care while struggling for food and rent. In contrast, countries with more equitable income and wealth distributions tend to have fewer people that are too impoverished to afford medical services. Income inequality may also negatively affect population health through two other mechanisms (Kaplan et al., 1996; Kawachi and Kennedy, 1997, 1999). First, income inequality may cause underinvestment in health-promoting resources, such as education, medical services, transportation, and environmental regulation. Second, it may lead to painful individual psychosocial processes and the erosion of social capital, causing detrimental physiological changes. We measure income inequality with the widely used *Gini coefficient.* A Gini coefficient, bounded between 1 and 0, indicates perfect income inequality at 1 and perfect equality at 0. We use the income inequality data collected by Deininger and Squire (1996), supplemented by the inequality data for the 1990s used in Ghobarah, Huth and Russett (2003). Following Easterly (1999) and Higgins and Williamson (1999), we use the decade average value of the Gini coefficient.

The level of democracy in a country may affect the mortality rate of its population. More democratic countries tend to have more equitable income distributions and faster growth in per capita income (Reuveny and Li, 2003; Przeworski et al., 2000). Low income groups that are typically ignored in autocratic countries can influence public policy in democratic countries by forming political parties, running for office, and casting their votes. They are able to acquire better health-care services for themselves in democratic states than under autocratic regimes. We measure the level of *democracy* using the Polity IV database (Marshall and Jaggers, 2000). The Polity data record the democratic and autocratic attributes of many countries on an annual basis from 1800 to 1999. The widely used measure for the level of democracy from Polity IV is the difference between the variable DEMOC and the variable AUTOC, ranging from -10 (strongly autocratic) to $+10$ (strongly democratic).

Urbanization often affects human mortality, but its effect may be ambiguous. On the one hand, urbanization often causes an influx of poor rural people into the cities, increasing the size of the urban low-income population and the pressures on urban health-care resources (Ghobarah, Huth and Russett, 2003). The mortality rate may rise. On the other hand, urbanization may bring about economic expansion, leading to more service industries and creating more job opportunities. Urbanization also leads to the widespread use of modern amenities, improving the hygiene conditions of new residents from the rural area. Modern medical facilities in the city save lives that may have been lost in the rural area. Urbanization may thus reduce mortality. We capture the effect of urbanization using two variables, the percentage of the urban population in a country (*urbanization*) and the annual growth rate of the urban population (*urbanization rate*).

Another control variable is the growth of per capita income in a country. Income changes affect the mortality rate in a population. As per capita income increases, public investment in health also increases. More people can afford health-care services. Their health conditions are better monitored and maintained. In contrast, the decline in per capita income often occurs with difficult national economic and financial conditions, such as high unemployment. People are less able to afford health-care services. The state of the economy is found to influence most aspects of public health (Cockerham, 2003). For example, several studies (Brenner and Mooney, 1983; Brenner, 1973, 1987a,b) link economic downturns to the increased incidence of heart disease, stroke, kidney failure, mental illness, and even infant mortality in the United States and several Western European countries. Economic recession increases the amount of social, financial, and psychological stress on individuals, causing physiological stress reactions and a rise in mortality. Hence, we expect an increase in per capita income to reduce adult mortality. We use the annual percentage growth of GDP per capita (*GDPPC growth*) to measure per capita income changes. Data are from the World Bank's World Development Indicators (2002).

On average, medical technologies have improved over time across countries. Technological progress produces drugs that cure diseases that once may have been lethal. Scientific evidence on behavioral and environmental determinants of health has been disseminated in recent decades, contributing to the trend toward healthy lifestyles and disease prevention, especially across Western societies. Thus, the adult mortality rate may experience a declining trend over time. We use the *year* variable to control for this possibility.

The population age structure of a country can influence its adult mortality. People who are younger than 15 or older than 64 are typically dependants. In a country that has more dependants, the burden on their working-age population (those of ages from 15 to 64) is also higher. The overburdened adult population may experience a higher mortality rate. We capture the effect of the population age structure using the *age dependency* ratio of the dependent population over the working-age population. Data are from the World Bank's World Development Indicators (2002).

The dynamics of public health differ between developed and developing countries. Some scholars (e.g., Omran, 1971) further argue that countries that reach a certain threshold level of income (around $5,000 per capita in 1990) pass through the so-called "epidemiological transition" into a new phase, where non-communicable diseases rather than infectious diseases become the predominant causes of deaths. In addition, developed countries tend to be wealthier, more democratic, and have better health-care systems. In contrast, developing countries have less modern medical facilities and less generous social welfare programs. To control for this possible difference, we create the *OECD dummy* variable, coded 1 if a country is a member of the Organization for Economic Cooperation and Development and 0 otherwise. As the OECD countries are largely in North America and Western Europe, the OECD dummy also helps to control for the region-specific effects.

The tropical region is an area where many infectious diseases such as diarrhea and malaria are most likely to erupt and spread. People in tropical climates are more likely to catch infectious diseases and die. The variable *tropical dummy* is coded 1 if a country lies in the tropical region and 0 otherwise, based on the coding of Ghobarah, Huth and Russett (2003).

3.4. MISSING DATA SELECTION BIAS AND STATISTICAL METHODS

Murray et al. (2002) argue that military conflict often causes national health information systems to cease to function, producing missing values or numeric underestimates in vital registration data on the event and cause of death. This creates a selection bias problem for assessing the effect of conflict on mortality. Where conflict occurs, data on mortality may be missing or underestimated. The resultant data selection bias can be modeled statistically using the Heckman sample selection model (Heckman, 1979; Greene, 2003). Based on the argument of Murray et al. (2002), we specify the following selection mechanism and regression model of mortality:

Selection equation:

$$z^*_{it} = \gamma_0 + \gamma_1 \,\text{conflict}_{it} + \gamma_2 \,\text{conflict}_{i(t-1)} + u_{1it}, \quad \text{where} \quad z^*_{it} \text{ is the probability of observing mortality data for country } i \text{ in year } t, \quad \gamma_1 < 0, \gamma_2 < 0.$$

Regression equation:

$$\text{Mortality}_{it} = x_{i(t-1)}\beta + u_{2it}, \text{ observed only if } z^*_{it} > 0, u_{1it} \sim N(0, 1), \quad u_{2it} \sim N(0, \sigma), \text{corr}(u_{1it}, u_{2it}) = \rho.$$

Mortality data for country i in year t are observed only when the sample selection variable $z^*_{it} > 0$, and missing otherwise. The probability of observing mortality data z^*_{it} is a function of conflict involvement of a country. Hence, in the selection equation, the conflict variables are the number of any type of armed conflict in which a country is involved for years t and $(t-1)$, respectively. They are expected to reduce the probability of observing the mortality data, that is, $\gamma_1 < 0, \gamma_2 < 0$. In the regression equation, observed mortality for country i in year t is a function of a vector of independent variables x for country i in year $(t-1)$, except for the conflict history variables which are measured until year $(t-2)$, and the error term u_{2it}. The independent variables are lagged to control for possible reverse causality.

As denoted, the model assumes that the error terms from both equations are normally distributed, with zero means and correlation ρ. If the mortality regression and the selection equation are not independent from each other (i.e., $\rho \neq 0$), the mortality data suffer from the conflict-induced data selection bias. The mortality regression that ignores the bias produces biased results. The selection model allows us to estimate the mortality model while taking into account the selection effect, generating consistent and asymptotically efficient estimates.[3]

Statistical models for pooled time-series cross-sectional data may exhibit heteroskedasticity and serial correlation. While these problems do not bias the estimated coefficients, they often lead to biased standard errors for the coefficients, producing invalid statistical inferences. To deal with these potential problems, we estimate the Huber–White robust standard errors clustered over countries. These estimated standard errors are robust to both heteroskedasticity and to a general type of serial correlation within the cross-sectional unit (Rogers, 1993; Williams, 2000).

4. Empirical findings

We present the statistical results in Tables 2 and 3 for males and females, respectively. The top panel presents results from the selection equation; the bottom panel, from the mortality regression. The selection equation is based on a sample of about 160 countries from 1961 to 1998. The mortality regression is based on a sample of 84 countries from 1961 to 1998, covering about 85% of the 99 countries on which the WHO has human mortality data. Appendix A includes descriptive statistics for the variables. Appendix B compares the countries on which the WHO has mortality data and those included in estimating the mortality equation.

Each table presents six models. Among the mortality regressions, Model 1 examines the immediate effect of any type of conflict, while Model 2 evaluates its immediate and lingering effects. Model 3 focuses on the immediate effects of intrastate and interstate conflicts, while Model 4 presents their immediate and lingering effects. Model 5 provides the immediate effects of minor and severe conflicts, while Model 6 presents their immediate and lingering effects.

We start with the selection equation results. Across all models in both tables, the number of conflicts in which a country is involved during either year t or year $(t - 1)$ reduces the probability of observing mortality data. The hypothesis that the cross-equation correlation equals zero is rejected at the 1% level. The cross-equation correlation ρ is above 0.7, far greater than zero correlation. The use of the Heckman selection model is appropriate.

Now we discuss briefly the results of the control variables. As expected, per capita income growth, urbanization, urbanization growth, and national wealth reduce both the male and the female adult mortality rate. These results are robust across all models. Income inequality has a significant and positive effect on adult mortality for both sexes. Overall, the patterns for these variables are consistent with previous research findings in the public health literature, giving us more confidence in our findings.

The effects of democracy, age dependency ratio, and the tropical dummy differ interestingly between the two genders. Democracy, age dependency ratio, and the tropical dummy do not affect the male mortality, but they have a statistically significant effect on the female mortality in the expected directions. It is possible that development-related factors, such as the level of economic development and urbanization, exert more influence on male health than the nature of the political system and the size of the dependent population. In addition, women's rights tend to be better protected in democracies than in non-democratic countries, reducing the female mortality rate. Adult women typically are the main caregivers for the dependent population in a society. A large dependent population implies a greater physical and psychological burden for the adult female group, increasing their mortality

	2.1 aggregate conflict	2.2 aggregate conflict	2.3 conflict type	2.4 conflict type	2.5 conflict severity	2.6 conflict severity
Selection equation						
Number of conflicts$_t$	−0.0811*	−0.1264**	−0.0739*	−0.1270**	−0.0772*	−0.1150**
	(0.0550)	(0.0570)	(0.0519)	(0.0576)	(0.0541)	(0.0574)
Number of conflicts$_{t-1}$	−0.1811***	−0.1446**	−0.2034***	−0.1549***	−0.1877***	−0.1540***
	(0.0617)	(0.0615)	(0.0596)	(0.0583)	(0.0600)	(0.0592)
Constant	−0.3646***	−0.3700***	−0.3612***	−0.3677***	−0.3639***	−0.3705***
	(0.0942)	(0.0943)	(0.0938)	(0.0940)	(0.0941)	(0.0942)
ρ	−0.71	−0.71	−0.75	−0.76	−0.72	−0.73
Wald ($\rho = 0$)	7.33***	8.86***	10.53***	13.62***	8.46***	10.83***
Total *N*	5,196	5,174	5,196	5,174	5,196	5,174
Regression equation						
Conflict dummy$_{t-1}$	0.1699***	0.0759				
	(0.0654)	(0.0590)				
Conflict history$_{t-2}$		0.0024**				
		(0.0010)				
Interstate conflict dummy$_{t-1}$			0.1548***	0.0093		
			(0.0445)	(0.0395)		
Intrastate conflict dummy$_{t-1}$			0.2001***	0.1548**		
			(0.0750)	(0.0700)		
Interstate conflict history$_{t-2}$				0.0064***		
				(0.0013)		
Intrastate conflict history$_{t-2}$				−0.0006		
				(0.0009)		
Minor conflict dummy$_{t-1}$					0.0888	0.0701
					(0.0715)	(0.0570)
Severe conflict dummy$_{t-1}$					0.2549***	0.1486**
					(0.0593)	(0.0616)

(*Cont.*)

	2.1 aggregate conflict	2.2 aggregate conflict	2.3 conflict type	2.4 conflict type	2.5 conflict severity	2.6 conflict severity
Minor conflict history$_{t-2}$						−0.0017
						(0.0011)
Severe conflict history$_{t-2}$						0.0044***
						(0.0008)
Control variables						
Gini coefficient$_{t-1}$	1.1078**	0.9686**	1.1141**	0.9502**	1.1083**	0.9590**
	(0.4918)	(0.4735)	(0.4812)	(0.4494)	(0.4741)	(0.4377)
Urbanization$_{t-1}$	−0.0038**	−0.0038**	−0.0039***	−0.0036***	−0.0038**	−0.0034**
	(0.0015)	(0.0015)	(0.0015)	(0.0014)	(0.0015)	(0.0014)
Urbanization rate$_{t-1}$	−0.0718***	−0.0760***	−0.0729***	−0.0802***	−0.0718***	−0.0750***
	(0.0187)	(0.0185)	(0.0182)	(0.0182)	(0.0182)	(0.0179)
GDPPC growth$_{t-1}$	−0.0137***	−0.0137***	−0.0136***	−0.0140***	−0.0133***	−0.0128***
	(0.0024)	(0.0024)	(0.0024)	(0.0022)	(0.0024)	(0.0021)
Democracy$_{t-1}$	−0.0026	−0.0023	−0.0031	−0.0020	−0.0024	−0.0012
	(0.0041)	(0.0040)	(0.0040)	(0.0039)	(0.0040)	(0.0041)
Age dependency$_{t-1}$	0.2502	0.2674	0.2136	0.3222	0.2485	0.3543
	(0.2623)	(0.2624)	(0.2621)	(0.2559)	(0.2542)	(0.2446)
OECD dummy	−0.4018***	−0.4280***	−0.4086***	−0.4656***	−0.4061***	−0.4678***
	(0.0879)	(0.0827)	(0.0906)	(0.0833)	(0.0874)	(0.0834)
Year	0.0006	-7.5×10^{-6}	0.0004	0.0003	0.0008	0.0010
	(0.0025)	(0.0024)	(0.0024)	(0.0025)	(0.0024)	(0.0023)
Tropical dummy	−0.0370	0.0028	−0.0420	−0.0193	−0.0363	−0.0271
	(0.0727)	(0.0702)	(0.0729)	(0.0678)	(0.0717)	(0.0690)
Constant	−5.7763	−4.5248	−5.2684	−5.2282	−6.0975	−6.5975
	(4.9047)	(4.8056)	(4.8553)	(4.9592)	(4.7764)	(4.6447)
N	1,710	1,688	1,710	1688	1710	1688
Model Wald test	183***	196***	221***	299***	220***	224***

	3.1 aggregate conflict	3.2 aggregate conflict	3.3 conflict type	3.4 conflict type	3.5 conflict severity	3.6 conflict severity
Selection equation						
Number of conflicts$_t$	−0.0884*	−0.1340**	−0.0840*	−0.1398***	−0.0877*	−0.1290**
	(0.0505)	(0.0528)	(0.0473)	(0.0533)	(0.0504)	(0.0531)
Number of conflicts$_{t-1}$	−0.1901***	−0.1556**	−0.2135***	−0.1635***	−0.1923***	−0.1583***
	(0.0620)	(0.0627)	(0.0603)	(0.0606)	(0.0613)	(0.0615)
Constant	−0.3607***	−0.3657***	−0.3564***	−0.3628***	−0.3603***	−0.3662***
	(0.0940)	(0.0941)	(0.0937)	(0.0940)	(0.0939)	(0.0941)
ρ	−0.78	−0.78	−0.80	−0.81	−0.77	−0.77
Wald ($\rho = 0$)	13.41***	17.82***	18.62***	23.71***	12.94***	14.77***
Total N	5,196	5,174	5,196	5,174	5,196	5,174
Regression equation						
Conflict dummy$_{t-1}$	0.1349**	0.0480				
	(0.0538)	(0.0548)				
Conflict history$_{t-2}$		0.0022***				
		(0.0009)				
Interstate conflict dummy$_{t-1}$			0.1301***	−0.0152		
			(0.0504)	(0.0401)		
Intrastate conflict dummy$_{t-1}$			0.1551***	0.1125**		
			(0.0544)	(0.0551)		
Interstate conflict history$_{t-2}$				0.0065***		
				(0.0016)		
Intrastate conflict history$_{t-2}$				−0.0006		
				(0.0008)		
Minor conflict dummy$_{t-1}$					0.1069	0.0651
					(0.0664)	(0.0524)
Severe conflict dummy$_{t-1}$					0.1626***	0.0674
					(0.0483)	(0.0544)

(*Cont.*)

Table 3. (*Continued*)

	3.1 aggregate conflict	3.2 aggregate conflict	3.3 conflict type	3.4 conflict type	3.5 conflict severity	3.6 conflict severity
Minor conflict history$_{t-2}$						−0.0004
						(0.0009)
Severe conflict history$_{t-2}$						0.0036***
						(0.0011)
Control variables						
Gini coefficient$_{t-1}$	1.0016**	0.8543**	1.0050**	0.8177**	0.9997**	0.8434**
	(0.4107)	(0.4008)	(0.4005)	(0.3791)	(0.4049)	(0.3862)
Urbanization$_{t-1}$	−0.0040**	− 0.0039**	− 0.0041**	−0.0037**	−0.0040**	−0.0036**
	(0.0018)	(0.0017)	(0.0017)	(0.0015)	(0.0018)	(0.0016)
Urbanization rate$_{t-1}$	−0.0437***	− 0.0477***	−0.0442***	−0.0520***	−0.0437***	−0.0471***
	(0.0153)	(0.0147)	(0.0150)	(0.0137)	(0.0153)	(0.0147)
GDPPC growth$_{t-1}$	−0.0099***	−0.0102***	−0.0098***	−0.0106***	−0.0098***	−0.0097***
	(0.0025)	(0.0023)	(0.0024)	(0.0021)	(0.0024)	(0.0022)
Democracy$_{t-1}$	−0.0096**	−0.0093**	−0.0099**	−0.0088**	−0.0095**	−0.0086*
	(0.0045)	(0.0044)	(0.0044)	(0.0042)	(0.0045)	(0.0044)
Age dependency$_{t-1}$	0.7667***	0.7749***	0.7372***	0.8423***	0.7681***	0.8353***
	(0.2709)	(0.2591)	(0.2629)	(0.2278)	(0.2676)	(0.2471)
OECD dummy	−0.1954**	−0.2248***	−0.1998**	−0.2636***	−0.1966**	−0.2475***
	(0.0846)	(0.0830)	(0.0855)	(0.0822)	(0.0843)	(0.0828)
Year	−0.0029	−0.0035*	−0.0030	−0.0031	−0.0028	−0.0029
	(0.0022)	(0.0021)	(0.0022)	(0.0022)	(0.0022)	(0.0021)
Tropical dummy	0.1478**	0.1859***	0.1449**	0.1693***	0.1486**	0.1685***
	(0.0683)	(0.0671)	(0.0674)	(0.0635)	(0.0682)	(0.0647)
Constant	0.0791	1.3532	0.4331	0.5110	−0.0114	0.1522
	(4.3514)	(4.2121)	(4.3801)	(4.4518)	(4.3315)	(4.2426)
N	1,710	1,688	1,710	1,688	1,710	1,688
Model Wald test	359***	402***	397***	504***	416***	465***

rate. Tropical women experience a higher mortality rate than those in non-tropical regions. One possible reason is that tropical countries are less developed and tropical women are more exposed to infectious diseases and hard living conditions.

Next, we turn to discuss the effects of the conflict variables. The immediate effect of conflict involvement is quite significant for both men and women. Based on the coefficients in Models 2.1 and 3.1, the *conflict dummy* is associated with about 19%[4] and 14% increase in the adult mortality rate for males and females, respectively. Models 2.2 and 3.2 examine the immediate and lingering effects of conflict simultaneously. The significant immediate effect of conflict disappears after accounting for conflict history, whereas conflict history has significant effects for both men and women. Based on the coefficients in Models 2.2 and 3.2, a one-standard-deviation (one-SD) increase in conflict history is associated with about 7% increase in the adult mortality rate of males or females. Alternatively, the adult mortality rate increases about 22% if the conflict history variable rises from its average value in the dataset to its highest value. In addition, there is not much gender difference in terms of the magnitude and direction of the effect of aggregate conflict.

Models 3 and 4 in both tables examine the immediate and lingering effects of interstate and intrastate conflicts for males and females. Without controlling for conflict history, the immediate effects of both interstate and intrastate conflicts on adult mortality are statistically significant for both genders. Based on Model 2.3 or 3.3, *interstate conflict dummy* is associated with about 17% or 14% increase in the male or female mortality rate, while *intrastate conflict dummy* is correspondingly associated with about 22% or 17% increase. Simultaneously testing conflict involvement and conflict history produces different patterns for the two types of conflict. The immediate effect of interstate conflict becomes insignificant in the presence of interstate conflict history. The effect of *interstate conflict history* is significant and nearly identical between males and females. Based on Models 2.4 and 3.4, a one-SD increase in interstate conflict history is associated with about 8% increase in the male and the female adult mortality rate. Moreover, the adult mortality rate increases by 85% if interstate conflict history rises from its average value to its highest value. For intrastate conflict, its immediate effect appears more salient than its lingering effect. Controlling for intrastate conflict history, *intrastate conflict dummy* is associated with about 17% and 12% increase in the adult mortality rate for males and females, respectively (based on Models 2.4 and 3.4).

Based on Models 2.4 and 3.4, the Wald test statistics (3.38 and 4.66) for the difference in the immediate effect between intrastate and interstate conflict are statistically significant, for males and females. As expected, intrastate conflict has a larger immediate effect than interstate conflict. The test statistics (15.92 and 12.03) for the difference in the lingering effect between the two types of conflict are also statistically significant for both genders. Interstate conflict history is shown to have a larger effect than intrastate conflict history.

Models 5 and 6 in both tables test the effects of minor and severe conflicts. Severe conflict significantly raises adult mortality immediately, while the immediate effect of minor conflict is insignificant. Based on Models 2.5 and 3.5, *severe conflict dummy* increases adult mortality by about 29% for males and 18% for females. Once controlling for severe conflict history (Models 2.6 and 3.6), the severe conflict dummy still significantly affects the male mortality, but its effect on the female mortality becomes insignificant. Severe conflict increases the male mortality both immediately and over time after conflict. Based on Model 2.6, severe conflict causes a rise of about 16% in the adult male mortality immediately. A one-SD increase in severe conflict history raises the adult male mortality rate by about 9%. Based on Model 3.6, a one-SD increase in severe conflict history leads to a 7% increase in the adult female mortality rate. If severe conflict history rises from its average value in the dataset to its highest value for males and females, the adult mortality rate increases by 48% and 38%, respectively.[5,6]

5. Conclusion

This research investigates systematically the effect of armed conflict on the adult male and female mortality rates across countries over time. Our theoretical argument specifies how adult mortality is affected by aggregate conflict, interstate and intrastate conflicts, and conflict severity, both immediately and over time after conflict. Using a Heckman selection model to account for the conflict-induced data-selection bias, we find broad empirical support for our theoretical expectations between the two genders. To the best of our knowledge, our analysis is the first longitudinal analysis of the effect of military violence on mortality using a pooled time-series cross-sectional design.

Nevertheless, this work has several limitations. First, this research focuses on people aged 15 to 64. While this population group is an important marker of productivity and economic development, future research should seek to collect more detailed age-distribution data and evaluate our hypotheses for other age groups. Second, other population health indicators, such as cause-specific mortality, are also worth exploring. It would be particularly interesting if specific patterns are detected for specific causes of deaths. It is possible that death rates from infectious diseases are more sensitive to the immediate effect of conflict, whereas mortality from non-communicable diseases is more sensitive to the lingering effect. The development of diseases such as heart disease and cancer is more likely affected by behavioral factors and social stressors that contribute to morbidity over an extended period. Further analysis is warranted to test these disease-specific effects. Third, we theorized several mechanisms driving the effects of conflict on health, but we did not directly test these mechanisms. These issues need further research.

That being said, our analysis produces several interesting findings. First, this study confirms that armed conflict has both immediate and lingering effects on adult mortality. The lingering effect of conflict appears more robust than the immediate effect.

Second, intrastate conflict has a very large immediate effect on both male and female mortality rates, but it does not have strong or robust lingering effects for both genders. In contrast, interstate conflict has a robust lingering effect on both males and females. The immediate effect of civil conflict appears stronger than that of the interstate conflict, while the reverse applies to the lingering effect.

Third, the effect of conflict severity exhibits a clear pattern. For either gender, neither the immediate effect nor the lingering effect of minor conflict is statistically different from zero. In contrast, severe conflict affects male mortality both immediately and over time after conflict, while such conflict raises female mortality mainly in the long run.

Fourth, between the two genders, where armed conflict affects men, it almost always affects women. Men typically suffer higher immediate mortality than women, at least in intrastate conflict and severe conflict. This makes sense because it is mostly men who are engaged in actual fighting. Women, however, are affected adversely over time following conflict to about the same extent as men.

Finally, we find a strong selection bias in the mortality data, induced by military conflict. Adult mortality data are likely to be missing during the conflict year and the year immediately following the conflict onset. Statistical analysis that fails to correct for the data-selection bias may cause biased estimates and invalid inferences. Future pooled time-series cross-sectional analysis of mortality and conflict should adopt a similar empirical strategy.

These findings suggest several important implications for society at large. Military violence involves quantifiable and severe human costs. That military conflict can still kill, even after actual fighting stops, highlights the imperative for negotiating peace. Armed conflict not only directly kills military personnel and civilians but also raises human mortality by depleting health-promoting resources and introducing health-compromising hazards. Special attention should be devoted to changing the vulnerable position of women in military conflict, particularly over the long run. Peace, however short lived and feeble, saves human lives. Ideally, it is prolonged peace that is truly beneficial for improving human conditions. But in the absence of any feasible, final solution to armed conflict, simply preventing a contest from escalating into a severe conflict can produce noticeable gains in saved human lives. Adult mortality is much lower in minor conflict than in severe conflict. Hence, international efforts, such as the United Nations peacekeeping missions, by minimizing conflict escalation and creating even just an ephemeral ceasefire, have probably saved more lives than people generally recognize.

Notes

* Equal authorship implied. An earlier version of this article was presented at the IUSSP Seminar on the Demography of Conflict and Violence, held in Oslo, Norway, 8–11 November 2003 and at the annual meeting of the Population Association of America, April 2004, Boston, MA. We thank Helge Brunborg, Nils Petter Gleditsch, Michael Timberlake, Patrick Heuveline, Marwan Khawaja, William Seltzer, and several anonymous referees for helpful comments and suggestions. We thank Bruce Russett for help with data. We thank Young Hum Kim, Tatiana Vashchilko, and San Gon Nam for research assistance. We also thank the World Health Organization for providing the mortality data and Doris Ma Fat at WHO, Geneva for addressing our data questions. The authors are responsible for analyses, interpretations, and conclusions in the article. Data employed in this article can be obtained at http://www.prio.no/jpr/datasets. Statistical analysis is conducted using Stata8.

[1] See e.g., Li and Sacko (2002) for the effect of war on trade; Tilly (1992), Mitchell, Gates and Hegre (1999), Thompson (1996) for the effect on democracy; and Organski and Kugler (1980) for the effect on national economy.
[2] Reported as official statistics from national vital registration system, the age-specific mortality data are available in the WHO Mortality Database. We choose to use direct standardization to adjust for population age structure. This method is more commonly used when the age-specific rates are known (Preston, Heuveline and Guillot, 2000). We use, as the standard, the average age distribution of the countries and years available in the study combined (McGuire and Harrison, 1995).
[3] For robustness check, we re-estimate the model including year dummies in the selection equation. The statistical results are robust.
[4] The coefficient of the conflict dummy is 0.1699 in Model 2.1. Because we log transformed the dependent variable, the effect size of the conflict variable corresponds to $\exp(0.1699) = 1.1852$ for men. So the conflict dummy is associated with a rise of about 19% in the male mortality rate.
[5] One may be concerned that models including both the conflict dummy variable(s) and the conflict history variable(s) may be affected by high collinearity among them, causing certain conflict variables to be statistically insignificant. The Variance Inflation Factor (VIF) diagnostics for these models show that the average VIF statistic for any of the models never exceeds 2.5, and the VIF statistic for any single variable never exceeds 4.5. The values are much below the threshold value (10 for any single variable) that renders collinearity a concern (Weisberg, 1980).
[6] Acknowledging the fact that the death rate is an uncertain estimate of a parameter in a model for mortality, one could apply weighted least squares, using as weight the inverse of $\mathrm{Var}(\sum_i w_i M_{it}) = \sum_i (w_i)^2\ \mathrm{Var}(M_{it})$, where i is age group, t is time/country, w_i is the weight of age group i in the standard population, and M_{it} the death rate for age group i and time/country t. We did not pursue this alternative modeling approach and hence do not know how large its effects would have been.

Appendix A: Variable descriptive statistics

Variable	*N*	Mean	*SD*	Min.	Max.
Age-standardized male death rate	2,211	0.009	0.005	0.002	0.035
Age-standardized female death rate	2,211	0.005	0.002	0.001	0.024
Conflict dummy	5,441	0.2	0.4	0	1
Conflict history (%)	5,378	18.7	27.1	0	100
Interstate conflict dummy	5,441	0.1	0.2	0	1
Intrastate conflict dummy	5,441	0.2	0.4	0	1
Interstate conflict history (%)	5,378	5.6	11.3	0	100
Intrastate conflict history (%)	5,378	13.0	23.0	0	100
Minor conflict dummy	5,441	0.1	0.3	0	1
Severe conflict dummy	5,441	0.1	0.3	0	1
Minor conflict history (%)	5,378	8.2	15.7	0	100
Severe conflict history (%)	5,378	10.5	18.8	0	100
Gini coefficient	6,878	0.4	0.1	0.18	0.6
Urbanization	6,723	44.3	24.0	0	100
Urbanization growth rate	6,690	3.7	2.7	−44.2	23.4
GDPPC growth	5,153	1.7	6.4	−52.1	79.7
Democracy	5,133	−0.4	7.6	−10	10
Age dependency	6,201	0.8	0.2	0.4	1.2
OECD	6,878	0.1	0.3	0	1
Year	6,878	1979	11.0	1961	1998
Tropical dummy	6,878	0.5	0.5	0	1
Number of conflicts	5,500	0.3	0.8	0	8

Appendix B: Lists of countries

List A based on available WHO data		List B for mortality regression	
Albania	Kuwait	Albania	Mexico
Antigua-Barbuda	Kyrgyz Republic	Argentina	Moldova
Argentina	Latvia	Armenia	Netherlands
Armenia	Lithuania	Australia	New Zealand
Australia	Luxembourg	Austria	Nicaragua
Austria	Macedonia	Azerbaijan	Norway
Azerbaijan	Malta	Bahrain	Panama
Bahamas	Mauritius	Belarus	Papua New Guinea
Bahrain	Mexico	Belgium	Paraguay
Barbados	Moldova	Brazil	Peru
Belarus	Netherlands	Bulgaria	Philippines
Belgium	New Zealand	Canada	Poland
Belize	Nicaragua	Chile	Portugal
Bosnia and Herz.	Norway	China	Romania
Brazil	Panama	Colombia	Russia
Bulgaria	Pupua New Guinea	Costa Rica	Singapore
Canada	Paraguay	Croatia	Slovakia
Chile	Peru	Cuba	Slovenia
China	Philippines	Czech Republic	Spain
Colombia	Poland	Denmark	Sri Lanka
Costa Rica	Portugal	Dominican Republic	Sweden
Croatia	Romania	Ecuador	Switzerland
Cuba	Russia	Egypt	Syria
Czech Republic	Sao Tome-Principe	El Salvador	Tajikistan
Denmark	Seychelles	Estonia	Thailand
Dominica	Singapore	Fiji	Trinidad and Tobago
Dominican Republic	Slovakia	Finland	Turkmenistan
Ecuador	Slovenia	France	Ukraine
Egypt	Spain	Georgia	United Kingdom
El Salvador	Sri Lanka	Germany	United States
Estonia	St. Kitts-Nevis	Greece	Uruguay
Fiji	St. Lucia	Guatemala	Uzbekistan
Finland	St. Vincent	Guyana	Venezuela
France	Surinam	Honduras	
Georgia	Sweden	Hungary	
Germany	Switzerland	Iceland	
Greece	Syria	Ireland	
Grenada	Tajikistan	Israel	

(Cont.)

Appendix B: *(Continued)*

List A based on available WHO data		List B for mortality regression
Guatemala	Thailand	Italy
Guyana	Trinidad and Tobago	Jamaica
Honduras	Turkmenistan	Japan
Hungary	Ukraine	Jordan
Iceland	United Kingdom	Kazakhstan
Ireland	United States	Korea, South
Israel	Uruguay	Kuwait
Italy	Uzbekistan	Kyrgyz Republic
Jamaica	Venezuela	Latvia
Japan	Yugoslavia	Lithuania
Jordan		Luxembourg
Kazakhstan		Macedonia
Korea, South		Mauritius

References

American Psychiatric Association, 1994. *Diagnostic and Statistical Manual of Mental Disorders.* Washington, DC.

Berkman, Lisa F., Thomas Glass, Ian Brissette and Teresa E. Seeman, 2000. "From social integration to health: Durkheim in the new millennium", *Social Science and Medicine* 51(6): 843–857.

Brenner, Harvey M., 1973. *Mental Illness and the Economy.* Cambridge, MA: Harvard University Press.

Brenner, Harvey M., 1987a. "Economic change, Alcohol consumption and disease mortality in nine industrialized countries", *Social Science and Medicine* 25(2): 119-132.

Brenner, Harvey M., 1987b. "Relation of economic change to Swedish health and social well-being, 1950–1980", *Social Science and Medicine* 25(2): 183–196.

Brenner, Harvey M. and Annie Mooney, 1983. "Unemployment and health in the context of economic change", *Social Science and Medicine* 17(16): 1125–1138.

Brunner, Eric and Michael Marmot, 1999. "Social organization, stress, and health", in Michael Marmot and Richard G. Wilkinson (eds), *Social Determinants of Health.* New York: Oxford University Press (17–43).

Chan, Steve, 1986. "Military expenditures and economic performance", *World Military Expenditures and Arms Transfers.* Washington, DC: Arms Control and Disarmament Agency (29–38).

Cockerham, William C., 2003. *Medical Sociology.* Upper saddle river, NJ: Prentice Hall.

Deininger, Klaus and Lyn Squire, 1996. "A new data set measuring income inequality", *World Bank Economic Review* 10(3): 565–591.

Durkheim, Emile, 1951. *Suicide.* New York: Free Press.

Easterly, William, 1999. "Life during growth", *Journal of Economic Growth* 43(3): 239–275.

Ghobarah, Hazem A., Paul Huth and Bruce Russett, 2003. "Civil wars kill and maim people—long after the ahooting stops", *American Political Science Review* 97(2): 189–202.

Gleditsch, Nils Petter; Peter Wallensteen, Mikael Eriksson, Margareta Sollenberg and Håvard Strand, 2002. "Armed conflict 1946–2001: A new dataset", *Journal of Peace Research* 39(5): 615–637.

Greene, William H., 2003. *Econometric Analysis.* Upper Saddle River, NJ: Prentice Hall.

Heckman, James J., 1979. "Sample selection bias as a specification error", *Econometrica* 47(1): 153–162.

Heijdra, Ben J. and Jenny E. Ligthart, 1997. "Keynesian multipliers, direct crowding out, and the optimal provision of public goods", *Journal of Macroeconomics* 19(4): 475–492.

Higgins, Matthew and Jeffrey G. Williamson, 1999. *Explaining Inequality the World Round: Cohort Size, Kuznets Curves, and Trade Openness.* Cambridge, MA: National Bureau of Economic Research.

Kaplan, George A., Elsie R. Pamuk, John W. Lynch, Richard D. Cohen and Jennifer L. Balfour, 1996. "Inequality in income and mortality in the United States: Analysis of mortality and potential pathways", *British Medical Journal* 312(7307): 999–1003.

Kawachi, Ichiro and Bruce P. Kennedy, 1997. "Health and social cohesion: Why care about income inequality?", *British Medical Journal* 314(7086): 1037–1040.

Kawachi, Ichiro and Bruce P. Kennedy, 1999. "Income inequality and health: Pathways and mechanisms", *Health Services Research* 34(1 Part II): 215–227.

Keynes, John M., 1963. *Essays in Persuasion.* New York: Norton.

Knight, Malcolm, Norman Loayza and Delano Villanueva, 1996. "The peace dividend: Military expenditure cuts and economic growth", *IMF Staff Papers* 43: 1–37.

Kunovich, Robert M. and Randy Hodson, 1999. "Civil war, social integration and mental health in Croatia", *Journal of Health and Social Behavior* 40(4): 323–343.

Li, Quan and David Sacko, 2002. "The (IR) relevance of interstate militarized disputes to International Trade", *International Studies Quarterly* 46(1): 11–44.

Link, Bruce G. and Jo Phelan, 1995. "Social conditions as fundamental causes of disease", *Journal of Health and Social Behavior* (Extra): 80–95.

McGuire, Tim and Joel A. Harrison, 1995. "sbe11: Direct standardization", *Stata Technical Bulletin* 21: 5–9. Reprinted in *Stata Technical Bulletin Reprints* 4: 88–94.

Marshall, Monty G. and Keith Jaggers, 2000. "Polity IV project: Political regime characteristics and transitions, 1800–2000 dataset users manual", data available at http://www.bsos.umd.edu/cidcm/inscr/polity/index.htm#data.

Mirowsky, John, Catherine E. Ross and John Reynolds, 2000. "Links between social status and health status", in Chloe E. Bird, Peter Conrad and Allen M. Fremont (eds), *Handbook of Medical Sociology.* Upper Saddle River, NJ: Prentice Hall (47–67).

Mitchell, Sara McLaughlin, Scott Gates and Håvard Hegre, 1999. "Evolution in democracy-war dynamics", *Journal of Conflict Resolution* 43(6): 771–792.

Montgomery, Scott M., Derek G. Cook, Mel. J. Bartley and Michael E. J. Wadsworth, 1999. "Unemployment in young men pre-dates symptoms of depression and anxiety resulting in medical consultation", *International Journal of Epidemiology* 28(1): 95–100.

Morris, Joan K., Derek G. Cook and Gerald A. Shaper, 1994. "Loss of employment and mortality", *British Medical Journal* 308(6937): 1135–1139.

Moser, Kath A., Jeffrey A. Fox and D. R. Jones, 1984. "Unemployment and mortality in the OPCS longitudinal study", *Lancet* 324(8415): 1324–1329.

Murray, Christopher J. L., Gary King, Alan D. Lopez, Niels Tomijima and Etienne G. Krug, 2002. "Armed conflict as a public health problem", *British Medical Journal* 324(7333): 346–349.

Omran, Abdel R., 1971. "The epidemiologic transition: A theory of the epidemiology of population change", *Milbank Quarterly* 49(4): 509–538.

Organski, A. F. K. and Jacek Kugler, 1980. *The War Ledger.* Chicago, IL: University of Chicago Press.

Preston, Samuel H., Patrick Heuveline and Michel Guillot, 2000. *Demography: Measuring and Modeling Population Processes.* Oxford: Blackwell.

Preti, Antonio and Paola Miotto, 1999. "Suicide and unemployment in Italy, 1982–1994", *Journal of Epidemiology and Community Health* 53(11): 694–701.

Pritchard, Colin, 1990. "Suicide, unemployment and gender variations in the western world 1964–1986. Are women in Anglophone countries protected from suicide?", *Social Psychiatry and Psychiatric Epidemiology* 25(2): 73–80.

Przeworski, Adam; Michael Alvarez, Jose Antonio Cheibub and Fernando Limongi, 2000. *Democracy and Development: Political Institutions and Well-Being in the World, 1950–1990.* Cambridge: Cambridge University Press.

Reuveny, Rafael and Quan Li, 2003. "Economic openness, democracy and income inequality: An empirical analysis", *Comparative Political Studies* 36(5): 575–601.

Rogers, William H., 1993. "Regression standard errors in clustered samples", *Stata Technical Bulletin* 13: 19–23.

Thompson, William R., 1996. "Democracy and peace: Putting the cart before the horse?", *International Organization* 50(1): 141–174.

Tilly, Charles, 1992. *Coercion, Capital and European States, AD 990–1990.* Cambridge: Blackwell.

Warr, Peter B., 1984. "Job loss, unemployment and psychological well-being", in Vernon L. Allen and Evert van de Vliert (eds), *Role Transitions.* New York: Plenum (263–285).

Weisberg, Sanford, 1980. *Applied Linear Regression.* New York: Wiley.

WHO, 2004. *The World Health Organization's Mortality Database*, data available at http://www.ciesin.org/IC/who/MortalityDatabase. html.

Wilkinson, Richard G., 1992. "Income distribution and life expectancy", *British Medical Journal* 304(6820): 165–168.

Wilkinson, Richard G., 1996. *Unhealthy Societies: The Afflictions of Inequality.* London: Routledge.

Williams, Rick L., 2000. "A note on robust variance estimation for cluster-correlated data", *Biometrics* 56(2): 645–646.

World Bank, 2002. *World Development Indicators 2002 CD-ROM.* Washington, DC.

PART III. COUNTING VICTIMS FOR THE PROSECUTION OF WAR CRIMES

CHAPTER 8. INTERNATIONAL HUMANITARIAN LAW AND COMBAT CASUALTIES

WILLIAM J. FENRICK
Office of the Prosecutor (OTP), International Criminal Tribunal for the Former Yugoslavia (ICTY), The Hague, The Netherlands

Abstract. The purpose of the article is to provide an overview of the law regulating combat in order to assist in determining whether casualties inflicted in combat should be classified as victims of war or victims of war crimes. The boundaries and the content of International Humanitarian Law are indicated. A brief statement of the law regulating combat is given. The concepts of military objective and of proportionality are analyzed. The scope of an unlawful attack is addressed as is the relationship between unlawful attack offences and other offences in International Humanitarian Law. The article concludes with a discussion of when combat casualties are war crimes victims.

1. Introduction

War inevitably involves death and destruction. The only way to avoid death and destruction in war is to avoid war. The fundamental purpose of International Humanitarian Law (IHL) is to reduce net human suffering and net damage to civilian objects in armed conflict. It is essential to develop legal standards for application in armed conflict which take account of the realities of armed conflict, particularly the military realities, and which endeavour to, at best, stretch the envelope of good military practice. Setting legal standards which are impossibly high because they ignore what is militarily practicable will bring the law into disrepute. It will increase human suffering in armed conflict because military personnel, if they believe they will inevitably violate the law even if they wish to comply with it, will simply ignore legal constraints. The inevitable and unfortunate fact is that there are both lawful and unlawful casualties in armed conflict.

The purpose of this article is to provide a legal framework which will assist in determining into which category particular victims of war fall when they are killed or injured as a result of combat activity. Regrettably, it is not practicable to provide a usable review of all aspects of international humanitarian law which are relevant to demographers within the confines of this article.

IHL has been defined by the International Committee of the Red Cross (ICRC) to mean "international rules, established by treaties or custom, which are specifically intended to solve humanitarian problems directly arising from international

This chapter was previously published in *European Journal of Population*, vol. 21, no. 2–3, 2005, pp. 167–186.

Helge Brunborg et al. (eds.), The Demography of Armed Conflict, 179–196.

or non-international armed conflicts and which, for humanitarian reasons, limit the right of Parties to a conflict to use the methods and means of warfare of their choice or protect persons and property that are, or may be, affected by conflict" (ICRC Commentary on Additional Protocols of 1977; hereafter "ICRC Commentary"; in Sandoz et al. (eds), 1987).[2] For the purposes of this article, IHL will be regarded as also including crimes against humanity and genocide. Although crimes against humanity and genocide, which may be regarded as the supreme crime against humanity, may be committed in times of peace as well as during armed conflict, they are particularly likely to occur during armed conflict. There will be no further discussion of crimes against humanity, in particular persecution/ethnic cleansing, or of genocide here because this article focuses exclusively on crimes in combat. For the reasons given in Section 7 below, for all practical purposes, all persons who may be regarded as the victims of serious violations of IHL occurring in combat (including victims of crimes against humanity or of genocide) must first be classified as victims of an unlawful attack. If they are victims of an unlawful attack, they may, depending on whether they meet other criteria, also be regarded as victims of other offences such as crimes against humanity or genocide. If there is no unlawful attack as a condition precedent, however, no offence has been committed.

IHL is a body of law which has been developed with military input. As a result, it is not acceptable for military personnel to suggest that they are entitled to violate the law because of military necessity or because of imperative military requirements. Military necessity is not an excuse for violation of the law. At the present time the legally relevant scope of military necessity is limited to:

(i) areas of law which are not adequately addressed in existing treaty law—at present such areas of law are relatively limited although earlier these areas were much broader. For example, during World War II, there was virtually no treaty law concerning the conduct of aerial bombardment. When and where such gaps continue to exist, military necessity must always be balanced against humanitarian imperatives in a crude proportionality equation and it is only when military necessity outweighs humanitarian imperatives that an action is permissible;
(ii) certain specific provisions in treaties which explicitly allow certain activities, for example the destruction of certain types of property when it is justified by military necessity.

2. Content of IHL

The body of IHL applicable to international armed conflicts, that is, conflicts in which there are one or more states involved on each side, is much more elaborate than the body of IHL applicable to internal armed conflicts basically because, for the most part, international law is developed by the representatives of states and states have, traditionally, been much more willing to accept limitations on how they engage in conflict with other states and much less willing to accept external limitations on how they treat rebel forces on their own territory. The main treaties applicable to international armed conflict are listed below. Detailed references are included in the list "Treaties and Treaty-like Instruments of International Law" at the end of this article. The text of all the more important treaties is also available from Roberts and Guelff (2000):

- Hague Convention IV (Laws and Customs of War on Land) of 1907;
- Geneva Convention I (Wounded and Sick) of 1949;
- Geneva Convention II (Maritime) of 1949;
- Geneva Convention III (Prisoner of War) of 1949;
- Geneva Convention IV (Civilians) of 1949;
- Additional Protocol I (AP1) of 1977.

Virtually all states are parties to (legally bound by) all of these treaties except for AP1. Most states are also parties to AP1 but some major states, including the USA, are not. All states are also bound by customary international law, and many of the provisions of AP1, including the attack provisions, are regarded as part of customary law.

The treaty law provisions applicable to internal armed conflict are much more skeletal, basically they consist of Article 3 common to the Geneva Conventions and Additional Protocol II (AP2) of 1977. Common Article 3 is regarded as a mini-version of the Geneva Conventions, and is considered to embody minimum standards applicable in all armed conflicts. AP2 is a truncated version of AP1 and it does not apply to all internal conflicts. There is also a body of customary law applicable to internal conflicts but its content and boundaries are not well defined. Since genocide and crimes against humanity may, as a matter of general international law, occur independent of peace or war, they may be committed in any type of conflict.

The Appeals Chamber of the International Criminal Tribunal for the Former Yugoslavia (ICTY), in the "*Tadić* Jurisdiction Decision" (*Prosecutor v. Duško Tadić*, 1995), its first decision, held that there was a body of customary international law which applied to all conflicts. The ICTY Office of the Prosecutor (OTP) has relied on that decision to argue insofar as it is practicable that the law is substantially similar for both international and internal conflicts, particularly in relation to combat activities such as lawful or unlawful attacks. This approach has been adopted for both reasons of principle (it is a good idea to make both bodies of law more similar) and practicality (it is awkward and very time-consuming to devote time to proving the nature of the conflict in every case). It has done so primarily by focusing on a single sentence which is common to both AP1 (Article 51(2); AP1 of 1977) and AP2 (Article 13(2), AP2 of 1977) as the basis for its unlawful attacks on civilians charges. That sentence is "The civilian population as such, as well as individual civilians, shall not be the object of attack." The OTP has argued, successfully to date, that the single sentence encapsulates the legal obligation and that other provisions in AP1 which elaborate upon that sentence can also be relied upon, at the least as best practice standards, applicable to all conflicts. This approach will be elaborated upon later in this article. Whether or not the common core of customary law approach will be followed elsewhere remains to be seen. It must be observed that the ICTY can adopt this approach because not all of its offences are enumerated in the Statute and because it can make substantial use of customary law. That option is not open to the International Criminal Court (ICC) because all of its offences are enumerated in the Statute.

3. Law for the legally sensitive combat commander

The principle of distinction is the basic principle which underlies all of IHL applicable to combat situations, with the exception of the rules which prohibit or limit the use of particular weapons or methods of war. This principle is contained in AP1 Article 48:

> In order to ensure respect for and protection of the civilian population and civilian objects, the Parties to the conflict shall at all times distinguish between the civilian population and combatants and between civilian objects and military objectives and accordingly shall direct their operations only against military objectives.

The remainder of the law is essentially an amplification of this principle. The resume of legal obligations related to combat which follows is rooted primarily in AP1 and therefore, strictly speaking, applies only to the military forces of a country which is party to AP1 and engaged in an international conflict. AP1 also reflects best practices which are applicable to all armed forces engaged in an armed conflict, regardless of classification:

- Weapons and methods of war which are prohibited shall not be used. When there are restrictions which apply to particular weapons and methods of war, these restrictions are complied with.
- All military operations, including attacks, must be directed against military objectives (Article 48, AP1 of 1977).
- When attacks are launched against military objectives, precautions must be taken to identify and locate the objective correctly and to ensure it will be at the aim point when the projectile arrives, to identify and assess the risk to civilian persons and objects in the vicinity of the aim point, and to minimize incidental civilian casualties and damage to civilian objects (Article 57, AP1 of 1977).
- If it is apparent before an attack is launched that the risk to civilian persons or objects is excessive, the attack should not be launched, if it becomes so apparent after the attack is launched, it should be aborted (*Ibid.*).
- Indiscriminate attacks, that is, attacks which are not or cannot be directed at specific military objectives are prohibited (Article 51(4), AP1 of 1977).

- As a subset of indiscriminate attacks, attacks directed against military objectives which may be expected to cause excessive or disproportionate injury or death to civilians or to civilian objects in relation to the concrete and direct military advantage anticipated from the attack are prohibited (Article 51(5)(b), AP1 of 1977).
- When a choice is possible between several military objectives for obtaining a similar military advantage, the objective to be selected shall be that on which the attack may be expected to cause the least injury to civilian lives or damage to civilian objects (Article 57(3), AP1 of 1977).
- Defending forces have an obligation not to use the presence or movements of the civilian to shield military objectives from attacks or to shield, favour or impede military operations. Whether or not the defending force complies with its obligations, the attacking force is still required to comply with all of its obligations including the requirement to comply with the principle proportionality (Article 57(7) and (8), AP1 of 1977).

4. What is a military objective?

Military objectives may be people or things. In so far as people are concerned, military objectives are combatants and civilians directly participating in hostilities. Combatants are members of the armed forces of a Party to a conflict other than medical personnel and chaplains (Article 43(2), AP1 of 1977). Combatants have the right to participate directly in hostilities (shoot at the enemy) at any time and, for that reason, they may also be attacked at any time, sleeping, eating, marching to the rear, unless they have surrendered or are injured and have ceased to take part in hostilities. Wounded combatants who continue to fight may be lawfully attacked. Although, strictly speaking, the concept of combatant status is legally relevant only during international armed conflicts, as is the related concept of prisoner of war status, it is the opinion of the author, which is probably widely agreed, that the concept is applicable by analogy to internal conflict. As a result, the members of the armed forces of all parties to an internal conflict (other than medical personnel and chaplains) would also be subject to lawful attack at all times unless they have surrendered or are injured and have ceased to take part in hostilities.

The concept of civilians directly participating in hostilities is much more contentious and also much more complicated. Armed forces of many western states in particular have begun to outsource to meet many of their requirements so that private contractors may provide both specialist services (such as technical representatives for the maintenance of complicated weapons systems) and more routine services (logistical support and provision of food services) which had previously been provided by military personnel. After a fashion, this is a return to the beginning of the modern period when specialists, even artillery personnel, were civilians. Further, quite clearly, some key civilian personnel, defence scientists for example, may be much more important to the war effort than most military personnel. In the territory of the former Yugoslavia an additional complicating factor was the fact that, at least in the early stages, new states were emerging and these were required to create new armed forces as the conflict went on. Although the matter is not beyond dispute, it is submitted that the concept of civilians participating directly in hostilities should be narrowly construed. Hostile acts "should be understood to be acts which by their nature and purpose are intended to cause actual harm to the personnel and equipment of the armed forces" (ICRC Commentary, para 1942; in Sandoz et al. (eds), 1987). "Direct participation in hostilities implies a direct causal relationship between the activity engaged in and harm done to the enemy at the time and place where the activity takes place" (*Ibid.*, para 1679). "There should be a clear distinction between direct participation in hostilities and participation in the war effort. The latter is often required from the population as a whole to various degrees. Without such a distinction the efforts made to reaffirm and develop international humanitarian law could become meaningless" (*Ibid.*, para, 1945). Civilians are military objectives only while they are taking a direct part in hostilities, not before or after. When making targeting decisions, in case of doubt whether a person is a civilian, that person shall be considered to be a civilian. The above comments reflect customary law and are codified in AP1 (Articles 43(1), 50(1), 51(2) and (3), AP1 of 1977). Essentially the same standard applies to internal conflicts as a result of AP2 (Article 13, AP2 of 1977) and Article 3 common to the four Geneva Conventions of 1949, although the latter uses the expression "persons taking no active part in hostilities" which, it is submitted, is synonymous with taking no direct part in hostilities.

Article 52(2) of AP1 states in part:

> In so far as objects are concerned, military objectives are limited to those objects which by their nature, location, purpose or use make an effective contribution to military action and whose total or partial destruction, capture or neutralization, in the circumstances ruling at the time, offers a definite military advantage.

The following paragraph goes on to indicate that in case of doubt whether an object which is normally dedicated to civilian purposes is being used to make an effective contribution, it shall be presumed not to be so used. The definition has two elements:

(a) the nature, location, purpose or use of the object must make an effective contribution to military action, and
(b) the total or partial destruction, capture or neutralization of the object must offer a definite military advantage in the circumstances ruling at the time.

States which have ratified AP1 and most other states would accept the AP1 definition of military objective as a reasonably accurate definition applicable as a matter of customary law to all conflicts. The definition is supposed to provide a means whereby informed objective observers (and decision makers in a conflict) can determine whether or not a particular object constitutes a military objective. It accomplishes this purpose in simple cases. Everyone will agree that a munitions factory is a military objective and an unoccupied church is a civilian object. When the definition is applied to dual-use objects which have some civilian uses and some actual or potential military uses (communications systems, transportation systems, petrochemical complexes, manufacturing plants of some types), opinions may differ. The application of the definition to particular objects may also differ depending on the scope and objectives of the conflict. Further, the scope and objectives of the conflict may change during the conflict. Although representatives of the United States Government have at times indicated the AP1 definition of military objective does reflect customary law, it should be noted that the United States adopted a substantially broader definition of military objective:

> "Military objectives" are those potential targets during an armed conflict which by their nature, location, purpose, or use, effectively contribute to the opposing force's war-fighting or war-sustaining capability and whose total or partial destruction, capture, or neutralization would constitute a military advantage to the attacker under the circumstances at the times of the attack (Article 5D, Military Commission Instruction of 30 April 2003; see US Department of Defence, 2003).

Certainly the reference to "war-sustaining capability" appears to be an extension beyond the AP1 definition.

A number of issues remain unresolved in connection with the military objective issue, including:

(1) Should more or fewer things be regarded as military objectives by the intervening side during a humanitarian intervention or by the "good" side during an international armed conflict?[3]
(2) Is civilian morale a military objective?[4]
(3) Is the political leadership a legitimate target?[5]

To a considerable extent, the debate concerning what should constitute military objective has yet to be joined. Fortunately for us at the ICTY, since we have been concerned primarily with ground combat, identification of military objectives has normally been a relatively simple task since the objectives are usually troop concentrations or weapons emplacements.[6]

5. Proportionality

The concept of proportionality is linked to the principle of distinction which is the fundamental legal principle underlying combat activities. Although the concept has been a part of IHL for a long time, it does not appear in treaty texts until the development of AP1 in 1974–1977. The concept is important because military objectives, civilians, and civilian objectives are too frequently located in the same area. Civilians and civilian objects do not have absolute immunity from the effects of combat. Attacks directed against military objectives are lawful unless they cause disproportionate civilian losses. It is not practicable to determine whether civilian casualties are lawful or unlawful until there have been prior determinations of whether the attack which caused the civilian casualties was directed against a military objective and whether, if the answer was yes, disproportionate civilian casualties were anticipated or resulted. The word proportionality is not used in AP1 but it is implicitly contained in several provisions of AP1 (Articles 51(5)(b), 57(2)(a)(iii), 57(2)(b) and 85(3)(c), AP1 of 1977), all of which refer to a prohibition on attacks which

> "may be expected to cause incidental loss of civilian life, injury to civilians, damage to civilian objects, or a combination thereof, which would be *excessive* in relation to the concrete and direct military advantage anticipated (Articles 51(5)(b), 57(2)(a)(iii) and 57(2)(b), AP1 of 1977; emphasis added; also, see Article 85(3)(c), AP1 of 1977)."

"Excessive", considered in context, is synonymous with "disproportionate".[7] In the context of the law related to unlawful attacks, proportionality is relevant simply for assessing the relative values of two essentially unlike concepts, notions or entities, military advantage and civilian losses. Since the relative values are of essentially unlike concepts, precise valuation is difficult. It is not a simple number crunching exercise. The best one can say is that if similar things are being measured, such as human lives, usually each life must be given a similar value.

Proportionality is not a legally relevant concept for other measurements of combat activity. The word "proportionality" may be used in various other contexts, such as disproportionate use of force when one side has or uses more military resources in a particular situation. Use of the expression may be factually accurate but it is also legally irrelevant. There is nothing unlawful about using more or better equipment or troops than an opponent. Armed conflict is not a sporting contest. The rules must be obeyed but there is no legal requirement to have a level playing field. Military forces strive to have a technological advantage and to inflict more combatant casualties than the other side. Measuring own side casualties against civilian losses on the other side is of no legal significance. Compliance or non-compliance with weapon expenditure norms is equally irrelevant. If military doctrine prescribes the use of X number of projectiles of a certain type to neutralize a military objective to Y extent, whether or not an attacker uses all the projectiles authorized by doctrine to neutralize the objective may be interesting from the point of view of doctrine. It is of no significance, however, when attempting to assess whether or not civilian losses are disproportionate relative to military advantage.

Although, unfortunately, it is not possible to provide simple answers concerning the application of the concept of proportionality to concrete military situations because of a lack of examples in legal decisions or legal literature, the following provides a rough frame of reference. First, who decides whether an action is disproportionate? One of the ICTY Trial Chambers held in the *Galić* case that the decision maker should be regarded as "a reasonably well-informed person in the circumstances of the actual perpetrator, making reasonable use of the information available to him or her" (*Prosecutor v. Stanislav Galić* (2003), para 58). Second, what is compared? The comparison is between the *anticipated* concrete and direct military advantage and the *anticipated* incidental loss of civilian life, injury to civilians, damage to civilian objects, or a combination thereof. The actual results of the attack may assist in inferring the intent of the attacker as he or she launched the attack but what counts is what was in the mind of the decision maker when the attack was launched. Third, what is the standard? The attack is prohibited if it is anticipated it will result in *excessive* civilian losses. Fourth, what is the scope of "concrete and direct military advantage anticipated"? The *Galić* Trial Chamber referred to several sources in addressing this point (*Prosecutor v. Stanislav Galić* (2003), para 58, at footnote 106):

> The *travaux préparatoires* of Additional Protocol I indicate that the expression "concrete and direct" was intended to show that the advantage must be "substantial and relatively close" and that "advantages which are hardly perceptible and those which would only appear in the long term should be disregarded" (ICRC Commentary, para 2209). The Commentary explains that "a military advantage can only consist in ground gained or in annihilating or in weakening the enemy armed forces" (ICRC Commentary, para 2218).

The military advantage gained by a successful attack on a military objective may vary somewhat depending on circumstances. For example, a successful attack on a military objective such as an artillery emplacement always gives the attacker a military advantage but the extent of the direct and concrete direct military advantage gained may vary depending on factors such as location of the objective and its current or potential use. It should also be noted that all civilians who are not participating directly in hostilities should be included in the civilian losses side of the equation. Civilians, who work in war factories, are still civilians. So are civilians who place themselves or are placed by others in the close vicinity of military objectives.

Fifth, what scale should be used in assessing proportionality? Should proportionality be assessed on the basis of an attack on a single military objective, on the basis of a battle, a campaign or a war? Several states made statements of understanding concerning the application of "military advantage" considered in the context of Article 51, 52, and 57 (see, for example, Statements of Interpretation by Belgium, Canada, Germany, Italy, Netherlands, New Zealand, Switzerland, and the United Kingdom in Roberts and Guelff (2000), pp. 499–512). The Statement by Canada is representative:

> "It is the understanding of the Government of Canada in relation to Article 51(5)(b), 52(2), and (57(2)(a)(iii) that the military advantage anticipated from an attack is intended to refer to the advantage anticipated from the attack considered as a whole and not from isolated or particular parts of the attack" (*Ibid.*, p. 503).

These Statements of Understanding notwithstanding, it is suggested that proportionality can be determined using a variety of scales ranging from the tactical (military objective by military objective) level to a much bigger scale as long as the more general context is also taken into account. The military objective scale is commonly used in modern state practice, particularly in assessing the legitimacy of aerial attacks (see Baker (2002), pp. 7–18; also, see the various incident studies referred to in the OTP Report on NATO). It was also used by the *Galić* Trial Chamber (*Prosecutor v. Galić* (2003), para 387).

No tribunal to date has ever explicitly determined in a well articulated manner in a close case that disproportionate damage was caused during an attack on a military objective. The *Galić* Trial Chamber was, however, compelled to grapple with the issue in its discussion of one shelling incident, the shelling of the Dobrinje football tournament on 1 June 1993. In that incident, about 200 spectators, including women and children, were watching a football game in the corner of a parking lot which was bounded on three sides by six-storey apartment blocks and on the fourth by a hill. Two shells exploded in the parking lot killing between 12 and 16 persons and wounding between 80 and 140 persons. The players and many of the spectators were military personnel and, as such, military objectives. The Commander of the Army of Bosnia and Herzegovina (ABiH) 5th Motorized Dobrinja Brigade, to which the soldiers belonged, filed a report indicating there were 11 killed and 87 wounded (6 combatants killed and 55 wounded, 5 civilians killed and 32 wounded; *Ibid.*, para 376). Although assessing proportionality is not a simple exercise in number crunching, it would be difficult to conclude that, in this incident, there were disproportionate civilian casualties unless one makes the arbitrary determination that civilian lives count for more than military lives. The majority of the chamber finessed a requirement to assess the proportionality of the result by focusing on the *mens rea*[8] of the perpetrators and on the fact that civilian casualties were caused.

> "... Although the number of soldiers present at the game was significant, an attack on a crowd of approximately 200 people, including numerous children, would clearly be expected to cause incidental loss of life and injuries to civilians excessive in relation to the direct and concrete military advantage anticipated ..." (*Prosecutor v. Stanislav Galić* (2003), para. 387).

6. What is an unlawful attack

The ICTY OTP has prosecuted unlawful attack charges in five cases to date. Trial judgements have been rendered in *Blaškić, Kordić/Čerkez*, and *Galić*. A judgement is awaited in *Strugar* and a trial is currently underway *in Milošević. Blaskić* and *Kordić/Čerkez* were trials involving Bosnian-Croat accused and incidents in the Lašva River Valley in Bosnia, in particular, the Ahmići massacre, in which many of the inhabitants of a small Bosnian village were killed when it was overrun by Bosnian-Croat forces. Galić was the commander of Bosnian-Serb forces involved in a protracted shelling and sniping campaign against the inhabitants of Sarajevo. Strugar was the commander of Yugoslav National Army Forces engaged in what the prosecution alleges was the unlawful shelling of the Old Town of Dubrovnik on 6 December 1991. Milošević is charged with responsibility for a wide range of offences, including offences related to what happened in Sarajevo and in Dubrovnik. By far the most elaborate and thoughtful judicial decision ever rendered in connection with unlawful attacks to date is the *Galić* decision.

As opposed to the ICC Statute, the ICTY Statute does not list unlawful attacks against civilians as enumerated offences. As a result, we at the ICTY must charge unlawful attacks as unenumerated offences under Article 3. Further, since the *Tadic* Jurisdiction Appeal Decision has provided us with the basis for arguing that certain offences have a substantially similar legal content in both international and internal conflicts, we have developed and defended unlawful attack charges which are common to all conflicts. To give our most recent example, in the *Strugar* case, where a judgement is pending, our charges include:

> **Count 3**: Attacks on civilians, a **Violation of the Laws or Customs of War**, as recognized by Article 51 of Additional Protocol I and Article 13 of Additional Protocol II to the Geneva Conventions of 1949, punishable under Articles 3 and 7(1) and 7(3) of the Statute of the Tribunal (*Prosecutor v. Pavle Strugar* (2003), para 18).

In order to evade the conflict classification issue, the ICTY OTP has rooted its unlawful attack on civilians charges in identically worded provisions of AP1 and AP2. AP1 Article 51(2) and AP2 Article 13(2) both state in part: "The civilian population as such, as well as individual civilians, shall not be the object of attack." AP1, however, goes on to refer to other forms of unlawful attack. In particular, Article 51 refers to indiscriminate attacks, including disproportionate attacks, and refers to five forms of such attack, all of which are prohibited. In addition, Article 85 contains grave breach provisions relating to unlawful attacks. By contrast, AP2 has no provisions related to unlawful attacks on civilians beyond the single sentence in Article 13(2) quoted earlier. ICTY OTP practice has been to focus on the common sentence in AP1 Article 51(2) and AP2 Article 13(2) and to argue that proof of the occurrence of the various types of indiscriminate attacks, including disproportionate attacks, may provide an evidentiary basis for the Trial Chamber to draw an inference that the attacks were, in substance, directed against the civilian population. In other words, we argue that the essential substance of the detailed AP1 provisions concerning unlawful attacks applicable to international conflicts is also contained in the single relevant sentence in AP2 which is applicable to internal conflicts. This is a conscious effort on our part, successful to date, to argue that the law concerning unlawful attacks against civilians is, in substance, the same in both international and internal conflicts.

In *Galić*, the Trial Chamber accepted that the mental element for the offence of unlawful attack was "wilful" and accepted that the approach taken in the grave breach provisions of AP1 was appropriate. Specifically, it held:

> ... The Commentary to Article 85 of Additional Protocol I explains the term as follows (ICRC Commentary, para 3474; in Sandoz et al. (eds), 1987):

> *Wilfully*: the accused must have acted consciously and with intent, i.e., with his mind on the act and its consequences, and willing them ('criminal intent' or 'malice aforethought'); this encompasses the concepts of 'wrongful intent' or 'recklessness', viz., the attitude of an agent who, without being certain of a particular result, accepts the possibility of it happening; on the other hand, negligence or lack of foresight is not covered, i.e., when a man acts without having his mind on the act or its consequences.
>
> The Trial Chamber accepts this explanation, according to which the notion of "wilfully" incorporates the concept of recklessness, while excluding here negligence. The perpetrator who recklessly attacks civilians acts "wilfully". (*Prosecutor v. Stanislav Galić* (2003), para 54).

The Chamber then goes on to decide that the elements for the charge are the elements common to offences under Article 3 of the ICTY Statute and the following specific elements (*Ibid.*, para 56):

1. Acts of violence directed against the civilian population or individual civilians not taking direct part in hostilities causing death or serious injury to body or health within the civilian population.
2. The offender wilfully made the civilian population or individual civilians not taking direct part in hostilities the object of those acts of violence.

It then goes on to indicate that "indiscriminate attacks, that is to say, attacks which strike civilians or civilian objects and military objectives without distinction, may qualify as direct attacks against civilians" (*Ibid.*, para 57).

Generally speaking, unlawful attack cases will involve multiple incidents of shelling or sniping. In the *Galić* case, hundreds of civilians were killed or wounded in Sarajevo by shelling or sniping during the period covered by the indictment, 1992–1994. Quite obviously it would be impossible to treat each incident of killing as a separate murder case. Some way must be developed to get from the specific incident at the micro level to what was alleged to be an unlawful shelling or sniping campaign at the macro level. Indeed, the link from the micro to the macro level was essential to the case. If, for example, the prosecutor can prove with a degree of precision in a manageable time that 20 sniping incidents have occurred over a two-year-period when the accused is responsible for 15,000 soldiers in the front lines, in the absence of direct evidence of relevant orders being given, would a reasonable court conclude that the commander bears command responsibility for the sniping or that he must have ordered such acts? On the other hand, if the prosecutor can establish both the occurrence of the 20 Incidents and an adequate link to what appears to be a much broader crime base, it is much easier for the court to reach such conclusions. Presumably the preferred approach would be to determine in some scientifically valid fashion the entire apparent crime base, for example, it appears from sound medical evidence that 1000 civilians have been killed by sniper fire from forces under the command of X, and then to pick a statistically valid sample on something like a random numbers basis for more detailed examination. Detailed evidence concerning all cases in the sample group would then be put before the court. If that is done, or if the prosecutor makes the court aware of cases in the sample group which do not indicate unlawful acts occurred, then, perhaps, the court can conclude, for example, that 70% of the cases in the sample group constitute crimes therefore 70% of the larger group also constitute crimes therefore a campaign of unlawful sniping occurred.

Desirable as the mathematical/scientific approach might be, it is not always practicable and it was not practicable in the *Galić* case. The *Galić* prosecution team listed scheduled sniping and shelling incidents as "representative allegations" in annexes to the indictment. These incidents were not chosen on any scientific or random numbers basis. They were chosen because they were perceived to be the best from a prosecution point of view. The prosecution also introduced evidence of unscheduled incidents, survey or impressionistic evidence, and solid demographic evidence which could adequately establish cause of death or injury but which could not, of itself, establish whether the death or injury was the result of unlawful acts.

The majority of the Trial Chamber held that a campaign of military actions in the area of Sarajevo involving widespread or systematic shelling and sniping of civilians resulting in civilian death or injury existed alongside a lawful military campaign directed against military objectives (*Ibid.*, para 583). Civilians were directly or indiscriminately attacked and, at a minimum, hundreds of civilians were killed and thousands of others were injured (*Ibid.*, para 591). The reasons for this finding included:

(a) no civilian activity and no areas of Sarajevo held by the ABiH seemed to be safe from sniping or shelling attacks from SRK-held territory (*Ibid.*, para 584),
(b) indeed specific areas of the city became notorious as sources of sniper fire directed at civilians (*Ibid.*, para 585),
(c) although civilians adapted to the environment by taking precautionary measures, they were still not safe from deliberate attack (*Ibid.*, para 586),
(d) the evidence of residents of Sarajevo and of victims was supported by the evidence of international military personnel (*Ibid.*, para 587),
(e) although there was some evidence that ABiH forces attacked their own civilians to attract the attention of the international community, that stray bullets may have struck some civilians, and that some civilians were shot in the honest belief they were combatants, "The evidence in the Trial Record conclusively establishes that the pattern of fire throughout the city of Sarajevo was that of indiscriminate or direct fire at civilians in ABiH-held areas of Sarajevo from SRK-controlled territory not that of combat fire where civilians were accidentally hit" (*Ibid.*, para 589) and
(f) fire into ABiH-held areas of Sarajevo followed a temporal pattern (*Ibid.*, para 590).

In cases brought under the ICC Statute, the analogous offences to ICTY unlawful attack offences would be Article 8(2)(b)(i) (intentionally directing attacks against civilians in international conflicts), Article 8(2)(b)(iv) (intentionally launching an attack in an international conflict in the knowledge that it will cause incidental losses "which would be clearly excessive in relation to the concrete and direct overall military advantage anticipated"), and Article 8(2)(e)(i) (intentionally directing attacks against civilians in internal conflicts). These offences and their related elements are not precisely the same as those for the ICTY. In particular:

(a) the mental element differs—the ICTY, derived from the APs, is "wilful" whereas the ICC is "intentional";
(b) the physical elements differ—the ICTY, derived from the APs, require proof of loss, whereas ICC does not, although, presumably, in most cases a charge would not be brought unless there was actual loss and, in any event, proof of loss is usually very helpful in proving the mental element;
(c) the ICC proportionality standard "*clearly* excessive in relation to the concrete and direct *overall* military advantage anticipated" appears to be higher than the ICTY standard which omits the underlined words; and
(d) on the face of the Statute, the ICC does not appear to have a way to charge for disproportionate attacks in internal conflicts.

Of course, over time, the ICC may find that its mental element and its proportionality standard are, in practice, similar to those of the ICTY. Since, all too often, military objectives, civilians, and civilian objects are located side by side, the ICC may also find that the ICTY argument that disproportionate attacks can become attacks directed against civilians may become quite helpful for cases involving unlawful attacks in internal conflicts.

7. The relationship between unlawful attack offences and other IHL offences

We do not contribute to the viability of IHL by indulging in creative reclassification so that an act which is regarded from one perspective as lawful can be regarded as unlawful because we changed the label. Where the crime base consists of shelling or sniping incidents in a combat environment, it is essential to prove that death, injury or damage was caused by an unlawful attack, that is, one directed against civilians or civilian objects or one directed against a military objective which may be expected to cause disproportionate incidental losses, before moving on to determine whether the additional elements necessary to establish the commission of other offences have also been established. If the attack was not unlawful then the resultant death, injury or damage is not unlawful. If a civilian is killed or injured during an attack on a military objective which was not expected to result in civilian casualties or damage to civilian objects disproportionate to the expected military advantage then no crime has been committed. This is so even if there is an expectation that, unfortunately, some civilians will be killed or injured during the attack. There is no basis for a crime against humanity charge because the attack was directed against a military objective, not against civilians or civilian objects. There is no basis for a war crimes charge of murder because the *mens rea is* lacking. The unlawful attack foundation is essential to the assessment of legality even if there is no unlawful attack charge relating to a particular combat-related incident.

We cannot avoid the issue by simply avoiding the charge. Quite clearly there can be incidents in which it is so clear that the attack is directed against civilians that one can proceed with a persecution count or a war crime or crime against humanity count of murder. Even in such circumstances, however, it is essential that the prosecutor and the chamber take into account the unlawful attack elements, at least implicitly, before coming to the conclusion that counts charged have been proven.

The *Galić* Trial Chamber applied the approach that goof of an unlawful attack was a prerequisite for proof of other offences related to shelling or sniping but it did so without enthusiasm (*Prosecutor v. Stanislav Galić* (2003), para. 144):

> The Prosecution submits that, in the context of an armed conflict, the determination that an attack is unlawful in light of treaty and customary international law with respect to the principles of distinction and proportionality is critical in determining whether the general requirements of Article 5 have been met. Otherwise, according to the Prosecution, unintended civilian casualties resulting from a lawful attack on legitimate military objectives would amount to a crime against humanity under Article 5 and lawful combat would, in effect, become impossible. It therefore submits that an accused may be found guilty of a crime against humanity if he launches an unlawful attack against persons taking no active part in the hostilities when the general requirements of Article 5 have been established. The Trial Chamber accepts that when considering the general requirements of Article 5, the body of laws of war plays an important part in the assessment of the legality of the acts committed in the course of an armed conflict and whether the population may be said to have been target as such.

Although the endorsement of the ICTY OTP approach is tepid at best, we think this approach is legally sound and contributes to the continued viability of IHL.

8. Conclusion: When is a combat casualty a war crime victim?

All persons killed or injured in combat may be victims of a war crime if they are killed or injured by the use of unlawful weapons or as a result of treachery. Article 3(b) of the ICTY Statute indicates that violations of the laws or customs of war include "employment of poisonous weapons or other weapons calculated to cause unnecessary suffering". This offence has never been the subject of a charge before the ICTY. There have been no allegations of the use of poisonous weapons. There is no general agreement on a list of weapons calculated to cause unnecessary suffering. The ICC Statute contains analogous provisions prohibiting the use of poison or poisoned weapons, asphyxiating or poisonous gases, dum-dum bullets, and weapons which are of a nature to cause superfluous injury or unnecessary suffering or are inherently indiscriminate provided they appear in an annex to the Statute yet to be developed (see Article 8, Rome Statute of the ICC, 1998). In addition, Article 8(xi) of the ICC Statute prohibits "killing or wounding treacherously individuals belonging to the hostile nation or army" and, presumably, treacherous killing could also be the basis for an unenumerated offence under Article 3 of the ICTY Statute. Although there are no judicial precedents for killing persons by the use of unlawful weapons, one could envisage charges for the use of chemical weapons by Iraq during the Iran–Iraq Conflict from 1980–1989 and anyone killed in these incidents, even combatants, would be victims of a war crime.

As a general statement,[9] however, the following categories of persons who may be killed or injured as a result of combat activities are not regarded as victims of war crimes:

(a) combatants who have not surrendered or who have not ceased to take part in the fighting because they are disabled;
(b) civilians who are taking a direct part in hostilities for so long as they are so doing; and
(c) civilians who are killed or injured as a result of an attack directed against a military objective which is not anticipated to cause disproportionate civilian losses.

The fact that people are killed or injured as a result of combat activities does not automatically mean that a crime has been committed. In order to evaluate whether or not a war crime has been committed, it is necessary to determine the status of the individuals killed or injured (combatants or civilians), what they were doing at the time they were killed or injured (for combatants—had they surrendered or were they disabled and out of the fighting, for civilians—were they taking a direct part in hostilities), and the surrounding circumstances (was the attack in which the individuals were killed or injured directed against a military objective, if yes, was the attack one in which the anticipated losses to civilians and civilian objects was proportionate or disproportionate). In some circumstances it may be readily apparent that the persons killed or injured were or were not victims of war crimes. In others, however, a detailed analysis of the context may be necessary.

List of Abbreviations

ABiH: Army of Bosnia and Herzegovina;
AP1: Additional Protocol I to the Geneva Conventions of 1949;
AP2: Additional Protocol II to the Geneva Conventions of 1949;
ICC: International Criminal Court;
ICRC: International Committee of the Red Cross;
ICTY: International Criminal Tribunal for the Former Yugoslavia;
IHL: International Humanitarian Law;
OTP: Office of the Prosecutor

Notes

[1] The views expressed in this article do not necessarily reflect either the views of the Prosecutor or the views of the International Criminal Tribunal for the Former Yugoslavia of the United Nations.
[2] Treaties impose legal obligations on states which have agreed to be bound by them, either by accession or ratification. Customary law, which is often difficult to find and define, imposes legal obligations on all states except those few which are persistent objectors.

[3] The author tends to be a bit reluctant to distinguish between the good and the bad side for the purposes of applying IHL but see Dunlap (2000), pp. 4–12.

[4] For a vigorous statement of the view that enemy civilian morale has traditionally been a legitimate military objective and that the AP1 definition of military objective should be interpreted to encompass attacks on morale targets, see Meyer (2001), pp. 143–182.

[5] See the extended discussion of practical aspects of targeting Saddam Hussein in Human Rights Watch (2003), pp. 21–40.

[6] The one exception to this rule, which in the event did not involve litigation, was the ICTY's report on NATO bombing ("OTP Report on NATO"; see ICTY (2000), pp. 1257–1283). See, in particular, the contentious discussion of the NATO attack on the headquarters and studios of Serbian state television and radio (RTS) in central Belgrade on 23 April 1999.

[7] Article 8(2)(b)(iv) of the Rome Statute for the International Criminal Court (Rome Statute for the ICC (1998), pp. 1002–1069) contains an analogous expression "clearly excessive".

[8] Mens rea [L = guilty mind] Law. The state of mind accompanying an illegal act which makes the act a crime; criminal state of mind. Excerpted from Oxford Talking Dictionary (1998).

[9] Military medical and religious personnel may become victims of unlawful attacks and therefore war crimes in the same circumstances as civilians.

References

Treaties and Treaty-like Instruments of International Law

Hague Convention IV (Laws and Customs of War on Land) of 1907: Hague Convention Respecting the Laws and Customs of War on Land, including Regulations Respecting the Laws and Customs of War on Land annexed thereto, printed in International Committee of the Red Cross, *International Law Concerning the Conduct of Hostilities; Collection of Hague Conventions and Some Other International Instruments*, Geneva, pp. 13–27.

Geneva Convention I (Wounded and Sick) of 1949: Geneva Convention for the Amelioration of the Condition of the Wounded and Sick in Armed Forces in the Field of August 12, 1949, printed in International Committee of the Red Cross, *The Geneva Conventions of August 12, 1949*, pp. 23–47.

Geneva Convention II (Maritime) of 1949: Geneva Convention for the Amelioration of the Condition of Wounded, Sick and Shipwrecked Members of Armed Forces at Sea of August 12, 1949, printed in International Committee of the Red Cross, *The Geneva Conventions of August 12, 1949*, pp. 51–72.

Geneva Convention III (Prisoner of War) of 1949: Geneva Convention Relative to the Treatment of Prisoners of War of August 12, 1949, printed in International Committee of the Red Cross, *The Geneva Conventions of August 12, 1949*, pp. 75–134.

Geneva Convention IV (Civilians), of 1949: Geneva Convention Relative to the Protection of Civilian Persons in Time of War of August 12, 1949, printed in International Committee of the Red Cross, *The Geneva Conventions of August 12, 1949*, pp. 153–214.

Additional Protocol I (AP1) of 1977: Protocol Additional to the Geneva Conventions of 12 August 1949, and Relating to the Protection of Victims of International Armed Conflicts (Protocol I), printed in International Committee of the Red Cross, 1977, *Protocols Additional to the Geneva Conventions of 12 August 1949*, Geneva, pp. 3–73.

Additional Protocol II (AP2) of 1977: Protocol Additional to the Geneva Conventions of 12 August 1949, and Relating to the Protection of Victims of Non-International Armed Conflicts (Protocol II), printed in International Committee of the Red Cross, 1977, *Protocols Additional to the Geneva Conventions of 12 August 1949*, Geneva, pp. 89–101.

Statute of the International Criminal Tribunal for the Former Yugoslavia, printed in American Society of International Law, 1993, *International Legal Materials*, Vol. 32, Washington, DC, pp. 1192–1201 ("*ICTY Statute*").

Rome Statute for the International Criminal Court (ICC), printed in American Society of International Law, 1998, *International Legal Materials*, Vol. 37, Washington, DC, pp. 1002–1069. ("*ICC Statute*").

Judgements, Indictments, and Decisions of the ICTY

Prosecutor v. Stanislav Galić, Case No. IT-98-29-T, *Judgment and Opinion*, 5 December 2003.
Prosecutor v. Pavle Strugar, Case No. 1T-01-.42-PT, *Third Amended Indictment*, 10 December 2003.
Prosecutor v. Duško Tadić, a/k/a "Dule", Case No. IT-94-1-AR72, *Decision on the Defence Motion for Interlocutory Appeal on Jurisdiction*, 2 October 1995, The Hague ("*Tadić Jurisdiction Decision*").

Other Publications

Baker, J. E., 2002. *Legal and Ethical Lessons of NATO's Kosovo Campaign* 'Judging Kosovo: The legal process, the law of armed conflict, and the commander in chief, in A. E. Wall (ed), Newport: Naval War College.
Dunlap, C. J., 2000. 'The end of innocence: Rethinking non-combatancy in the post-Kosovo era', *Strategic Review* (Summer 2000) 4: 4–12.
Human Rights Watch, 2003. *Off Target: The Conduct of the War and Civilian Casualties in Iraq.* Brussels, New York. Washington, DC, London.
International Criminal Tribunal for the Former Yugoslavia (ICTY), 2000. 'Final report to the Prosecutor by the Committee established to review the NATO bombing campaign against the Federal Republic of Yugoslavia', in: *American Society of International Law, International Legal Materials*, Vol. 39, Washington, DC, pp. 1257–1283 ("OTP report on NATO").
Meyer, J. M., 2001, 'Tearing down the façade: A critical look at the current law on targeting the will of the enemy and Air Force doctrine', *Air Force Law Review* 51: 143–182.
Oxford Talking Dictionary. Copyright © 1998 The Learning Company, Inc. All Rights Reserved.
Roberts, A. and Guelff, R., 2000. *Documents on the Laws of War*, 3rd ed. Oxford University Press, Oxford.
Sandoz, Y. et al. (eds), 1987. *Commentary on the Additional Protocols of 8 June 1977 to the Geneva Conventions of 12 August 1949.* Geneva: International Committee of the Red Cross/Martinus Nijhoff Publishers ("ICRC Commentary").
US Department of Defence, 2003. Military Commission Instruction No. 2, 2003. Washington DC: The US Department of Defence, 30 April 2003 ("*Military Commission Instruction*").

CHAPTER 9. ACCOUNTING FOR GENOCIDE: HOW MANY WERE KILLED IN SREBRENICA?*

HELGE BRUNBORG
Senior Research Fellow, Statistics Norway

TORKILD HOVDE LYNGSTAD
Sociologist, Statistics Norway Oslo (PRIO)

HENRIK URDAL
Research Fellow, International Peace Research Institute, Oslo (PRIO), Norway

Abstract. The takeover of the UN 'safe area' of Srebrenica by Bosnian Serb forces in July 1995 was followed by the killing of a large number of male Bosnian Muslim civilians, in what has been characterized as the worst massacre in Europe since World War II. This article is based on a report submitted as evidence to the UN International Criminal Tribunal for the former Yugoslavia (ICTY) in the case against General Radislav Krstić, who became the first person to be convicted of genocide at this Tribunal. This case also forms part of the genocide charges against Slobodan Milošević, Radovan Karadžić. To our knowledge, this report is unique among genocide studies in its approach, using individual-level data to identify every victim in order to arrive at a highly reliable minimum estimate of the number of people killed. This was possible because of efforts by humanitarian organizations to register people who disappeared during the war as well as the availability of both pre-and post-conlict data on individuals. We conclude that at least 7,475 persons were killed after the fall of Srebrenica. We also present estimates of the probability of being a victim: more than 33% for Muslim men who were enumerated in Srebrenica in 1991.

1. Genocide accounting

Accounting for genocide is not an exact science. Reliable sources on the number of casualties are often rare, resulting in more or less qualified 'guesstimates'. Most often, the parties to a conflict have an interest in either exaggerating or playing down the magnitude of atrocities, and objective sources may be hard to find. Methods used for estimating the number of people killed in genocides most often include critique of historical sources, primarily governmental archives, witness statements, and public documents. By such an approach one may be able to map pieces together to establish reasonable estimates of total casualties.

Demographic estimation techniques may also be employed to account for genocide. McCaa (2001) conducted a study comparing censuses taken before and after the Mexican revolution and estimated what the population development would have been in the absence of that conflict, assuming normal levels of mortality, fertility and migration. He used this to estimate the demographic consequences of that conflict. While this method of determining over-all population consequences may be

---

This chapter was previously published in *European Journal of Population*, vol. 19, no. 3, 2003, pp. 229–248.

Helge Brunborg et al. (eds.), The Demography of Armed Conflict, 197–215.

central to demography, it cannot usefully establish the number of war or genocide victims since it fails to separate direct victims from those 'missing' because of abnormally increased mortality, reduced fertility and increased migration. In a similar study aimed at directly estimating the victims of the Cambodian civil war and of the Khmer Rouge regime, Heuveline (1998) used data from a pre-conflict census and a post-conflict electoral list to arrive at estimates of 'excess' mortality in the 1970s. Heuveline attempts to separate violent deaths from mortality caused by harsh living conditions.

A quantitative approach that has received much attention is the work of Rudolph J. Rummel (1994, 1997). Rummel's methodology is not based on demographic estimation techniques, but rather on using a large number of historical sources to identify low to high ranges for different "democides", and then assert a 'most likely' mid-estimate. While the method is certainly controversial, Rummel has received praise for his thorough and well documented studies.

As described below, our study uses a very different approach. The expert report on which most of this article is based (Brunborg and Urdal, 2000), was submitted as evidence in the case against Radislav Krstić in the International Criminal Tribunal of the former Yugoslavia (ICTY). The nature of the project made it necessary to be as specific and reliable as possible about the identities of the genocide victims from Srebrenica, which required that we present a list of names. It was also necessary to take a conservative approach, i.e., only including victims about whose identity we were virtually certain. This article exemplifies the technique of using individual-level data collected for other purposes to estimate the number of victims of an armed conflict. Moreover, the article describes how other types of data on individuals, e.g. censuses and electoral registers, can be used to corroborate the identified victims.[1]

2. Prosecuting genocide

Why do individuals, groups or governments engage in genocide? Bookman (1997) points to the importance of demographic characteristics, arguing that many ethnic conflicts can be understood within the framework of a demographic struggle for power. She focuses on the relative strength of ethnic groups, and states that "the relationship between the size of an ethnic group and its economic and political power is usually positive" (p. 17). In Bosnia and Herzegovina, the most heterogeneous of the republics of the former Yugoslavia, the demographic struggle for power became vivid following the process leading to independence in 1992. The 1991 Bosnian population consisted of 44 percent Bosnian Muslims, 31 percent Serbs and 17 percent Croats. The relatively stronger growth of the Muslim population in the 1980s caused concern among Serbs of being 'outnumbered', and was used as an argument for a secession of the Serb areas by Bosnian-Serb leaders such as Radovan Karadžić, Ratko Mladić and Momčilo Krajišnik (Urdal, 2001). These ethno-nationalist leaders used such tools of 'demographic engineering' as targeted and arbitrary killings, rapes, destruction of houses, and expulsion to create ethnically homogenous areas in Bosnia and Herzegovina.

To date, the world has seen only a few ad hoc tribunals prosecuting persons for genocidal acts: The International Military Tribunals at Nuremberg and Tokyo after World War II, the International Criminal Tribunal for the former Yugoslavia (ICTY) in 1993, and the International Criminal Tribunal for Rwanda (ICTR) in 1994.[2] In July 2002 the UN General Assembly established a permanent International Criminal Court (ICC), following the ratification of the ICC Statute by 60 UN members.

There is often a question about numbers in war crime trials, especially in connection with genocide: How many people were killed? Article 4 of the ICTY Statute defines genocide as "*acts committed with intent to destroy, in whole or in part, a national, ethnical, racial or religious group*" (ICTY, 2000). A crucial issue is thus how many victims must be established to convict someone of genocide.

The war in Bosnia and Herzegovina started in the spring of 1992 and ended with the Dayton Peace Accords in November 1995. The total number of casualties in the armed conflicts in Bosnia and Herzegovina is contested. It is generally believed that approximately 200,000 of the pre-war population of around 4.3 million were killed as a result of war activities, but there are other estimates ranging from 20,000 to 328,000 deaths (Brunborg, 2001:230). The demographic consequences of the conflict lasting from 1992 to 1995 were, however, not limited to the relatively high death tolls. The 'ethnic cleansing' of large territories, in particular areas claimed by nationalist groups of Bosnian Serbs and Bosnian Croats, also caused substantial population displacements, both internally and externally. More than two million Bosnians were displaced by thewar.[3] Of all the atrocities committed during the war, the attempt to eradicate the male Muslim population following the capture of Srebrenica represents the gravest and most obvious example of genocide during the wars in the former Yugoslavia and has been characterized as the worst massacre in Europe since World War II (Honig and Both, 1996; Rohde, 1997).

All of Eastern Bosnia was occupied by the Bosnian Serb Army after 1992, except for a few areas, including Goražde, Žepa and Srebrenica (see appendix map). These areas, together with Sarajevo, were declared 'safe areas' by the UN Security Council in April 1994. In 1995, Srebrenica had been isolated for several years and the living conditions of the population, which included thousands of refugees from surrounding areas, were harsh. A Dutch contingent (DUTCHBAT) was posted in Srebrenica as peacekeepers, but it was small and lightly armed, and its mandate was unclear (NIOD, 2002).[4] On 6 July 1995 the Bosnian Serb army (VRS), under the command of general Ratko Mladić, started shelling Srebrenica. The requested NATO air support was too late and too little and DUTCHBAT, which had neither the power nor the mandate to stop the attacks, also failed to protect the civilian population (NIOD, 2002). Fearing what would happen when the VRS took over the enclave, a group of men, numbering perhaps as many as 15,000, mainly of 'military age',[5] started walking through the forested hills towards territories controlled by the federal Bosnian army. The long columns of these men were shelled and ambushed, many were killed as they were fleeing, while others were rounded up and taken away for execution. Those who remained in Srebrenica until the fall of the enclave were forced to walk to the UN compound in nearby Potočari, where the men were separated from their families, taken away and executed. The exact number of victims from Srebrenica is unknown.[6] By 1999, ICTY exhumations had uncovered about 1,900 bodies, of which only a few have been identified.

The war crimes committed in Srebrenica have lead to several serious indictments by the ICTY. These indictments called for a thorough analysis of the magnitude of the atrocities in Srebrenica, evidence that would stand the scrutiny of the court. The research questions that guided the demographic project on Srebrenica were defined by the Office of the Prosecutor as:

- What was the minimum number of victims from Srebrenica who were killed by the VRS after the fall of the enclave on July 11 1995 who can be identified by name?
- What is the reliability of this list of victims?

The latter research question was added because of allegations that persons listed as Srebrenica victims were either fictive persons (i.e., they never existed), or that such listed victims had actually survived the war. The findings from this study (Brunborg and Urdal, 2000) were reported to the court in June 2000 in the trial against General Radislav Krstić. Krstić was sentenced to 45 years imprisonment in August 2001 for a number of charges, including genocide.[7] The Srebrenica atrocities are also part of the indictments against Slobodan Milošević, Radovan Karadžić and Ratko Mladić.

In addition to the two research questions posed by the Office of the Prosecutor, we also want to assess the magnitude and demographic impact of the massacre. The following questions are concerned with these matters:

- What was the magnitude of the massacre relative to the pre-war population?
- From whence came the missing men to Srebrenica before the fall of the enclave?

3. Data sources and methods[8]

Several international and local organizations have collected data on persons missing after the fall of Srebrenica, including the International Committee of the Red Cross (ICRC) and Physicians for Human Rights (PHR). ICRC registered missing persons throughout the war period 1992–1995 "to help families establish the fate of their relatives who remain missing" (ICRC, 1998). Similarly, the American-based PHR registered missing persons with extensive detail to assist in identifying exhumed bodies, and to help families find out what happened to their missing relatives. Their list, the "Ante-Mortem database", is essentially a compilation of data on people believed to be dead.

The data collection procedures of the two organizations were somewhat different. Hence some victims are only registered in one of the two lists. ICRC started the registration soon after the fall of the enclave, primarily to register persons believed to be in detention. At that time the memories of the people escaping from Srebrenica were still fresh. On the other hand, the family members were very distressed, suffering from emotional and physical fatigue, and usually not in possession of identification papers or other detailed documentation of the disappeared persons. Because of the chaotic situation some people reported as missing were later found to be living, and, therefore, ICRC removed such cases from the list of missing persons.[9] PHR started its registration process about one year later, in July 1996, at a time when many Srebrenica survivors had resettled elsewhere in Bosnia and Herzegovina or had left for other countries. The PHR questionnaire included very detailed questions about the missing persons, such as particular physical characteristics and clothing, which was often emotionally difficult for the informants to answer. At the same time, the informants were often well prepared for the interview situation, with many providing identification papers for the missing persons.

Although the objectives and the procedures for the two registration activities seem somewhat different, it is our conclusion that the types of cases registered were very similar. Both activities were conducted to trace missing persons; more than 95 percent were registered by close relatives; and registration of persons known to be dead was accepted in several cases. The PHR list has fewer cases than ICRC. The main explanation for this is most likely that PHR started later and worked actively to register persons in only two areas (Tuzla and Sarajevo).

Fully four versions of the ICRC list of missing persons for Bosnia and Herzegovina have been published, the versions used by us, numbers 3 and 4, were released in January 1997 and July 1998, respectively. We merged these two, as well as a list of dead persons published together with version 4 of the ICRC list,[10] and arrived at 19,403 persons for all of Bosnia and Herzegovina, after correcting for a few obvious inconsistencies. The PHR Ante-Mortem Database made available to us was updated in July 1999 and this was combined with additional information received from PHR in May and October 1999, for a total of 7,269 victims for Srebrenica.

Both organizations collected data on surname, first name, father's name, sex, date and place of birth, date and place of disappearance. Some information was only recorded by ICRC, such as municipality of disappearance, and other information only by PHR, such as ethnicity. In both lists there is a substantial amount of missing data. In the ICRC list the least frequently complete items are date of birth (65.4% complete) and date of disappearance (89.6% complete). However, the *year* of these events is included for almost everybody. For the PHR list the least complete items are date of birth (78.2%) and place of disappearance (80.7%). The other variables are recorded for almost everybody—but that does not necessarily mean that they are always correct. Errors are particularly common in the spelling of names of persons and places. Moreover, by comparing the two lists we know that although there are many errors, they are mostly small, in variables such as date of birth. Such errors are common all over the world in data collected through questionnaires in surveys and censuses.

Both organizations collected information on missing persons from a greater spatial and temporal domain than only from the fall of Srebrenica. ICRC covered all of Bosnia and Herzegovina for the whole period of armed conflicts, while PHR worked mainly on Srebrenica but collected information also on persons who disappeared elsewhere in Eastern Bosnia earlier in the conflict. A major challenge for the project was to separate out just persons who went missing in connection with the fall of Srebrenica in July 1995.

Both ICRC and PHR collected some information that could be used to identify Srebrenica victims. ICRC did not pose any precise question on this to the families but their own definition of Srebrenica-related disappearances was based on the stories told by the informant, which usually started with: "During the fall of Srebrenica" or "After the fall of Srebrenica". This information was not made available to the authors, however. PHR asked a specific question on the fall of the enclave: "Did he/she disappear after the fall of Srebrenica in July 1995?" This information was used in conjunction with data as to the place and date of disappearance for each person,[11] then to define the Srebrenica victims. Both lists provide information on the place and date of disappearance and the authors were assisted by experts on the Srebrenica investigations to define the exact places from where Srebrenica victims could have disappeared on different dates.

To arrive at a total number of victims, the two lists of missing persons were merged.[12] In this process we investigated whether there were records in the two sources that represented the same individual. Items that were used as criteria for defining whether two records were for the same or for different persons were surname, first name, father's name, date of birth, place of birth, and to the extent possible date and place of disappearance. Due to misspellings and missing information, this was not a straightforward task. In cases that were impossible to distinguish due to lack of data, we decided to take a cautious approach not to inflate the number, thus assuming that they were for the same person.

We further investigated how the records of missing persons matched pre-and post-conflict information for each individual. Since the ICRC list contained persons whose fate was still unknown, we wanted to examine whether people on the list of missing persons showed up in registers of survivors of the war. One major register of survivors was available to us: the OSCE Voters' register for the 1997 and 1998 elections. This register contained information on some 2.8 million individuals living in Bosnia and Herzegovina or abroad, who actively registered to vote in these elections. The two lists were matched based on surname, first name, date of birth, and to some extent place of birth. Two items that would have made it easier to match the two lists were only available in one or the other source: the Father's name was only available in the lists of missing persons and the unique ID number[13] was only recorded in the Voters' register.

The lists of missing persons were also matched with the 1991 Census records. This was first done to counter allegations that persons registered as missing had never existed, but it has also been used to compute more accurate descriptive statistics on the victims. Because of the war, the records of the 1991 Census had not been checked and revised after the optical scanning of the enumeration forms, and a plethora of errors existed in the files. Nevertheless, a comparison of the census files with the consolidated list of missing persons succeeded in identifying 87% of the missing persons in the 1991 Census. The failure to match the remaining 13% was primarily due to data quality. The matching was conducted on the basis of information on surname, first name, father's name, date and place of birth, and place of disappearance.

To investigate whether our minimum estimate of victims was likely to be far off the actual number of persons killed, we applied a method referred to as dual (or multiple) systems estimation. The method, which will be described in more detail in section 5 below, is suitable to estimate the size of the actual population when we know the degree of overlapping between two or more independently collected data sets.

4. Arriving at a minimum number of Srebrenica missing

After merging the ICRC and the PHR lists, we arrived at a *consolidated list of missing persons* for all of Bosnia and Herzegovina, including all ICRC and PHR records, but with only one record for each person.[14] 7,490 records on the consolidated list are Srebrenica-related, according to the strict criteria that were applied (Table 1). In addition to expanding the total number of missing persons, the combination of the two sources corroborated the available data as well as provided additional information when data were missing in one of the sources. For example, 75.5 percent of the Srebre-nica-related records on the consolidated list have full date of birth, compared to 53.5 percent and 79.1 percent on the ICRC and PHR lists, respectively.

The comparison of the list of missing persons and the Voters' register 1997/98 resulted in a total of nine Srebrenica-related matches. The identities of these nine persons were checked with the 1991 Census for Eastern Bosnia and we are convinced that these matches are matches of the same people and not a mix-up of persons with the same name and identical or similar date of birth. These matches

Table 1. Srebrenica-related missing and dead persons

	Number of records
On both ICRC and PHR lists	5,712
On ICRC list only	1,586
On PHR list only	192
Srebrenica-related missing persons registered by ICRC and/or PHR	*7,490*
Found in Voters' Registers 1997 and 1998	−9
Srebrenica-related victims, excluding persons found in the Voters' Registers	*7,481*
Found alive by ICRC since Jan. 1997 (identities unknown to us)	−6
Srebrenica-related victims	***7,475***

imply that these nine persons either survived Srebrenica, or that their identities have been misused when registering to vote. Six of the nine persons were reported independently *both* to ICRC and PHR, decreasing the likelihood that the inconsistencies are due to fraudulent registration of missing persons—and increasing the likelihood that they are due to fraudulent registration to vote. In any case, the number of such inconsistencies is very small, only 0.1 percent of the approximately 7,500 missing persons. This indicates that there was no large-scale campaign to register living persons as missing or to misuse missing persons' identities to vote.

To be conservative, we have subtracted the nine missing persons found on the OSCE Voters' register from the total number. Moreover, we have also subtracted six missing persons from Srebrenica who have been found to be alive since ICRC published its version 3 in January 1997, but whose identities have not been disclosed to us. However, some or all of the six may be among the nine found in the Voters' register. Thus, the number of investigated cases where persons registered as missing may be alive is a minimum of 9 and a maximum of 15.

At least 7,475 persons have been found to be dead or missing after the fall of Srebrenica, according to our conservative criteria. This number does not, however, include 148 cases of missing persons who may be Srebrenica-related according to either the ICRC or the PHR lists, but where the information is inconsistent or incomplete with regard to date and place of disappearance.

Moreover, the number does not include an unknown number of persons *not* reported as missing. This situation could arise for a number of reasons: there was nobody left to report the missing because the entire family had been killed; family members were too sick or too old to be able to do the reporting or too disillusioned to find it worthwhile to do so; family members may have left the Tuzla area before the registration process was underway. There may also have been cases where persons were not reported as missing because their families were convinced that they were dead and therefore not meeting the registration criteria. Lastly, some persons may not have been identified as Srebrenica-related because the information contained in the lists was lacking or incorrect.

Thus, the actual number of Srebrenica victims is likely to be somewhat higher than 7,475. But the authors have not, during fact-finding missions and other sources, come across virtually any cases of persons missing or killed after the fall of the enclave that have not been reported. A further indication of the high degree of completeness of the ICRC list is that PHR registered only 192 Srebrenica-related persons not already on the ICRC list. Also, only a couple of the about 60 bodies which had been identified among those exhumed in Srebrenica-related graves by late 1999, were not already on the ICRC and PHR lists.[15]

5. Estimating the likely number of victims

Fully 5,712, or 76 percent, of the missing persons were found on *both* lists, which can be regarded as two independent samples of the total population of missing persons.

Moreover, each individual is uniquely identifiable so that we know whether he or she is present in each sample. This enables us to make an estimate of the number of disappearances not appearing on any of the two lists, by applying multiple systems estimation (Sekar and Deming, 1949; Marks et al., 1974), also called the capture-tag-recapture technique (Bishop et al., 1975).[16] Ball et al. (2002) have used a similar approach to estimate the number of victims in Kosovo in 1999.

The two samples can be assumed to be independent since the data were collected at different times, by different people, via different questionnaires, and for different purposes. The only link between the two samples that we are aware of is that PHR entered the ICRC registration number of a missing person when a person was registered with the same name and date of birth as a person on the ICRC list, which was public and widely available.

Let $N(I)$ be the number of persons in the ICRC list, $N(P)$ be the number of missing persons in the PHR list, and $N(B)$ be the number of persons who appear on both lists. Then, under independence, the maximum likelihood estimator of the total number $N(T)$ of missing persons is, after deleting the 9 persons found in the Voters' Registers:

$$N(T) = \frac{N(I) * N(P)}{N(B)} = (5,706 + 1,584) * (5,706 + 191)/5,706 = 7,534.$$

This number is only marginally higher, 53 persons or 0.71 percent, than the minimum number given in Table 1, 7,481.[17]

However, aggregation may have concealed effects of differential reporting for different age groups. To investigate this we stratified the population into 5-year age groups for men and into two age groups for women (below 50 years and 50+). In this case the maximum likelihood estimator is

$$N(T) = \sum_{i=1}^{17} \frac{N_i(I) * N_i(P)}{N_i(B)} + \sum_{j=1}^{2} \frac{N_j(I) * N_j(P)}{N_j(B)},$$

where $i = 1, \ldots, 17$ denotes age group of men and $j = 1, 2$ denotes age group of women.

This barely affected the total estimate, which increased by only 2 persons to 7,536. It is interesting to note, however, that the estimate of missing persons increased relatively more for older men (1.4 percent for men over 50) than for younger men (0.5 percent for men under 30), and more for women (3.4 per cent) than for men (0.7 percent). This could indicate that young men had more surviving family members to report their disappearance and that women who went missing often had missing husbands as well, implying that it was less likely that they were reported as missing.

Table 2. People missing from Srebrenica by sex and age group

Age group	Number	Percent
Men <16	76	1.0
Men 16–60	6,727	89.9
Men >60	629	8.4
Men, age unknown	1	0.0
Women <16	2	0.0
Women 16–60	20	0.3
Women >60	26	0.3
Total	7,481	100.0

The table includes six missing persons known to have survived according to ICRC, but with ages and identities unknown to us.

6. Who were the Srebrenica victims?

Only 48 of the missing persons are women, and a total of 753 persons (10.1%) are either women and children or elderly, i.e. not men of 'military age' (Table 2). The youngest are two girls, who were aged 8 and 9 when they disappeared. The age distribution of the missing men is shown in Figure 1.

Ideally we would have liked to know the proportion of people killed of all who resided in the enclave at the time it fell. This could show that the atrocities were of a genocidal character. But such an operation proved difficult. The people who stayed in the town of Srebrenica in July 1995 came from the Srebrenica municipality itself as well as from surrounding municipalities. There were large flows of displaced

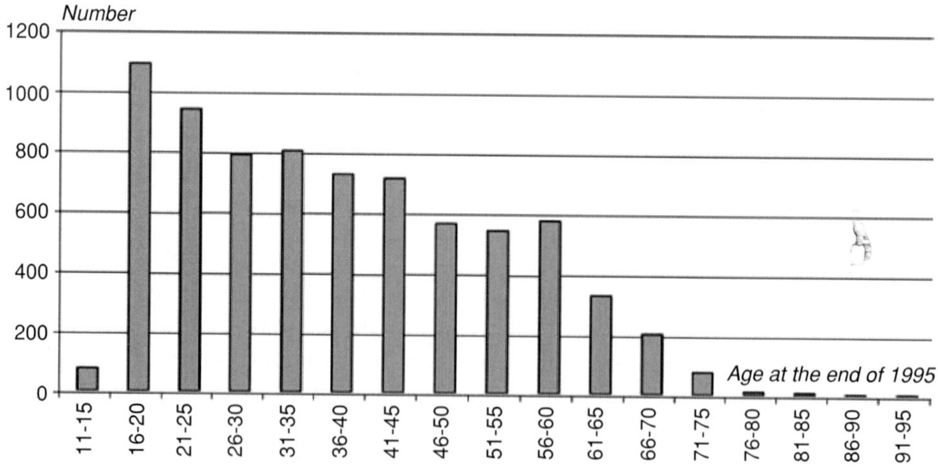

Figure 1. Number of missing men from Srebrenica by age at disappearance.

people in and out of Srebrenica between the outbreak of the war in April 1992 and the fall of Srebrenica in July 1995, due to the war going on in the surrounding areas. Local authorities and international humanitarian organizations are said to have compiled lists of the people who were present in the enclave prior to its fall, but the authors have not been able to locate such lists and we doubt their existence. It is assumed that about 40,000 people were in the town of Srebrenica before it fell, but the exact size of this population and its distribution is not known. The lack of data on the population at risk made it difficult to calculate proper fatality rates, so we had to opt for another approach.

The second-best solution to this problem was to use information on place of residence in 1991, according to the census, i.e., before the armed conflict started.

We obtained such information from the matching of the missing persons with the 1991 census records. A total of 6,431 (or 87 percent) of the missing men were matched with records in the census.[18] This provided us with census information for these persons, including municipality of residence and ethnicity. It seems reasonable to assume that the matched persons constitute a fairly representative sample of the total population of missing persons.[19] Consequently, the aggregate numbers presented below have been adjusted on the assumption that the residency and age distribution is the same for the records that were not matched as for those that were.

As expected, we found that in 1991 more than 90% of the persons who later went missing lived in Srebrenica municipality or in one of the two municipalities of Bratunac and Vlasenica that were captured by Serb forces early in the war (Table 3). The shares of the victims originating from non-neighbouring municipalities decline with their geographic distance from Srebrenica. Bratunac, the municipality with the second highest proportion of missing persons, has a long border with Srebrenica,

Table 3. Missing men by municipality of residence in 1991

Municipality	Absolute number	Percent
Srebrenica	4,146	55.8
Bratunac	1,775	23.9
Vlasenica	911	12.3
Zvornik	393	5.3
Han Pijesak	103	1.4
Other	105	1.4
Total	7,433	100

The numbers have been adjusted for 1,002 records of missing men (13 percent) that were not matched with the 1991 census records, assuming that the distribution of municipality of residence in 1991 is similar to the distribution of the matched records.

whereas Zvornik and Han Pijesak are farther away. Muslim refugees from Zvornik in particular were more likely to flee to other Muslim-held areas in Bosnia.

To get a better picture of the scale of the atrocities, we have computed the 'missing probability', i.e., the proportion of men that went missing in relation to the fall of Srebrenica relative to the number of Muslim men enumerated in the 1991 Census, broken down by age and pre-war municipality. We assume that all missing persons were Muslims, since there is only one non-Muslim (a Serb) among the 5,556 persons on the PHR list with data on ethnicity. Information from the 1991 Census corroborates this. Table 4 shows the proportions of missing Muslim men enumerated in these four municipalities in 1991 by birth cohort and municipality. As expected, Srebrenica has the highest missing rate. More than a third of all Muslim men born in Srebrenica between 1905–1984 as enumerated in the 1991 Census, disappeared in connection with the fall of the enclave in July 1995. The missing rates for men enumerated in neighbouring municipalities are also very high (Table 4).

Table 4. Proportion of Muslim men enumerated in 1991 who went missing from Srebrenica in 1995, by birth cohort and municipality of residence in 1991 (percent)

Birth cohort	Approximate age in 1995	Municipality of residence in 1991				
		Srebrenica	Bratunac	Vlasenica	Han Pijesak	Zvornik
1905–1909	86–90	5.1	0.0	0.0	0.0	0.0
1910–1914	81–85	15.7	0.0	0.0	0.0	2.1
1915–1919	76–80	14.9	8.9	7.3	11.3	0.9
1920–1924	71–75	25.3	7.7	12.9	4.5	2.3
1925–1929	66–70	29.3	19.1	14.3	1.8	3.2
1930–1934	61–65	37.8	25.9	15.8	9.9	2.6
1935–1939	56–60	46.3	23.5	22.0	12.1	3.4
1940–1944	51–55	46.8	31.4	16.6	6.1	2.8
1945–1949	46–50	50.4	27.0	21.0	12.5	2.8
1950–1954	41–45	44.9	24.8	15.5	10.7	3.3
1955–1959	36–40	38.5	22.2	11.9	12.1	1.7
1960–1964	31–35	38.1	21.2	9.4	4.2	1.6
1965–1969	26–30	31.2	17.5	8.4	7.6	1.7
1970–1974	21–25	33.4	19.9	9.7	6.8	1.5
1975–1979	16–20	37.0	21.0	12.8	15.5	1.5
1980–1984	11–15	2.6	1.4	1.0	0.0	0.1
1905–1984	11–90	33.7	18.9	11.2	8.0	1.8

The numbers have been adjusted for the missing men that were not matched with the 1991 census records and for 2.5 percent of men without data on the year of birth in the census, assuming a similar distribution on age and municipality of residence in 1991 as for the matched records.

The missing proportions should be considered as low estimates because of demographic changes between the census on 31 March 1991 and the fall of the enclave on 11 July 1995, which reduced the population at risk of disappearing. These factors include deaths from natural causes, especially among the elderly; deaths from war-related causes, especially among young men; people migrating or fleeing from Srebrenica; and the likelihood that men of military age were engaged in fighting elsewhere in the country. On the other hand, there is hardly any upwards bias in the rates, as people who came to Srebrenica from other municipalities are included in the population at risk for the municipalities from which they originated.

Only a few young children from the five municipalities reported in Table 4 went missing, but the rates are very high for young men, fully 37 percent for Srebrenica men aged 16–20 in 1995 (those born in 1975–1979). The rate is highest for middle-aged men 46–60 years, with about 50 percent missing. This may seem surprising, since middle-aged men should be less likely to be suspected of being soldiers and singled out for execution. A main explanation may be that the middle-aged men were less likely to leave Srebrenica because they had families in the enclave. Also, younger men are generally healthier, which increased the likelihood that they would attempt to trek the approximately 70 kilometres through the woods to Tuzla, and succeed in doing this. Consequently, younger cohorts probably experienced a lower risk of being victims. However, the population at risk in the enclave was probably significantly lower for cohorts of younger men, especially those in their 20s, than what we have suggested here, potentially causing a bias in the fatality rates. Younger men from Srebrenica were more likely than older men to be engaged in fighting elsewhere in the country and to have been killed or captured earlier in the war. The youngest boys, aged 16–20 in 1995, were less likely to be in the army, which may explain their elevated risk of disappearance compared to the preceding cohorts.

Ideally, we would have liked to control for factors such as normal mortality and migration when calculating the missing probabilities. We have no information about migration flows but we have attempted to adjust for normal mortality. To do this we projected the male Muslim Srebrenica population from 31 March 1991 (census day) to 1 July 1995 (immediately before the fall of Srebrenica), assuming the pre-war mortality level for Bosnia and Herzegovina 1985–1990, i.e. a life expectancy at birth of 69.2 years (UN, 2001).

As it is more convenient to use single years of age, and since one-year death rates are not easily available, we used the period life table for Norway 1948 (Mamelund and Borgan, 1996), with a life expectancy of 69.4 years, very close to the pre-war life expectancy for Bosnian males. The difference in the age structure of mortality between Srebrenica Muslim men before the war and Norwegian men in 1948 is not likely to be as large as to cause very different results. This is a modest approach as the mortality of Srebrenica Muslim men during the period April 1991– July 1995 was probably much higher than that corresponding to a life expectancy of 69.2 years, due to considerable hardship in the isolated enclave caused by lack of food,

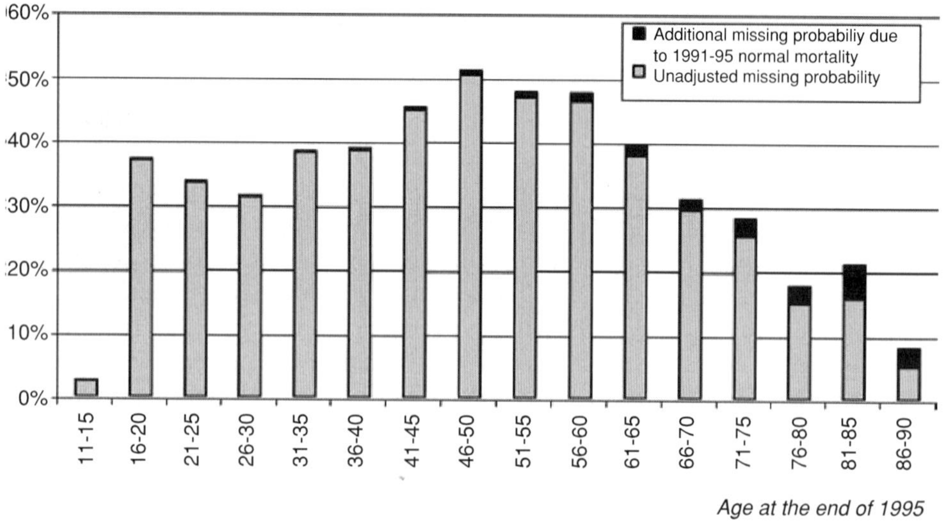

Figure 2. Probability of going missing in 1995 for Muslim men enumerated in Srebrenica in 1991, by age in 1995.

proper medical treatment and firewood, in addition to people being killed directly and indirectly in war-related activities.

Figure 2 shows that the adjustment of the population at risk for 'normal' mortality does not affect the estimates of the missing probabilities very much, only increasing the total estimate by about 0.5 percentage point. For old men the adjustment is striking, however. For the very oldest, born 1905–1914, the missing rate increased by almost one half, from 10.4 to 14.9 percent. The real fatality probability for very old men may be even higher since the excess mortality is likely to have been most severe for the elderly.

7. Are the missing persons really dead?

As stated initially, a major task for the project was to present evidence of the likelihood that the persons listed as missing actually had died. While this is the assumption made by most observers,[20] the project engaged in several activities to support such a conclusion. Major evidence for this view is our finding that only nine Srebrenica-related missing persons were found on the Voters' Register for the 1997 and 1998 elections. Also, only 22 Srebrenica-relevant persons of a total of 7,421 persons have been found to be alive by ICRC since they started registering Srebrenica victims in July 1995. Only six persons missing from Srebrenica have been found alive since January 1997, in spite of strong efforts by ICRC to find survivors.

In addition, we have compared our findings with results from ICTY exhumations. The age distributions of the Srebrenica-related missing persons and the exhumed bodies are very similar (Figure 3), indicating that the exhumed bodies are a

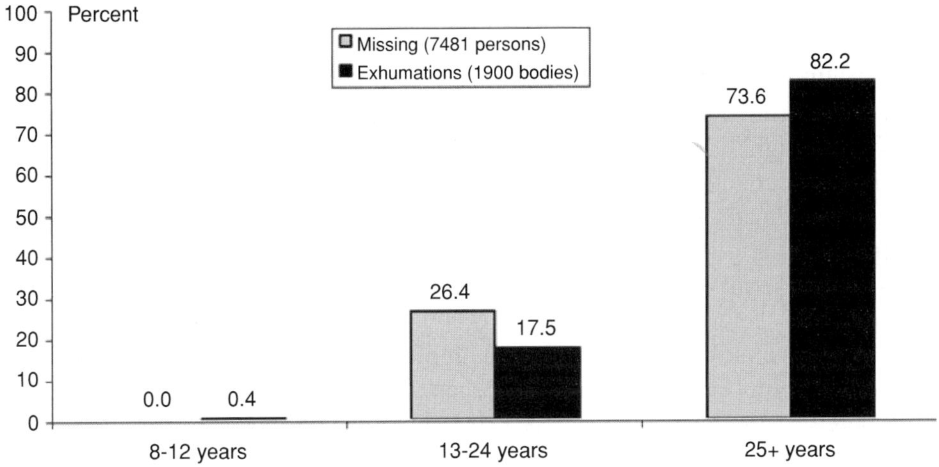

Figure 3. Age distribution of Srebrenica-related missing persons and of bodies exhumed by ICTY (percent).

random sample of the persons assumed to be killed after the fall of the enclave. It is not surprising that there are some differences between the distributions, however, considering the uncertainties involved in estimating the age of an exhumed body, especially since the estimates are often based on fragments of bodies, in addition to the sample variance. The bias towards older age groups for the exhumed bodies may also reflect the likelihood that more middle-aged and older men were taken to Potočari and later executed, while younger men to a larger degree attempted to flee through the forests towards Tuzla. Most mass graves consist of victims that were taken away for execution in groups. In sum, these findings support a conclusion that the persons missing in connection with the fall of Srebrenica are actually dead.

8. Conclusions

The aim of this article has been to present the results and the methods used by the authors to establish a minimum estimate of the victims of the genocide in Srebrenica based on individual-level data. It also provides descriptive statistics that elaborate on the magnitude of the genocide of Muslim men in this former UN 'safe area'. The methods used here, if appropriate, may be applicable to other cases of genocide. In many conflict areas, humanitarian organizations like the ICRC collect information on people who have disappeared in order to establish their fate. This may enable researchers to conduct further studies of genocide and war crimes at the individual level.

In this study we compiled a list of missing persons from two lists that were collected independently, and compared a consolidated list of missing persons with the 1991 Census and the OSCE Voters' register for the 1997 and 1998 elections. The comparison with pre-and post-conflict registers was primarily conducted in order to (a) establish that persons registered as missing were existing and alive in 1991 and (b) investigate whether people registered as missing could be found to be alive after the end of the war. The comparison with these data also provided us with information that enabled us to say more about who the missing persons were, and of the magnitude of the genocide.

The study concludes that at least 7,475 persons have been reported as missing and are presumed dead after the fall of the Srebrenica enclave on 11 July 1995, according to our conservative criteria. Also, an unknown number of persons were probably not reported as missing, for various reasons. Our estimate is lower than the commonly referred to range of 8–10,000 killed persons. As previously stated, ours is a conservative estimate based on highly reliable data. The actual number of genocide victims is likely to be higher than 7,475 and thus, this figure should be considered a *minimum estimate*. By using multiple systems estimation we found the likely estimate for the total number of victims to be only slightly higher, 7,536.

Estimates of the proportions of the 1991 population that disappeared in specific age groups show the great magnitude of the atrocities in Srebrenica. More than a third of those born between 1920 and 1979 and who lived in Srebrenica municipality in 1991 went missing from the enclave after its fall. Almost all of the missing persons are men (99.4 percent). A substantial number are young boys under 16 (76 persons) or older men above 60 (629 persons). Women comprise only 48 of these missing persons, the youngest female being 8 years old at the time of her disappearance.

There is no evidence that any significant number of the Srebrenica-related missing persons have survived. On the contrary, all available information indicates that the overwhelming majority of those listed as missing are actually dead. Using comparison with the 1991 census, our study further undermines the argument presented by some that persons registered as missing were fictive individuals, registered solely for propaganda purposes.

The judgement on Radislav Krstić makes several references to the demographic evidence presented in our report to the court, including: "The correlation between the age and sex of the bodies exhumed from the Srebrenica graves and that of the missing persons support the proposition that the majority of missing people were, in fact, executed and buried in the mass graves" (para. 82). The Trial Chamber concluded that it had been established beyond a reasonable doubt that "In July 1995, following the take-over of Srebrenica, Bosnian Serb forces executed several thousand Bosnian Muslim men. The total number of victims is likely to be within the range of 7,000–8,000 men (para. 84)" (para. 427) (http://www.un.org/icty/krstic/TrialC1/judgement/krs-tj010802e.pdf).

We believe that the large scale of the tragedy, comprising more than a third of all Muslim men in Srebrenica before the war, including about 50 percent of all middle aged men (41–60 years of age), meets the ICTY genocide criteria: "... acts committed with intent to destroy, in whole or in part, a national, ethnical, racial or religious group ...". In the ICTY trial against General Radislav Krstić, the court ruled in accordance with this view.

Acknowledgements

We are grateful to William Seltzer, Patrick Ball, Nico Keilman, Nils Petter Gleditsch, Michael Hofmayer and Ann Tilton for comments on drafts of this article.

Notes

* All authors have formerly been with the UN International Criminal Tribunal for the former Yugoslavia (ICTY). They share equal responsibility for this article. The views expressed in the article are those of the authors and not necessarily those of the United Nations, Statistics Norway or the International Peace Research Institute, Oslo (PRIO).

[1] In a study on Kosovo done after the Srebrenica report was written Ball et al. (2002) used a similar approach, i.e. merging several lists with individual-level data on victims, to estimate the total number of victims. They did not, however, have pre and post conflict individual-level data at their disposal.

[2] Several people have been sentenced to life imprisonment for genocide and other war crimes by ICTR, including the former Prime Minister Jean Kambanda (http://www.ictr.org).

[3] Human Rights Watch World Report 1998 (http://www.hrw.org/worldreport/Helsinki-05.htm #P357_89852).

[4] The Srebrenica massacre is still a very sensitive topic in the Netherlands. The NIOD report caused Prime Minister Wim Kok and his cabinet to resign in April 2002, seven years after the events took place (*Time*, 29 April 2002: 33).

[5] In the former Yugoslavia this commonly meant all men between the ages of 16 and 60.

[6] The NIOD report suggests that of the total number of 7,500 missing persons, "[. . .] approximately 1,500 people died on the road to Tuzla, whether under gunfire, in combat, killed by mines, suicide or starvation" and 6,000 were taken by the Bosnian Serb Army (VRS) as prisoners of war and later executed (NIOD, 2002).

[7] The evidence presented to court in this report and in the testimony appears to have formed an important basis for the judgement, see http://www.un.org/icty/krstic/TrialC1/judgement/krs-tj010802e.pdf. The judgment was appealed by the defendant and is still undergoing legal proceedings.

[8] A more detailed description of the problems encountered in the matching process between the different lists is described in Brunborg and Urdal (2000).

[9] The "total number of persons for whom a tracing request regarding Srebrenica's fall was opened by the family" is 7421. Of these the fate has been clarified for 85, with 22 determined to be alive and 63 to be dead. Source: Tracing requests Missing in BiH (updated on 29/09/99), International Committee of the Red Cross, Sarajevo.

[10] "Part 2 which is printed on different colour paper to facilitate usage, is the list of persons for whom ICRC has received information on death and whose relatives have been informed. The mortal remains of these persons have not yet been recovered by their families" (ICRC, 1998). These deaths have been established on the basis of eyewitness accounts and/or evidence provided by the family. Prior to the publication of version 4 of the ICRC list, families had the opportunity to register missing relatives that were not assumed to have survived, as dead.

[11] The date of disappearance could either be the date the informant her/himself last saw the person alive, or a date based on information provided by an eyewitness through the informant. The same applies to the place and date of disappearance.

[12] In the merging and matching process of the different lists we used the database utilities in Microsoft Access. The matching process was done electronically based on specified criteria, and then inspected manually.

[13] The unique ID number, *matični broj*, was introduced in all of the former Yugoslavia in 1981.

[14] The consolidated list includes 19,692 persons missing from all of Bosnia and Herzegovina, where 6,980 records are found on both lists, 12,423 on the ICRC list only, and 289 found on the PHR list only.
[15] A registration in either the ICRC or the PHR list probably makes identification more likely. The main reason for not being identified, however, is that there are no personal characteristics on the bodies that make identification possible.
[16] We are grateful to Patrick Ball and William Seltzer for advice on this.
[17] Since we do not know whether the six survivors on the ICRC list are also on the PHR list, we use the total of 7,481 persons as the basis for this estimation.
[18] Because of the relatively low number of female victims, we do not present further statistics on females broken down by municipality and age.
[19] A counter-argument is that some of the missing persons we failed to match may have been enumerated in Yugoslav republics other than Bosnia and Herzegovina (or abroad), particularly in Serbia that is only a few kilometres away from Srebrenica. The number of such persons is not likely to have been very high, however.
[20] One example is the ICRC itself: "In February 1996, the ICRC's conclusions were made public for the first time: that the vast majority of the missing men had been killed after capture and that many others had been killed in armed con-frontations while fleeing the enclave or in lieu of arrest". Source: ICRC Special Report, *The issue of missing persons in Bosnia and Herzegovina, Croatia and the Federal Republic of Yugoslavia*. The date of publication is not given but it is probably 1 February 1998.

Appendix

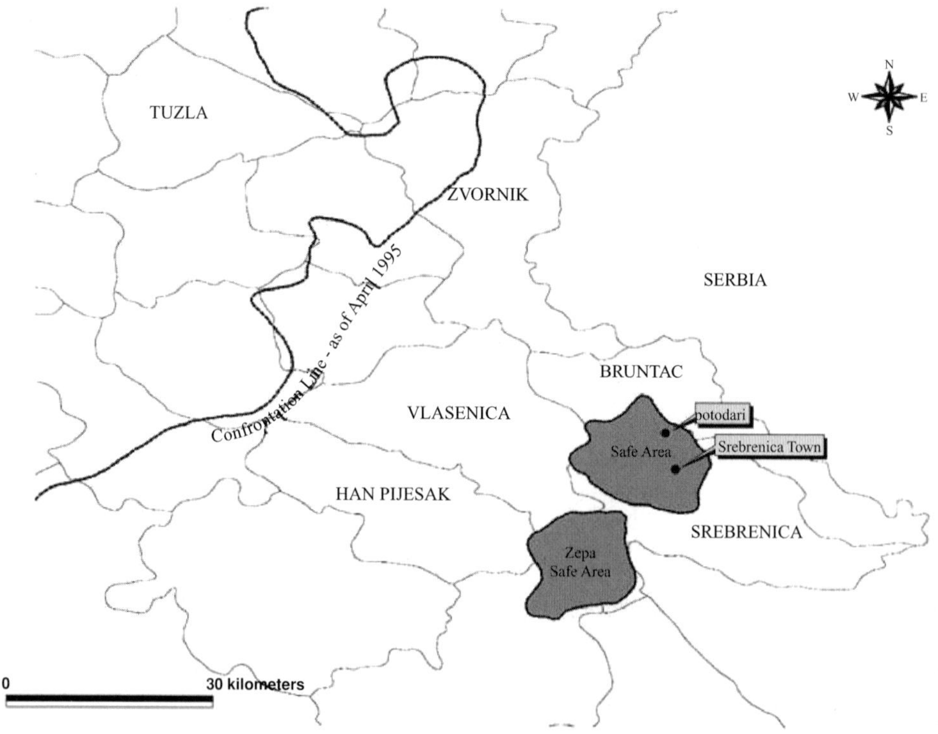

Figure Map.

References

Ball, P., Betts, W., Scheuren, F., Dudukovich, J. and Asher J., 2002. *Killings and Refugee Flow in Kosovo March–June 1999*. A Report to the International Criminal Tribunal for the Former Yugoslavia. American Association for the Advancement of Science and the American Bar Association—Central and East European Initiative. Available at http://hrdata.aaas.org/kosovo/ icty_report.pdf.

Bishop, Y. M. M., Fienberg S. E. and Holland, P. W., 1975. *Discrete Multivariate Analysis. Theory and Practice*. MIT Press, Cambridge.

Bookman, M. Z., 1997. *The Demographic Struggle for Power: The Political Economy of Demographic Engineering in the Modern World*. Frank Cass, London.

Brunborg, H. 2001. 'Contribution of statistical analysis to the investigations of the International Criminal Tribunals', *Statistical Journal of the United Nations Economic Commission for Europe* 18: 227–238.

Brunborg, H. and Urdal, H., 2000. *Report on the Number of Missing and Dead from Srebrenica*. Office of the Prosecutor, International Criminal Tribunal for the former Yugoslavia, 12 February.

Heuveline, P., 1998. 'Between one and three million': Towards the demographic reconstruction of a decade of Cambodian history (1970–1979)', *Population Studies* 52(1): 49–65.

Honig, J. W. and Both, N., 1996. *Srebrenica: Record of a War Crime*. Penguin, London.

ICRC (International Committee of the Red Cross), 1998. *Missing Persons on the Territory of Bosnia and Herzegovina*, Fourth edition issued on 30.06.1998—by alphabetical order. International Committee of the Red Cross, Sarajevo.

ICTY, 2000. *Statute of the Tribunal*. The Hague: International Criminal Tribunal for the former Yugoslavia. Available at http://www.un.org/icty/basic/statut/stat2000_con.htm.

Marks, E. S., Seltzer W. and Krotki, K. J. 1974. *Population Growth Estimation: A Handbook of Vital Statistics Measurement*. The Population Council, New York.

Mamelund, S.-E. and Borgan, J.-K., 1996. 'Cohort-and period mortality in Norway 1846–1964', *Reports* 96/9. Statistics Norway, Oslo.

McCaa, R. 2001. 'Missing millions: The Mexican revolution, a demographic catastrophe', paper presented to the Population Association of America's Annual Meeting. Washington, DC, 29–31 March.

NIOD, 2002. *Srebrenica, een 'veilig' gebied. Reconstructie, achtergronden, gevolgen en analyses van de val van een Safe Area* [*Srebrenica, a 'Safe' Area. Reconstruction, Background, Consequences and Analyses of the Fall of a Safe Area*]. Nederlands Instituut voor Oorlogsdocumentatie, Amsterdam. Available at http://www.srebrenica.nl/en/a_index.htm.

Rohde, D., 1997. *Endgame. The Betrayal and Fall of Srebrenica: Europe's Worst Massacre Since World War II*. Farrar, Straus and Giroux, New York.

Rummel, R. J. 1994. *Death by Government*. Transaction, New Brunswick, NJ.

Rummel, R. J. 1997. *Statistics of Democide: Genocide and Mass Murder Since 1900*. Center for National Security Law, University of Virginia, Charlottesville, VA.

Sekar, C. C., and Deming, W. E. 1949. 'On a method for estimating birth and death rates and the extent of registration', *Journal of the American Statistical Society* 44: 101–115.

UN, 2001. *World Population Prospects: The 2000 Revision. Volume I: Comprehensive Tables*, ST/ESA/SER.A/198. United Nations, New York.

Urdal, H. 2001. 'Nasjoner som kategorier: En analyse av folketellingene i Bosnia-Hercegovina [Nations as categories: An analysis of the population censuses of Bosnia-Herzegovina]', *Tidsskrift for Samfunnsforskning* 42(4): 571–589.

CHAPTER 10. WAR-RELATED DEATHS IN THE 1992–1995 ARMED CONFLICTS IN BOSNIA AND HERZEGOVINA: A CRITIQUE OF PREVIOUS ESTIMATES AND RECENT RESULTS[1]

EWA TABEAU
Demographic Unit, Office of the Prosecutor (OTP), International Criminal Tribunal for the former Yugoslavia (ICTY), The Hague, The Netherlands

JAKUB BIJAK
Demographic Unit, Office of the Prosecutor (OTP), International Criminal Tribunal for the former Yugoslavia (ICTY), The Hague, The Netherlands
Central European Forum for Migration Research

Abstract. In this article, we provide a critique of previous estimates of war-related deaths from Bosnia and Herzegovina and propose an analytical framework and a new estimate of such deaths. Our assessment is concentrated on civilian victims, whose death (or disappearance) can in a straightforward manner be linked with war operation. The estimate is based on carefully selected sources analysed jointly at the level of individual records, allowing for identity verification of victims, elimination of duplicates within the sources and exclusion of records overlapping between the sources. Although we can argue that our estimate is much better founded than any other estimate ever obtained, it is still incomplete and should be seen as work in progress.

1. A general framework[2] for assessment of war-related deaths of the Bosnian conflict

In 1991, Bosnia and Herzegovina (BH) was still one of the six constituent republics of Yugoslavia, the one having the most mixed ethnic composition. The population of Bosnian Muslims was in 1991 the largest among all ethnic groups (1.9 million, 44% of all). The second largest were the Serbs (1.4 million, 31%). Bosnian Croats (760,000) and Others (all remaining ethnicities jointly: 350,000) comprised, respectively, 17 and 8 percent of the 1991 population of Bosnia, enumerated in the census of the 31st March. All other republics had a clear majority group, for example mainly Croats lived in Croatia, and Slovenes in Slovenia. In June 1991, it was obvious that the Serbian president Slobodan Milošević began to increase the dominance of Serbs in the former Yugoslavia. Especially three republics, Bosnia, Croatia and Slovenia, felt directly threatened by Serb nationalism and the perspective of Greater Serbia carved out of the territories mainly in Bosnia and Croatia, with Slovenia providing the Serbs with cheap resources. The republics of Slovenia and Croatia were

This chapter was previously published in *European Journal of Population*, vol. 21, no. 2–3, 2005, pp. 187–215.

Helge Brunborg et al. (eds.), The Demography of Armed Conflict, 217–244.

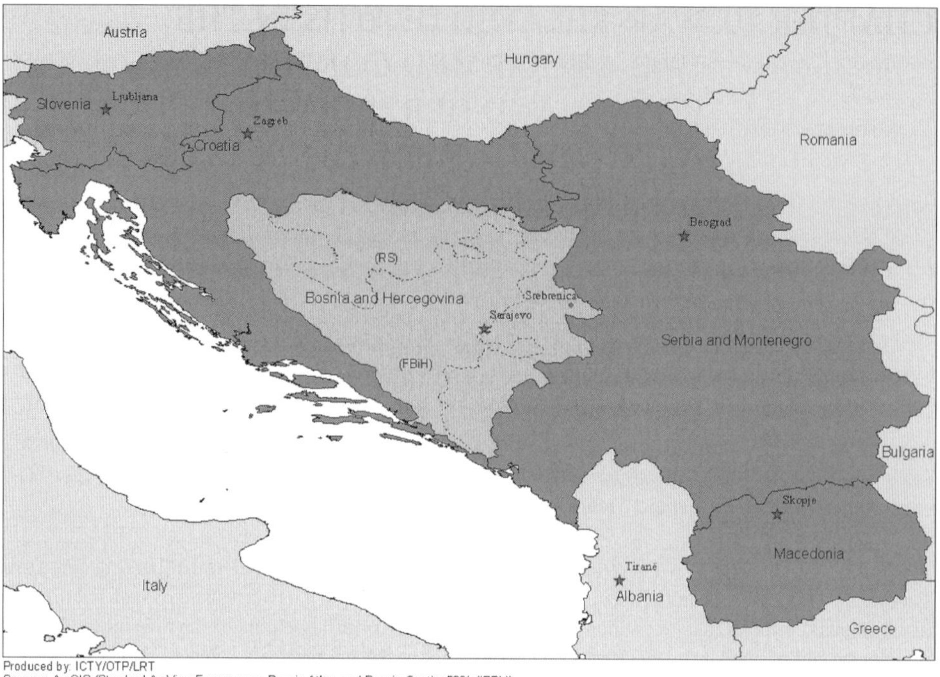

Figure 1. Map of the former Yugoslavia.

the first ones to break away from the socialist Yugoslavia, Slovenia after a short ten-day relatively painless war with the Yugoslav National Army (JNA), practically representing the interests of Serbia, and Croatia after seven-month fights with JNA and Serbia. After the recognition of Croatia by the international community and the first seven-month war episode, the Croatian war with Serbia had its continuation in the period 1992–1995, when the Croats fought for the territories they lost to the Serbs in the first months of war. Noteworthy is that the first episode of the Croatian war provided the world with the images of Croatian civilians from the towns, such as Vukovar and Dubrovnik, shelled by the Serb artillery and exposed to Serb air strikes for months in late 1991. The late stages of the war in Croatia produced quite opposite images of the Croatian Serbs brutally cleansed from the territories the Serbs acquired in the beginning of the war (the Republic of Serb Krajina and Western Slavonia) (Figure 1).

The situation in Bosnia was far more complex than in Slovenia or Croatia, due to the mixed ethnic composition with two large majority groups, Bosnian Muslims (called Bosniaks) and Bosnian Serbs, a strong minority group, Bosnian Croats, aided by Croatia, and the absence of a single ethnic Muslim republic in the former Yugoslavia. The most essential observation of the Bosnian population at the outbreak of the 1990s conflict is that while there were Bosnians in a geographical sense (i.e. all peoples in Bosnia), there were hardly any Bosnians in a political sense. Bosnian Muslims, Serbs and Croats existed as politically distinguished groups who happened to live in one country. Political goals of these groups were too distinct to allow for a peaceful settlement. Bosnian Serbs, and later also Bosnian Croats, fought (often through ethnic cleansing and terror campaigns) to take and control territories that otherwise would be subject to the rule of Bosnian Muslims from Sarajevo. The Muslims fought for these territories as they believed they did not have much choice. If Bosnian Muslims remained in the post-1991 Bosnia that would belong to the rump Yugoslavia, their educational or job opportunities would be severely limited by the dominance of Serbs. Their fate in the already independent Croatia would not be much different. But breaking away from Yugoslavia put Bosnian Muslims in a particularly difficult position, as they were left with no support other than the one expected from the international community. And the international community did not rush with the recognition of Bosnia's independence. The issue was obviously complicated. The European Community (EC) and United States finally granted their recognition to Bosnia in April 1992, which, however, did not stop the Bosnian conflict. The war in Bosnia lasted until November 1995 and comprised several episodes, including such as those with Serb perpetrators and Muslim (or Croat) victims, with Croat perpetrators and Muslim (or Serb) victims, as well as with Muslims perpetrators and Serb (or Croat) victims. At one point, there was even a Muslim–Muslim conflict. All these episodes took place in various time periods and territories throughout the war lasting from April 1992 to November 1995. The war ended leaving the country divided into two political entities, the Federation of Bosnia and Herzegovina (FBH; Bosnian Muslims and Croats) and Republika Srpska (RS; Bosnian Serbs). Noteworthy, the ethnic cleansing of the Bosnian Muslims by Serbs brought, in consequence, the most casualties and, most importantly, an extraordinary migration (both internal and external) of mainly Muslim population that resulted in the dramatic changes in the size and ethnic composition of the pre-conflict population of the country. The population of Bosnian Muslims suffered the greatest losses during this war.

Even though the migration movements were the most significant demographic consequence of the Bosnian war, the subject of this article is the number of war-related deaths of the 1992–1995 conflict in Bosnia. The issue is not new, but remains unresolved until the present. This does not mean that no estimates have been produced and presented to a broader audience. On the contrary, quite a number of sometimes extreme figures are available. We are, however, strongly convinced that none of the previously made estimates is well founded. Therefore in this article we provide a critique of a selection of the previous numbers and propose an analytical framework and a new estimate of war-related deaths in Bosnia.

Note that our research results were obtained from a project somewhat different from the usual statistical and academic work. Our perspective was in line with that of expert reports submitted to the Trial Chambers at the International Criminal Tribunal for the former Yugoslavia (ICTY) as part of the (prosecution) evidence.

The goal of such reports is to provide the Chambers with high-standard war-related population statistics satisfying the requirement of being 'beyond reasonable doubt' and consistent with the framework of the International Humanitarian Law. The first prerequisite implies that questionable, deficient, incomplete sources and/or individual death cases are excluded from our statistics. Secondly, particular attention is paid in our research to the civilian-military status of victims, and causes and circumstances of death. Only those death cases that come from reliable sources and that are complete and consistent with our pre-determined requirements are included as war-related deaths; otherwise they are not reported at all. This research approach is more restrictive than the usual statistical and academic work and results in rather conservative estimates.

Let's begin by noting that among all demographic events, death occurs to everyone with certainty. Questions that remain unanswered in the course of people's lives are when and how. Both the timing and the cause of death are generally determined by an individual's age, sex, health and its genetic component, lifestyle, living and working conditions, and sometimes violent factors. Shortly after the occurrence of death, statistical agencies take a record of it, based on the compulsory notification from the family of the deceased. For statistical purposes, every death is described in terms of date, place, and cause of death. Personal details, such as the first and family names, date and place of birth, place of residence, education, profession, etc. are reported as well. A physician, other trained medical personnel, or a coroner must declare the cause of death as a medical category on the basis of the International Classification of Diseases and Conditions Leading to Death (ICD) provided by the World Health Organisation. Currently, the 10th revision of the classification is used throughout the world. The ICD allows us to distinguish between diseases, or fatal health conditions, and external causes of death (i.e. accidents).

The ICD is not the only classification of diseases that exists, though it is the only one officially in use. Demographers and epidemiologists have proposed several alternative classifications, one of the most informative being the etiological classification, in which causes of death are expressed as particular lifestyles responsible for certain types of medical conditions leading to death. The best known example of an etiological cause of death is smoking behaviour, which is a widely recognised risk factor in frequent causes of death, such as cardiovascular diseases (most importantly, coronary heart disease and stroke), lung cancer, and chronic lower respiratory diseases. Analogously, drinking behaviour, improper diet, or lack of physical activity are the next best examples of etiological causes.

The awareness of the existence of different classifications of causes of death is the key to the proper understanding of the size and causes of mortality that occurred in Bosnia and Herzegovina in 1992–1995. Causes of death taken into account must distinguish in this case between *regular causes of death* and causes responsible for *excess deaths* in this period. Among the regular causes, indeed the usual disease-, ageing-, or accidents-related medical categories should be considered. Among the causes of excess deaths, we must think of exclusively conflict-related causes, in particular excess deaths of civilians *due to war operations* or due to *harsh living and working conditions during the war.* Mortality of the military personnel should be seen as a separate conflict-related category.

The components of the total number of deaths in Bosnia and Herzegovina in 1992–1995, as in any other conflict, must distinguish between the following death categories:

(a) Regular deaths caused by disease, old age or war-unrelated accidents
(b) Deaths (of mainly civilians) due to severe living conditions during war
(c) Deaths of civilians due to war
(d) Deaths of soldiers/other military personnel due to war[3]
(e) Missing persons (both civilians and soldiers)

The assessment of war-related deaths must be concentrated on the civilian victims, whose death (or disappearance) can in a straightforward manner be linked with war operations[4] (categories b, c and the civilian component of e). A reliable estimate of war-related deaths must be based on carefully selected sources that ideally should be analysed jointly at the level of individual death records.

In the following parts of this article we give an overview of selected previous estimates of the 1992–1995 war-related deaths from Bosnia (Section 2), and discuss our latest estimates obtained in the Office of the Prosecutor (OTP) at the ICTY (Section 3). In the final Section 4, we summarise our critique regarding previous estimates and try to formulate general guidelines as to how one should proceed in order to obtain a fair estimate of the number of war-related deaths for a country such as Bosnia and Herzegovina.

2. An overview of previous estimates

The discussion of the total number of victims of the war in Bosnia and Herzegovina started during the war and has continued until present. It is striking that no reliable estimate has been produced so far. Estimates presented by various authors range from about 25,000 to 329,000 deaths. This lack of meaningful results is partly caused by the lack of reliable sources of information, but largely it is also because of unclear, non-transparent approaches applied to produce the total estimate. In order to explain the above points, we collected several estimates published between 1993 and 1999 and made an overview of their numerical values and methodological foundations.

We distinguish between two groups of estimates: those made in Bosnia or Croatia, and those made outside the region of the former Yugoslavia. The distinction is quite necessary, as particularly the local estimates were frequently biased by the historical knowledge, political views, and individual war experience of the authors. Another reason for the distinction is that practically all local estimates are based on one single source, while the estimates made at the international arena have usually been obtained from more sources used jointly.

2.1. ESTIMATES MADE IN BOSNIA AND CROATIA

All studies made in Bosnia or Croatia are based on data collected by the Institute for Public Health (IPH) in Sarajevo. This governmental institute was active throughout the war years 1992–1995 collecting systematic reports from those municipalities in Bosnia and Herzegovina, which were accessible to them. These were the municipalities controlled by the Bosnia and Herzegovina government, thus the Serb-controlled areas were not covered. The reporting may therefore be biased towards Muslim victims. Finally, duplicates are likely included in the IPH statistics, as no personal details were collected but only aggregate numbers.

IPH published two overviews of victims in Bosnia and Herzegovina in 1992–1995 (IPH, 1996a and 1996b; see Table 1). The preliminary total number of killed and disappeared persons (156,824) was shown on 1 January 1996 and the final total of killed, disappeared and died in 'another way' (but war-related) persons (278,800[5]) on 25 March 1996. Both totals apparently cover civilians and soldiers jointly. Ethnicity is shown in the March estimate. Of the two totals, the first one seems to be related to 'direct' victims and the second to the 'direct and indirect' victims. As any specific definition of an indirect victim is missing, and it is impossible to propose any definition of such victims from the Institute's reports, it is better to restrict the use of this source to the category 'killed and disappeared' who can be considered direct victims.

The two overviews published by the Institute were used by several authors, notably by Prof. Bošnjović and Prof. Smajkić,[6] a demographer and a public health scientist from Sarajevo. They produced an estimate of 258,000 (direct and indirect) victims (Bošnjović and Smajkić, 1997; see Table 1). On his own, Bošnjović suggested several figures, the latest one, presented at an international conference in Sarajevo in 1999, was as high as 270,000 victims (Bošnjović, 1999; see Table 1). It is striking that this total includes some 17,800 indirect victims and 252,200 direct victims (i.e. killed and disappeared). All these figures seem to be highly overestimated. The estimation method of Bošnjović and Smajkić is likely adding up the weekly figures of the Institute.

Vladimir Žerjavić is a Croatian demographer who studied the numbers of Yugoslav victims of World War II, and questioned the heavily overestimated numbers of casualties of the Jasenovac concentration camp and Bleiburg massacre (produced under Tito's regime). Recently he made a similar study of the victims of the Bosnian war, 1992–1995 (Žerjavić, 1998). According to Žerjavić, there were in total 220,000 war-related deaths in the 1992–1995 armed conflicts in Bosnia, of which 160,000 Muslims, 30,000 Croats, 25,000 Serbs and 5000 other ethnicities (Žerjavić, 1998; see Table 1). The numbers he produced for Bosnia were obtained from studying the IPH statistics. It is unclear what method he used; likely he studied the IPH documentation and took a simple sum of the (ethnicity-specific) numbers found in the source. The same source was also used by Bošnjović and Smajkić (1997), Bošnjović (1999), and Prašo (1996). Surprisingly, even though they all

Table 1. Estimates of war-related deaths in Bosnia and Herzegovina in 1992–1995: An overview of Yugoslav sources[a,b]

Sources	IPH[c] (1996a)	IPH[c] (1996b)	Bošnjović and Smajkić (1997)	Bošnjović (1999)	Žerjavić (1998)	Prašo (1996)
Killed and Disappeared	156,824	278,800	258,000	252,200	220,000	329,000
Other excess death[d]:	Excluded	Included	Included	17,800	Included	Included
Muslims	na	140,800	138,800	153,000	160,000	218,000
Croats	na	28,400	19,600	31,000	30,000	21,000
Serbs	na	97,300	89,300	72,000	25,000	83,000
Others	na	12,300	10,300	14,000	5000	7,000
Total in BH	156,824	278,800	258,000	270,000	220,000	329,000

Note. na: not available.
[a] All estimates cover the period from April 1992 to December 1995.
[b] All estimates *presumably* include both civilians and soldiers.
[c] IPH stands for the Institute for Public Health in Sarajevo.
[d] 'Other excess deaths' should be seen as indirect war victims, who died *mainly* due to severe living conditions during the war.

apparently used one and the same source, each of these authors ended with a different estimate. The results of their studies are: 220,000, 258,000, 270,000, and 329,000 victims, respectively. Žerjavić's number is indeed the lowest among all four presented, but this does not yet guarantee that it is close to reality. It has all deficiencies of the estimates obtained from a single source containing exclusively summary statistics, not individual records.

Yet other aspects of Žerjavić's work suggest that we should take his results with much hesitation. For example, he presented a specific distribution of the overall totals for every ethnic group by the perpetrators that caused these deaths:

- Muslim victims: 158,000 died due to the Serb aggression and 2000 by the Croat perpetrators,
- Croat victims: 28,000 died due to the Serb aggression and 2000 due to the Muslim perpetrators,
- Serb victims: 12,500 (50%) died due to the Muslim perpetrators and another 12,500 (50%) were caused by the Croat perpetrators.
  The above-mentioned distribution would require all fatal incidents to be known, which is largely unavailable in the original source.

The next author who used the same source is Prašo (1996; see Table 1). The 1992–1995 population loss is the central theme of his 1996 article, which is mainly devoted to demographic projections of the population in Bosnia and Herzegovina at the end of 1995. The 1992–1995 population loss, and in particular the dead and disappeared population, plays a central role in obtaining the 1995 population. In the first step Prašo projects the 1995 population under 'no conflict' and 'stable ethnic composition' assumptions, thereafter this estimate is adjusted by subtracting the presumed 1992–1995 (ethnicity-specific) population loss. No explanations are given regarding the presumed numbers of dead and disappeared. It seems that the total of 329,000 includes all categories of deaths, i.e. those killed or lethally wounded, excess deaths due to harsh life conditions and probably those who died of regular causes of mortality. Both civilians and military personnel are included in this total. It is unclear how many deaths out of 329,000 were killed or disappeared. The total of Prašo is extremely high. Also worth noting is the fact that Prašo is an economist and had no previous experience in demography. He very much relied on his personal experience and stresses his numbers are approximate.

2.2. ESTIMATES MADE OUTSIDE THE FORMER YUGOSLAVIA

The estimates made by international observers of the Bosnian conflict were based on more sources than just one, however frequently it is unclear what sources were used and how they were used in producing these estimates. The resulting estimates are generally lower than the estimates produced in Bosnia and Croatia.

Cherif Bassiouni was a professor of law at DePaul University and the president of the International Human Rights Law Institute. In 1993, he was appointed the chairman of the UN Commission of Experts investigating the war crimes in the former Yugoslavia, and in particular in Bosnia and Herzegovina. The Commission operated until the end of April 1994. Bassiouni concluded his studies mid-1995, with extensive reports of in total 3,500 pages (and a 100-page summary) and his testimony in the US Congress at a hearing before the Commission on Security and Cooperation in Europe (Bassiouni, 1995).

The Commission used funding from the UN as well as grants received from foundations, such as Soros and McArthur. Also individual countries contributed to the work of the Commission by donating funds for groups working in the region. Bassiouni and his associates spent 2 years between 1992 and 1994 in the former Yugoslavia, collecting documents, searching for and visiting mass graves, detention or concentration camps, interviewing witnesses, collecting all kinds of facts and indications on the crimes committed in the region. The Commission developed a database, which accumulated 65,000 documents and 300 tapes. This source material was used for writing the reports and producing estimates of war crimes,[7] in particular the number of war-related deaths in the Bosnian conflict, 200,000 individuals (Table 2). The number covered all types of victims in Bosnia and Herzegovina in 1992–1995. The number (very high) was in use in the last stage of the war and in the years thereafter. It is, however, unlikely that Bassiouni's Commission was able to establish individual-level statistical databases and check the individual death records as to how reliable and unique they were. The approach of the Commission was rather based on summary statistics on killing and missing, reported in the many documents they were able to collect.

Table 2. Estimates of war-related deaths in Bosnia and Herzegovina in 1992–1995[a] :Sources other than from the former Yugoslavia[b]

Source	Bassiouni (1995)	SIPRI[c] (1993)	Boyle (1997)	Thomas (1993)	Kenney (1995)
Killed and disappeared	200,000	169,100	Na	40,000 to 70,000	25,000 to 60,000
Muslims	na	128,000	139,000	na	na
Croats	na	11,100	na	na	na
Serbs	na	30,000	na	na	na
Others	na	na	na	na	na
Total BH	200,000	169,100	139,000	40,000 to 70,000	25,000 to 60,000

Notes:
[a] Except of SIPRI, all other estimates cover the period from April 1992 to December 1995.
[b] All estimates *presumably* include both civilians and soldiers.
[c] SIPRI is the Stockholm International Peace Research Institute. na: not available.

Table 3. Estimates of the killed and wounded population from Bosnia and Herzegovina, status as of August 1993

Population	Serbian	Croat	Muslim	Others	Total
As of 6 April 1992	1,442,560	829,472	1,780,660	455,308	4,508,000
Mobilized	150,000	124,420	130,000	na	404,420
In active fights	90,000	50,000	70,000	na	210,000
Killed soldiers	10,000	5,100	28,000	na	43,100
Wounded soldiers	33,000	40,000	32,000	na	105,000
Killed civilians	20,000	6,000	100,000	na	126,000
Wounded civilians	5,000	12,000	163,000	na	180,000
Refugees and IDPs	100,000	250,000	800,000	na	1,150,000

Source: Stockholm International Peace Research Institute (1993).

SIPRI is the Stockholm International Peace Research Institute, which engaged in producing an estimate of the total number of war-related deaths in Bosnia and Herzegovina in 1993 (SIPRI, 1993; see also Riedlmayer, 2000; Tables 2 and 3). Several original sources were investigated in a great detail. Only the 16 first months of conflict were covered by this project (April 1992 to July 1993) but the result is already striking: they estimated 169,100 Muslim, Croat and Serb victims (civilians and soldiers). Deaths of other ethnic groups (Other) are not stated, and regular deaths are excluded. The Institute has a good professional image in the field of peace research; their results are widely respected. But as regards statistical and demographic standards, it is hard to assess how reliable their estimates are.

Francis Boyle, an American lawyer lobbying for years for Bosnian Muslim authorities, stated in 1997 after a local doctor[8] from Sarajevo that some 139,000 victims of Muslim ethnicity (direct and indirect, civilians and militaries) died during the war (Boyle, 1997; see Table 2). His total, coming obviously from the work of others, most likely was an overestimation.

Raju Thomas from the Political Science department, Marquette University, Milwaukee, Wisconsin, produced the second lowest estimate of the total number of victims in Bosnia and Herzegovina, 40,000–70,000 deaths (quoted by Tosić, 2000; see also Thomas, 1993; Table 2). The sources he used included the International Committee of Red Cross (ICRC) and SIPRI. It is hard to believe that these totals cover all types of victims as the SIPRI alone shows much higher figures. Either a bias or misunderstanding of his totals is an explanation for the very low values of these results.

Finally, George Kenney published in 1995 his standpoint about the Bosnian casualties: between 25,000 and 60,000 war-related deaths (regular deaths excluded; see Kenney, 1995; Table 2). The author is a former State Department official who resigned in protest over the American policy regarding Bosnia and Herzegovina. The sources he used for his estimate include information from ICRC, CIA, State Department Bureau of Intelligence and Research, European military intelligence officers, and relief workers. The author believes the sources are reliable. As we already have collected more than 100,000 *unique* death records in our ICTY archive, we believe that Kenney's figure is largely underestimated.

3. The latest estimates made at ICTY

3.1. SOURCES AND METHODS

Since 1997, the Demographic Unit (DU, at the OTP—ICTY) has been conducting data collection and analytical projects intended to improve the knowledge of demographic consequences of the conflicts in the former Yugoslavia. The consequences of the Bosnian war have been central in demographic analyses conducted at ICTY, due to the most dramatic nature of this particular conflict, in comparison with the conflicts in Slovenia, Croatia, and Kosovo. The demographic sources collected for Bosnia are much more exhaustive than for all other conflicts.

In our work on mortality we applied an approach that can be seen as a reconstruction of war-related deaths, with elements of statistical estimation and using assumptions about a few missing sources of information. Our goal was to collect *all* death records from the territory of Bosnia and Herzegovina in the years 1992–1995. Only individual-level sources were collected. The names and other particulars of the deceased allowed for elimination of duplicates within each source and for comparing the sources in order to exclude the overlapping records.[9] The third reason for using individual records was the need of confirmation of persons' identities and their survival status. The 1991 population census served as a basis for the validation of the deceased. Also the 1997/1998 and 2000 registers of voters were used to verify the reliability of reporting of disappearances or deaths. This was done to exclude cases from the analysis where persons reported as dead or missing might have survived the conflict, as indicated by the fact that they appear on the electoral rolls from the post-war period. Having eliminated the duplicates, overlap, and inconsistent cases, we made a list of individuals whose deaths took place in Bosnia and Herzegovina in the period from April 1992 to December 1995 and were all war-related (in a direct or indirect way). The list was used as a basis for producing statistics such as the overall number of war-related deaths in Bosnia, or the number of civilian and military victims.

Worth noting is the fact that the sources selected for this project are an essential element of our method. We believe that the reliability of these sources is relatively high and their coverage is large (3 out of 10 sources are complete, 6 are largely complete, and only 1 is rather incomplete). One important source is, however, missing altogether and we had to make assumptions about its size. The reliability of the sources is fairly satisfactory, although it is not comparable with that of regular statistical sources. Our sources cover particularly well three major episodes of the Bosnian war: the 1992 initial conflict in the Autonomous Region of Krajina (min. 3,000, likely about 6000 *estimated* deaths), the 1992–1995 siege of Sarajevo (min. 7700, likely 10,000), and the 1995 fall of Srebrenica (min. 7,500, likely 8,000). On the other hand, war-related deaths from the territory controlled by the VRS (the army of Republika Srpska) are weakly represented in our sources. The major RS source, deaths registered in the local vital events offices, are not available. Also persons, whose bodies had been exhumed and not yet identified, are not included in our sources. These two sources should yet become available in the future.

The following mortality sources were available and have been used in producing our estimate of war-related deaths in Bosnia:

- military records of fallen soldiers of the BH Government Army (ABiH), 1992–1995. Acquired in 2001 from the Ministry of Defence of the Federation of Bosnia and Herzegovina. Coverage: *complete*, entire country, 28,027 records, all war-related.
- military records of fallen soldiers of the Republika Srpska Army (VRS), 1992–1995. Acquired in 2001 from the Ministry of Defence of Republika Srpska. Coverage: *complete*, entire country, 14,237 records, all warrelated.
- military records of fallen soldiers of the Croatian Defence Council (HVO), 1992–1995. Acquired in 2002 from the Ministry of Defence of the Federation of Bosnia and Herzegovina. Coverage: *complete* entire country, 6689 records, all war-related.
- the ICRC and PHR lists of Missing Persons for Bosnia and Herzegovina, 1992–1995, established by the International Committee of Red Cross and a non-governmental American organisation Physicians for Human Rights (PHR). Both lists were acquired at first in 1998, the ICRC list was updated in 2002. Coverage: *largely complete*, entire country, 20,621 unique records on the two lists merged, all records war-related.
- the FIS Mortality Database, 1992–1995, established by the Federal Institute for Statistics (FIS) in Sarajevo through a centralisation and computerisation of individual death records available from the vital events registration system in the territory of the Federation of Bosnia and Herzegovina. The collection of war-time death records, although disturbed and incomplete, took place in local offices of the vital events registration already during the conflict. After the war more forms were completed retrospectively and added to the local archives. The retrospective collection of war-time death registration forms continues also at present, although at a lower pace. The collected forms were stored locally until the Federal Statistical Office decided in late 2001 to engage in processing of this information. This decision was made in response to the request made by the OTP (ICTY), and approved by the Bosnian government.

In the first half of 2002, all available forms were computerised. The OTP (ICTY) acquired the FIS database in mid-2002 from the Federal Institute for Statistics in Sarajevo. Coverage: *largely complete* the FBH territory, 74,402 death records, of which 25,103 are war-related.

- the HSS-94 Mortality Database, 1992–1994, (HSS-94 stands for the Households Survey of Sarajevo conducted in mid-1994), established at the OTP (ICTY) in 2002 from the original survey questionnaires collected in mid-1994 through interviewing approximately 85,000 households (equivalent to about 340,000 persons) living at that time on the territory within the front lines in Sarajevo. The survey was designed and conducted by the Research Institute for War Crimes and International Law in Sarajevo. Coverage: *largely complete*, the within-front-lines territory of Sarajevo as of mid-1994, 12,860 death records, of which 7879 are war-related.
- the MAG Mortality Database of War Victims, 1992–1995, established by a non-governmental Bosnian organisation Muslims Against Genocide (MAG).[10] First acquired in 1998, the latest version of the MAG database supplemented at the OTP (ICTY) in 2003. Coverage: *largely complete*, entire country, 34,378 records of dead and missing persons, all war-related.
- death records of the Bakije Funeral Home in Sarajevo, 1992–1995, the largest and oldest Muslim funeral home in the city. Acquired in 1996. Coverage: *largely complete*, the within-front-lines territory of Sarajevo as of 1992–1995, 12,866 death records, of which 5,449 are considered war-related (only those records matched with the war-related records from other sources).
- exhumation records of the identified bodies from the Autonomous Region of Krajina (ARK), RS territory. Coverage: *rather incomplete*, status as of 2000: 2,705 records, all war-related.
- *Knjiga nestalih općine Prijedor* (Prijedor Municipality Book of Missing, KNP). Coverage: *largely complete*, 3,146 records acquired in 1998, supplemented in 2001, all considered war-related.

Statistics produced in the former Yugoslavia, as in several other similar countries, were characterised by the presence of duplicates. The 1991 population census likely contains several thousands duplicated records. These refer to persons who were reported by their parents as household members of the parental household, and at the same time these persons reported about themselves from their own households. Students, newly married couples, children of divorced couples are a few examples justifying the presence of duplicates.

Duplicates are not unusual in statistical surveys, and therefore during the 1991 census in Bosnia this problem received the necessary attention too. And thus, the municipal census commissions searched for and eliminated the duplicates within municipalities. In the next step, the Republican Statistical Office was supposed to clean the duplicates observed between municipalities. However, because of the outbreak of the conflict, the 1991 census records have never been cross-compared between municipalities, leaving some duplicates in the data. All in all, despite of the fact that many duplicates had been eliminated directly after the census and before releasing the first preliminary results of the census, duplicated records are still included in the census files. In addition to the efforts of the Bosnian statistical authorities, we recently found another 8,500 duplicated records and eliminated them from the data files.

Duplicates are also included in the lists of dead persons, especially in the sources where only summary statistics are mentioned. Generally, individual level sources should have priority above summary sources. However, when the data situation is bad (as for BH in the period 1992–1995), each source may add to the knowledge of the phenomenon.

The next difficulty with data on war-related deaths is that persons reported in certain sources as dead or missing sometimes could have survived without their families notifying the appropriate authorities. Only a few sources can be taken as safe and sound, for instance records from death certificates, court decisions proclaiming persons dead, and death records of armed forces from the archives of the Ministry of Defence.

Another serious problem with the figures on deaths is the overlap of sources. For instance, three basic sources on war-related deaths in Sarajevo in 1992–1995 are Muslims Against Genocide, the Bakije Funeral Home, and the 1994 Sarajevo Household Survey. Each of the three groups collected their data independently and produced estimates from about 9,400 to 12,800 deaths. The simple sum of the three totals would result in some 30,000 deaths for Sarajevo in this period, an obvious mistake of overestimation. At the same time, we must realise that no single source is ever complete. After excluding the duplicates and the overlap, the obtained number of unique records is an underestimation due to missing information.

Finally, not all sources include information about ethnicity. Moreover, ethnicity reported in different sources may be inconsistent, which would bias the outcome of the analysis. We therefore used the links of every source with the 1991 population census and compiled our statistics according to the self-reported ethnicity from the census.

All in all, the method used for estimating war-related deaths should take the following principles into account:

- individual-level information should be preferred above summary sources,
- sources are hierarchical; some are more informative and reliable than others,
- identity of the deceased must be ensured,
- ethnicity must be reported consistently in all sources,
- distinction between conflict-related and regular causes of death must be made,
- control for duplicates must be carried out in every single source,
- overlap of the sources must be eliminated, only the best-quality unique records are to be included as a basis for producing estimates.

The above-mentioned principles underlie the approach applied for producing statistics on war-related deaths by the Demographic Unit:

- to use individual-level records with personal details included; summary sources serve merely as a reference for our results,
- the identity of the deceased is confirmed through a verification procedure in which each mortality source is cross-examined against the 1991 population census,
- the sources are required to contain specific information not only on the date and place of death, but also on the cause of death,
- checking for duplicates and eliminating overlap are inherent parts of data examination,
- the definition of ethnicity is always the same: as reported in the 1991 census, this is possible by establishing links between the census and all mortality sources.

As mentioned before, we matched information about individuals from the 1991 census with records of these individuals from other sources. When comparing various lists with data on individuals we used the MS Access database management system to search for records on one list that match records on the other list. If key variables are identical in two lists the matched records are assumed to represent the same person, otherwise not.

Matching two lists always starts with searching for records with identical personal identification numbers (if available), names and date of birth. Only exceptionally would two different persons have identical names and be born on exactly the same date, especially if we only consider the population of a limited area, such as a single municipality. Quite often, however, names are spelled differently or the date of birth is recorded slightly differently—or missing altogether in one or both lists. Consequently, for persons not matched in the first round we make the search criteria gradually broader for one or more variables, for example by including only the year (and not the full date) of birth, or only the initial of the first name, in addition to the surname. The results of such matches have, however, to be inspected visually before deciding whether different records are likely to refer to the same person or not, by looking at other available information, such as the municipality and place of birth or residence. For difficult cases we checked the 1991 census for additional information, e.g. information about family members of the person in question.

The final matching result is that on average 80% of the original source records are linked with the census. So, some 20% of the records reported in the original source are 'lost' and excluded from the minimum numbers. The excluded information can be recovered in the stage of producing the overall numbers of war-related deaths, by adjusting the minimum numbers for the incomplete matching rate. Some more information may be added later, when new sources become available and new records are linked between the sources.

3.2. MINIMUM NUMBERS

As of 15 June 2003, the fate of 53.1% of the pre-war (census) population of Bosnia and Herzegovina was established by linking with the other sources: 2,212,052 individuals (50.6% of those reported in the 1991 census) were found on the electoral lists and are presumed to be alive, while 107,395 persons (2.5% of the census population) were found on various lists of dead, killed or missing persons. Moreover, for 1923 individuals the evidence was inconsistent as they were found both on an electoral list and among the war-related deaths. As we are not able to determine their fate, they have been excluded from further analysis and from the calculation of the total estimate of war-related deaths in Bosnia and Herzegovina. An overview of current population statistics is shown in Table 4.

Out of the total of 107,395 deaths and disappearances 67,530 are considered war-related. These are all records from the military sources (ABiH, VRS and HVO), missing persons lists (ICRC-PHR, KNP), exhumations from the ARK and the MAG 2002 database of war-related deaths. From the FIS death registration and HSS-94 databases only those records are taken that are explicitly mentioned as war-related, unless they also appear in another of the above-mentioned sources. From the Bakije funeral lists only those individuals mentioned in other war-related sources are considered to be of relevance for the purpose of this study. By combining all these lists (and controlling for duplicates), we obtain a *minimum estimate* of war-related deaths in Bosnia and Herzegovina (67,530) as the number of unique individual records, matched with the 1991 population census (i.e. having confirmed identity) and matched with neither of the

Table 4. Overview of matching statistics with the 1991 population census for deceased, missing and survivors from Bosnia and Herzegovina, 1992–1995, status as of mid-2003

Data source category	Absolute size (matched)	% of unique census records	Unmatched records	Percent unmatched
Pre-war population: 1991 census	4,377,032	–	–	–
–of which unique (not duplicated)	4,368,514	100.00%	–	–
Survivors–post-war voters*	2,212,052	50.64%	*548,507*	*19.86%*
Deaths and disappearances**	107,395	2.46%	*24,982*	*18.87%*
Inconsistent evidence	1,923	0.04%	–	–
Unknown fate	2,047,144	46.86%	–	–

* Figures on voters refer to the 1997–1998 voters registers only. They do not include the 2000 voters.
** Deaths statistics cover war-related and war-unrelated causes of death.
Status as on 15 June 2003.
Source: Demographic Unit, OTP.

Table 5. Minimum war-related death ratios, by ethnicity, status as of mid-2003

Ethnicity	Serbs	Muslims	Croats	Others	Total
Total Pop. 1991	1,361,814	1,896,009	758,585	352,106	4,368,514
Killed	12,642	45,980	5,629	3,279	67,530
Percentage	*0.93*	*2.43*	*0.74*	*0.93*	*1.55*
Civilians	2130	22,225	986	1241	26,582
Percentage	*0.16*	*1.17*	*0.13*	*0.35*	*0.61*
Soldiers	10,512	23,755	4643	2038	40,948
Percentage	*0.77*	*1.25*	*0.61*	*0.58*	*0.94*

Status as on 15 June 2003.
Source: Demographic Unit, OTP.

post-war electoral rolls. For the matched records, we can take the indicator of ethnicity from the 1991 census and show the distribution of this minimum total number of victims by ethnic affiliation, differentiating whether the victims were civilian or military. These distributions are shown in Table 5 and Figures 2 and 3, with percentages of the pre-war total population, taken from the 1991 census.

For Muslims, the rates turn out to be substantially higher than those for the other ethnic groups. On the one hand, this may reflect the real differences in war-inflicted

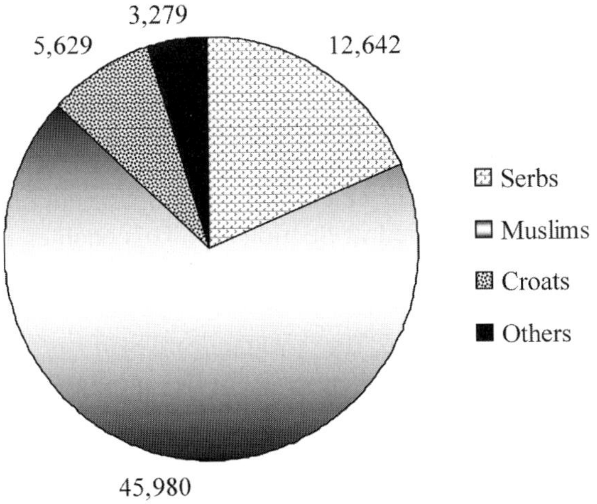

Figure 2. A minimum number of persons killed in the Bosnian war, by ethnicity, status as of mid-2003. Overall Minimum Number of All Killed: 67,530. Coverage: Civilians (26,582) and Soldiers (40,948), BH, 1992–1995.

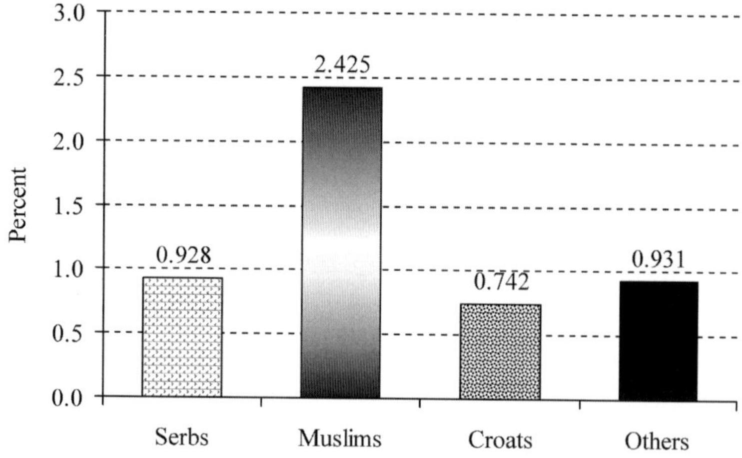

Figure 3. Minimum war-related death ratios, by ethnicity, status as of mid-2003. *Note*: Ratios are obtained by dividing the numbers of war-related deaths by the 1991 population. All numbers are taken by ethnicity. The outcomes are multiplied by 100 (%).

mortality, but on the other, it may also be a result of not including enough sources describing mortality of the RS part of the population. For example, we could not include the regular RS mortality registers, which are still unavailable; RS mortality might therefore be underrepresented in our sources.

Apart from the incomplete matching, this also indicates that the true number of war-inflicted deaths is higher than the mentioned minimum figure of 67,530 victims. An attempt to adjust the results to overcome the above-mentioned problems is made in the next part of this study.

3.3. OVERALL NUMBERS

Due to the data quality problems, the matching of particular sources was never complete. On average 81.1% of the records were matched with the 1991 census. Therefore, to obtain a more accurate estimate, an adjustment has to be applied to the minimum estimate mentioned in Section 3.2. This enables the elimination of inconsistent evidence and overcoming the problems associated with incomplete matching.

In the last column of Table 6, the *estimated numbers of records from every source* are obtained by correcting (i.e. dividing) the number of *consistent* matches from a given source by the matching rate achieved for this particular source. (Note that '*consistent matches*' are the *unique* records *matched* with the 1991 census). For example, for the ABiH collection of military deaths, the number of 25,031 consistent matches divided by the matching rate of 0.9011 gives the estimate of 27,778 ABiH soldiers killed in the conflict. In the second step, the overlap of sources

Table 6. Estimated overall numbers of war-related deaths from Bosnia and Herzegovina in 1992-1995, status as of mid–2003

Source	Total	Matched	Percent	Consistent	Estimated
ABiH	28,027	25,255	90.11	25,031	27,778
VRS	14,237	11,166	78.43	10,981	14,001
HVO	6,689	5,904	88.26	5,365	6,078
Less overlap of sources				(429)	(498)
Military			86.46	40,948	47,360
ICRC'2002	20,621	16,888	81.90	13,281	16,217
FIS	25,103	21,791	86.81	9,355	10,777
Sarajevo	7,879	5,761	73.12	2,968	4,059
MAG'2002	34,378	26,243	76.34	10,286	13,475
Bakije	5,449	3,945	72.40	1,564	2,160
ARK	2,705	2,180	80.59	1,748	2,169
KNP	3,146	1,953	62.08	1,770	2,851
Less overlap of sources				(14,390)	(18,200)
Known civilians			79.33	26,582	33,508
Other civilians (assumed 50% of known civilians for RS and 5,000 more unique records of missing persons from the 1CMP)					21,754
Estimated total civilians					55,261
Estimated total					102,622

The estimated total does not include excess deaths due to harsh living conditions
Status as on 15 June 2003, overlap corrected 18 August 2003.
Source: Demographic Unit, OTP.

is calculated[11] and corrected (i.e. divided) by applying the average matching rate for the whole group (combatants/civilians). Then, for every group, the military deaths and the civilian deaths, the sum of *estimated deaths* is calculated over the available sources and the *estimated overlap of sources* is subtracted from the sum of the components (i.e. sources). The total for civilians is further increased by including two additional components, one compensating for the underrepresented RS module and one for the exhumations' records, largely unavailable in the OTP (ICTY) databases at present but likely to be soon incorporated thanks to the efforts of authorities advancing the identification of exhumed bodies (among others: the International Commission for Missing Persons (ICMP)).

The final estimate constructed in this way (see Table 6) consists of three components: the number of military deaths from the three warring factions (already in the OTP (ICTY) database, complete), the number of civilian deaths already listed in the database and the assumed number of civilians whose records are not yet obtained from authorities in Bosnia and Herzegovina (from the ICMP and the statistical registration of RS deaths). The last, unknown RS component was subjectively *assumed* to be equal to 50% of the number of known civilian war-related deaths,[12] plus 5000 more unique records expected from the identification process of exhumed bodies from Bosnia (work-in-progress of the ICMP for Bosnia). This assumption can be easily verified once the missing data sources will be obtained.

The estimates of military and civilian victims obtained in this way are *minimum numbers of unique records*, ensuring that each individual casualty of the conflict is counted only once, no matter in how many sources this person is mentioned. These minimum numbers can be further improved when new sources and new matching results will become available.

In conclusion, applying the above-mentioned methodology to the available sources, the number of war-related deaths in Bosnia and Herzegovina can be estimated as 102,622 individuals, of which 47,360 (46%) are military victims and about 55,261 (54%) are civilian war-related deaths. The calculation is done under the assumption that a majority of the records of civilian victims is already in the possession of the OTP (ICTY) and incorporated into the current (as of mid-2003) version of the database, and a small portion of war-related deaths is still missing. The missing part needs to be obtained in the future from the relevant authorities, in order to complete the task of estimating the total number of war-related deaths of the 1992–1995 war in Bosnia and Herzegovina.

4. Discussion

High-standard information sources available for estimation of war-related deaths from Bosnia are scarce, fully reliable and complete sources do not exist, and the sources that exist are all incomplete and deficient. This is related to several reasons, some of which are mentioned below.

The most serious obstacle for producing reliable and exhaustive estimates of war-related deaths for Bosnia is that the statistical institutions producing statistics on vital (births, deaths) and other demographic events (marriages, divorces, migration, etc.) did not function normally during the conflict, or had no access to the territories they used to report about. The statistical registration system was largely down, attempting to maintain their normal functions but the overwhelming chaos of war did not allow the system to operate properly. As a consequence, regular statistical sources are largely unavailable for the war period in Bosnia.

A related obstacle was the wanton or accidental destruction of vital records collected by the statistical authorities. Especially, when the front lines were moving from one side to the other, offices and documentation were burned out to prevent the enemies to capture these materials.

Another reason for difficulties in producing war-time statistics on deaths (and migration) is that most of the existing records were (until recently) only available on paper, in the form of registration questionnaires submitted by the population. A complex analysis of duplicates and of overlap of sources, and validation of persons' identity requires that *all existing material* is computerised and standardised. These requirements were difficult to fulfil and practically no attempts have been made to produce serious in-house estimates of war-related deaths.

International organisations operating in Bosnia, such as for example ICRC, ICMP, and UNHCR,[13] made considerable contributions to the process of collecting information about war-time missing persons, deaths, identification of victims, and internal and external migration. The mandates of these organisations have, however, other major objectives than producing statistical information about casualties of war. Their contributions can therefore not be seen as a substitute of the outcomes of regular statistical activities normally conducted in peace time.

The contributions of (local and international) non-governmental organisations operating in Bosnia, being meaningful and important, can for the same reasons not be considered as replacements for regular statistics.

Due to the incompleteness and deficiencies of the existing sources, no local or international statistical authorities have ever engaged in producing estimates of the victims in Bosnia and Herzegovina during 1992–1995. It is clear from Sections 2.1 and 2.2 that only scholars, politicians, and journalists have made such estimates. They have exploited the existing sources only to a very limited extent. Most authors of the published estimates do not use all or a majority of existing sources jointly. Many authors base their estimates on just one single source, i.e. IPH statistics, a summary source that did not include the necessary personal details for verification of identity and elimination of duplicates.

The estimates presented by politicians and journalists are usually not transparent, and their sources and methods are not clearly explained (or even explicitly addressed). The scholars usually are more specific, but far from being fully clear about what they really did.

When producing our estimate we tried to be as specific as possible. The most essential part of our estimate is related to the sources, their selection, use of sources by individual records and jointly controlling for duplicates in every single source and for overlap of sources. We also verified the identity of the individuals reported in all mortality sources by comparing their records with those from the 1991 population census for Bosnia and the voters registers from 1997 and 1998. Death records linked with records of survivors (i.e. the 1997–98 voters) were excluded from the analysis. Having completed all these steps, we made a list of unique records of war-related deaths that occurred in Bosnia in 1992–1995. This list provided us with a minimum number of confirmed deaths, which could be shown according to place, date and cause of death. The records of fallen soldiers made it possible to distinguish between civilians and soldiers.

In the second stage, we corrected the minimum numbers for the incomplete matching rate (about 20% information loss), added our 'guesstimates' of two missing components (RS and exhumations), and we ended with estimates of the unknown overall number of war-related deaths of the Bosnian war: in total 102,622 persons. Of these 102,622 deaths some 55,261 were civilians and 47,360 militaries at the time of death.

The above mentioned numbers are, however, still incomplete, since death records of those who moved out of Bosnia during the conflict are not included in our estimates. Two components weakly represented in our estimate are the records from Republika Srpska and from exhumations, still far from being known, and therefore taken only as a 'guesstimate' in our numbers discussed here. Thus, even though we can argue that our estimate is much better founded than any other estimate ever obtained, it is still not complete.

Finally, one general problem needs to be addressed, the large forced and voluntary (but war-related) out-migration from Bosnia, which at present remains an obvious obstacle for obtaining *complete* statistics on war-related deaths from this country.

Mortality among refugees and other conflict-related migrants[14] might be high, especially in the periods directly after they had left their homes (often in panic and chaos) and travelled to arrive at their destination. Mortality of Bosnian refugees (mainly Bosnian Muslims) has up until now not yet been measured. Measuring it would require obtaining their death records from receiving countries in and outside Europe or conducting sample surveys among the refugee populations in these countries.

The size of emigration from Bosnia (forced and voluntary) at the end of the Bosnian war has been estimated by UNHCR at approximately 1.2 million persons (i.e. approximately 27% of the 4.4 million pre-war inhabitants reported in the 1991 census, see Table 7). The estimate for the end of 1992 is even higher: 1.8 million (about 41% of the 1991 population, Table 7). The number of deaths in populations of this size must be high, amounting to several thousands a year. However, only a (rather small) fraction of these deaths should be considered as related to war-operation. These deaths are of course excluded from the estimates presented for Bosnia so far.

Deaths among refugees are beyond the estimates of war-related deaths made for use in International Criminal Courts, as they occurred outside the conflict-affected territory of Bosnia, and sometimes outside the conflict time frame. This argument is not necessarily valid if one would take the pre-war population as the basis for estimating the size of all demographic consequences of war. In this case, all war-related deaths, in and outside the country, all internal and external migration, and even disturbances in the reproduction process, should be considered as components of war-related distortions of population development.

Table 7. Refugees (Refs) and internally displaced (IDPs) persons from Bosnia and Herzegovina according to UNHCR estimates

Country of Destination	Nov-92 06.11.92	Apr-96 01.04.96	Dec-97 01.12.97
Bosnia	810,000	1,000,000	816,000
Croatia	714,000	170,000	255,839
Serbia, Montenegro	495,000	330,000	253,387
Slovenia	52,000	19,000	33,429
Macedonia	19,000	6,300	4,989
Outside SFRY	536,840	686,533	776,900
Total Refugees	1,816,840	1,211,833	1,324,544
Total IDPs and Refugees	2,626,840	2,211,833	2,140,544

Notes: The 1st row ('Bosnia') contains the numbers of Bosnian IDPs, the following rows-numbers of refugees.
Sources: Morokvasić (1992, 1993); United Nations High Commissioner for Refugees (1996); Humanitarian Issues Working Group UNHCR (1997).

Acknowledgements

This article summarises the Bosnia and Herzegovina casualties part of the research on demographic consequences of the 1990s wars in the former Yugoslavia conducted since 1998 in the Demographic Unit of the International Criminal Tribunal for the former Yugoslavia. This research would not have been possible without the generous contribution of the Norwegian government that gave impact to the creation and development of this project and without the establishment of two regular posts for demographers within the Office of the Prosecution. We want to express gratitude to our sponsors for the opportunity to continue this work. Research results discussed in this article were presented at the seminar organized under the auspices of the International Union for the Scientific Study of Population (IUSSP) on the Demography of Conflict and Violence in Jevnaker, Norway, 8 to 11 November 2003. We also thank Helge Brunborg, Evert van Imhoff (†), Robert Hayden, and Gijs Beets for their careful reading, thoughtful observations and most helpful comments on an earlier version of this article.

List of Abbreviations

ABiH: Army of Bosnia and Herzegovina, i.e. armed forces of the BH government, pro-Muslim orientation

ARK: Autonomous Region of Krajina; i.e. a North-Western part of Bosnia and Herzegovina that Bosnian Serb leaders declared as one of the first Serbian autonomous regions in Bosnia in 1991

BH: Bosnia and Herzegovina, i.e. since April 1992 an independent country, before this date one of six constituent republics of Yugoslavia

DU: Demographic Unit (at OTP—ICTY)

FBH: (Muslim-Croat) Federation of Bosnia-Herzegovina

FIS: Federal Institute of Statistics; i.e. Statistical Office of the (Muslim-Croat) Federation of Bosnia and Herzegovina

HIWG: Humanitarian Issues Working Group of the United Nations High Commissioner for Refugees

HSS-94: Household Survey Sarajevo—1994

HVO: Army of the Croatian Defence Counsel; i.e. armed forces of the Bosnian Croats affiliated with the Bosnian branch of the Croatian Democratic Union party (HDZ)

ICD-10: International Classification of Diseases and Conditions Leading to Death, 10th edition

ICMP: International Commission for Missing Persons

ICRC: International Committee of Red Cross

ICTY: International Criminal Tribunal for the former Yugoslavia

IDP: Internally displaced person; i.e. a person who involuntarily moved inside their own country; this movement may be due to a variety of reasons, including human made disasters, armed conflict, or a situation of generalized violence (Inter-Parliamentary Union and United Nations High Commissioner for Refugees, 2001); a related term is a refugee (see below)

IPU: Inter-Parliamentary Union

IPH: Institute for Public Health in Sarajevo, Bosnia and Herzegovina

IUSSP: International Union for the Scientific Study of Population

JNA: Yugoslav National Army

KNP: Book of Missing from Prijedor; Prijedor as a municipality located in the ARK region in Bosnia and Herzegovina

MAG: Muslims Against Genocide

OTP: Office of the Prosecutor (at ICTY)

PHR: Physicians for Human Rights

Refugee: A person who has a well-founded fear of persecution based on race, religion nationality, membership in social groups, or political opinions; is outside his/her own country; and is unable or unwilling to avail himself/ herself to protection of that country, or to return there, for the fear of persecution (Inter-Parliamentary Union and United Nations High Commissioner for Refugees, 2001)

RS: Republika Srpska

SIPRI: Stockholm International Peace Research Institute

TWRA: Bosnia and Herzegovina news directory; available from the BosNet news bulletin complied by the Balkan Institute; accessible through the Hellenic Resources Institute from Cambridge: http://www.hri.org/news/balkans/ bosnet/
UN: United Nations
UNHCR: United Nations High Commissioner for Refugees
VRS: Army of the Republika Srpska

Notes

[1] The views expressed in this article are of the authors alone and do not necessarily express the views of the International Criminal Tribunal for the former Yugoslavia or the United Nations.
[2] The historical background of the Bosnian war can be found in several books, for example: Burg and Shoup (1999), Central Intelligence Agency (2002), or Power (2003).
[3] This category consists of members of the army, police, other forces of the Ministry of Defense, and supporting military personnel. Paramilitaries are usually not reported as part of official records on combatants, but among civilians.
[4] A clear distinction between the various categories of deaths is not always possible. In particular, separating deaths from regular causes and deaths related to harsh living conditions during conflict is very difficult. Based on the reported causes, the latter deaths are usually seen as regular mortality and excluded from counting of war-related deaths. Another problem is the civilian vs. military status of victims, which can be seen differently depending on circumstances of death. A soldier shot dead when (s)he was *not* participating in combat (e.g. while on leave) must be seen as a civilian. And a civilian shot in a fighting in which (s)he used a gun and thus was engaged in combat would be a combatant. Despite of these problems, a majority of deaths have unambiguous causes which allow for clear classification.
[5] In his article "Schindler's Fate" Hayden (1996; see also "TWRA Press, Sarajevo" from March 29, 1996, http://www.hri.org/) noted the number of 278,800 war victims proclaimed by the IPH, and in particular its components: 140,800 Muslims, 97,300 Serbs, 28,400 Croats and 12,300 Others, are almost identical to those reported by Belgrade, in the regime controlled journal *Politika* on 12 November 1994 (p. 4), as having been published by the Greek *Elefterotipija*, as results of the work of prof. Bošnjović from Sarajevo. The author further notes that the ratio of war-related deaths to the pre-war populations of Muslims and Serbs in Bosnia are almost the same: 7.4% for Muslims and 7.1% for Serbs. This observation suggests a political motivation of these estimates and emphasizes reservations regarding their reliability.
[6] Smajkić was the director of the Institute for Public Health during the war and was involved in collecting the weekly reports that were used in producing the widely known overviews.
[7] The Bassiouni Commission not only came up with the overall number of killed persons in Bosnia (200,000), but also with other statistics: 800 prison camps and detention facilities, and about half a million of people who stayed there during the war, 50,000 tortured persons, 20,000 (estimated) cases of rape, 151 mass graves, some containing up to 3,000 bodies, etc. The materials collected by Bassiouni were very rough (sometimes contested) estimates. Nevertheless, they were handed over to the ICTY which further investigated these crimes.
[8] The nameless doctor from Sarajevo is most likely prof. Bošnjović or prof. Smajkić (authors' comment).
[9] Duplicates are identical or very similar personal records appearing more than once in a given source. If several sources are studied jointly, duplicates can additionally relate to multiple records of the same person reported in different sources. This type of duplicates is referred to as 'overlapping records' or 'overlapping sources'. Irrespective of the nature of duplicates, searching for and deleting duplicates

is always meant to eliminate those records which are redundant and to keep unique records. Before deleting duplicates, the non-duplicated small *pieces* of information are usually moved from the deleted record to the record remaining in the database.

[10] The MAG database has been up-dated and expanded by the BH Commission for Gathering Facts about War Crimes, which recently changed their name and status (from governmental to non-governmental). The commission is known now as the Research and Documentation Centre in Sarajevo. Mirsad Tokača has been in charge of this project. Hopefully, some new and additional records become soon available from this work.

[11] 'Overlap of sources' refers to records of the same persons reported in more than one source. In Table 6 the overlap is reported jointly as the number of records repeated more than one time. If only three sources were used (1, 2, and 3), the 'formula' for calculating the size of overlap would be the following: $(1\cap 2) + (1\cap 3) + (2\cap 3) - 2 \times (1\cap 2\cap 3)$. Note the part $1\cap 2\cap 3$ is common to overlap of every two sources.

[12] According to RS statistical authorities (communication with Slavko Šobot, director of the RS Statistical Office in Banja Luka, March 2002), there were approximately 50,000 deaths recorded in local vital events offices on the territories controlled by VRS during the years 1992–1995. Records of these deaths exist as entries in the local vital statistics offices in RS. The number of similar records from the Federation-controlled territories is approximately 75,000 (see the source called FIS), of which about 1/3 (25,000) were war-related. Applying the same fraction (1/3, which most likely is too much) to the 50,000 RS deaths resulted in about 16,700 (expected) war-related deaths in the RS part of Bosnia. Because RS sources are weakly represented in our study (except in VRS and ICRC lists), we assume that no overlap is observed with other sources, which is not necessarily fully correct. We further assume that all these deaths occurred to civilians, and this again is not entirely true. Many of them were soldiers not yet reported in the VRS records. The number of 16,700 deaths coincides with 50% of our number of known civilians (Table 6: 50% of 33,508 equals 16,754) and for simplicity we refer to our 'guesstimate' for RS mortality as '50% of known civilians'.

[13] The ICRC is mandated to register and trace missing persons all over around the world. ICMP is mainly responsible for the identification of persons reported as missing. Finally, UNHCR carries out the responsibility to monitor and coordinate the flows of refugees in the world.

[14] Mortality among refugees, after they have settled down in receiving countries, is actually relatively low. This conclusion however only holds for the period beginning after they have arrived at their destination. Before this time, the refugees and voluntary conflict-related migrants are exposed to increased risks of illness and death due to the stress, fatigue and uncertainty about their future fate.

References

Bassiouni, Ch., 1995. Genocide in Bosnia and Herzegovina Hearing before the Commission on Security and Cooperation in Europe. One Hundred Fourth Congress, Commission on Security and Cooperation in Europe, [CSCE 104-X-X], 4 April 1995, Washington DC. (On-line) transcript of the hearing: http://www/house.gov/csce.

Bošnjović, I., 1999. Population of Bosnia and Herzegovina in the 2nd Half of the 20th Century. Unpublished paper, presented at the International Conference: Changes in 1990s and the Demographic Future of the Balkans, October 1999, Sarajcvo.

Bošnjović, I. and Smajkić, A., 1997. 'Chapter', in: A. Smajkić (ed), *Health and Social Consequences of the War in Bosnia and Herzegovina—Rehabilitation Proposal, 4th edition.* Sarajevo: Svjetlost and the Institute of Public Health of Bosnia and Herzegovina, 3–6.

Boyle, F., 1997. Re: Statistics. An (on-line) commentary, in: *Buffalo Archives of the Tribunal Watch, 23, 24 and 25 May 1997*, http://listserv.acsu.buffalo.edu/archives/twatch-l.html.

Burg, S. L. and Shoup, P. S., 1999. *The War in Bosnia and Herzegovina: Ethnic Conflict and International Intervention.* M.E. Sharp, Inc., Armonk, New York, London, England.

Central Intelligence Agency, 2002. *Balkan Battlegrounds: A Military History of the Yugoslav Conflict, 1995–1996.* Central Intelligence Agency Office of Public Affairs, Washington.

Hayden, R.M., 1996. 'Schindler's fate: genocide, ethnic cleansing, and population transfers'. *Slavic Review* 55(4): 727 (Winter 1996).

Humanitarian Issues Working Group UNHCR, 1997. 'Bosnia and Herzegovina: repatriation and return operation 1998', HIWG *Bulletin* No. 97/7, 10 December 1997, Geneva.

IPH—Institute for Public Health, 1996a. *Bulletin* No. 01.01.1996, Sarajevo: Institute for Public Health.

IPH—Institute for Public Health, 1996b, *Bulletin* No. 25.03.1996, Sarajevo: Institute for Public Health.

Inter-Parliamentary Union (IPU) and United Nations High Commissioner for Refugees (UNHCR), 2001. *Refugee Protection: A Guide to International Refugee Law, Research Report.* IPU and UNHCR, Geneva.

Kenney G., 1995. 'The Bosnia calculation', *New York Times Magazine*, April 23, 1995.

Morokvasić, M., 1992. *Krieg, Flucht und Vertreibung in ehemaligen Jugoslavien*, Demographie Aktuell, no. 2. Humbold University, Berlin.

Morokvasić, M., 'Krieg, Flucht und Vertreibung im ehemaligen Jugoslawien', *Journal für Sozialfors-chung*, 33(3): 273–292.

Power, S., 2003. *A Problem From Hell. America and the Age of Genocide.* New York: Perennial, An Imprint of Harper Collins Publishers.

Prašo, M., 1996. 'Demographic consequence of the 1992–95 war'. *Most*, No. 93, March–April 1996, Mostar, Bosnia and Herzegovina. Re-printed in: Bosnia Report, Newsletter of the Alliance to Defend Bosnia and Herzegovina, No. 16, July–October 1996.

Riedlmayer, A., 2000. 'Re: Request for information on death statistics'. An (on-line) commentary', in: *Buffalo Archives of the Tribunal Watch, 2 Aug 2000*, http://listserv.acsu.buffalo.edu/archives/twatch-l.html.

SIPRI - Stockholm International Peace Research Institute, 1993. 'Casualty estimate of the war in Bosnia and Herzegovina', *Nedjelna Dalmacja*, 4 August 1993, Croatia.

Thomas, R., 1993. 'Dehumanizing a nation. The Balkan conflict and international reaction'. 'Excerpts from R. Thomas' report on a fact-finding mission to Yugoslavia in April 1993. On-line article: http://www.srpska-mreza.com/library/facts/dehumanizing.html.

Tosić, P., 2000. 'Re: Request for information on death statistics. An (on-line) commentary', in: *Buffalo Archives of the Tribunal Watch, 2 Aug 2000*, http://listserv.acsu.buffalo.edu/archives/twatch-l.html.

United Nations High Commissioner for Refugees, 1996. 'BH Refugees in other countries of former Yugoslavia', Information Notes, Bosnia and Herzegovina, Croatia, the Federal Republic of Yugoslavia and Slovenia, No. 3–4/96, (March–April 1996) UNHCR Office of the Special Envoy Zagreb, p. 11.

Žerjavić's, V., 1998. 'Great Serbia: tragic outcome'. *Globus*, 9 January 1998, Croatia.

Sources

1. Military records of fallen soldiers of the BH Government Army (ABiH), 1992–1995, Ministry of Defence of the Federation of Bosnia and Herzegovina
2. Military records of fallen soldiers of the Republika Srpska Army (VRS), 1992–1995, Ministry of Defence of Republika Srpska
3. Military records of fallen soldiers of the Croatian Defence Council (HVO), 1992–1995, Ministry of Defence of the Federation of Bosnia and Herzegovina
4. The ICRC (2000) and PHR (1999) Lists of Missing Persons for Bosnia and Herzegovina, 1992–1995, International Committee of Red Cross (ICRC) and Physicians for Human Rights (PHR)
5. The FIS Mortality Database, 1992–1995, Vital Events Registration, Federal Institute for Statistics (FIS), Sarajevo

6. The HSS-94 Mortality Database, 1992–1994, mid-1994 Households Survey of Sarajevo, Research Institute for War Crimes and International Law, Sarajevo
7. The MAG Mortality Database of War Victims, 1992–1995, Muslims Against Genocide (MAG), Sarajevo
8. Death records of the Bakije Funeral Home in Sarajevo, 1992–1995
9. Exhumation records from the ARK—Autonomous Region of Krajina, RS territory
10. *Knjiga nestalih općine Prijedor* (Prijedor Municipality Book of Missing, KNP)

PART IV. DEMOGRAPHIC CONSEQUENCES OF CONFLICT: CASE STUDIES

CHAPTER 11. CAMBODIA: RECONSTRUCTING THE DEMOGRAPHIC STAB OF THE PAST AND FORECASTING THE DEMOGRAPHIC SCAR OF THE FUTURE

RICARDO F. NEUPERT
Center for Population Studies, Royal University of Phnom Penh, United Nations Population Fund (UNFPA), Phnom Penh, Cambodia

VIRAK PRUM
Center for Population Studies, Royal University of Phnom Penh, United Nations Population Fund (UNFPA), Phnom Penh, Cambodia

Abstract. Cambodia went through 5 years of violent internal conflicts (1970–1975), including the spread of the American–Vietnamese war into the country, followed by four more years of brutal and chaotic Khmer Rouge government (1975–1979). The result was almost 2 million deaths.This article attempts to contribute to the reconstruction of the demographic history of Cambodia. This is done in three ways. First, by analysing *scars* in the pyramids corresponding to the recent past, present and future; second, by estimating major demographic events during the 1970s, especially excess deaths; and third, by comparing the size and composition of a simulated *normal* population with the real population.

1. Introduction

After almost a century of being a French protectorate, Cambodia gained full independence under the leadership of Prince Norodom Sihanouk in November 1953. However, under his reign, internal political conflicts continued and in March 1970 a military coup led by General Lon Nol overthrew Prince Sihanouk. After 5 years of civil war and the spill over of the American—Vietnamese conflict into the country, on April 1975, the Khmer Rouge ousted the Lon Nol government and took control of the country. Just after taking power, the radical new regime forced the whole population of the capital city and provincial towns to leave for the countryside where they were placed in mobile teams and worked as forced labourers in the field for 12 or more hours a day. Cut off from the rest of the world, Cambodia went into a dark period or *year zero society*, as all former national institutions were completely eradicated. In January 1979, Vietnam invaded Cambodia and, with the support of Cambodian anti-Khmer Rouge forces, defeated the regime. In May 1993, free elections took place under the close supervision of the United Nations Transitional Authority in Cambodia (UNTAC), with a turnout of 89.6%. Since then the country has been proclaimed as the Kingdom of Cambodia with a system of constitutional

This chapter was previously published in *European Journal of Population*, vol. 21, no. 2–3, 2005, pp. 217–246.

Helge Brunborg et al. (eds.), The Demography of Armed Conflict, 247–277.

monarchy. At present, Cambodia is relatively stable in political, economical and social terms (see, for example, Chandler, 1996).

As might be expected, the events of the 1970s resulted in a substantial increase in mortality, a decline in fertility and significant emigration. These trends induced by the atypical political and economic situation experienced by the country, especially during the second half of the 1970s, lasted only so long as that situation continued. With the normalisation of the situation in the early 1980s, fertility experienced a substantial increase before a major decline started. Mortality underwent a significant reduction, although it is still high in comparison with other Southeast Asian countries.

The demographic consequences of the political and social turmoil of the 1970s form a clear *indentation* in the population pyramid based on the most recent census (1998). Since there is no reliable registration, the volume of the losses is under discussion. Estimates go from 1 million to as high as 3 million direct and indirect deaths. Several quantifications of the dramatic mortality of the 1970s have been conducted. The approaches have been 2-fold. The first begins with a backward count of deaths in a sample obtained from grave excavations, or survivors' oral communications. The sample number is then extrapolated to the population of the country. These estimates have been from 1.5 million to 2 million (Sliwinski, 1995; Kiernan, 1996). The reliability of these calculations cannot be evaluated reasonably because of the limited information on the population being sampled. Also, the data are difficult to verify (Heuveline, 1998). The second approach is based on demographic analysis. It has produced lower estimates of deaths, from 0.7 to 1.2 million (Kiljunen, 1984; Ea, 1987; Vickery, 1988). Banister and Johnson (1993) and Heuveline (1998) have probably done the most thorough demographic analyses. The last,author used electoral list collected by the UNTAC in 1992 in preparation for the 1993 election (see the following section) and a balance equation method. The latter authors utilised a cohort component projection method based on a 1980 administrative population count and a 1982 demographic survey.

The purpose of this study is to also reconstruct the population dynamics of Cambodia during the 1970s. This exercise is justified because it reconstructs the demography of the tragic 1970s using data collected more recently through conventional demographic instruments, which are more reliable than previous unconventional counts or estimates. The basic data utilised for the present study are the 1998 General Population Census of Cambodia (NIS, 1999) and the 2000 Cambodian Demographic and Health Survey, CDHS (NIS, DGH and ORC Macro, 2001).

The general strategy used to estimate the 1970s excess deaths can be briefly described as follows. Population by age and sex was estimated at two different moments: 1980 and 1970. The 1980 population was attained by a backward projection component method applied to the adjusted 1998 Census population. Deaths, births and migrations were estimated with data from the 1998 Census and the 2000 CDHS. The 1970 population was obtained from an available projection based on the 1962 Population Census (Siampos, 1970), although assumptions regarding mortality were modified.

For the 1970–1980 period, which covers the tragic decade, the projection based on the 1962 population was continued forward, though using other estimates of the components. Fertility was estimated using an indirect method. Net international migration was taken from a study by Banister and Johnson (1993). Based on the 1960s mortality trend estimated for the 1962 projection, *normal mortality* was projected for 1970–1980. The difference between the size of the population in 1980 according to this forward projection and the population according to the backward projection yielded an estimate of a residual population change, which corresponds to excess deaths. This procedure is explained in detail in Section 6.

Although the main purpose of this study is to reconstruct the demography of the 1970s, other aspects are also included. First, the present and future demographic consequences of the traumatic events of the 1970s are examined. Second, we estimate what the population would have been now and in the future two decades if no conflict had taken place.

After presenting a brief account of the main events that preceded the genocide, the population of Cambodia is examined according to the 1998 Census. The emphasis is on the analysis of irregularities in the respective population pyramids caused by the events in the 1970s. In the same section the population is projected up to the year 2020 in order to analyse how, as time passes, the irregularities move through the pyramid. In the following section, the 2000 population is retrospectively projected back to 1980, while in the subsequent section the population from the 1962 Census is projected to 1970. As mentioned above, these two estimates are the pivots for evaluating the demographic trends in the 1970s. In the next section, the excess of deaths and the deficit of births are estimated for that decade by using the 1970 and 1980 estimated populations and the estimated number of net migrants. Finally, the 1970 population is projected to 2020 under the assumption that the conflicts of the 1970s did not occur. The results of this projection are compared with those obtained from ordinary projections.

Therefore, this article attempts to contribute to the reconstruction of the demographic history of Cambodia in three ways. First, by analysing *scars* in the pyramids corresponding to the recent past, present and future; second, by estimating major demographic events during the 1970s, especially excess deaths; and third, by comparing the size and composition of a simulated *normal* population with the real population.

2. Toward the disaster*

Cambodia is in the heart of Indochina, surrounded by Vietnam in the east, Thailand and Laos in the north, Thailand in the west and the Gulf of Thailand in the south (Map 1). Modern Cambodia is the descendant state of the Khmer empire, which was one of the greatest kingdoms in South East Asia during, the Angkorian period (from the 9th to the 14th century). Previously Cambodia was a set of competing kingdoms, ruled by ineffectual and weak kings. Early in the 9th century, Jayavarman II unified

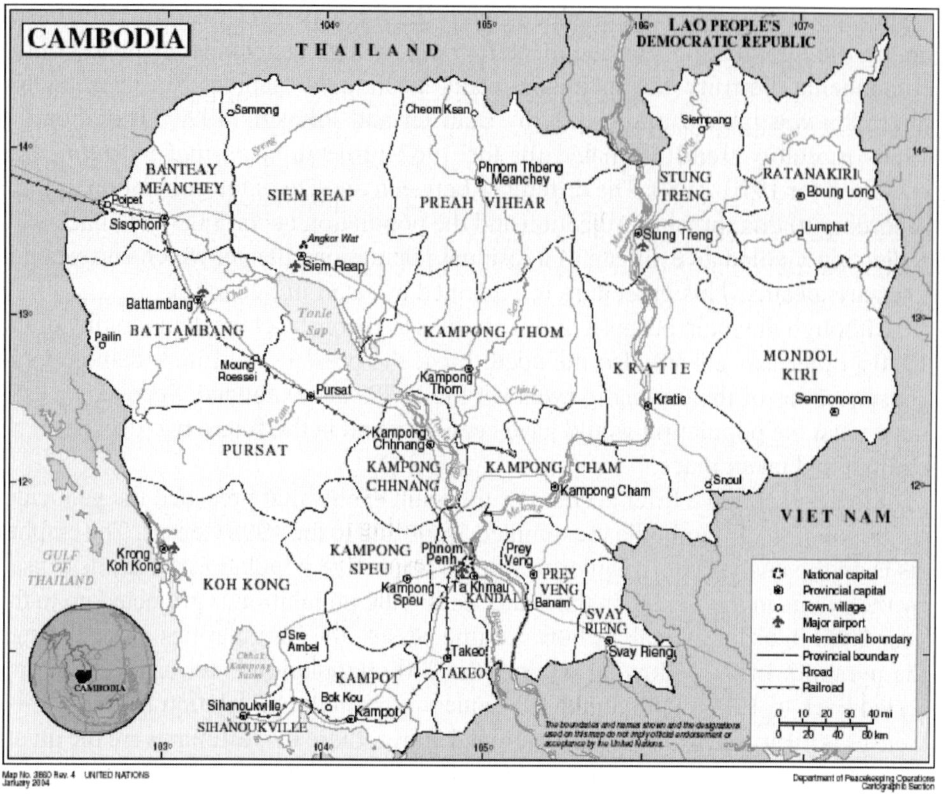

Map 1. Map of Cambodia.

the territories of Cambodia mainly through alliances, proclaiming himself king in the process. He was the first of a long sequence of kings who ruled Cambodia and much of what is now Vietnam, Laos and Thailand. By 1400, the Angkor kingdom came to an end and, until the arrival of the French in 1863, the country was governed by a series of weak kings who frequently requested protection from either Thailand or Vietnam because of continual internal royal family conflicts. This protection was provided at a price, usually territorial payments. This situation ended with the French controlling of the country.

The French forced King Norodom to sign a protectorate treaty. The French control of Cambodia paralleled the French colonisation of Vietnam. At first France had relatively little direct interference in Cambodia's affairs of state, but in 1884 Norodom was compelled to sign a treaty that made his country virtually a colony. After World War II and the Japanese invasion of the country, the French returned, making Cambodia an autonomous state within the French Union, but maintaining actual power and control in reality. After 1945, several political groups of diverse ideological tones appeared and political conflicts began to develop.

In January 1953, King Sihanouk, placed in the Cambodian throne upon the death of King Monivong, made a decisive move: he dissolved the parliament, declared martial law and embarked on a 'royal crusade', which consisted of a travelling campaign directed to gain international support for Cambodia's independence.

On 9 November 1953, independence was declared. The Geneva Conference of May 1954, which ended the French control of Indochina, recognised Cambodia as an independent country. As a consequence of a set of conflicts between Sihanouk and his internal opponents, severe internal political turmoil continued. Sihanouk regarded the two allies of the USA (which he considered as a natural opponent) in the region, South Vietnam and Thailand, the greatest threats to Cambodia's security and even survival. Although he also felt threatened by North Vietnam during the early 1960s, he declared Cambodia neutral in the South Asian conflict. In May 1965, Sihanouk broke diplomatic relations with the USA because of suspicion of a conspiracy against him and came closer to North Vietnam, the Viet Cong and China. In addition, he agreed that the North Vietnamese army and the Viet Cong could use Cambodian territory in their fight against the USA.

Sihanouk became isolated from rightist elements due to his position in the Indochina conflict and the adoption of socialist economic policies, but also from the left because of internal repression of dissidents. A rural uprising broke out in 1967, leading him to believe that the main enemy was the left. Compelled by the army, he violently repressed left wingers. In 1968, the Cambodian Communist Party, led by Saloth Sar, later known as Pol Pot, began an armed opposition to the regime.

In 1969, the USA started to carry out the infamous secret program of bombing suspected communist bases within Cambodian territory. Up to August 1973, when the bombing was halted by the US Congress, large areas in the east of the country were carpet-bombed by US B-52s, killing large numbers of civilians and creating huge refugee movements.

In March 1970, while Sihanouk was in France, General Lon Nol and Prince Sisowath Matak, Sihanouk's cousin, overthrew him, apparently with US support. Sihanouk moved to Beijing, where he formed a government in exile nominally in control of the Cambodian revolutionary movement, that he named Khmer Rouge.

On 30 April 1970, Cambodia was invaded by US and South Vietnamese troops in order to get rid of Viet Cong and North Vietnamese bases. The result of the invasion was that the Vietnamese communists moved deeper into Cambodia. At the same time, the new government was becoming increasingly ostracised by the people as a result of mounting corruption. Intense fighting quickly involved the entire country, affecting millions of Cambodians. Many left the rural areas for the capital city Phnom Penh and provincial capitals.

During the following few years the Lon Nol regime was seriously threatened by Khmer Rouge, since its role became increasingly more important. It received substantial help from the Vietnamese, although afterwards the Khmer Rouge leadership never acknowledged this support.

Although Lon Nol received massive US military and economic aid, he lost the war against the Khmer Rouge. Large parts of the countryside were won and became controlled by the rebels. Later on, many provincial capitals were also secured and cut-off from Phnom Penh. On 17 April 1975 Phnom Penh was taken by the Khmer Rouge, 2 weeks before the fall of Saigon.

Just after taking Phnom Penh, the Khmer Rouge carried out one of the most extreme and brutal restructuring of a society ever. All towns and cities were forcibly evacuated. About 2 million people, including children, the elderly and sick, were coerced into rural areas to work in the fields. A main principle of the Khmer Rouge doctrine was that peasants and manual workers were the only valuable and useful members of society. Many Cambodians did not survive the exodus and many of those linked to the previous regime were executed. Money, markets, organised religious schools, private property and freedom of movement were abolished. The *angkar*, or *organisation*, a few unseen Khmer Rouge officials, controlled the whole country and the lives of the people. In 1976, in simulation of an election, a person known as Pol Pot became the prime minister of Democratic Kampuchea, the official new name of the country. After a year, outsiders were able to recognise him as Saloth Sar, leader of the Cambodian Communist Party.

Pol Pot and his most close followers attempted to implement a set of unconvincing Utopian policies directed to achieve communism in Cambodia by skipping the socialist stage and, therefore, more rapidly and comprehensively than anywhere else in the world. The effects of these ideas on the Cambodian population were malnutrition, overwork, wrongly treated diseases and executions. There was a sort of 4-year plan, which aimed at doubling Cambodia's rice output and other agricultural products for the external market, directed to funds for financing industrialisation. The plan was a naïve copy of plans designed and implemented in socialist countries. Needless to say the plan turned out to be a disaster. It was irrational for the party bureaucracy to expect a planned production increase without more capital-intensive methods, while the labour force was internally displaced, demoralised and malnourished. The Khmer Rouge transformed wishful thinking into a plan and by doing so they almost destroyed Cambodia. Agricultural surpluses were all taken by the state leaving insufficient amounts for local consumption. Poorly planned and badly built irrigation works resulted in thousands of worker deaths. Medical treatments were almost non-existent. Many were executed for being able to speak foreign languages or for saving food for themselves or their families. The regime was unable to accept these losses and disasters as ideological or political errors and, since it was committed to stay in power no matter at what costs, they blamed *traitors* inside the Party. By the end of 1976, brutal purges were carried out taking the lives of several thousands of party members accused of spying for or collaborating with foreign intelligence services to defeat the revolution.

From 1976 to 1978, the Khmer Rouge government set-off several border conflicts with Vietnam. In December 1978, Vietnam invaded Cambodia, deposing the

Pol Pot government. The Khmer Rouge took refuge in the jungles and mountains on both sides of the border with Thailand. The fight, widespread famine, and uncertainty about the Vietnamese occupation caused a massive migration of Cambodians to Thailand in 1979 and 1980. Refugee camps were set up in Thailand with the support and protection of the United Nations.

The Vietnamese organised a government in charge of two former Khmer Rouge officers, Hun Sen and Heng Samrin, who shifted to the opposition before the fall of the regime. The social and economic disruption that followed the Vietnamese invasion resulted in a severe and widespread famine in 1979.

During the 1980s, Cambodia remained closed to most of the world, except for the presence of some aid agencies. The government was in fact under control of the Vietnamese, which resulted in Cambodia becoming part of the eastern block.

In 1985, most of the Khmer Rouge retreated to Thailand after the Vietnamese crackdown of the major rebel camps inside Cambodia. The response of the Khmer Rouge was a guerrilla warfare intended to demoralise its opponents. During the 1980s Thailand backed the Khmer Rouge and the other opposition factions in order to counterweight the Vietnamese power in the region. In addition, as a strategy to harass and isolate Hanoi, the USA provided about US$ 15 million a year to the non-communist factions of the Khmer Rouge-headed coalition and helped it to keep its seat at the UN.

In September 1989, Vietnam completely withdrew all of its troops from Cambodia. The opposition coalition, still dominated by the Khmer Rouge, launched a series of offensives, generating a huge number of internally displaced persons. However, diplomacy overcame violence and a civil war was avoided. In September 1990, the Phnom Penh government and the three factions of the resistance alliance accepted a plan agreed upon in Paris by the five permanent members of the UN Security Council. According to the plan, a coalition of all factions, called The Supreme National Council, was to be formed under the presidency of Sihanouk. The UNTAC (United Nations Transitional Authority) in Cambodia was given the mandate to supervise the administration of the country and to create an adequate climate so that free elections could take place. On 25 May 1993 elections were conducted, with a 89.6% turnout.

The following period, up to the present decade, has been far from quiet. The remnants of the Khmer Rouge continued to threaten the stability of the country for some time, but by December 1998 almost all the remaining Khmer Rouge guerrillas laid down their arms in return from amnesty. The Khmer Rouge ceased to be a military organisation. However, internal political conflicts, including a coup, continued to affect the political stability of Cambodia. These disputes and tensions did not involve mass violence, however. Recent internal political conflicts are quite complex but a discussion of them goes beyond the aim of this article. However, it is important to state that Cambodia is plagued by the divisions of its past. Uncontrolled corruption and bad government affect the country. Cambodia's economy is gradually improving and some social progress is evident, but many observers are pessimistic about the future unless major political reforms are carried out.

3. The present and the future: 2000–2020

The last population census in Cambodia was taken in 1998. Just after the results of the census were ready, the National Institute of Statistics (NIS) prepared population projections by age and sex at the national, provincial and rural–urban level (NIS, 1999). A standard cohort method was used for the projection. However, the NIS decided to update those projections using the new and more reliable fertility and mortality estimates from the 2000 CDHS. The information presented in this section is from this updated or revised projection (NIS and CPS, 2004).

The enumerated 1998 census population was adjusted according to several assessments, which are presented in Appendix A.

The assumptions regarding the three components (mortality, fertility and migration) used in this projection are presented in Appendix B. In general, the assumptions were proposed using trends from the recent past and other available relevant information.

Table 1 summarises the demographic development of Cambodia from 1960 to 2020. It shows the estimated and projected population, as well as the main population parameters that we utilised in the calculations. The data is explained and discussed in the different sections of the article.

Figure 1 shows the population pyramids in absolute numbers corresponding to years 2000, 2010 and 2020. The most recent pyramid (year 2000) depicts a population with a young age composition, with a typical triangular form, although with some major irregularities.

The first and most evident abnormality of the 2000 pyramid is the small size of birth cohort aged 20–24 years as compared to adjacent age groups, especially the bars corresponding to birth cohort aged 0–19 years (patterned bars), which indicates a much smaller population than expected. The reason for this is that persons in age groups 20 and older were alive or were born during the 1970s, particularly during the Khmer Rouge period (April 1975 to January 1979). As mentioned above, during this time mortality rates were extremely high, due to political violence as well as harsh living and working conditions. Fertility rates were also low. In addition, numerous people emigrated and have not returned. These issues are examined comprehensively in Section 6.

The second irregularity refers to the length of the bars corresponding to the birth cohort aged 40–74 years (light grey). The number of males is markedly smaller than the number of females. During the Khmer Rouge period, most of this population was 20–54 years of age. The pyramid suggests that adult males were more targeted by political violence than were women, children, teenagers and the elderly. Their excess deaths were caused by combat and political executions. Violent mortality certainly affected the whole population during the 1970s but it seems that the main

Table 1. Estimated and projected population, and components of population change, 1960–2020

Year	Population	Annual rate of growth		
1960	5,329,770	–		
1970	7,411,637	3.30		
1980	6,803,168	−0.86		
1990	9,653,624	3.50		
2000	12,573,580	2.64		
2010	15,268,588	1.94		
2020	18,724,315	2.04		
		Life expectancy at birth		
Quinquennium	TFR	Male	Female	Net migration
1960–1965	6.9	50.2	52.3	-
1965–1970	6.9	52.7	54.8	-
1970–1975	6.0	..	..	−349.000
1975–1980	4.8	..	..	−218.000
1980–1985	6.1	56.5	60.2	−30.209
1985–1990	5.9	57.9	62.0	18.000
1990–1995	5.8	54.0	60.5	110.000
1995–2000	4.0	53.1	59.2	26.000
2000–2005	3.8	55.8	62.0	-
2005–2010	3.5	59.3	65.6	-
2010–2015	3.3	62.7	69.1	-
2015–2020	3.1	66.2	72.6	-

– not applicable.
- amount negligible.
.. data is not available.

victims were adult males. In most countries there are more females than males over age 60. Thus, the sex difference over age 60 in 2000 is probably not only the result of an excess of male deaths during the Khmer Rouge period but also of lower female mortality.

Initially, the main targets of the Khmer Rouge executions were personnel from the Lon Nol regime and later on suspected *traitors* within the party (Heuveline, 1998). Harsh living conditions and lack of health services may also have affected the mortality of these age groups but violent deaths appear to have played a major role for the small population size in the respective birth cohorts.

Notice, however, that in the 2000 pyramid the male and female bars corresponding to age groups 20–39 are similar in length (dark grey). These birth cohorts were born during the 1970s or were children at that time. The excess mortality seems to

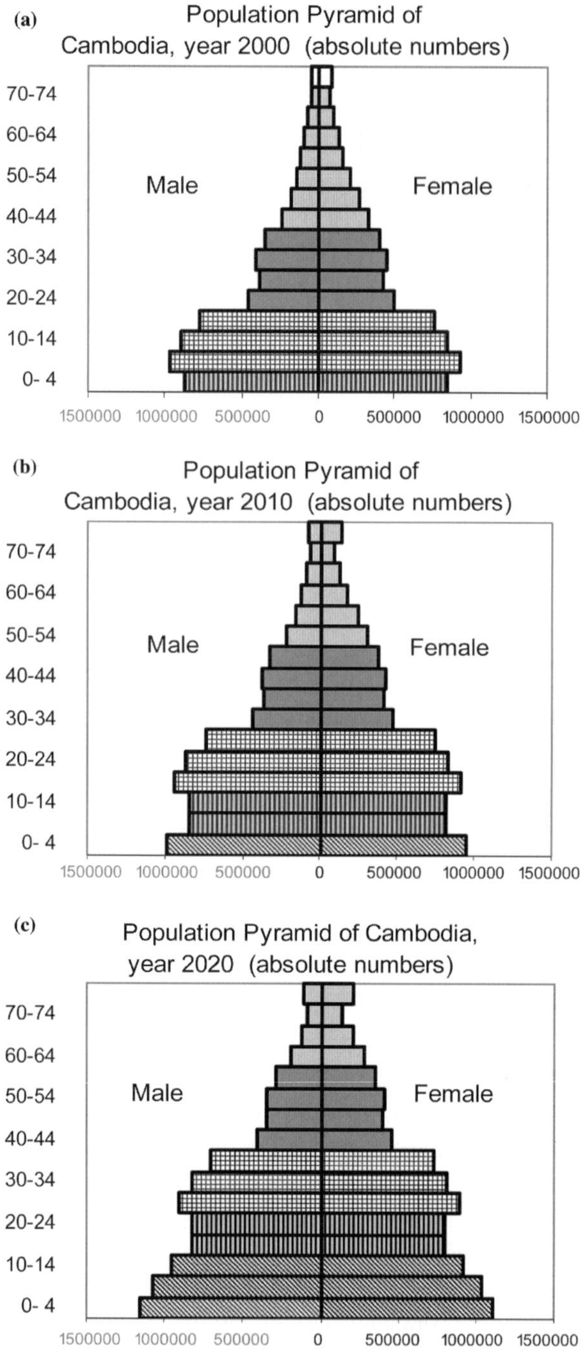

Figure 1. (a) Population Pyramid of Cambodia, year 2000 (absolute numbers). (b) Population Pyramid of Cambodia 2010 (absolute numbers). (c) Population Pyramid of Cambodia 2020 (absolute numbers).

have affected both sexes similarly in these birth cohorts. Indirect mortality associated with poor nutrition and a deterioration of health conditions may have affected their survival. These indirect mortality causes do not seem to discriminate much between the sexes. They may also have experienced some violent deaths, especially those older than 15 years of age in the 1970s, but in general, excess deaths in these birth cohorts were caused mainly by indirect causes.

It is also important to notice that the birth cohorts born during the 1970s (20–24 and 25–29 years old in 2000) are of a size similar to those born during the previous decade (1960–1969) and who are 30–39 years old in 2000. Considering the level of fertility during the 1960s, the total fertility rate (TFR) declined substantially during the 1970s (see Table 1). Assuming that the elevated mortality similarly affected the four birth cohorts under consideration, we would have expected longer bars for age groups 20–24 and 25–29 if fertility had remained constant or experienced only a minor decline during the 1970s. However, the respective bars are not much longer than the previous two (30–34 and 35–39 years old that were born during the 1960s). This pattern suggests a significant fertility decline during the 1970s, which is discussed further in Section 6.

The three birth cohorts corresponding to the population aged 5–19 years (checked bars in the pyramid) were born after the 1970s, that is, between 1980 and 1995. Their sizes suggest that after the Khmer Rouge period a *baby boom* took place (Desbarats, 1995; Dasvarma and Neupert, 2002). Considering the length of the bars corresponding to age groups 20–39 years in the 2000 pyramid, the larger size of ages 5–19 appear to be the result of both a mortality decline and an increase in fertility. Actually, during the period from the early 1980s to the mid-1990s, fertility seems to have declined slightly as compared to pre-conflict levels, but it was much higher than during the 1970s (see Table 1).

As pointed out before, starting in the second half of the 1990s, fertility substantially declined: 3.99 for the period 1996–2000. This decline is quite clear in the 2000 pyramid. The 0–4 bars are shorter than the previous bars corresponding to ages 5–9. Between 1991–1995 and 1996–2000 the TFR declined by 31%.

The year 2010 pyramid (Figure 1b) shows the 2000 pyramid's birth cohorts 10 years later. The cohorts that were born after 1980, aged 0–39 (patterned bars) are moving up in the pyramid, replacing those who experienced the hardship and violence of the 1970s and that are 40 years and older (plain grey bars). Notice that the first bar in the 2010 pyramid, for birth cohort aged 0–4 years (bar with diagonal line), is longer than those corresponding to the two older birth cohorts. These bars, corresponding to age groups 10–14 and 5–9 (grey bars with lines), are mainly the children of the 1960s and 1970s generations (dark grey bars) but the birth cohorts aged 0–4 years are the children of parents born after the 1970s (checked pattern bars). Fertility is assumed to decline among those birth cohorts in the projection; the assumption is that it will continue to fall throughout the projection period. The reason for the longer bars for the 0–4-years-old is that they mainly represent the children of the population born after 1980 (checked pattern bars), which is larger than the cohorts born during the 1960s and 1970s (because of lower mortality). Thus, the larger post-1980 birth cohorts gave birth to a larger number of children than the smaller cohorts born in the 1960s and 1970s that were affected by the mortality excess and low fertility. This is even more evident in the 2020 pyramid (Figure 1c). The children of the 1960s and 1970s birth cohorts are represented by shorter bars (grey bars with vertical lines), producing a sort of indentation in the pyramid. The three bars at the bottom are the children of the *baby boom* cohort (bars with diagonal lines).

Finally, it is worth stating that the annual rate of population growth for the decade 2000–2010 is lower than that corresponding to 2010–2020 (Figure 1b and c, and Table 1), in spite of the fact that fertility is assumed to decline. The reason is the comparatively larger birth cohorts that were born after the Khmer Rouge period (1980–1995) under a demographic regime of relatively high fertility and a sudden improvement in survival probabilities.

4. The recent past: 1980–2000

The 2000 Cambodian Demographic and Health Survey (2000 CDHS) included questions designed to construct birth histories and, therefore, obtain fertility and early-age mortality rates for the past 20 years (NIS, DGH and ORC Macro, 2001). Using that information, 1998 Census migration data and other available sources, as well as the year 2000 population by age groups and sex, a backward projection was conducted in order to estimate the population by age and sex from 2000 back to 1980. In other words, the year 2000 population was retrospectively projected back to 1980. The assumptions used for this are presented in Appendix B. According to this method the total population for 1980 was estimated at 6.8 million people (Table 1).

The population estimate for 1980 is particularly important because of the economic and political situation that Cambodia was experiencing. It is relevant to point out that other estimates are available for the 1980 population. Precisely in 1980, the Government of the People's Republic of Kampuchea conducted a population count with a result of 6.4 million (Banister and Johnson, 1993; cited by Huguet, 1997; Heuveline, 1998). This effort was an administrative count based on the population registered by village chiefs and aggregated by administrative officers in the country's 19 provinces. The central government in Phnom Penh at that time expected a figure around 5.8 million. Therefore, the result was a surprise for the national government and international observers. It was suspected that the number of people counted at local levels was inflated by the local officers in order to get a larger piece of governmental and international resources after the 1979 famine (Heuveline, 1998).

Banister and Johnson (1993) assumed a population of 6 million for 1980 in a *low population scenario* for a projection of the Cambodian population. The main justification for reducing the observed 1980 administrative count was the overestimates mentioned above. However, in a *high population scenario* they made an opposite assumption. They assumed a 1980 population of 7 million with the argument that to count a traumatised population after the 1970–1980 catastrophic decade is extremely difficult and that many people were just ignored. The 2002 United Nations revision of estimates and projections reports that the 1980 population of Cambodia's is 6.6 million (United Nations, 2003). Huguet (1997), using the 1996 Demographic Survey of Cambodia (NIS, 1996) and employing several indirect demographic techniques and a reverse projection method, arrived at an estimate for 1980 of 6.6 million. Heuveline (1998), utilising the number of voters registered by the UNTAC at the end of 1992 and various demographic data and methods, estimated that the total population for 1980 was about 10% higher than the 1980 administrative count. The United States Bureau of the Census (1983) estimated the mid-year 1980 population at 5.7 million. This low figure reflects the distrust of the census count. The estimate appears to be based on a 1980 study by the CIA (Heuveline, 1998). Compared to the other estimates, this figure clearly underestimates the population.

The population size for 1980 obtained by us, 6.8 million, is only 5.9 percent higher than that obtained by the 1980 administrative count, which is comparable to the coverage error of a modern census. Our estimate is 2.9 per cent higher than the United Nations and Huguet's estimates, and 3.5 per cent lower than Heuveline's estimate. Such differences can be expected considering the utilisation of different methodologies and sources of data. It is important to mention that the suspicion that the 1980 population count was highly overestimated might not be justified. This is consistent with the argument of Banister and Johnson (1993) for using a 1980 population of 7 million for their projection scenarios.

It is relevant to repeat that the merit of the population size and composition estimated in the present study is that they were obtained mainly with conventional demographic sources (namely the 1998 Census and the 2000 CDHS), which can be considered more reliable than unconventional sources such as voters' lists or fragmentary registers. Starting with this assumption the present results validate the 1980 administrative count, the United Nations estimate, and Huguet's and Heuveline's estimates on the basis of the 1996 Demographic Survey of Cambodia and the UNTAC electoral data, respectively. However, given possible uncertainties inherent in backward projections, the results obtained here may be subject to errors and, therefore, also validated by previous estimates.

Figure 2 shows the pyramids corresponding to the estimated populations of 1980 and 1990. Notice that for comparative purposes they have the same scale as the previous pyramids (years 2000, 2010 and 2020).

Pyramids 2a and 2b are consistent with the 2000 pyramid. Among the population 20 to 54 (light grey) there is a larger number of females. The explanation of these trends was given in the previous section when the projected 2000, 2010 and 2020 pyramids were examined, and these cohorts were much older. It is important to emphasise the length of the bars corresponding to age groups 0–19

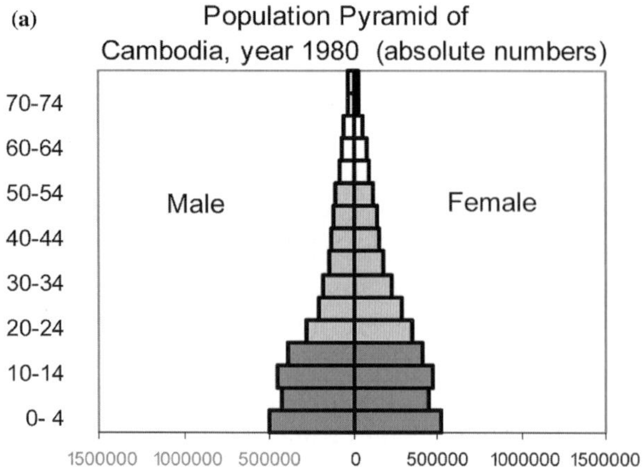

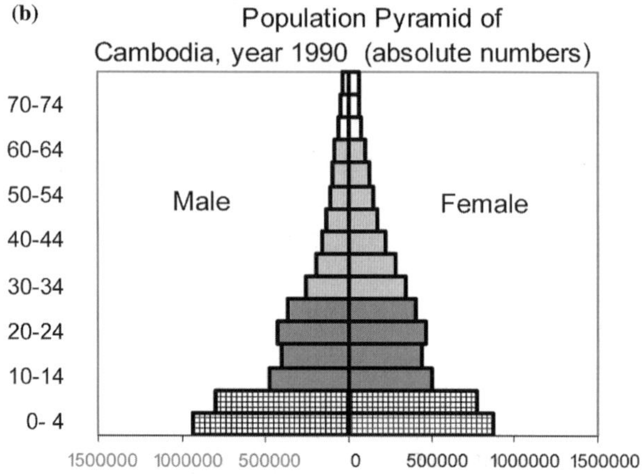

Figure 2. (a) Population Pyramid of Cambodia 1980 (absolute numbers). (b) Population Pyramid of Cambodia 1990 (absolute numbers).

in the 1980 pyramid. The fact that the respective bars are not arranged in a series of ascending steps with a clear slope suggests a fertility decline during the 1970s.

Note that in the pyramid representing the 1990 population, the two cohorts born after the Khmer Rouge period ended (checked pattern bars), 0–10 years, are represented by much longer bars than older age groups. As pointed out above, these are the *baby boom* cohorts; in addition, their members did not experience the harsh conditions that resulted in the excess of death of the previous decade.

5. The pre-conflict period: 1960–1970

The only census before 1998 was conducted in 1962. We used that census to estimate the 1965 and 1970 populations. The total population that we obtained

(a)

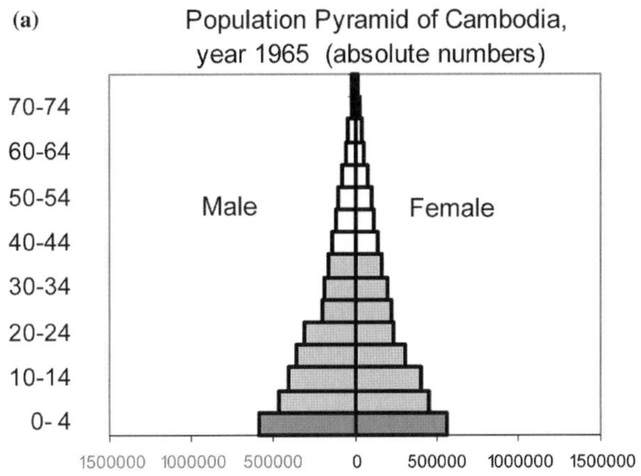

(b)

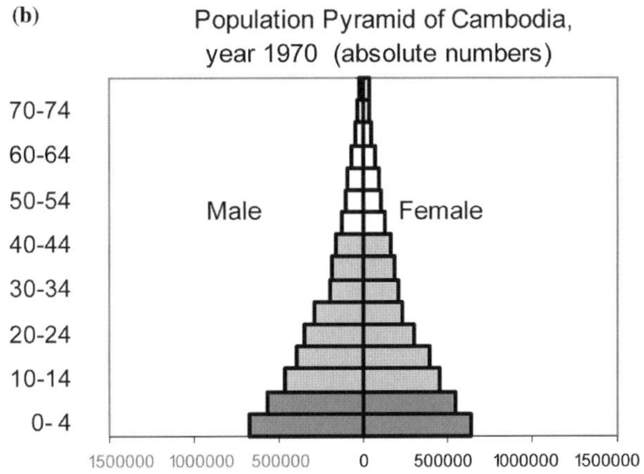

Figure 3. (a) Population Pyramid of Cambodia 1965 (absolute numbers). (b) Population Pyramid of Cambodia 1970 (absolute numbers).

for 1970 was 7.4 million. A projection conducted by Siampos (1970) estimated the 1970 population at 7.3 million. Heuveline (1998) also projected the 1970 population on the basis of the 1962 Census but his paper did not include his projection results. Banister and Johnson (1993) estimated a population of about 7 million in 1970. The United Nations population estimate for 1970 is 6.9 million (United Nations, 2003). The technique and assumptions that we utilised in this exercise, as well as those used by the other authors, are discussed in Appendix B.

The pyramids representing the 1965 and 1970 populations are shown in Figure 3. Note that the cohorts that were examined in the previous pyramids begin to appear in these figures.

It should be mentioned that these pyramids are *normal*, that is, they have the regular triangular shape of a young population with high fertility and mortality rates, with no important irregularities. It is also relevant to notice that the differences between males and females are much smaller than in the pyramids for 1980 and later. For example, in 1970, the sex ratio is 100.3 men per 100 women, but in 1980 it is 86.9. In the year 2020, the sex ratio will return to normal with a value of 96.5, according to the projection. The sex ratio for age group 20–54 is 105.1 males per 100 females in 1970, but in year 1980 the ratio has dropped to only 77.8. For the same years, the sex ratios for age group 0–19 are 103.4 and 94.2, respectively. These data confirm that during the 1970s there was an excess of male deaths, especially among the adult population. For children and teenagers the difference is much smaller. As suggested above, this is likely to be related to the fact that adult deaths were predominately caused by violence, while children and adolescents deaths were related to indirect causes such as poor nutrition and lack of health services, which do not discriminate by sex.

6. The tragic decade: 1970–1979

Until now, the populations corresponding to the periods 1965–1970 and 1980–2020 have been projected forward or backwards. In this section, an attempt is made to estimate the excess deaths and deficit of births during the 1970–1980 period. For this purpose, the 1970 population was projected to 1980 using a standard cohort component method. The size of the births cohorts aged 0–4 and 5–9 years in 1980, obtained from the 1998 Census backward projection, suggest that fertility in the 1970s was much lower than in the period before the crisis (6.85 children per woman). In fact, an indirect estimate based on the relationships between the numbers in the age groups 0–4 and 5–9 and women in the reproductive age range suggest a TFR of 6.0 for 1970–75 and 4.8 for 1975–80 (see Appendix B and Table 1). Banister and Johnson (1993) also suggest that during the first half of the 1970s, fertility did not change much, with the TFR remaining at 7.0 children per woman. For the Khmer Rouge period they suggest a TFR of 4.6 children per woman. Their article does not provide much explanation of how they reached their values, however, but considering the size of the two youngest age groups in 1980, their estimates seem reasonable.

The number of net migrants for our projection was obtained from Banister and Johnson (1993). Based on diverse sources they proposed a net migration of −567,000 persons for the whole decade (see Appendix B and Table 1). During this decade, migration in Cambodia mainly consisted of refugee movements. Most of these movements were to and from Thailand and Vietnam.

We assumed that during the 1970s the mortality level followed the same trend as for the previous decade, i.e. an increase of 2.5 years per quinquennium, which can be considered a *normal* mortality trend.

The 1980 population obtained by this hypothetical projection refers to the population that remained in the country, with reduced fertility, but on the assumption that it was subject to *normal* mortality levels and trends. It is a theoretical or *expected* population resulting from crisis-affected migration and fertility but not mortality. If the population projected backward from the 1998 Census is subtracted from this *expected* population, the excess deaths are obtained. Table 2 shows the *expected* and *observed* populations, as well as the excess deaths by sex and age groups.

According to this estimate, the number of excess deaths during the 1970s was almost 2 million. Disaggregated by sex, the number of male deaths during the tragic decade was 1.3 million and that of female deaths 0.7 million (not including normal deaths).

An alternative variant to estimate the *expected* population has been produced. In this alternative projection, we assume *normal* fertility but mortality as estimated for the 1970s. In fact, a slow decline was proposed for the 1970s (see Appendix B). If the births obtained in this projection are compared with those obtained in the *expected* projection, the deficit of births can be infered. We estimated that for the period 1970–1975 the deficit was 206,746 births and for 1975–1980 it was 495,044 births. Notice that these deficits are caused not only by a fertility decline but also by deaths and emigration of women in reproductive ages.

It would have been important to calculate also a measure of mortality. The main problem is that a temporal distribution of deaths can impossibly be made with the method of demographic reconstruction that we used to estimate the excess deaths. An additional problem is the calculation of the population for the middle of the decade which should be used as denominator in the calculation of mortality rates. For these reasons, life expectancies at birth for the quinquennia 1970–1975 and 1975–1980 are not presented in Table 1. It is important to mention, however, that the 2002 United Nations revision of estimates and projections reports life expectancies at births of 39.0 years for males and 41.7 years for females in 1970–1975. For 1975–1980 life expectancies at births are 30.0 and 32.5, respectively. Unfortunately, the method used to estimate these values is not presented (United Nations, 2003) and, therefore, impossible to evaluate.

It is interesting to examine the excess deaths by broad age groups. This can be done by a simple sum of the 5-year conventional age groups in Table 2. The excess deaths of children 0–14 years old was 783,187 during the decade. The 15–64 years old population suffered excess deaths of 1,097,029 and those 65 years and older of 72,868. The excess mortality among children suggests a deterioration of living conditions during the 1970s. The excess death of small children, 0–4 years old, is 235,672 during the decade. About 45% of the excess deaths are for people 0–14 years old and 60 years or more. As suggested earlier, most of these deaths are not due to combat casualties or political executions but are the effect of the hardship conditions that the country experienced, especially during the Khmer Rouge government. For example, young children and the elderly are the most vulnerable segments of the population regarding health conditions. This is not to say that violence did not produce deaths in these age groups, but most casualties seem to have occurred indirectly considering the low probability of these groups to be involved in violent conflicts. On the other hand, most of the excess deaths among the population 15–59 were probably *violent deaths*.

Table 2. Estimated number of excess deaths, 1970–1980

Age	1980 expected population (Normal mortality)			1980 observed population (Backward projection)			Estimated number of excess deaths		
	Male	Female	Total	Male	Female	Total	Male	Female	Total
0–4	642,710	611,156	1,253,866	496,086	522,108	1,018,194	146,624	89,048	235,672
5–9	617,044	583,624	1,200,668	421,971	448,923	870,894	195,073	134,701	329,774
10–14	584,174	552,081	1,136,255	445,725	472,789	918,514	138,449	79,292	217,741
15–19	509,769	485,061	994,830	390,297	418,850	809,147	119,472	66,211	185,683
20–24	411,417	403,226	814,643	277,494	356,144	633,638	133,923	47,082	181,005
25–29	345,910	350,139	696,049	206,483	291,081	497,564	139,427	59,058	198,485
30–34	303,797	264,341	568,138	177,448	228,785	406,233	126,349	35,556	161,905
35–39	260,493	203,110	463,603	146,241	183,679	329,920	114,252	19,431	133,683
40–44	163,754	183,874	347,628	126,381	156,531	282,912	37,373	27,343	64,716
45–49	154,861	164,263	319,124	112,766	137,633	250,399	42,095	26,630	68,725
50–54	132,516	137,297	269,813	98,781	117,714	216,495	33,735	19,583	53,318
55–59	103,668	109,396	213,064	82,817	96,049	178,866	20,851	13,347	34,198
60–64	80,040	86,049	166,089	71,150	79,628	150,778	8,890	6,421	15,311
65–69	61,741	67,372	129,113	49,695	58,384	108,079	12,046	8,988	21,034
70–74	40,818	45,397	86,215	31,041	36,425	67,466	9,777	8,972	18,749
75+	44,266	52,888	97,154	28,627	35,442	64,069	15,639	17,446	33,085
Total	4,456,978	4,299,274	8,756,252	3,163,003	3,640,165	6,803,168	1,293,975	659,109	1,953,084

These considerations do not attempt to give precise estimates of violent vs. non-violent or indirect deaths, but to show how the brutality of an authoritarian government can result in a genocide, which was caused not only by violence but by irresponsible economic and social measures that indirectly killed large numbers of children and old people. The question is: In a globalised world, would the international community allow the existence of a similar genocidal regime? The evidence from recent decades does not show an optimistic picture (Rwanda, Bosnia, Sudan, etc.). It is true that the international community has reacted to the atrocities in these countries, for Bosnia and Rwanda by establishing the international criminal courts and indicting and arresting the political leaders, and for Sudan by peace negotiations that were finally signed on 9 January 2005. However, the real issue is to what extent has the international community the capacity to avoid genocidal actions? In other words, is the international community establishing institutions, structuring plans and developing a logistic to avoid mass murder and genocide? We are not optimistic and we surely are not alone.

7. Comparison

As suggested above, the most careful studies of the demographic reconstruction of the 1970s in Cambodia are those conducted by Banister and Johnson (1993) and Heuveline (1998). The former authors estimated the number of excess deaths at 1.3 million. The latter author's estimate ranges from 1.2 to 3.4 million, but he did not consider the mortality of the births that took place during the 1970s. Including that, the excess deaths would have been 1.4 million, according to our estimates.

The estimate of the 1980 population using the 1998 Census, 2000 CDHS data and a retrospective projection, yields a number quite similar to that from administrative counts and the electoral register used by the previously mentioned authors. The main differences are to be found in the estimate of the 1970 population and/or the projection assumptions.

Banister and Johnson's excess deaths estimate is 0.7 million lower than the number obtained here. They used a smaller initial population, which explains part of the difference. However, this difference might be compensated by the fact that they used higher fertility, especially for the early 1970s. Since we used the same net migration here, the main explanation of the difference must be mortality. In fact, they assume that mortality did not increase very much during the first half of the 1970s. Unfortunately, they do not provide much information on the demographic components and the techniques used for their projection. Their estimate of excess deaths is 275,000. For the next 4-year period their estimate increases to 1.05 million, which is a plausible and convincing estimate. However, the mortality level assumed for the early 1970s seems extremely low considering the heavy North American bombing and the escalating civil war. For this period other authors have estimated the excess number of deaths to be between 600,000 and 800,000 (Kiljunen, 1984; Albin and Hood, 1987; Ea, 1987), but support for these estimates is not provided or is very weak. The methodology used in the present study is different and does not allow for assessing the temporal distribution of excess deaths within the decade, but the age composition for 1980 and later years suggest that mortality was higher in 1970–1975 than Banister and Johnson assumed.

Heuveline (1998) worked with three hypotheses regarding the components of the projection of the initial population (1970), the level of *normal* mortality, and the volume of net migration. The number of excess deaths (without considering the population born during the decade) estimated by us (1.4 million) falls within his range (1.2–3.4 million). If only his medium hypothesis is considered (2.5 million), the excess deaths estimated in the present study is more than 1 million smaller. That can partly be explained by the smaller volume of net migration assumed by Heuveline, but more important is that he used a lower normal mortality level for the 1970s. For the beginning of the decade he assumed lower mortality than estimated here and he also assumed a smaller gain in life expectancy at birth throughout the decade. In addition his 1970 population was larger than the one estimated by us.

It is possible to conclude that the main source of uncertainty behind the estimates of the excess deaths during the 1970s is the assumption about fertility and mortality under *normal* conditions. Another source of uncertainty could be the size of the 1980 population, but three independent estimates give similar numbers. The estimate of the 1970 population is yet another source of uncertainty together with international migration, but although relevant they are not as important as the assumed *normal* mortality and fertility during the tragic decade. The trends of normal mortality and fertility utilised in the present exercise are reasonable given past trends and the experience in other developing countries. Therefore, our estimate of 1.4 million excess deaths is probably not far from the actual number.

8. Simulations

The final exercise is directed towards assessing the population size up to year 2020 if the tragic events of the 1970s had not occurred. The *expected* population as projected for 1980 was projected forward for another 40 years, and compared with the *observed* population for 2000 and the projected population for later years. The results are presented in Figure 4, and also in Table 3. Each figure shows two curves. The upper curve corresponds to the *simulated* population (assuming no conflict in the 1970s) and the lower curve is the *standard* projection (based on the estimated mortality parameter).

Two aspects are worth commenting. First, there is a distinct dent in the curve corresponding to the *standard projection*, which reveals the excess deaths, the deficit of births and the emigration experienced by the two five-year birth cohorts born during the 1970s. The line corresponding to the *standard projection* shows a *scar*

(a)
(b)
(c)

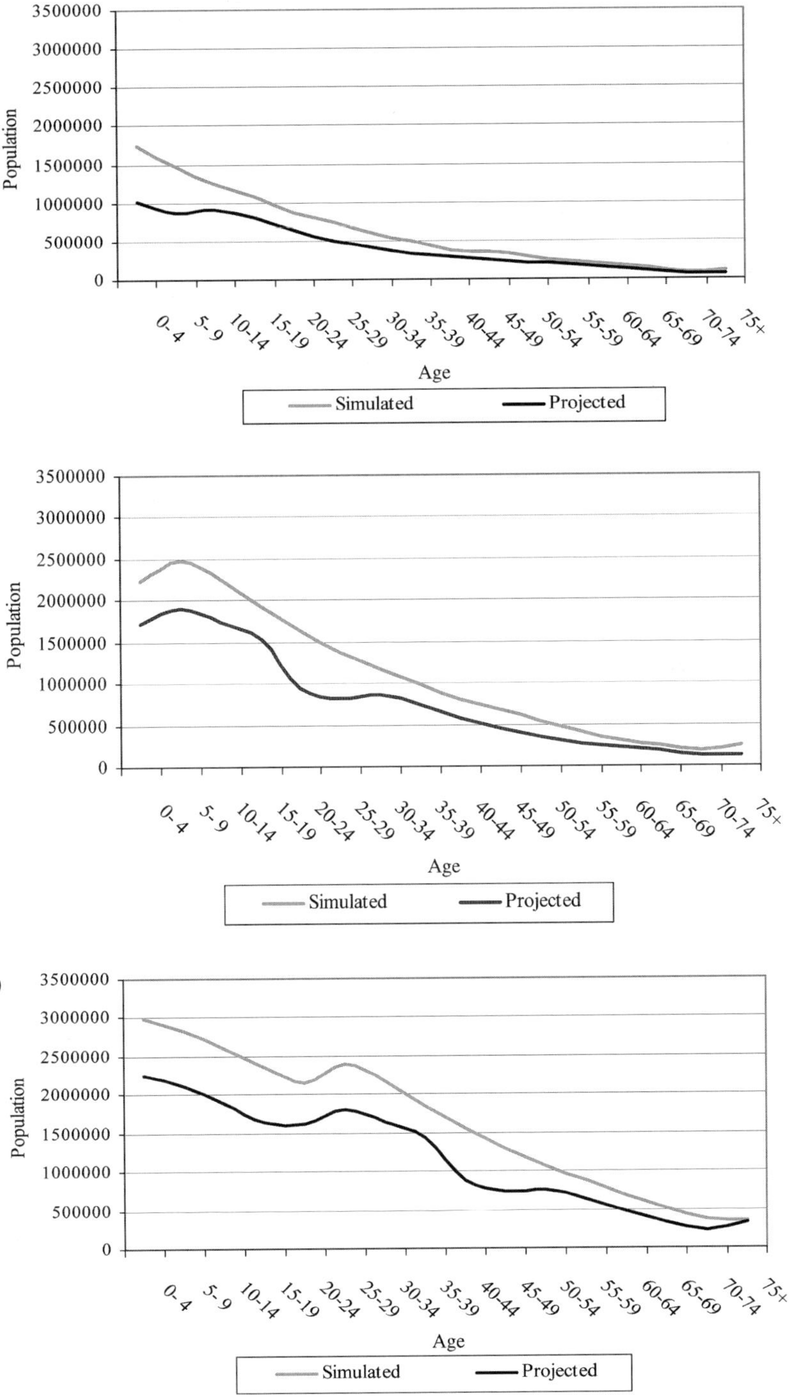

Figure 4. (a) Projected (retrospectively) and simulated population of Cambodia, 1980. (b) Projected and simulated population of Cambodia, 2000. (c) Projected and simulated population of Cambodia, 2020.

Table 3. Projected and simulated population of Cambodia, 1980–2020

	1980		2000		2020	
Age	Simulated	Projected	Simulated	Projected	Simulated	Projected
0–4	1,722,863	1,018,194	2,205,548	1,719,671	2,905,094	2,261,118
5–9	1,450,731	870,894	2,445,417	1,901,630	2,732,579	2,110,871
10–14	1,236,497	918,514	2,173,249	1,744,740	2,477,154	1,883,609
15–19	1,059,890	809,147	1,870,017	1,540,633	2,209,848	1,632,104
20–24	871,161	633,638	1,585,509	949,426	2,091,863	1,621,618
25–29	746,837	497,564	1,339,560	816,272	2,327,780	1,801,833
30–34	561,970	406,233	1,127,855	853,667	2,050,187	1,639,112
35–39	427,619	329,920	952,660	746,181	1,744,037	1,431,117
40–44	381,985	282,912	771,210	578,372	1,460,799	871,963
45–49	339,076	259,399	649,176	445,490	1,214,836	736,565
50–54	286,969	216,495	475,359	352,407	998,620	752,754
55–59	226,529	178,866	346,783	273,902	814,572	634,599
60–64	176,208	150,778	290,437	219,781	625,715	468,328
65–69	135,850	108,079	231,790	174,271	485,099	330,496
70–74	89,819	67,466	164,423	125,308	310,247	225,929
75+	82,595	64,069	170,791	131,829	347,048	322,299
Total	9,796,599	6,803,168	16,799,684	12,573,580	24,795,478	18,724,315

that will be visible for a long time. Obviously, this indentation does not appear in the *simulated* curve. Second, the distance between the two curves suggests that the entire population obtained in the *standard projection* is smaller than the *simulated* one as a result of the excess deaths and the small number of births supplied by the small 1970 cohorts. It is also relevant to point out that the *standard projection* curve has a second, more recent indentation, but that is the result of the recent fertility decline. This indentation is also present in the curve corresponding to the *simulated* population since fertility decline was also assumed in that projection. However, the two curves maintain the distance mainly caused by the excess of deaths and deficit of births in the 1970s.

9. Conclusions

Demographic reconstructions are hindered by the reliability of measurement of each population component, which is compounded in the estimate of the residual component. One of the strengths of the present estimates is that the information to estimate the 1980 population of Cambodia is reasonably reliable (the 1998 Census and the 2000 CDHS). It is also worth mentioning that other studies, using independent sources, reach similar results regarding the size and structure of the 1980 population. The uncertainty of the estimates comes from the lack of data for the period 1963–1979. However, reasonable assumptions and appropriate methods produce acceptable estimates of the mortality balance of a tragic period of the history of Cambodia. The demographic traces from the 1970s will continue to be present in the composition of the Cambodian population far into the future.

Irrespective of the uncertainties of demographic reconstruction carried out about Cambodia, all of these reveal the tragic consequences of the events that took place during the 1970s. It is also important to point out that excess deaths are only part of the burden of the decade and in particular the Khmer Rouge period. Non-returning migrants, the birth deficit, and age composition distortions complete the present and future legacy of those 4 years.

It is also important to repeat that most of the almost 2 million excess deaths that took place during the tragic decade, and in particular during the Khmer Rouge regime, are not casualties but direct or indirect victims of genocide. As shown above, 40% of the excess deaths were children below 15. How was this possible?

In most terrorist dictatorships, the theoretical knowledge that guides the organisation of the society, the function of institutions, policies, etc., appears to be discarded because it is no longer useful for the personal plan of the leader. This plan is usually a Utopian deviation of a political doctrine or ideology. If the implementation of this plan goes against usual or traditional forms of life, it must be based on terror and has to be accepted and practised not only by the leader and close colleagues but also by all the members of the revolutionary organisation or party. This seems to occur only if the capacity of the State to act over the people cannot be limited by a legal system and a set of ethic principles. This *flexibility* appears to take place only when a leader (or party/organisation) emerges with a subjective capacity to act with cruelty and to be above conventional ethics. It is also necessary to take away the individuality of revolutionary organisation members, or even the common people, by discipline or abjection. It seems that these were the conditions that made the Cambodian genocide possible.

Acknowledgements

The views expressed in this article are those of the authors and do not necessarily reflect the views of the Royal Government of Cambodia, the Royal University of Phnom Penh or the United Nations Population Fund. The authors are indebted to the UNFPA, the Royal University of Phnom Penh and the National Institute of Statistics for their support and co-operation. We also would like to express our gratitude to Dr. Chiev Khus and Mr. Bjarke Oxlund for their many valuable suggestions and comments. Finally, we would also like to thank the anonymous referees for their excellent comments and to the editors for their contribution to substantially improve our article.

Note

This brief accountant of the main events of the history of Cambodia is taken from Albin and hood (1987), Kiernan (1996) and Chandler (1996).

10. Appendix A. 1998 Census adjustments

The following adjustments were done to the population enumerated in the 1998 census (see NIS, 1999 and NIS-CPS, 2004):

(a) A post-enumeration survey found that the net census undercount was 1.78% of the total population. Thus, the total population size was increased by this percentage. The adjustment was applied equally to each sex and age group (prorating).

(b) At the time of the census (March 1998) it was not possible to enumerate the population of four small areas of the country for security reasons: the district of Antong Veaeng in Otdar Mean Province, the village of Ou Bei Choan in Banteay Mean Chey Province, the district of Samlot in Bat Dambang Province, and the district of Veal Veaeng in Pousat Province. Exact estimates of the population in these areas are not available, but it was estimated that their total population was 45,000 persons. For the national projection, this number was added to the national census population by age and sex.

(c) In March 1998 there were 60,000 Cambodians temporarily displaced in camps in Thailand due to conflicts near their villages. Since all of them were supposed to return to Cambodia within a few months after the census, they were included in the population of the country for projection purposes. It was assumed that 30,000 returned to Banteay Mean Chey Province and 30,000 to Bat Dambang Province. Hence, the national population was increased by 60,000 and it was assumed that the returnees had the same age and sex distribution as the national population.

(d) In most censuses there is under-enumeration and age misreporting for age group 0–4. In order to correct data for this age group the following procedure was carried out. We assumed that fertility had been constant for 5 years prior to the census with a TFR of 3.99. The census female population was reverse-projected by single years. The age-specific fertility rates for 1996–2000 from the 2000 CDHS were applied to the backward projection of women in order to obtain the number of births in each of the 5 years prior to the census. These were disaggregated by sex assuming a sex ratio at birth of 105 males per 100 females. Survivals of those numbers of birth were then added to the census date using the infant mortality rates estimated from the 2000 CDHS. These calculations suggest that the number of males aged 0–4 years, enumerated by the census should be increased by a factor of 1.2713 and the number of females aged 0–4 by a factor of 1.2859. These adjustment factors were applied to the census population after it had been adjusted for the three types of under-enumeration mentioned above.

11. Appendix B. Assumptions and estimates of the components for the four projection periods

11.1. PERIOD 1998–2020

11.1.1. *Method*

Cohort component method using Rural–Urban Projection (RUP), a program developed by the US Bureau of the Census (see Arriaga, 1994).

11.1.2. *Base population*

Adjusted 1998 Census population.

11.1.3. *Mortality*

The level of mortality, in terms of life expectancy at birth, for 1998, was estimated at 53.1 years for males and 59.2 years for females. Mortality levels were projected assuming that by the year 2020 they would be equal to those observed in Phnom Penh in 1998, that is, 68.4 years for males and 74.8 years for females. Life expectancies for each quinquennium between the base and the final year of the projection period were estimated linearly. The life tables corresponding to the projected life expectancies were produced using the software MORTPAK (United Nations, 1988). Table 1 shows life expectancies by quinquennium as they were used in the projection.

11.1.4. *Fertility*

TFR for the four quinquennia before 2000 were obtained from the 2000 CDHS (see Table 1). The data clearly shows that Cambodia is experiencing a substantial decline in fertility. It was considered that a logistic curve is the most appropriate function to project future fertility. The application of this function requires four values: an upper asymptote, that should indicate the historical high and stable fertility level; a lower asymptote, that should indicate a level of fertility expected for the distant future, usually the level corresponding to replacement (a TFR of 2.1); and two intermediate TFRs with values between the upper and lower asymptotes.

In the present projections, a TFR of 6.85 children per woman was used as the upper asymptote and 2.10 as the lower asymptote. The upper asymptote was estimated by applying a Brass-type method to the 1962 Census. The result was consistent with those found by other authors before (Siampos, 1970; Heuveline, 1998). The P/F ratios decline as age increases (these are the correction factors to correct fertility levels and structure); this trend indicates a constant fertility in the past, which is an important assumption when a Brass-type method is utilised. In other words, the Brass method seems to work well with the 1962 Cambodian data. The estimated TFR corresponds to the 5-year period before the census, i.e.

1958–1962, or to the mid-year 1960. Since the estimates suggest that fertility has not declined we assume that 6.85 is the historical fertility level of Cambodia and, therefore, it was used as the upper asymptote.

For the lower asymptote the replacement level fertility (2.1) was used. This is common practice in this type of fertility projections. The TFR of 3.99 estimated by the 2000 CDHS for 1998 was used as the first intermediate value of the logistic curve. As the second intermediate value, a TFR of 3.0 children per woman in year 2020 was proposed. This value was based on two considerations. First, according to the 2000 CDHS, the ideal number of children reported by women at the start of their reproductive carrier (aged 15–19 years) is 3.1. Second, also according to the 2000 CDHS, women with secondary education or more had a TFR of 2.9 children in 2000. In many countries a decline of the overall fertility level toward the fertility among the most educated women has been observed. Therefore, it is reasonable to expect a TFR of 3.0 by the year 2020 (or 3.1 for 2015–2020, see Table 1).

11.1.5. *Net migration*

Net migration is assumed to be negligible during the projection period.

11.2. PERIOD 1980–2000 (*RETROSPECTIVE PROJECTION*)

11.2.1. *Method*

Cohort component method using PRODEM, a program developed by the Latin American Demographic Center (see CELADE, 1992).

11.2.2. *Base population*

Adjusted 1998 Census population.

11.2.3. *Mortality*

We derived life expectancies from the infant mortality rate which was estimated at 84.6, 78.8, 91.1 and 95.0 for the quinquennia 1980–1985, 1985–1990, 1990–1995 and 1995–2000, respectively (NIS, DGH and ORC Macro, 2001). Using the program MORTPAK (United Nations, 1988) and the *model* life table constructed for the 1998–2020 projection, life expectancies at births and life tables were obtained. The life expectancies, by quinquennia, used in the retrospective projection are presented in Table 1.

11.2.4. *Fertility*

Total fertility rates were also estimated from the 2000 CDHS. The respective values are shown in Table 1.

11.2.5. *Net migration*

The 1998 Census included a question on place of residence which yielded the number of immigrants by age and sex. This information was obtained from 1979 to 1997. For the whole period we estimated a total immigration of 194,438 persons. Regarding emigration, we considered that 72,000 people left the country between 1980 and 1985. This number was estimated by Huguet (1997) from data provided by the United Nations High Commissioner for refugees (UNHCR) in Bangkok. It was also assumed that those emigrating had the same sex and age composition as the population of the country at the time. It was assumed that by the second half of the 1980s the emigration was zero (Heuveline, 1998). The total net migrants for the quinquennia from 1980–1985 to 1995–2000 are presented in Table 1.

11.3. PERIOD 1960–1970

11.3.1. *Method*

The method to conduct this projection was also the cohort component method, using the program RUP (Arriaga, 1994).

11.3.2. *Base population*

We used the 1962 Census population as adjusted by Siampos (1970) to carry out a projection based on that census.

11.3.3. *Mortality*

Siampos applied a Brass-type indirect method to the 1962 Census and the results indicate a very rapid mortality decline during the 1950s. Using information from a 1958–1959 demographic survey, he found that mortality began to decline by 1945 from an approximate constant life expectancy at birth of 35.0 years. For the present projection, 1962 Census data, a Brass-type of indirect mortality estimate technique was also used with the 1962 Census data (Trussell technique, see United Nations, 1983 and 1988). Using Mortpak and the *Cambodian model life table* (see Period 1998–2020), life expectancies at birth were calculated for mid-1958 at 48.0 years for males and at 49.8 years for females. According to these estimates, life expectancy at birth would have increased by about 1 year per calendar year. To assume that mortality would continue to decline at this pace during the 1960s seems too optimistic, since it is more difficult to sustain an increase of 1 year per year when life expectancy reaches 50 years or more. For this reason, we estimated that from 1960 to 1970, life expectancy at birth increased by half a year per year. Therefore, according to the present estimates, life expectancy at birth is 50.2 years for males and 52.3 years for females for the period 1960–1965; and 52.7 and 54.8, respectively for 1965–1970 (Table 1). This estimate is consistent with that obtained by other authors. Siampos estimated a life expectancy at birth of 51 years in 1961.

He assumed the same level for 1960–1965. For the next quinquennium (1965–1970) he accepted an increase of 2.5 years, but with a greater improvement for males than for females. His results are similar to those estimated here. Heuveline (1998) also estimated life expectancy at birth using the 1962 Census and an indirect method, obtaining 51 and 53 years for males and females, respectively. He proposed three mortality scenarios (levels and decline) for projecting the 1970 population. His medium scenario assumes a life expectancy at birth of 53.0 years for males and 55.5 years for females for 1962–1967 and 54.5 and 57.5 years, respectively for 1967–1970. He assumed an increase of 1.5 and 2.0 years per quinquennium for males and females, respectively. We considered that his projection is too pessimistic, taking into account the substantial decline estimated from 1945 to the late 1950s. It is important to mention that the different life expectancies obtained in this study for the late 1950s as compared with those calculated by Siampos and Heuveline are mainly the result of the use of the previously mentioned *Cambodian mortality model* (PDPST, 2002; NIS and CPS, 2004), instead of a Coale-Demeny model. An exception is the estimate of the United Nations: life expectancy at birth for 1960–1965 and 1965–1970 were 42.0 and 44.0 for males and 44.9 and 46.9 for females (United Nations, 2003). The procedure to estimate these values quite different from other estimates is not described.

11.3.4. *Fertility*

The TFR was assumed to be 6.85 children per woman during the whole projection period (see Period 1998–2000). For his medium projection, Heuveline used a TFR of 6.7 children for the complete period and Siampos an initial TFR of 7 children and a 5 to 10% decline during the 1960s.

11.3.5. *Net migration*

Net migration is assumed to be negligible during the period 1960–1970. We did not consider it necessary to propose different demographic scenarios to project the 1970 population, as the available information on mortality, fertility and net migration was reliable enough to make the projection with only one set of components.

11.4. PERIOD 1970–1980 (PROJECTION OF THE *EXPECTED POPULATION*)

11.4.1. *Method*

The cohort component method using the software RUP.

11.4.2. *Base population*

The 1970 population projected in the exercise corresponding to the period 1960–1970.

11.4.3. *Mortality*

The same trends as assumed for the period 1960–1970 were assumed here, that is, an increase of 2.5 years in life expectancy at birth per quinquennium. In terms of life expectancy at birth we assumed that the *normal* mortality for 1970–1974 would be 55.2 and 57.3 years for males and females, respectively; and for 1975–1980, 57.7 and 59.8 for males and females, respectively. It must be remembered that the purpose of this exercise was to estimate excess mortality, which was done by comparing the 1980 population obtained with this projection (*expected*) with the 1980 population calculated with the backward projection (*observed*).

11.4.4. *Fertility*

The population 0–4 and 5–9 years old, as well as the female population 15–49 years old, estimated by the retrospective projection for 1980 was used to estimate fertility during the 1970–1980 period. Fertility was obtained using the Rele indirect technique, which is based on an analysis of child-woman ratios (see Arriaga, 1994). For the period 1970–75 we estimated a TFR of 6.00 children per woman and for 1975–1980 a much lower value (4.80) (see Table 1).

A second fertility assumption was proposed in order to estimate the deficit of births. *Normal* fertility for the 1970–1975 and 1975–1980 periods was estimated at 6.61 and 6.37 children per women, respectively, under the assumption that fertility would start a slow decline during that decade. A comparison between births obtained with the projection conducted to obtain the *expected* population and the same projection with normal fertility provides the deficit of births.

11.4.5. *Net migration*

Based on diverse sources, Banister and Johnson (1993) proposed a net migration figure of −567,000 persons. This number was distributed throughout the 1970s (see Table 1). We disaggregated this number by sex and age, assuming that migrants had the same sex and age composition of the country's population at the time.

11.5. SIMULATION (PROJECTION OF THE *SIMULATED POPULATION*)

11.5.1. *Method*

Cohort component method and software RUP.

11.5.2. *Base population*

The 1970 population projected in the exercise corresponding to the period 1960–1970.

11.5.3. *Mortality*

For 1970–80 we used the same normal mortality as we used to estimate the excess mortality. From 1980 and 2010, life expectancy at birth was increased by 2 years per quinquennium; from 2010 and 2020 it was increased by 1.5 years per quinquennium.

11.5.4. *Fertility*

From 1970 and 1980 we assumed that fertility began to decline slowly from an historical TFR of 6.85 children per woman to 6.61 in 1970–75 and to 6.37 in 1975–80. After that, the same assumptions as for periods 1980–2000 and 2000–2020 were applied.

11.5.5. *Net migration*

It was assumed that net migration was negligible for the entire projection period.

References

Albin, D. and Hood M.S. (eds), 1987. *The Cambodian Agony.* Sharpe, New York.

Arriaga, E., 1994. *Population Analysis with Microcomputers (PAS).* U.S. Bureau of the Census, USAID, UNFPA, Washington, D.C.

Banister, J. and Johnson, E.P., 1993. 'After the nightmare: The population of Cambodia', in: B. Kiernan (ed), *Genocide and Democracy in Cambodia: the Khmer Rouge, the United Nations and the International Community, Monograph Series 41, Southern Asian Studies.* New Haven: Yale University, 65–139.

Chandler, D., 1996. *A History of Cambodia*, 2nd edn. Westview Press Inc, Boulder, Colorado.

CELADE (Latin American Demographic Center), 1992, PRODEM Version 2 CELADE Santiago.

Dasvarma G., Neupert R., 2002. Fertility Trends in Cambodia, Paper presented at the 2002 IUSSP Regional Population Conference, Bangkok, 10–13 June, 2002.

Desbarats, J., 1995. *Prolific Survivors: Population Change in Cambodia, 1975–1993.* Arizona State University, Tempa, Arizona.

Ea, M.T., 1987. 'Recent population trends in Kampuchea', in: D. Albin and M. Hood (eds), *The Cambodian Agony.* New York: Sharpe, 3–15.

Heuveline, J.H., 1998. 'Between one and three million: Towards the demographic reconstruction of a decade of Cambodian history (1970–79)', *Population Studies* 52, 49–65.

Huguet, J.W., 1997. *The Population of Cambodia, 1980–1996, and Projected to 2020.* National Institute of Statistics, Phnom Penh.

Kiernan, B., 1996. *The Pol Pot Regime.* Yale University Press, New Haven.

Kiljunen, K., (ed), 1984. *Kampuchea: The Decade of Genocide. Report of a Finish Inquiry Commission:* Zed Books: London.

NIS (National Institute of Statistics), 1996. *Demographic Survey of Cambodia 1996. General Report.* National Institute of Statistics, Phnom Penh.

NIS (National Institute of Statistics), 1999. *Population Projections 2001–2021. Report 6.* National Institute of Statistics, Ministry of Planning, Phnom Penh.

NIS (National Institute of Statistics) and CPS (Center for Population Studies—Royal University of Phnom Penh), 2004. *First Revision. Population Projections for Cambodia, 1998–2020.* National Institute of Statistics, Phnom Penh.

NIS (National Institute of Statistics), DGH (Directorate General for Health) and ORC Macro., 2001. *Cambodian Demographic and Health Survey.* NIS, DGH, ORC Macro, Phnom Penh, Cambodia and Calverton, Maryland.

PDPST (Population and Development Policy Support Team). 2002. *Mortality in Cambodia: a Technical Note, Technical Note # 1, Population and Development Policy Support Team.* Ministry of Planning, Phnom Penh.

Siampos, G.S., 1970. 'The population of Cambodia', 1945–1980, *Milbank Memorial Fund Quarterly* 48, 317–360.

Sliwinski, M., 1995. *Le génocide Khmer Rouge: une analyse démographique.* L'Harmattan, Paris.

United Nations. 1983. *Manual X. Indirect Techniques for Demographic Estimation.* United Nations, New York.

United Nations, 1988. *MortPak-The United Nations Software Package for Mortality Measurement.* United Nations, New York.

United Nations, 2003. *World Population Prospects: The 2002 Revision.* United Nations, New York.

United States Bureau of the Census, 1983. *World populations, 1983: Recent Demographic Estimates for the Countries and Regions of the World.* United States Government Printing Office, Washington D.C.

Vickery, M., 1988. 'How many died in Pol Pot's Kampuchea?', *Bulletin of Concerned Asian Scholars* 20, 70–73.

CHAPTER 12. ANALYSING LOW INTENSITY CONFLICT IN AFRICA USING PRESS REPORTS

PHILIPPE BOCQUIER
Institut de Recherche pour le Développement (IRD), DIAL, France

HERVÉ MAUPEU
Centre de Recherche et d'Etude sur les Pays d'Afrique Orientate (CREPAO), UFR Droit, Economie et Gestion, Université de Pau et des Pays de l'Adour, France

Abstract. In the absence of reliable and unbiased sources in most African countries, press reports can serve to evaluate some specific causes of death, on condition that a political analysis of the relation between the press and the political power is conducted. Tested on data collected from a leading Kenyan newspaper, the method proposed here is used to conduct a historical and geographical analysis of deaths due to police violence, community clashes and banditry. It also helps to point out the discrepancies between the press discourses on insecurity and political violence, and the reality of deaths reported by the very same press.

1. Introduction

This study originates from a concern for persistent violence that surrounds the political scene in Kenya since the return to a multiparty system in the early 1990s. After taking power in 1978, President Moi imposed an authoritarian regime and progressively reduced the spaces of liberty that could threaten his ruling. At the beginning of the 1990s, alliances in the political opposition and popular upheavals led to the return to the multiparty system. However, the ruling party took advantage of a divided opposition to win the 1992 elections. In order to exclude parts of the population opposed to the regime from the Rift Valley where the most fertile lands are situated, members of the ruling party organised ethnic cleansing, with the help of militias and police special units. The 1997 elections generated violence but it was more sporadic and scattered in several regions than in 1992. Once again, President Moi gathered a minority of the popular votes (less than 40%) but, thanks to the electoral system and to the incapacity of the political opposition to unite, this was enough to win the elections. The 1990s will be remembered as a period of increasing criminalisation of the state, when the political elite looted public resources through an extended system of corruption, amplifying if not causing a sustained economic crisis. In 2002, a coalition of the opposition parties at long last won the elections. However, the new regime of President Kibaki is divided and is still not able to conduct the structural reforms needed to boost the economy.

This chapter was previously published in *European Journal of Population*, vol. 21, no. 2–3, 2005, pp. 321–345.

Helge Brunborg et al. (eds.), The Demography of Armed Conflict, 279–301.

In the last 15 years, Kenya has been going through a period of high sensitivity to, and exasperation with, violence that newspapers' headlines reflect every day. But when there is no reliable source on violence, subjective perception forestalls any objective analysis of the phenomenon. This article shows how to use press reports, which are often the only information source available on violent crime in Africa, to monitor collective violence[1] in the context of low intensity conflict. The article focuses on immediate fatalities only, i.e. on deaths. But deaths are obviously not capable of representing all dimensions of violence. Most notably, the magnitude of wounding acquired in violent incidents cannot be assessed through the analysis of deaths. Also the fatalities/wounded ratio is not necessarily the same for all types of violence. Finally, casualties of violence, including both the wounded and the dead, are not reliably captured in the press reports. Before explaining the sociological framework of our study and the political context of Kenya, the present introduction explains why we cannot rely on other data sources and have to study press reports to learn about collective violence in Kenya.

In Kenya there is no exhaustive death registration system that could become a basis for conducting a study on causes of mortality resulting from violent crime, neither at the national nor at the local level, not even for Nairobi (Bocquier, 2003). Among the reasons for the incapacity of the existing administration to keep an exhaustive and continuous record of deaths is the fact that birth and death registration is not a priority for allocating human and financial resources to the territorial administration, and that in Kenya a serious under-reporting of vital events by families exists. Births and deaths certificates are not always used and concern mainly urban dwellers. The families do not simply have the habit of reporting births and deaths to the authorities. All this implies that the usual demographic sources, such as the births and deaths registration system, are not reliable enough to conduct a study of mortality by cause.

Other potentially exhaustive sources are population censuses or police and mortuary records. Besides problems of under-reporting, the census only asks about deaths in the preceding year and not about the various causes of deaths. Police and mortuary records are made available to the public only in aggregate format and indicate obvious under-reporting as well. In particular, deaths occurring in hospitals have more chance of being reported than deaths at home, especially for children.

In the absence of an effective registration system, the demographic surveys are an indisputable alternative. The Demographic and Health Surveys (DHS) (National Council for Population and Development et al., 1989, 1994) and the Nairobi Child Survival Survey (APHRC, 2002) are valuable sources of information on infant and child mortality but do not cover adult mortality. Only in the DHS-1998 women were asked about the death of their sisters in the 15–50 age brackets. However, causes of death were not reported (National Council for Population and Development et al., 1999).

Considering the scarcity of statistical information and the overwhelming perception of intense violence in Kenya, it seems perfectly justifiable to collect specific data on mortality due to conflict and violence. A first attempt was made by the Safer Cities Programme of the United Nations Centre for Human Settlements (UN-Habitat, 2002) to collect data on violent crime through a victimisation survey conducted in Nairobi in 2001. The declared objective of this programme was to convince the local (and later national) urban authorities to adopt measures to improve security of the citizens. The survey followed the methodology developed by the Durban Victim Survey in 1997 (Robertshaw et al., 2001) and the Cape Town Victim Survey in 1998 (Camerer et al., 1998). Other victimisation surveys included Johannesburg (Louw et al., 1998) and Dar es Salaam (UN-Habitat, 2000).

However, the results published from the Victimisation Survey of Nairobi (VSN-2001) cast doubt on the validity of the methodology used. Of the 1,000 respondents aged 18 and over, 38 declared that at least one member of their family was murdered in the year preceding the survey, i.e. from July 2000 to June 2001 (UN-Habitat, 2002, pp. 118–119). Such a rate is unreasonably high, knowing that the crude death rate for the entire population of Nairobi is about 15 for 1,000 inhabitants, all causes of death included (Bocquier, 2003). In Dar es Salaam, 12 murders were reported by 1000 respondents. It is a much lower rate than in the VSN-2001, but it is still much too high with regard to the overall mortality, which is about the same as in Nairobi (15 for 1,000). Why is there such a gross overestimation of murders in the UN-Habitat Victimisation Surveys?

The use of quotas is probably the origin of the problem. This sampling method, widely applied in opinion polls and market research, does not ensure a representative sample of the population. The clusters might have been chosen appropriately using random sampling at the first stage but the quota method used at the second stage to interview respondents was a source of huge, immeasurable biases. The procedure was as follows, quoting from the Dar es Salaam report:[2] "1,000 respondents were approached. In this survey the same 20 ward areas were selected. [...] The Ward Executive Officer supplied each fieldworker with a list of the plot and flat numbers in their respective areas. The field worker was then able to randomly choose which households would be approached and in a block of flats only two households were to be interviewed. In each ward area 50 respondents were interviewed in three age categories [18–30, 31–50 and 51 and over, for males and females]. A respondent selection technique ensuring that the selection process was both random and rigorously implemented was constructed." (UN-Habitat, 2000).

This 'selection technique' is not mentioned in the document but it is clear that as many households as necessary were interviewed to reach the required 50 respondents distributed in the six age-sex categories. This led to strong cluster effects, since there is a high probability that all adults in the households were interviewed, except for the last, in order to attain 50 respondents exactly. According to this procedure, also known as 'convenience sampling', a question such as "Was any of your immediate family members residing with you [in Nairobi/Dar es Salaam] murdered in the last 12 months?" leads to a predictable problem of overestimation. A murder in a household will be reported as many times as members of the household are interviewed. The same cluster effect will occur for any kind of event that is not uniquely related to a particular member of the household, such as a burglary. On average bigger households will also have higher chances of being victims of a murder or a burglary, simply because the crime will be multiplied by as many members as there are in the household. On the opposite, when the victim of a murder lived alone, there is nobody to report the crime. The quota sampling thus leads to systematic biases that are almost impossible to measure.

Clearly, the victimisation survey cannot help us to measure homicides in Kenya, even by restricting the analysis to Nairobi. What other sources could be used to evaluate at least the number of homicides in the country? The World Health Organisation (WHO) in its report on violence and health gives estimations for the year 2000 (WHO, 2002). Translated from the average rate of 18.1 per 100,000 inhabitants computed by WHO for Africa, the total number of homicides in Kenya would have been 5,600 in 2000. Using the average rates of South Africa, the only country in Africa where statistics are available on the subject, for the years 1999–2001 (11.6 per 100,000 inhabitants), which were particularly deadly compared to the years before and after this period, Kenya would have had 3,600 homicides. Crime in South Africa has been, however, much better controlled than in most other African countries, including Kenya, even during the peak of homicides that South Africa experienced in 1999 (Statistics South Africa, 2002). The homicides extrapolated from the South African rates would represent a minimum value for Kenya. In the absence of other sources, we are unable to offer a more accurate estimate of homicides in Kenya.

Considering the scarcity of data on homicides, contrasting with the rising concern about violence in Kenya, it is necessary to find alternative ways of estimating the variation in violent deaths and distinguishing among their causes. Because all residents in Kenya are daily informed about violence mainly through the newspapers, we thought of adopting a systematic approach to study this source of information. Using press reports to analyse homicides might look unorthodox to social scientists, but we believe that, in the absence of more exhaustive and reliable sources, newspapers can be used for evaluating collective violence, provided that a critical analysis of press practices and opinions is conducted. Despite of biases inherent in press reports, they actually are a valuable alternative source of information on collective violence, and complement other existing sources that also appear nonexhaustive, incomplete or biased.

The methodology presented here is not suitable either to analyse major armed conflicts or, at the opposite end, domestic or inter-personal violence. It is meant to serve as an alert system, similar in aim but methodologically not as rigorous as an epidemiological surveillance system. The methodology is not suitable for thorough analysis of determinants of collective violence but it certainly helps to monitor policies against violence or to pinpoint upsurges of violence at a fairly low geographical level, provided that the coverage of press reports is critically assessed. In this study, we do not pretend to offer a complete analysis of violence as we analysed here only the press reports from one leading Kenyan newspaper. A systematic analysis of several newspapers in Kenya would certainly help to improve the completeness of this study. Here, we focus on the methodology that can be generalised to other newspapers and to other countries.

2. Conceptual framework

The proposed method does not aim at explaining violent deaths. It is mainly a surveillance system presenting two advantages: firstly, it helps to conduct a salutary critic of the prevalent paradigms of violence in Kenya; secondly, it allows taking a historical record of violence and analysing its underlying factors.

2.1. THE NECESSITY OF A SURVEILLANCE SYSTEM OF VIOLENT DEATHS IN KENYA

In East Africa frequently two paradigms of violence are used: the paradigm of the proliferation of small arms and the culturalist paradigm. Although both these paradigms are very popular, they emphasise a selection of particular factors, which prevents from capturing the variety of other factors and, even more so, from showing the evolution of violent deaths, their numbers and forms, in the region.

The paradigm of the proliferation of small arms is the most caricature-like and seeks to demonstrate that insecurity is mainly caused by the proliferation of small arms. This theory is less accepted by the scientific community but much favoured by numerous NGOs and Western Embassies (e.g. in Kenya, the Security Research and Information Centre (SRIC); see also Section 3). According to it, all African conflicts are linked, if not caused, by trade of small arms. This school of thought is one of the last expressions of the dependence theories explaining all African tragedies mainly by a single international factor, namely the trade of small arms. Some case studies showed, however, situations where certain communities were able to re-establish a strong social control of the youth, thus considerably decreasing the number of violent deaths in spite of a great number of small arms still in circulation (Heald, 2002). Besides, it is difficult to relate the variations in violent deaths to arrival of arms since many murders and other violent deaths in East Africa were often perpetrated using machetes.

The culturalist paradigm is more convincing. This anthropological approach tries to explain the violence by looking at the social structure of the society. The masterly study on violence in the Gisu ethnic group in Kenya by Heald (1989) is a good example of the heuristic capacities of this mode of analysis. Heald showed that the refusal by the elders to let the younger generation rule disorganised the generational system which was the core of their political organisation. In order to make their decisions more acceptable, the elders tried to increase social control over the youth, which in turn elevated the anger of the latter, resulting in periodical strong outbursts of violence. This approach explains not only the reasons for violence but also the forms that it takes and why some social actors are more likely to resort to violence. However, anthropologists tend to consider communities as isolated whereas communities actually interact with neighbouring communities. In addition to that, they all have to deal with the state which is often a major actor of violence.

Given the limits of the common paradigms of violence in Kenya, a quantitative analysis of violent deaths as reported by the press over a relatively long period of time (1990–2004) appears as a complementary approach. The analysis might be particularly useful in displaying the historical evolution of different kinds of violence, and in particular, of violence caused by the state. The quantitative analysis contributes, therefore, to create a historical record of violent mortality. It also helps to map violence to show that some regions and estates in the cities are more affected than others. This approach is conducive to a political analysis of violence, as journalists are particularly conscious of the political factors of violence in Kenya.

2.2. THE JOURNALISTIC ETHOS AND POSSIBLE BIASES IN REPORTING VIOLENT DEATHS IN KENYA

The Kenyan press played a minor role in the conquest of independence. In the first post-colonial decades, the role of the media was reduced to that of a spokesman for the official forces of the country's nationalism. Since the rebirth of a multiparty system in 1991, the direct censure was not applied anymore, but journalists remained under surveillance.

The role of the press in the so-called 'second democratisation', from the early 1990s onwards (see Section 3), was more prominent and active, although the press operated in circumstances of tension and limited liberty. This led to the emergence of a public space where media and civil society questioned decisions of political structures and negotiated with the political elite in an unequal dialog. The pluralism of media improved. The privatisation of electronic media (private TV stations and FM radio) greatly opened up the country to the world. The urban middle class, more than ever before, turned their attention to the rest of Africa (especially towards South Africa) and towards the West. The number and influence of opinion newspapers increased. Their critique of the Kenyan reality, although often partisan, led to a freedom of expression and greater demand for investigation that forced the dailies to deliver precise high quality news.

The increased freedom of press brought the promotion of a renewed civil society. Without a close collaboration with journalists, some prominent lawyers in the 'Democracy and Governance' sector of NGOs in Kenya (referred to in this paper as DG NGOs) would never have achieved as much impact as they had in the country in the 1990s. The success of the ideology of human rights can be directly linked to the new power of the media in Kenya. Journalists sought to improve their professionalism by associating with the civil society. This allowed them to break away from the control of the political elite. The media became a resonance chamber for the civil society, which in return fed the newspapers with precise data and defended the freedom of the press.[3] This close proximity of the human rights NGOs and the media was also seen in the value system to which journalists frequently referred.

Two researchers recently studied the beliefs and attitudes of Kenyan journalists. Using different methods, Opiyo (1994) and Gituto (2002) came to surprisingly similar conclusions in an eight-year interval. Despite the diversity of beliefs among the journalists, both authors showed that a vast majority of them are reformists. They are very critical about the sociopolitical situation that, they suggest, must change. This leads them to a cynicism concerning the political sphere. In this context, Gituto (2002, p. 87) speaks even of an "antipolitical bias". Most journalists (80%) not only are very sceptical about the government, but also about the opposition parties that do not offer viable alternatives (77%). For two-thirds of the journalists, politicians belong to an elite or a clique that has no interest in public issues. Sometimes their scepticism extends to the civil society, even though most journalists have confidence in the church.

With regard to issues concerning their profession, journalists call for more democracy in their work. They feel that the selection of events to deal with is beyond their control. Therefore, almost 69% among them agree with the declaration that "many journalists are familiar with cases of corruption or governance problems but they cannot write about them or even investigate them" (Gituto, 2002, p. 156). Additionally, they share a strong feeling of not only job insecurity but also of threats for their physical well-being. They often consider their work as dangerous. To protect themselves, they develop adaptation strategies. "Journalists are doubly imaginative in order to withstand and face this situation of insecurity, by seeking to place themselves at the centre of news production, either by underhand dealings or by subterfuge" (Gituto, 2002, p. IX). It is in this context of insecurity that the evolution of the journalists' sensitivity to violent deaths should be analysed. Sometimes, speaking about these deaths allows one to indirectly discuss bad governance and, in particular, unreliability of the police. Newspapers would basically report these deaths according to the level of press freedom at the time and according to the sensitivity of the political power to given events.

In Kenya, four dailies and a number of weekly and monthly publications are available on the press market. Among them, the *Daily Nation* has its own, uncontested position: it is the most respected and popular newspaper in the country and that is why we chose it first for testing the methodology developed here for the analysis of violence.

Its position can be partly attributed to the negative impact of the political affiliation of its competitors. The *Kenya Times* is the press organ of the Kenya African National Union (KANU), the political party that ruled over the country for about 40 years until it was defeated in the 2002 elections. During the last decade, its share of the press market reduced to negligible at present. Most Kenyans consider it as propaganda. The *People* belongs to Kenneth Matiba, a former minister and candidate to the 1992 presidential elections. Since his defeat, this businessman ceased from politics but still used his newspaper to express his political views. In the 1990s, the *People* personified some kind of resistance of the Kikuyu ethnic group to oppressions by President Moi. However, the journal's bad management (an example of which being that journalists were not always paid at the end of the month) and the recent take-over by the opponents of the Moi regime led many of its readers to abandon it. Some readers would turn to the *East African Standard*, which claims to be one of the older newspapers in East Africa. It is, after the *Daily Nation*, the second best daily. However, it belongs to businessmen close to former President Moi, and during electoral periods it echoes its master's voice.

In this context, the *Daily Nation* stands out as the only daily with a lasting reputation of objectivity, which during some critical moments of the Moi regime stayed notably neutral. Belonging to the Aga Khan Group, it can afford neutrality. It is part of an international media group that comprises a weekly magazine (*The East African*), other dailies in English in Uganda and in Kiswahili in Tanzania, radios in the three East African countries as well as a TV Channel in Kenya (Nation TV). Collaborations between those different organs and a large network of reporters ensure the *Daily Nation* an unchallenged coverage.

The *East African Standard*, which belongs to the same media group as KTN TV (Kenya Television Network), is the only daily which could contest the *Daily Nation* position. We compared the violent deaths reported for one month by the two newspapers and obtained about the same number of deaths. However, we found that in a majority of cases, they do not report on the same events, which indicates firstly that the network of journalists is quite different from one newspaper to the other, and, secondly, that the actual number of deaths could be twice as many as reported in only one of the two newspapers. This is yet another proof that newspapers cover a limited number of violent deaths and that not surprisingly they do not aim at completeness of reporting. Further on, the urban bias of African daily newspapers must be kept in mind. The Kenyan newspapers employ very few reporters from outside the capital city. Generally, journalists are urban dwellers who mainly write for readers from urban areas, in particular from Nairobi. The dissemination of the press in the provinces, although recently increased, is far from adequate. A violent death that occurs in Nairobi has a higher chance of being reported to the readership than violent deaths in the provinces. There, a major event must occur to send out a team to the field. Otherwise, the newspaper has to rely on official data from the administration or on news from the civil society, mostly from Christian organisations (Peace and Justice Commissions in each diocese, NGOs with local projects, etc.).

Bearing in mind the above-mentioned biases of the journalism in Kenya, we must draw up a methodology capable of pulling out the maximum of reliable news from the data collected and published by the press. Considering the selection bias of events reported by the press, we will be mainly interested in the variations in violent deaths rather than in the absolute level of reported violent mortality.

3. Background information: second democratisation, politicised human rights and 'judicialisation' of politics in Kenya

To date, press reports have been mostly used by organisations belonging to what is collectively referred to as the civil society. From the press, the civil society draws quantitative analyses, which claim to be neutral, accurate and scientifically valid. However, does the civil society use press reports objectively? To answer this question, it is necessary to understand the role of the civil society and how it acted in the 'second democratisation' in Kenya, i.e. the return of the multiparty system (as stated by political scientists, obtaining independence was the 'first democratisation'). The 'second democratisation' emerged in a context of a strong belief in the democratic potential of civil society.

In Kenya, as in other countries, the opening up of politics (i.e. the multiparty system largely stimulated from outside), allowed the emergence of an influential civil society. However, contrary to other African countries, Kenyan Christian churches and also numerous NGOs lawyers, who were well organised and well-versed in human rights even before the democratisation process, were politicised[4] during the process itself. These two spheres of the Kenyan civil society sought to use press reports on violent deaths in achieving their own political objectives.

In Kenya service associations (service NGOs) are generally distinguished from defence associations (DG NGOs), although the distinction is not obvious. As a matter of fact, all NGOs do oscillate between these two types. For example, a majority of the defence NGOs, which are discussed in this article, also provide services. This is the case with the Kenya Human Rights Commission (KHRC) and the National Council of Churches of Kenya (NCCK), whose use of press reports is discussed here as well. The former organisation is involved in education, election monitoring and propagation of community policing. The latter puts a lot of effort into the education and health care systems as well as into rural development. Like a majority of service associations, the defence NGOs are also obliged to co-operate with state organs, in particular with the state administration. These organisations have no desire to radically change the existing regime. They have a moderate reforming agenda.

In the whole of Africa, the civil society has very little standing among the masses. It is mostly an urban phenomenon and in the case of human rights associations clearly linked to the middle class, whose development has lately been very weak. Even if urbanisation makes progress at the present time, it does so at a much slower rate than in the 1970s and 1980s. The economic crisis of the last two decades reduced the proportion of the middle class in the population. This occurred in spite of a high literacy rate in Kenya, and a higher number of secondary and university graduates than in the rest of Africa. Nevertheless, the DG NGOs clearly represent the aspirations of this particular social class, the class which feels particularly threatened by the excesses of a populist and ideologically pro-rural regime.

Pommerolle (2003) wrote the history of the leading Kenyan human rights NGO, the Kenya Human Rights Commission (KHRC). She showed that since its inception in 1990, two generations of militants successively appeared in KHRC, the 'activists' who later were replaced by the 'administrators'. The KHRC tried to 'nationalise' human rights, firstly by broadening them beyond the defence of civic and political rights and additionally addressing economic rights and inequalities created by the current land tenure, and secondly by using original kinds of mass mobilisations, e.g. theatre, street funerals, etc. The second generation of KHRC militants institutionalised their approach without renouncing the principles that made the organisation a success. They consequently attempted to be accessible at the grassroots level and to co-operate more with the state in order to facilitate their influence on public policies. From a radical movement of protesters involving mainly former political prisoners, they evolved into a classical pressure group.

The civil society has 'politicised' the human rights but at the same time the state has 'judicialised' its politics. Unfortunately, the state has not been successful in doing so, and the 'second democratisation' has often been perceived as a failure (because of ethnic cleansings, criminalisation of the state etc.). Some people refer to the 1990s as a lost decade (the Moi regime was defeated only in 2002). This afro-pessimism is excessive because the legalisation of a multiparty system was expected to bring many positive consequences. Despite that the discourse of human rights became legitimate, the practices of the ruling elite did not always follow the rule of law. Human rights NGOs placed therefore the need for a constitutional reform on their political agenda in order to better protect the rights of individuals and to create a mechanism for control and counter balance against a (too) strong executive power. In these circumstances, the civil society needss to collect accurate valid data on violent deaths in order to advance political reforms through the law.

Influences of DG NGOs on the Kenyan civil society are unquestionable. Kenya is one of a very few African countries which succeeded several times in massively mobilising the lumpmen proletariat of the capital city (in 1991, 1992 and especially 1997; Throup and Hornsby, 1998). In this context it becomes much clearer how eager the civil society is to produce and digest reliable statistics on violent deaths in Kenya. Civil society organisations focus on violent deaths in Kenya because they need them for the politicised conception of human rights they developed and because of a specific political situation in Kenya. The unreliability of oficial statistics (victims do not report offences to authorities and the police manipulates the available data) forces the NGOs to use press reports as the only remaining source on violent deaths. Unfortunately, each NGO collects and interprets the data according to its own agenda. One thing is common among all NGOs: they are mainly interested in studying two kinds of violent deaths, ethnic cleansing and extra-judicial executions.

The KHRC was the first organisation to study extra-judicial executions, defining it as "all deadly illegal and deliberate act perpertrated by a government agent, on order or by complicity and negating all right of life or impartial judgement to the victim" (Pommerolle, 2003). The term is used to characterise a common practice in the Kenyan police to shoot without warning at any suspect of a crime or an offence, even when they (the suspects) do not threaten them. This policy of 'zero tolerance', also advertised as the 'shoot to kill policy' by the police, was supposed to be the most efficient way to deal with violent banditry, intolerable to the authoritarian regime as much as to the people. However, the numerous collateral damages that resulted from this policy, contributing to the feeling of insecurity and adding to an endemic corruption, only succeeded in making the police, and by extension the regime, even more unpopular. In the cities, the understaffed police forces are unable to fight delinquencies. As the forces are also underpaid, they live of the population. According to Transparency International, Kenyans believe that the police are the most corrupt structure of the state (Transparency International, 2002, 2004). Also, a great number of policemen arrested or killed while committing crimes gives the impression that strong links exist between the police and criminals. Many of the police staff are policemen by day and criminals by night. The KHRC puts the emphasis on extra-judicial executions because demanding police reform is a means to advance their agenda of more global modifications of governance through human rights. It is a way to emphasise the pathologies of the economically liberal but politically authoritarian Kenyan state, which reacted to the rise of the opposition by using the army, police and justice to serve partisan interests.

The Nairobi Central Business Association (NCBA) is another NGO which showed interest in extra-judical exeutions. This association of businessmen is seeking to demonstrate that the growing insecurity in the city centre creates a negative environment for business and is not conducive to hosting offices of big corporations and embassies. In order to create conditions for renewed economic dynamism of the city centre threatened by the development of highly secured suburban malls, the NCBA is willing to develop constructive co-operation with the police forces through programmes of community policing (Pommerolle and Ruteere, 2003). Their aim is also to expel informal traders, who are regarded as exercising an unfair competition, from the city centre. The association therefore requires sociologists to demonstrate that crime is mainly located in the streets where the informal traders ply their wares.

The Security Research and Information Centre (SRIC; UN-Habitat, 2002) nurtures another agenda when studying the violent deaths caused by police or other actors. This association seeks to demonstrate that insecurity is mainly caused by the proliferation of small arms and tries to lobby for international agreements aimed at forbidding trade and export of small arms. The SRIC belongs to a vast pan-African movement whose leader is Safer Africa based in Pretoria. Their simplistic perception of the African conflicts seems to be favoured by many western embassies, in particular the British Department for International Development (DFID) and the Embassy of Norway, which have generously sponsored the Victimisation Survey of Nairobi referred to in the introduction.

The measurement of ethnic massacres through newspapers was done by KHRC (Kenya Human Rights Commission, 1998), NCCK, Institute for Education in Democracy (IED) and Catholic Justice and Peace Commission (CJPC) (Institute for Education in Democracy et al., 1998), among others. In the short term, these organisations hope to distribute, especially abroad, exact information about these deaths. In the mid-term, they seek to demonstrate the necessity of effective counter powers capable of watching over and limiting the excesses of an all-powerful executive. Their objective is in fact a grassroots constitutional reform achieved on the initiative and systematic efforts of the civil society. This objective is rooted in deep scepticism towards the political elite who is viewed as being incapable of breaking free from the dominant authoritarianism. Because of its capacity for mobilisation, the Kenyan civil society has a tendency to forget that the route to democracy involves a political society, which comprises political parties, elections and a leadership. This is actually one of the drifts of the contemporary conception of the human rights observed by Gauchet (2002, p. 326): "It is not only that human rights do not suffice to define a policy. By housing the active conscience of democracies, human rights have simultaneously been representing the political difficulty of being of democracies." Kenyan DG NGOs belong to this political reduction movement, especially when its leaders, like Mutunga, advocate for 'a civilian coup'. In Kenya, a strong civil society coexists with a particularly institutionalised political society. The aims of NGOs do not necessarily invalidate their analyses of violent deaths in Kenya, but their political objectives lead these organisations to lose interest in the methodology. They seek arguments for their political aims and forget about scientific standards required for valid statistics. This situation is worsened by the proximity of civil society and the media.

4. The study: an illustration based on one leading newspaper

As we mentioned earlier there are no reliable sources of data on causes of death, let alone homicides. Although press reports are neither more exhaustive nor less biased than official sources, we believe that they constitute a valuable source of information if used in a systematic way. In this section we first identify the possible biases in press reports, and then explain how the database was established and how it should be analysed. After this, we describe how a historical and geographical approach of violent deaths in Kenya should be conducted. The results presented here are, however, more illustrative than substantive as the coverage of collective homicides through one newspaper only is merely indicative of the possible trends.

4.1. GENERAL PRINCIPLES OF THE QUANTITATIVE APPROACH

A database on violent deaths was established from an extensive collection of press reports published in the *Daily Nation* from January 1990 up to September 2003. About 5,700 fatal incidents were reported in the whole period (almost 14 years), i.e. 35 incidents a month, after elimination of double entries. These incidents made up a total of 15,300 deaths, i.e. a mean number of 93 deaths per month (Table 1).

This number of reported violent deaths is obviously a tiny proportion of all deaths. In Kenya it is estimated that around 4.5 million deaths occurred in the same period for all ages and from all causes, of which about 1.5 million died of HIV/AIDS. For homicides only, by comparison with WHO estimates cited in introduction, it would appear that the press largely underreports violent deaths. The *Daily Nation* would be very far from reality since it reported 'only' 7,400 homicides for the entire 14 years period (Table 1) compared to the 5,600 yearly homicides extrapolated from the 2000 WHO rate for Africa. Extending the data collection to several newspapers would certainly not suffice to cover all violent deaths in Kenya.

It is clear that press reports are no reasonable substitutes for a statistical death registration system or police records, assuming that these sources would be well maintained. The press not only underreports violent deaths, its reports are also biased towards the most extreme events. The average number of deaths is 2.7 per incident (2.3 for homicides and 3.2 for accidents). There is obviously a higher chance of being on headline news when one dies in a bus with many others rather than alone, driving one's car straight into an electric pole. On the other hand, the road accident, in which the future President Kibaki was involved in December 2002, made the headlines, not necessarily because of the two resulting deaths but because of possible consequences of this accident on the fate of the country.

Road accidents are actually the most frequent cause of violent deaths appearing in press reports, irrespective of the location of occurrence (rural or urban). Road accidents are only reported in exceptional circumstances, e.g. deaths of well-known persons, highly fatal accidents etc. Through reporting road accidents, the press provides the public opinion with a message that the state is incapable of dealing with road safety. On the other hand the homicides are commonly mentioned by opinion leaders as a major telltale of the incapacity of the state. The importance of homicides is more qualitative than quantitative. Homicides are the main reported cause of violent deaths only by combining deaths due to banditry, community clashes and state violence (the latter being mainly police violence). Because they are of particular concern to journalists, our hypothesis is that their reports on such manifestations of violence should cover most of the actual magnitude of the phenomenon. Facts should not be too biased even if they are subjected to all kinds of interpretation. Journalists have a vested interest in reporting on the failure of the state in controlling crime. They are also keen to point out the roots of political and community violence and the drift of the state towards criminal activities. On the other hand, journalists play down deaths due to mob justice against alleged thieves because they generally back the common opinion that 'those thugs deserve it' (Darbon and Du Bois de Gaudusson, 1997; Rodriguez-Torres, 1998).

There is a tendency in the unwritten 'rules of procedure' for journalistic news to marginalise or even shift away the 'scientific' accuracy of registration of certain deaths by the media. For example, sometimes newspapers are less interested in certain deaths, especially those which are common, because some other 'bigger' news already occupies the headlines. In this way, relatively ordinary deaths, such as those resulting from mob justice, will be relegated to news briefs, reported on another day, or simply forgotten. On the other hand, spectacular deaths could

Table 1. Percentage distribution of violent deaths by cause and by area as reported by the *Daily Nation*, January 1990–September 2003

	Accidents			Homicides						
	Road accident	Natural elements	Other accident	Banditry	State (police)	Commu-nities	Mob justice	Personal and family	Total	% by area
Rural	35.9	7.6	6.6	21.8	8.6	10.2	4.8	4.6	100	76.8
Nairobi	31.3	2.3	10.9	14.6	26.3	3.7	7.5	3.4	100	14.7
Other urban	53.1	19.2	5.0	7.7	8.0	0.5	4.8	1.8	100	8.6
Kenya	36.7	7.8	7.1	19.5	11.1	8.4	5.2	4.2	100	100
Deaths (1)	5,615	1,190	1,079	2,989	1,704	1,284	794	642	15,297	–
Incidents (2)	1,517	471	464	1,223	777	263	487	466	5,668	–
(1)/(2)	3.7	2.5	2.3	2.4	2.2	4.9	1.6	1.4	2.7	–

capture the attention of the media for several days and newspapers would repeatedly comment on the same violent deaths.

The classification of incidents can also introduce biases. Journalists do not always use the same criteria for violence caused by communities, militias, vigilante groups or ordinary bandits. For this reason, we have to create an exhaustive database of all violent incidents reported in the press and analyse them in relation to each other. It is the simultaneous analysis of different categories of incidents, as classified by the journalists, that allows us to understand and properly code the actual reality of violence. This is particularly true for deaths due to banditry, community clashes and state violence that often depend on each other, either by reaction, e.g. police forces reacting to an upsurge of banditry, or by co-action, e.g. militias joining forces with the police to crush squatters.

The following paragraphs explain how the analysis of homicides is conducted and why it should be put in both a historical and geographical perspective. Accidents are discarded: they could be the subject of a separate analysis. This article shall focus on four actors of collective violence: bandits, state (mainly the police), communities (including the infamous ethnic clashes) and mob justice. The latter is a minor reported actor of violence and is sometimes joined with communities. These deaths represent more than 45% of all deaths reported by the *Daily Nation*, i.e. approximately 500 deaths a year from 1990 to 2003. The homicides studied here exclude domestic violence and inter-personal violence at large. For ease of reference, the terms 'collective violence' and 'collective homicides' will be used for violent deaths studied in this article. We excluded from this analysis 257 deaths resulting from the terrorist attack on the US Embassy in 1998, which is classified as 'other'.

4.2. THE METHOD TO ESTIMATE THE VARIATION OF REPORTED DEATHS

Measuring the rate of collective homicides is not our main objective here. We are more concerned with the variation of homicides resulting from collective violence than with the level of this violence, even though its high level is particularly distressing in Kenya. Let us suppose that the homicide rate for the whole country is constant over time. The expected homicides would then increase according to the growth of the population. Most of those homicides would be domestic and interpersonal, and their intensity would probably slowly vary over time. Even if the rate of domestic and inter-personal homicides was not exactly constant, it would not change much from one year to another. The total number of homicides would follow a slow upward trend together with the total population in Kenya. Our hypothesis is that collective homicides reported in the press are more subjected to variation over time. Although they comprise a small proportion of all homicides, they contribute more to the overall variation.

To analyse in detail the variation of homicides over time, we cannot simply use the yearly number of deaths, as the actual observations showed considerable

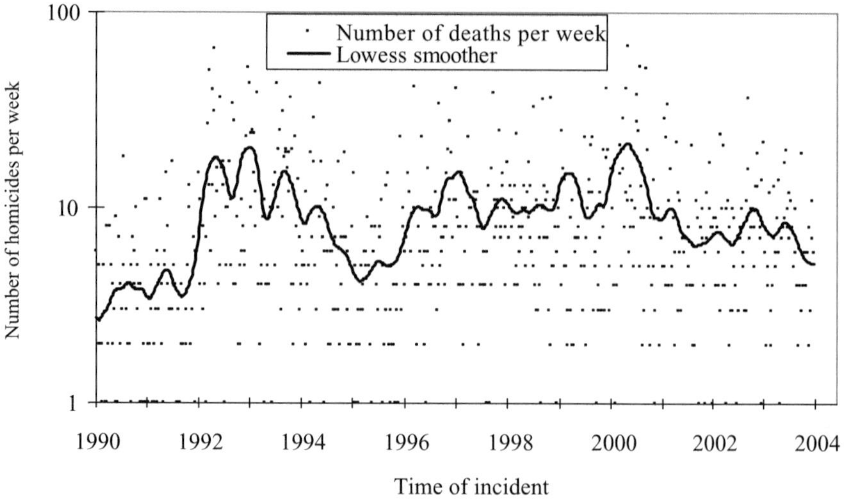

Figure 1. Number of weekly homicides and Lowess smoother.

variation within each given year. At the same time, daily or even weekly numbers would be too detailed and variation patterns confusing. Figure 1 illustrates the need for smoothing the observed data. Each dot in the graph represents the number of homicides in a week. Any interpretation is almost impossible. To facilitate the interpretation, we used the Lowess smoother, a technique that estimates a locally weighted regression of the number of deaths at each point in time. The smooth values are represented as a curve in Figure 1.

4.3. ILLUSTRATION OF HISTORICAL AND GEOGRAPHICAL APPROACH TO COLLECTIVE HOMICIDES

The use of smooth curves is best illustrated by comparing the different causes of homicides, i.e. the different offenders. Figure 2 shows the variations of homicides from 1990 to 1995. The increase of the number of homicides around the elections (December 1992) appears quite clearly. This example illustrates the need to cautiously interpret the causes of homicides as reported by journalists. From Figure 2, it would appear that gangsters are the main cause of homicides during the elections period. But one notices that for the same period, journalists declared fewer homicides due to community clashes, contrary to the period before (first half of 1992) and after (second half of 1993). How can we interpret such variations?

Journalists are very willing to give an accurate image of violence in Kenya as it allows them to express some of their criticism towards the regime. However, in spite of their professionalism, their presentation of violent deaths is always influenced by some degree of manipulation by authorities, which is often difficult to eliminate. Obviously, media coverage of violence is restricted by numerous

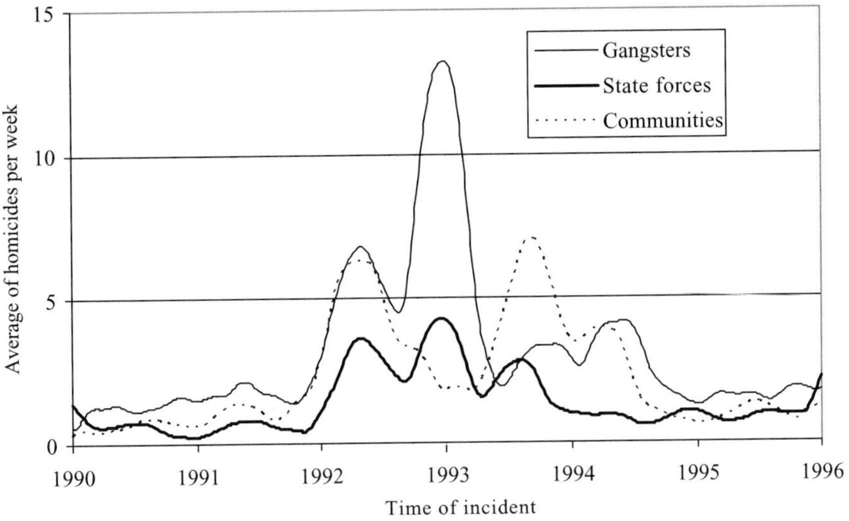

Figure 2. Average number of homicides per week in rural areas, Lowess smoother, 1990–1995.

reverse factors. In the framework of our survey, this led to the difficult problem of how the deaths reported by the press should be labelled. The most obvious example is that of the Rift Valley massacres in the 1990s (Médard, 1999). At the moment when they were triggered off in 1991, the media spoke of acts of violence by bandits, thus making use of official police categories. A few months later, during the electoral campaign of 1992, the rhetoric changed. According to the ruling body, ethnic tensions would appear following the rebirth of the multiparty system (1991), which would revive the community gaps that the single party era had put under a bushel. Already at that time, journalists were suspicious that these acts of violence were related to ethnic cleansing directly involving the leaders of the state. But they had no proof, and it would be too risky to accuse the most influential ministers of ethnic massacres. The press was under the pressure of the government and preferred to use the official rhetoric of violence. The homicides that resulted from ethnic tensions were attributed to bandits by the police. Some could have even been disguised as accidents. The very same incidents appeared later, as assessed by different parliamentary commissions set up in the middle of the 1990s under the pressure of the civil society, to be ethnic cleansing, in which the party in power (KANU) was closely involved. For this reason the incidents could not be reported as such at the time they occurred. At that time, the journalists had to continue using the official labelling, but parallel they disseminated results of surveys carried out by local and international human rights NGOs and eventually, for the most part they were able to prove the role played by the governmental elites. Only then the press could change the labelling of violent deaths and speak clearly of ethnic cleansing.

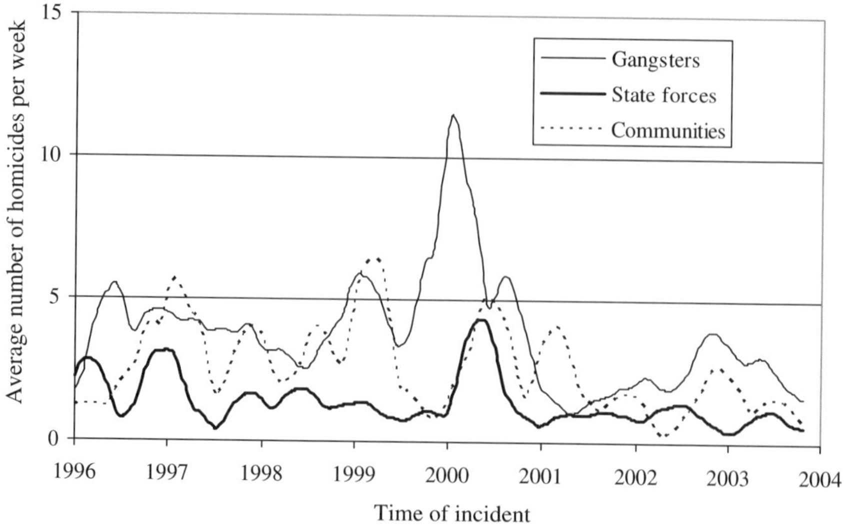

Figure 3. Average number of homicides per week in rural areas, Lowess smoother, 1996–2003.

Were the elections a major time for collective violence, as most journalists, and also human rights and religious organisations, claim? From the data collected from the *Daily Nation*, the first elections under the multiparty regime in 1992 showed a bad example (Figure 2). However, irrespective from how keen journalists were to report on violence at the time of the next elections in 1997, they were unable to show as much violence in 1997 as in the 1992 elections (Figure 3 for rural areas, to compare with Figure 2). Truly the number of homicides was on average particularly low in 1995 and increased in the years 1996–1998. But homicides did not particularly increase around the elections of December 1997, thus contradicting the allegations of the journalists themselves. In reality, from 1996, the political violence was less concentrated in the Rift Valley and more diffused in the whole country (Throup and Hornsby, 1998). Most ethnic cleansing occurred in the 1992–1993 election period. Violence was more sporadic and less fatal in 1997–1998. Actually, our data show that the years 1999–2000 were more fatal though in the mid–term between two elections. The December 2002 elections seem to have triggered violence at a much lower level than previously seen.

The comparison of homicides attributed to state forces (mainly the police) in rural areas and in Nairobi (too few cases were observed in other urban areas) illustrates the kind of monitoring of violence that can be done at a more local geographical level. The comparison helps to identify a change in the state policy regarding law and order in Nairobi. In Figure 4, we rescaled the (Y) axis associated with the state homicides in rural areas, so that it better reflects the actual size of the overall rural population, which is about 12 times as large as the population in Nairobi agglomeration. First of all, it can be clearly seen from Figure 4 that except for 1992, the *Daily Nation* journalists attributed much more deaths due to police

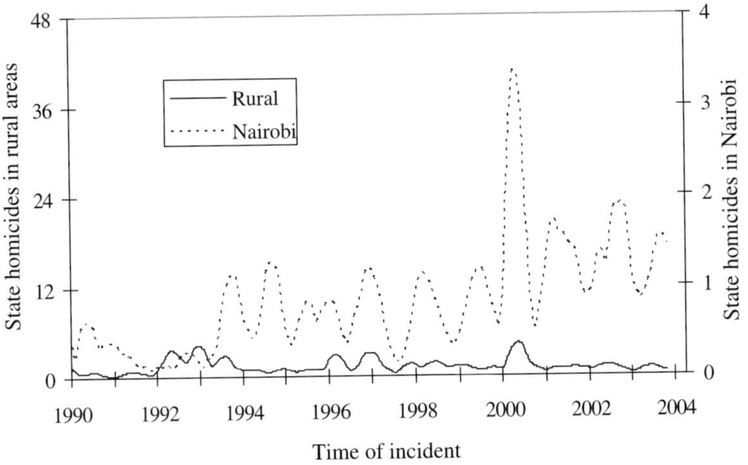

Figure 4. Average number of homicides per week due to State forces in rural areas (left-hand scale) and in Nairobi (right-hand scale), Lowess smoother, 1990–2003.

violence to Nairobi than to rural areas, subject to the population size in both areas. Second, there was a peak in early 2000 both in rural areas and in Nairobi. Third, in 2001 and 2002, the average number of deaths due to police violence hovers between 1 and 2 per week as against 0 and 1 per week from 1993 to 1999. There was a rise of homicides before the December 2002 elections but a drop in the period during and after the elections. Fourth, the average level of homicides remains high in 2003, despite the recent reform in the police, which was supposed to reconsider its 'shoot-to-kill' policy. This last observation illustrates the use of the database (that can be compiled daily) as a monitoring system.

The state is the first cause of collective homicides in Nairobi, with 3.6 deaths a month according to the *Daily Nation*. By comparison, banditry causes 'only' 2 deaths a month, whereas community clashes and mob justice cause 1.5 deaths a month. The media perceives this situation as a pathology of the police. It could merely be a characteristic of a neo-colonialist state. But that does not explain why the brutality of the police increased in recent years in Nairobi. The reported homicides also increased for banditry (+29%) and for communities (+40%) between the two periods, but not as much as for police (+97%). In other words, 71% of the overall increase of the collective homicides in Nairobi reported in the *Daily Nation* is due to state forces. The number of bandits killed by the police increased by a factor of 1.8 in recent years. However, an analysis of the victims of police violence in this city indicates the growing importance of 'collateral damage' and mob justice. The innocent victims caught in the middle of police-gangsters gun battles appeared in the press reports from 1999 only. The victims of such battles (gangsters and other people) represent now 7% of the victims while the number of so-called 'suspects' tripled and now represent 14% of the victims (9% before 2000). The consequence is that while the bandits represented three quarters of all victims of police violence before 2000, they now represent 'only' two thirds of the victims. A comparison with data collected from other newspapers should confirm whether this is to be attributed to a systematic bias from the *Daily Nation* reports or whether it is a reflection of the actual phenomenon.

5. Conclusion: the potential of press reports to analyse low intensity conflicts

The monitoring of violence that we proposed in this study should obviously be perfected through a systematic collection of reports over the entire press spectrum. This preliminary study, aimed mainly at showing the potential of the proposed method, is based on a single Kenyan newspaper data, the *Daily Nation*. We expect much more robust results from a full coverage of the press reports. Once this is done, there is much more to analyse than what we exemplified in this study, simply by comparing trends for different causes of deaths, by region and nationally. Variables other than the date and place of incidents and types of offender are contained in our database as well but were not analysed here: physical agent of death (firearm, blade, explosion, vehicle, etc.), number of victims by sex and whether they are adults or not (press reports usually do not give more details on age). We also collected victims' characteristics (usually their profession) but this information is not systematic as press reports do not usually make a description of each victim when there are many.

Clearly, the press reports cannot provide data for a precise epidemiology of violent deaths. They are obviously subjected to some non-measurable biases, depending on the press freedom in a country and on the interest of journalists and their involvement in the political debate. However, we believe that, if properly analysed, press reports can certainly serve as a surveillance system of violence, especially when it is collective. Press reports help measuring the trend of collective violence over time and/or at a sub-national level. The method is particularly appropriate to analyse low intensity conflicts, which persist over decades and are typical of violent political cultures, very common in contemporary sub-Saharan Africa. The quantitative approach also helps to put the violence into perspective and to avoid conventional wisdom on violence, which usually presents violence as increasing. For example, our analysis indicates that violence may have decreased in rural areas, and that the 1997 and 2002 elections do not appear as fatal as previously thought. The quantitative approach also helps in monitoring recent trends. The increase in state violence in Nairobi, if it is confirmed by data collected from other newspapers, is an indication that something is wrong in the way the police is handling crime in the capital city, despite of the lack of parallel increase of death due to banditry.

Finally, more sophisticated analytical tools could be used to analyse our data. In this article, we used fairly simple descriptive tools, such as percentages, rates and graphs. Time series analysis is an obvious option. The difficulty will be to introduce in the model the relevant independent variables. In particular, changes in politics and political actions in general are not easily dated. Testing the interactions between different series of violent deaths is also worth trying.

Glossary

Collective violence: In this article, this term covers violence resulting from conflicts between groups or between a group and (an) individual(s) identified as belonging to a group. It excludes inter-personal violence (such as domestic violence) and includes the following:

Mob justice: lynching of suspected or alleged criminals, usually by a crowd and in a public space (street, market).

State (police) violence: abuse of violence by state forces against individuals or groups. This violence can take the form of extra-judicial executions (see section 3 of this article).

Violence due to banditry: violence perpetrated by bandits against the victims during a robbery, carjacking, etc.

Violence due to community clashes: violence resulting from the conflicts between communities, usually neighbouring ethnic groups.

Acknowledgements

The authors would like to thank Dr. Ewa Tabeau and anonymous reviewers for their useful comments, the French Institute for Research in Africa (IFRA), Nairobi, for its support in data collection, and the *Daily Nation* editorial board and journalists for their indirect contribution to the research.

List of Abbreviations

DG NGO: Democracy and governance non-governmental organisation;
DHS: Demographic and Health Survey;
KANU: Kenya African National Union;
KHRC: Kenya Human Rights Commission;
NCBA: Nairobi Central Business Association;
NCCK: National Council of Churches of Kenya;
NCSS: Nairobi Child Survival Survey;
NGO: Non-governmental organisation;
PJC: Peace and Justice Commission;
SRIC: Security Research and Information Centre;
VSN: Victimisation Survey of Nairobi;
WHO: World Health Organisation

Notes

[1] This term is explained in Section 4.1 and in the glossary at the end of this article.

[2] The Nairobi report is not sufficiently precise on sampling but indicates that the methodology is the same as in Dar es Salaam.

[3] Defending the freedom of press took often place in courts of law, where several DG NGOs lawyers specialised in the rights of press. Additionally, the freedom of press was emphasized in various civil society publications, see for instance Kabatesi (1996).
[4] The politicisation of the civil society was not obvious to all Kenyan social scientists. From the mid-1990s, some sociologists, e.g. Ndegwa (1996), indicated that many NGOs did not wish to be involved in politics.

References

APHRC, 2002. *Population and Health Dynamics in Nairobi's Informal Settlements.* African Population and Health Research Centre (APHRC), Nairobi.

Bocquier, P., 2003. 'La mesure de la mortalité à Nairobi: mais oú les morts ont-ils disparu?', in: Y. Droz and H. Maupeu (eds), *Les figures de la mort à Nairobi—Une capitale sans cimetières.* Paris: L'Harmattan—IUED-IFRA-CREPAO. 7–16.

Camerer, L., Louw, A., Shaw, M., Artz, L. and Scharf, W., 1998. *Crime in Cape Town—Results of a City Victim Survey.* Institute for Security Studies, Cape Town, Pretoria.

Darbon, D. and Du Bois de Gaudusson, J. (eds.), 1997. *La création du droit en Afrique.* Karthala, Paris.

Gauchet, M., 2002. *La démocratie contre elle-même.* Gallimard, Paris.

Gituto, B.M., 2002. The relationship between journalist orientation, newsroom politics and journalist attitudes towards the crisis over reviewing the constitution in Kenya. Unpublished M.A. dissertation. Mass Communication Department, Daystar University, Nairobi.

Heald, S., 1989. *Controlling Anger. The Anthropology of Gisu Violence.* Manchester University Press, Manchester.

Heald, S., 2002, 'Domesticating Leviathan: Sungusungu groups in Tanzania', in: *Crime in Eastern Africa: Past and Present Perspectives,* Conference proceedings, BIEA-IFRA, Naivasha, Kenya.

Institute for Education in Democracy (IED), Catholic Justice and Peace Commission (CJPC), and National Council of Churches in Kenya (NCCK), 1998. *Report on the 1997 General Elections in Kenya.* IED, CJPC, NCCK, Nairobi.

Kabatesi, K., 1996. 'Mass media sectors: assessing the current situation, in: K. Kibwana, S. Wanjala and O. Owiti (eds). *The Anatomy of Corruption in Kenya: Legal. Political, and Socio-economic Perspectives.* Nairobi: Center for Law and Research International—Claripress.

Kenya Human Rights Commission (KHRC), 1998. *Killing the Vote. State Sponsored Violence and Flawed Elections in Kenya.* KHRC, Nairobi.

Louw, A., Shaw, M., Camerer, L. and Robertshaw, R., 1998. *Crime in Johannesburg: Results of a City Victim Survey.* Institute for Security Studies, Cape Town, Pretoria.

Médard, C., 1999, Territoires de l'ethnicité: encadrement, revendications et conflits territoriaux au Kenya. Doctorat, UFR de géographie, Université de Paris 1—Panthéon-Sorbonne.

National Council for Population and Development and Institute for Resource Development, 1989. *Kenya Demographic and Health Survey, 1989. Nairobi and Columbia.* NCPD, Ministry of Home Affairs and National Heritage. Macro International, Inc, Maryland.

National Council for Population and Development, Central Bureau of Statistics, and Macro International Inc, 1994. *Kenya Demographic and Health Survey, 1993. Nairobi and Calverton.* NCPD. CBS, Office of the Vice-President and Ministry of Planning and National Development. Macro International Inc, Maryland.

National Council for Population and Development, Central Bureau of Statistics, and Macro International Inc., 1999. *Kenya Demographic and Health Survey, 1998. Nairobi and Calverton.* NCPD. CBS, Office of the Vice-President and Ministry of Planning and National Development. Macro International Inc. Maryland.

Ndegwa, S. N., 1996. *The Two Faces of Civil Society: NGOs and Politics in Africa.* Kumarian Press, West Hartford, Connecticut.

Opiyo, B. A., 1994. The press and Kenyan politics: a study of newswaking in a newly democratic state. Unpublished PhD dissertation, Mass Communication Department, University of Iowa, Iowa city.

Pommerolle, M.-E., 2003. 'Droits de l'Homme et politique: l'institutionnalisation paradoxale d'une ONG kenyane', in: *Gouvener les institutions africaines—Acteurs et institutions*, Conference proceedings, CEAN, Bordeaux.

Pommerolle, M.-E. and Ruteere, M., 2003. 'New wine old skins? Community policing and public policy in Kenya', in: *Crime in Eastern Africa: Past and Present Perspectives.* Conference proceedings, BIEAIFRA, Naivasha, Kenya.

Robertshaw, R., Louw, A., Shaw, M., Mashiyane, M. and Brettell, S., 2001. *Reducing Crime in Durban, a Victim Survey and Safer City Strategy.* Institute for Security Studies, Cape Town, Pretoria.

Rodriguez-Torres, D., 1998. 'La justice expéditive à Nairobi. Informalité ou formalité juridique?', *Journal of Legal Pluralism* 42, 179–198.

Statistics South Africa, 2002. *Causes of Death in South Africa 1997–2001: Advance Release of Recorded Causes of Death.* Statistics South Africa, Pretoria.

Throup, D. W. and Hornsby, C., 1998. *Multy-party Politics in Kenya. Oxford, Nairobi.* James Currey, EAEP, Ohio University Press, Athens.

Transparency International, 2002. *Kenya Urban Bribery Index.* Transparency International Kenya, Nairobi.

Transparency International, 2004. *Kenya Urban Bribery Index.* Transparency International Kenya, Nairobi.

UN-Habitat, 2000, *Crime in Dar es Salaam: Results of a City Victim Survey and in Depth Interviews on Violence against Women.* Safer Cities Series, Dar es Salaam.

UN-Habitat, 2002, *Crime in Nairobi: Results of a Citywide Victim Survey.* Nairobi: Safer Cities Series.

WHO, 2002. *Report on Violence and Health.* World Health Organisation, Geneva.

CHAPTER 13. MIGRATORY COPING IN WARTIME MOZAMBIQUE: AN ANTHROPOLOGY OF VIOLENCE AND DISPLACEMENT IN "FRAGMENTED WARS"

STEPHEN C. LUBKEMANN
Anthropology Department, George Washington University, USA; and Watson Institute, Brown University, USA

Abstract. Current frameworks for analyzing conflict in developing nations usually focus on the agendas of national-level parties to conflicts. This article draws heavily on the author's own ethnographic work in central Mozambique to demonstrate how political alignment during the Mozambican civil conflict (1977–92) was regarded by local actors as a tool for engaging in family- and community-level political struggles. Comparing findings from his own work in the district of Machaze to that of other ethnographic researchers who focused on wartime experiences elsewhere in Mozambique, he shows how the means of violence of national-level parties during the civil conflict were appropriated by local actors in service to local forms of social struggle. He proposes the concept of "fragmented war" to describe such contexts in which national "civil wars" take on a large degree of local character and in which there is considerable variation in that local character as a result of sociocultural and ethnic diversity within a country. The article then documents how wartime migration—as one of the most visible and consequential strategies for reacting to violence—was organized primarily as a response to such micro-level political struggles rather than merely to the state of hostilities between national-level political actors. Different local "logics of violence" thus produced different patterns of wartime displacement throughout Mozambique. Some of the key historical conditions that made wartime violence in Mozambique susceptible to "fragmentation" are reviewed, in order to reflect more broadly on what general conditions might produce "fragmentations of violence" in other war contexts. The article concludes with a discussion of how anthropological approaches can contribute to the demographic analysis of forced migration in culturally diversified war zones.

1. Introduction

Processes of prolonged conflict and consequent displacement have assumed mounting importance in the political, social, and demographic reorganization of many developing countries, particularly in Africa. Current frameworks for analyzing conflict in developing nations usually focus on the agendas of national-level parties to conflicts. In this article, I draw heavily on my own ethnographic work in south central Mozambique to demonstrate how political alignment during the Mozambican civil conflict (1977–92) was shaped largely by family- and community-level struggles rather than national politics. Through a comparison of my own findings to that of other ethnographers who have researched wartime experiences elsewhere in Mozambique, I demonstrate how the means of violence of the two national parties to the civil conflict were appropriated by local actors in service to their own

This chapter was previously published in *Journal of Peace Research*, vol. 42, no. 4, 2005, pp. 493–508.

Helge Brunborg et al. (eds.), The Demography of Armed Conflict, 303–320.

agendas. I propose the concept of "fragmented war" to describe such contexts, in which national civil wars take on a large degree of local character, and in which there is considerable variation in that local character as a result of sociocultural and ethnic diversity within a country.

This article then proceeds to document how Mozambican wartime migration was organized primarily as a response to such micro-level political struggles rather than merely to the state of hostilities between national-level political actors. I detail how specific forms of social antagonism and cultural beliefs in the district of Machaze significantly shaped wartime violence, assessments of risk, and consequent migratory reactions during the conflict. By then comparing Machaze to other areas of Mozambique, I demonstrate how different forms of local social conflict ultimately produced very different patterns of displacement throughout the country. Thus, in Gaza province, displacement was organized along ethnic lines that pitted the Ndaus against the Shangaans; in Manica and Sofala provinces, intra-familial conflict led to the dissolution of family units; while in Nampula province, ethnic tensions between the Erati and Macuane resulted in entire villages migrating together.[1] I briefly outline some of the critical historical conditions that allowed wartime violence in Mozambique to become fragmented.

In conclusion, I hypothesize what general conditions might produce "fragmentations of violence" in other civil war contexts and suggest that these are worthy of further empirical and comparative investigation. I also outline key premises that should inform the demographic analysis of forced migration in "fragmented war" contexts. Finally, I discuss how anthropological approaches can inform such analysis.

2. Theorizing wartime violence

As a form of "political violence", war is typically understood and analyzed as a phenomenon that is organized by the interests and agendas of state-level actors—that is, governments and/or insurgencies that are contesting state power. In such formulations, violence is understood as an instrumental expression of the interests of those who have the means to technically perpetrate it. There is consequently a tendency for analysts of conflict to explain the specific ways in which violence is organized (its forms, its timing, who enacts it, who suffers from it) in terms of the interests of those who control the means for violence. Such assumptions have certainly informed much of the analysis of the Mozambican conflict.

Thus, in the Mozambican case, several analysts have attempted to explain the savagery of RENAMO's wartime tactics against civilians in certain parts of the country as tactics for controlling local dissent (Geffray, 1989; Vines, 1991; Finnegan, 1992). In other cases, such savagery has been explained as an attempt by a nominally weak military force to use terror in order to gain influence it could not achieve on the battlefield (Africa Watch, 1992; Gersony, 1988; Hanlon, 1984; Wilson, 1992; Nordstrom, 1997).

Similarly, it is generally assumed that those who experience or suffer from violence also understand it to be a direct and unmediated expression of the political interests of the military forces and political factions that perpetrate it. In other words, when a rural Mozambican who refused to comply with the government's (FRELIMO) demand that locals resettle in fortified villages was confronted by a government patrol that burned his house, killed or forcibly recruited his sons, and moved his family to the village by force, it is assumed by many analysts that he understood his suffering to be the consequence of his violation of the government's publicized interests (Lubkemann, 2000a). In such frameworks, violence is seen as perpetrated in service to, and given its particular form by, the interests of the parties who have military forces in the field, and who generally are contesting state-level power. Similarly, such approaches assume that individuals expect to be targeted for violence primarily if they challenge or oppose the interests of one of these parties to the conflict (though they may clearly expect to suffer inadvertently if caught in the crossfire as well).

In contrast, this article demonstrates how wartime violence in the district of Machaze, in the central Mozambican province of Manica, was significantly shaped by local-level social tensions and micro-political goals, defined and operating at the community and even family level. I demonstrate how residents of Machaze managed to appropriate the means of violence of the government (FRELIMO) and the insurgency (RENAMO)—the two national parties to the civil war—in their pursuit of local social struggles whose dynamics were defined by culturally distinct logics. By and large, these micro-political objectives were entirely unrelated to the contest for state power. Understandings of wartime violence, assessments of risk, and consequent migratory reactions thus often had very little to do with the political programs or pretensions of either of the national parties to the war. Rather, residents of Machaze calculated risk and reacted to it primarily in terms of the logic of local social conflicts.

3. The Mozambican civil war

Mozambique gained independence from Portugal in 1975, after more than a decade of anti-colonial struggle. Shortly thereafter, Mozambique closed its borders with Rhodesia to support the Zimbabwe African National Liberation Army (ZANLA) led struggle against Ian Smith's apartheid regime in Rhodesia. Reacting against such support, the Smith regime drew on Mozambican political dissenters to establish a military movement that would support Rhodesian efforts against ZANLA guerrillas based in Mozambique and help to destabilize Mozambique politically and economically. That military movement later came to be known as the Mozambique National Resistance Movement, or RENAMO (an acronym for the name in Portuguese). When the Smith regime capitulated in 1980, South Africa's apartheid regime took over the role as RENAMO's patron. Foreign support remained vital for RENAMO and greatly influenced its early strategy and operations (Hall and Young, 1997).

However, RENAMO's eventual success in extending the insurgency to the whole country and in prosecuting a civil war that lasted until 1992 ultimately depended on more than its initial external backing. Most specifically, the policies pursued by the post-colonial FRELIMO government after independence from Portugal was achieved in 1975 amplified deeply ingrained sentiments of mistrust against any and all forms of central political authority in many areas of the country.

Within the first two or three years that followed independence, rural populations in areas such as Machaze quickly became disillusioned with the new post-colonial government, largely as a result of a significant decline in their economic well-being and standard of living. This decline resulted in large part from government policies designed to recast Mozambique's economy in a socialist mold (Wuyts, 1984, 1985). In Machaze, FRELIMO's policies raised new obstacles to long-established patterns of international labor migration by establishing new pass laws that restricted movement (Lubkemann, 2000a). The war with Rhodesia also restricted migration trip options for young unmarried men, who traditionally undertook one or two shorter trips to work on the plantations in Rhodesia in order to earn the money needed for beginning a migratory career to more distant destinations in South Africa (Lubkemann, 2000a). FRELIMO also imposed unpopular mandatory collective agriculture programs, instituted price controls and a state monopoly on the sale of local agricultural surplus, and nationalized the rural shop network. These measures reduced local earnings and restricted the availability of commodities for purchase in rural areas. The new post-colonial government's drastic social engineering policies disenfranchised local social elites, particularly the traditional authorities who played an important role in land distribution and local governance in rural areas such as Machaze. FRELIMO's policies also placed many of those who had been socially and economically marginalized in new positions of power and influence in local government (Lubkemann, 2000a; Alexander, 1994).

Machaze is a district in Manica province, not far from the district of Manhica, where RENAMO made its first appearance in 1977. By early 1979, Machaze had witnessed its first incursions by RENAMO forces. RENAMO's early actions in Machaze were directed against visible and unpopular symbols of the government's policies—such as the government-run *lojas do povo* (people's shops). Through visible public actions such as the burning of these *lojas* and through its propaganda, RENAMO articulated a simple political agenda: the expulsion of FRELIMO and the demise of the unpopular social and economic changes the FRELIMO government had instituted after decolonization. The fact that it articulated no alternative national program did not prevent it from garnering considerable local sympathy.

The arrival of RENAMO in Machaze led the FRELIMO government to pursue draconian measures meant to prevent RENAMO from benefiting from any popular support. Taking a page directly from the politico-military strategy of the Portuguese during the recently ended war for independence, FRELIMO sought to forcibly move all the residents of the district into guarded communal villages (Coelho, 1998; Hall and Young, 1997; Lubkemann, 2000a). Few residents of Machaze complied willingly with this directive for a variety of reasons. Many did not trust the FRELIMO government and wished to avoid unnecessary contact with central authorities. Most importantly, subsistence in Machaze was dependent upon a pattern of slash and burn agriculture that required relatively large parcels of land for each household and thus had long been characterized by a highly dispersed settlement pattern (Lubkemann, 2000a).

Most district residents resisted the government's resettlement scheme for these reasons rather than because they were active supporters of RENAMO. However, the generalized reluctance of the population to resettle was interpreted by FRELIMO as default evidence of support for RENAMO. This interpretation led FRELIMO to even more violent measures against those who did not obey this order. At one point, FRELIMO began to systematically lob long-range mortar and artillery fire into the bush areas in an effort to drive the population into the "safety" of the villages. Patrols began to burn houses outside the villages in order to discourage their inhabitants from leaving the communal villages and going home (Lubkemann, 2000a) (see Figure 1).

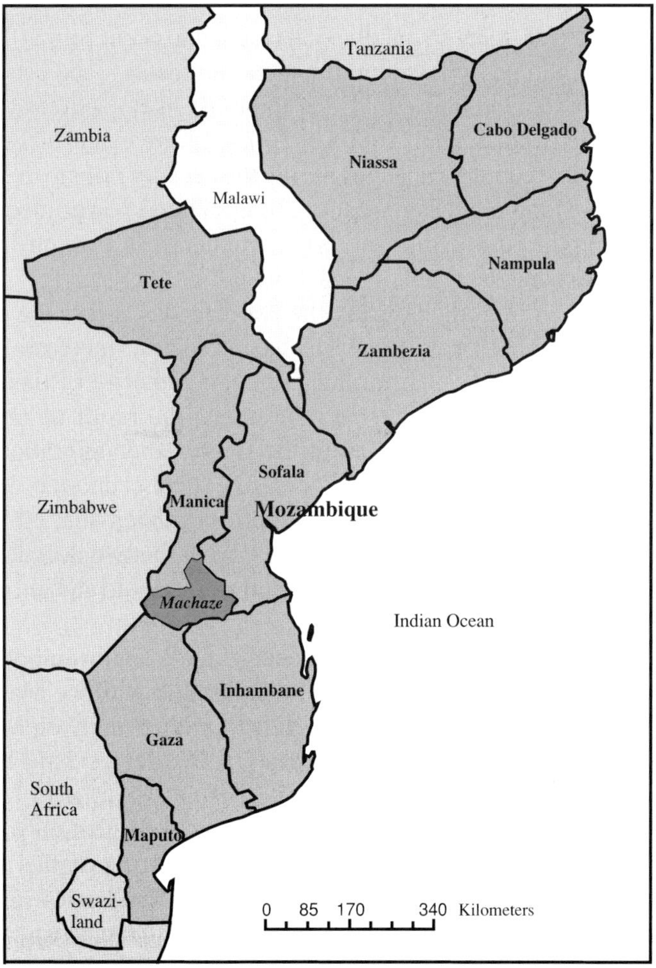

Figure 1. Map of Mozambique.

It is important to note that although many district residents were sympathetic with RENAMO's agenda and many were highly resentful of FRELIMO's social and economic engineering policies, such sentiments did not translate immediately into active mobilization in support of RENAMO. For the most part, Machazians were primarily interested in avoiding *both* military parties and in continuing to practice their traditional forms of subsistence agriculture that presumed highly dispersed settlement patterns. However, by 1980, it had become increasingly hazardous to pursue such strategies. Both FRELIMO and RENAMO soldiers began to treat those who would not resettle into the zones that were securely under their control as supporters of the other side to be targeted for capture or for death. It is in this context that long-standing forms of local social antagonism increasingly affected the dynamics of military violence in the district.

4. Local social conflict and wartime violence in machaze

Historically in Machaze, local social divisions tended to occur primarily within kinship groups. Ndau cultural beliefs identify social intimates—and especially members of one's own extended household—as the most likely sources of rivalry and jealousy. Elsewhere (Lubkemann, 2000a,b, 2002), I have extensively documented how significant socio-economic changes during the decades prior to the civil war had accentuated socio-economic differentiation, redistributed power inequality within households, and produced a significant rise in witchcraft as an expression of social tension and antagonism.

Specific changes in migration during the two decades before the civil war had generated new intergenerational rifts in Machazian society. Increasingly, labor migration had allowed younger men to challenge the authority of their fathers and senior kinsmen. Differential success in migration—the result of changes in the structure of employment opportunities in the major labor migration destination (South Africa)—had also significantly increased socio-economic differentiation within extended households and local communities (Lubkemann, 2000a). In short, a series of significant socio-economic changes during the two decades prior to the civil war had substantially amplified forms of intra-household and intra-community strife in Machaze.

It is important to realize that particularly early in the civil war, both FRELIMO and RENAMO troops and commanders were unfamiliar with the Machaze area in which they had been deployed. They thus tended to rely heavily on locals to guide them and to identify enemy cadres or collaborators. District residents became adept at using accusations of "collaboration with the enemy" in order to further private agendas. Fairly early on in the war, Machazians figured out that they could further their personal interests by suggesting to one of the warring parties that personal opponents were partisans of the other side in the conflict.

In one particularly illustrative case that was reported to me, a man who had been a particularly successful migrant and consequently had started several grinding mills was the subject of intense jealousy on the part of older brothers who had not been as successful in their own migratory careers. He actually was a RENAMO sympathizer and had thus chosen to move to a remote area in order to be farther from the FRELIMO villages. However, his brothers convinced RENAMO troops that he was taking grain into the villages and giving it to government soldiers. As a consequence, he was shot by RENAMO troops—ironically enough the very party he actually sympathized with!

In another case described to me, a man and his wife who had moved into the village had been involved in a long dispute with a neighbor over a honeycomb bordering their two homesteads. The neighbor, who was also resettled in the village, actually managed to obtain a landmine through a family member who was a part of the government militia, and planted it near the honeycomb. The other man and his wife were both hit by the landmine when they visited the honeycomb. The man died instantly and the woman was fatally injured. She died later the same day after crawling back to the village.

In a third case, one of two junior wives of a man I interviewed reported to FRELIMO soldiers that the son of a rival co-wife was about to join RENAMO. As a result, the rival wife and her children were forcibly removed to the village and the son in question was detained. He later died under interrogation.

Such accounts were typical rather than exceptional in my in-depth life-history interviews with members of over 120 different Machazian households conducted in 1996 and 1997. Such cases exemplify the way that local social agendas strongly influenced the deployment of violence by FRELIMO and RENAMO from the very outset of the conflict. The violence of the national parties to the conflict was, more often than not, diverted to serve local micro-political, rather than national macro-political, ends. While a small minority of local FRELIMO party cadres and early RENAMO sympathizers may have been motivated by the political projects of the contenders for national power, most residents of Machaze reacted to the way in which that power itself was manipulated and deployed in local social struggles.

5. Cultural shapings of violence in machaze

Machazian interest in using wartime violence for private ends was also encouraged by the ways in which Ndau religious beliefs amplified local social antagonism (Lubkemann, 2002). Machazians believed that those who suffered violent deaths were likely to become *mfukwas*. Among the Ndau, the spirits of the dead are believed to continue to interact with and affect the lives of the living, in both helpful and harmful ways. Ancestral spirits were believed to be largely benevolent, while those who died particularly violent deaths or who had been severely wronged were believed to take on a vengeful state that made them particularly deadly. Spirits in such a state were called *mfukwas* and were particularly feared.

The death of soldiers who were "outsiders" and had died violent deaths in the bush raised the specter of a proliferation of dangerous unknown *mfukwas*, who could randomly intervene to cause death. A more predictable, yet also more constant, threat was posed by the intimate relative whose violent death was believed to provoke them to take on the dreaded *mfukwa* state.

Although wrongful death obligated the living to seek redress, the culturally prescribed institutions for pursuing redress had been decimated by post-colonial government policies. Soon after independence, FRELIMO had launched a national campaign that specifically targeted the traditional ritual specialists (in Machaze known as *nyangas* and *nhammossos*) who were regarded within Ndau society as intercessors with the spirits of the dead. Initially, FRELIMO had acted against these specialists because it viewed them as obstacles to its vision of socialist modernization (Hall and Young, 1997). However, as RENAMO became more active, the government began to view these ritual specialists as the segment of the population most likely to aid and abet the insurgency. FRELIMO therefore instituted even more focused and repressive measures against these ritual specialists. While many were imprisoned or fled from FRELIMO-held areas, those who remained in the government's communal villages were forbidden (or simply too fearful) to practice their ritual specialization.

Consequently, those Machazians in the communal villages often felt they had no effective means for peacefully interceding and negotiating with angered ancestral or other spirits. Moreover, the impossibility of interacting with the guilty parties (often unknown or else unreachable in the opposing force's area of control) made the negotiation of a settlement with a *mfukwa* all the more difficult if not impossible, even if a ritual intercessor could be found. Sometimes even proper burials were impossible—another ritual failure thought likely to provoke ancestral virulence. Not only did Machazians believe that a *mfukwa* could threaten its own family members, but a *mfukwa* in the family could place relationships in the broader community at risk as well. Any form of conflict with a family plagued by a *mfukwa* was believed to be particularly dangerous.[2]

Lacking the possibility for redress, revenge was upheld as the very lowest level of action believed capable of deflecting the ancestral wrath of those violently slain in war. This belief in conjunction with the crippling of "peaceful" forms of resolution led many Machazians to perpetrate radically violent actions of revenge in what amounted in part to a form of "socio-spiritual defense". Each act of violence inevitably gave motive for reactive acts of at least the same magnitude, thus multiplying the number of accusations and violent deaths in a viciously escalating and ever more socially inclusive spiral.

Such analysis (see Lubkemann, 2002, for more details) shows how the social antagonism that shaped much of the wartime violence in Machaze was related to social processes and cultural logics that predated the war itself. These antagonisms were largely unrelated to the larger political agendas of the national parties to the war. The prosecution of these social struggles was dictated by cultural logics rather than strategic military ones.

6. Mozambique as a "fragmented war"

Comparative analysis of ethnographic work in different areas of Mozambique clearly demonstrates the degree to which the war itself was interpreted and constructed in highly variable and culturally specific terms throughout the country. The means of violence were shaped to serve the ends of specific forms and expressions of local conflict. Consequently, from the perspective of those actors embroiled in the day-to-day violence of the Mozambican civil conflict, what the war was about in one area was often something that was entirely different from what the war was about elsewhere.

For example, in the northern province of Nampula, the anthropologist Christian Geffray (1989) reported on how forms of social tension very different from those that shaped violence in Machaze informed wartime political alignments among the Macuane and the Erati ethnic groups. The Erati and Macuane had a long history of warfare and antagonism that predated colonial conquest. The politically centralized Erati had been more readily co-opted into the Portuguese system of indirect rule. Consequently, they came to occupy an intermediary position of privilege between the Portuguese and the subordinate Macuane during the colonial era. When independence arrived in 1975, the Erati continued to occupy most bureaucratic positions in local government, while the Macuane remained marginalized.

Meanwhile, the Macuane had retained a generalized stance of distrust and disengagement with central authority throughout the colonial period. They had also suffered from the post-colonial governments' attempts at forced villagization and to divest traditional authorities of legitimacy. They thus proved receptive to the anti-government insurgency when it arrived in Nampula in the mid-1980s. In particular, the Macuane saw in RENAMO a way to simultaneously restore local autonomy vis-à-vis the central state, and to simultaneously react against the perceived and resented ethnic dominance of the Erati.

In response to the almost universal adherence of the Macuane to RENAMO, the Erati then reacted by seeking support from FRELIMO. Thus, in Nampula, the war took on ethnic characteristics quite different from those evidenced in Machaze. In Nampula, entire communities tended to align as a whole with either FRELIMO or with RENAMO (Geffray, 1989). This pattern of community cohesion and inter-ethnic violence contrasts sharply with the patterns in Machaze, where ethnicity was irrelevant in the shaping of wartime violence. Rather than violence occurring *between* communities as in Nampula, in Machaze violence primarily occurred *within* communities and quite often among actual household members.

In yet an entirely different area of the country—the southern province of Gaza—local social tensions were primarily structured by yet another ethnic dynamic with its own particular history (Roesch, 1992). The atrocities committed by RENAMO troops (who in this area were predominantly Ndau) against civilians (who were predominantly Shangaan) were particularly noteworthy for their savagery (Gersony, 1988; Roesch, 1992; Hall, 1990; Minter, 1994). RENAMO originated in the Ndau-speaking center of the country, and its leadership was initially largely Ndau. In contrast, much of the leadership of FRELIMO was originally from the Shangaan-speaking south.

There has been a long history of contention between Shangaan speakers and other ethnic groups from north of the Save river. This rivalry predated the advent of colonial rule, extending back to the late 1800s and the northward military expansion and domination of the Gaza empire first under Shoshogane and later under Gungunhanna (Newitt, 1995). Antagonism between Shangaans and Ndaus persisted throughout the colonial period as a result of labor migration policies that attempted to prohibit those from north of the Save from engaging in labor migration to South Africa. Such policies forced many Ndau speakers from the central provinces of Manica and Sofala to attempt to "pass" as Shangaans from the southern province in Gaza in order to work in South Africa. Ndau speakers often had to enter into subordinate relations with local Shangaan chiefs or individuals in Gaza that involved payoffs in order to succeed in this strategy. Many Ndau labor migrants resented this form of exploitation as well as what they perceived to be a Shangaan sense of superiority (Lubkemann, 2000a). It is thus not surprising that Ndau combatants in Gaza, many of whom had most likely previously been Ndau labor migrants passing through Gaza, sought violent redress for grievances that stemmed from the subordination they experienced before the war.

What such comparisons suggest *when viewed together* is the degree to which local social tensions, rather than national political projects, shaped the deployment and understanding of violence in the Mozambican civil war as a whole. Such conflicts can be described as "fragmented wars". Such wars are "fragmented" in that violence is likely to be organized in service to very different, largely local rather than national, agendas throughout a country suffering from civil strife. What the "war is about" is likely to vary widely throughout the country, as very different forms of culturally informed social antagonisms inform the ways in which local populations appropriate, assess, and react to violence.

7. Wartime migration in fragmented wars

The notion of "fragmented wars" is significant to theorizations of demographic change in conflict environments, most specifically to the theorization of wartime population movements. Migration is perhaps the most dramatic response to violence or the threat of violence in wartime. In fragmented war contexts, in which the violence of military actors is appropriated and deployed in the service of local-level social conflicts, reactions to violence—migratory or otherwise—will tend to reflect the logic of those social conflicts. In short, wartime migration behavior in fragmented wars will be primarily a reaction to the use of violence in struggles with local social and cultural logics.

By extension, variation in the social organization of forced migration will occur to the degree that the national space of a civil war is fragmented by different primary forms of local social organization and micro-political conflict. Within a single national space, different local "conflict logics" will result in different patterns of violence and thus in different patterns of migratory reaction to violence, producing in turn different demographic outcomes with respect to wartime population redistribution.

In the Machazian case, cultural logics of local social conflict clearly shaped the social organization of wartime migration—namely, with whom individuals fled, when they chose to flee, and where they chose to go. As the war intensified in Machaze, more and more people opted to flee from their homes, not when they themselves were targeted for violence but soon after hearing that a significant social rival had been captured or targeted by one faction. Upon hearing that a social rival had been captured by one faction, individuals or households often chose to move in exactly the opposite direction into areas controlled by the other faction. Such moves were pre-emptive measures, since it was feared that under duress those who had been forcibly relocated would readily identify their own social rivals to their captors as sympathizers with the "other side". Similarly, when a social rival was known to have suffered violence, it was often deemed wise to relocate. The assumption was that the one's social rival would seek to identify the perpetrator of the witchcraft believed to have caused or permitted the violent episode. That search could be expected to focus on the victim's known social rivals, who would then be likely targeted for revenge in turn. Under such an assumption, movement to a new, and if possible undisclosed, location made good sense.

By contrast, in Nampula migration did not generally involve the fragmentation of households into individuals or small groups. Rather, migration tended to occur in large groups, as entire communities moved all together or in large factional groups. Thus, Erati villages moved primarily into FRELIMO areas and Macuane communities into RENAMO ones (Geffray, 1989). Such patterns of wartime migration contrast sharply with those witnessed in Machaze, where displacement typically involved the atomization of families, domestic units, and communities.

Wartime migration patterns in Gaza also reflected the ways in which local ethnic tensions structured wartime violence. Whereas in Machaze, an ethnically Ndau area, a majority of civilians fled from the government forces into RENAMO-controlled areas, throughout rural Gaza (a predominantly Shangaan area) the reverse pattern held true (Roesch, 1992; Hall, 1990). This difference can be attributed to the fact that in Machaze RENAMO was primarily identified as simply an "anti-central government force", whereas in Gaza it was perceived as an "ethnically Ndau force". In each of these three cases, very different patterns of wartime migration resulted from the way in which local social struggles shaped the interpretation of wartime violence. Resulting differences in the social organization of wartime migration thus reflected the highly differentiated dynamics of local social strife throughout war-torn Mozambique.

8. "Local political cultures of disengagement"

It is worth briefly considering both the historical trajectories and the more immediate political and economic conditions that rendered the Mozambican conflict susceptible to "fragmentation". In large part, the fragmentation of the Mozambican conflict's meaning and the capacity of local social dynamics to "hijack" and redirect the means of violence of national parties to the war can be traced to a history that created a pervasive culture of local "disengagement" (Azarya, 1988) from central political authority. In Machaze, central government strategies for articulating local power exhibited strong similarities throughout pre-colonial, colonial, and immediate post-colonial eras. These strategies of central governance relied primarily on periodic intrusive action based on shows of force and less on more systematic and more comprehensive bureaucratic means. The primary local "political logic" that was produced by this history was governed by the desire to minimize involvement with and the interference in everyday life of central authorities.

Throughout much of the 20th century, the weakness of the Portuguese colonial authorities throughout significant parts of Mozambique—both in administrative and financial terms—led to practices of governance at a local level that were sporadically intrusive and heavy-handed (Lubkemann, 2000a; Isaacman, 1983, 1996; Newitt, 1995). Consequently, the central state's actions and intention came to be seen by local actors as suspect by default. The state was thus viewed as a source of unwanted attention to be evaded (Lubkemann, 2000a; Chingono, 1996; Geffray, 1989; Baptista-Lundin and Machava, 1995; Hall and Young, 1997).

Rather than employing overt resistance or forming grassroots political movements to change the state's policies, rural Mozambican reactions to colonial rule were characterized by less overt yet nevertheless highly effective forms of resistance. These included mass illegal labor migration across international borders, flight from forced labor, evasion of tax collectors, and a multitude of other strategies of passive resistance including non-compliance, absenteeism, and petty vandalism (Isaacman, 1996). These strategies proved highly effective in defending local interests against the far more powerful colonial state, particularly since that power was not so great that it could be exercised in a sustained and uniform manner across space and time.

Thus, throughout the colonial era, a political culture of "disengagement" (Azarya, 1988) developed throughout much of rural Mozambique, in which the primary objective became to minimize the presence of the state in everyday local life. This very same historical trajectory simultaneously strengthened the legitimacy of many local social institutions in locations such as Machaze, some of these precisely because they allowed for the more effective evasion of the central state's presence in everyday life.

In the immediate colonial aftermath, FRELIMO's own radical attempts to create a centrally planned and managed economy and its efforts to institute a "command society" arguably intensified the alienation of large portions of the Mozambican population, particularly in rural areas. FRELIMO's policies not only reinforced an already established culture of disengagement from central authority, but also significantly amplified local forms of social antagonism by challenging the established local sociopolitical order and contributing to economic crisis. Despite its pretensions to broad social change, FRELIMO's governance capacity remained highly circumscribed and dependent upon those locals it co-opted into its own program. Many of these locals had been previously marginalized and were not drawn from already locally legitimized authority (Hall and Young, 1997; Lubkemann, 2000a, 2001).

Under these circumstances, a majority of Machazians eventually proved receptive to RENAMO after it arrived in the district in 1979. However, this was not because RENAMO articulated any positive alternative vision (to FRELIMO's) of how central authority or the "nation" should be constituted. Rather, RENAMO attracted a following because it directed its violence against the most onerous symbols of central authority's presence in local lives. The fact that RENAMO also did not articulate an alternative vision that included any significant presence of central authority in local lives resonated resoundingly with the local terms of "legitimacy" that had been historically forged in Machaze.

It is important not to overgeneralize the character of local political culture, much less views of FRELIMO or of RENAMO that may have prevailed in Machaze, to all of Mozambique. Clearly, in certain areas of the north where the anti-colonial struggle had been most successful, in larger urban areas, and among certain educated elites (Isaacman, 1996), political consciousness may have been formulated with greater reference to the "national order of things" (Maalki, 1995). However, in the light of a long history of central power's uneven reach, yet frequently coercive projection, it is perhaps even more problematic to assume that local political imaginations throughout Mozambique were organized around the assumption that "engagement" (Azarya, 1988) was the best, inevitable, or most desirable strategy for coping with national-level central authorities. At the very least, there is sufficient ethnographic and case-study evidence available (Roesch, 1991; Geffray, 1989; Wilson, 1992; Alexander, 1994; Wilson and Nunes, 1994; Baptista-Lundin and Machava, 1995; Englund, 1995; Nordstrom, 1997; Chingono, 1996; Gengenbach, 1998; McGregor, 1998; West, 1998) to suggest that the Machazian tendency towards disengagement was a widely subscribed strategy throughout the country prior to and during the war.

9. Theorizing fragmented wars and their displacement

In most social science and policy analyses of displacement, and of the conflicts that produce it, violence is generally analyzed and understood as a phenomenon organized by the principles and agendas of the highest level at which political legitimacy is being militarily contested. Typically, this involves a focus on the actions and agendas of parties with national-level political aspirations. However, the empirical evidence from Mozambique indicates that the violence experienced in the conflict was not solely, or perhaps even primarily, shaped by the two national-level parties (FRELIMO and RENAMO) who were contesting political legitimacy at the national government level.

Comparative ethnographic analysis of conflict and forced migration in Mozambique demonstrates that "violence" was an experience problematized and fundamentally shaped by the social formations and micro-political matrixes in which it took place. Violence was thus not a singular phenomenon whose meaning was pre-established by larger forces and brought unaltered into local contexts. Rather, violence was significantly reshaped by a highly differentiated terrain of local social tensions and cultural currencies. In this sense, it can be argued that there was no singular war—no monolithic experience or understanding of violence—in Mozambique. Rather, as seen from the perspective of the local actors who had to formulate strategies for reacting to conflict—what the war "was about" in one area of the country had little to do with what it was about elsewhere.

Based on the Mozambican case-study, I offer the following as hypotheses about which historical and precipitating conditions may more generally lead to the susceptibility of wartime violence becoming "fragmented":

Historical conditions:

(1) a national context characterized by significant sociocultural and socio-economic variation;
(2) in which historical conditions have produced a generalized political culture that revolves around efforts at local disengagement from central authority;
(3) in which local forms of social authority are regarded as more legitimate than supra-local forms of national central authority;
(4) in which national strategies of governance are sporadic, based on coercive force, and involve dependence on local agents (in former colonial contexts we may speak of a form of perpetuation of "indirect rule")—a result of the central government's lack of instrumental power;

Precipitating conditions:

(5) an environment in which economic policies or conditions amplify already existing forms of local social antagonism and competition;
(6) the implementation of policies of governance that directly challenge the established local sociopolitical order;
(7) the emergence of political movements whose primary political agenda is the articulation of grievances against central authority (rather than stating an alternative vision of it), and that have access to sufficient means of violence (weapons) so as to mount a publicly credible challenge to the government's exercise of power at the local level.

Drawn from the limited Mozambican experience, these conditions are primarily suggested as hypotheses worthy of testing through further empirical case-based comparative investigation and analysis. Conflicts such as Afghanistan (Marsden, 1999; Donini, Niland and Wermester, 2004), Somalia (Besteman, 1999; Brons, 2001), and possibly Liberia (Sawyer, 1992; Ellis, 1999) may be particularly promising cases in which to explore and test whether these conditions produce a "fragmented war" dynamic.

The dynamic of "fragmented wars" is hypothesized to be quite distinct from that of "ethno-nationalist" wars (such as those in Eritrea, Kosovo, or Chechnya), in which ethnic minorities aspire to the creation of independent states. The dynamics of "fragmented wars" are also hypothesized to be distinct from that of "ethnic civil wars" (such as in Rwanda, Burundi, Ivory Coast, and Sri Lanka), in which different ethnic groups are contesting state-level power and political predominance. By contrast, in the environments in which the conditions listed above predominate, the "political logic" that organizes violence may be characterized as "localist". It is "localist" in the sense that local actors are unlikely to be animated by projects that aim to replace one set of central authority actors with another. They are, however, likely to mobilize around projects that resist all forms of central authority presence in local affairs. In such environments, the primary objective may not be to capture or control the state, but indeed to minimize its everyday presence in local lives.

In contexts in which the notion of the state is not the predominant trope for organizing the political imagination, analytical approaches that assume wartime violence and migration are primarily shaped by state-level political processes and agendas are likely to require revision. An understanding of strategies for coping with violence (be they migratory or otherwise) is likely to require a much more fine-grained analysis of how local-level social organization and ideologies shape violence itself. Other social agendas, relationships, and formations, largely unrelated to those of national parties, may play a far more central role in the organization of violence and reactions to violence in such "fragmented wars".

10. Anthropology and the analysis of displacement in "fragmented wars"

In conclusion, it is also important to consider what analytical approaches may prove most fruitful for analyzing forced migration in "fragmented wars". As this study shows, displacement in "fragmented wars" is affected by many local forms of social struggle, each potentially informed by very different cultural logics. Consequently, many of the specific variables that shape forced migration decisionmaking in one location may not apply in other corners of the same theater of war. Elsewhere (Lubkemann, 2004), I have suggested that approaches to analyzing forced migration that take cultural processes seriously should avoid attempting to explain migratory behavior solely through reference to universally applicable variables. The social factors and logics that shaped wartime violence and migratory reactions in Machaze were clearly not the same ones that operated in Nampula, despite the fact that these were both contested theaters in the same civil war. In Machaze, the jealousy of one's own kin had to be monitored and guarded against, while in Nampula it was the "ethnic other" in the village down the road whose intentions and actions were feared. The religious beliefs that led people in Machaze to interpret, participate in, and react to wartime violence in particular ways were not the same beliefs or social dynamics that shaped violence and migration in Gaza and Nampula.

In anthropological approaches to studying demographic outcomes, the determination of the range of sociocultural variation within the field of study (in this case the theater of war) is the standard point of departure for analysis. Thus, the necessary first task of analysis becomes the identification of the terms by which local actors formulate their life projects and understand their social world. By extension, the study of wartime migration and population redistribution must be embedded in, and merely a part of, a broader study of the culturally defined social processes that give migration meaning as an effective strategy in social struggles.

Such an approach will allow analysts of displacement to avoid the fallacy of acting as if the demographic consequences of behavior (such as migration) were the ultimate ends of that behavior itself. After all, people do not move in war just to move, but rather they migrate in order to accomplish other goals. Wartime migration is thus ultimately a "side-effect" of other projects undertaken by agents whose goals and aspirations are shaped by culturally specific worldviews rather than universally uniform utility functions. It is this range of specific social projects and their cultural milieus that anthropological demographers take as the prerequisite object of inquiry in wartime migration research. By carefully examining how complex patterns of social and cultural variation inform uses, experiences, and understandings of violence, anthropological approaches may provide particularly illuminating analysis of wartime migration and population redistribution in culturally diversified warscapes.

Notes

[1] It bears mentioning, for those unfamiliar with the social and cultural geography of Mozambique, that there are at least 16 major ethno-linguistic groups in Mozambique; a variety of matrilineal systems in the north, and patrilineal ones in the south; all manner of religious persuasions including Islam, a broad gloss of Christian beliefs, and many variations in local forms of ancestral veneration (Newitt, 1995).

[2] For example, individuals might be very reluctant to choose a spouse from a family believed to be plagued by a *mfukwa*.

References

Africa Watch, 1992. *Conspicuous Destruction: War, Famine and the Reform Process in Mozambique.* New York: Human Rights Watch.

Alexander, Jocelyn, 1994. "Terra e Autoridade Politica no Pós-Guerra em Mocambique: O Caso da Provincia de Manica" [Land and political authority in post-war Mozambique: The case of the Province of Manica], *Arquivo* 16(3): 5–94.

Azarya, Victor, 1988. "Reordering state–society relations: Incorporation and disengagement", in Donald Rothchild and Naomi Chazan (eds), *The Precarious Balance: State and Society in Africa.* Boulder, CO: Westview (3–21).

Baptista-Lundin, Irae and F. J. Machava (eds), 1995. *Autoridade e Poder Tradicional* [Traditional power and authority]. Maputo: Centro de Estudos Estrategicos, Instituto Superior de Relacoes Internacionais.

Besteman, Catherine, 1999. *Unraveling Somalia.* Philadelphia, PA: University of Pennsylvania Press.

Brons, Maria H., 2001. *Somalia: From Statelessness to Statelessness?* Utrecht: International.

Chingono, Mark, 1996. *The State, Violence and Development.* Aldershot: Avebury/Ashgate.

Coelho, João B., 1998. "State resettlement policies in post-colonial rural Mozambique: The impact of the communal village programme on Tete Province, 1977–1982", *Journal of Southern African Studies* 24(1): 61–91.

Donini, Antonio, Norah Niland and Karin Wermester (eds), 2004. *Nation Building Unraveled? Aid, Peace, and Justice in Afghanistan.* Westport, CT: Kumarian.

Ellis, Stephen, 1999. *The Mask of Anarchy: The Destruction of Liberia and the Religious Dimension of an African Civil War.* New York: New York University Press.

Englund, Harri, 1995. "Brother against brother: The moral economy of war and displacement in the Malawi–Mozambique borderland", unpublished *PhD Dissertation*, Department of Social Anthropology, University of Manchester.

Finnegan, William, 1992. *A Complicated War: The Harrowing of Mozambique.* Berkeley, CA: University of California Press.

Geffray, Christian, 1989. *A Causa das Armas: Antropologia da Guerra Contemporanea em Mocambique* [The Cause of Arms: Anthropology of the Contemporary War in Mozambique]. Lisbon: Afrontamento.

Gengenbach, Heidi, 1998. "'I'll bury you in the border!': Women's land struggles in post-war Facazisse (Magude District) Mozambique", *Journal of Southern African Studies* 24(1): 7–36.

Gersony, Robert, 1988. *Summary of Mozambican Refugee Accounts of Principally Conflict-Related Experience in Mozambique.* Washington, DC: US State Department.

Hall, Margaret, 1990. "The Mozambican national resistance movement (RENAMO): A study in the destruction of an African country", *Africa* 60(1): 39–67.

Hall, Margaret and Tom Young, 1997. *Confronting Leviathan: Mozambique Since Independence.* Athens, OH: Ohio University Press.

Hanlon, Joseph, 1984. *Mozambique: The Revolution Under Fire.* London: Zed.

Isaacman, Allen, 1983. *Mozambique: From Colonialism to Revolution 1900–1982.* Boulder, CO: Westview.

Isaacman, Allen, 1996. *Cotton is the Mother of Poverty.* Portsmouth, NH: Heinemann.

Lubkemann, Stephen, 2000a. "Situating wartime migration in central Mozambique: Gendered social struggle and the transnationalization of polygyny", unpublished *PhD Dissertation*, Department of Anthropology, Brown University.

Lubkemann, Stephen, 2000b. "The transformation of transnationality among Mozambican Migrants in South Africa", *Canadian Journal of African Studies* 34 (1): 41–63.

Lubkemann, Stephen, 2001. "Foreign aid, local capacity and civil society in the reconstruction of Mozambique's National health system", in Ian Smillie (ed.), *Patronage and Partnership: Local Capacity Building in Humanitarian Crisis.* West Hartford, CT: Kumarian (77–106).

Lubkemann, Stephen, 2002. "Where to be an ancestor? Reconstituting socio-spiritual worlds and post-conflict settlement decision-making among displaced Mozambicans", *Journal of Refugee Studies* 15(2): 189–212.

Lubkemann, Stephen, 2004. "Situating migration in wartime and post-war Mozambique: A critique of forced migration research", in Simon Szreter, A. Dharmalingam and Hania Sholkamy (eds), *Categories and Contexts: Anthropological Studies in Critical Demography.* Oxford: Oxford University Press (371–400).

Maalki, Liisa, 1995. *Purity and Exile: Violence, Memory, and National Cosmology Among Hutu Refugees in Tanzania.* Chicago, IL: Chicago University Press.

McGregor, Jo Ann, 1998. "Violence and social change in a border economy: War in the Maputo Hinterland, 1984–1992", *Journal of Southern African Studies* 24(1): 37–60.

Marsden, Peter, 1999. *The Taliban: War and Religion in Afghanistan.* London: Zed.

Minter, William, 1994. *Apartheid's Contras: An Inquiry into the Roots of War in Angola and Mozambique.* London: Zed.

Newitt, Malyn, 1995. *Mozambique: A History.* Indianapolis, IN: Indiana University Press.

Nordstrom, Carolyn, 1997. *A Different Kind of War Story.* Philadelphia, PA: University of Pennsylvania Press.

Roesch, Otto, 1991. "Migrant labour and forced rice production in Southern Mozambique: The colonial peasantry of the lower Limpopo Valley", *Journal of Southern African Studies* 17: 239–270.

Roesch, Otto, 1992. "RENAMO and the peasantry in Southern Mozambique: A view from Gaza Province", *Canadian Journal of African Studies* 26(3): 462–484.

Sawyer, Amos, 1992. *The Emergence of Autocracy in Liberia: Tragedy and Challenge.* San Fransisco, CA: Institute of Contemporary Studies Press.

Vines, Alex, 1991. *Renamo: Terrorism in Mozambique.* London: James Currey.

West, Harry, 1998. "'This neighbor is not my uncle!': Changing relations of power and authority on the Mueda Plateau", *Journal of Southern African Studies* 24(1): 141–160.

Wilson, Ken B., 1992. "Cults of violence and counter-violence in Mozambique", *Journal of Southern African Studies* 18: 527–582.

Wilson, Ken B. and Jovito Nunes, 1994. "Repatriation to Mozambique: Refugee initiative and agency planning in Milange district, 1988–1991", in Tim Allen and Hubert Morsink (eds), *When Refugees Go Home.* London: James Currey (167–236).

Wuyts, Marc, 1984. *Money and Planning for Socialist Transition: The Mozambican Experience.* Aldershot: Gower.

Wuyts, Marc, 1985. "Money, planning and rural transformation in Mozambique", *Journal of Peasant Studies* 22(1): 180–207.

PART V. POST-CONFLICT DEMOGRAPHIC RESPONSES: CASE STUDIES

CHAPTER 14. FORCED MIGRATION AND UNDER-FIVE MORTALITY: A COMPARISON OF REFUGEES AND HOSTS IN NORTH-WESTERN UGANDA AND SOUTHERN SUDAN*

KAVITA SINGH
Measure Evaluation, Carolina Population Center, USA

UNNI KARUNAKARA
Médecins Sans Frontières

GILBERT BURNHAM
The Johns Hopkins University, Bloomberg School of Public Health, USA

KENNETH HILL
The Johns Hopkins University, Bloomberg School of Public Health, USA

Abstract. Millions of people around the world live as displaced persons, often for lengthy periods of time. Little, however, is known about the correlates of health outcomes in displaced populations. This research article used data from north-western Uganda and southern Sudan to understand if and how forced migration and resulting residential arrangements impact under-five mortality for long-term displaced and corresponding host populations. Multivariate logistic regression revealed that over the long-run forced migration and residential arrangement did not significantly impact under-five mortality.

1. General introduction

1.1. NUMBERS OF DISPLACED PERSONS

Each year new accumulations of people are forcibly displaced from their homes as long-standing problems within or between countries remain unresolved and new problems emerge. Some displaced persons will return home quickly but the world is increasingly seeing more and more long-term displacement. Most of today's displacements have resulted from intense and long-standing conflicts that remain largely unresolved. Underlying causes for these conflicts are a complex interplay of political, economic, ethnic and environmental pressures (Loescher, 1993; UNHCR, 1993).

Estimates of the numbers of refugees by the United States Committee for Refugees (USCR) and the United Nations High Commissioner for Refugees (UN-HCR) are 13.0 million and 10.4 million in 2003 (USCR, 2003; UNHCR, 2003).

This chapter was previously published in *European Journal of Population*, vol. 21, no. 2–3, 2005, pp. 247–270.

Helge Brunborg et al. (eds.), The Demography of Armed Conflict, 323–345.

The difference in numbers illustrates the difficulty in counting displaced persons. The USCR also estimated the number of internally displaced persons to be 21.8 million in 2003. Approximately 30 million people around the world are displaced.

1.2. STUDY OBJECTIVES

Despite the large number of those displaced and the often lengthy periods of displacement, little is understood concerning the health status of long-term displaced populations.[1] Quality data on displaced populations is lacking, which has made it difficult to study correlates of health outcomes. It is likely that factors that are associated with health outcomes in developing countries are also significant in long-term displaced populations, but there are several factors specific to migrant situations that have never before been thoroughly researched. Displaced persons find themselves in a variety of situations in their countries of asylum—some are settled in large transit camps, others reside in more permanent settlements and many settle on their own. Some refugees are clearly visible, while others are indistinguishable from the host population. Some displaced persons receive relief aid while many more do not. The type of settlement of displaced persons and whether or not they receive any relief aid may also impact the host population. Particular interest in the humanitarian field has concerned the effect of residential arrangement upon the well being of displaced persons and the effect of the presence of refugees upon the host population. Such research is important in determining how policy can be used to improve health outcomes in displaced populations. This article researches these issues by comparing under-five mortality in southern Sudan and north-western Uganda among 'stayees' (those who did not leave home), settled refugees, self-settled refugees, hosts living in the presence of settled refugees, hosts living in the presence of self-settled refugees and hosts living in the absence of refugees. Under-five mortality was chosen as the outcome of interest because it is often used as an indicator of a country's health status.

2. Conceptual framework

2.1. CORRELATES OF INTEREST

To study under-five mortality the Mosley and Chen (1984) proximate determinant framework was used as a guide. The underlying premise of the framework is that distal (or social and economic) determinants of child health operate through a common set of biological or proximate determinants to impact child mortality. The distal determinants are individual, household and community factors. The five groups of proximate determinants are maternal factors, environmental contamination, nutrient deficiency, injury and personal illness control.

Forced migration changes residential arrangement, which may act through the distal determinants to influence child mortality. This article studies the possibility that forced migration and residential arrangement impact under-five mortality even after other proximate and distal factors have been controlled.

A key focus of this research is the separation of individual and household factors from community factors because of different policy implications. Associations of community factors with child mortality would call for much different changes than associations with individual and household factors. For example if it is found that residential arrangement or community factors are significant correlates, then drastic policy changes may be needed. If it is found that individual and household factors are most important, however, then programs targeting individuals within their existing residential arrangements may be emphasised.

2.2. THE IMPORTANCE OF RESIDENTIAL ARRANGEMENT

There has been a debate in the humanitarian aid field concerning the effect of settlement versus self-settlement upon refugees and concerning the effect of refugees upon the host population. Many relief organisations prefer that refugees settle in camps or assisted settlements because they are easier to count and are more visible. Camp arrangements and assisted settlements may also facilitate the provision of services and some degree of security (Harrell-Bond, 1994). The refugee camp has been the standard approach for settling displaced persons. A particularly successful example of this approach is the handling of the 10 million refugees who fled from former East Pakistan to India in 1971. The refugees were placed in 1,000 camps along the border and returned home to Bangladesh 10 months later (Gardner et al., 1972; Seaman, 1972; van Damme, 1995). The Bangladeshi refugee crisis was successfully managed because the refugees were spread over many small camps and the problem was of relatively short duration (van Damme, 1995). Today, however, it is not uncommon to find people who have been refugees well over 10 years and who live in camps or settlements with tens of thousands of other refugees.

The UNHCR has three durable solutions for refugees: voluntary return to the country of origin; settlement in the country of first asylum; and resettlement in a third country. The preferred option is voluntary return, but when this is an inviable solution settlement in the country of first asylum is the next choice. Camps are meant to be a short-term solution, but when repatriation becomes elusive the question of how long to keep refugees in camps becomes important. Harell-Bond (1994) and van Damme (1995) have suggested that keeping refugees in camps may be detrimental to their health because of resultant dependency, passivity and over-crowding. A comparison of acute malnutrition during the emergency phase of several crises lends some support to their argument. The prevalence rates of acute malnutrition were lowest in the two populations where refugees were self-settled in rural villages rather than placed in camps (Toole, 1993), but selection effects could have also played a role.

Countries of asylum may prefer camps for safety reasons. Sometimes refugees themselves include persons who may have perpetrated violence as was the case for many Rwandan refugees in the Democratic Republic of the Congo (Virmani, 1996; Zolberg et al., 1989). Even a suspicion of violence performed by refugees can give impetus for the host country government to be vigilant. After the 1981–1982 exodus of refugees from Arua District to Yei River District, Sudanese officials wanted the Ugandans to stay in camps so that their activities could be monitored. It was feared that because the refugees included some of Idi Amin's ex-soldiers, they might be plotting an attack against the Ugandan government for which the Sudanese government could be blamed (Virmani, 1996).

Kibraeb (1991) has called the debate between settlement and self-settlement the most sustained controversy in African refugee studies. A simple dichotomisation, however, is detrimental to a deeper understanding of the life situation of refugees (Virmani, 1996). For example many of the Sudanese refugees studied in this article have members of their household who spend part of their time in a settlement and part of their time outside looking for work. Other families register at the settlement to receive food rations but usually live as 'self-settled refugees'. These families often will not admit this for fear of losing food rations. Though it is important to study child mortality differences between settled and self-settled refugees, the distinction is not always clear.

2.3. HOST POPULATIONS

Despite the increasing attention given to refugees, the needs of the host population are often neglected. The developing world hosts the majority of the world's refugees. The impact of refugees on the host country is particularly important because receiving states are often resource poor. Though the better off among the hosts may gain from the services provided to refugees, the poorer hosts can lose out from competition for food, work, wages, services and common property resources (Chambers, 1986). A large refugee influx could immediately and negatively affect the environment and physical resources, local administrative units, the local economy, health and social services and transport and communication systems (Simmance, 1987). Over longer periods of time it is perceivable that the attention refugees bring to an area could result in the improvement of services and infrastructure if humanitarian organisations work to build the capacity of the local population. There is some indication that self-settled refugees have the potential to benefit the overall host population. Refugees from Liberia and Sierra Leone spontaneously settled in border villages and medium sized towns in Guinea. Instead of creating camps, UNHCR provided support to villages that welcomed refugees. The results were that refugees boosted rice production, and the health care facilities in the refugee-affected areas were the best in the country and served both the host and refugee populations (van Damme, 1995).

3. Background information

3.1. SUDAN—THE HOME OF THE WORLD'S LONGEST CIVIL WAR

Sudan, the largest country in Africa, covers nearly one million square miles. The Nile River flowing from south to north traverses a country varied in both landscape and ethnic and cultural composition. The land varies from arid desert in the north to savanna and grassland in the centre to forests and lush, fertile land in the south. The north covers two-thirds of the area, but the majority of the natural wealth (i.e. gold, lumber and fertile land) is found in the south. Throughout history leaders in the north have exploited the wealth of the south, and this exploitation is one of the underlying causes of the current civil war.

Sudan has a population of approximately 38 million and is one of the most sparsely settled countries in the world. Within Sudan there are more than 450 ethnic groups who speak 133 different languages. Much of the diversity is found in the 9–10 million persons originating from the south (Peterson, 1999; Virmani, 1996). Islam is the state religion, but only 60% of the Sudanese are Muslims. Christians account for approximately 4–5% of the population, and the remainder follows traditional religions (Human Rights Watch, 1996; The Economist Intelligent Unit, 1995). The Northerners are mostly Muslim and identify themselves as Arab or African-Arab. The Southerners are composed of Nilotics, Bantu and a small percentage of Sudanic people.

Civil war first broke out in 1955, 1 year prior to independence and lasted until 1972. A period of peace lasted for 10 years, after which civil war resumed in 1983 and has been ongoing since. The key factors in the war had been the Khartoum government's desire to impose Islam including sharia law upon the south and their desire for the South's resources. In efforts to obtain oil-rich or fertile land, the Khartoum government has conducted extermination campaigns to drive Southerners away from their villages. The southern cause has been led by the Sudan People's Liberation Army (SPLA), however, dissent within the SPLA has resulted in many factions of this rebel group fighting among themselves. The tension is largely based upon tribal identity, and the Khartoum government has exploited age-old antagonisms between tribes in an attempt to create even more division. The result is that all sides in this civil war have intended to destroy the livelihoods of communities deemed to be supporters of their enemies. All sides in this war have been guilty of killing civilians, manipulating relief aid, conscripting young men and children, raping women, burning villages and stealing livestock. At the end of 2003 approximately 475,000 Sudanese were refugees mostly in Uganda, the Democratic Republic of Congo, Ethiopia and Kenya and up to four million were internally displaced, making Sudan the country with the largest number of internally displaced persons (IDPs) (USCR, 2003). USCR has estimated that 1.9 million people have died between 1983 and 1998 because of the civil war.

With immense international pressure for peace, a formal peace agreement was signed on January 9, 2005 in Nairobi, Kenya by the Khartoum government and the SPLA. A sign of hope looms for Sudan.

3.2. UGANDA—TURMOIL IN THE NORTH

Like Sudan, Uganda has seen its share of turmoil. Many Ugandans were killed or forced to flee the country during the reigns of Idi Amin, the second President

(1971–1979), and Milton Obote, who was both the first (1966–1971) and third President (1980–1985). Both dictators are estimated to have been responsible for the deaths of 100,000–500,000 persons during their time in power. Both Amin and Obote were from the North, but from different tribal groups Amin was a Kakwa (Sudanic tribal group) from what was then West Nile. Obote was a Langi (Nilotic tribal group) from what was then Acholi. Many of the people killed or displaced during Amin's reign were from the Nilotic tribes, but as Amin became more paranoid and sensitive to criticism he targeted anyone he felt could be a threat to his power, including Uganda's intellectuals. During Obote's second term in power his army attacked civilians in the West Nile region in an effort to take revenge on 'Amin's people'. More refugees were created during Obote's term as his weak and ill-organised army struck at civilians instead of the many active guerrilla groups (Amaza, 1998; Minority Rights Group, 1984). In Sudan alone there were estimated to be at least 300,000 refugees by 1984 mostly from the West Nile District (Harrell-Bond, 1986). Obote was removed from power by the National Resistance Army (NRA), which also played an instrumental part in removing Amin from power. The NRA was led by Yoweri Museveni, a Bantu from south-western Uganda, who has been president since 1986.

Today Uganda has a population of about 25 million and is considered to have one of the fastest growing economies in Africa. Though most of Uganda is peaceful, parts of the North remain under turmoil. In Obote's home area the rebel group, the Lord's Resistance Army (LRA), hopes to overthrow Museveni and rule Uganda according to the Ten Commandments. The LRA is known for brutal attacks against civilians from their own tribal groups and has been responsible for the internal displacement of between 600,000 and 700,000 Ugandans in northern Uganda and 20,000 Sudanese in Sudan (USCR, 2003). The LRA often hides and trains in remote areas of South Sudan. Thus a peace deal in Sudan could also bring hopes of peace for northern Uganda.

3.3. THE UGANDA–SUDAN BORDER

The Uganda–Sudan border was a boundary created with little regard for the people it separated (Kabwegyere, 1995). The border is approximately 270 miles long and has been a source of instability for at least the past 100 years (Taha, 1978). Both countries have shared some similar internal problems. The political isolation of the southern Sudanese and northern Ugandans has resulted in a great deal of cross border activity (Woodward, 1991). Post-independence relations between the two countries have vacillated between peace and confrontation with the later prevailing (Ofransky, 2000). The Khartoum government holds the belief that the Ugandan government supports the SPLA. The Ugandan government holds the belief that the Khartoum government supports the LRA. Despite the Ugandan and Sudanese governments' hatred for one another, Uganda and Sudan have always harboured each other's refugees, and they tend to co-operate on refugee matters.

Many relief organisations that work in Sudan have bases in Uganda. There are an estimated 170,000 Sudanese refugees in northern Uganda (USCR, 2000). Many Ugandans have been refugees in South Sudan during the turmoil surrounding the reigns of Amin and Obote. Refugees in both countries have received warm welcomes, largely because of shared tribal identities. Many Sudanese who had hosted Ugandan refugees in the 1980s would themselves become refugees in Uganda in the 1990s (Amaza, 1998; Ofransky, 2000).

4. The study: summary and results

4.1. FIELDWORK

Data for this study came from the Demography of Forced Migration Project (DFMP), a study aiming to document mortality, fertility and health outcomes in the refugee and national populations of Arua District, Uganda, and Yei River District (Otogo Payam), Sudan (see Figure 1). Fieldwork for this project was conducted between September 1, 1999 and March 4, 2000. The Uganda–Sudan border has seen many mass movements of people over the past few decades. Many of the Ugandans in Arua were formerly refugees in Yei River District, Sudan in the 1980s. Most have repatriated back to their homes so in a sense they have a complete migration history (from home to exile and back to home).[2] Now many Sudanese from Yei River District have become long-term refugees in the Arua District, so the former hosts have now become the hosted. Because the Sudanese have been in Arua for many years it was possible to study the effects of post-emergency residential arrangement on mortality, fertility and health outcomes.

The study employed a retrospective and cross-sectional survey approach to obtain information on fertility, mortality, migration and other individual, household and community factors. The questionnaire had eight modules: (1) background/household economics, (2) pre-migration history, (3) migration history, (4) post-migration, (5) child health, (6) reproductive health, (7) security and the (8) security migration history. Modules were asked to both men (20–55) and women (15–49) except for the child health module, which was only administered to women.

A major limitation of this study in general is survivor bias. Information was collected only from surviving men and women. This is a limitation in terms of this particular study because information concerning orphans was not available. It is likely that the under-five mortality rates for orphans differ from non-orphans.[3]

4.2. STUDY POPULATION

This study captured information from different groups of Ugandan nationals and Sudanese refugees allowing for comparisons between nationals and refugees, self-settled and settled refugees,[4] nationals living in the presence of refugees and

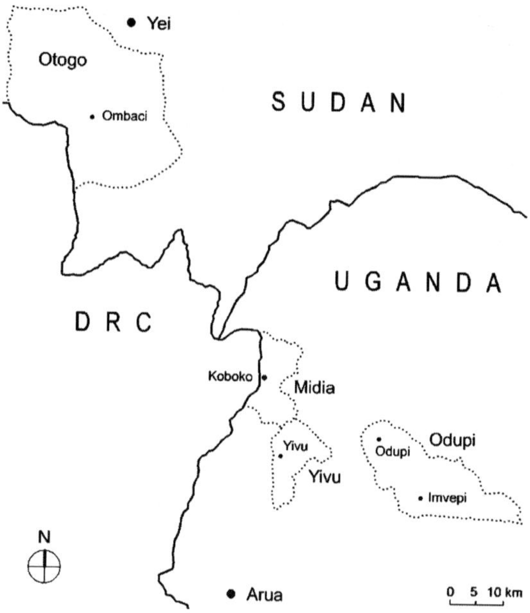

Figure 1. Map of the study population.

nationals living in the absence of refugees, and refugees and those remaining in their country of origin. The six study populations (or strata) were the following:

(1) Ugandans living in the absence of refugees (Yivu)
(2) Ugandans living in the presence of settled refugees (Odupi)
(3) Ugandans living in the presence of self-settled refugees (Midia)
(4) Sudanese refugees living in a settlement (Imvepi)
(5) Sudanese refugees who are self-settled (Koboko)
(6) Sudanese currently in Sudan (Yei)

In order to capture persons from each of the six desired study populations, this study employed a multi-stage sampling frame. These six categories also indicated persons living in specific counties or geographic areas. Within the counties clusters at the village level were randomly selected, and within the villages households were randomly selected. A total of 2525 women and 814 were interviewed in Lugbara (spoken by the Ugandan study populations) and Juba-Arabic (spoken by the Sudanese study populations). Interviews were carried out by men and women from the study population areas.

4.3. ANALYSES

Stata statistical software was used to clean and analyse the data. The analysis presented in this study was a means to assess how proximate and socioeconomic factors such as individual, household and community factors impact child mortality for long-term displaced and affected national populations. The impact of forced migration and residential arrangement was studied after controlling for individual, household and community factors. Analysis was restricted to 2252 children who were born within 5 years of the time of the survey.

4.4. DESCRIPTION OF THE MODEL

Logistic regression was used to model the probability of dying for children born in the 5 years since the time of the survey. Logistic regression was suitable because the outcome, the probability of dying, has a binomial distribution. Stata's 'svy' or survey command was used to account for intra-cluster correlation within the multistage sampling design of the study (Stata Corporation, 1999).

4.5. OUTCOME VARIABLE

The outcome variable was whether or not a child born in the last 5 years (since January 1995) was alive at the time of the survey. There were 197 deaths to 2252 children.

Because none of the children completed exactly 5 years of age, these data were right censored. In order to account for the censoring, age spells were treated as units of observation rather than children. The age spells used were 0–1, 2–3, 4–11, 12–23, 24–35 and 36–47 months to reflect the neonatal period, early infancy, late infancy and early and late childhood. The interval of 48–60 months was excluded because no children in the child health section of the survey completed exactly 5 years of age.

Adjusting for censoring and expansion of the data sets there were 153 deaths and 8,051 observations. The small number of deaths and large number of observations mean that the analysis had low power. Thus, the analysis can only indicate large differences within categories of the covariates and small differences would not been detected.

4.6. EXPLANATORY VARIABLES: INDIVIDUAL

The individual/household variables that were studied were education, occupation, child's age, child's gender and mother's marital status. Because levels of education were so low in this population, education was studied as a dichotomous variable with the categories of no education versus some education. The occupation variable had five categories—agriculture, trading, brewing alcohol, contract labour and professional/artisan. The categorisation was important because families involved in these occupations had different access to cash. Those with a steady access to cash might find it easier to purchase medicines for sick children or obtain the necessary transportation to seek care. As mentioned earlier children contributed observations to age spells of 0–1, 2–3, 4–11, 12–23, 24–35 and 36–47 months. Child's gender was included to study whether there was a sex differential in mortality. Mother's marital status was included to understand whether being in a formal partnership was protective in terms of child mortality.

4.7. EXPLANATORY VARIABLES: PROXIMATE

The explanatory variables studied were parity, mother's age at birth and tetanus immunisation. The parity variable reflected the birth order of the child and was categorised into birth order 1, 2–4 and 5+. Mother's age was studied as her age at the time of the birth of the child and not her age at the time of the interview. Tetanus immunisation was also studied as a dichotomous variable. A limitation of the variable was that there is no distinction between the number of doses received.

4.8. EXPLANATORY VARIABLES: HOUSEHOLD

The household variables that were studied were separate room for cooking, toilet, water source, ownership of a radio, and sex of household head. Poor air quality can lead to environmental contamination so whether or not a household has a separate room for cooking is an important variable. Toilet was a dichotomous variable indicating whether or not a respondent's household had a toilet facility (all households with toilet facilities had a pit latrine or shared a pit latrine with a neighbour). A limitation of this variable is the mere presence of a toilet does not automatically make a household more hygienic. Water source was classified as either good quality or poor quality. Source of water does not imply anything about how water is handled or whether drinking water is boiled, but this variable does make a crucial distinction between those who have access to clean water and those who do not. The ownership of a radio variable served two purposes. It served as an indicator of wealth and was also used to represent a household's access to information. Sex of household head was studied because female-headed households are often considered more vulnerable in settings of conflict. The variable was included in the analysis to determine if the consequences of this vulnerability transfer to child mortality.

4.9. EXPLANATORY VARIABLES: COMMUNITY

Two community variables were studied—time to the nearest health centre, and time to school. Time to the nearest health centre represents access to health care services. This variable was dichotomised into 30 min or less and greater than 30 min. The areas sampled for this research were extremely rural with very little infrastructure (no paved roads, no running water and no electricity) so time to the nearest school was used as an indicator of development in the community. Families closer to schools also may have more access to information concerning child health. This variable was also dichotomised into 30 min or less and greater than 30 min.

4.10. EXPLANATORY VARIABLES: MIGRATION

Three migration variables were studied—migration/reproductive history, place of current residence, and migration-child. They are described in the following paragraphs.

The 'migration/reproductive history' variable was a classification of women based upon the correspondence of reproductive years and their migration history. To study the impact that migration has upon long-term child mortality, women were divided into several categories based upon where they spent most of their reproductive years. The categories were based upon their migration history and upon their answers to the following two questions:

Q308. Now, I would like to ask you about your home and the places you have lived in. Have you always lived in (name of current place of residence) since birth?

Q309. Do you consider (name of current place of residence) to be your home?

Home is a concept that is difficult to define in many cultures, so what constituted 'home' was left largely to the respondents. From qualitative research it was discovered that 'home' was generally considered the place where a person spent his or her childhood and where his or her parents were settled. Women were first dichotomised by whether or not they had ever left home.[5] The categories were further broken down according to the places women spent most of their reproductive years (ages 15–49). A simple differentiation between 'home' and 'away from home' was made. Many women have made multiple moves during their lifetimes but because the sample size is not large enough, the number of movements was not used to classify women.

This variable may make it possible to understand if and how migration impacts cumulative child mortality. Based upon the classification scheme presented in the previous paragraph, women were classified into five categories: 'stayees', 'displaced before age 15', 'returnees before age 15', 'returnees after age 15' and 'displaced after age 15'. A description of the categories is the following:

(1) 'Stayees' are women who never migrated. All their reproductive years were spent at home
(2) 'Displaced before age 15' are women who migrated and had all their reproductive years after leaving home (these women are currently refugees)
(3) 'Returnees before age 15' are women who migrated, repatriated and had all their reproductive years after repatriating
(4) 'Returnees after age 15' are women who migrated and had reproductive years at home, were then away from home and finally at home again
(5) 'Displaced after age 15' are women who had reproductive years at home and away from home (these women are currently refugees).

The 'place of current residence' variable referred to where a respondent was living at the time of the survey and captures several interesting issues because all respondents interviewed in one place represent Sudanese in one type of residential arrangement or Ugandans with a specific exposure or non-exposure to refugees. As mentioned in Section 4.2, for Sudanese respondents there were three separate categories to determine whether they were currently living in Sudan, living in a settlement or living in a self-settlement. For the Ugandan population there were three categories to represent no exposure to refugees, exposure to settled refugees and exposure to self-settled refugees. The variable also captures nationality and follows the stratified sampling frame of the study population. So the variable represents a distinct area and perhaps may capture community differences between the six areas in addition to settlement pattern for Sudanese and exposure to refugees for the hosts. The breakdown of categories is the following:

Yivu: Ugandans living in the absence of refugees
Odupi: Ugandans living in the presence of settled refugees
Midia: Ugandans living in the presence of self-settled refugees
Imvepi: Sudanese refugees living in a settlement
Koboko: Sudanese refugees who are self-settled
Yei: Sudanese who were living in Sudan at the time of the survey.

The 'migration-child' variable represents whether a child ever forcibly migrated or not. Information for this variable was obtained by comparing how long the mother lived in the current place of residence with the child's birth date.

5. Results

5.1. THE BIVARIATE ANALYSIS

Results from the univariate and bivariate analyses are presented in Table 1. It must be mentioned that what is presented is not a true bivariate analysis because age of the child is always controlled for. Some of the standard errors are rather large reflecting the low power in this study.

Of the individual variables only one category of the occupation variable and three of the child age categories were significant. Women whose families were involved in agricultural activities have children with higher mortality than women whose families are involved in non-agricultural activities. The negative difference in log odds is only statistically significant for women in families who brew alcohol compared to those in agriculture.[6] Three categories of the child's age variable were significant. The odds ratio was 0.51 for children 2–3 months compared to 0–1 months ($e^{B} = \exp(-0.689) = 0.51, p < 0.01$)[7] which fits with the knowledge that risks of mortality tend to be highest for children under 1 month in most populations. Mortality of children 4–11 months and 12–23 months, however, was significantly higher than for children in the neonatal period. These intervals are much longer than the 0–1 and 2–3 month intervals so these findings are also not surprising. Child's

Table 1. Univariate and bivariate analysis of under-five mortality of children born in the past 5 years

Covariate	N	Coefficient	Std. err.
Individual			
Education			
None	3,603	–	–
Some	4,444	−0.283	0.174
Occupation			
Agriculture	5,150	–	–
Trading	780	−0.034	0.322
Brewing alcohol	871	−0.531**	0.228
Contract labour	900	−0.327	0.274
Professional/artisan	321	−1.234	0.763
Child's gender			
Female	3,976	–	–
Male	4,042	−0.131	0.160
Child's age			
0–1	2,221	–	–
2–3	2,006	−0.689***	0.280
4–11	1,642	0.674**	0.235
12–23	1,152	0.729**	0.255
24–35	701	−0.327	0.328
36–47	329	0.306	0.553
Mother's marital status			
Single/widowed/divorced	931	–	–
Married	7,051	0.074	0.245
Proximate determinants			
Parity (birth order)			
1	1,249	–	–
2–4	3,586	−0.007	0.225
5+	3,216	−0.167	0.184
Mother's age at birth			
10–19	354	–	–
20–24	643	0.208	0.238
25–29	666	0.516**	0.218
30–34	343	0.126	0.290
35+	235	0.290	0.359
Tetanus immunisation			
No	747	–	–
Yes	7,210	−0.776***	0.217

(cont.)

Table 1. (continued)

Covariate	N	Coefficient	Std. err.
Household factors			
Separate room for cooking			
No	20,625	–	–
Yes	5,413	−0.104	0.162
Toilet			
No facility	831	–	–
Shared or own pit latrine	6,963	−0.141	0.285
Water source			
Poor quality	2,794	–	–
Good quality	4,995	−0.501**	0.192
Ownership of a radio			
No	5,375	–	–
Yes	2,442	0.031	0.148
Sex of household head			
Female	927	–	–
Male	7,214	−0.006	0.305
Community factors			
Time to health centre			
>30 min	6,469	–	–
<= 30 min	1,582	−0.276	0.240
Time to school			
>30 min	3,448	–	–
<= 30 min	4,603	−0.503***	0.157
Residential arrangement			
Migration-child			
No migration/voluntary migration	5,795	–	–
Forced migration	2,226	−0.153	0.275

*$p < 0.10$; **$p < 0.05$; ***$p < 0.01$.

gender was not significant, thus indicating no apparent sex differential in mortality. Mothers with some education had children with lower mortality than mothers without an education but this finding was not statistically significant. Marital status had a high standard error and was therefore left out of the multivariate analysis.

Of the proximate determinants mother's age at birth and tetanus immunisation were significant. All categories of mother's age at birth were positively associated with mortality compared to mothers 10–19, though only the association for the category 25–29 was significant. Most women in the 10–19 category, however, were 17–19 so they are not as young as the category name seems to indicate. Tetanus immunisation was a protective factor with an odds ratio of 0.46 for children whose mothers were immunised compared to those who were not ($e^{B} = \exp(0.776) = 0.46$, $p < 0.01$). Tetanus immunisation and the age spell 0–1 were interacted to understand if immunisation was most important for protecting children in the neonatal period (since this is when most deaths due to tetanus occur). This interaction was insignificant with a coefficient of 0.673 and a standard error of 0.439. This suggests that tetanus immunisation is serving as proxy for some selection factors, which make children whose mothers received tetanus immunisation different from those who do not.

The household factors of separate room for cooking, toilet, ownership of a radio, and sex of the household head were all insignificant. The variables, toilet and ownership of a radio, had high standard errors and were therefore left out of the multivariate analysis. Having a clean source of water proved to be a protective factor with an odds ratio of 0.61 ($e^{B} = \exp(-0.501) = 0.61$, $p < 0.05$).

The community factor, time to school, was significant. Those living 30 min or less from a school had children with only one third the mortality risks of those living more than 30 min from a school ($e^{B} = \exp(-0.503) = 0.61$, $p < 0.05$). Time to health centre was not significant.

The migration-child variable was not significant, but the place of current residence and migration/reproductive history variables were significant depending upon what was used as reference. The reference categories for the place of current residence and migration/reproductive history variables were altered so that each category served as the reference. These results are presented in Figures 2 and 3. Based upon these findings it is apparent that the risks of child mortality were lowest in Koboko where the self-settled refugees reside, and highest in Midia where the Ugandans exposed to the self-settled refugees reside. All categories of Sudanese children had significantly lower mortality than Ugandan children in Midia. Ugandan children in Odupi (exposed to settled refugees) and Midia (exposed to self-settled refugees) and the Sudanese in Yei had significantly higher risks than self-settled

	REFERENCE CATEGORY					
Comparison	Yivu	Odupi	Midia	Imvepi	Koboko	Yei
Yivu	---------	Lower	Lower	Higher	Higher	Higher
Odupi	Higher	---------	Lower	Higher	Higher**	Higher
Midia	Higher	Higher	----------	Higher**	Higher***	Higher*
Imvepi	Lower	Lower	Lower**	-----------	Higher	Lower
Koboko	Lower	Lower**	Lower***	Lower	---------	Lower**
Yei	Lower	Lower	Lower*	Higher	Higher**	----------

*p<.10 **p<0.05 ***p<0.01

Note: Yivu (Ugandans not exposed to refugees); Odupi (Ugandans exposed to settled refugees); Midia (Ugandans exposed to self-settled refugees); Imvepi (settled Sudanese refugees); Koboko (self-settled Sudanese refugees); Yei (Sudanese living in Sudan) (See Figure 1 for map of the study population).

Figure 2. Matrix of direction and significance of comparisons of 'place of current residence'.

REFERENCE CATEGORY					
Comparison	Stayees	Displaced before 15	Returnee before 15	Returnee after 15	Displaced after 15
Stayees	---------------	Higher	Lower	Lower	Higher
Displaced before 15	Lower	--------------	Lower**	Lower***	Lower
Returnee before 15	Higher	Higher**	--------------	Lower	Higher*
Returnee after 15	Higher	Higher***	Higher	-----------	Higher**
Displaced after 15	Lower	Higher	Lower*	Lower**	------------

*p<.10 **p<0.05 ***p<0.01

Figure 3. Matrix of direction and significance of comparisons of 'migration/reproductive history'.

refugee children in Koboko. Comparisons among Ugandans with differing exposures to refugees were not significant.

The analysis also suggested that children of women 'displaced before age 15' have the lowest mortality risks, but only comparisons with 'returnees before age 15' and 'returnees after age 15' were significant. 'Returnees after age 15' had children with the highest mortality risks, but only comparisons with those 'displaced before age 15' and 'displaced after age 15' were significant.

5.2. THE MULTIVARIATE ANALYSIS

Three multivariate models were tested in order to study the theory behind the conceptual framework. Model 1 presents only the individual, proximate and household factors. Model 2 adds community factors to understand if these factors are significant net of individual, proximate and household factors. Model 3 adds migration factors to understand if migration is important after all other factors are controlled. The significance or lack of significance of these factors could be essential in determining appropriate policy. These models are presented in Table 2.

In Model 1 the only statistically significant individual variables were the dummy category of brewing alcohol and some of the child age intervals. Children in the 2–3 month interval have lower mortality than in the 0–1 month interval, but children in the 4–11 and 12–23 month intervals had higher mortality. Education and child's gender were both insignificant.

In Model 1 the dummy category of birth order 5+ gained significance. Children of birth order 5+ had an odds ratio of 0.48 compared to children of birth order one ($e^{B} = \exp(-0.731) = 0.48,\ p < 0.01$). Children of birth orders 2–4 also had a lower odds of mortality, but this finding was not statistically significant. The mother's age at birth categories of 25–29 remained positively associated with mortality with an odds of 2.17 compared to mothers age 10–19 ($e^{B} = \exp(0.774) = 2.17,\ p < 0.01$). Tetanus immunisation remained protective for all children. Children of immunised mothers had an odds of mortality of 0.49 compared to children of unimmunised mothers ($e^{B} = \exp(-0.710) = 0.49,$

Table 2. Multivariate analysis of under-five mortality of children born in the past 5 years

	Model 1		Model 2		Model 3	
	Coeff.	Std. err.	Coeff.	Std. err.	Coeff.	Std. err.
Sample size	7605		7605		7501	
Constant	−3.050***	0.465	−2.957***	0.463	−2.643***	0.755
Individual						
Education						
None	–	–	–	–	–	–
Some	−0.233	0.181	−0.238	0.177	−0.217	0.186
Occupation						
Agricultural	–	–	–	–	–	–
Trading	0.089	0.314	0.105	0.317	0.267	0.352
Brewing alcohol	−0.456*	0.229	−0.402	0.250	−0.320	0.236
Contract labor	−0.263	0.293	−0.227	0.322	0.035	0.382
Professional/artisan	−1.151	0.796	−1.131	0.808	−0.958	0.831
Child's gender						
Female	–	–	–	–	–	–
Male	−0.122	0.142	−0.117	0.138	−0.098	0.135
Child's age						
0–1	–	–	–	–	–	–
2–3	−0.786**	0.304	−0.787**	0.305	−0.794**	0.303
4–11	0.696***	0.231	0.697***	0.233	0.669**	0.239
12–23	0.788***	0.255	0.786***	0.255	0.750***	0.258
24–35	−0.227	0.331	−0.231	0.333	−0.230	0.339
36–47	0.378	0.547	0.370	0.547	0.382	0.565
Proximate determinants						
Parity (birth order)						
1	–	–	–	–	–	–
2–4	−0.313	0.250	−0.319	0.252	−0.351	0.244
5+	−0.731***	0.252	−0.741***	0.252	−0.735***	0.246
Mother's age at birth						
10–19	–	–	–	–	–	–
20–24	0.243	0.282	0.263	0.270	0.236	0.268
25–29	0.774***	0.267	0.804***	0.262	0.752***	0.261
30–34	0.505	0.350	0.529	0.340	0.420	0.330
35+	0.516	0.459	0.540	0.448	0.418	0.460
Tetanus immunisation						
No	–	–	–	–	–	–
Yes	−0.710**	0.250	−0.693**	0.247	−0.673**	0.250

(cont.)

Table 2. (continued)

	Model 1		Model 2		Model 3	
	Coeff.	Std. err.	Coeff.	Std. err.	Coeff.	Std. err.
Household factors						
Separate room for cooking						
No	–	–	–	–	–	–
Yes	−0.234	0.182	−0.231	0.180	−0.226	0.177
Water source						
Poor quality	–	–	–	–	–	–
Good quality	−0.471**	0.207	−0.364*	0.210	−0.434	0.259
Sex of household head						
Female	–	–	–	–	–	–
Male	−0.032	0.279	−0.033	0.302	−0.220	0.259
Community factors						
Time to health center						
>30 min			–	–	–	–
<= 30 min			−0.056	0.278	0.037	0.294
Time to school						
(>= 30 min)			–	–	–	–
<= 30 min			−0.346*	0.173	−0.296	0.174
Residential arrangement						
Migration/reproductive history						
Stayees					–	–
Displaced before age 15					0.234	0.711
Returnees before age 15					0.187	0.284
Displaced after age 15					0.296	0.244
Returnees after age 15					0.344	0.719
Current place of residence						
(Yivu)–Ugandans unexposed to refugees					–	–
Odupi—Ugandans exposed to settled refugees					0.205	0.402
Midia—Ugandans exposed to self-settled refugees					0.278	0.456
Imvepi—settled Sudanese refugees					−0.491	0.795
Koboko—self-settled Sudanese refugees					−0.722	0.796
Yei—Sudanese in Sudan					−0.362	0.504
Migration—child						
Forced migration					–	–
No migration/voluntary migration					−0.254	0.296

$^{*}p < 0.10$, $^{**}p < 0.05$, $^{***}p < 0.01$.

$p < 0.05$). The only significant household factor was having a clean water source which resulted in an odds of mortality of 0.62 for households with a clean source compared to those with a poor source ($e^B = \exp(-0.471) = 0.62$, $p < 0.05$). Neither having a separate room for cooking nor the sex of the household head were significant.

In Model 2 brewing alcohol fell slightly below significance, but the other covariates that were statistically significant in Model 1 retained their significance. The p-value for water source, however, rose from $p < 0.05$ to $p < 0.10$. Time to health centre was not significant, but children who lived close to school had significantly lower mortality than those who lived far away ($e^B = \exp(-0.346) = 0.62$, $p < 0.05$).

In Model 3 none of the migration variables were statistically significant. Table 2 only presents results with Yivu as the reference for place of current residence and 'stayees' as the reference for the migration/history variable, but all categories of both variables were alternated as the reference to study comparisons of specific groups. No significant comparisons were found except that children in Yei had lower mortality than children in Midia ($e^B = \exp(-0.640) = 0.52$, $p < 0.01$). The bivariate analysis had also revealed that Ugandan children in Midia had the highest mortality.

The community variable of time to school and the household variable of water source become just marginally insignificant both at $p < 0.11$. Tetanus immunisation remained protective with an odds ratio of 0.51 for children of mothers immunised for tetanus compared to children whose mothers' were not immunised ($e^B = \exp(-0.673) = 0.51$, $p < 0.05$). The proximate determinant variables of mother's age of birth category of 25–29 and birth order 5+ retained the significance levels they had in Models 1 and 2. The child age intervals of 2–3, 4–11 and 12–23 also retained their significance.

6. Conclusion

6.1. DISCUSSION OF THE ANALYSES

The lack of significance of the migration variables presented in this analysis is quite revealing. The findings seem to suggest that there is not much difference in being a stayee, refugee or host in terms of recent child mortality after controlling for other factors. The long-term consequence of being displaced is not dire in terms of recent child mortality. Much of this study population has been living in their current place of residence for at least 3–4 years so once the physical effects of the actual migration have diminished and individuals begin building new homes in their place of asylum, being a refugee in and of itself is not necessarily negative. These findings provide an alternative view to the frequent image of all refugees as helpless and passive. Refugees and displaced persons have suffered intolerably yet despite what they have suffered many have shown an incredible resiliency and a capacity to rebuild their lives. Given enough time and support, it seems that even people who have gone through incredible hardship are able to move forward. Thus, to view refugees as helpless and passive is not a fair assessment.

A key reason for the similarity between the stayees, refugees and hosts in terms of child mortality is that the Ugandan hosts are poor, the Sudanese in Sudan are poor and the Sudanese refugees are poor. The media and sometimes humanitarian organisations as well often focus attention on refugees not realising that host populations and people in the country of origin often face the same issues as refugees in settlements—lack of infrastructure and facilities, lack of health care access and malnutrition. Some studies of displaced populations focus on the findings of high under-five mortality rates without seeming to realise that in many non-displaced populations in developing countries children under-five also suffer high mortality. The possible indicators in the data that children in Midia may suffer higher mortality than refugee populations may be a specific cause for concern because these children are living in the presence of self-settled refugees who do not receive food aid or much assistance from relief organisations. This population may be suffering the negative consequences of refugees such as crowding and competition for jobs but not benefiting from some of the positive consequences such as attention from relief agencies. On the other hand it is quite possible that there are factors other than the presence of refugees inherent in the place of current residence variable which may be elevating the risks.

The settled and self-settled refugees did not differ in terms of child mortality. As mentioned previously there is much overlap between the refugees in these two places of residence and perhaps the issue of settlement and self-settlement is too complicated to be studied as a simple dichotomy. Many families had some relatives who stayed in Imvepi but other relatives who lived in Koboko. Because of the extended family network in Africa, relatives often help one another. The distance between Imvepi (the settlement) and Koboko (the self-settlement) is not great (about 3 h by vehicle) so perhaps it would have been more ideal to study a settlement and self-settlement that were much further apart.

The lack of significant differences in the migration/reproductive health variable is not surprising. A woman's entire migration history should not heavily affect the mortality of her most recent children if she has been living in the same place of residence for some time. Only about 27% of the interviewed women had migrated due to force after the birth of the index child. The lack of significance of the migration-child variable suggests that migration is not necessarily a negative event. Of course the actual migration event is often traumatic, but over the long run being able to flee may be more beneficial than remaining behind in dire situations of war and conflict.

The factors that were significant included proximate determinants, individual, household and community factors. Having access to cash, immunisation services and clean water are important for children's health. Development and information about child health also appeared to be significant as evidence by the importance of being close to a school. Some policy and programmatic suggestions can be made from these findings. Relief organisations should not narrowly focus on refugees to the exclusion of hosts and stayees. All populations need access to these basic services.

6.2. FINAL THOUGHTS

This is one of the first studies of its kind concerning the impact of forced migration upon long-term child mortality. Some of the substantive findings from the multivariate analysis may not be generalisable to other displaced populations, but the methods are intended for use in any long-term displaced population.

Several proximate and distal factors were correlated with mortality and as mentioned previously could be key policy targets. Overall the migration variables were often not significant in this study, but they should be studied in the future because each forced migration setting is unique. Despite the limitations of this study, it is hoped that this research has added to what little is known concerning the correlates of child mortality in displaced populations.

Acknowledgements

The authors would like to thank Médecins Sans Frontières (MSF)-Holland for logistical support and the hardworking survey team who climbed hills and waded through swamps to follow the sampling frame. The authors are especially grateful to the Ugandan and Sudanese respondents for sharing their experiences with us and hope this research will benefit displaced and host populations.

Notes

* The authors wish to thank the United States Agency for International Development (USAID), The Hewlett and Andrew Mellon Foundations and The National Institute of Child Health and Human Development (NICHD). The research for this article was carried out while the primary and secondary authors were students at The Johns Hopkins University School of Public Health.

[1] Long-term is taken to mean 6–12 months because this is when the emergency phase of forced migration settings typically ends.

[2] The Arua District has been peaceful in recent years and has not been affected by LRA activity. The Arua District was formerly part of the West Nile District and was also the birthplace of Idi Amin.

[3] Possible ways to include orphaned children in a future study would be to ask adults taking care of the orphans about the survival status of the orphan's siblings. Alternatively, orphaned children could be included in a birth history analysis along with a respondent's biological children. Yet another option would be to ask respondents about the survival of their siblings and about all children ever born to sisters who reached the age of 15.

[4] In this study population settled refugees received food rations while self-settled refugees did not receive food rations.
[5] Respondents who moved but considered their new place of residence to be home were not included in this analysis. These respondents moved for voluntary reasons.
[6] This finding may seem curious but families who brew alcohol typically sell it for cash. It would be dangerous to advocate brewing alcohol as a profession, however, because of negative repercussions that could result from the profession. Qualitative interviews in Uganda revealed that excessive alcohol consumption by men is considered a serious problem in terms of their work and family life.
[7] In the equation B represents the coefficient to be exponentiated.

References

Amaza, O., 1998. *Museveni's Long March from Guerrilla to Statesman.* Fountain Publishers, Kampala.

Chambers, R., 1986. 'Hidden losers? The impact of rural refugees and refugee programs on poorer hosts', *International Migration Review* 20(2): 245–263.

Gardner, P., Rohde, J. and Majumdar, M., 1972. 'Health priorities among Bangladesh refugees', *The Lancet*: 834–836.

Harrell-Bond, B., 1986. *Imposing Aid: Emergency Assistance to Refugees.* Oxford University Press, Oxford.

Harrell-Bond, B., 1994. 'Pitch the Tents. An Alternative to Refugee Camps'. *New Republic*, 15–19.

Human Rights Watch, 1996. *Behind the Red Line.* New York.

Kabwegyere, T., 1995. *The Politics of State Formation and Destruction in Uganda.* Fountain Publishers, Kampala.

Kibraeb, G., 1991. *The State of the art Review of Refugee Studies in Africa.* Uppsala Universitet, Uppsala.

Loescher, G., 1993. *Beyond Charity. International Cooperation and the Global Refugee Crisis.* Oxford University Press, London.

Minority Rights Group, 1984. *Uganda and Sudan.* London.

Mosley, W. H. and Chen, L., 1984. 'An analytic framework for the study of child survival in developing countries', *Population Development Review (suppl)* 1: 25–45.

Ofransky, T., 2000. 'Warfare and instability along the Sudan-Uganda border: a look at the 20th century', in: J. Spaulding and S. Beswick (eds), *White Nile Black Blood.* Lawrenceville: The Red Sea Press, Inc.

Peterson, D., 1999. *Inside Sudan.* Boulder: Westview Press.

Seaman, J., 1972. 'Refugee work in a refugee camp for Bangladesh refugees in India', *The Lancet*: 866–870.

Simmance, A., 1987. 'The impact of large-scale refugee movements and the role of UNHCR', in: J. Rogge (ed), *Refugees: a Third World Dilemma.* Totowa, NJ: Rowman & Littlefield.

Stata Corporation, 1999. *Stata Reference Manual Release 6.* Texas: Stata Corporation, College Station.

Taha, F., 1978. 'The Sudan-Ugandan boundary', *Sudan Notes and Records* 59: 1–23.

The Economist Intelligence Unit, 1995. *Sudan: Country Profile*, 1994–1995. London.

Toole, M., 1993. 'The public health consequences of inaction: lessons learned in responding to sudden population displacements', in: K. Cahill (ed), *A Framework for Survival: Health, Human Rights and Humanitarian Assistance in Conflicts and Disasters.* New York: Harper Collins, 144–158.

UNHCR., 1993. *The State of the World's Refugees. The Challenge of Protection.* Penguin Books, Geneva.

UNHCR, 2003. *Refugees and others of concern to UNHCR: 1999 statistical overview.* Registration and Statistical Unit, Programme Coordinational Section. Geneva: United Nations High Commissioner for Refugees.

USCR., 2000. *World Refugee Survey.* D.C.: Immigrant and Refugee Services of America, Washington.

USCR., 2003. *World Refugee Survey.* D.C.: Immigrant and Refugee Services of America, Washington.

Van Damme, W., 1995. 'Do refugees belong in camp? Experiences from Goma and Guinea', *The Lancet* 346: 360–362.

Virmani, A., 1996. *The resettlement of Ugandan Refugees in Southern Sudan, 1979–86.* Ph.D. Dissertation. Department of Political Science, Northwestern University, Evanston.

Woodward, P., 1991. 'Uganda and southern Sudan 1986–9: new regimes and peripheral politics', in: H. Hansen and M. Twaddle (eds), *Changing Uganda.* Kampala: Fountain Publishers.

Zolberg, A., Suhkre, A. and Aguayo, S., 1989. *Escape from Violence: Conflict and Refugee Crisis in the Developing World.* Oxford University Press, New York.

CHAPTER 15. CHILD SURVIVAL AND FERTILITY OF REFUGEES IN RWANDA

PHILIP VERWIMP
Poverty Research Unit at Sussex, United Kingdom, German Institute of Economic Research in Berlin, Germany and Households in Conflict Network

JAN VAN BAVEL
Department of Sociology, Catholic University of Leuven, Belgium and Postdoctoral Researcher of the Fund for Scientific Research—Flanders, Belgium

Abstract. In the 1960s and 1990s, internal strife in Rwanda has caused a mass flow of refugees into neighbouring countries. This article explores the cumulated fertility of Rwandan refugee women and the survival of their children. To this end, we use a national survey conducted between 1999 and 2001 and covering 6,420 former refugee and non-refugee households. The findings support old-age security theories of reproductive behaviour: refugee women had higher fertility but their children had lower survival chances. Newborn girls suffered more than boys, suggesting that the usual sex differential in child survival observed in most populations changes under extreme living conditions.

1. Introduction

The last decade of the 20th century was probably the most turbulent Rwanda has ever seen. A combination of economic crisis, civil war, genocide, internal displacement, mass emigration, political transition and return of refugees ravaged the country. Every Rwandan household was affected by at least one of these events. These events have scarred the Rwandan population at multiple levels: loss of family members through violent death, rape, disease, hunger, loss of dignity, loss of property, loss of land, fleeing to neighbouring countries, renewed onslaught, absence of respect for human rights, imprisonment. It is not farfetched to ask if a country or a population can overcome such a devastating decade.

The scare inflicted on the population of a country engulfed in violent conflict is reflected in its mortality pattern. This is a well-researched area of inquiry for the case of Rwanda as well as for other countries. Less researched is the effect of violent conflict on the reproductive behaviour of affected populations. That is the topic that we want to address in this article by studying fertility of refugee women and analysing survival chances of their children in Rwanda during the 1990s. More specifically, we compare the reproductive pattern of women who lived and stayed in their own residence in Rwanda during their entire life with the reproduction of women who either were forced to flee Rwanda, fled voluntary, were internally displaced or came to Rwanda for the first time after 1994.

This chapter was previously published in *European Journal of Population*, vol. 21, no. 2–3, 2005, pp. 271–290.

Helge Brunborg et al. (eds.), The Demography of Armed Conflict, 347–365.

2. Forced migration, fertility, and child survival

According to the 1951 UN Convention, refugees are persons who are outside their country of nationality due to a well-founded fear of being persecuted for reasons of ethnicity, religion, nationality, membership in a particular social group, or political opinion. Conventionally, they are distinguished from internally displaced persons (IDP's). The latter include people who have fled or left their homes as a result of armed conflict and violence, but who have not crossed an internationally recognised state border (see UN OCHA, 1998). Both refugees and IDP's fall under the more general heading of forced migration.

The available literature mentions contradictory theoretical positions about the impact of forced migration on fertility. One relevant line of demographic theory is the risk-insurance or old-age security approach, which emphasises the insurance role of children under conditions of economic insecurity. This theory implies that fertility rises among refugees as a response to lower child survival: high child mortality entails a pressure to replace deceased children. The opposite stance is that fertility falls because the stress and uncertainties of refugee life are not conducive to childbearing. According to this hypothesis, couples will try to delay births in response to sudden declines in income or increased uncertainty (Lindstrom and Berhanu, 1999; McGinn, 2000).

The old-age security approach is advanced in the literature on the reproductive behaviour of rural populations in peacetime as well. It is assumed that children contribute to the economic and social well-being of parents, especially when they get older. Nugent (1985) writes that the absence of well-functioning financial, product, and labour markets increases the importance of children as old-age support. Clay and Vander Haar (1993) find support for this in Rwanda. Using the 1988 Non-farm Strategies Survey of Rwanda, they find that 69% of parents in the sample with children living outside the household report that they receive support from their children. Support is received in the form of labour, in kind or in cash. In the study, sons were more likely to give support in cash, whereas daughters gave support in terms of labour or gifts in kind. This suggests that Rwandan parents improve their social security by having more children, male as well as female. Together with this economic rationale for having many children, May et al. (1990) report that social norms and attitudes of Rwandan women are very pro-natalist. They consider it their duty to transmit life. Having a lot of children gives honour and prestige to the family.

A number of empirical studies have found increased fertility among refugee populations. This is the case for Afghan women in refugee camps in Pakistan (Yusuf, 1990), Palestinian refugees living in Gaza and the West Bank (Al-Qudsi, 2000), and Indochinese refugees resettled in the United States (Weeks et al., 1989). In these cases, high fertility is associated with low reproductive health: Sachs (1997) argues that dislocation, inadequate shelter, minimal food rations, poor sanitation and physical danger typical of refugee life make safe motherhood almost impossible. One should be cautious, however, of deriving general observations from case studies. Reproductive health in general, and fertility behaviour in particular, may vary a lot in refugee situations depending on the overall conditions in the camps, the length of stay, the access to health care and so on. In a comparative study of more than 600,000 people living in 52 post-emergency phase camps in seven countries, Hynes et al. (2002) found better reproductive health outcomes (lower fertility, lower neonatal mortality, lower maternal mortality, and higher birth weight) among refugees and internally displaced populations in these camps compared to the populations in their respective host country and country-of-origin populations. They attribute their findings to better access of camp residents to preventative and curative health care services, and to food and non-food items, as well as improvements in water supply and sanitation.

In a non-refugee setting, Clay and Johnson (1992) used the 1988 survey held among Rwandan households and found that households with larger farms have more children. They also found that it is not the demand for labour that drives fertility, since the farm size was unrelated to the number of household members of labour force age. The causal mechanism appears to be that a larger farm makes it possible to afford a higher supply of children. One must add that Rwandan customary law, before 1994, divides the land owned by the father equally over all sons. Daughters and wives could not own land (exception made for special circumstances). This is not unrelated to Nugent's (1985) assertion that the loyalty of children to provide support to their parents depends on the amount of land and other wealth that they will inherit.

In times of violent conflict and forced migration, physical capital (fixed assets which have to be abandoned during refuge), such as the size of a household's farm, may play a less important role in reproductive behaviour compared to the social capital, education and relationship status of the mother, among other variables. On top of this, traditional methods of birth control used by Rwandans, such as birth spacing, may be more difficult to practice in the stressful, unhealthy and coercive situations refugees are living in (May et al., 1990). A short time span between two births impairs the survival chances of the last born child because this one has to be weaned early, risking illness, malnutrition and psychological distress.

Research on the health situation of displaced populations finds excess mortality, especially among children under age five, as a prime fact (Médecins sans frontières—MSF, 2003). In a survey held among former UNITA members (900 households, 6,599 family members) in refugee camps, MSF found malnutrition, fever or malaria, and war or violence as the three most frequently reported causes of death. The Danish Epidemiology Science Centre (1999) found severe malnutrition and high mortality in a survey of 422 refugee children in Guinea-Bissau. They report higher malnutrition and higher mortality for children living in a non-camp setting, compared to children living in a camp. The Goma epidemiology group (1995) found high prevalence of child mortality as well as acute malnutrition among children in refugee camps in Eastern Zaire, especially in female-headed households.

Apart from the living conditions, Mbago (1994) uses the 1988 Tanzanian census to examine other factors associated with child mortality in three regions populated with refugees from Burundi. He finds that low levels of maternal schooling are associated with high child mortality for both the Tanzanian nationals and the refugees. Mother's employment affected child mortality among the Tanzanian population but was statistically insignificant among the refugees.

Was fertility of Rwandan refugee mothers higher than fertility of their non-refugee counterparts? And how was child survival related to the fertility of refugee mothers? Before Section 4 introduces the data we have used in order to answer these questions, the next section (Section 3) first outlines the historical background of civil war, genocide, and mass migration in Rwanda. Section 5 presents the results of our study and Section 6 summarises the findings.

3. Civil war, genocide and mass migration in Rwanda

Between April and July 1994, at least 500,000 Tutsi (Des Forges, 1999),[1] or about 75% of the Tutsi population, together with many Hutu who were known to be opponents of Habyarimana, were killed by the Rwandan military forces (Forces Armées Rwandaises, FAR), local police, national guard and militia called Interahamwe. A few years before, in October 1990, a group of rebels consisting of Tutsi refugees who had left Rwanda during the 1959–1962 revolution, together with their offspring, attacked Rwanda from Uganda. What followed was a civil war between the Rwandan armed forces (FAR) and the rebel army (Rwandan Patriotic Front, RPF), in which the civilian population in the north of Rwanda was the main victim. While the RPF claimed to fight against the dictatorship of president Habyarimana, the latter claimed to represent the majority of the people. The battles between both armies were paralleled by peace negotiations and third party interventions. In order to understand the drama of this period, it is essential to know its history.

The ethnic composition of the population had been a major issue in Rwandan politics since the time of colonisation. The Belgian coloniser had first favoured the Tutsi ruling class because they were considered racially superior to the Hutu, who were known as a people of cultivators. In the 1950s, with the spread of anti-colonial and independence movements, the ruling Tutsi began to claim the independence of Rwanda. At that time a Hutu counter-elite was given the chance to study at catholic seminars. With Belgian military and political aid, this new elite of Hutu leaders succeeded in overturning the ruling Tutsi regime and replaces it by the leadership of the *Parmehutu*, the party for the emancipation of the Hutu. Grégoire Kayibanda, a seminarian, became the first president. The ethnic divide, however, remained and was even strengthened. The new rulers, at the national as well as at the local level established their power by removing all Tutsi from positions of power. Ordinary Tutsi, who were not associated with political power, were also targets of reprisal and murder. For detailed treatment of the history of Rwanda, books written, among others, by Newbury (1988), Reyntjens (1994), Prunier (1995), De Lame (1996) and Chrétien (2000) can be recommended.

In 1973 a group of army officers around Juvénal Habyarimana took power by a coup d'État. They were frustrated by the monopolisation of power by the group around Kayibanda, whose base was the central prefecture of Gitarama. The group around Habyarimana, originating from northern Rwanda, saw all benefits of power going to the people from Gitarama. After the coup d'état, Habyarimana became the new president. He established the MRND (Mouvement Révolutionnaire National pour le Développement), the only party that every Rwandan was supposed to belong to by birth. Aided by high prices of coffee, the country's main export crop, and generous donor support in the late seventies, Habyarimana was liked, or at least not contested, by a large part of the population. He did not abolish the ethnic identity cards, however, and he also forbade officers and soldiers to marry Tutsi wives. In order to control population movements, he set up a detailed system of registration and reporting of demographic changes at the local level. He also had every adult participate in the *Umuganda* (weekly communal labour), and institutionalised weekly animation sessions in honour of himself (Verwimp, 2003).

A key characteristic of the Habyarimana regime was its doctrine on the relation between population and land. The president had never been an advocate of a family planning policy. On several occasions he declared that children were the wealth of every Rwandan family. Groups set up by the Ministry of the Interior attacked pharmacies that sold condoms. The president was fully supported by the Catholic Church, which was omnipresent in Rwanda. The fertility rate of Rwandan women was among the highest in the world and the average size of cultivated land per family was shrinking rapidly from 1.2 ha in 1984 to 0.9 ha in 1990 (National Agricultural Survey, 1984 and Agricultural Household Survey 1989–1991). Many families did not have enough land to earn a living and feed their families. In 1986, when discussing the fate of the 1959–1962 refugees, the Central Committee of the MRND concluded that their return was not possible because the country was over-populated.

During the civil war preceding the genocide (1990–1994), a number of local massacres occurred, in which a total of 2,000 Tutsi were killed. These massacres were not a spontaneous outburst of violence from a poor peasant population but were organised by the national power elite. On April 6th, 1994, Habyarimana's plane was shot down. After that, the genocide broke out.

A substantial part of the FAR, together with several hundreds of thousands of civilian refugees fleeing the war, were pushed into neighbouring Zaire, Tanzania and Burundi. For 2 years, a mix of civilian refugees and warrior-refugees (ex-FAR) resided in refugee camps along the border between Zaire on the one hand and Uganda, Rwanda and Burundi on the other hand. The Goma Epidemiology Group (1995) estimated that between 6% and 10% of all refugees died during the first month of their arrival in eastern Zaire, 85–90% of them because of diarrhoeal disease. Such a death rate is two to three times higher than the highest previously reported rates among refugees in Sudan, Somalia or Thailand. In November 1996, the Rwandan patriotic army (RPA, successor of the RPF) attacked the Zairian camps thereby killing both thousands of armed ex-FAR soldiers as well as unarmed civilians. The majority of the surviving refugees then returned to Rwanda. A sizeable part of ex-FAR forces, Interahamwe and genuine refugees fled deeper into Zairian territory. During the subsequent years, 1997–2000, the most remaining refugees had either died or were repatriated.

4. Data and methods

4.1. DATA SOURCES

In order to investigate the effect of these subsequent refugee crises, we used a nationally representative household survey, conducted in Rwanda between 1999 and 2001. The Household Living Conditions Survey, also known under its French acronym EICV (Enquête Intégrale des Conditions de Vie), was conducted by the Statistics Department of the Government of Rwanda and covered 6,420 households in rural areas, in small cities as well as in the capital Kigali. The survey was multipurpose and collected information on education, health, family composition, migration, employment, agricultural and non-agricultural activities, expenditures and transfers from over 32,000 household members. The sample of households was selected by stratified, two-stage cluster sampling. First, primary sampling units (zones in cities, cells in rural areas) were selected with probability proportional to size. From a complete list of households in the selected units, a systematic sample was drawn. The demographic and health data in the EICV are not of the same depth as one sees in the well-known Demographic and Health Surveys. For example, information on the date of birth of deceased children is missing, making it impossible to analyse birth spacing or to measure the direct impact of child mortality on fertility. Also, the survey did not include a retrospective mortality count of family members.Entire families of men, women and children who all died in Rwanda or abroad were not taken into account. Given these limitations, the coverage of the migration pattern of households and individuals in this survey makes it very suitable for our present purpose, which is to see what difference a woman's refugee status makes for her reproductive behaviour. The Statistics Department of the Rwandan Ministry of Finance compared the data with other data sources and checked for internal consistency. They conclude that one can have a good degree of confidence in the overall quality of the data (Ministry of Finance of Rwanda, 2002).

Table 1 presents a comparison of the demographic profile of Rwandan women at the start and at the end of the decade. High levels of fertility combined with decreasing levels of mortality in the seventies and eighties made Rwanda a case of an exceptional high level of population growth (3.7% per year, May et al., 1990). Given the scarcity of land, this population growth led to an equally exceptional level of population density (300 persons per square km in the early 1990s). At the end of the decade, fertility remained high, even though there was some decline.

Table 1. Demographic profile of Rwandan women aged 15–49 years

Demographic indicator	1992	2000
Percent of women with no education	38.0	29.4
Total fertility rate	6.2	5.8
Median age at first marriage	20.0	20.7
Median age at first birth	21.5	22.0
Mean ideal number of children	4.2	4.9
Percent of women who want no more children	36.0	33.0
Median breastfeeding duration (months)	27.9	30.6
Infant mortality rate (per thousand)	85.0	107.4
Under-five mortality rate (per thousand)	150.8	196.2

Source: Demographic and Health Survey 1992 and 2000, Final Reports.

Infant and child mortality went up, but this is probably only temporary due to the aftermath of the genocide, civil war and mass migration.

4.2. RECONSTRUCTION OF REFUGEE STATUS

The EICV featured several questions on the migration history of households. We combined these questions to arrive at five categories currently composing the Rwandan population according to their migration and refugee status. Table 2 gives an

Table 2. Migration history of Rwandan women aged 15–49 years

Categories	Count (N)	Percent	Mean age	Children born alive	Percent of children still alive
(1) Never migrated	4,968	60.1	26.8	2.36	80.9
Refugees after 10/1990:					
(2) Refugees or IDP's <6 months	1,522	18.4	27.8	2.48	81.9
(3) Refugees or IDP's >6 months	1,103	13.4	27.3	2.66	79.0
Refugees before 10/1990:					
(4) Returned before or after April 1994	180	2.2	34.8	4.40	76.3
(5) Never lived in Rwanda before	468	5.7	25.7	2.03	87.5
Migration history missing	19	0.2	na	na	na
Total	8,260	100.0	na	na	na

Source: Authors' calculation based on data from the EICV, 1999–2001.

overview of the categories that we distinguished and the number of women in each category.

In the first category are women who never migrated, neither voluntary nor forcefully. The second group consists of short term, temporary migrants, i.e. those who were displaced in Rwanda for less than 6 months or who found themselves abroad for less than 6 months after 1990. A large majority of the women in this group sought shelter elsewhere in Rwanda for a short period of time, often a few weeks, in order to escape violence in their home region. They were not considered refugees in the EICV. Categories three and four are women who fled for a considerable period, i.e. for at least 6 months. Category three consists of women who were internally displaced or who fled Rwanda for at least 6 months after 1990. Many women from northern Rwanda, for example, were first displaced in camps around Kigali for several months prior to the genocide and then fled to Zaire in July 1994. The fourth group is the so-called old caseload refugees. These people, practically all Tutsi, were expelled from Rwanda in the sixties. They lived in neighbouring countries and returned to Rwanda before or after 1994. The fifth and last group of women is new to Rwanda: they are the offspring of refugees who lived in the Diaspora and came to Rwanda after 1994.

Figure 1 presents the migration history of old and new caseloads (categories (3) and (4) in Table 2) taken together. It is the duration of their flight (at least 6 months), which distinguishes this group from the other groups. The large majority among them was refugee in the Congo, Tanzania, Burundi or Uganda. A limited number of persons in these two categories were internally displaced persons.

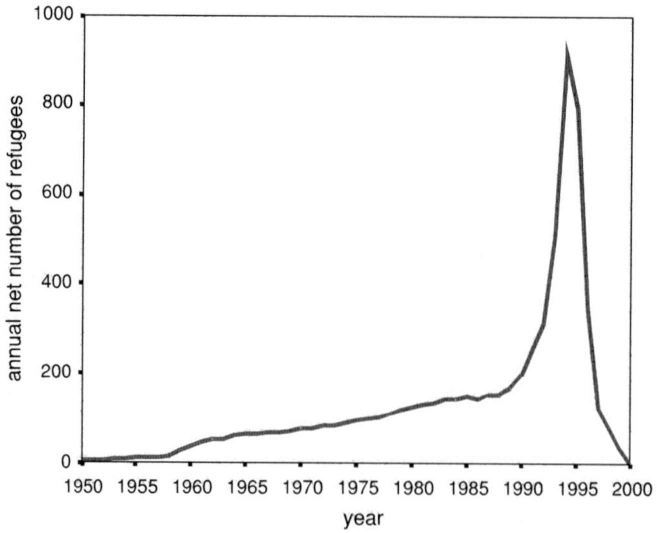

Figure 1. Number of women aged 15 to 49 years who were a refugee or internally displaced for at least 6 months (old and new caseloads), $N = 1283$

Table 3. Descriptive statistics on fertility and child survival of Rwandan women, 1999–2001

	Age						
Variables	15–19	20–24	25–29	30–34	35–39	40–44	45–49
(1) Number of women	2,488	1,553	1,104	874	806	812	539
Not refugee	2,171	1,342	925	735	691	656	457
Refugee	317	211	179	139	115	156	82
(2) Number of children ever born alive							
Mother not refugee	0.04	0.74	2.10	3.37	5.04	6.43	7.05
Mother refugee	0.02	1.00	2.22	3.84	5.36	6.69	7.38
(3) Children still living in % of born alive							
Mother not refugee	91.9	86.3	85.9	83.0	79.7	77.4	73.3
Mother refugee	72.2	85.0	82.4	80.2	78.9	73.4	68.1

Source: EICV, 1999–2001.

However, the data do not allow distinguishing between refugees and internally displaced persons. In the subsequent analysis therefore, we consider categories 3 and 4 as 'refugees.' One sees a gradual but steady increase of refugees from 1960 to 1990. These are Tutsi, also called old caseload refugees, who fled the Hutu Republics under presidents Kayibanda and Habyarimana. The refugee flow continued in the 1990s with a peak in 1994 when 13.4% of all women between 15 and 49 years old in our sample fled Rwanda. This time, Rwandan Hutu fled the country in mid-1994 when the RPF was gaining control. They were to become the new caseload refugees. From mid-1994 onwards, we get a return of old caseload refugees, followed by, from the end of 1996 onwards, a mass return of new caseloads.

An overview of fertility and child survival by age and refugee status is presented in Table 3. Panel (2) of the table shows that refugee women had higher cumulated fertility than non-refugee women: at all ages above 20, Rwandan women who had been a refugee for part of their lives, reached a higher parity on average than women who did not flee. However, refugee women lost a higher proportion of their children, as panel (3) shows.

These descriptive data seem to support the risk-insurance approach. The main reason for the insurance-hypothesis to predict higher fertility among refugees seems to apply: mothers who were forced to flee from Rwanda lost more children. This raises three questions. First: is the difference in fertility between refugee and non-refugee women really due to their forced migration history, or is this a spurious effect? Second: are the lower survival chances of refugee children due only to adverse living conditions or is there also an effect of their mothers' fertility? Third: do the differences in fertility and child survival depend on the different circumstances of their migration or life in exile, more specifically on whether or not they were new or old caseload refugees?

4.3. MODELING FERTILITY AND CHILD SURVIVAL

The survey data do not include the dates of all births, but the number of children ever born (B_i in the following) is available for each woman. Because this is a count variable, the natural approach then is to assume that it has a Poisson distribution. The Poisson regression model assumes that the observed number of events B_i is determined by an underlying, unobserved rate μ_i, so that B_i has a conditional mean that depends on a vector of women's characteristics X_i.

A critical assumption of the Poisson model is that the probability of an event occurring is constant within a given time unit, and independent of other events during the same period. If this assumption is true, the variance of the count variable will be equal to its mean. However, due to contagion, this assumption rarely holds in social sciences. Contagion means that the likelihood of an event occurring is influenced by the occurrence or nonoccurrence of another event. As a result, the variance may be bigger than the mean number of counts or the variance may be lower. In the first case, we will observe more high and low counts than expected in the Poisson model. This is known as overdispersion. In the second case, when the variance of the count is smaller than its mean, we will observe a greater number of births right around the mean. This is known as underdispersion (McCullagh and Nelder, 1989).

It is possible to account for over- and underdispersion with respect to the Poisson model by introducing a dispersion parameter φ that captures the difference between the mean μ_i and the variance (McCullagh and Nelder, 1989).

$$\text{var}(B_i/X_i) = \mu_i\varphi = \exp(\beta X_i)\varphi \qquad (1)$$

When $\varphi = 1$, model (1) reduces to the Poisson model. Underdispersion implies that $\varphi < 1$, while $\varphi > 1$ indicates overdispersion. McCullagh and Nelder (1989) suggest to estimate the value of the dispersion parameter φ as a ratio of the deviance to its associated degrees of freedom. This is the approach taken here.

Our dataset includes women between ages 15 and 49. The exposure time varies accordingly from close to zero for the youngest women to the maximum of 35 years for the oldest. We therefore need to use the exposure time as an offset variable in the Poisson regression. We have calculated the exposure time for all women by subtracting 14 years from the current age. So the real dependent variable in our regression is not the number of live births B_i, but'a fertility rate, i.e. the number of live births divided by the length of the risk interval. What we are doing is to model women's average yearly fertility rate under the assumption that the risk interval starts at the age of 14. This amounts to the classic approach to fertility rates in demography. So the model we actually fitted can be written as:

$$\log \hat{\mu}_i = \log \left[\frac{B_i}{\text{age}_i - 14} \right] = \beta X_i + \varepsilon_i \Rightarrow \log(B_i) = \log(\text{age}_i - 14) + \beta X_i + \varepsilon_i \tag{2}$$

The vector of predictor variables X_i includes woman's age, civil status, schooling, occupational sector, place of residence, and migration history. First, age is included in the form of five dummies for six age categories in order to allow for a non-linear relationship between age and the number of children ever born. Second, we do have information about current relationship status, but not about when the relationship started. We use women who are currently married as a reference category, and compare them with single, unmarried but cohabiting, divorced or separated, and widowed women. Unfortunately, the data provide only information about the civil status at the survey time and not during women's previous migration and fertility history. Third, the woman's educational status is measured in number of years of schooling. Fourth, we distinguish between women who report the cultivation of their own farm as their principal occupation and all other occupations. Because of the importance of the rural-urban divide in the literature, we also incorporate residential dummies.

In order to assess the net effect of the migration history on child survival, we estimated a logistic regression model with the proportion of surviving children as the dependent variable. Technically, we count the number of live births as 'trials', and the number of currently surviving children as binomially distributed 'successes' (see Long, 1997). In addition to the covariates used in our fertility model, we added the average fertility rate to the list of covariates of child survival because the level of fertility is known to be an important determinant of infant and child mortality (Reher, 1999). The fertility rate was, of course, the endogenous variable in the Poisson model, while it is treated as exogenous in the analysis of child survival.

5. Results

5.1. IMPACT OF MIGRATION ON FERTILITY

Table 4 reports the estimates of the Poisson regression model. The fact that Bayesian Information Criterion (BIC, at the bottom of the table) is negative is usually taken as an indicator of a good fit (Long, 1997). This is confirmed by the ratio of the deviance to the number of degrees of freedom being 0.67, which is close enough to one to indicate that the model fits the data reasonably well (Pedan, 2001). This ratio is also the estimate of the dispersion parameter. The fact that it is lower than one

Table 4. Poisson regression of cumulated fertility, Rwanda 1999–2001

Variable	Coeff.	S.E.
Age (ref = 14–24)		
25–29 years	0.103***	0.029
30–34 years	0.148***	0.028
35–39 years	0.213***	0.028
40–44 years	0.225***	0.027
45–49 years	0.142***	0.028
Relationship status (ref = married)		
Cohabitating	−0.033**	0.016
Divorced	−0.335***	0.026
Single	−2.319***	0.048
Widow	−0.178***	0.015
Education and occupation		
Years of schooling	−0.024***	0.002
Principal occupation is farming	0.050*	0.028
Paid work in the last 12 months	−0.004	0.017
Displacement/Refuge/migration (ref = never displaced)		
Short term IDPs or refugees (cat.2)	−0.016	0.016
New caseloads (cat.3)	0.041**	0.017
Old caseloads (cat.4)	0.040	0.030
New to Rwanda (cat.5)	0.077***	0.028
Place of residence (ref = rural area)		
Residing in Kigali	−0.089***	0.031
Residing in a small city	−0.067**	0.029
Constant	−1.566***	0.039
Dispersion parameter	0.669	n.a.
N observations	8,089	
Deviance	5,406.0	df = 8,070
BIC [Deviance—df-ln(N)]	−67,210	

***sign. at the 1% level, **at the 5% level, *at the 10% level.

indicates that our data are underdispersed. This implies that the number of births predicted by the model for any particular combination of the independent variables is strongly concentrated around the mean $E(B_i|X_i)$. Possibly, this is the result of compelling reproductive values and norms in Rwanda.

Turning immediately to the estimated impact of migration history, which is the main issue in this article, one can see in Table 4 that the new caseload refugees had significantly higher fertility than women who never migrated, even after controlling for the other variables in the model. To repeat, the new caseload refugees are the women who were internally displaced or became refugees after 1990 for a relatively long period of time (at least 6 months). The exponentiated effect parameters can be interpreted as factor effects, so $\exp(0.041) = 1.04$ means that the expected fertility rate for the new caseload refugees is 1.04 times the mean rate for the reference group.

Women who were new to Rwanda after the genocide had significantly higher fertility than the reference group as well. For women who never lived in Rwanda before, the estimated factor effect is $\exp(0.076) = 1.08$. After controlling for the other covariates, the fertility of short term IDP's or refugees and of the old caseload refugees were not significantly different from the fertility of women who never migrated inside or outside Rwanda.

Age has the expected effect in the regression: older women have significantly higher cumulated fertility than younger women have. As women approach the age of menopause, the number of additional births declines, making the average number of births during the overall risk interval (defined to start at age 14) decrease again.

With respect to relationship status, the estimates indicate that married women had the highest and single women the lowest fertility. Marriage in Rwanda, as in other countries, is an important determinant of fertility. The numbers of years spent in school as well as the practise of farming as one's principal occupation also have a profound and statistically significant effect on fertility. More educated mothers have fewer children. Farming women have, all else equal, $\exp(0.05) = 1.05$ times more children compared to non-farming women.

One could argue that multicollinearity between farming and residence in the rural areas could be a problem in this regression. Econometric theory tells us that multicollinearity becomes a problem when the data set has very few cases in which the two correlating variables have different values (Wooldridge, 2003). This is not the situation in our data. In case of substantial overlap between variables, as in our data set, including all variables helps to identify which one actually mattered. In this case, both farming and place of residence had an independent and statistically significant effect on fertility. Measured against residence in the rural areas as a reference category, a woman living in Kigali or in one of the other urban centres of Rwanda has significantly fewer children.

The off-farm variable, measuring the fact whether or not the women have performed paid work outside the family farm for the last 12 months, is not statistically significant. The off-farm variable is a very broad category, including wage work on someone else's farm as well as the management of business, small or large.

So far, our multivariate analysis shows that the migration history of refugees had the effect of raising their fertility. The descriptive statistics in Table 3 indicated, however, that fewer children of refugee mothers survived. The next section analyses the covariates of child mortality with multivariate logistic regression.

5.2. CHILD SURVIVAL AND REFUGEE STATUS

Table 3 already showed that Rwandan refugees (categories 3 and 4) saw more of their children die than non-refugees. This is no surprise, although higher mortality among refugee children should not be taken for granted (see Khawaja, 2004).

In most populations, infant and child mortality for boys is higher than for girls under normal conditions. However, when conditions are extremely bad and mortality is very high, the sex differential in mortality may become smaller or even disappear. There is evidence of this in the Rwandan data: among refugees, 23.6% of the sons and 21.8% of the daughters had died at the time of the survey, which is a difference of 1.8 percentage points. The figures for non-refugee sons and daughters are 21.0% and 17.6%, respectively, which is a difference of 3.4 percentage points. *Excess* mortality in response to bad living conditions seems to have been higher among girls than among boys, thereby effectively reducing the sex differential. This finding is reminiscent of sex differences in infant and child mortality before the mortality transition in Europe: as a consequence of improving living conditions, the mortality difference between boys and girls increased during the nineteenth century (Pinnelli and Mancini, 1997).

The results in Table 5 show that new caseload refugees suffered a significantly larger loss of children than any other category. However, this only holds for the mortality of daughters. There was no statistically significant effect of refugee status on the survival of sons. One possible interpretation for this sex difference is the following. Given the adverse living conditions in terms of health as well as stress and violence during their refuge in Eastern Congo, Burundi or Tanzania, refugees were not able to keep all their offspring alive. When choices about food, health and bare survival had to be made in these extreme conditions, Rwandan refugees chose to spend the scarce resources on the survival of their sons more than on their daughters. Unfortunately, we have no data on the allocation of food and other resources within refugee families, so we cannot test this interpretation directly. The effect for short duration refugees and IDP's is significant but smaller than the effect for the long-term refugees.

A mother's relationship status significantly affects the survival of her children. Although not all widowed, divorced or single women are at the same time head of households, our findings correspond with those of the Goma Epidemiology Group (1995). In their study in Eastern Congo, they found a greater loss of children in female-headed households. This also corresponds to Mbago's findings (1994) on Burundian refugees in Tanzania.

Table 5. Logistic regression of the proportion of live births currently surviving, by sex of the live births

	All children		Daughters		Sons	
Variables	Coeff.	S.E.	Coeff.	S.E.	Coeff.	S.E.
Age (ref = 15–24)						
25–29	−0.227**	0.097	−0.256*	0.144	−0.197	0.131
30–34	−0.330***	0.093	−0.363***	0.138	−0.306**	0.126
35–39	−0.441***	0.090	−0.464***	0.134	−0.424***	0.122
40–44	−0.531***	0.089	−0.552***	0.132	−0.518***	0.120
45–49	−0.723***	0.091	−0.728***	0.136	−0.722***	0.123
Relationship status (ref = married)						
Civil union	−0.222***	0.047	−0.208***	0.069	−0.247***	0.065
Divorced	−0.332***	0.077	−0.296**	0.116	−0.351***	0.102
Single	−0.297*	0.156	−0.533**	0.208	−0.048	0.237
Widow	−0.350***	0.043	−0.347***	0.063	−0.355***	0.059
Education and occupation						
Years of schooling	0.060***	0.007	0.069***	0.010	0.053***	0.009
Principal occup. (farming = 1)	−0.381***	0.090	−0.238*	0.132	−0.510***	0.126
Paid work in the last 12 m	−0.044	0.051	−0.119	0.073	0.023	0.071
Mothers fertility						
Average fertility rale	−1.303***	0.177	−1.056***	0.250	−1.536***	0.251
Displacement/Refuge/migration (ref = never displaced)						
Short term IDPs or refugees	−0.064	0.047	−0.126*	0.070	−0.001	0.064
New caseloads	−0.172***	0.048	−0.274***	0.070	−0.082	0.067
Old caseloads	0.004	0.089	0.003	0.129	−0.006	0.122
New to Rwanda	0.284***	0.095	0.270*	0.142	0.308**	0.128
Place of residence (ref = rural area)						
Residing in Kigali	0.300***	0.107	0.453***	0.156	0.143	0.148
Residing in a small city	0.105	0.091	0.181	0.138	0.037	0.123
Constant	2.361***	0.142	2.231***	0.208	2.40**	0.195
Numbers of observations	4,600		3,919		3,921	
Deviance (−2 Log L)	21,048.5		9,937.8		11,038.6	
df		4,581		3,900		3,902
BIC	−17.586		−22,329		−21,246	

***sign. at the 1% level. **at the 5% level, *at the 10% level.

Finally, the regression shows that a high number of births during the reproductive span had a negative and statistically significant effect on child survival, for boys as well as for girls.

6. Conclusion

This article has explored the repercussions of forced migration of Rwandan mothers on their fertility and on the survival chances of their children. Essentially, our analysis was comparative in nature: since our data included women who never left Rwanda, we were able to compare these women with several groups of refugee women. Unfortunately, our data do not allow us to analyse the timing of birth and death of deceased children, because the survey we used only mentions the number and sex of deceased children. The main strength of our data lies in its relatively detailed recording of individual migration histories.

As a result of several Rwandan conflicts, including revolution, massacres and exile in the 1960s, followed by civil war, genocide and mass migration in the 1990s, the population of Rwanda has known several waves of refugees seeking refuge in the neighbouring countries. Our data allowed us to distinguish between these groups and analyse the difference in their reproductive behaviour. Of course, fertility and child survival are not only determined by a persons' refugee status but also by a series of exogenous characteristics. We applied multivariate regression analysis in order to control for the effects of these characteristics.

From the regressions, a clear pattern emerged that allowed us to shed light on the reproductive behaviour of different waves of refugees. Two groups stand out, meaning that their demographic history is significantly different from the non-refugees. The first group is the so-called new caseload refugees: mostly Rwandan Hutu who had fled the country in mid-1994. From our fertility and child survival analysis we derive that these refugees, at all ages, have given birth to more children than non-refugees. This, together with our results showing significantly higher mortality of children of this group of refugees, is in line with the risk-insurance theory of reproductive behaviour: given high excess mortality during their stay in the refugee camps in Eastern Congo, the refugees compensate the loss of children by having more children. The result for the refugee category stands, even after controlling for the speed of childbearing, which has by itself an independent negative effect on child survival.

Furthermore, for the same group of refugees, the analysis of child survival shows that girls suffered more than boys from the crisis conditions refugee mothers were living in: the survival chances of daughters of refugee mothers were significantly lower than the survival chances of daughters of mothers who did not have to flee. There was no such difference for boys. This suggests that parents may have been investing more in new-born boys than in girls, possibly in order to insure that at least one son would survive. This could be an effect of paternal inheritance rights, especially the inheritance of land. Until 1994, women and daughters could not inherit land, though exceptions were made in special circumstances.

Note that the data did not allow us to test directly for intra-household allocation of resources and thus for a possible sex discrimination during crisis. However, the negative and statistically significant effect for daughters is also visible in the analysis of child survival for mothers who sought short-term (less than six months) shelter from violence. The estimated effect is smaller than the effect for the long-term refugees, but its significance in relation to the reference group of non-refugees offers additional support for our interpretation.

Mothers in the fifth group, who have not resided in Rwanda before the genocide, form a second interesting group with features that are significantly different from women who never migrated. We recall that we did not consider this group as refugees. These women had more children and lost fewer of them than the women in the reference group. This applies to boys as well as to girls. At first sight, the risk-insurance explanation for reproductive behaviour does not seem to apply to this group: they have more children even if fewer of them die. In contrast to this intriguing result, the old caseload refugees are not significantly different from the reference group of non-migrants. Neither fertility nor child survival do stand out in this group. These old caseload refugees were mostly Rwandan Tutsi who fled Rwanda between 1955 and 1990. Apparently, they took with them the reproductive behaviour that they had known, seen or experienced in Rwanda long before they came back.

It seems to us that the women who came to Rwanda for the first time only after the genocide, i.e. the daughters of the old caseload refugees, followed the same fertility strategy as their mothers. Yet, they eventually came to live under less adverse conditions. As a result, they had somewhat higher fecundity and natural fertility. At the same time and for the same reason, they were able to keep more of their offspring alive than they had expected.

Acknowledgement

The authors thank Evert van Imhoff (†July 2004), Gijs Beets and the two guest editors of this special edition of the European Journal of Population, Ewa Tabeau and Helge Brunborg, for their extensive, thoughtful and very useful comments on an earlier version of this article. The authors only are responsible for the views expressed in this article. None of its content can be attributed to the institutions where the authors are affiliated with.

Note

[1] Other scholars, such as Prunier (1995), put the death toll between 500,000 and 800,000.

References

Al-Qudsi, S. S., 2000. 'Profiles of refugee and non-refugee Palestinians from the West Bank and Gaza', *International Migration* 38(4): 79–107.

Chrétien, J. P., 2000. *Afrique des Grands lacs: deux mille am d'hisloire.* Aubier, Paris.

Clay, D. and Johnson, N., 1992. 'Size of farm or size of family: which comes first?', *Population Studies* 46(3): 491–505.

Clay, D. and Vander Haar, J., 1993. 'Patterns of intergenerational support and childbearing in the third world', *Population Studies* 47(1): 67–83.

Danish Epidemiology Science Centre, 1999. 'Nutritional status and mortality of refugee and resident children in a non-camp setting during conflict: follow-up study in Guinea-Bissau', *British Medical Journal* 319(7214), 878–881.

De Lame, D., 1996. *Une colline entre mille ou ee calme avant la tempête, transformations et blocages du Rwanda rural.* Tervuren: Musée Royale de l'Afrique Centrale.

Des Forges, A., 1999. *Leave None to Tell the Story.* Human Rights Watch, New York.

Goma Epidemiology Group, 1995. 'Public health impact of Rwandan refugee crisis: what happened in Goma Zaire, in July 1994?', *The Lancet* 345(8946): 339–344.

Hynes, M., Sheik, M., Wilson, H. and Spiegel, H., 2002. 'Reproductive health indicators and outcomes among refugees and internally displaced persons in post-emergency phase camps', *Journal of the American Medical Association, August* 288(5): 595–603.

Khawaja, M., 2004. 'The extraordinary decline of infant and childhood mortality among Palestinian refugees', *Social Science and Medicine* 58, 463–470.

Lindstrom, D. P. and Berhanu, B., 1999. 'The impact of war, famine, and economic decline on marital fertility in Ethiopia', *Demography* 36, 247–261.

Long, J. S., 1997. '*Regression Models for Categorical and Limited Dependent Variables*'. Advanced Quantitative Techniques in the Social Sciences 7, London: Sage.

May, J. F., Mukamanzi, M. and Vekemans, M., 1990. 'Family planning in Rwanda: status and prospects', *Studies in Family Planning* 21(1): 20–32.

Mbago, M. C., 1994. 'Some correlates of child mortality in the refugee populated regions in Tanzania', *Journal of Biosocial Science* October 26(4): 451–467.

McCullagh, P. and Nelder, J. A., 1989. *Generalized Linear Models.* Chapman and Hall, New York.

McGinn, Th., 2000. 'Reproductive Health of War-Affected Populations: What Do We Know?', *International Family Planning Perspectives* 26(4): 174–180.

Médecins sans frontières, 2003. 'Mortality among displaced former UNITA members and their families in Angola: a retrospective cluster survey', *British Medical Journal* 327(7416): 650–660.

Ministry of Finance of Rwanda, 2002. *A Profile of Poverty in Rwanda, an Analysis Based on the Results of the Household Living Conditions Survey.* Kigali: Ministry of Finance and Economic Planning, Republic of Rwanda.

Newbury, C., 1988. *The Cohesion of Oppression: Clientship and Ethnicity in Rwanda, 1860–1960.* Columbia University Press, New York.

Nugent, J. B., 1985. 'The old-age security motive for fertility', *Population and Development Review* 11, 75–97.

Pedan, A., 2001. 'Analysis of count data using the SAS system'. The 26th Annual SAS Users Group International Conference, Paper 247–26. Long Beach, California, 22–25 April 2001.

Pinnelli, A. and Mancini, P., 1997. 'Gender mortality differences from birth to puberty', in C. A. Corsini and P. Viazzo (eds), *The Decline of Infant and Child Mortality—The European Experience: 1750–1990.* Netherlands: Martinus Nijhoff: Dordrecht.

Prunier, G., 1995. *The Rwanda Crisis, History of a Genocide.* University of Columbia Press, New York.

Reher, D., 1999. 'Back to basics: mortality and fertility interactions during the demographic transition', *Continuity and Change* 14, 9–31.

Reyntjens, F., 1994. *L'Afrique des Grands Lacs en crise.* L' Harmattan, Paris.

Sachs, L., 1997. 'Safe motherhood in refugee settings', *African Health* May 19(4): 24–25.

UN OCHA, 1998. *Guiding Principles on Internal Displacement.* United Nations Office for the Coordination of Humanitarian Affairs, Geneva.

Verwimp, P., 2003. *Development and Genocide in Rwanda: a Political Economy Analysis of Peasants and Power under the Habyarimana Regime.* Economics Department, Catholic University of Leuven, Leuven (Doctoral Dissertation).

Weeks, J. R., Rumbaut, R. G., Brindis, C., Korenbrot, C. C. and Minkler, D., 1989. 'High fertility among Indochinese refugees', *Public Health Report.* March–April 104(2): 143–150.

Wooldridge, J. M., 2003. *Introductory Econometrics. A Modern Approach.* Thomson/South-Western, Mason (Ohio).

Yusuf, F., 1990. 'Size and socio-demographic characteristics of the Afghan refugee population in Pakistan', *Journal of Biosocial Science* July 22(3): 269–279.

Sources

Demographic and Health Survey, 1992, National Office of Population, Kigali, Rwanda.

Demographic and Health Survey, 2000, National Office of Population, Kigali, Rwanda.

Enquête Intégrale des Conditions de Vie (EICV), 1999–2001, Statistics Department, Ministry of Finance, Kigali, Rwanda.

CHAPTER 16. THE DEMOGRAPHIC CONSEQUENCES OF CONFLICT, EXILE AND REPATRIATION: A CASE STUDY OF MALIAN TUAREG

SARA RANDALL
Department of Anthropology, University College London, United Kingdom

Abstract. A framework outlining the potential impacts of conflict on demographic behaviour is used to analyse the post-conflict demography of Malian Tuareg after substantial conflictinduced social, political and economic changes. A remarkable stability in both fertility and marriage leads to the conclusion that an important demographic consequence of persecution and conflict may be an entrenchment of demographic behaviour which reinforces the population's demographic identity particularly with respect to reproduction. The importance of unique historical, political and cultural experiences of a population in responding to conflict precludes the development of a 'demography of conflict', suggesting we should be pursuing the 'demography of conflicts'.

1. Introduction

'The demography of conflict' conjours up the human costs in terms of deaths on battlefields or in bombed out cities. Looking beyond the immediate mortality costs of conflict there are myriad other short term demographic consequences: forced and voluntary migration; increased mortality through destruction of health and sanitary infrastructure; decreased fertility as a result of spousal separation or psychological stress. Indeed it is hard to delimit where the demographic consequences of conflict stop, since conflict reconfigures the social and political landscape as well as generating economic deprivation; subsequent social change will be associated with changing demographic behaviour in all spheres of demography: fertility, mortality, migration and nuptiality and subsequent intergenerational echoes in the age-sex structure.

Conflict is part of the human condition and therefore should be integral to all analysis and interpretation of demographic behaviour. Yet it is possible to focus in on particular situations and events in order to establish more specific conflict-induced demographic responses with the aim of developing our theoretical understanding of the particular role of conflict in shaping demography. Immediate consequences of conflict (deaths, migration, births averted) may be difficult to measure because of social disorder and priorities for humanitarian relief rather than data collection and although we should recognise that such consequences represent a huge human cost, ultimately they may be of less intrinsic importance to an understanding of the demography of conflict than the medium to long term changes that conflict

This chapter was previously published in *European Journal of Population*, vol. 21, no. 2–3, 2005, pp. 291–320.

Helge Brunborg et al. (eds.), The Demography of Armed Conflict, 367–395.

generates in the surviving population because the latter forms the basis for the emergent society with its population dynamics.

Few studies have focused on the longer-term impact of conflict on demographic dynamics in contemporary developing countries—although much demographic research has been undertaken in populations involved in or recently emerged from conflicts (many Demographic and Health Surveys) where demography is inevitably shaped by not only the conflict but post-conflict political and economic reconstruction. Agadjanian and Prata's (2002) analysis of Angolan fertility is an exception in their use of time periods and regions which are likely to have experienced different intensity of conflict. Contrary to their expectations, the capital Luanda, which had least direct experience of conflict, had the strongest fertility response. This could be interpreted two ways—that "advanced urbanisation made residents more responsive to changes . . . and at the same time better able to control their fertility" (p. 227), the other being that the fertility decline in Luanda was largely unrelated to the conflict. Lindstrom and Berhanu's (1999) analysis of Ethiopian data also focuses on probability of births in particular time periods known to have had intense conflict. Such periods also tended to be times of drought and it is hard to separate the two but there seems to be a fertility depressing effect of conflict. More long-term consequences are not considered although they consider whether "the experience of fertility limitation under the duress of political and economic crises may have increased couples' awareness of the real and opportunity costs associated with each additional child and the benefits of reduced fertility" and thus have contributed to subsequent fertility decline. On the other hand one could equally well anticipate a pronatalist response, with children perceived not as costs but as longer term security as well as being increasingly vulnerable to death. Such pronatalist responses to conflict are particularly evident for Palestinians whose fertility is substantially higher than would be expected from their level of socio-economic development (Courbage, 1995, 1999; Khawaja, 2000, 2003; Pedersen, Randall and Khawaja, 2001; DellaPergola, 2001).

Neither of the above African studies considers the impact of conflict on nuptiality, which is unfortunate since, in low contraceptive prevalence communities—such as most conflict-affected populations in Africa—nuptiality is the major determinant of fertility differentials, the primary arena for reproductive decision making and far more pertinent to the fertility of disenfranchised rural populations than contraceptive use, showing remarkable elasticity (Chojnacka, 1995). Nuptiality responses to conflict are critical not only for their impacts on fertility but because marriage remains the principal forum for recruitment to and reproduction of the social group. Conflict frequently threatens specific social groups. Disruptions to or substantial changes in patterns of couple formation are indicative of both individual and community psychological responses to the perceived or real threats to the group. These could take the form of positive attitudes to population reconstruction and rebuilding; retrenchment towards marriage behaviours which reinforce a specific ethnic or lineage identity through endogamy and consanguinity; expansion of marital networks in order to maximise strategic alliances in case of future conflicts. The potential for nuptiality responses to conflict may be ultimately more far-reaching than those of mortality or fertility, because they have not only demographic consequences but also profound cultural and political meanings.

2. A framework for conceptualising demographic consequences of conflict

A framework developed for conceptualising the impacts of forced migration on fertility (Randall 2004) can be expanded to include both mortality and nuptiality and the wider connotations of conflict (Figure 1). This framework considers the demographic consequences of conflict in different stages, each building upon and reacting both with pre-conflict demographic regimes and different groups' perceptions of their own demographic dynamics and those of neighbouring populations. The different forces will vary in importance as the phases of conflict and post-conflict advance: speculation about the weight of each force on fertility is represented by the thickness of the arrows in Figure 1.

The pre-conflict demographic regime should not be conceptualised as a static state generated by that population's cultural values. For all populations conflict just adds a further element or accelerant of change into a dynamic demographic scenario which could have been relatively stable or changing rapidly in the years preceding the conflict. In a demography of conflict we need to understand how conflict may act as a catalyst to demographic change or have predictable impacts on the particular

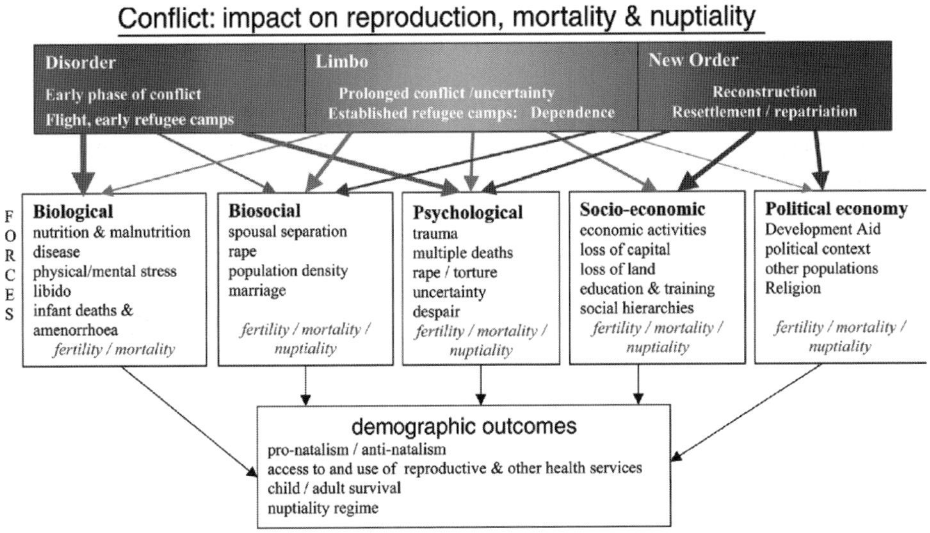

Figure 1. Conceptualisation of phases of forced migration or conflict on demography.

manifestations of demographic change. However, in all cases, long-established cultural values have shaped both the pre-conflict demographic parameters of a population and the potential for change. Religion, class hierarchies, normative gender roles, values, belief systems all contribute to determining observed demographic behaviour of populations and the range of demographic choices for individuals within that population, but ecology, environment, production and the political and economic context are equally important. Neither cultural values nor the other external factors remain constant and conflict is likely to accelerate changes. It is essential not to think of culture as a simple monolithic determinant (Hammel, 1990; Lockwood, 1995; Coast, 2003) while recognising that traditions, norms and accepted values will certainly contribute to the marking of the boundaries of acceptable demographic responses at the individual level. The framework below attempts to disentangle the different components of these boundaries.

Three basic periods of conflict and forced migration can be identified whilst recognising that each specific situation will have its own complexities.

Disorder at the beginning of conflict may include flight or movement, and early responses to a different environment. During *Limbo*, conflict is established, people have learnt how to cope but the future is totally uncertain. Refugees are not yet able to rebuild their lives but immediate acute danger may be past, and for them at least, the basic logistic problems of health-care and sanitation have often been resolved. The same is not true for people who remain in conflict zones in a limbo of uncertainty with productive economic activities often restricted. This phase may be very short or may last for many years. *New Order* is the post-conflict reconstruction of an independent economic life and the re-establishment of social and political order which, for refugees is contingent upon resettlement or repatriation. This is not a return to the past: "the return process is not about going home or back in time to regain something that once existed, it creates an entirely new situation" (Haug, 2002: 71) and this is as true for demography as for social, political and economic relations.

In each phase of conflict, demography will be influenced by many voluntary and involuntary forces which can be grouped broadly into five categories (Figure 1) each of which will have a different degree of importance in terms of impact on pre-crisis demographic norms.[1] During *Disorder* biological impacts will often resemble those in famine situations: nutritional crisis, disease, stress, loss of libido, infant deaths and curtailed breast-feeding (Ashton et al., 1984; Watkins and Menken, 1985; Dyson, 1991; National Research Council, 2004). Biosocial impacts on fertility and nuptiality will be a consequence of spousal separation or lack of privacy; the risk of rape may be important. Individual level psychological factors may have a major impact at this stage.

In *Limbo* all five forces operate with different intensities and outcomes according to the particularities of the situation; biosocial and psychological factors usually being more important than biological or those of the political economy. The latter, along with socio-economic impacts, generally dominate fertility and nuptiality in the *New Order.* All impacts on fertility in each of the phases will operate through the proximate determinants but in terms of conceptualising the specific impact of conflict it is essential to consider the specific modifying forces in each situation.

Using this framework I will analyse the particular case of the Kel Tamasheq in western Mali to show the importance of community history, past experiences and pre-conflict relationships with other populations for understanding the trajectory of post-conflict demographic responses. It will become clear that one cannot just consider 'the demography of conflict'. Every conflict-affected population will interpret the causes and consequences of conflicts according to their prior experience and will respond accordingly, usually within the culturally accepted range of possibilities. Each population will be subject to unique conflict-generated socio-economic changes which are predicated upon the pre-conflict social organisation, political context and international responses to the conflict. It will be shown how conventional demographic understanding of both mortality and fertility transitions may need to be reconsidered in both the immediate and longer-term post-conflict reconstruction.

3. Background

Kel[2] Tamasheq live across Northern Mali, southern Algeria, Niger and northern Burkina Faso and most used to be archetypal nomadic pastoralists, herding goats, sheep, cattle and camels according to the local environment. Two populations were studied in 1981 and 1982 (Randall, 1984, 1996) when western Kel Tamasheq spent the dry season using pastures in the inner Niger delta (see map), leaving in the wet season to move north and west into drier areas. This transhumance pattern was itself relatively recent with the Kel Tamasheq first entering the delta in substantial numbers after the 1913 drought, a movement that frequently engendered local conflicts between different groups.[3] The surveyed populations were all nomadic pastoralists practising no agriculture and were socially heterogeneous with representatives of all the different Tamasheq social classes; warriors, religious groups, vassals, lower status groups, blacksmiths, and Bella—slaves and ex-slaves.[4]

In contemporary Mali 'Tuareg' refers to the warriors, religious groups and vassals descended from Berbers and Arabs who crossed the Sahara in the 15th and 16th centuries (although originally 'Tuareg' just referred to the warrior minority). Tamasheq is a Berber language and physically most of these higher status Kel Tamasheq are light skinned Berbers and are variously referred to both by themselves and other Malians as red (*rouges*).[5] Like in many West African communities, slavery was a well established institution in pre-colonial times and most Kel Tamasheq slaves were originally captured in raids on sedentary farming communities. Bella are black African and although all speak Tamasheq, they clearly have different genetic origins to the Berber Tuareg. Many Bella were liberated in the colonial period and after independence, although de facto ownership of slaves still continued at the time of the 1981–1982 surveys with many Tuareg having resident Bella to do most domestic and herding work. The 1981–1982 surveys included both dependent and long-freed independent Bella.

The 1980s surveys showed the Kel Tamasheq to be demographically unusual for sub-Saharan African populations. Heterogeneity in terms of production, environment and social organisation within the Malian Kel Tamasheq population means that we cannot generalise about their demography—but some of the specificities almost certainly apply elsewhere.[6] The demographic regime was typified by low(ish) fertility,[7] largely a function of the monogamous nuptiality regime with frequent divorce and substantial spousal age differences, and unusual patterns of mortality differentials. Higher status (and usually wealthier) Tuareg children had much higher mortality than lower status blacksmith and Bella children (Hill and Randall, 1984; Randall, 1984). Tuareg women had higher mortality than Bella women but the opposite was the case for adult men. Although extra-marital childbearing was more acceptable for Bella, overall their total fertility was similar to that of the Tuareg (Randall and Winter, 1985).

Culturally determined gender roles had a major impact on the demographic regime (Randall, 1984; Fulton and Randall, 1988). In this region Tuareg women were expected to do little or no work except making and repairing the leather tents. This was possible because of the existence of the dependent slave population. Class based differences in behaviour were reinforced by force feeding rich high status girls and young women and their subsequent obesity limited physical activity. Most Tuareg women were expensive to maintain—often contributing little to the household economy, housework and even childcare.[8] In the total absence of access to effective health services, childcare patterns were partially responsible for differential mortality between social classes (Randall 1984; Hill and Randall, 1984).

Nevertheless, there was substantial diversity over both time and space. The extent of both force-feeding and slavery had been declining for at least two decades before the 1981–1982 demographic surveys but in the populations studied they were still quite frequent. Elsewhere in Mali, Kel Tamasheq had become less nomadic as a consequence of herd loss in the 1973 drought and the domestic slave population had declined, with Bella moving to urban areas, becoming independent herders or turning to agriculture. In the 1980s there was a small urban minority of educated Kel Tamasheq, but in both the populations studied everyone was nomadic, few had been to modern school and there was little contact with health services. Most people lived in relatively small isolated camps (20–50 people) and although men had contact with the outside world through travel and markets, most women led very socially restricted lives.

The 1984–1985 drought led to substantial herd losses, population movements, food aid and a mushrooming of international and local Non Governmental Organisations (NGO). Dependent Bella left their owners who could no longer afford to support them, people moved temporarily to the towns and some groups started to sedentarise (Randall and Giuffrida, in press). Those who remained nomadic became less isolated, with increased knowledge about the outside world and contact with development projects.

3.1. CONFLICT

In 1990 rebellion first broke out in Niger and was followed by a Tuareg attack in east Mali. Thereafter small bands of armed Tuareg attacked military and administrative posts—sometimes killing the incumbents, usually stealing vehicles. The MPLA (Mouvement Populaire pour la Libération de l'Azawad) was created with the aim of liberating Tuareg territories in the north. The Malian Army responded at first by patrolling the areas and then clashed with the rebels. Despite negotiations mediated by the Algerians, the rebel attacks increased in intensity throughout early 1991 and gradually expanded westwards towards Tombouctou and the Mema (see map). As the rebel attacks increased so did those of the Malian army on the Tuareg and Maures with men, women and children being killed in camps, villages and towns. The Malian population became incited against the 'reds' and there were attacks and raids on shops owned by Tuareg and Maures throughout northern and central Mali. Skin colour and physical appearance was a major factor identifying those who were attacked and after the '*massacre de Lere*' in May 1991, Tuareg in the Delta and Mema areas fled en masse to Mauritania[9] (elsewhere people fled to Algeria, Niger and Burkina Faso), just across the border. Some took their herds and tried to

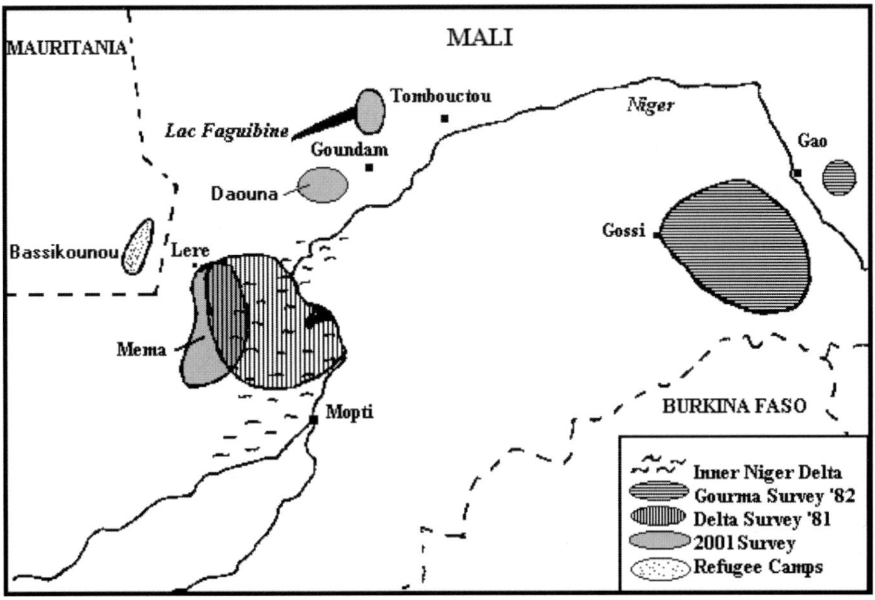

Map. Mali and Mauritania detailing survey sites and refugee camps.

continue their mobile pastoralism in Mauritania—facing major problems of access to water and wells. Others left everything behind or consumed most of their animals during the flight.

UNHCR (United Nations High Commission for Refugees), WFP (World Food Programme) and NGOs responded rapidly to the huge influx of people and three refugee camps were set up. Conditions were poor at first because of the scale of the crisis and the isolation of the area. People continued to flood into the refugee camps through 1991–1993 and into 1994. The majority stayed until 1996, having spent 4 or 5 years there, although spontaneous repatriations occurred throughout the period. Nevertheless the main waves into the Mauritanian refugee camps were in 1991–1992 and the main wave out was in 1996 under a repatriation programme run by UNHCR and GTZ (Deutsche Gesellschaft für Technische Zusammenarbeit) after the signing of various peace agreements. Although the majority of camp residents had previously been nomadic pastoralists, there were also people who had sedentarised after the 1985 drought, along with civil servants, teachers, traders, craftsmen and students. A few domestic Bella fled with their masters but black Tamasheq were not persecuted and many stayed in Mali, some with the animals, some leaving the pastoral sector altogether. Many changes were experienced by former nomadic pastoralists in the refugee camps: forced immobility with large numbers of people with heterogeneous former experiences; rudimentary health care provision developed into immunisation programmes, free health and maternity care; boreholes provided clean tap water in contrast to previous experience of river and marsh water; young people enjoyed a more varied and active social life. In later years schools were set up in the refugee camps and some women received training to facilitate economic independence after repatriation.

Repatriation compounded changes to life-style. Part of the reconciliation and repatriation package developed by the Malian government with UNHCR and other international organisations (République du Mali, 1995) included promises to build schools, drill boreholes and develop infrastructure in the refugees' destinations as well as in other northern communities. For repatriated refugees infrastructure was to be proportional to the population registered in a specific site. This encouraged sedentarisation and has led to a proliferation of wells surrounded by small settlements (Randall and Giuffrida, in press). People with few or no animals no longer needed to be nomadic and many of those who retained animals claim to have seen the physical benefits of a sedentary lifestyle although there are also clear political aspects (see section 4.2.1) to this transformation.

Thus in 2001, four years after repatriation, much of the population is sedentary, fewer are totally dependent on a pastoral economy, unpaid domestic labour is rarely available and Tuareg women are thinner and more active. Formal education and modern health care are more acceptable and available and good quality water is usually close by. The population is highly politicised and feels vulnerable about being physically conspicuous in Mali with many believing there could be future violence against them.

3.2. DEMOGRAPHIC ASPECTS OF THE CONFLICT

Although it would be fallacious to think that this conflict was underpinned by demographic causes, past migrations, population dynamics and spatial distribution of populations certainly contributed to some of the underlying tensions. Tuareg and Maures had migrated southwards across the Sahara in previous centuries and their racial distinctness combined with traditions of raids and slave capture among the black African cultivating populations mean that there is a culture of racially determined suspicion. This is exacerbated by the fact that many Tuareg persist in denigrating black Malians with what they see as slave-like qualities—stupidity, ugliness, inferiority. In the early 1980s two Tuareg women expressed total incomprehension about how a black government could possibly be capable of running a country and they mourned the passing of the French (although the archives testify to substantial Franco-Tamasheq conflict). According to Berge (1993) ". . . many Tuaregs however now feel that the Malian government rather than France, is the main cause of their troubles". This racial prejudice was more at a population level than between individuals. Many Tuareg men had excellent individual reciprocal relationships with Songhay and Peul whom they encountered over negotiations about pastures and in the market. These relationships were essential for survival in the zone. Marty (1999) explains how in pre-colonial and colonial times the only way the hugely variable Sahelian environment could be effectively exploited was through the co-existence of populations with economic specialisations appropriate to different ecological niches who could exchange goods, produce and services. Marty makes the point that in the early 20th century the French tried to sever the mutually beneficial economic, social and political links between the sedentary and the nomadic populations who had long evolved an effective (although not conflict-free) co-existence and interdependence. Nevertheless distrust of the 'other' was always present and this flared up in 1990 once the conflict between the army and the rebels was established. From the Tuareg perspective, an element of this distrust was an ever-present perception that they were a demographic minority who had never had their fair share of political, administrative and military power and that they were constantly discriminated against by the Malian government. They also believed (correctly) that the black populations were growing faster than they were because of higher fertility and lower mortality. It is unclear to what extent this perception arose out of intellectual Tuareg reading the colonial archives[10]—which consistently portrayed Tuareg as a declining population with very low fertility—and to what degree it was an accurate observation of the polygamous Songhay, Bambara and Peul populations maintaining most reproductive age women continuously married and reproducing.

Over recent decades, driven by population growth and by drought induced economic transformation, the expansion of agriculture along the banks of the Niger and into areas which were previously dry season pastures is very evident. In the increased competition for natural resources, especially water and productive land, mobile pastoralist groups have lost out. One of the original aims of the rebellion was a separate land for the Tuareg which may have been as much a plea for inalienable land rights as one for political autonomy.

These demographic undertones to the conflict are particularly relevant to understanding some of the demographic repercussions and responses but contemporary Tamasheq demography cannot just be interpreted in the light of the conflict which this population has endured. This study was undertaken nearly ten years after the start of the conflict and over 4 years after repatriation. In these ten years Mali underwent democratisation and decentralisation which have serious implications both for demographic outcomes but also for deliberate manipulation of demographic behaviour.

4. This study

4.1. DATA

In both 1981 and 2001 demographic data were collected using a single round retrospective survey and birth histories for women (Table 1). In 2001 marriage histories were also collected for women aged 12–55 and for present men. For absent and elderly women summary data were collected on numbers of living and dead children.[11] In 1981 we attempted a total enumeration of the Tamasheq population who spent the dry season in and on the periphery of the Niger inland delta (see map). By 2001 most of this population no longer transhumed into the delta and the aim was to enumerate all the Tamasheq population living in or transhuming around the

Table 1. Population characteristics 1981, 2001

	1981	2001
De jure population	6,125	8,270
Sex ratio	0.98	1.04
Tuareg (red)	1.07	1.06
Bella and blacksmiths (black)	0.88	0.96
Individual interviews	*All women 15–50*	*Ever married women 12–55*
	1289 interviews done	1313 interviews done[a]
	89% eligible women	79.1% eligible women
		Ever married men
		739 interviews
		54.7% eligible
Percentage Tuareg	53%	76.5%

[a] + 23 interviews with women over 55.
Source: Demographic surveys 1981, 2001.

sites[12] to the west of the delta (the Mema) where most of the groups enumerated in 1981 were known to live. In 2001 we also enumerated both sedentary and nomadic communities in the Daouna further north, some of whom had previously transhumed in the delta, and some communities north of Goundam which included nomadic groups who had not fled during the rebellion. A linked anthropological study into the demographic consequences of the rebellion was undertaken in these northern communities.

4.2. FERTILITY

A population level comparison of parity and age-specific fertility shows little change over the last twenty years (Figures 2 and 3). This is a population where age reporting is poor and where surveys encounter substantial suspicion. The anomalies can largely be explained by reporting problems such as the deficit of children for older women in 1981 and the outliers for older cohorts (Figure 3).

This stability is remarkable when one considers all the crises that this population has endured: drought, forced migration, repatriation; economic transformation from nomadic pastoralism to semi-sedentary living in a more diverse economy; for rich families the quasi-total loss of unpaid domestic labour and a general impoverishment of a substantial majority of the population alongside substantial declines in child mortality (see section 4.4).

This stability in the face of conflict suggests that fertility responses to crisis are not homogenous. Conflict may engender very different responses to an economic slump. In urban West Africa, faced with major economic problems, fertility has fallen rapidly, largely through postponement of marriage (Antoine and Djire, 1998), yet this rural Tamasheq population which has faced more intense economic,

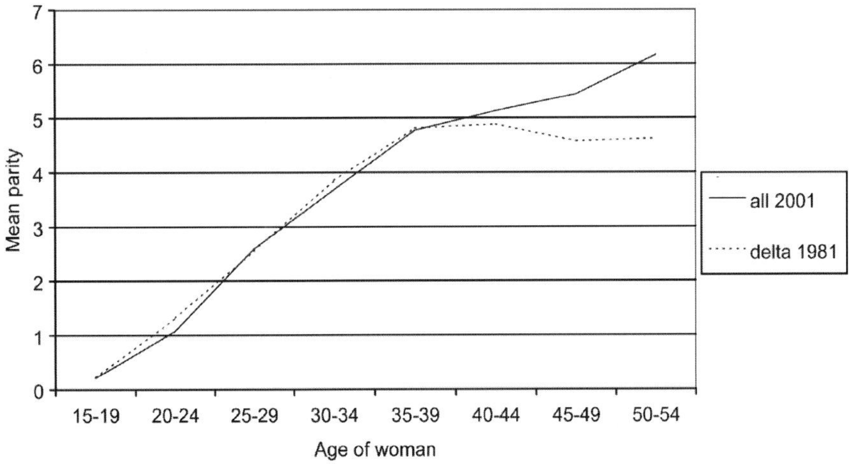

Figure 2. Tamasheq parity by age 1981, 2001.

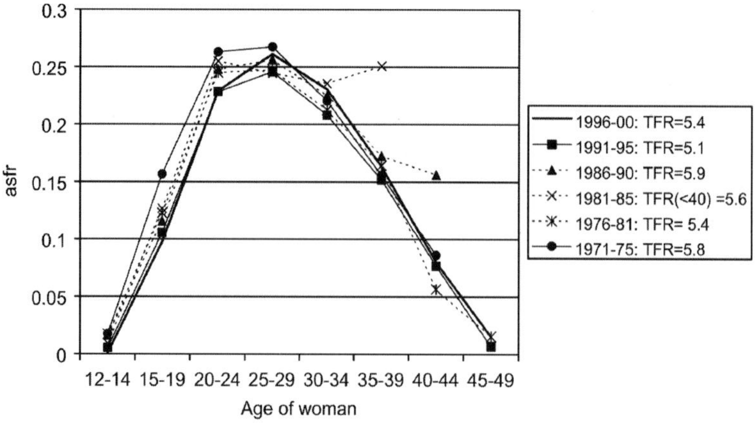

Figure 3. Age specific fertility rates (asfr) by period: Total population using 2001 and 1981 data.

social and political crisis responds not by fertility decline but by stability. The general consensus is that fertility transition is stimulated by some (although not necessarily all) of modernisation, education, a move away from subsistence production, exposure to mass media, declining infant and child mortality (Bulatao and Casterline, 2001). All these have occurred in these Tamasheq populations over the last few years, although the starting point was so low that the enormous social and economic transformations may only be visible to those who knew this population twenty years ago.

In fact, the low level of socio-economic development coupled with the substantial social change gave good reason to anticipate an increase in fertility. In 1981 total fertility was around 5.5, total marital fertility around 10. Fertility was low compared to the rest of rural Mali largely because of the marriage regime (see below)—although there was some evidence of slightly raised levels of primary and secondary infertility and subfertility (Randall, 1996). Although Muslim, most Kel Tamasheq are monogamous in a country where other populations are highly polygamous: 42.6% of Malian women were in polygamous unions, rising to over 50% for women over 35 (République du Mali, 2001: Table 6.2), whereas only 0.5% Tuareg women and 5.5% Bella women were in polygamous unions. There are substantial spousal age differences (median 10 years) and a general inclination to divorce with no stigma attached. These characteristics, alongside young female age at first marriage and high male adult mortality mean that a substantial proportion of reproductive aged women are unmarried at any one time (Randall, 1984; Randall and Winter, 1985; Fulton and Randall, 1988; Randall and Giuffrida, 2003), reducing fertility significantly. Yet two simple changes in the marriage dynamics would allow a substantial increase in proportions of reproductive aged women married and thus in fertility: a reduction in male age at first marriage (Singulate Mean Age at Marriage (SMAM) 1981 = 28.1, 2001 = 29.4) or the adoption of polygamy. The first would increase the supply of potential husbands and the second is religiously acceptable because they are Muslims and polygamy is ubiquitous in surrounding populations. Tuareg men do attempt polygamy from time to time, but with the exception of one lineage where it is said to be acceptable, and where three cases of polygamy were observed during fieldwork, few men attempt it and even fewer women accept it.

4.2.1. *Expectations of conflict induced fertility change*

Using my framework it becomes clear that there are many reasons why one might expect conflict-induced increases in Tamasheq fertility in the *New Order* phase.

Biological and biosocial factors. These will have most impact on fertility in the *Disorder* and *Limbo* phases of conflict (see Randall, 2004) rather than post-conflict.

Psychological factors. Psychological impacts must be considered at both the individual and the group level, although at times it may be hard to distinguish between the two with individual responses conditioned by group attitudes. The Tuareg studied in 1981–1982 believed themselves to be a minority who were being outpaced demographically by other (black) Malian populations.[13] The conflict, with its racial overtones and forced migration reinforced this self-perceived vulnerability. The period spent in the refugee camps allowed for plenty of exchanges between traditional rural pastoralists, modern, educated 'intellectuals' and young radical rebels and time to reflect on the Tuareg position vis à vis Mali (and Mauritania). The exile occurred simultaneously with the world-wide popularisation of fundamentalist Islam. Improved communications and contacts with the many former migrants to Libya, Algeria and Saudi Arabia certainly facilitated the spread of some fundamentalist Muslim ideas including that a good Muslim has many children to increase the Muslim population, and that God will provide for all. The melting-pot in Mauritania of intellectuals, nomads, religious leaders and returned migrants combined with militant rebels campaigning for a separate Tuareg state, was almost certainly a fertile discussion-ground for a development of pronatalist attitudes. Yet in the anthropological study, such pronatalism was really only expressed by a few intellectuals and not the mass of refugees. Many men and women believe that it is a sin to control fertility within marriage[14] and some women clearly felt a personal conflict of interest, being personally terrified of childbirth through observations of horrendous maternal deaths[15] and not wanting too many children yet believing that fertility control was *haram* (forbidden), but this is just the traditional interpretation of Islam and unrelated to the conflict. Thus, there were many reasons why leaders might take a determined pronatalist stance, but other than that associated with interpretations of Islamic doctrine, such pronatalism does not appear to have materialised in individual behaviour or discourse. On the other hand, in neither the anthropological study nor the demographic data was there any evidence of an anti-natalism consequent upon despair and trauma as documented among some urban Tuareg by Canut and Iskova (1996).

Socio-economic factors. The socio-economic impacts of the conflict were substantial for most rural Kel Tamasheq, continuing the process of herd loss, impoverishment and loss of dependent labour which started in the droughts of the 1970s. In the process of flight many households lost much livestock: abandoned in panic, consumed en route, sold to pay the extortionate price that Mauritanians asked for access to wells. Not all animals were lost. Some people managed to maintain herds outside the refugee camps in Mauritania, some were able to build up herds of small stock through trade and investment in the later days of exile. Some families—especially in the north—never left during the rebellion and maintained their herds and a highly nomadic lifestyle in hidden inaccessible places in the mountains. In general though, it seems there has been a substantial decline in wealth and herd size (although some of the rich have probably become richer). This impoverishment appears to have no impact on reproductive decision-making. Children are not perceived as consumers who must now be fed from a smaller pot. God is seen to be the ultimate provider and within most communities there are poor households partially or totally supported by richer kin. Substantial resources are flowing into the area through NGOs and their associated projects, and although these projects do produce infrastructures, some of the inflowing resources may be converted into assets and cattle for rich people with the right networks. Traditions of kinship support networks remain strong and can mitigate temporary absence of resources. Their very strength motivates people to want children, because children are the basis for future networks and are seen (sons at least) as far more of an asset than a cost.

A further conflict-related motivation for high fertility might have been the final erosion of social hierarchies and dependent (slave) labour. In 1981 there were some dependent (unpaid) Bella in every Tuareg camp surveyed, although there were also independent Bella camps. By 2001 most Bella living in mixed communities were either independent Bella who had chosen to live in there, or paid servants. Most Tuareg women had to do substantially more domestic labour than before and one might imagine that both women and children as sources of labour would be more valued. However, observations in the sedentary sites indicate that many older children (especially boys) have little economic, or other, role to play, with many just hanging about. There are too few animals for them to learn herding and little in the way of other economic activities. Many men also spend much of their time sitting around talking,[16] although herd owners, blacksmiths and those working as masons building the many new houses, work extremely hard. Thus, although conflict-induced diversification of economic activities and the loss of slave labour might have led children to become more desirable for their labour—in fact there is little evidence of this because such diversification is not very evident.

The conflict and exile transformed demand for and participation in education. Schools were set up in the refugee camps and many children attended for one to three years (see the increase in the proportions of younger children declared literate in Table 2). Attitudes to formal education have changed. In the refugee camps those

Table 2. Percentage literate in French by age 1981, 2001

	Women		Men	
Age	1981	2001	1981	2001
10–14	0.3	15.3	0.3	15.3
15–19	0	7.5	0	11.5
20–24	0.3	3.6	2.5	13.2
25–29	0.4	1.5	4.1	2.7
30–34	0	0	0.5	6.5
35–39	0	1.5	1.2	7.3
40–44	0	1.6	1.1	7.5
45–49	0	1.3	2.8	9.3
50–54	0	0	0	6.9
55–59	0	0	1.1	6.0
60–64	0	0	0	1.0
65–69	0	0	0	9.0

Source: Demographic surveys 1981, 2001.

who had any schooling were easily able to get paid employment with the NGOs and UNHCR and education is now seen as one path to employment and future security. Provision is now easier; modern education and a nomadic lifestyle are practically incompatible whereas now that many people are sedentarised and have few animals, education is not competing with traditional animal husbandry training. The repatriation package for larger sites included the construction of schools (Papandiek et al., 1999), some of which have teachers supported by the government and others which are community schools. Many more teachers in local schools are now Tamasheq, some trained in the refugee camps, others attracted by life in a sedentary Tamasheq milieu. Elsewhere in Africa, increased educational participation has driven fertility decline because of the costs to parents, but here the minimal costs of schooling are not yet a brake on fertility with material costs often met by NGOs or rich kin. School attendance remains low by international standards but high compared to 1981.

If a substantial proportion of girls goes through primary school there may be future repercussions for fertility. Only 17 of 1,110 women had ever used modern contraception and only 22 had used traditional methods (4 both). Literacy in French or Arabic was significantly associated with contraceptive use, as was having lived in a town or village; having been a refugee was not. The conflict has transformed Kel Tamasheq socio-spatial distribution. In 1981 the few educated people left the area and pastoralism in order to use their education in appropriate urban occupations. Decentralisation and sedentarisation—both linked to the conflict—have

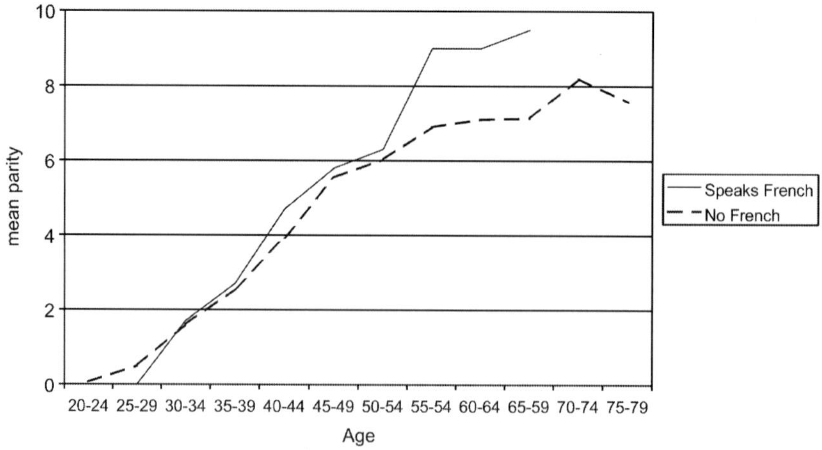

Figure 4. Male parity by age and ability to speak French.

attracted back some educated former urban dwelling men, accompanied by their cosmopolitan wives and daughters (see Table 2 for literate women aged 35–49). They have chosen to be based in the sedentarised communities—where there is now more appropriate employment because of the schools, the NGO projects and the administrative posts in the new decentralised communes. This increased educational heterogeneity may eventually contribute to fertility decline—although comparing parity distributions of French-speaking men (6.9% of over 20s) with non-French speaking suggests not in the near future (Figure 4).

Political economy. The post-conflict political economy has substantial potential for an impact on fertility through pro-natalist agendas. This is particularly the case in Mali where democratisation and decentralisation emerged partly as a consequence of the conflict. Decentralisation and more local financial and development autonomy were a concession to the original demands for a Tuareg state. In practice, the decentralised communes in the North are often tiny because each group wants autonomy; many are likely to be unviable in terms of tax collection, provision of services and in paying the salaries of the elected office holders. Future fertility and population growth is likely to become an issue since all these communes need to attract more people. Again one would expect the changes engendered by the conflict to trigger pro-natalist attitudes but this certainly had not manifested itself in increased fertility by the time of the survey.

Another consequence of the rebellion and the subsequent peace process is the huge amount of development aid being siphoned into the area (Giuffrida and Randall, 2003; République du Mali, 1995). To the outside observer, it is not clear where all these resources are going, but a substantial population with few visible means of support is thriving. In visiting over 50 communities, few obviously malnourished babies or children were observed and although women are no longer seriously obese, many would be classed as overweight in Europe. If, as seems likely, many of these 'development' resources are subsidising the survival of individuals and communities, then this too will influence perceived costs and benefits of reproduction in favour of pronatalism.

Thus in terms of demographic logic and the socio-economic and political changes consequent upon this conflict, one would have expected Tamasheq fertility to increase. Yet there is no evidence for this at all. Does this mean that our predictions were wrong or do other consequences of conflict counteract or inhibit changes in fertility? Given that nuptiality was the major determinant of Tamasheq fertility in 1981, an examination of the dynamics of the marriage regime before, during and since the conflict contribute to our understanding of why conflict crisis may induce different responses to economic crisis.

4.3. NUPTIALITY

Both in 1981 and 2001 Tamasheq were monogamous, with early but variable age at first marriage for women, late male first marriage, high frequency of divorce and widowhood and substantial numbers of currently unmarried women usually living with close male kin; 5–10% women never married. This is very different from the rest of Mali (Figure 5) where most women marry in their teens, polygamy is frequent, marriage is universal and most women are married throughout their reproductive years. The uniqueness of the Tamasheq marriage system is compounded by their very high levels of consanguineous marriage. Most rural Malian populations have marriage preferences for close kin but the Tamasheq encourage all forms of cousin marriage (in contrast to Bambara for whom only cross cousin marriage[17] is acceptable) with half of all first marriages being between first degree cousins or once removed. Parallel patrilateral cousins are preferred spouses but cross cousin and

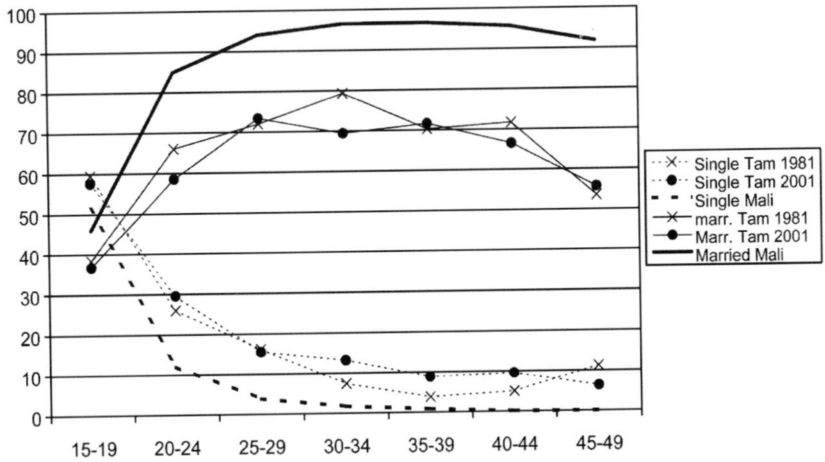

Figure 5. Percentage women currently single and married Tamasheq 1981, 2001, Mali 2001 (DHS).

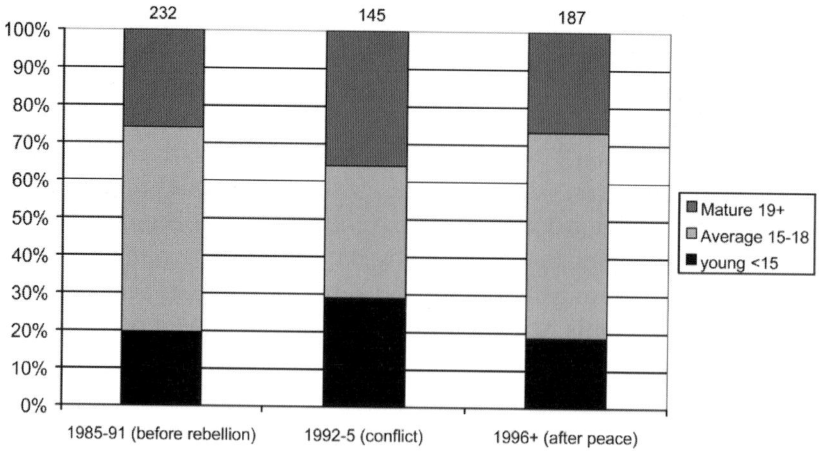

Figure 6. Tuareg women-percentage distribution of age at first marriage by conflict period.

matrilateral parallel cousin marriages are quite frequent. Because of previous consanguineous marriages most spouses can trace their kin links in various different ways.

With the exception of the biological, all the different forces outlined in Figure 1 influence nuptiality in the different phases of conflict. However, it is difficult to disentangle them and consider each discretely because of the complex nature of the influences on and consequences of marriage.

Other than migration, marriage is the demographic behaviour over which people have most control. It can therefore be manipulated in an attempt to secure various ends, some of which may be conflict related. In a situation of conflict, marrying off one's daughters or sisters secures alliances, reinforces bonds and may also increase women's safety, although in this conflict there is no evidence that rape was a problem. During the conflict the proportion of first marriages of very young girls (under 15) and of older women (aged 19+) increased (Figure 6) reverting to the pre-conflict distribution after the end of the conflict.

This marital response could be interpreted as a pronatalist strategy of moving women, who might normally have remained unmarried, into reproductive situations; this might have been the case for the older women. The large numbers of people in the refugee camps allowed for matching of couples who might otherwise have had problems in finding a spouse. It could also have been protection for women. In the refugee camps parents lost much control over their unmarried daughters who attended the frequent marriage celebrations. Accounts of camp life by young unmarried girls show that they had a lot of freedom and enjoyed themselves considerably. Premarital pregnancies are totally unacceptable for Tuareg and one way of protecting daughters is to marry them off. Both of these explanations could account for the increased proportions of young and old marrying. A third possibility is that the conflict and the refugee camps provided both the

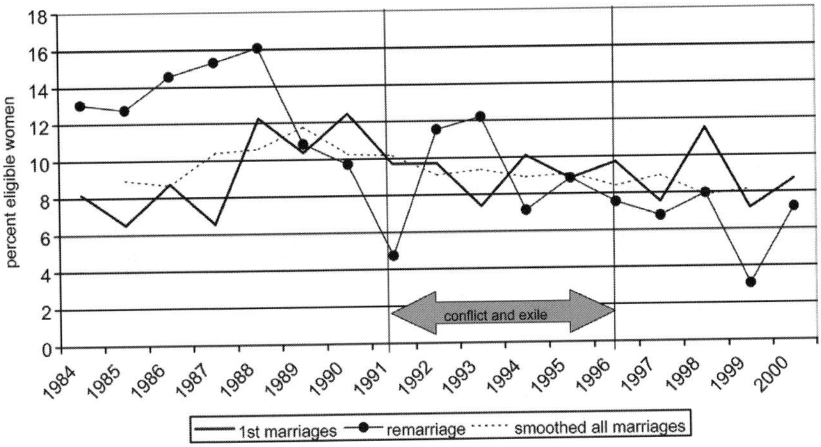

Figure 7. Annual first and remarriage rates: Tuareg.

opportunity and the need to reinforce old alliances and create new ones. Many people commented that in the refugee camps they met kin whom they had known about but had never met before. Marriage has long been a Tamasheq strategy to generate alliances and networks and during the rebellion there was probably more need of these than ever before. However, this would imply an increase in marriage rates during the period of conflict and exile for which we have no evidence (Figure 7). It seems, therefore, that both young girls and older women were married off in the conflict period with a concomitant decline in proportions of women aged 15–18 marrying, but not that there was an excess of marriages in a pronatalist fervour.

An examination of the choice of spouse can also indicate particular priorities in a conflict. From women's marriage histories we have data on the kinship link with husband—recorded using Tamasheq terminology—from which it can be seen that the kinship distance of first spouses remained fairly constant from the pre-conflict, through the conflict and then post conflict (Figure 8).

First marriages are usually organised by parents and the motives may be political alliances, economic networks, a desire or an obligation to please close kin. The couples themselves often have strong expectations of love. Sometimes either or both of the couple do not want the marriage at all but go through with the proceedings to conform to their family's wishes, divorcing a few months later, although many close kin first marriages do succeed (Randall and Giuffrida, 2003). A woman generally has more say in choosing a spouse for second and subsequent marriages but many still prefer to marry close kin. Kinship bonds are seen as being much stronger than marital bonds—therefore the strong love which, for Tuareg, is seen to be inherent between close kin, will contribute to making a marriage strong. A closely related husband cannot mistreat his wife because of the kinship links, and she cannot insult her in-laws because they are also kin. Although substantial bridewealth may be

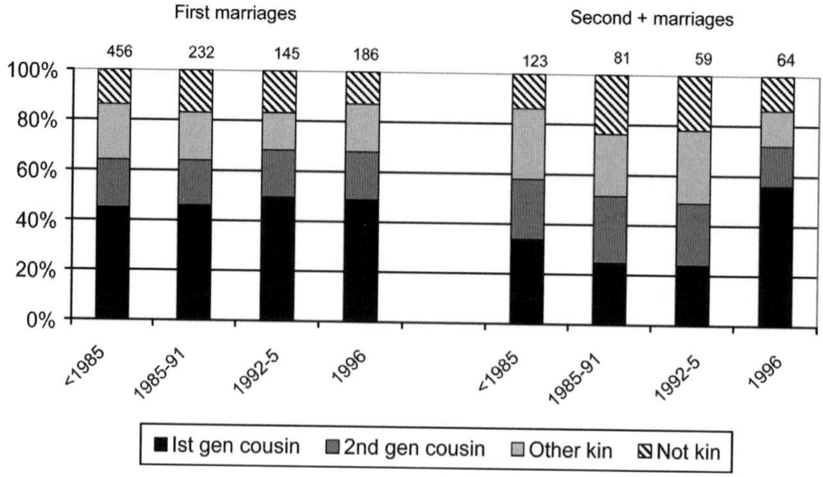

Figure 8. Percent Tuareg marriages by period and kinship distance.

declared for a marriage—either in cash or animals—it seems that, in the case of close kin marriage much of this bridewealth is never actually exchanged.

The pattern of spouse choice for second marriages (Figure 8) has changed considerably since the end of the conflict with a substantial increase in the proportion of close kin marriages. This is clearly a response to the post-conflict situation but from the demographic data we cannot tell whether more second marriages are being arranged as strategic alliances or whether women are choosing close kin in an atmosphere where kin are more certain than somebody more distant. Given that remarriage rates have declined (Figure 7) the decrease may just be an overall reduction in marriages to distant kin and non-relatives with no concomitant increase in close kin. Whatever the case the population appears to be turning inwards.

These marriage patterns can be seen as a particular 'Tuareg' response to this conflict through the maintenance of traditional marriage behaviour reinforcing an identity far apart from 'others' in the conflict. Monogamy is an important identifying characteristic of being Tuareg in Mali and one which can be maintained in the post-conflict era. Consanguineous marriage is frequently used to reinforce links between different *tiwsaten* (the patrilineages), where the *towsit* is another important element of people's identity. People are Tuareg but more importantly they belong to a specific *towsit.* Many other characteristics which contributed to Tuareg identity in the past have had to be or have been largely abandoned: nomadic pastoralism; most of the material culture associated with the tent and pastoral production; fat women who could be admired as expensive objects but who need not do any work; traditional values of hospitality and generosity, undermined by loss of resources and conflict generated suspicion of others; the social hierarchy. Monogamous marriages with close kin are an element that can be retained, that the conflict and social change has been unable to destroy. Such marriages can simultaneously serve a purpose reinforcing alliances, guaranteeing the pedigree of the next generation, demonstrating a solid Tuareg front to the outsiders, and reinforcing links and networks within the society that can provide some security to the impoverished and develop power and influence for certain individuals and groups.

Traditionally in Africa marriage serves political and economic ends, generating or consolidating alliances usually validated through the children born to the couple. Marriage is the means of legitimising reproduction which is an important goal for both men and women and usually the unmarried adult (or the childless adult) is a social anomaly. This is only true of Tuareg marriage to an extent, in a culture where reproduction is rarely given the primordial position that it is in other societies. The importance of the links and networks and obligations created by Tuareg marriages should not be underestimated and may go a long way towards understanding why the conflict seems to have consolidated traditional marital behaviour rather than leading to change. Around 20% marriages are with girls aged 14 or less, few of whom have reached menarche and clearly where immediate reproduction is not the goal (preservation of virginity is not the main aim of these marriages either since virginity is not a particularly sought after virtue in Tuareg society (Nicolaisen, 1997)). These precocious marriages are often quite brief and may even be unconsummated; the girls are not interested in having children, finding such thoughts totally shameful. The motives for these marriages are about the links and obligations they generate at the time, not about future fertility. This reinforces the idea that the stability of Tuareg marriage in the face of this conflict and concomitant socio-economic changes is because marriage is not serving primarily fertility functions, but is reinforcing aspects of Tuareg society and identity which the conflict has made ail the more important to demonstrate to others.

4.4. MORTALITY

The immediate and longer-term impact of conflict on mortality is self-evident and operates largely through biological forces. There were massacres and attacks which resulted in death, and the epidemics and poor conditions in the early days in the refugee camps also resulted in increased infant and child mortality (Randall, 2001). Nevertheless, on the scale of many African conflicts excess deaths were probably not substantial, although that is not to deny the trauma caused by those that did occur and the conditions under which they happened. According to individual biographies, specific attacks and massacres were frequently the trigger for flight into Mauritania. Estimation of the impact of the rebellion on adult mortality is difficult because the indirect methods available make assumptions about time related patterns of mortality, which may not apply in conflict. Direct measures of child mortality from birth histories are more robust and demonstrate the role of biological factors in the *Disorder* phase of conflict (Figure 9) having most impact on infants but also interrupting the mortality decline for children aged 2–5. This ties in with accounts

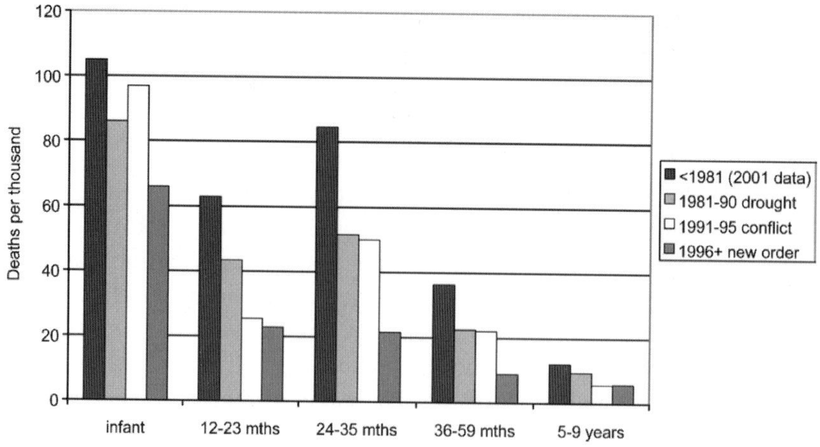

Figure 9. Infant and child mortality from birth histories.

of epidemics at first in the refugee camps followed by the development of free health care and vaccination campaigns.

Ultimately however the social change for which the conflict was a catalyst was largely beneficial in terms of infant and child mortality if one looks at the substantial decline between the 1980s and the late 1990s with child mortality now lower than elsewhere in Mali.[18]

There are several reasons why this should be so, with the biological risks influenced by both socio-economic and political forces. Although many people have lost livestock and become poorer, ironically this has had beneficial consequences for children's health. With fewer livestock, and changing residence patterns most children no longer transhume into the inland Niger delta where they all spent the hot season in the 1970s. The water in the delta was atrocious—marsh and river water—and malaria was a constant problem. Now, in the drier Mema and Daouna where most people now spend most of the year, malaria is less intense, and water quality is improved with wells, boreholes and water pumps, many created as part of the reconciliation and repatriation package (République de Mali, 1995: Papandiek et al., 1999). High status women are now thinner and more active, leading to more continuity of childcare. Observations suggest that children are washed much more frequently than in 1981–1982, and with soap. All the children who had been in the refugee camps were immunised, and at the time of the survey there was a new mobile immunisation campaign. Primary health care workers have been trained in the refugee camps, and although they have little in the way of drugs, people do consult them and are prepared (and able) to travel to health centres if they feel it is necessary because communications and transport are much improved.

Thus the social change caused by the conflict has generally led to changes with positive impacts on infant and child health and mortality, particularly compared to elsewhere in rural Mali (Table 3). However, there is one exception related to

Table 3. Child mortality—Kel Tamasheq and Rural Mali

	Neonatal	${}_{1}q_{0}$[c]	${}_{4}q_{1}$	${}_{5}q_{0}$
Rural Mali 1991–2001[a]	71.0	131.9	139.8	253.2
Kel Tamasheq 1991–2001	50	82	119	166
Kel Tamasheq 1971–81 (1981 data)	(34)[b]	114	165	260

[a] Source République du Mali, 2001 (Table 6.2).
[b] There was substantial underreporting of necnatal deaths in 1981.
[c] ${}_{1}q_{0}$ = probability of dying between birth and first birthday.
${}_{4}q_{1}$ = probability of dying between 1st and 5th birthday.
${}_{5}q_{0}$ = probability of dying between birth and 5th birthday.
Source: Demographic surveys 1981, 2001.

the marriage patterns outlined above. Consanguineous marriages have deleterious health and mortality consequences for the offspring (Bittles. 1994) and Tuareg have extremely high levels of consanguinity. Table 4 shows that children born to closely related parents have higher mortality than those of unrelated parents, although the differences are only statistically significant for the earliest and most recent period and are most marked since repatriation. Given that only about 30% of the couples are in the low risk group, the maintenance of consanguineous marriage strategies will have an important impact on child survival.

The consequences of conflict for Tamasheq child mortality therefore can be summarised as favourably influenced by biological factors with a generally improved physical environment and maternal health, but deleteriously influenced by biosocial factors through increased consanguinity. Socio-economic and political changes are ultimately responsible for the improved physical environment with livestock loss and impoverishment one of many motives for sedentarisation. However NGO and UNHCR policies both in the refugee camps and in the conditions

Table 4. Proportion of children surviving to age 5 by period and relatedness of parents

Period of birth	1st cousin and once removed (1)	2nd/3rd cousin and once removed (2)	Distant kin or unrelated (3)	p (between kin (1 & 2) and not kin) (3)
<1981	0.717	0.702	0.776	0.058
1981–90	0.789	0.787	0.801	not significant
1991–95	0.835	0.815	0.871	not significant
1996+ (to age 3)	0.807	0.871	0.937	$p < 0.0001$

Source: Demographic survey 2001.

for repatriation also contributed to new attitudes towards health services alongside increased provision and access.

4.5. SPATIAL DISTRIBUTION

The most visible demographic impact of the conflict has not been on population dynamics but on the spatial distribution. Although the survey methods are not appropriate for considering this in the same detail as population dynamics, some observations are possible.[19] Whereas in the early 1980s the surveyed Kel Tamasheq were all nomadic pastoralists, living in small flexible camps, now over half the population are semi or permanently settled in fixed communities with houses built of mud bricks. Even the more nomadic households tend to remain close to a site for much of the year to use the well or borehole. Some of this sedentarisation occurred before the conflict as a result of drought but the rate accelerated after repatriation for many reasons—economic, political, and a response to policies of development agencies,[20] and all were directly influenced by the conflict (see Randall and Giuffrida (in press) for detailed discussion) and by the social change generated by the refugee camp period. However, alongside the socio-economic and political changes, sedentarisation, or at least the building of permanent settlements, also has a psychological dimension, which is grounded in the conflict. People are very aware that mobile pastoralists living in tents were somewhat invisible with little evidence that they had ever been in Mali after they had fled. Many likened themselves to birds—when birds have flown away you cannot tell they have ever been there. Fear of future conflicts and a determination to render themselves much more visible is one of the dimensions behind the rapid construction of mudbrick houses—if forced to abandon them in the future there is hard evidence that people lived there. This determination to make their mark upon the landscape may have some grounds in their experience of access to land. In Mali throughout the colonial and Independence periods those who claimed rights over land had to exercise a *'mise en valeur'* which effectively meant cultivating the land. Pastoralists who merely grazed the land had few rights and these had gradually been eroded throughout the 20th century. Building houses in sites is a way of physically demonstrating one's presence and one's use of the land. Many sites have also attempted cultivation—although it is not clear with how much success.

5. Conclusions

Aspects of both sedentarisation and nuptiality can be seen as part of the same range of responses to conflict—attempts to make the Tuareg population visible and readily identifiable in case of future conflicts, so that they are unable to disappear from Mali. The maintenance or even exaggeration of traditional marital behaviour, much of which distinguishes this population from other rural Malian groups, is part of consolidation of group identity as Tuareg. The tendency for conflict and crisis to reinforce interethnic divisions and delimit identities (Marty, 1999) is clearly evident both in the creation of these solid Tuareg communities and in the retention of monogamy, the rejection of polygamy and the frequency of close kin marriage.

How can this case study contribute to a conceptualisation of the demography of conflict? It seems unlikely that one will ever be able to generalise about a demography of conflict, save that in the short term mortality is inevitably going to rise. In order to understand or even predict responses in any situation it is essential to have a historical perspective—conflict does not emerge from nowhere—there are past tensions, past relationships, past conflicts which contribute to the range of responses (Berge, 1993). In the north west Mali tensions between different ethnic groups, between groups using different modes of exploiting the natural resources, were documented in the French archives throughout the twentieth century—although it is true that many of these tensions may have themselves been generated by the French colonial administration (Marty, 1999). The same archives also document substantial conflicts *within* ethnic groups, between different lineages and the groups behind different chiefs. Nevertheless, the tensions between Tuareg and Maures and other ethnic groups were very real by the 1990s and demographic responses to the conflict include attempts to respond to those tensions through reinforcing identity as Tuareg or more usually in terms of the *tiwsaten*—the lineages. One must never forget that fertility is the primary mode of recruitment to most social groups and marriage is the legitimisation of fertility. Thus, when a group feels itself under threat, a frequent response is going to be one where the boundaries between the aggressor and the threatened are clarified, delimited and strengthened—in this case by reinforcing marriage rules and conventions, by constructing communities that are both visible and unambiguously Tuareg, and by consolidating networks between those who are known to be part of the same group.

This account documents the demographic responses of one group to the conflict they experienced. We cannot predict that other conflicts emerging out of different historical situations and with different patterns of power, economic adaptation and disruption and in different environments will respond in similar ways. In Mozambique Lubkemann (2003) demonstrates the variety of migration responses manifested by different groups during the same conflict. The variability of patterns of who moves, where and how they move and whether families fission or whether communities consolidate, is interpreted in terms of pre-existing social fault-lines and tensions—themselves conditioned upon historical experience. As with this Tuareg study, Lubkemann's work suggests that in the field of demography and conflict, generalisations and predictions are probably futile because conflict's causes, meanings and responses are so diverse and so embedded in historical relations. The framework outlined in this study can contribute to our understanding of the complexity of demographic responses to conflict, but is unlikely ever to permit prediction of outcomes. We should be wary of attempts to develop 'a demography of conflict' but should move towards 'a demography of conflicts' or even 'demographies of conflict'.

Acknowledgements

The ESRC funded the 2000–2001 demographic and anthropological study of repatriated Tamasheq refugees (Grant No. R000238184), which was undertaken in collaboration with ISFRA, Université du Mali, Bamako. Alessandra Giuffrida undertook the anthropological component of this study and provided valuable contributions to this article. The 1981 demographic survey of the Delta Tamasheq was financed by ILCA as part of their socio-economic research programme directed by Jeremy Swift. Further work on Tamasheq demography in 1982 was financed by the Population Council. An anonymous reviewer suggested the contrast between 'demography of conflict' and 'demography of conflicts' for which I am grateful.

Notes

[1] These norms can themselves been seen as a complex and dynamic product of history (including previous conflicts), cuiture, environment and economics.
[2] Kel Tamasheq means the people who speak Tamasheq.
[3] Eg. 32 Tamasheq killed by Peul (another pastoralist ethnic group) in 1931 in the delta (République du Mali, 1931). The Peul had managed and exploited the pastoral resources of the delta for centuries.
[4] The Tamasheq term for the ex-slave class is *iklan* but this has pejorative overtones and although still used by high status Tamasheq it is often unacceptable. The Songhay term 'Bella' is frequently used in Mali.
[5] The terminology of Bella (black) and Tuareg (red) will be used here since physical differences largely determined different Tamasheq roles and fates during the rebellion. For simplicity and because of small numbers, blacksmiths will usually be combined with the Bella although in terms of the traditional Tamasheq class groups they are 'free', not captives. Most blacksmiths are black African, they were not persecuted during the rebellion and their women have always been economically active.
[6] Bella formed a much higher proportion of the Tamasheq population in southern areas—around 50% of the Gourma and Delta populations surveyed in 1981–1982. In the far north (Kidal) Bella were rare and Tuareg women much more active.
[7] TFR between 5 and 6 compared to over 7 for other rural Malian populations.
[8] Some women were however very rich in terms of livestock ownership through inheritance, gifts and successful herd growth. Their animals though were always managed by male kin or husbands.
[9] Most people in the Mema left because there was nowhere there to hide. Further north, around Goundam and Tombouctou, some fled but others hid with their animals in the mountains and the desert. The massacres in the North were later (1993–1994) and more people fled then.
[10] Some intellectuals have clearly read the archives and quote them to researchers. It is likely they have also discussed them with other Tuareg.
[11] For full details of survey methodology see Randall (2001).
[12] A 'site' is a sedentarised community of former nomads.
[13] This idea was enunciated both by women in nomadic camps and by educated intellectuais. The latter may have been influenced by reading the colonial archives which regularly stressed Tuareg low fertility and low growth rates although with little reliable quantitative evidence.

[14] Although not necessarily sinful before marriage and in adulterous relations where there is heavy petting and possibly coitus interruptus (Nicolaisen, 1997).

Interview from the anthropological study IZ35vf03:
I: And what happens if the [married] woman gets a child with her lover?
R: It's impossible that her lover has children with her. Is that possible? . . . There are lots of sorts of love. The woman's body also has lots of parts. It's not just because a man follows you and courts you that you have to have children with him. As your body has lots of parts you can give him the parts which give him pleasure. It's because of this pleasure that they are united and her lover respects her because of this pleasure, but they don't need to have children.

[15] The estimated lifetime risk of maternal mortality was 1 in 8!

[16] The same was true in the 1980s.

[17] Cross cousin marriage is that between a man and either his mother's brother's daughter or his father's sister's daughter. Parallel cousin marriage is between a man and his mother's sister's daughter or his father's brother's daughter.

[18] Tamasheq child mortality may be underreported because people dislike talking about dead children, but also because of high adult female mortality. From the men's marriage histories (men 60 and under who are likely to have wives of reproductive age) marriages which ended in the death of the wife included 8.6% of all children born but 14.3% of all dead children. These children have no mother to report their births or deaths.

[19] To study this transformation in detail would be very data-demanding because of the seasonal and annual mobility of communities, households and individuals within households. It is uncertain whether the bascline data exist. Census data for nomads in Mali are grouped by administrative affiliation rather than spatial distribution and cannot take account of seasonal movement patterns and inter-annual variability.

[20] GTZ subsidised the house building, by providing free doors and windows and transporting the wood (Papandiek et al., 1999).

References

Agadjanian, V. and Prata, N., 2002. 'War, peace and fertility in Angola', *Demography* 39(2): 215–231.

Antoine, P. and Djire, M., 1998. 'Un célibat de crise', in: D. Ouedraogo, P. Antoine and V. Piché (eds.), *Trois générations de citadins au Sahel: trente ans d'histoire sociale à Dakar et à Bamako.* Paris: Harmattan.

Ashton, Basil, Hill, K., Piazza, J. and Zeitz, R., 1984. 'Famine in China 1958–1961', *Population and Development Review* 10(4): 613–645.

Berge, G., 1993. 'The Tuareg conflict in Mali in natural resources and social conflicts', Proceedings from the Sahel Workshop Denmark: Sandbjerg Manor, 1–17.

Bittles. A., 1994. 'The role and significance of consanguinity as a demographic variable', *Population and Development Review* 20(3): 561–584.

Bulatao R. and Casterline J., (eds.), 2001. *Global Fertility Transition.* Supp to Population and Development Review 27.

Canut, C. and Iskova, I., 1996. 'Langues et identités en question: le cas des Touaregs en milieu urbain', in: H. Claudot-Hawad (ed.), *Touaregs et autres Sahariens entre plusieurs mondes.* Edisud: Aix-en Provence.

Chojnacka, H., 1995. 'The role of nuptiality in the demographic transition, the case of Africa: a conceptual essay', *Genus* LI (3–4): 117–150.

Coast, E., 2003. 'An evaluation of demographers use of ethnographies', *Population Studies* 57(3): 337–346.

Courbage, Y., 1995. 'The population of Palestine', *Population: An English Selection* 7, 210–220.

Courbage. Y., 1999. 'Economic and political issues of fertility transition in the Arab world—answers and open questions', *Population and Environment* 20(4): 353–379.

DellaPergola, S., 2001. *Demography in Israel/Palestine: Trends, Prospects, Policy Implications.* Paper Presented at IUSSP General Conference. Salvador, Brazil.

Dyson, T., 1991. 'On the demography of South Asian famines parts I and II', *Population Studies* 45(1): 5–25 and 45(2): 279–297.

Fulton, D. and Randall, S., 1988. 'Households, women's roles and prestige as factors determining nuptiality and fertility differentials in Mali', in: J. Caldwell, A. Hill and V. Hull (eds.), *Micro Approaches to Demographic Research.* London: Kegan Paul International, 191–211.

Giuffrida A. and Randall S., 2003. Economic and political implications of forced migration: the case of returned Tuareg refugees in north-west Mali. Unpublished paper presented at International Association for the Study of Forced Migration Biennial conference, Chiang Mai, Thailand, January 2003.

Hammel, E., 1990. 'A theory of culture for demography', *Population and Development Review* 16(3): 455–485.

Haug, R., 2002. 'Forced migration, processes of return and livelihood construction among pastoralists in Northern Sudan', *Disasters* 26(1): 70–84.

Hill, A. G. and Randall, S., 1984. 'Différences géographiques et sociales dans la mortalité infantile et juvénile au Mali', *Population* 39(6): 921–946.

Khawaja, M., 2000. 'The recent rise in Palestinisn fertility: permanent or transient?', *Population Studies* 54(3): 331–346.

Khawaja, M., 2003. 'The fertility of Palestinian women in Gaza, the West Bank, Jordan Lebanon', *Population E* 58(3): 273–302.

Lindstrom D. and Berhanu, B, 1999. 'The impact of war, famine and economic decline on marital fertility in Ethiopia', *Demography* 36(2): 247–261.

Lockwood, M., 1995. 'Structure and behaviour in the social demography of Africa', *Population and Development Review* 21(1): 1–32.

Lubémann S., 2003. *The Anthropological Demography of Violence and Displacement in Fragmented Wars* Paper presented at IUSSP Seminar on the Demography of Conflict and Violence, Oslo.

Marty, A., 1999. 'La division Sédentaires-Nomades. Le cas de la Boucle du Niger au début de la période colòniale', in L. Holtedahl, S. Gerrard, M. Njeuma and J. Boutrais (eds.), *Le pouvoir du savoir de l'Arctique aux Tropiques.* Paris: Karthala, 289–306.

National Research Council, 2004. 'War, humanitarian crises, population displacement and fertility: a review of evidence', in: K. Hill (ed.), *Roundtable on the Demography of Forced Migration.* Committee on Population Washington, DC: National Academies Press.

Nicolaisen, J.I., 1997. *The Pastoral Tuareg: Ecology, Culture and Society.* Thames and Hudson, London. Papandiek B., Papandiek H. and ag Mohamed Ali Y., 1999. Rapport d'activités septembre 1998-juillet 1999. GTZ/KfW Programme Mali-Nord, Bamako.

Pedersen, J., Randall, S and Khawaja, M., (eds.), 2001. *Growing Fast: the Palestinian Population in the West Bank and Gaza Strip.* Fafo, Oslo.

Randall S., 1984. *A Comparative Demographic Study of Three Sahelian Populations: Marriage and Childcare as Intermediate Determinants of Fertility and Mortality.* Unpublished PhD thesis, London University.

Randall, S., 1996. 'Whose reality? Local perceptions of fertility versus demographic analysis', *Population Studies* 50(2): 221–234.

Randall S., 2001. Rapport sur l'Enquête Démographique en Milieu Tamasheq www.ucl.ac.uk/Anthropology/HERG/.

Randall, S., 2004. *Fertility of Malian Tamasheq Repatriated Refugees: Expected Change and Observed Stability.* Occasional Paper: Roundtable on the Demography of Forced Migration. National Academy of Sciences. Washington DC.

Randall S. and Giuffrida A., 2003. *Mariage et ménages chez les Kel Tamasheq du Mali: bouleversements socio-économiques et continuité démographique.* Paper presented at Cinquièmes Journées Scientifiques du Réseau Démographie de IAUF, Marseille.

Randall S. and Giuffrida A., in press. 'Forced migration, sedentarisation and social change: Malian Kel Tamasheq', in: D. Chatty (ed.), *Nomadic Societies in the Middle East and North Africa.* Leiden: Brill.

Randall, S. and Winter, M., 1985. 'The reluctant spouse and the illegitimate slave: marriage, household formation and demographic behaviour among Malian Kel Tamasheq', in: A. Hill (ed.), *Population, Health and Nutrition in the Sahel.* London: Kegan Paul International.

République du Mali, 1931. Archives Nationales, Rapport Politique, IE 18.

République du Mali, 1995. Rencontre Gouvernement-Partenaires sur le Nord-Mali, Annexe, Bamako.

République du Mali, 2001. *Enquête Démographique et Santé, Mali* 2001, Direction Nationale de la Statistique et de l'Informatique, Bamako, Mali; Macro International, Calverton, Maryland.

Watkins, S. and Menken, J., 1985. 'Famines in historical perspective', *Population and Development Review* 11(4): 647–675.